The Historical Encyclopedia of

WORLD SLAVERY

VOLUME II
L-Z

The Historical Encyclopedia of

WORLD SLAVERY

VOLUME II
L-Z

Junius P. Rodriguez
General Editor

ABC-CLIO

Santa Barbara, California
Denver, Colorado
Oxford, England

Library of Congress Cataloging-in-Publication Data

The Historical encyclopedia of world slavery / Junius P. Rodriguez,
    general editor.
        p.   cm.
    Includes bibliographical references and index.
    ISBN 0-87436-885-5 (alk. paper)
    1. Slavery—Encyclopedias. I. Rodriguez, Junius P.
    HT861.H57 1997
    306.3'62'03—dc21   97-42839

02 01 00   10 9 8 7 6 5 4 3

ABC-CLIO, Inc.
130 Cremona Drive, P.O. Box 1911
Santa Barbara, California 93116-1911

This book is printed on acid-free paper ∞.
Manufactured in the United States of America

❧CONTENTS❧

Maps, ix

The Historical Encyclopedia of
WORLD SLAVERY

⫷MAPS⫸

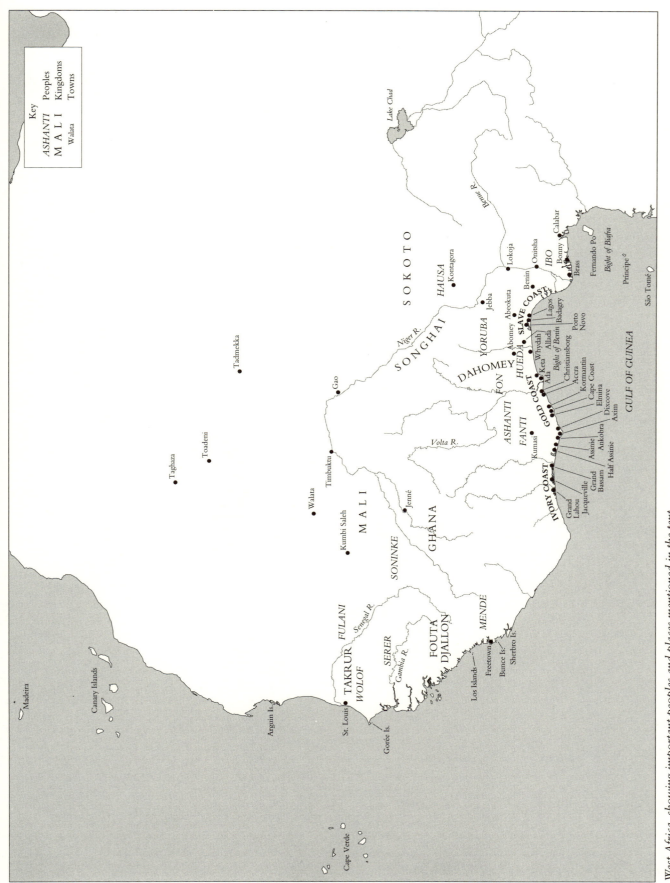

West Africa, showing important peoples and places mentioned in the text.

Key

ASHANTI Peoples
M A L I Kingdoms
Walata Towns

Madeira
Canary Islands
Arguin Is.
Cape Verde
Goree Is.
St. Louis

TAKRUR
FULANI
WOLOF
SERER
Senegal R.
Gambia R.
FOUTA
DJALLON
MENDE
Los Islands
Freetown
Bunce Is.
Sherbro Is.

SONINKE
GHANA
Kumbi Saleh
Walata
Jenné
Volta R.
Timbuktu
Toadeni
Taghaza
Tadmekka

M A L I
Gao
Niger R.
SONGHAI

SOKOTO
HAUSA
Kontagora
Benue R.
Lake Chad

Jebba
YORUBA
Abeokuta
Lokoja
Benin
IBO
Onitsha
Calabar
Bonny
Brass
Fernando Po
Bight of Biafra
Principe
São Tomé

ASHANTI
FANTI
Kumasi
FON
DAHOMEY
HUEDA
Abomey
Allada
Whydah
Keta
Ada
Badagry
Lagos
Porto
Novo
SLAVE COAST
Bight of Benin
Christiansborg
Accra
Kormantin
Cape Coast
Elmina
Dixcove
Axim
GOLD COAST
GULF OF GUINEA

IVORY COAST
Grand
Lahou
Jacqueville
Grand
Bassam
Assinie
Ankobra
Half Assinie

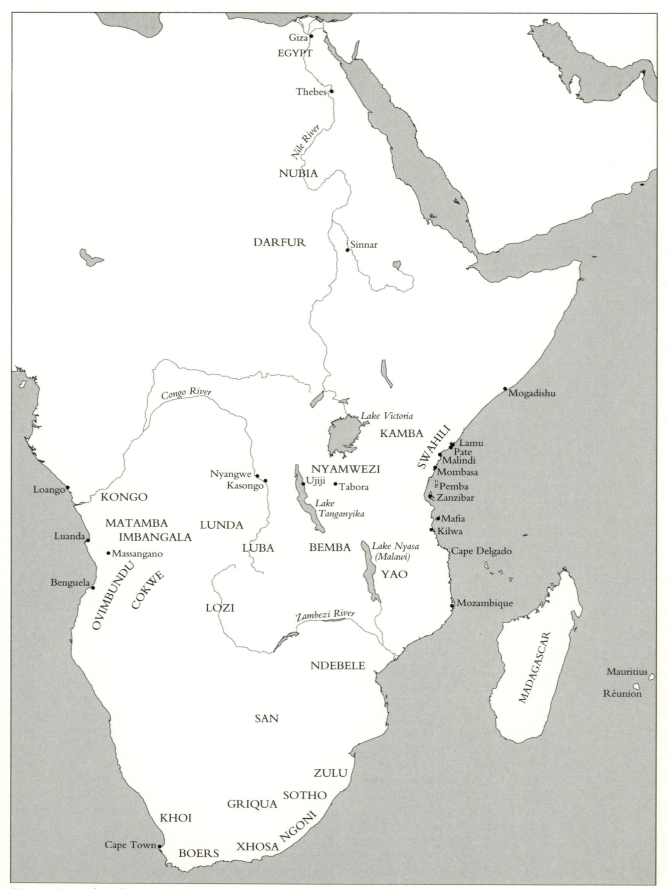

Eastern, Central, and Southern Africa, showing important peoples and places mentioned in the text.

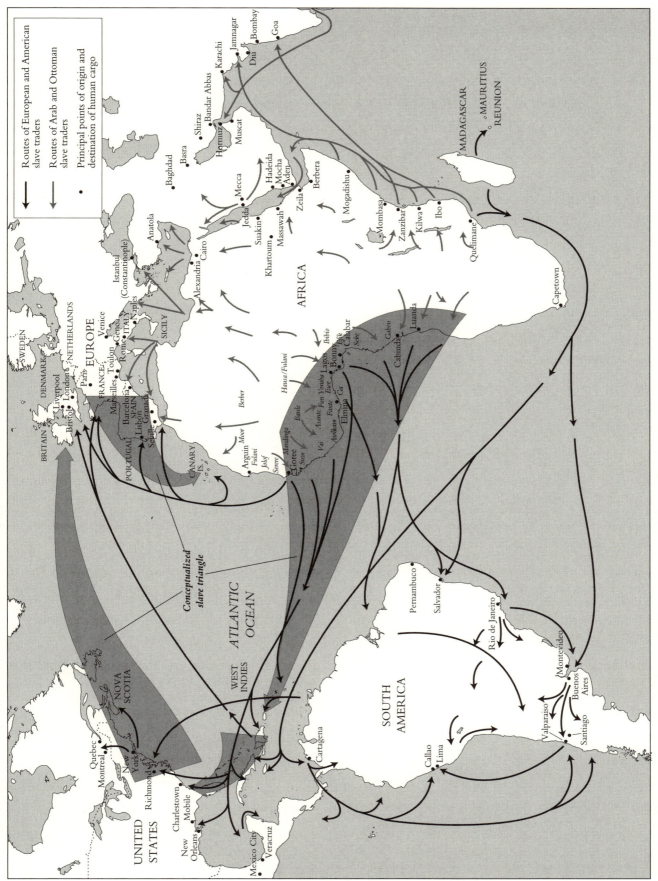

The African Diaspora. Courtesy of Joseph E. Harris.

Routes of European and American
slave traders

Routes of Arab and Ottoman
slave traders

Principal points of origin and
destination of human cargo

Conceptualized
slave triangle

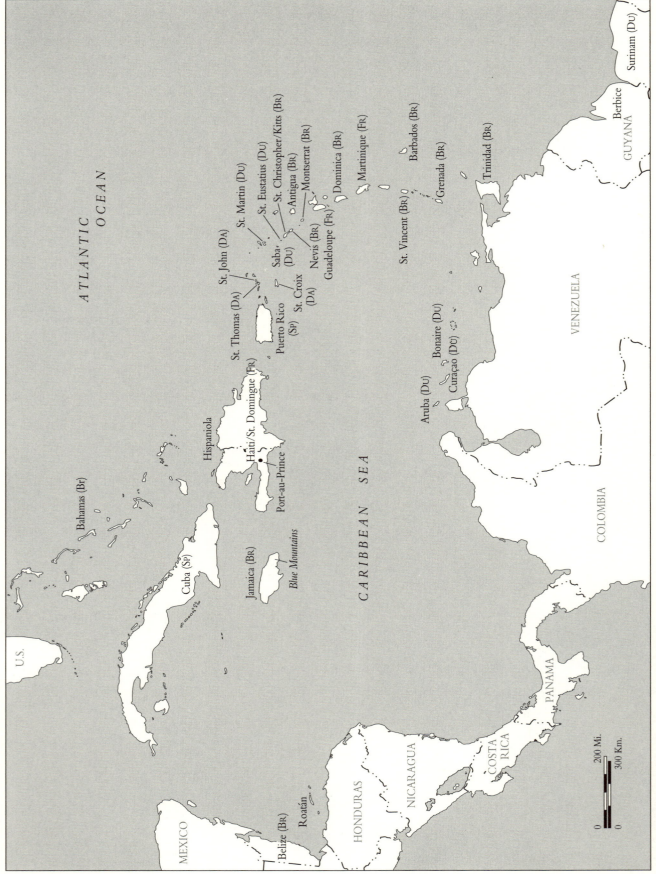

The Caribbean, late eighteenth century (present-day boundaries of countries in Central and South America shown for reference).

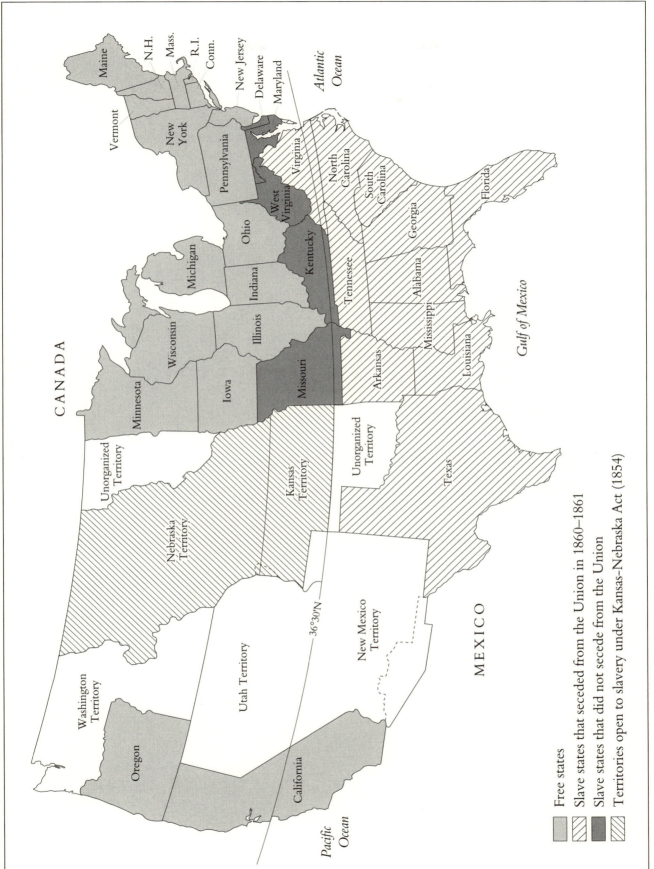

CANADA

Maine

N.H.

Mass.

R.I.

Conn.

Vermont

New York

New Jersey

Delaware

Maryland

Atlantic Ocean

Pennsylvania

Virginia

West Virginia

Ohio

North Carolina

South Carolina

Georgia

Florida

Michigan

Indiana

Kentucky

Tennessee

Alabama

Wisconsin

Illinois

Missouri

Mississippi

Minnesota

Iowa

Arkansas

Louisiana

Gulf of Mexico

Unorganized Territory

Kansas Territory

Unorganized Territory

Texas

Nebraska Territory

36°30'N

New Mexico Territory

MEXICO

Washington Territory

Utah Territory

Oregon

California

Pacific Ocean

Free states

Slave states that seceded from the Union in 1860–1861

Slave states that did not secede from the Union

Territories open to slavery under Kansas–Nebraska Act (1854)

The United States, 1860–1861.

The Historical Encyclopedia of

WORLD SLAVERY

VOLUME II
L-Z

LADIES' NEW YORK CITY ANTI-SLAVERY SOCIETY (1835–1840)

The Ladies' New York City Anti-Slavery Society circulated petitions to Congress and the Presbyterian Church's General Assembly, distributed antislavery tracts, and collected funds for the national society. Additionally, a special auxiliary sewed antislavery articles for sale. In 1836, the group sponsored a series of parlor lectures featuring the Grimké sisters in an effort to widen the society's audience. Besides organizing this lecture series, the members hosted a four-day national convention of antislavery women in May 1837 and sent 18 delegates and 80 corresponding members to the meeting.

The society represented the most homogeneous of the autonomous female antislavery societies in the United States. All of the women belonged to evangelical denominations, and unlike either the Boston Female Anti-Slavery Society or the Philadelphia Female Anti-Slavery Society, the New York women did not attempt to integrate their society.

The Second Great Awakening, a religious revival movement of the early-nineteenth century, had encouraged women to participate in many moral reform movements, including antislavery. Members of the New York antislavery organization considered slavery a moral and domestic evil, which motivated their efforts toward emancipation. In addition to being deeply religious, the New York women also believed strongly in the "woman's sphere," an ideology that placed women's activities within their homes and left public actions to men. The society's documents bear witness to the fact that, its more radical cause aside, the Ladies' New York City Anti-Slavery Society looked and operated similarly to other benevolent and moral reform societies.

In 1839 and 1840, during a debate within the American Anti-Slavery Society over the role of women in the abolitionist movement, the members of the male New York City Anti-Slavery Society, led by Lewis Tappan, walked out of the American Anti-Slavery Society's convention and formed the American and Foreign Anti-Slavery Society. The Ladies' New York City Anti-Slavery Society members walked out with the men, many of whom were husbands and fathers, and shortly thereafter declared themselves an auxiliary of the newly formed organization. After 1840, no record exists of further organizational activity by this women's group, although many members' names later appear on the rolls of more conventional reform societies.

The Ladies' New York City Anti-Slavery Society thus operated for only five years. Its members took up abolition based on their religious beliefs and with the encouragement of their ministers, and they left the movement for the same reasons they entered it. Although the New York City women were mostly conservative abolitionists in their beliefs and actions, they surpassed most of the city's women in their understanding and commitment to action outside the domestic sphere. In addition, most contemporary women shared their conservative ideology, which probably contributed to the climate's being favorable to antislavery and made New York one of the first states to put abolition on the ballot.

—*Sydney J. Caddel*

See also
Grimké, Angelina; Grimké, Sarah Moore; Second Great Awakening; Women and the Antislavery Movement
For Further Reading
Swerdlow, Amy. 1994. "Abolition's Conservative Sisters: The Ladies' New York City Anti-Slavery Societies, 1834–1840." In *The Abolitionist Sisterhood: Women's Political Culture in Antebellum America*. Ed. Jean Fagan Yellin and John C. Van Horne. Ithaca, NY: Cornell University Press.

LAGOS

Located on the first major inlet along the lower Guinea coastline from the Volta estuary to the Niger Delta, Lagos was historically the most important entrepôt of the slave trade on West Africa's Slave Coast. Established by Awori, Ijebu, Egba, and other migrants from the Yoruban hinterland, its many names reflect its varied past. To early Yoruban settlers, it was Eko, a name derived from their word for farm *(oko)*. To the Edo of Benin, who established hegemony over it in the mid-sixteenth century, it was a war camp *(eko)*; and to the outside world it is Lagos, a contraction of the Portuguese word for "lagoon."

Geography and history, internal and external trades, and politics interacted to establish Lagos's commercial supremacy. Its lagoon and natural harbor, with an extensive system of inland waterways, made Lagos an ideal berthing and landing spot for European shipping. Although a notoriously shallow bar and narrow tidal range made access difficult and dangerous for ships with a draft over 12 feet, smaller ships could navigate the bar, and bigger ones could connect with the inland waterways by boats and canoes. A lack of space and poor sandy soil made agriculture difficult for the inhabitants of the islands of Lagos, forcing them to become dependent on mainland neighbors for food and ensuring an intensive exploitation of the rivers and coastal waters. Thus, they became great fishermen before becoming great traders. They sold fish inland and sent sea salt to Benin in exchange for food products and clothes. In the early-sixteenth century, slaves began to come from the interior to Lagos, where they were sold "for twelve or fifteen bracelets each."

The slave trade through Lagos apparently remained inconsiderable until the 1760s when the reigning *oba* ("king") Akinshemoyin invited a group of Portuguese and Brazilian traders to establish their business at his capital. Soon other factors were encouraging the new trade in human cargo. This was the period when the demand for slaves in the American market was at its height. European wars provoked by the French Revolution affected the number of slaves exported through the French-dominated port of Whydah (Ouidah), and after about 1800, the Oyo Kingdom's power declined, and its trade routes to Porto Novo and Whydah became vulnerable to incessant Dahomean attacks. These factors collectively resulted in the gradual shift of the slave trade eastward from Whydah to Lagos, which soon became the most thriving slave port on the Slave Coast, stimulating an increased demand for slaves from the Yoruban hinterland.

At the peak of this trade in the 1820s, and despite the abolitionist acts passed by the major European states, well over 10,000 slaves were exported annually from Lagos. The pervasive and devastating state of warfare dominating nineteenth-century Yoruban power politics accelerated the process, sending many slaves to the coast and ensuring that the Yoruba would constitute the single largest West African ethnic group sold as slaves, exported to the Americas, or resettled in nineteenth-century Sierra Leone.

Transformed by the transatlantic slave trade from an obscure dependency of Benin to a metropolis of wealth and power, Lagos became a center and a magnet of converging interests. Determined to extirpate the "abominable traffic" in humans for which Lagos had become notorious, eager to stimulate legitimate trade in palm products, and hoping to foster the Christian missionary enterprise in Yoruba territory, the British began to intervene in Lagos's political economy. Supported by missionaries, European merchants, the Christianized Yoruban elite, and returned freed slaves from Sierra Leone, and exploiting a perennial fratricidal succession struggle, the British in December 1851 bombarded the city and made it a British protectorate. In August 1861, facing stiff resistance from indigenous authorities, the British annexed Lagos, making it a crown colony.

That action initiated the gradual colonization and creation of modern Nigeria. In 1960, Lagos became Nigeria's first postindependence capital, a status it maintained until December 1991. It is still Nigeria's first and major seaport; the key terminus of its railway; the country's leading cultural, industrial, and commercial center; and one of Africa's most boisterous, cosmopolitan, and populous cities (1990 estimate, 7 million).

—*Funso Afolayan*

See also
Benin; Crowther, Samuel Ajayi; Dahomey; Portuguese Slave Trade; Slave Coast; The Yoruba
For Further Reading
Adefuye, Ade; Babatunde Agiri; and Jide Osuntokun, eds. 1987. *History of the Peoples of Lagos State*. Ikeja, Nigeria: Lantern Books; Aderibigbe, A. B., ed. 1975. *Lagos, the Development of an African City*. London: University Press; Smith, Robert S. 1979. *The Lagos Consulate, 1851–1861*. Berkeley: University of California Press.

LAS CASAS, BARTOLOME DE (1474–1566)

*T*he sixteenth-century friar Bartolomé de Las Casas was a spokesman for Native American peoples and a critic of Spain's New World conquest. In 1514, this well-educated priest radically changed a previous stance and began advocating colonial reform. Renouncing his own *repartmiento* (tribute grant) of Indians and the colonial system, he promoted an alternative plan of conversion.

As "protector of the Indians," Las Casas traveled throughout the New World and Spain preaching the proper responsibilities of the Catholic Church and the Spanish crown. He stated that the papal grant of America to the crown of Castile required the conversion of the Indians and stressed that it did not support forced servitude or confiscation of Indian land. His

A late-nineteenth-century engraving of Bartolomé de Las Casas "bewailing the cruelty of the Spaniards."

reform program called for suppressing all *encomiendas,* liberating Indians from all servitude, and restoring the ancient Indian states and rulers. His plan allowed for a small voluntary tribute to the crown as repayment for its gift of Christianity.

Las Casas used his New World influence to gain access to the Holy Roman emperor Charles V (King Charles I of Spain), and as his humanitarian adviser, Las Casas influenced colonial policy. In 1520, the government declared the Indians freemen to be Christianized. Later in 1542, Charles V wrote new laws that prohibited Indian enslavement and limited the inheritability of *encomiendas.* Under the *encomienda* system, Indian families were entrusted to Spanish colonists. The Spaniards could extract tribute and labor from the Indians and were obliged to provide religious instruction and protection in exchange. The orders to control and eradicate the *encomienda* system were not enforced, and the system spread.

To strengthen his position, Las Casas administered peaceful conversion projects. In 1521, he attempted to colonize Venezuela's northeastern coast. The failed plan included Spanish farmers living with and working beside Indians. Another notable experiment in the late 1530s included the peaceful Christianization of an unconquered region, Guatemala's "land of war." Las Casas and other Dominican friars actually introduced Christian doctrine there, won over the chiefs, and effectively converted the region in a few months. The changes were transitory, but they did result in the region's receiving a new name, "true peace."

In 1543, Las Casas became bishop of Chiapas in southern Mexico and apostle of the Indians. He spent the remainder of his life extolling the virtues of the Indians and highlighting the cruelty of the Spaniards. While in a Dominican monastery he devoted more than a decade to writing numerous tracts that condemned the cruelty of the conquest. His campaigns stimulated caution and increased sensitivity to the conquest in Spain, and his advocacy led the monarchy to halt all conquest in 1550 while a royal court heard testimony and later issued humanitarian reforms. The harshness of the toil in New World mines and the continued desire for profits resulted in a search for new labor. Initially, Las Casas advocated the introduction of Negro slaves, as he felt they could withstand the heavy work, but he later took a stand against all slavery.

—*Yolandea Wood*

See also
Encomienda System; Sepúlveda, Juan Ginés de
For Further Reading
Gibson, Charles. 1966. *Spain in America.* New York: Harper Torchbooks; Hanke, Lewis. 1949. *The Spanish Struggle for Justice: In the Conquest of America.* Philadelphia: University of Pennsylvania Press; Rawley,

James A. 1981. *The Transatlantic Slave Trade: A History.* New York: Norton; Shafer, Robert Jones. 1978. *A History of Latin America.* New York: Heath.

LATIFUNDIA

*L*atifundia were large ancient Roman estates. The name derives from the Latin words *latus* ("wide" or "extensive") and *fundus* ("estate"). Modern scholars use the word *latifundia* to describe the formation of large Italian estates with an area of more than 250 hectares (61,776 acres) worked by gangs of chained slaves from the early-second century B.C. The extensive latifundia engaged in numerous economic activities, including specialized slave handicrafts, and they supposedly originated from an allocation of public lands and amalgamation of small peasant farms.

Originally it was thought that the Second Punic War (218–201 B.C.), which devastated much of southern Italy, and continuous overseas wars caused a deterioration in the economic situation of many free smallholders who were called away for military service. The resulting agrarian reorganization arising from systematic land investment and massive slave importation forced impoverished peasants to sell their land to elite buyers and move to Rome. That view is now considered a gross oversimplification and has been revised because of new archaeological information about Roman agriculture and a scholarly hesitation to generalize from fragmentary data and modern analogies.

Most of the recent archaeological field surveys in Italy have shown that peasant smallholdings existed at a later period and in greater numbers than previously supposed. Farms and medium-sized estates were the norm until late-second century A.D., but regional divergences were profound. Large ranches involved in large-scale pasturage and sheep rearing existed in southern Italy, but huge estates dedicated to specialized cash crops or arable farming also existed, especially in Sicily, Roman North Africa, and the eastern provinces, where very different rural socioeconomic conditions prevailed.

There is little evidence for the use of the word *latifundia* by Latin authors, and no ancient definition survives. The term occurs only about 10 times in moral and satirical texts of the mid-first century A.D. and never in the works of the Roman agricultural and legal writers. Pliny the Elder said in his *Natural History* that "large estates have been the ruin of Italy" (18.35: *latifundia perdidere Italiam*) and added that six landowners owned half of Roman North Africa when the Emperor Nero put them to death. The strongly polemical and rhetorical passage about land concentration is a moralizing anachronism with a wider purpose, which is also found in other parts of Pliny's *Natural History*: the contrast between Nero with his personal excessive consumption and the moderate emperor Vespasian.

But the situation Pliny described must surely contain some element of fact: the accumulation of land in still-fewer hands in the early part of the Roman Empire. The large landholdings of the Roman elite and the emperor were normally created by the acquisition of medium-sized estates with a mixed economy and were located in different regions of Italy and the provinces. They were not monolithic, centralized managerial blocks of property but were run as independent units entrusted by the absentee owners to slave bailiffs or freedmen. The status of the workforce and the organization of production depended on various factors, including the estate's location and local traditions. Tenancy was an alternative, increasing in importance in the early and later periods of the empire to the slave-run estates, but the pattern of scattered holdings continued.

Latifundia should therefore only be used loosely in the meaning of "large estates" or "landholdings of the Roman elite" and should be avoided in describing the types of estates in and/or production of Roman agriculture. Latifundia is sometimes used to describe large, extensively cultivated estates worked by dependent labor or sharecroppers in later periods. The term applies to some parts of preindustrial Italy, Spain, and Latin America but has also been used in Hungary and England to characterize marginally profitable plantations with landlords dominating the societies socially and economically.

—*Jesper Carlsen*

See also

Agricultural Slavery; *Coloni;* Latin America; Roman Empire; Roman Republic

For Further Reading

Du latifundium au latifondo. Un héritage de Rome, une création médiévale ou moderne? 1995. Paris: Centre Pierre Paris; Hopkins, Keith. 1978. *Conquerors and Slaves: Sociological Studies in Roman History.* Cambridge: Cambridge University Press; Kuziscin, Vasilij Ivanovic. 1984. *La grande proprietà agraria nell'Italia romana II secolo a.C–I secolo d.C.* Rome: Editori Riuniti; White, Kenneth Douglas. 1967. "*Latifundia.*" *Bulletin of Institute of Classical Studies* 14: 62–79.

LATIN AMERICA

Enslaved labor was used in the Americas prior to Columbus's arrival in the Bahamas on October 12, 1492. The Portuguese and the Spaniards altered and expanded the preexisting institution of slavery from a war-produced and ceremonially related practice involving Amerindians to indigenous and then African slavery on a massive scale throughout Brazil, the Caribbean, and other parts of Latin America. The transatlantic slave trade, which lasted for more than three centuries, involved the shipping of 8–10 million blacks across the Atlantic. The effects of this African diaspora would influence the demography, economy, independence, and liberalism of the region.

The "Columbian exchange," named after the admiral because of the significant changes that followed his first voyage to the New World, initiated a trend toward "biological homogeneity" that continues to this day. Perhaps the most dramatic example of this transoceanic connection was the destruction of the Amerindian population by the illnesses that the Europeans took with them to the newly "discovered" lands. For instance, Sherburne F. Cook and Woodrow Borah have argued that the population of the Valley of Mexico dropped from 25 million inhabitants in the early 1500s to about 16 million by mid-century (Crosby, 1972).

The demographic disaster was aggravated by harsh forms of labor such as the *encomienda* (the allotment of a group of Indians to a Spaniard who, at least nominally, was to instruct them in Christianity), *mita* (a rotational draft system), and outright slavery. The enslavement of natives was common in the sixteenth-century Viceroyalty of New Spain, where "there was such haste to make slaves that they poured into Mexico City from all directions . . . like sheep to be branded" (Zorita, 1963).

African slaves, who filled the "labor demands not met by the Indian population," were essential to the plantations of Latin America because sugar production required numerous hands in the fields and mills (Palmer, 1976). In fact, approximately 90 percent of the African slaves had settled in the circum-Caribbean by the mid-nineteenth century (Crosby, 1972). *Palenques* (settlements of runaway slaves, or *cimarrones*), like the one near Veracruz, which was populated by almost 500 bondsmen in 1608, were established in New Spain and Peru by "slaves [who] were quick to exploit the advantages that the physical environment offered them" (Palmer, 1976).

On the other hand, blacks were not as evident where "seasonal labor needs made the use of negro slaves difficult and costly" (MacLeod, 1973). Such was the case with the harvest of indigo, which was not as labor intensive as sugar, in colonial Central America. Indian workers were the mainstay of that region since "involuntary servitude was never so critical to the Central American economic system" (Rout, 1976).

Slavery was affected by the Spanish-American revolutions because of the economic havoc they caused in the region in the early 1800s. Furthermore, the use by insurgents and royalists of black soldiers who were promised emancipation in return for military service raised African expectations of freedom once the fighting ended and undermined the legitimacy of the institution in the eyes of many people.

Simón Bolívar was one of those individuals, and he advocated the "confirmation of the absolute freedom of the slaves [which he had already decreed], as I would plead for my very life and for the life of the Republic" (Rout, 1976) when he addressed the Congress in Angostura that established Gran Colombia (Colombia, Ecuador, and Venezuela) in 1819. Bolívar wrote the Bolivian constitution and submitted it to the national legislature in 1826. In submitting the document to the legislators, he described bondage as the "negation of all law" and a "crime." The Venezuelan had freed his own slaves years beforehand.

Church and state relations, federalism, and individual liberties were important concerns of liberals after the independence period. Many Latin American intellectuals of the nineteenth century viewed slavery as an obstacle to development along European lines. They realized the "need for modernization and a rational approach to economic problems as the utilitarian influence" of Jeremy Bentham and others illustrated (Woodward, 1985).

Demographic, economic, ideological, and political considerations motivated several countries to outlaw the practice of slavery in their constitutions. Thus, the Central American Federation (Costa Rica, El Salvador, Guatemala, Honduras, and Nicaragua), established on June 29, 1823, abolished slavery in 1824. In this case, liberalism triumphed over conservatism because of the scant number of bondsmen in the area. For example, there were only 100 African slaves in Costa Rica and 800 in Guatemala when abolition became the law of the federation (Rout, 1976).

The Indian and African experiences in the Americas have been affected by the legacy of slavery and related forms of labor in the region. The exclusion of both groups from mainstream Latin American society was one result of the existence of the "peculiar institution" throughout several centuries. That is why, "culturally and racially, the Central American insists on depicting himself as Spanish" according to one source (Rout, 1976). Naturally, this observation can be applied to South Americans as well. In effect, the centuries-long exploitation scarred the collective identity of Latin America, and one cannot understand its history without coming to terms with this fact.

—*Fidel Iglesias*

See also
Bolívar, Simón; Central America; Columbus, Christopher; New Spain

For Further Reading
Crosby, Alfred W., Jr. 1972. *The Columbian Exchange: Biological and Cultural Consequences of 1492.* Westport, CT: Greenwood; MacLeod, Murdo J. 1973. *Spanish Central America: A Socioeconomic History, 1520–1720.* Berkeley: University of California Press; Palmer, Colin A. 1976. *Slaves of the White God: Blacks in Mexico, 1570–1650.* Cambridge, MA: Harvard University Press; Rout, Leslie B., Jr. 1976. *The African Experience in Spanish America: 1502 to the Present Day.* Cambridge: Cambridge University Press; Woodward, Ralph L., Jr. 1985. *Central America: A Nation Divided.* New York: Oxford University Press; Zorita, Alonso de. 1963. *Life and Labor in Ancient Mexico: The Brief and Summary Relation of the Lords of New Spain.* New Brunswick, NJ: Rutgers University Press.

LATIN AMERICAN LAW

*I*n 1502, the Spanish government legalized the importation of African slaves into the New World. The legal basis for the introduction of African slaves originated with the Siete Partidas (Seven Protectors), a body of laws drawn up from 1263 to 1265 that eventually applied to all of Spanish America. A brief experiment with Native American slaves in the Caribbean had failed, and since Spanish officials were already using Africans on the Iberian Peninsula, they had familiarity with dark-skinned slaves.

With the Siete Partidas in place, slave traders carried several cargoes of African slaves to the Spanish Caribbean between 1502 and 1506. The early slave trade introduced so many slaves that the Spanish government soon prohibited additional shipments into Cuba. Although Siete Partidas ultimately resulted in the enslavement of millions of Africans, it nevertheless afforded them some protection.

Siete Partidas gave slaves the right to marry, enabled them to inherit property, and provided avenues to freedom through manumission, especially if they were victims of extreme cruelty. In addition, the Catholic Church sometimes intervened on behalf of slaves and thus gave them some added rights. But slaves were usually at the mercy of their masters, and neither Siete Partidas nor the Catholic Church could prevent the cruel treatment of African slaves. Thus, slaves were worked from sunrise until sunset on sugar, tobacco, cacao, cotton, and coffee plantations with little fear of recrimination on the part of the Spanish authorities.

The entry of other European counties into the Caribbean and the presence of the Portuguese in Brazil resulted in the implementation of additional laws. The French developed the Code Noir to apply to their bondspeople in the Caribbean. This 1685 body of laws regulated the institution throughout the French possessions, including Haiti, Grenada, Guadeloupe, Martinique, and later Louisiana. Code Noir mirrored Siete Partidas in providing some protection to slaves, and the evidence suggests that the French permitted more manumissions.

Native American slavery lasted much longer in Brazil than elsewhere, but by the mid-sixteenth century, African slaves were beginning to replace the indigenous population on sugar plantations. Unlike the Spanish, the Portuguese left the legal sanctions to local officials rather than attempting to implement and enforce laws from a distance. Some Brazilian slaveholders developed their own laws concerning slavery, including rules for manumission.

In contrast to Spain, France, and Portugal, England did not create a legal foundation for slavery in Latin America but left it to their North American colonies to develop a significant body of legislation. In the Caribbean, the English government gave nearly complete authority to their subjects, including control over slaves. Other countries, such as the Netherlands, used statutes rather than a body of laws to legalize slavery in the New World.

During the sixteenth century, then, and coinciding with the start of the transatlantic slave trade, most European nations developed extensive bodies of laws to regulate slavery in the Caribbean and their mainland colonies. These copious bodies of legislation remained in place until the abolition of slavery and provided the foundation for more than three centuries of African slavery in Latin America and the Caribbean.

—*Jackie R. Booker*

See also
Code Noir; Dutch Caribbean; Spain; Spanish Borderlands

For Further Reading
Conniff, Michael L., and Thomas J. Davis. 1994. *Africans in the Americas.* New York: St. Martin's; Keen, Benjamin. 1966. *A History of Latin America.* Boston: Houghton Mifflin; Lockhart, James, and Stuart B. Schwartz. 1983. *Early Latin America: A History of Colonial Spanish America and Brazil.* Cambridge: Cambridge University Press.

LATINO, JUAN
(1516–1599)

Juan Latino was the most important and widely known of three African-born intellectuals active in early modern Europe. After he had been taken from Guinea to Baen, Spain, as a slave at age 12, a noblewoman purchased him to work in her household. When he demonstrated a strong interest in his master's studies, she allowed him to attend the cathedral school where he excelled and ultimately became his master's tutor. He learned Greek but was especially fond of Latin and changed his slave name, Juan de Sessa, to Juan Latino (or, occasionally, Joannes Latinus). His first major translation was of Horace into Castilian. After obtaining bachelor's and master's degrees at the University of Granada, he began a long professorial career there in 1557.

A favorite of students, and with the support of an admiring dean, Latino became Chair of Grammar, and the apogee of his university work occurred in 1565 when he delivered the Latin oration to open the academic year. His quick wit, sophistication, proficiency with musical instruments, and ability to sing madrigals provided access to members of Granada's wealthy and ruling class, who held him in high esteem. His remarkable courtship of Dona Ana de Carlobal, daughter of the governor of his former master's estates, inspired a play, *Juan Latino* (1652), by Diego Jimenez de Enciso and mention by Lope de Vega in his play *La Dama Boba* (1613). Perhaps no greater testimony to Latino's genius exists than the following poetic lines by Miguel de Cervantes in *Don Quixote:*

> Since Heaven it hath not pleased on thee
> Deep erudition to bestow.
> Or black Latino's gift of tongues,
> No Latin let thy pages show.

Latino cultivated the friendship of Austria's Don Juan, son of Emperor Charles V and victor of the Battle of Lepanto (1571). Captivated by the celebratory fervor sweeping Europe at the time, Latino wrote his masterpiece, *Austuriad,* a lengthy Latin poem praising his close comrade, Don Juan, and honoring Prince Ferdinand of Spain and Pope Pius V. Written in elegiac couplet, the poem's 160 pages contain numerous references to classical mythology and Catholic dogma. Latino also wrote *Translatione* (1576), a solemn work of 600 lines dedicated to the reinterment of royal remains at El Escorial. He penned his last poetic endeavor in 1585, a 12-page poem honoring his patron, Don Gonsalvo Fernando de Cordova.

Although Latino flourished among the educated, rich, and powerful of European society, his attitudes toward Africa, religious proselytizing there, and slavery were as progressive and empathetic as anyone might expect in the context of that era. One passage in the *Austuriad* mocks the white man's narcissism: "If our black face, O King, seems ugly to your ministers, Ethiopians find your egg-white faces equally so."

Because dogmatic racism was not prevalent in sixteenth-century Europe, Latino's accomplishments were, at the time, not considered racially ascribable. Centuries later, his success is deemed proof of an African's intellectual competence and potential to benefit from (Western) civilizing influences. Unlike the cases of Jacobus Eliza Johannes Capitein (1717–1747) of the Netherlands and Anton Wilhelm Amo (1703–1753?) of Germany, who were both stolen from Ghana and enslaved, Latino's benefactors neither viewed nor intended his youthful education as a racial "experiment."

—*Robert Fikes, Jr.*

For Further Reading
Fikes, Robert. 1980. "Black Scholars in Europe during the Renaissance and the Enlightenment." *Negro History Bulletin* 43 (July–September): 58–60; Maso Vazquez, Calixto. 1973 *Juan Latino: Gloria de Espana y su raza.* Chicago: Northeastern Illinois University; Spratlin, Valaurez. 1938. *Juan Latino: Slave and Humanist.* New York: Spinner Press.

LAURENS, JOHN
(1754–1782)

Born into a well-respected South Carolina family, John Laurens earned distinction as a Revolutionary War soldier and diplomat. His father, Henry Laurens, was a planter, Continental Congress delegate, and diplomat. Young John enrolled in school in London in 1771, but after a year, he and two brothers traveled to Geneva, Switzerland, to attend a liberal-minded institution there. In September 1774, Laurens returned to London to study law and returned to America in April 1777.

Using family influence, he joined George Washington's staff as an aide-de-camp. Young, ambitious, and brave to the point of rashness, Laurens fought at Brandywine, Monmouth, and Germantown, where he was wounded. His continental education served him well as his fluency in French made him a valuable liaison. Laurens returned to South Carolina in May 1779, where he was both an elected official in the state assembly and a soldier. Although captured when Charleston fell in May 1780, he was paroled in a prisoner exchange.

Laurens shifted his career when Congress appointed him special minister to the Court of Versailles in late 1780. Although unconventional, Laurens successfully negotiated French aid and returned to America in August 1781 with ships, supplies, and money for the cause of independence. Laurens immediately joined Washington's force at the Yorktown siege, and he helped negotiate the surrender terms for Cornwallis's British army.

Returning to South Carolina, Laurens was again elected to the state assembly. He maintained his military commission and commanded revolutionary forces near Charleston. In a meaningless and insignificant skirmish with a superior British unit at Chehaw Neck on the Combahee River (August 17, 1782), Laurens was killed, a result of his rash behavior as a military commander.

Laurens was a product of his age and his education. He was essentially a republican and a progressive, a believer in the rights of man. As early as 1776, he advocated emancipating blacks for their participation in military service. Washington's Continental Army utilized whatever troops the states provided, and any reluctance to use blacks as troops disappeared because of impending shortages. On March 29, 1779, Congress recommended that Georgia and South Carolina form separate black battalions, 3,000 troops in all. Slaveowners would be compensated up to $1,000 per able-bodied male up to age 35. The troops would be outfitted at government expense, freed at the war's end, and paid $50 each.

Congress selected Laurens to elicit South Carolina's support for the idea, and he was the ideal choice. When his father had earlier mentioned freeing his slaves, John had written to him in 1778 suggesting raising a troop of blacks to fight as a unit. Young Laurens found South Carolina's planters horrified by the thought of black soldiers, but a key shortage of available soldiers in South Carolina led Gen. Benjamin Lincoln to support using blacks in his ranks, and Gen. Nathanael Greene shared his view.

In early 1782, when Laurens was back from his French mission and serving in the state legislature, the state assembly took two votes on enrolling black troops. Despite the presence of the popular and gregarious Laurens, the measures failed. Georgia also refused the request, even when facing superior British forces. Slaveowners and planters had spoken, proving that fear of the British paled in comparison to the idea of blacks earning their freedom through military service.

—*Boyd Childress*

For Further Reading
Bailey, N. Louis, and Elizabeth Ivey Cooper, eds. 1981. "John Laurens." In *Biographical Directory of the South Carolina House of Representatives.* Columbia: South Carolina University Press; Quarles, Benjamin. 1961. *The Negro in the American Revolution.* Chapel Hill: North Carolina University Press.

LEAGUE OF NATIONS

When the League of Nations was founded in 1920, the slave trade was no longer an important international issue. Colonial powers had ended slave raids in all but their remoter territories and had outlawed the slave traffic and ended the legal status of slavery in most possessions. At the end of World War I, the victorious powers had abrogated the only comprehensive treaty against the African slave trade—the Brussels Act—claiming that it was no longer needed. However, one of the treaties signed in 1919 bound the victorious powers not only to end the slave trade but to "secure the complete suppression of slavery in all its forms," and Article 23 of the Covenant of the League of Nations bound members to "secure and maintain fair and humane conditions of labor" and the "just treatment of the native inhabitants under their control."

These commitments went beyond those of the Brussels Act since they were not limited to Africa and they included the suppression of slavery, other labor abuses, and the slave trade. However, "fair and humane conditions of labor" were not defined, no time limit was set for compliance, no concrete measures were mandated, and there was no mechanism for enforcing the treaties. None of the colonial powers wanted to be bound to take action or have any international supervision of their labor policies.

Thus, the slavery question might never have been brought before the League of Nations if the secretary of the British-based Anti-Slavery and Aborigines Protection Society (ASAPS), John Harris, had not realized that the League could be used to pressure governments to protect indigenous peoples. He was spurred into action by reports of slave raiding on the frontiers of Ethiopia, where slavery and the slave trade were still legal, and of a flourishing traffic across the Red Sea to the newly independent Hejaz. When he found the British government unwilling for political and economic reasons to release information about slaving in Ethiopia—where Britain, France, and Italy were competing for influence—he got the New Zealand delegate, Sir Arthur Steel-Maitland, to ask the League Assembly in September 1922 to institute inquiries. In response, the League launched an investigation into slavery everywhere and asked all governments to furnish information.

When the replies were inadequate, the League appointed a Temporary Slavery Commission (TSC) in 1924 to review the evidence on "slavery in all its forms" and suggest measures to end it. The TSC consisted of eight experts who were appointed by the League and were not answerable to their governments. However, six of them were nationals of the most interested colonial powers (Britain, France, Italy, Portugal, Belgium, and Holland), and three distinguished colonial officials, Frederick Lugard, Maurice Delafosse, and Alfredo Freire D'Andrade represented Britain, France, and Portugal, respectively. There was also a delegate from the International Labour Organization and a Haitian member, appointed because he was black, "moderate," and able. To limit its powers, the colonial powers insisted that the TSC was to be a temporary and purely advisory body and could take evidence only from nongovernmental organizations approved by their own governments. To curb its only weapon—publicity—it was to meet in private and only its report, not its evidence, was to be published.

Nevertheless, the TSC set important precedents for the future. It interpreted slavery "in all its forms" to include the slavery practiced by Africans (with which the colonial rulers had no wish to interfere for fear of disrupting local economies and alienating elites) as well as peonage, debt-bondage, pawning, the sale of children for domestic service, the sale of brides under guise of dowry payments, and the forced retention of concubines. To the dismay of the colonial powers, the TSC also included forced labor, which was practiced in many colonies and was often more exploitative than the remaining vestiges of slavery. Furthermore the commission objected to indirect methods of forcing indigenous peoples into wage labor by devices such as taxation and vagrancy laws. The result was to extend the concept of slavery to include forms of exploitation not previously considered at the international level. Finally, the TSC recommended the negotiation of a convention for their suppression.

Lugard forced the hand of a reluctant British government by sending the British a draft convention, which they watered down and presented to the League, where it was further weakened but became the Slavery Convention of 1926, which is still in force. Slavery was vaguely defined as "the status of a person over whom all or any of the rights attaching to ownership are exercised," and signatories were bound to suppress it in "all its forms" but only "progressively and as soon as possible." Forced labor was to be used only for public purposes; its private use was to be ended only progressively. The slave trade was to be suppressed, but, because France and other powers would not concede the right to search, a separate convention was to be negotiated to cover the maritime traffic.

The treaty had serious flaws. Since no final date was set for abolition, even countries in which slavery was legal could sign it. The various forms of slavery were not spelled out. There was no mechanism for enforcement or even for monitoring results, and the maritime convention was never signed. Nevertheless, the treaty focused attention on a wide range of forms of exploitation, and to complete the work, the League invited the International Labour Organization to negotiate a treaty against compulsory labor. This led to the signature of the Forced Labor Convention of 1930—the first of several treaties for the protection of colonial labor. Moreover, some colonial governments, particularly in the British Empire, passed more stringent antislavery laws and took stronger action to ensure that slaves who wished to do so might claim their freedom.

Slavery remained legal in Ethiopia and on the Arabian peninsula, including the British satellites on the Gulf and the Aden Protectorate. In China and in Britain's Far Eastern territories, little girls, known as *mui tsai,* were still sold into domestic service. Slave raiding and trading continued in Ethiopia. Slaves were still exported to Arabia from Africa, across the Gulf from Baluchistan and India, and, under cover of pilgrimage, from all parts of the Muslim world. Slaves captured in Liberia were sent as "contract" labor to the Spanish island of Fernando Po in the Bight of Biafra and to the French colony of Gabon.

Small-scale trading continued in parts of Africa, where unknown numbers, although legally free, remained with their former owners in what was called "voluntary" servitude. Peonage was widespread in the Americas. Debt-bondage kept people in lifelong, even hereditary, servitude in the Indian subcontinent and other areas, and various forms of involuntary labor were exacted by local rulers and chiefs in Africa and elsewhere. Forced labor under different guises was also widely practiced, particularly in French and Portuguese territories.

In 1929, the British government, pressed by the ASAPS and unable to get the support of other colonial powers even to protest the continuing raids in Ethiopia, proposed that the League of Nations appoint a small, permanent body of experts to collect and publish information on slavery. This proposal was no more welcome to the British Colonial and India Offices than it was to the other colonial powers, but, because none of them wanted to risk the odium of rejecting a humanitarian proposal, they eventually agreed to an even more emasculated League body—the Committee of Experts on Slavery (CES), which met in 1932 for one year only. It was only to consider the working of the 1926 convention and suggest ways in which the League might assist countries who asked for help; it was not to discuss forced labor. Again the committee met in private and could take only evidence submitted by or through governments.

All European colonial powers—Britain, France, Portugal, Spain, Belgium, Italy, and the Netherlands—were represented on the CES, and its meetings were highly politicized. For instance, the French attacked Britain for failing to suppress slavery in all its territories and fended off criticism of Ethiopia, where Emperor Haile Selassie, fearing positive action by the League, had introduced new antislavery measures. Liberia was not discussed although its government, under pressure from the United States, had invited the League to investigate slavery in 1931 and then rejected its recommendations as threatening its sovereignty. The CES, however, had one positive outcome. It recommended the establishment of a small, permanent League slavery commission.

This proposal, supported by Britain, resulted in the appointment of the Advisory Committee of Experts on Slavery (ACE) in 1934. France and Portugal, fearful of any supervision of their colonial policies, insisted that it was to be purely advisory, collect evidence only from governments, and meet biennially if necessary. The seven experts came from each of the European colonial powers, and most either were serving as or were retired colonial officials.

As a group, the experts were neither distinguished nor committed, but the British delegate, Sir George Maxwell, forced the pace. Tireless and dedicated, he engineered annual meetings and found ways to conduct his own investigations, demanding information from his government on all forms of exploitation in the British Empire, including debt-bondage, child labor, servitude in Bechuanaland, and bride wealth (goods exchanged between the family of the groom and the family of the bride) in Africa. He wanted an investigation into why slaves had stayed with their owners after the legal status of slavery was abolished and suggested that slaves be given land credit to speed up their emancipation. He tried to force reluctant officials to take action by incorporating his criticisms into the committee's reports.

Since Maxwell's colleagues were more concerned with defending national interests than with ending slavery, the result, to the dismay of his government, was that the ACE's reports dealt almost entirely with the shortcomings of Britain's antislavery policy while those of other powers were barely mentioned. By 1937, the British Foreign Office had decided that the committee had outlived its usefulness.

By this time chattel slavery was disappearing, and its legal status had ended almost everywhere outside the Arabian peninsula. Changes in the economic sphere were creating a growing mobile wage-labor force, presenting both slaves and masters with new options. New forms of capital and new status symbols were replacing slaves, which were becoming more expensive as taxes were imposed. Rail and road transport were replacing human porterage, and the colonial rulers were introducing new methods of mobilizing and exploiting labor.

In the political arena, Italy had conquered Ethiopia in 1936 and had outlawed slavery there. When Italy failed to get international approval for its conquest, it withdrew from the League and the Italian delegate left the ACE. Ibn Saud had conquered the Hejaz and had established his rule over most of Arabia in the 1920s; in 1936, he signed a treaty with Britain undertaking to end the importation of new slaves and regulate the sale and manumission of those already in the country. Since Saudi Arabia was not a member of the League and Italy was now in control of Ethiopia, both of the areas where classic slavery and slave trading continued most openly were beyond the jurisdiction of the League. Moreover, the British, increasingly nervous of rising Italian power in the Red Sea area, were now anxious to play down the slavery issue. They had little incentive to support a committee that was openly critical of their policies while failing to show up the shortcomings of others.

By 1938, the ACE was dying of attrition as tensions rose in Europe. Its Spanish member withdrew on the outbreak of civil war in Spain, and the Portuguese delegate ceased to attend meetings. Maxwell hoped to hold a final session in 1939 to wind up the committee's affairs and pass its functions to a more prestigious body, such as the International Labour Organization or the League's Social Questions Committee. The final session, however, was canceled, and the outbreak of World War II in September 1939 sealed the fate of the ACE. Although not formally dissolved, it never met again.

The most important achievement of the antislavery activities of the League of Nations was the negotiation of the 1926 convention. For all its shortcomings, this treaty began the process of extending the definition of slavery to include a wide range of forms of exploitation. It became the basis of the United Nations Supplementary Convention on the Abolition of Slavery, the Slave Trade, and Institutions and Practices Similar to Slavery of 1956, which supplemented it. Moreover, the three League committees, although hampered by international politics, focused public attention and generated information on slavery, causing some governments to take more vigorous action to suppress it. They were thus a factor, although doubtless less important than changing economic and political conditions, in the decline of slavery and the slave trade in the interwar period.

—*Suzanne Miers*

See also
Brussels Act; United Nations Ad Hoc Committee on Slavery; United Nations Protocol of December 7, 1953
For Further Reading
Atchebro, Dogbo Daniel. 1990. *La Société des nations et la lutte contre l'esclavage 1922–1938*. Geneva: Mémoire of the Institut Universitaire des Hautes Études Internationales.

LECLERC, CHARLES VICTOR EMMANUEL (1772–1802)

Charles Victor Emmanuel Leclerc commanded the ill-fated French expedition sent by Napoleon Bonaparte to reestablish slavery in Saint Domingue. A volunteer in the Republican army, Leclerc rose quickly through the ranks, distinguishing himself in 1793 at Toulon, where he first met Bonaparte. He came under Bonaparte's command in the Army of Italy in 1796, married Bonaparte's sister Pauline in 1797, and accompanied the leader in his rise to power during the next years. He commanded the soldiers who dispersed the Conseil des 500 (Council of 500) during Bonaparte's 1799 coup and served as a general in Germany, Egypt, and Spain.

In 1801, Bonaparte placed him in command of an expedition being prepared to wrest Saint Domingue from Toussaint Louverture's control and solidify French presence in the Americas. Bonaparte had decided to maintain slavery in those islands, recently returned to France, where it had never been abolished, but he had announced that he would not restore slavery where it had been abolished in Saint Domingue and Guadeloupe. Yet secret instructions given to Leclerc stipulated that initial promises about the preservation of liberty were meant to coax Louverture and his generals into accepting the arrival of the French troops. After Leclerc had landed, he was to wage war against the generals on the island, disarm the blacks, and return them to plantation slavery to reestablish the prerevolutionary colonial economy.

When Leclerc's expedition arrived at Le Cap (Cap Haitien) on Haiti, Louverture's general, Henri Christophe, demolished the city and its defenses before retreating. Leclerc managed to entice many of Louverture's soldiers to the French side and won battles against those who resisted. Finally, after even Christophe had abandoned him, Louverture surrendered command of his troops. Leclerc invited him to a meeting, captured him, and sent him to prison in France where he died in 1803.

Leclerc meant to follow Louverture's capture with a generalized disarmament of colonial blacks. He encountered continued resistance, however, and yellow fever increasingly decimated his troops. When news of the violent reestablishment of slavery in Guadeloupe arrived in Saint Domingue, the French intention to reestablish slavery—still denied by Leclerc—was unmasked. Resistance, rooted among Maroons (communities of runaway slaves) who had consistently fought the French, spread as black and mulatto soldiers who had rallied to Leclerc changed sides. Desperate, Leclerc wrote to Bonaparte that the only way to force

Saint Domingue to submit was to purge all blacks who had profited from freedom and all who had had a command in the army, in whatever capacity.

In the last month of his life, Leclerc inaugurated terror tactics, which were pushed to new extremes by his successor, Gen. Jean-Baptiste-Donatien de Vimeur, comte de Rochambeau. Leclerc died in November 1802 of yellow fever; like most of the soldiers who accompanied him, he did not live to see France again or to witness the failure of Napoleon's plans for Saint Domingue when the colony became independent Haiti.

—*Laurent Dubois*

See also
Haitian Revolution; Louverture, Toussaint; Napoleon Bonaparte
For Further Reading
Fick, Carolyn. 1990. *The Making of Haiti: The Saint Domingue Revolution from Below.* Knoxville: University of Tennessee Press; Mezière, Henri. 1990. *Le General Leclerc, 1772–1802 et l'expédition de St. Domingue.* Paris: Tallandier.

LECOMPTON CONSTITUTION

The Lecompton Constitution was drawn up in 1857 by proslavery Kansans to admit the territory into the United States as a slave state. The Kansas-Nebraska Act (1854) had established that slavery in the area would be decided by popular sovereignty, which led to anti- and proslavery forces battling in Kansas over the slavery question. Kansas's proslavery party met from September 7 to November 7, 1857, at Constitution Hall in Lecompton, the territorial capital of Kansas, to frame the Lecompton Constitution.

The constitution stated the functions of the state government and included provisions for slavery. It maintained that the legislature could not deny owners property rights to their slaves, nor could it emancipate slaves without compensation to owners or prevent immigrants from bringing slaves into the area. It also protected the legal and civil rights of slaves with provisions for trial by jury and protection against brutal punishment.

The vote on the Lecompton Constitution was not a choice between accepting or rejecting the constitution. The choice was between adopting the Lecompton Constitution "with slavery" or "with no new slavery." With no slavery meant that "slavery shall no longer exist in the territory of Kansas, except that the right of property in slaves now in this Territory shall in no

manner be interfered with." In short, whatever the outcome of the vote, slavery would still exist in Kansas.

Angered by this deception, Kansans who opposed the extension of slavery into the territory boycotted the polls, so that on December 21, 1857, the constitution "with slavery" was ratified by a vote of 6,226 to 569 (2,720 of the votes for the constitution were fraudulent). Another vote on January 4, 1858, this one involving both the free-state contingent and the proslavery faction—but largely boycotted by the proslavery people—denounced the Lecompton Constitution 10,226 to 162.

President James Buchanan was reluctant to accept the apparently clear mandate, and on February 2, 1858, he recommended to Congress that Kansas be admitted under the Lecompton Constitution. Perhaps his decision was partly the result of the Supreme Court's *Dred Scott v. Sandford* (1857) decision, which stated that Congress could not pass a law depriving persons of their slave property. The U.S. Senate passed Buchanan's legislative recommendation, but Illinois Democrat Stephen A. Douglas denounced the Lecompton Constitution and prevented it from passing in the House of Representatives.

Partly to avert further division in the Democratic Party, the English Bill (named after its author, William H. English of Indiana) was proposed as a compromise, and it offered Kansans a third vote on the slavery issue. Although not directly confronting the slavery issue and to save Buchanan embarrassment, the English Bill attached an issue regarding voting. Kansans would vote either to accept or reject a federal land grant of 4 million acres of land for new states, seen by many people as a congressional bribe to encourage support of the proslavery constitution.

On August 2, 1858, in a strictly supervised election, Kansans voted 11,300 to 1,788 to reject the land grant offer, and indirectly to repudiate the Lecompton Constitution. This renunciation of the Lecompton Constitution demonstrated Kansans' preference to remain a territory rather than become a slave state. Kansas was finally admitted as a free state in 1861.

The Lecompton Constitution split the country on several levels. Kansans first battled each other over the legality of slavery in their territory. The Topeka (antislavery) and Lecompton (proslavery) factions clashed in a local war that alerted the rest of the country to the divisiveness of the slavery question. The national Democratic Party and the U.S. executive and legislative branches also passionately debated the validity of the Lecompton Constitution, further demonstrating the unsettled state of the nation over the slavery issue. The conflict that the Lecompton Constitution provoked foreshadowed the U.S. Civil War.

—*Julieanne Phillips*

For Further Reading
Connelley, William E. 1918. *A Standard History of Kansas and Kansans*. Chicago: Lewis; Stampp, Kenneth M. 1990. *America in 1857: A Nation on the Brink*. New York: Oxford University Press; Wilder, Daniel W. 1875. *The Annals of Kansas*. Topeka, KS: G. W. Martin.

LEI AUREA
(1888)

Lei Aurea, the Golden Law, of May 13, 1888, put an end to more than three centuries of slavery in Brazil. The brief text declared, "From this date slavery is declared extinct in Brazil," and a second article revoked all contrary provisions. This law was, in reality, just the formal accomplishment of a development that had already destroyed slavery in Brazil. It was meant to stop a wave of social unrest that swept the core areas of slavery in São Paulo and Rio de Janeiro, causing thousands of slaves to leave their plantations, crowd highways, and march against the cities. The law has also been considered a part of a liberal project to secure the future of the monarchy in Brazil, but the reforms came too late and were too limited. The military establishment had little difficulty in imposing the republic less than two years after the abolition of slavery.

Emancipation arrived gradually in Brazil. It was inevitable after slave importation from Africa had stopped in 1850, but the slaveowners resisted until the end. Emancipation progressed through three successive laws. In 1871, the Law of the Free Womb (Rio Branco Law) stated that offspring of slave mothers should be freed when they reached the age of 21. In 1885, the Sexagenarian Law freed all slaves over the age of 65 and stipulated that slaves over 60 should work only three more years for their masters before being freed. Finally, the Golden Law abolished slavery in 1888.

The final years of slavery in Brazil were marked by internal dissolution, and it became evident that emancipation was only a question of time. In 1884, the northern provinces of Ceará and Amazonas abolished slavery. In 1886, the public whipping of slaves was prohibited, and this innovation was rightly seen as a severe blow to the institution of slavery as slaves did not work without the threat of punishment.

The key to Brazilian slavery was the constant labor shortage, and the paradox is that slavery was the major impediment to the creation of a free labor force. Neither free Brazilians nor immigrants wished to share the conditions of slaves. When slaveowners in the coffee districts finally understood that the days of slavery were numbered and that immigration was the only way to get sufficient manpower to expand production, their resistance to abolition soon faded away. When the provincial government of São Paulo began supporting immigration in 1887, most producers changed their mind about slavery. At the same time, a social upheaval among the slaves caused apprehension. The slaves, often assisted by abolitionists, left the farms and moved to *quilombos* (communities of runaway slaves) near the larger cities.

At the opening of the legislature on May 3, 1888, the regent, Imperial Princess Isabel, spoke warmly in favor of the abolition of slavery. The Golden Law was approved almost unanimously 10 days later. However, the abolitionist ideal that abolition should be followed by educational and agrarian reform was not realized.

—*Birgitte Holten*

See also
Abolitionist Confederation; Brazilian Anti-Slavery Society
For Further Reading
Conrad, Robert. 1972. *The Destruction of Brazilian Slavery*. Berkeley: University of California Press; Costa, Emilia Viotti da. 1985. *The Brazilian Empire: Myths and Histories*. Chicago: University of Chicago Press; Holloway, Tom. 1977. "Immigration and Abolition: The Transition from Slave to Free Labor in the São Paulo Coffee Zone." In *Essays Concerning the Socio-Economic History of Brazil and Portuguese India*. Ed. Dauril Alden and Warren Dean. Gainesville: University Press of Florida; Toplin, Robert Brent. 1992. *The Abolition of Slavery in Brazil*. New York: Atheneum.

LEX POETELIA PAPIRIA

Lex Poetelia Papiria was a Roman law prohibiting debt-bondage and imprisonment for private debts. It is thought that it was named after Gaius Poetelius Libo Visolus and Lucius Papirius Cursor, the consuls of 326 B.C., but a different ancient tradition dates the law to 313 B.C. when Poetelius was dictator.

According to the earliest written Roman law codes, the Twelve Tables, which date from the mid-fifth century B.C., defaulters were liable to be sold into slavery outside Roman territory by their creditors. The Twelve Tables also refer to an older legal institution of servitude, *nexum* (from *necto*, "to bind"), which has an obscure nature. *Nexum* was apparently a formal contract into which the debtor entered voluntarily, but it is unclear whether the debtor pledged his own person as security or whether the creditor had the right, without a court judgment, to enslave the defaulter until the debt was satisfied. *Nexum* was a debt-bondage system, but the debt-bondsman retained his Roman citizenship and continued to live in his place of residence. In economical sense *nexum* was similar to slavery, and it provided wealthy Roman landowners with dependent labor in great numbers.

Debt caused considerable social and political tensions in Rome in the fifth and fourth centuries B.C. and was the object of much legislation that attempted to weaken the Twelve Tables' harshest provisions. The Lex Poetelia Papiria formally abolished *nexum*, freed the debt-bondsmen, and guaranteed that loan security would be in property and not the person of the borrower. This law marked an important victory for Roman plebeians, and the Roman historian Livy in the first century called the law "a new beginning of freedom" (*History of Rome*, 8.28).

Yet Livy's description of enslavement for debt is similar to the overthrow of Athenian tyranny in the sixth century as social tensions led to a relaxation of policy. His account relates an anecdote about homosexual maltreatment of a debtor but ignores the economic and social factors behind the discontent. Rome's abolition of debt-bondage, even if it persisted in other parts of Italy until later, meant that an internal dependent labor force disappeared and that chattel slaves replaced debt-bondsmen on many estates of rich Roman landowners. The numbers of slaves increased greatly because of Rome's continuous warfare, and the Roman "slave economy" may have originated in the late-fourth and early-third centuries B.C.

—*Jesper Carlsen*

See also
Roman Republic
For Further Reading
Brunt, Peter A. 1971. *Social Conflicts in the Roman Republic*. London: Chatto and Windus; Cornell, Tim J. 1995. *The Beginnings of Rome*. London: Routledge; Finley, Moses I. 1981. "Debt-Bondage and the Problem of Slavery." In *Economy and Society in Ancient Greece*. Ed. B. D. Shaw and R. P. Saller. London: Chatto and Windus; MacCormack, G. 1973. "The Lex Poetelia." *Labeo* 19: 306–317.

THE LIBERATOR

The *Liberator* (Boston, 1831–1865) was a radical abolitionist weekly newspaper owned and edited by William Lloyd Garrison. It provides an excellent record of Garrison's views on slavery, antislavery, national politics, contemporary events, women's rights, nonresistance, institutional religion, and racism over the antebellum period and prints many of his speeches, most of which have not been published elsewhere. Its accounts of antislavery meetings animate the passion and range of ideas within the antislavery movement.

The paper describes the activities of the Garrisonian antislavery societies, in particular the American Anti-Slavery Society, the Massachusetts Anti-Slavery Society, and smaller affiliated groups. It reports the speeches and experience of both prominent and lesser known abolitionists, and it is a useful source of proslavery, antiabolitionist, and non-Garrisonian antislavery texts and Garrison's responses to them. Equally as significant, the *Liberator*—or Garrison speaking through it—helped set the terms of the antislavery debate; the paper's astute deployment of the American Revolution's patriotic language and the religious language of apocalypse and its oppositional stance forced others to respond in kind. Although neither the first antislavery newspaper nor the one with the largest subscription list, it was the best known, longest lived, and most influential.

Garrison began the paper to advocate abolition to both North and South, for he believed the entire nation was implicated in the sin of slavery. Most of the paper's subscribers lived in the North and West and in the first 10–15 years were predominantly free blacks, but the subscription lists do not accurately depict the *Liberator*'s influence. In 1831, for instance, the paper was exchanged with some 100 Southern newspapers. For Southerners and many Northerners as well, the *Liberator* embodied abolitionist propaganda, reliably printing the very worst ideas (according to Southern readers) in consistently extreme language. Southern newspaper editors printed excerpts from the *Liberator* along with attacks upon both it and Garrison, and they and their readers wrote letters to him. Garrison published these letters in the front-page feature, "The Refuge of Oppression," the more scurrilous the better.

The *Liberator*'s reputation was made in 1831 when a Southern newspaper editor, trying to explain Nat Turner's violent uprising, claimed Turner had been incited by abolitionist propaganda and specifically by the *Liberator*. Clearly, Turner did not need abolitionists to identify the cruelty and injustice of slavery, and the *Liberator* was a new, struggling, and obscure paper, one of which few Americans were aware. Even so, the claim stuck. Since even moderate or nominal abolitionists received similar accusations, Garrison functioned as a representative abolitionist for the South as his newspaper was an easily identified target. The language of the *Liberator* was not moderate; Garrison believed he needed strong language to win the war against slavery.

Garrison made the *Liberator* a powerful propaganda

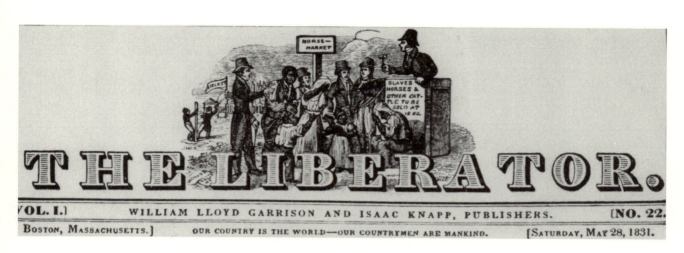

The masthead of the abolitionist paper the Liberator, 1831.

tool by exploiting the newspaper's form and meaning. The outstanding character of a newspaper, particularly the tremendously popular penny papers, which first appeared in the 1830s, is variety. The *Liberator* offered speeches, proslavery gibes, clippings from Southern papers, editorials, descriptions of abused slaves, reports about Congress's doings, poems, and, for a time, small illustrations in addition to the paper's large and impressively illustrated masthead. Although Garrison wanted to "diversify the contents of the *Liberator* so as to give an edge to curiosity" (January 1, 1831), he also kept the reader focused on a small body of abolitionist truths. Hence, the paper fell between the new kind of popular newspaper and the older sort of political paper, which made no pretensions to express anything other than a partisan opinion.

In fact, Garrison turned his newspaper into a pulpit, imbuing it with the language and moral force of the sermon, following a long tradition of joining the sacred and the secular in the press and pulpit. A vigorous religious press had begun in the 1820s, and the pulpit had always been a place to comment on vital secular topics and to urge congregations to carry sacred lessons into the world. The substitution of page for pulpit was essential for Garrison, who was mild mannered and, unlike some other abolitionists or the charismatic revivalist preachers, an ineffective orator. The *Liberator*'s sermon-speeches and editorials have all the fire and force his oral delivery lacked. Through his newspapers, Garrison's words gave him a moral and social stature, even heroism: just because he published the *Liberator*, he was hailed as a modern Martin Luther or John the Baptist and became a catalyst for inciting mobs and riots. In a sense, Garrison became the *Liberator;* as a poem on the first page of the first issue (January 1, 1831) put it:

My name is LIBERATOR! I propose
To hurl my shafts at freedom's deadliest foes!
My task is hard—for I am charged to save
Man from his brother!—to redeem the slave!

Although most of Garrison's early subscribers were free blacks, he directed much of the *Liberator* at a white audience or else at "Americans," who were implicitly white. Perhaps he did not feel a need to appeal to free blacks because he believed they already sympathized with his cause. But this focus on a white audience also assumed that black Americans lacked the power to end slavery, that they needed white "liberators."

Garrison published the *Liberator* every week for over 30 years, an astonishing record for any antebellum newspaper and more so for one that constantly rested on the edge of financial collapse. In the early years Garrison did much of the work himself—writing, setting type, printing, and even delivering the papers to Boston-area subscribers. In later years other prominent abolitionists assumed editorial duties, among them Oliver Johnson and Maria Weston Chapman. The *Liberator* finally suspended publication on December 29, 1865; with the Civil War over, Garrison believed the *Liberator* had accomplished its task.

—*Andrea M. Atkin*

See also
Garrison, William Lloyd
For Further Reading
Atkin, Andrea M. 1995. "Converting America: The Rhetoric of Abolitionist Literature." Ph.D. dissertation, Department of English, University of Chicago; Merrill, Walter M. 1963. *Against Wind and Tide: A Biography of William Lloyd Garrison*. Cambridge, MA: Harvard University Press.

LIBERIA

Settled in 1822 by freed slaves from the United States, Liberia's organizers intended to fight the slave trade being conducted along the western coast of Africa as colonists spread the Christian religion and "civilization" among the indigenous population. Under white governors appointed by the American Colonization Society, the colonists had little success in persuading Africans to abandon either domestic slavery or the coastal sale of slaves.

Even after gaining independence in 1847, the Americo-Liberians continued dressing in European clothes, speaking English, and modeling their government and society after their "mother" country. Their stated policy toward the African population was assimilation, but they maintained almost complete separation despite a system of apprenticeship that brought children into their homes as servants. They did mix somewhat more with the 5,000 "Congoes," Africans freed by the U.S. Navy from slave ships captured before reaching the Americas. The native African population considered the Congoes Americo-Liberian slaves, but the Congoes adopted Christianity and English and became a buffer between the 15,000 Americo-Liberians and the 2 million natives.

Using trade goods supplied by U.S. and European donors, the Americo-Liberians purchased control of 600 miles of coastline, but they made little impact on the hinterland before 1900. Pressured by British and French expansion during the late 1800s, the Americo-Liberians claimed as much of the interior as possible and adopted the British strategy of indirect rule for its governance, but they had no way of imposing their will until the founding of the Liberian Frontier Force (LFF) in 1908.

Relying on U.S. assistance, they established the LFF but never adequately paid or disciplined its members. The LFF pillaged, raped, and enslaved hinterland peoples who did their best to escape its depredations. The national government imposed a "hut tax" in 1916 and used the LFF and taxes to saddle the interior with district commissioners, who used their official positions to establish plantations manned by forced labor, to smuggle various goods, and to extort rice from the local people. Complaints by the chiefs and missionaries led to the hiring of white commissioners from the United States in an effort to reform local government. When a U.S. commissioner arrested a slaveowning district commissioner and had him marched in chains to Monrovia, the Americo-Liberians reacted with indignation at the American's racism, and by 1921, they had forced all foreign commissioners out of the country.

Market farming in the interior proved unprofitable because there were no roads to transport products to the coast, so the Americo-Liberians turned to exporting labor. The government sold licenses to the Germans and later to the Spanish to allow them to recruit workers. A scandal ensued when the Spanish employed Americo-Liberians as agents to produce labor for the unhealthy cocoa plantations on Fernando Po, a Spanish island in the Bight of Biafra. The League of Nations investigated and found that both fraud and later the LFF had been used to capture Liberians for export. The vice-president of Liberia had been the principal organizer—both he and the president resigned.

Domestic slavery was outlawed in the 1930s, but there was little basic change following the scandal. Firestone Tire Company established a massive rubber plantation and, bowing to the pressure of Americo-Liberian planters, accepted the forced-labor system, paying chiefs to "recruit" labor. As late as 1965, one-quarter of all wage laborers in the country were forced workers.

After World War II, the Liberian government dropped assimilation in favor of a unification policy and established a Bureau of Folkways to generate respect for indigenous cultures, but that policy made little difference in ethnic relationships. The International Labour Organization found that Liberian laws did not meet the standards set by the 1930 international labor convention and that forced labor remained legal. In response to international condemnation, in 1961, the government made it illegal for chiefs to use force or threats to recruit labor but still retained that right for the state. In 1962, Liberia repealed the forced-labor and cultivation laws, and Firestone stopped paying chiefs for labor recruitment. Nevertheless, in the mid-1960s, a U.S. group, Growth Without Development, reported that "recruitment" continued.

The Americo-Liberians remained in control of the government, exploiting most of the population, until 1980 when Sgt. Samuel Doe, an African, overthrew and murdered the Americo-Liberian president in a coup. Rebellion and ethnic warfare followed. Despite U.S. support, Doe was overthrown and murdered, and one-third of the population fled the country, which remains in a state of anarchy.

—*Dennis J. Mitchell*

See also
Africa; American Colonization Society
For Further Reading
Akpan, M. B. 1973. "Black Imperialism: Americo-Liberian Rule over the African Peoples of Liberia, 1841–1964." *Canadian Journal of African Studies* 7 (2): 217–236; Gershoni, Yekutiel. 1985. *Black Colonialism: The Americo-Liberian Scramble for the Hinterland.* Boulder, CO: Westview Press; Shick, Tom W. 1977. *Behold the Promised Land: A History of Afro-American Settler Society in Nineteenth-Century Liberia.* Balti-

more: Johns Hopkins University Press; Sundiata, I. K. 1980. *Black Scandal: America and the Liberian Labor Crisis, 1929–1936.* Philadelphia: Institute for the Study of Human Issues.

LINCOLN, ABRAHAM
(1809–1865)

As president of the United States during the Civil War, Abraham Lincoln issued the Emancipation Proclamation (1863), which freed African American slaves in parts of the Confederacy unoccupied by Union forces and laid the legal groundwork for the eventual eradication of slavery in the United States. Lincoln is often associated with giving freedom to an enslaved people and restoring the values of equality contained in the Declaration of Independence to the forefront of the American experience.

Economic issues rather than slavery dominated Lincoln's thinking during his early career as an attorney and a leading Illinois politician, particularly the problems of ensuring equal opportunities for white Americans in an increasingly complex national economy. He absorbed his father's antislavery attitudes, and he never publicly defended slavery. Yet he said little about the institution while serving in the Illinois state legislature (1834–1840) or the U.S. Congress (1846– 1848). As a lawyer, he defended rights of slaveholders and runaway slaves alike with no apparent moral qualms.

By the early 1850s, Lincoln had concluded that slavery's degradation of free labor and entrepreneurship was anathema to his ideals of equal economic opportunity for all citizens. The period's national political crises also propelled the problems associated with slavery to the forefront of Lincoln's political consciousness. The repeal of the Missouri Compromise line by the Kansas-Nebraska Act (1854), which opened newly acquired western territories to slavery, and the proslavery language of the Supreme Court's Dred Scott decision (1857) led Lincoln to believe that some white Southerners and Northern white Democrats were engaged in a secret plan to make slavery a national institution. Searching for a constitutional and political basis to combat this plan, he concluded that the Declaration of Independence contained an antislavery ideal that the Constitution's language and provisions should fulfill. By setting the Declaration's high ideals of equality as the moral goal toward which the republic must always strive, Lincoln believed the Founders had placed slavery "in the course of ultimate extinction."

Lincoln carried his ideas with him when he joined the fledgling Republican Party in 1856. He avoided the radical plans of some Republicans and abolitionists for an immediate and possibly violent end to slavery, calling instead for preventing slavery's spread into western lands while leaving it untouched to die of its own accord in the South. He also supported colonization schemes to ship ex-slaves to Africa, and he expressed doubts as to whether the two races could ever live together in peace. Lincoln was keenly aware of the virulent prejudice exhibited by many of his white neighbors toward African Americans, and he was sometimes compelled to cater to those prejudices to win votes. During an unsuccessful campaign for the U.S. Senate in 1858, for example, he stated, "I have no purpose to introduce political and social equality between the white and the black races" (Donald, 1995).

Once elected president in 1860 and facing the country's subsequent dissolution, Lincoln declared that he had no intention of making war on slavery. "My paramount object in this struggle is to save the Union," he wrote, "and is not to either save or destroy slavery" (Donald, 1995). He quashed early emancipation schemes by Union generals John Frémont and David Hunter and was ambivalent toward congressional legislation, such as the Confiscation Acts, that appeared to be legal precursors of emancipation.

Lincoln began a gradual movement toward emancipation in 1862 for several reasons. Abolitionist leaders like Frederick Douglass and Charles Sumner constantly pressured Lincoln to end slavery, the war itself created tremendous pressures on the institution as thousands of African Americans escaped into Union-held territory and their presence demanded clarification of their legal status, and a manpower shortage compelled Lincoln to contemplate the unprecedented employment of African American soldiers, which would necessarily be accompanied by the promise of freedom. Primarily, Lincoln himself achieved a deeper and more profound understanding of the war's ultimate meaning as he began to realize that Americans required a loftier goal than restoration of the Union to justify the war's dreadful cost. He believed that what was at stake was nothing less than the future of all of mankind's free institutions.

On January 1, 1863, Lincoln issued the Emancipation Proclamation. Ever mindful of public opinion, he crafted the document carefully to avoid antagonizing Northerners on such a sensitive subject. The proclamation freed only those slaves in areas of the Confederacy that were not yet occupied by Union forces and was devoid of the inspirational eloquence that characterized the Gettysburg Address and other speeches. But Lincoln's proclamation ended the national legal protection that had been afforded human bondage in America for over two centuries and paved the way for the Thirteenth Amendment's final eradication of slavery. Lincoln believed the Emancipation Proclamation was his greatest achievement as president.

With emancipation came a variety of related policies and measures from Lincoln's administration designed to hasten slavery's demise. Chief among these was the recruitment of African American soldiers, which Lincoln encouraged to help freedmen erase slavery's stigma. He also tried quietly to persuade leaders of the conquered South to allow African Americans limited legal and political rights. Lincoln's assassination in 1865 cut short whatever further efforts he may have made on behalf of the freedmen; we will never know what his policies might have been concerning slavery's legacy.

Lincoln's actions concerning slavery have been debated ever since his death. Generations of Americans, white and black, have revered him as the Great Emancipator. Beginning in the 1960s, however, some Americans began questioning this reputation, arguing that he freed the slaves because of wartime necessity rather than any internal antislavery or egalitarian values. Perhaps Frederick Douglass provided the best assessment of Lincoln's legacy in this regard. "Viewed from the genuine abolition ground, Mr. Lincoln seemed tardy, cold, dull, and indifferent," Douglass declared, "but measuring him by the sentiment of his country, a sentiment he was bound as a statesman to consult, he was swift, zealous, radical, and determined" (Cox, 1981).

—Brian Dirck

See also
Abolition, United States; Bleeding Kansas; Civil War, United States; Confiscation Acts; Douglass, Frederick; *Dred Scott v. Sandford*; Emancipation Proclamation; Thirteenth Amendment; U.S. Constitution

For Further Reading
Cox, LaWanda. 1981. *Lincoln and Black Freedom: A Study in Presidential Leadership*. Urbana: University of Illinois Press; Donald, David. 1995. *Lincoln*. New York: Simon and Schuster; Johannsen, Robert. 1991. *Lincoln, the South, and Slavery: The Political Dimension*. Baton Rouge: Louisiana State University Press.

LITERATURE

Slavery was abolished in law, at least in Britain and the United States, by the emancipation of slaves in the British colonies (1834–1838) and by the Emancipation Proclamation (1863) and the Thirteenth Amendment (1865) in the United States. Yet the subject is far-reaching, and its discourse in literature is detectable in texts as diverse as Aphra Behn's *Oroonoko; or, The History of a Royal Slave* (1678), Jane Austen's *Mansfield Park* (1814), and Richard Wright's *Native Son* (1940).

Whenever one enters London's Tate Gallery, built on the proceeds from British sugar plantations, or sings "Amazing Grace," written by John Newton, a slave-ship captain who underwent a conversion to abolitionism, one recognizes the all-pervasive nature of slavery and oppression.

Slavery often appears in literature, not as subject, but as a sensational backdrop to a story that is essentially about other things, as in Margaret Mitchell's *Gone With the Wind* (1936). Literary texts also use the subject to articulate other concerns about the power structures of the day. Thus Behn's *Oroonoko* comments specifically on female oppression and the struggle for political power in seventeenth-century England, and in Austen's *Mansfield Park,* Sir Thomas Bertram's departure for interests in the West Indies precipitates a moral collapse in the comfortable and respectable nineteenth-century English country home, leaving only the heroine, Fanny, to raise the issue of slavery. She does so through an underlying question of the text: that of the nature of the patriarchy under which the weak and the powerless live. Charlotte Brontë's *Jane Eyre* also uses slavery as a metaphor for male tyranny, by Jane's cousin at the beginning of the text and later, if one is aware of the Creole blood of Bertha, by Rochester's wife, as a signifier of that dark other which is to be both feared and oppressed.

In the nineteenth century, a perceived analogy between British factory workers and the slaves of the Americas was exploited in factory novels like Francis Trollop's *Michael Armstrong, the Factory Boy* (1839), and Elizabeth Gaskell's *Mary Barton* (1848). Harriet Beecher Stowe's *Uncle Tom's Cabin* (1852) and her second novel, *Dred* (1865), were used by the British to build support for the Reform Act of 1867, which began the emancipation of British labor. The analogy was strenuously refuted, most famously by James Baldwin in *Notes of a Native Son* (1955), in which he argued that Uncle Tom wore his badge upon his face and could not, therefore, better his lot via education and social mobility.

More directly, pro- and antislavery literature abounded during the eighteenth and nineteenth centuries. Proslavery literature, given a traditional association of darkness with evil in Western culture, commonly used the myth of barbarism to assert its arguments. Thus, Thomas Jefferson, in *Notes on the State of Virginia* (written in 1781–1782), compares the American slave to the Roman slave and, after commenting on the artistic and intellectual capacities of the latter, concludes that it is nature, not slavery, which creates the distinctions between black and white. Some writers used biblical and providential arguments to justify slavery while others, like Edward Long in *The History of Jamaica* (1714), searched for a scientific and anthropological rationale, prefiguring

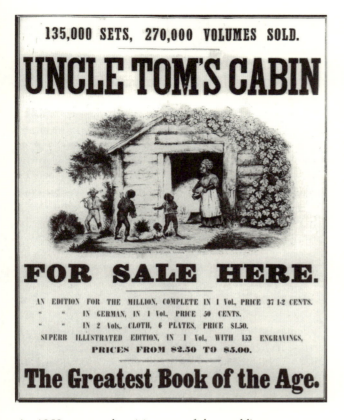

An 1859 poster advertising one of the world's great bestsellers, Uncle Tom's Cabin *by Harriet Beecher Stowe, first published in 1852. Little read today, the book was credited with a major role in the antislavery movement because of its popularization of the harsh and inhumane treatment of slaves in the American South.*

the nineteenth-century pseudoscientific justifications perpetrated by Josiah Nott and others.

The almost continuous denials of the relationship between blackness and slavery in the antislavery literature indicate the degree to which these ideas were associated. Many writers insisted that it was slavery, not skin pigmentation, that was responsible for the African's condition. The colonial claim, prior to the American Revolution, that all men were created equal merely extended the argument in writings such as James Otis's *The Rights of the British Colonies Asserted and Proved* (1764) and David Cooper's *A Serious Address to the Rulers of America* (1773), while a mischievous footnote to John Trumbull's *M'Fingal* (1775), pondering the nature of liberty, insists that the 13 stripes on the new American flag are to be associated with neither prison bars nor the stripes on the backs of slaves. Trumbull, like other American satirists such as Artemus Ward and David Ross Locke, wrote against slavery, but the author of the most famous antislavery novel, *Uncle Tom's Cabin,* was able to draw the "facts" of the book from the vast quantity of slave literature circulating at the time in narratives, histories, tracts, and pamphlets.

Many slave narratives used their undoubted sensationalist appeal—gruesome tales of cruelty, beatings, and lynchings—to turn public opinion against slavery. Because it was illegal to teach a slave to read or write, many of the narratives were transcribed or indeed written by white abolitionist editors, as was Harriet Ann Jacob's *Incidents in the Life of a Slave Girl* (1861). Others were written by African Americans themselves, the most famous being the narratives, essays, and works of Frederick Douglass, the escaped slave and activist who established the antislavery newspaper, the *North Star.* Douglass's *Narrative of the Life of Frederick Douglass* (1845), besides relating the story of his escape to freedom, finds common ground with other period literature through its essentially questioning (as Emerson and Thoreau did) what it is that separates the human being from the animal and in what forms, therefore, does human freedom exist.

For Ralph Waldo Emerson, the question was esoteric. Henry David Thoreau was involved with the antislavery movement, and he did take a political and moral stand. He delivered speeches, such as his "Slavery in Massachusetts" speech in 1854, and, profoundly stirred by his meeting with John Brown at Emerson's home in 1857, three lectures: "A Plea for Captain John Brown," "The Last Days of John Brown," and "After the Death of John Brown." For Douglass, questions of human freedom were not abstract but vital. His capacity to "think himself free" empowered his emancipation.

The African American voice on slavery in literature, however, was at best marginalized and at worst silent. It was an oppressive silence, broken only sporadically during the centuries of slavery and then by slaves like the poet, Phillis Wheatley (c. 1755–1784), who had been taught by her "owners" to read and write and did not, in any direct sense, question her servitude, regarding it as the price paid for bringing her to God. In the period following emancipation, recuperation began. Charles Waddell Chesnutt wrote *The Conjure Woman* (1899), a series of dialect stories about slavery told by an African American gardener to his Northern employers that denied the plantation's romanticism and slavery's glorification and emphasized the divisions between black and white. The poet Paul Lawrence Dunbar blended the use of African American dialect and refrains with a rich mixture of pathos and humor in his collected poems, *Lyrics of Lowly Life* (1896). There were others, but it was with the age of the Harlem Renaissance and writers such as Jean Toomer (who published *Cane* in 1924), the poets Langston Hughes and Countee Cullen, and the novelist Zora Neale Hurston that writers began to rid literature of the connotations of slavery.

The Harlem Renaissance, fueled by the interest in jazz, was not a school and the aims of its writers differed, but a popular term at the time described these self-assertive and racially conscious African Americans as the "new Negro." The term marked the shift of the black intellectuals from the agrarian South to the urban North, and a movement from the world of Booker T. Washington to that of W. E. B. DuBois. These writers created characters and perspectives that considered African Americans as people; as subjects in their own literature rather than as the objects of other peoples' literature, which their depiction as the passive Uncle Tom in *Uncle Tom's Cabin* or as the singing and dancing caricatures of the minstrel shows had imagined them to be.

The writers of the Harlem Renaissance did not, on the whole, deal directly with stories of slavery. It exists in their texts as a brooding and inevitable presence—in the laconic question in Countee Cullen's poem of the same name, "What is Africa to me?" or in the attitudes and actions of Janie and her grandmother, who was born into slavery, in Hurston's *Their Eyes Were Watching God* (1937). Janie is bullied into marrying a staid and much older man because that will keep her "safe" from the atrocities common to her grandmother's experience. Later works like Richard Wright's *Native Son* (1940), Ralph Waldo Ellison's *Invisible Man* (1952), and the poetry of Gwendolyn Brooks confront the social and psychological problems inflicted by the racism, bigotry, and stereotyping that was the legacy of slavery.

It has been the present generation of writers who have confronted the silence of the past by remembering the lives of the people whose existence as slaves meant that their stories could not be told. On a popular level, Alex Palmer Haley wrote *Roots: The Saga of an American Family* (1975), which traced his own slavery background back to Africa. The stunning television series that followed demonstrated to people throughout the world what it might mean for generations to come to lose country, home, language, freedom, even one's name. To be, in short, enslaved. Toni Morrison's *Beloved* (1987) similarly explores the nature of possession and freedom through the generations. Beloved, the child she killed rather than allow her to be taken into slavery, returns to Sethe. The return brings little joy as Beloved takes possession, holding Sethe from life as her would-be lover, Paul D., is locked from life by the memory of slavery's atrocities. Ultimately, it is the black community itself that is empowered to free Sethe, and ultimately, too, it is among this community that depictions of slavery in literature have found their finest form.

—*Jan Pilditch*

LIVERPOOL AND THE SLAVE TRADE

iverpool, England, was a major slaving port, and its ships and merchants dominated the transatlantic slave trade from the mid- to late-eighteenth century. The town and its inhabitants derived great civic and personal wealth from the trade, which laid the foundations for the port's future growth.

Liverpool is situated on England's northwest coast at the mouth of the River Mersey. Originally only a small fishing village, by 1700 its ships were trading along the English coast, to Ireland and Europe, and increasingly to the Americas, including trade in white indentured labor.

The first Liverpool vessel to enter the slave trade, following the curtailment of the Royal African Company's monopoly in 1698, was *The Blessing,* which sailed for West Africa in August 1700. In the following years, growth of the trade was slow but solid. By the 1730s, about 15 ships a year were leaving for Africa, and the numbers grew to about 50 a year in the 1750s and to just over 100 in the early 1770s. Numbers declined during the American Revolution (1775–1783) but rose to a new peak of 120–130 ships annually in the two decades preceding the abolition of the slave trade in 1807. Probably three-quarters of all European slaving ships in the last two decades of the eighteenth century left from Liverpool, and overall, Liverpool ships transported half of the 3 million Africans carried across the Atlantic by British slavers.

The precise reasons for Liverpool's dominance of the trade are still debated by historians. Some suggest that Liverpool merchants were being pushed out of other Atlantic trades, like sugar and tobacco; others claim that the town's merchants were more enterprising than merchants elsewhere. A significant factor was the port's position as there was ready access via a network of rivers and canals to the goods traded for slaves in Africa—textiles from Lancashire and Yorkshire, copper and brass from Staffordshire and Cheshire, and guns from Birmingham.

Although Liverpool merchants engaged in many other trades and commodities, involvement in the slave trade was pervasive as nearly all the principal merchants and citizens of Liverpool, including many of its mayors, were involved. Several of the town's members of Parliament invested in the trade and spoke strongly in its favor in Parliament. Generations of families like the Tarletons, Earles, and Cunliffes organized slaving, and many were related by marriage. Some merchants like William Davenport organized the trade for others; during a career of over 40 years, he was involved in some 120 slaving voyages. Another prominent slave trader, Thomas Leyland, was three times mayor of Liverpool and founder of one of the town's major banks. When he died in 1827, he left over £736,000.

It would be wrong to attribute all of Liverpool's success to the slave trade, but it was undoubtedly the backbone of the town's prosperity. David Richardson (1994) suggests that slaving and related trades may have occupied one-third and possibly one-half of Liverpool's shipping activity in the period 1750–1807. The wealth acquired by the town was substantial, and the stimulus given to trading and industrial development throughout northwestern England and the Midlands was of crucial importance.

The last British slaver, *Kitty's Amelia,* left Liverpool under Capt. Hugh Crow in July 1807. There is no evidence that Liverpool traders engaged in the illegal trade, though they may have supplied goods for others and as late as 1860, a U.S. ship, *Nightingale,* which had been refitted in the port, was arrested for slaving.

However, even after abolition Liverpool continued to develop the trading connections that had been established by the slave trade. During the early-nineteenth century, Liverpool merchants used their contacts in West Africa to build up the palm oil trade, and many traders, like Sir John Tobin, who made a fortune in this new commodity had begun their careers as slave traders. More important, slave-produced cotton from the Southern states of the United States became the port's largest single commodity, and when the question of slavery came to crisis point in the United States, the long-standing connection ensured significant support for the Confederacy in the port. Several Confederate ships, including blockade runners and raiders, like the famous *Alabama,* were built on the Mersey.

Even today the influence of the slave trade is still present in Liverpool. It is reflected in some of the buildings and street names, and a gallery devoted to transatlantic slavery opened in the city's maritime museum in 1994.

—*Anthony Tibbles*

For Further Reading
Anstey, Roger, and P. E. Hair. 1976. *Liverpool: The African Slave Trade and Abolition.* Liverpool: Historic Society of Lancashire and Cheshire; Richardson, David. 1994. "Liverpool and the English Slave Trade." In *Transatlantic Slavery: Against Human Dignity.* Ed. Anthony Tibbles. London: HMSO; Williams, G. 1897. *History of the Liverpool Privateers and Letters of Marque with an Account of the Liverpool Slave Trade.* London: Heinemann.

LOCKE, DAVID ROSS
(1833–1888)

David Ross Locke was born in New York State and spent his working life as a free-lance printer and journalist, mainly in Ohio. During the U.S. Civil War he invented his famous pseudonym, "Petrolium V. Nasby, late pastor uv the Church uv the New Dispensation, Chaplain to his excellency the President, and p.m. at Confederate x roads, kentucky." The character he assumed was that of a dissolute and illiterate country preacher whose fervent support of any cause, but especially that of slavery, satirized that cause and brought it into disrepute.

Nasby's support took the form of a long series of misspelled letters and ludicrous arguments, after the manner of Artemus Ward or Seba Smith's Major Jack Downing letters. Although, it must be admitted that Locke's Petrolium V. Nasby is the most conniving, rationalizing, and generally appalling of all the writers of misspelled letters, and given that it is the satirist's duty to ridicule the vice and folly of humanity, it is perhaps no accident that this epitome of all cracker-barrel philosophers should emerge in the course of the misery that was the U.S. Civil War. The first Petrolium V. Nasby letter appeared in the Findlay, Ohio, *Jeffersonian* on March 21, 1861.

The misspelled letters made their point via a series of puns, ludicrous spelling, outrageous grammar, incongruous juxtaposition, and anticlimax. Thus, Petrolium V. Nasby, in asserting the superiority of his lineage, wrote: "My politiks hez ever bin Dimocratic, and I may say, without egotism, I hey bin a yooseful member uv that party. I voted for Jackson seven times, and for every succeedin Dimocratic candidate ez many times as possible." Or, despite his enthusiasm for the Confederate cause, Nasby is unable to fight. On reading in the newspaper that the government had instituted a draft, Nasby wrote on August 6, 1862: "I know not wat uthers may do, but ez for me, I can't go. . . . My teeth is all unsound, my palit aint eggsackly rite, and I hev hed bronkeetis 31 yeres last Joon. At present I hev a koff, the paroxisms uv wich is friteful to behold."

This appalling human frame embodies a collection of equally appalling values, supported by spurious appeals to God and nature. He reacts to an election occurring after the Fourteenth Amendment to the Constitution had been passed by rigging it. Nasby drags voters from jails and poorhouses: "One enthusiastic Dimekrat, who cost us $5, hed to be carried to the polls. He hed commenced early at one uv the groseries, and hed succumbed afore voting." The way in which misspelling reinforced the satire is evident in the spelling of Dimekrat. Elsewhere, Locke spelled the word "dimocrat," but here the issue of bribery is paramount—so that the voting rights of African Americans could be rendered worthless by the "liberty-lovin freemen uv Ohio."

If Harriet Beecher Stowe was the writer Lincoln credited with starting the Civil War, then David Ross Locke was the writer Lincoln credited with helping him to win it. He is said to have read the latest Nasby letter to his cabinet for comic relief before outlining the Emancipation Proclamation. *The Nasby Papers* were published in 1864, the first of many collections, and a political novel, *The Demagogue,* was published in 1891.

—*Jan Pilditch*

LOCKE, JOHN
(1632–1704)

*J*ohn Locke was an Englishman of many talents whose primary interest was practicing medicine. He performed successful operations when surgery was little short of butchery, and although Locke would probably have been happy spending his life as a physician, he was urged to write down his thoughts on politics and philosophy.

Locke is noted today, not for practicing medicine, but for his philosophical treatises. His "Thoughts on Education" is a primer for training educators, and his *Essay Concerning Human Understanding* is a seminal work in philosophy. Locke's *Second Treatise of Government* is, perhaps, the most important work in modern political philosophy and has been called the founding document of liberal political theory. It is in this work that we find Locke's most systematic treatment of slavery.

Locke's main argument in the *Second Treatise* may be stated briefly. Human beings originated in a state of nature, a condition where no duly constituted governmental authority existed. In that state of nature, individuals possessed natural rights to life, liberty, and property, but the absence of duly constituted authority made enjoyment of those rights uncertain. For this reason people united, forming a social contract. The social contract created a government, the sole purpose of which was to protect natural rights. Since all people are by nature free and equal, no one has a natural or God-given right to rule another. Governmental authority then, comes only from the consent of the governed. Whenever a government ceases to protect natural rights, the people are justified in altering or abolishing it and instituting another in its place. These are the central tenets of classical liberalism.

Chapter 4, "Of Slavery," is one of the shortest chapters of the *Second Treatise,* and Locke began it by distinguishing between freedom in the state of nature and freedom in civil society. In the state of nature, a person is free to do as he or she wishes within nature's law. This tenet teaches those who heed it "that no one should harm another in his life, health, liberty, or possessions." Nor should there be any subordination of one to another. Liberty in a civil society involves having standard rules to live by that all in society are equally obligated to obey. The citizen is free to make choices only when the law is silent, but no citizen should be subject to the inconstant, uncertain, or arbitrary will of anyone except the duly constituted authorities.

The right to self-preservation, or self-defense, is a natural right. It is not forfeited when citizens enter civil society but is, in fact, inalienable. It cannot legitimately be sold, bartered, or surrendered, and because the right to life is inalienable, slavery is generally unjust. To be a slave is to become "subject to the inconstant, uncertain, unknown, arbitrary will of another," and persons subject to such a will are by definition unable to exercise their right to self-preservation. Since one cannot voluntarily surrender the right to self-preservation, one cannot voluntarily become a slave.

Locke did not mean, however, that slavery is unjust under all circumstances. He believed a person might forfeit his or her life by committing an act that warranted death and that in the state of nature, the person to whom this right is forfeited may choose to spare the individual's life and make the person a slave instead. The slave may at any time thereafter choose death over slavery by resisting the master's will. Within civil society, when the government is the arbiter of personal disputes, the transgressor's life is forfeited to the government.

The idea that someone cannot become a slave by contract but may become one by committing a crime initially seems contradictory since committing a crime is ordinarily a voluntary act. But if one could not forfeit one's freedom by committing a crime, the innocent would be defenseless in both the state of nature and civil society. And there would be no reason for people in the state of nature to form a social contract to create a government.

Locke also recognized what might be termed "natural slavery." In Chapter 6 of the *Second Treatise,* "Of Paternal Power," Locke argued that parents have a right to rule their children while they are infants. This authority is justified because children are born "without knowledge or understanding" and are unable to discern what is good for themselves. Parental power should direct children to their proper interests until they can make such judgments for themselves. In the ordinary course of nature, occasionally some people do not come "to such a degree of reason that [they] might be supposed capable of knowing the law and so living within the rules of it." These persons can never become free but must remain under their parents' guidance, though parents or guardians do not have despotic power over these "natural slaves." Parents may not take their lives or mistreat them but must seek to procure their good.

Locke's *Second Treatise* was written three centuries ago, but its teaching is as pertinent today as it was in the 1680s. Locke argued decisively against enslaving the innocent and for a humane respect of individuals, on the part of both government and fellow citizens. His teaching provided the theoretical justification for the resistance of citizens to tyrants and of slaves to masters.

In 1790, a century after the publication of Locke's *Second Treatise*, only 3 nations—England, France, and the United States—could claim to be liberal democracies, or governments in which individual rights were respected and protected. Yet even those nations tolerated slavery within their borders or promoted it elsewhere. By 1990, the number of liberal democracies had risen to more than 60, none of which tolerated or promoted slavery. In the meantime, authoritarian and totalitarian rivals to liberal democracy had proved themselves to be dismal failures.

—*Wesley Phelan*

For Further Reading
Johnson, Merwyn S. 1978. *Locke on Freedom: An Incisive Study of the Thought of John Locke.* Austin, TX: Best Print; Schouls, Peter A. 1992. *Reasoned Freedom: John Locke and Enlightenment.* Ithaca, NY: Cornell University Press; Strauss, Leo, and Joseph Cropsey, eds. 1981. *History of Political Philosophy.* Chicago: University of Chicago Press; Welchman, Jennifer. 1995. "Locke on Slavery and Inalienable Rights." *Canadian Journal of Philosophy* 25 (1): 67–83.

LOPEZ, NARCISO
(1798–1851)

Narciso Lopez, a native of Venezuela who had married into a Cuban planter family, became involved with Cuban events in 1848. In that pivotal year, which saw the U.S. acquisition of the vast Southwest from Mexico, there also was great enthusiasm throughout the United States for the was annexation of Cuba—one of Spain's last colonial possessions in the Western Hemisphere—and Cuban revolutionaries issued a proclamation stating that the island's future lay with the rising nation to the north. Eager to promote trade with the United States, and determined to thwart Spanish efforts to abolish slavery, Cuban annexationists contended that admission to the Union would see the island's "farms and slaves . . . double their value" (Brown, 1980).

Led by Gen. Narciso Lopez, these patriots planned a revolt for June 29. Once a loyal Spanish soldier, Lopez had fought against the Latin American revolutionary Simón Bolívar and had served in the First Carlist War, a Spanish civil war in the 1830s fought over problems of succession. Although he had subsequently held several administrative posts in Spain and Cuba, he was apparently driven to support the island's anti-Spanish faction by serious financial reverses.

Ironically, Lopez and his followers were betrayed by the U.S. government, which, in the process of negotiating the purchase of the island, exposed the plot to Spanish authorities. Lopez barely escaped capture, fled to New York, and with the support of Cuban exiles and U.S. expansionists, raised a private army to liberate Cuba in 1849. However, President Zachary Taylor's strong stand against filibustering, coupled with legal and military precautions taken by federal officials, effectively thwarted Lopez's invasion plans.

When efforts to organize a second expedition were foiled by federal authorities, Lopez transformed his base of operations from New York to New Orleans. Strongly proslavery, Lopez was well known in Cuba for harsh sentences against free blacks while serving as president of a military commission in the early 1840s. Although Lopez failed to persuade prominent Southerners like Robert E. Lee and Jefferson Davis to lead a new expedition, he received substantial support from Governor John A. Quitman of Mississippi, who believed that the annexation of Cuba as a slave state would balance the recent admission of California to the Union as a free state.

"Cuba fever" spread rapidly through the South, and by spring 1850, Lopez had assembled an invasion force of nearly 600 men. Sailing from New Orleans, he landed on Cuba's northern coast on May 19 and captured the Spanish garrison at Cardenas. The local populace failed to rise, and Spanish reinforcements forced Lopez's "liberators" to reembark hastily and sail for Key West. Closely pursued by a Spanish warship, the filibusters scattered upon reaching Key West, narrowly avoiding arrest by local federal officials.

Lopez and 16 followers, including Quitman, were subsequently indicted by a federal grand jury for violating the Neutrality Law of 1818, which banned private military expeditions from U.S. soil against foreign nations. Released after three hung juries compromised the government's case, Lopez promptly organized a fourth expedition. Ignoring a proclamation by President Millard Fillmore, Lopez sailed for Cuba from New Orleans on August 3, 1851.

Lopez's 400 filibusters landed at Bahía Honda on the northwestern coast on August 11 and marched inland only to discover, as before, that Cuban support failed to materialize. Discipline soon fell apart, and Lopez's force was overwhelmed by Spanish troops. Col. William L. Crittenden of Kentucky and over 50 others were shot in Havana on August 16, and over 162 others were sent to Spain in chains. Hunted down by Spanish troops, Lopez himself was captured and publicly garroted in Havana on September 1.

The news of Crittenden's fate, which reached New Orleans prior to Lopez's capture, sparked anti-Spanish riots that wrecked the Spanish consulate in that city. However, the U.S. government was unwilling to protest Spain's harsh measures against what was regarded as an illegal expedition. Spain subsequently released all surviving prisoners after the U.S. Congress voted a $25,000 indemnity for the damage in New Orleans.

For many Cubans and Americans, Narciso Lopez died a martyr for liberty. However, as one historian contends, he was in reality "an agent of annexation" (May, 1973). Many of Lopez's followers subsequently participated in Quitman's abortive filibuster expedition against Cuba in 1855 and/or fought under William Walker in Central America in 1855–1860.

—*James M. Prichard*

See also
Filibusters; Quitman, John; Walker, William
For Further Reading
Brown, Charles H. 1980. *Agents of Manifest Destiny: The Lives and Times of the Filibusters.* Chapel Hill: University of North Carolina Press; May, Robert E. 1973. *The Southern Dream of a Caribbean Empire, 1854–1861.* Baton Rouge: Louisiana State University Press; Thomas, Hugh. 1971. *Cuba: The Pursuit of Freedom.* New York: Harper and Row.

LOUVERTURE, TOUSSAINT (1743–1803)

A former slave who emerged as the dominant figure in the Haitian Revolution, Toussaint Louverture is arguably the most important black leader in the history of the Americas. Even though he did not live to see an independent Haiti, Louverture (as he became known after the revolution) made independence possible. He became a formidable symbol of black power, dignity, and autonomy in the Americas, both for those who aspired to and for those who abhorred this possibility.

Tradition reports that Toussaint's father was a West

Toussaint Louverture

African Arada chief, but the future general and governor was very much a product of French colonial society. Born a slave in 1743 on the Bréda sugar estate outside of Saint Domingue's most dynamic city, Cap Français, Toussaint was not a field hand but a skilled worker, perhaps a coachman. By 1779, Toussaint de Bréda, as he was known before the revolution, was a freeman growing coffee on rented land with a leased team of about 12 slaves. After 30 years as a slave, he was taught to read and write by an ex-priest once he became free. A devout Catholic who outlawed voodoo in his armies, Toussaint was nevertheless a skilled folk healer, and his first known position in rebel slave armies was that of doctor.

There is no evidence of his participation in the early events of the slave uprising that began in the Cap Français hinterland on August 22, 1791. The slaves who planned that revolt were men much like Toussaint: skilled, born in the colony, and respected figures on their plantations. However, he was no longer a slave and is said to have saved the lives of the Bréda plantation manager and his family early in the revolt. The first record of his presence among the rebels is on December 4, 1791, in negotiations between white and black leaders.

The white colonists rejected the demands of the slave generals Jean-François and Biassou, under whom Toussaint served, and the revolt spread to other regions of the colony, where whites and free mulattoes were already fighting about how to interpret civil reforms decreed by the Paris revolutionaries. Toussaint became Biassou's chief lieutenant, and in 1793, they allied with the Spanish in Santo Domingo on the eastern side of the island.

Fighting under the banner of counterrevolution, Saint Domingue's slaves forced French revolutionary commissioners to abolish slavery in September 1793 in order to save the colony. In 1794, after Paris ratified this act, Toussaint, now calling himself Toussaint Louverture, changed sides and quickly became the leading black general under the French tricolor. He achieved notable success against his former comrades until the Treaty of Bayle (1795) between France and Spain.

By 1796, Louverture was a dominant figure in Saint Domingue. Revolutionary wars in Europe kept French armies out of the colony, and although a French-educated mixed-race elite aspired to colonial leadership, black generals confined mulatto control to the colony's southern peninsula. From 1796 to 1801, Louverture, using his army and his influence with ex-slaves, who composed 90 percent of Saint Domingue's population, achieved an unprecedented autonomy from metropolitan authorities. Acting variously as loyal protégé, virtuous republican, and powerful general, Toussaint engineered the return to France of Gen. Étienne Laveaux (1796), revolutionary commissioner Léger Félicité Sonthonax (1797), and Gen. Gabriel-Marie Hédouville (1798). In 1800, Toussaint arrested a French agent by the name of Roume as an enemy of the revolution.

In 1798, without authorization from French authorities, Toussaint negotiated with the British, who had invaded the colony in 1793, and by the end of the year, he had concluded a secret treaty providing for withdrawal of British troops, commerce with Jamaica, and the rehabilitation of pro-British colonists. Again without French permission, Toussaint entered into negotiations with the United States and signed a commercial agreement with that country in 1799.

This external support allowed him to end years of rivalry with his mulatto counterpart André Rigaud, who controlled Saint Domingue's southern peninsula. In the bloody "war of the south," which began in July 1799, Louverture and his lieutenant Jean-Jacques Dessalines pitted more than 45,000 soldiers against Rigaud's 15,000 troops. In August 1800, black troops took the mulatto capital of Les Cayes. By the end of the year, Louverture had conquered Spanish Santo Domingo, where slavery was still legal. He had launched this campaign despite explicit directions from Paris to treat the Spanish as allies.

In 1801, Toussaint consolidated his position as Saint Domingue's ruler with a new colonial constitution, which named him governor general for life, and he adopted a policy of forced plantation labor like that envisioned by white and mulatto leaders. After a decade of civil war, a black and mulatto elite replaced most white landowners, but the abolition of slavery devastated Saint Domingue's sugar and coffee exports. After 1801, Toussaint's army revived the plantation sector, hoping to generate commercial revenues for the regime.

For all his measures to ensure Saint Domingue's autonomy, Toussaint maintained a strong public attachment to French culture. His entourage included three white priests and several white advisers. He was known to ridicule blacks he considered ill-educated when they requested political or judicial posts, and his own children were schooled in France.

This fledgling cultural policy reflected Toussaint's colonial background, but it also illustrates his realization that he could not afford to antagonize the French. In a region where political and economic order was built on black slavery, Saint Domingue's black leader needed viable plantations to buy military supplies. As long as the French Republic opposed slavery, submission to France was an essential component of Saint Domingue's freedom.

But Bonaparte would not allow France's most valuable possession to go unexploited for long. In early 1802, a French military expedition arrived in Saint Domingue, and within six weeks, its commanding general Charles-Victor-Emmanuel Leclerc, Bonaparte's brother-in-law, had declared Louverture an outlaw. In June, after new French laws had reestablished slavery and the slave trade in Saint Domingue, the black ex-general was arrested for conspiracy and deported to France. In April 1803 he died in his cell at Fort Joux in the Alps.

—*John D. Garrigus*

See also
Dessalines, Jean-Jacques; Haitian Revolution; Rigaud, André

For Further Reading
Pluchon, Pierre. 1989. *Toussaint Louverture: Un révolutionnaire noir d'Ancien Régime*. Paris: Fayard.

LOVEJOY, ELIJAH P.
(1802–1837)

Abolitionist, antislavery activist and advocate, newspaper editor and publisher, Elijah P. Lovejoy earned a reputation as an uncompromising opponent of slavery who sacrificed his life to defend his conviction. He spent his life mobilizing resources—material, physical, and intellectual—to further the antislavery cause.

Lovejoy was born in Albion, Maine, on November 9, 1802. His parents, the Reverend Daniel Lovejoy and Elizabeth (Pattie) Lovejoy, were both of New England origin. A brilliant young man, Lovejoy attended Waterville (now Colby) College and graduated with honors in 1826. He taught school for about a year and then moved to St. Louis, Missouri, and continued teaching. Perhaps influenced by his father, young Lovejoy entered the ministry. He attended the Theological Seminary at Princeton and was licensed to preach in 1833 by the Philadelphia Presbyterian Church. He returned to St. Louis that same year, this time driven by a deep sense of mission and determined to contribute to the antislavery cause.

In November 1833, he began publishing and editing the *St. Louis Observer,* a Presbyterian weekly, and fired by an inner determination and a revulsion against slavery, he transformed the paper into a vocal antislavery organ. Early in his antislavery crusade, Lovejoy came under the influence of Garrisonian moral-suasionist ideology. Followers of the New England abolitionist William Lloyd Garrison embraced moral suasion and nonviolence and believed strongly that the most viable and effective weapon against slavery was the force of moral condemnation and exposition. Lovejoy accepted the creed and became a radical pacifist who rejected violence but persistently criticized and exposed slavery's evils. Such persistence, Lovejoy and other nonviolent abolitionists felt, would eventually influence public opinion against slavery, bringing down the institution in the process. Consequently, though his editorials were harsh and often fiery, Lovejoy remained a pacifist at heart.

But St. Louis proved intolerant of his antislavery activities, and opposition to Lovejoy developed, becoming increasingly militant and life-threatening. He was confronted with the choice of either moderating his criticisms or leaving the city completely. He chose the latter. He strongly believed in his constitutionally given right to protest and criticize slavery and vowed not to "give ground a single inch." His unpopularity deepened with his coverage of the public roasting of a St. Louis mulatto sailor in May 5, 1836, for killing a white deputy. The perpetrators were never punished. Lovejoy reported the incident in his paper, bitterly de-nouncing the perpetrators and the judge who was lenient on them. Enraged by Lovejoy's coverage, public sentiment against him turned violent, and fearing for his life and his family, his antislavery friends advised Lovejoy to leave the city. He relocated across the Mississippi River in Alton, Illinois, home to many antislavery New Englanders, but even there Lovejoy was not completely safe. An antiabolitionist mob from St. Louis followed him to Alton and destroyed his press as it stood on the dock.

Altonians initially welcomed Lovejoy and expressed regret over the destruction of his press, pledging to assist him in replacing it. They also made clear their discomfort with abolitionism, and Lovejoy allegedly promised to restrict the content of his newspaper to religious matters. Illinois was not quite an ideal haven for abolitionists. The state legislature recognized the constitutional right of Southerners to maintain slavery and had condemned abolition. Nevertheless, abolitionist sentiments were rising in the state, and Lovejoy felt at ease, believing that he had finally found a safe place to propagate antislavery ideas. He replaced his press, thanks to the generosity of antislavery friends in Ohio.

The *Alton Observer,* like its predecessor, assumed the character of a staunch opponent of slavery, and soon the tone of his writings and his activities became worrisome to Altonians. Lovejoy criticized and condemned slavery and gave wide publicity to antislavery activities, both local and distant. He supported abolitionists and began to advocate forming an abolitionist society in Alton. On July 4, 1837, the paper called for an antislavery meeting in Alton to consider establishing a state branch of the American Anti-Slavery Society. Opposition to his activities mounted, but after several deliberations, the society was finally formed on October 26.

That event brought the wrath of Altonians down on Lovejoy, and people began publicly discussing the possibility of violence to stop him. His press was destroyed by mobs three times, and each time a replacement arrived from Ohio. When the third press was destroyed, Lovejoy, with the concurrence of Alton's mayor, decided to arm himself in order to protect his family and press against further attacks. He thus abandoned pacifism, believing that self-defense was justified in such a situation of helplessness and vulnerability. Unfortunately, the townspeople were just as determined to end his editorial career permanently.

His fourth press arrived from Ohio, and just as in the past, a mob gathered to destroy it. Lovejoy stood his ground, beside a group of armed supporters, in defense of his new press. Tension mounted, and in the ensuing confrontation, shots were fired. Lovejoy was hit and fatally injured. He died on the spot, thus becoming a martyr of the antislavery cause—in fact, the

American Anti-Slavery Society proclaimed him the "first martyr of American liberty." Fellow pacifists bemoaned Lovejoy's decision to defend himself and seemed to blame him for his death.

His death strengthened the abolitionist movement. Angry meetings were held throughout the country to denounce his killing, and thousands of men and women were drawn to the antislavery cause. His death also reduced Northern antagonism to abolition, giving abolitionists a freer and more permissive atmosphere in which to meet, speak, publish, and agitate. Lovejoy's devotion to antislavery and the sacrifice of his life for the cause inspired generations of abolitionists, black and white. Perhaps the most outstanding was John Brown, who, at a memorial meeting in Ohio, vowed to dedicate his own life to the destruction of slavery.

—*Tunde Adeleke*

For Further Reading
Mabee, Carlton. 1970. *Black Freedom: The Nonviolent Abolitionists from 1830 through the Civil War.* London: Macmillan; Richards, Leonard L. 1975. *Gentlemen of Property and Standing: Anti-Abolition Mobs in Jacksonian America.* New York: Oxford University Press.

LUGARD, FREDERICK JOHN DEALTRY (1858–1945)

Frederick John Dealtry Lugard was a soldier, colonial administrator, forceful opponent of the African slave trade, founder of British Nigeria, and an author who defined the policy of indirect rule. Escaping an unhappy love affair by losing himself in East Africa in 1888, Lugard linked himself to the African Lakes Company to justify his wanderlust. Encountering Arab slave raiders, he risked his life in battle against them. After learning about the customs and laws governing indigenous slavery, he differentiated between local slavery and long-distance trade. A racist, Lugard believed most indigenous slaves were contented with their lot. As agent of the Imperial British East Africa Company in Uganda, he refused to disturb the slave system and only freed the Swahili, who had recently come under the protection of the British Crown as subjects of the sultan of Zanzibar.

Returning to England in 1892, he wrote a two-volume account of his African exploits, *The Rise of Our East African Empire,* and lobbied for both British annexation of East Africa and a policy to end slavery gradually by refusing to recognize the legal status of a slave in British colonies. He urged this tactic as the best way to end slavery without disrupting the local economy and social relationships. Modeled on a similar policy in India, the policy remained Lugard's core conviction throughout his long career.

In West Africa, Lugard served the Royal Niger Company in claiming territory for the British Empire. In 1900 he became high commissioner of northern Nigeria; Lugard ended slave raiding and used local law and custom to abolish slavery over time. He extended *murgu,* the practice of allowing slaves to buy their freedom, so that a master was required to set a purchase price, and he gave courts the right to issue decrees recognizing manumission. Additionally, he declared all children born after March 31, 1901, to be free. The reform worked, but slaves proved Lugard's assumptions about their contentment wrong when they escaped from their masters in large numbers.

As governor general of northern Nigeria, Lugard manipulated the tax system to make free labor more attractive and insisted that forced labor not replace slavery. Although other colonial powers employed forced labor to build roads and railways, Lugard insisted that wage labor was Nigeria's only option.

As an elder statesman and a peer, Lugard served on the League of Nations' temporary committee on slavery and produced that group's first slavery convention. Lugard studied slavery in Ethiopia and became an informal adviser to Haile Selassie, and working with the international Anti-Slavery Society, Lugard spoke often and wrote many articles against slavery. He also served from 1925 to 1941 as a member of the International Labour Organization's Committee of Experts on Native Labor. Eventually, Lugard outgrew his racist ideas and enjoyed the company of young Nigerians who visited him in retirement to discuss the future of their country in "liberal" terms.

—*Dennis J. Mitchell*

See also
League of Nations
For Further Reading
Lugard, Frederick D. 1968. *The Rise of Our East African Empire.* London: Frank Cass; Miers, Suzanne, and Richard Roberts, eds. 1988. *The End of Slavery.* Madison: University of Wisconsin Press; Perham, Margery F. 1956. *Lugard.* London: Collins.

LYCURGUS

Lycurgus was credited with creating all of the institutions of the Greek city-state of Sparta, one of the world's first slave societies, at some unverifiable time before the seventh century B.C.

He was worshiped as a god in Sparta and was regarded as a god before he was praised as a legislator in popular legend. He is mentioned in Herodotus's *Histories* and Xenophon's *Constitution of Sparta* and *History of Greece*, but neither author was able to say when Lycurgus might have lived. Plutarch, who wrote *Lycurgus a Life*, admitted that it was impossible to confirm that Lycurgus was a historical ruler or was responsible for the actions that the Spartans attributed to him.

The name Lycurgus may belong to an influential archaic family, or Lycurgus may merely be a mythical figure regarded as the source of the basic elements of Spartan society and its long-established laws. Archaeology places most of these developments at a little before 600 B.C., but their origin is still uncertain.

Of the institutions that bear his name, the landed bondage of Helots is the most important in the context of slavery. These serfs belonged to the state, only the state could set them free, and they could not be sold. The purpose of these agricultural slave workers was to farm the lands that supported the Spartiates, free citizens who were raised in communes from the age of seven and dedicated to military duties. The Helots could not travel from their appointed areas and were bound to work for their masters, but they were not owned by any individual. The state could redeploy Helots to state projects or command them to serve in the army.

Lycurgus was said to have established a system of checks and balances in Sparta to ensure that all property, planning, and administration remained communal. The measures included two kings, a senate of 28 citizens over the age of 60, an assembly of all citizens over the age of 30, and five ephors, who were elected from among the citizens. The ephors kept watch over the implementation of decisions made by the legislative bodies and could combine to overrule the kings, if that was in the best interests of Sparta as a whole. Iron bars were substituted for coinage, so amassing personal wealth was impossible. All land, goods, and resources were held in common; all meals were shared in large mess halls.

The Lycurgan ideology attracted philosophers, but most Athenians and other non-Spartan Greeks regarded the system of Spartan communism as state slavery for citizens, artisans and Helots alike. They saw restrictions on personal action, marriage, family life, child rearing, and travel outside Sparta as being bound, a compulsory way of life that reduced everyone under the rule of the state to no better than slave status.

The purpose of the system was equitable distribution of all to all and the maintenance of a military elite to protect Sparta from unwanted outside influences. Visitors from other city-states were not welcomed, unless on diplomatic missions, for fear that ideas contrary to the strict laws of Lycurgus should cause unrest among the Spartans. Sparta had no slaves as commodities, but neither did it enjoy what the cradle of democracy considered to be freedom.

—*Lindy J. Rawling*

See also
Helots; Plato's *Laws*
For Further Reading
Burn, Andrew R. 1977. *The Pelican History of Greece*. London: Pelican; Finley, Moses I. 1984. *Politics in the Ancient World*. Cambridge: Cambridge University Press; Kirk, Geoffrey S. 1986. *The Nature of Greek Myths*. London: Pelican; Moore, J. M., ed. 1975. *Aristotle and Xenophon on Democracy and Oligarchy*. London: London University Press.

M

MADISON COUNTY SLAVE WAR

The 1859 Madison County, Kentucky, "slave war" resulted from a series of misunderstandings and prejudices that occurred in and around the small settlement of Berea, Kentucky. Encouraged by the abolitionist Cassius M. Clay's emancipation of his slaves in Kentucky, followers of Rev. John G. Fee, a noted abolitionist, settled in the Berea area in 1855 and established a school and church where the principles of racial equality were taught. Clay became disenchanted with the teachings of those at Berea and gave them little support after 1856, but Fee continued his efforts to attract recruits and to raise money for the colony.

In October 1859, Fee traveled throughout New England to garner support for a proposed college at Berea, and while in the North, he was invited to speak to Henry Ward Beecher's congregation at the Plymouth Congregational Church in Brooklyn. During his speech, Fee invoked the name of the abolitionist, John Brown. The Kentucky papers reported the incident in a sensational manner, and calls for Fee and his followers to be driven out of Kentucky, or to be arrested, were numerous.

Madison County citizens were outraged at Fee's words. On December 5, 1859, a group of influential residents met in the courthouse at Richmond, Kentucky, to discuss the Berea community. Among their resolutions was a pledge to stop Fee and his followers by "fair and proper means and measures." On December 23, 1859, 60 men rode to Berea to warn the inhabitants to leave the state within 10 days or be forced out. Kentucky governor Beriah Magoffin refused to send the militia to protect them.

Fear of mob violence prompted a group of 10 families, consisting of 36 people, to leave their homes, and 20 of them went to Cincinnati and free territory. Although feelings among many slaveowners ran high against Fee and the Berea community, some Madison County residents did not feel completely negative about the Bereans, as at least one-third of the students at the Berea school were from slaveholding families.

The threat of violence did not end with the exodus of some of the Berea residents. In March 1860, a group of 25 armed men rode into the community to find that John C. Hanson, one of the former residents, had returned to settle some business and to sell his sawmill. This time the proslavery people met resistance, and shots were exchanged. The infuriated mob returned to Richmond to get reinforcements, and the following day, a force of over 200 returned to Berea and destroyed Hanson's mill. Cannons were ordered from Lexington to aid in the attack. Hanson escaped capture and fled the state, and because of continued threats and violence, in April 1860, some 60 additional members of the Berea community left Kentucky for the free states.

Madison County experienced, on a smaller scale, some of the same difficulties that had occurred in Kansas and Nebraska just a few years earlier. The clash of antislavery forces with proslavery forces gave the citizens of Madison County a foretaste of what Kentucky and the nation would endure with the coming of the U.S. Civil War.

—*Ron D. Bryant*

For Further Reading
Dorris, Jonathan T. 1936. *Old Cane Springs*. Louisville, KY: Standard Printing; Ellis, William. 1985. *Madison County: 200 Years in Retrospect*. Richmond, KY: Madison County Historical Society.

MALI

The greatest of the West African kingdoms of antiquity, Mali acquired imperial dominance following the thirteenth-century disintegration of the ancient and medieval Kingdom of Ghana in the western Sahara. Mali's eclipse of that once-great Sudanic empire in wealth and grandeur created a hegemony unequaled in the world at the time. Extending from the Senegal and Gambia Rivers to present-day Guinea in the west, extending southward from Tadmekka in the Sahara to include Timbuktu and Gao, and reaching almost to the shores of Lake Chad in present-day Nigeria in the east, Mali's bureaucratic domain was preeminent. The words of the great wayfarer and ancient historian Ibn Khaldun attest to Mali's triumph: "The power of Mali became mighty. All the nations of the Sudan stood in awe of Mali, and the merchants of North Africa travelled to his country" (Davidson, 1991).

Two central turning points provided the impetus for Mali's ascension. First, Ghana's prowess succumbed to persistent military onslaughts and subsequent invasion by the North African Almoravids, who finally sounded the death knell with the destruction of Kumbi, the capital city, in 1076–1077 under the leadership of one Abu Bakr. Second, following Abu Bakr's death, the Almoravid stronghold itself rapidly disintegrated as a result of internecine struggles for power coupled with continued resistance on the part of the Soninke people as they attempted to reassert Ghanaian influence. In the chaos, lesser states challenged the Soninke and Almoravids alike for autonomy with the wealth in slaves, mineral deposits, other natural resources going to the victor.

The kingdoms of Songhai, Mandinka (Mali), and Takrur (the last in far western Sudan, near modern-day Senegal) were more prominent and militarily capable of defying the Soninke. All had Islamic influence dating back centuries, and this influence had, over time, provided them with a fairly strong, centralized religious and political foundation (from a Qur'anic perspective) during their respective periods of Sudanic dominance. Muslim regimes of these and earlier periods were involved in slavery, but Islamic jurisprudence mitigated some aspects of the trade through imposition of Qur'anic inscriptions aimed at providing guidelines for the slaves' maintenance, treatment, and subsequent freedom.

The ancient state of Kangaba (Mali), founded before A.D. 1000, was the basis for Mali's development. The Mandinka people quickly asserted their ascendancy by defeating Sumanguru, the king of the Sosso (a Soninke group), in 1235. A famous military strategist who ruled for 30 years, Sundiata Keita, began Mali's imperialistic phase when he became king of Mali in 1230. Sundiata founded a new progressive empire, and its authority throughout the Sudan was uncontested and legitimized Mali's hegemony from Takrur in the west to present-day Guinea in the south.

Mali's imperial ascension was important for the continuance of Sudanic slavery. The slave trade was common even before Mali's dominance, and Kumbi controlled one of the largest slave markets in West Africa. Weaker ethnic groups on the frontiers of present-day Guinea were a major source of slave captives. Merchants from North Africa made the long and arduous journey across the Sahara to buy Sudanese captives to sell as slaves to Arabs and Islamic countries as well as to Europe and the Far East.

Mali's expansive territory required a centrally organized governance, and Sundiata proved worthy of the challenge. Pivotal to the annexation of new lands was

the management of an extensive labor force capable of supplying the empire with the wealth it needed for self-maintenance. Preexisting slave markets were expanded, and the capital was moved to Niani, where "Slaves were of prime importance in . . . economic, military, administrative and political spheres" (Fage et al., 1975). Thus, the slave trade continued to be lucrative and thrived in precolonial history under Malian leadership. It is important to note that this indigenous slavery, which was so familiar to Africans, changed radically with the advent of the European demand for African captives.

Mali's prosperity was heightened by maintaining the trans-Saharan trade route and its aggregate networks linking Mali to North Africa and countries to the east. The assertion of control over gold, salt mines, diamonds, and copper production assured Mali of economic prosperity. Unlike its predecessor, the Mali empire also made rapid agricultural advancements, and central to that economic output was a continuity of the slave-trading markets that supplied the labor for systemic agrarian production. Mali's artisans in wood carving, jewelry making, and ornament production and the cloth and textile industry all helped lead the empire to material greatness.

But, it was under the superb leadership of Mansa Musa that Mali achieved the zenith of its glory, fame, and expansion beyond ancient Ghana. The ascension of Musa enabled Mali to enjoy a long and prosperous tenure. Having expanded the empire through diplomacy and statesmanship, he consolidated Mali with unprecedented statecraft. Musa also greatly encouraged Islamic growth and learning among all his subjects. The Muslim world trekked to Timbuktu and Jenné, then the seat of learning and scholarship in Africa and the Islamic world.

Musa's most notable diplomatic feat was his famous pilgrimage to Mecca, on which he took an estimated 100 camels carrying 300 pounds of gold dust each and over 60,000 Africans. It is reported that his generosity disrupted the gold standard of Cairo for over 12 years. Musa was so revered throughout the known world that "in 1375, the Majorcan cartographer Cresques shows the lord of Mali seated in majesty upon his throne, holding an orb and scepter, while the traders of all North Africa march sturdily towards his markets" (Clark, 1991). By the time of Musa's death in 1337, Mali had become one of the largest empires in the world and by far the richest that Africa has ever known.

—*Au'Ra Muhammad Abdullah Ilahi*

For Further Reading

Ajayi, J. F. A., and Michael Crowder. 1976. *History of West Africa*. London: Longman; Clark, Leon E. 1991. *Through African Eyes: The Past, the Road to Indepen-*

dence. New York: Apex Press; Davidson, Basil. 1991. *Africa in History*. New York: Macmillan; Fage, J. D., Roland Oliver, and Richard Gray. 1975. *The Cambridge History of Africa: From c. 1660 to c. 1790*. New York: Cambridge University Press.

MAMLUKS

The name Mamluk derives from the Arabic *mamlūk*, meaning "slave" (literally, "[one who is] owned"). The word gradually came to refer specifically to slaves or freedmen serving as soldiers, with the exception of blacks who were generally called *'abīd* (singular, *'abd*). Mamluk also refers to regimes ruling Egypt (and parts of North Africa and Palestine) from 1250 to 1798.

The first military slaves used extensively were Turkish cavalry brought to Baghdad by the Abbasid caliph al-Mu'tasim (833–842). They were a personally loyal force used to offset other elements in the army and administration. Later caliphs became increasingly dependent on mamluks, who eventually came to wield considerable power. Military slaves of non-Turkish background—Slavs, Greeks, Europeans, and Africans—were also employed, particularly in Spain, North Africa, and Egypt.

The Mamluk regimes originated in the Fatimid period (969–1171), although military slaves were used by their predecessors. The Fatimids depended heavily on mamluks, and by the end of their dynasty, the balance had shifted toward Qipchak Turk and Circassian levies. These slaves were purchased or captured as children, converted to Islam, raised communally in barracks, educated in the arts of war and administration, and trained to be unflinchingly loyal to their masters. These bonds of loyalty and service continued even after manumission (which typically occurred at adulthood). Living together in ethnically homogenous and segregated communities, they were a close-knit group and remained a "foreign" element unassimilated by Egyptian society; many did not even learn Arabic. The mamluk corps was maintained through continued acquisition of new youths, both privately and under state supervision.

When the succession of the Ayyubid sultanate in Cairo faltered, 'Izz al-Dīn Aybak (r. 1250–1257) took the throne, which initiated the Bahrī ("river") Mamluk period that lasted until 1390. These Mamluk sultans were essentially autocrats, but they relied on peer support, a military oligarchy controlling all governmental aspects. Qipchak became the court language. The most notable of these Mamluk sultans were Baybars "the crossbowman" (r. 1260–1277) and Qalā'ūn (r. 1279–1290). Baybars thwarted the Mongol advance at 'Ayn Jalūt in 1260 and subdued much of Palestine. He was succeeded briefly by two of his sons. Qalà'ūn founded a more durable dynasty, which finally defeated the Crusaders; extended Mamluk hegemony from Syria to Libya; and established stronger trade relations with the West via Italy. Yet, from the mid-fourteenth century on, the Black Death (1347–1349) and shifting trade routes planted the seeds of Egypt's social and economic decline. Intermittent looting by bands of renegade mamluks, arbitrary taxation, confiscations, and the oppression of minorities discouraged economic stability.

The rule of the Circassian Burjī ("citadel") Mamluks began with Sultan Barqūq (r. 1382–1389, 1390–1399). Early in the Burjī period the idea of filial succession was abandoned, and sultans came to be chosen from among the most powerful mamluks; succession was actually restricted to those who had been recruited as youths. The mid- to late-fifteenth century saw something of a recovery, particularly with Qā'itbāy (r. 1468–1496), who struggled to bolster the Mamluk state economically and militarily. The recovery would not last. In 1517, sapped by internal conflicts and a series of weak sultans, the Ottoman sultan Selim I (r. 1512–1520) defeated the Burjī Mamluks.

Despite initial friction, which prompted Selim to execute some 800 mamluks, the Turks found themselves gradually enmeshed in the mamluk administrative class, which was indispensable to their continued rule. Eventually, a mamluk contingent emerged as the real power behind the Ottoman pashas (governors) sent to Cairo from Constantinople, and by the seventeenth century, this contingent's leaders, the Beys, were the acknowledged rulers of Egypt.

Factionalism and the power struggles that inevitably followed the death of each of the Beys inhibited the formation of a hereditary dynasty and were generally detrimental to the economy and to society. Intermittent plagues and famines were accompanied by a declining transit trade between India and Europe (owing to the opening of new spice routes) and the compression of the domestic manufacturing industry (with a greater dependence on European products). Outstanding Beys include Islam'īl Bey (r. 1707–1724) and 'Alī Bey (r. 1770–1771), the latter declaring himself sultan of an independent Egypt. After his death the Ottomans sought to curb Mamluk power until the rule of the Beys was finally ended by French occupation in 1798.

—*Brian Catlos*

See also
Janissaries; Ottoman Empire; *Šaqàliba*
For Further Reading
Ayalon, David. 1994. *Islam and the Abode of War: Military Slaves and Islamic Adversaries*. Aldershot, Eng.:

Variorum; Ayalon, David. 1979. *The Mamlūk Military Society*. London: Variorum; Irwin, Robert. 1968. *The Middle East in the Middle Ages: The Early Mamluk Sultanate, 1250–1382*. Carbondale: Southern Illinois University Press; Little, Donald. 1986. *History and Historiography of the Mamluks*. London: Variorum.

MANUMISSION LAWS

Throughout history, where there has been slavery there has been some mechanism for the manumission, or formal emancipation, of slaves. Most of the time, this took the form of simple ransom, purchase, or gift; that is, the slave or someone close to the slave could buy the individual's freedom, or the owner could confer it as a favor or in payment for some kind of personal obligation. Manumission by deed or by will was often the normal legal instrument. Slaves were generally considered to be real property, and the transmission of freedom passed along the same legal channels as the transmission of land.

In the English-speaking parts of the Americas, where slavery represented the combination of racism with substantial capital investment, a complex system of manumission laws developed toward the late-eighteenth century. These laws seem to have been the outcome of three interrelated and conflicting social movements. One, there was a genuine interest in manumission, which, through most of the eighteenth century was usually granted by deed or by special act of a legislature. Two, there were powerful interests in the Southern and middle states of the United States and in the British island colonies who were opposed to manumission in any form and who sought to make manumission as cumbersome and as difficult as possible. Three, this period marked a transition in the provision of what are called social services today, including the care of orphan children and indigent persons who had no responsible relations to care for them.

Movement toward a growing centralization of poor relief in the hands of government authorities merged with an increasing interest in abolition to distort that movement into a misshapen mockery of itself. Generally, manumission was recognized as the only decent way to deal with the problem of slavery, but easy manumission allowed irresponsible owners to divest themselves of the requirement that they feed and house slaves who were no longer useful for work.

Freed slaves often were simply too old or too worn out to support themselves. But a bevy of new "poor laws," which provided for institutional relief of indigent citizens in the United States, made these newly free persons with no means of support the responsibility, not of the owners who had used up their laboring years, but of the county or local jurisdiction. This arrangement was considered burdensome, and new manumission laws were enacted that were intended to shift the burden of the care of aged slaves back to the owner. As early as 1774, Jamaica required that anyone who was manumitting a slave or slaves to post a bond guaranteeing that each former slave would receive £5 a year toward his or her maintenance, which meant that less conscientious owners were held to their obligation to support their worn-out laborers in their old age.

In 1780, Pennsylvania passed a law that required the registration of all slaves and banned the creation of new slaves. Thereafter, children born to slaves were born free, although they were usually indentured at birth to the mother's owner. In the eyes of officialdom, indenture primarily provided that a free and legally responsible person could answer at law for the maintenance of a child. Efforts were made to make the status of indentured blacks more like the status of indentured white servants, but many indentured blacks were effectively kept in bondage much longer than white ones. In Delaware, white indentured girls were usually free at 18 or upon marriage, and boys at 21, but black indentured girls were seldom free until they were 25, and men 30.

A burst of manumissions followed the American Revolution in the former middle colonies, but the number slowed as revolutionary fervor waned. A new poor law was passed in Delaware in 1790 that modified the process of simple manumission by deed. Similar in many ways to the Jamaican law, this law required, among other things, that a slaveowner must indemnify the county against a manumitted slave eventually becoming a public ward. This law had the effect of slowing the manumission of adult slaves, but young indentured children continued to be manumitted very early, much like the process in Pennsylvania.

As the eighteenth century merged into the nineteenth, manumission laws in English-speaking America took two basic directions. One was the increasing adoption of a requirement that owners post a bond against a slave's future need for public care. The other was to restrict the circumstances under which a slave could be manumitted.

In the slave-dependent Southern states, simple restrictions limited manumission. In 1820, a South Carolina law limited manumissions to private legislative acts, and two years later, Mississippi restricted manumission to bequests upon the death of the owner. By the time of the outbreak of the Civil War, several states, including some border states, had outlawed manumission altogether.

In the British island colonies, manumission laws were largely formulated according to the indemnification model. Indemnification amounts ranged from a fairly reasonable £50 (Bermuda, 1806), to £100 (Grenada, 1796), to a prohibitive £300 (Leeward Islands, 1798) and an even more prohibitive £500 for native and £1,000 for imported slaves (St. Kitts, 1802). Jamaica was the most liberal of the island colonies. There, waiver of the manumission bond was permitted if the vestry of the parish could be convinced that the manumission was not intended to defraud the parish or to place the burden for care of an aged or infirm slave upon the public charge. Similar proof of a slave's ability to support himself or herself was required in Dominica, Tobago, and the Bahamas, but those areas did not allow a waiver of the manumission bond.

In all cases, a slave's status as property was considered superior to manumission by will, meaning that manumission was secondary to the need to pay the debts of an estate. If the settlement of the debts required the sale of a slave who had been manumitted by will, the manumission was disallowed. Only rarely, as in Grenada in 1818, was it possible for a slave freed by will to purchase his freedom by reimbursing the estate the amount of his appraised value toward the settlement of the debts of the estate.

—Louise Heite

For Further Reading
Friedman, Lawrence M. 1973. *A History of American Law.* New York: Simon and Schuster; Howard, John Henry. 1827. *The Laws of the British Colonies in the West Indies and Other Parts of America Concerning Real and Personal Property and Manumission of Slaves; with a View of the Constitution of Each Colony.* London: Joseph Butterworth and Son.

MARXISM

Debate over slavery's utility as a theoretical category at once confronts a lack of precision and consistency in utilizing the concept to distinguish historical forms of slavery from other types of noneconomically compelled labor. Karl Marx offered little indication of how to account for slavery's emergence *within* any society (a question of greater interest to Friedrich Engels); he was more concerned with slavery's role in the enforcement of unequal relations *between* societies, the appropriation of the surplus value of slave labor, and its conversion to exchange value.

What are the general historical forms of slavery? In *Capital,* Marx noted two types, each reflecting society's prevailing organization and relations of production. "Patriarchal" slavery was typical of early societies dedicated to producing the immediate means of subsistence (use value) in domestically oriented economies. In such preclass formations, slavery's role in the economy was restricted, and slavery existed alongside other less completely unfree forms of labor. But in ancient Greece and Rome, with the emergence of a commodity sphere, slavery would eventually dispense with the communal sphere and come to dominate the entire economy. Advanced capitalist production, while based systematically on wage labor, also had recourse to slavery to produce a surplus appropriated, commodified, and converted to capital by a distinct ruling class. It is this latter form to which Marx most often referred.

How is slavery to be defined? Through capture, sale, and threat of force, a slave is denied control and ownership of both his labor power and the means of production, and the entire product of slave labor is surrendered to a dominant, wealth-accumulating class. In return, a slave receives only the means of subsistence while the surplus value created through slave labor fuels the process of producing and reproducing slavery as a component of the prevailing social formation.

The slave also is denied effective membership in the society in which he labors. Legal depersonalization exposes the slave to real or potential exploitation, alienation, and exchange, both as a producer of commodities and as a commodity himself. So if slave capture and commerce approximate in abstract terms the alienability of commodities, such phenomena assume force only in the context of the already functioning social institutions that make the alienation of slaves possible.

But slavery reproduces itself institutionally, not simply via the legal assimilation of slaves as property or the appropriation of the surplus value of their labor and its circulation in the capitalist sphere. Internally, the process entails recognition of the variable competence of individual slaves as human beings and their susceptibility to internalizing an ideology of deference and obligation characteristic of every class of dependents. Actual slave-master relationships exhibit considerable individual variation in degrees of trust and conferral of privilege. These concrete relationships are more intimate than economic, and their personal everyday character conditions the practical indeterminacy of slave inequality as a legal abstraction. The slave's alienated status serves slaveowners primarily in a strictly formal sense as the owner deals externally with the broader capitalist formation.

Claude Meillassoux (1991) analyzes this circumstance by distinguishing between the state and the condition of a slave. Enslavement, the legal deprivation of social status, is the formal legal *state* of slaves as a social class, which is necessarily defined in relation to the market. But each slave's distinct and potentially mutable individual *condition,* if likewise defined in relation to the market, importantly reflects the individual's dynamic personal situation *within* the social relations of production and reproduction. Internally, then, slavery in the Americas retained the patriarchal character of other precapitalist formations, even as the institution at large served the external needs of capitalism.

Understanding slavery as a definite mode of production is complicated by the actual variety of historically specific types, especially in the New World where slavery arose in relation to the global capitalist market for the purpose of creating exchange value for it. A shift from seeing slavery as a distinct mode of production to a broader conception of the actual complexity of social formations reveals the possibility of a plurality of modes of production being broadly linked, so that one dominates the entire concrete historical and social assemblage. Unlike patriarchal slavery or that of classic antiquity, then, slavery in the Americas cannot be treated as an independent order of analysis, because it was a subsidiary institution of European colonial expansion. As Marx wrote in 1846:

> Direct slavery [in the Americas] is as much the pivot of our industry today as machinery, credit, etc. Without slavery, no cotton; without cotton no modern industry. It is slavery which has made the colonies valuable; the colonies have created world trade; world trade is the necessary condition of large-scale machine industry. . . . Slavery is therefore an economic category of the highest importance . . . [and as such] has existed in every nation since the world began. Modern nations have merely known how to disguise slavery in their own countries while they openly imported it to the New World. (Marx, 1975)

Hence, the productive relations governing slave labor were in the last instance conditioned by the prevailing wage-labor system of Western capitalism and the circulation of commodities that linked its various productive regimes and reproduced the overall system. But slavery in the Americas did not produce for an overseas market merely as one socioeconomic formation tied to another. European expansion created New World slavery precisely to meet capitalism's own peculiar requirements, and slavery must be analyzed as an integral if subordinate sector of the broader global capitalist socioeconomic formation.

—*Michael C. Stone*

For Further Reading
Engels, Friedrich. 1972. *The Origin of the Family, Private Property, and the State*. New York: International Publishers; Marx, Karl. 1906. *Capital: A Critique of Political Economy*. New York: Modern Library; Marx, Karl. 1975. "Letter to P. V. Annenkov, December 28, 1846." In *Marx-Engels Selected Correspondence*. Ed. S. W. Ryazanskaya. Moscow: Progress Publishers; Meillassoux, Claude. 1991. *The Anthropology of Slavery: The Womb of Iron and Gold*. Chicago: University of Chicago Press.

MASON-DIXON LINE

The Mason-Dixon Line was originally the southern boundary of Pennsylvania, but it became the symbolic division line between slave and free states. Charles Mason and Jeremiah Dixon were engaged by the proprietors of Maryland and Pennsylvania to settle a long-standing boundary dispute between the two colonies. When Mason and Dixon arrived in America on November 15, 1763, they brought with them sophisticated surveying technology and astronomical location-finding techniques that previously had been unknown in the colonies. They fixed the southern boundary of Pennsylvania at 39° 43′ 17.6″ north latitude, within 10 seconds of more recent calculations. By the time they finished their survey in 1767, the astronomers had set milestones or posts for 230 miles along the line.

Before Mason and Dixon, American land surveying had been primitive, and the sophisticated instruments and techniques they introduced revolutionized the mathematical professions in the United States. David Rittenhouse, a Philadelphia watchmaker who worked on the survey, went on to have a distinguished career as an instrument maker, astronomer, and president of the American Philosophical Society.

The Land Ordinance of 1785 established a point on the line where it crossed the Ohio River as the beginning point of a national quadrangular survey. The Mason-Dixon line was thereby perpetuated as the baseline for all General Land Office (now Bureau of Land Management) surveys, and the baseline was extended westward after the Louisiana Purchase in 1803.

The Kansas-Nebraska Act (1854) set the boundary between the two territories at 40° north latitude, roughly the Mason-Dixon Line. The Bleeding Kansas struggle followed in the wake of the congressional decision to allow the future residents of Kansas to determine whether their territory would be slave or free. Settlers from the adjacent slave state of Missouri clashed with free soil Northerners who rushed to settle the new territory.

In the East, the southern boundary of Pennsylvania marked the southern limit of the free Northern states. Fugitive slaves had a better chance of obtaining their freedom if they could get from Maryland to Pennsylvania across Mason and Dixon's line. After passage of the Fugitive Slave Act in 1850, the southern boundary of Pennsylvania became a bloody battleground between fugitives, their helpers, and enforcers of the law.

—*Edward F. Heite*

See also
Bleeding Kansas
For Further Reading
Bayliff, William H. 1951. *Boundary Monuments on the Maryland-Pennsylvania and the Maryland-Delaware Boundaries.* Annapolis: Maryland Board of Natural Resources.

MAURITIUS

Mauritius, an island of 720 square miles, is located in the southwestern Indian Ocean 500 miles east of Madagascar at latitude 20° south. Like the other two Mascarene Islands, Réunion (known as the Île de Bourbon until 1848) and Rodrigues, Mauritius was unknown to the larger world before the early-sixteenth century when it was visited by Portuguese and other European explorers.

The Mascarenes remained uninhabited until 1638 when the Dutch made initial attempts to colonize the island they named Mauritius. Abandoned by Holland in 1710, the island was claimed by France in 1715 and renamed Île de France. Settled in 1721 by colonists from the Île de Bourbon (occupied by France in 1670), the Îles de France and de Bourbon remained a French colony until captured by a British expeditionary force in 1810. The Treaty of Paris (1814) ceded the Île de France, once again called Mauritius, to Great Britain while the Île de Bourbon returned to French control.

Although the Dutch first introduced slaves onto Mauritius, slavery did not become entrenched until the eighteenth century when large numbers of servile laborers were imported from various regions of Africa, India, and Southeast Asia. An estimated 160,000 slaves reached the Mascarenes between 1670 and 1810, only 5,000 of whom arrived before 1729. During the next four decades, slave imports averaged 1,000 a year. Local demand for servile labor led to a dramatic expansion of the East African and Malagasy (Madagascar) slave trades during the late-eighteenth century, as 80,000 slaves arrived in the Mascarenes between 1769 and 1793. The Anglo-French wars of the revolutionary and Napoleonic eras periodically disrupted this trade, resulting in only 35,000 slaves reaching the islands between 1794 and 1810.

Slaves imported into the Mascarenes came from throughout the Indian Ocean world and beyond. It is estimated that of those arriving before 1810, 2 percent were of West African origin, 13 percent came from India and elsewhere in southern Asia, 40 percent were shipped from Mozambique and East Africa's Swahili coast, and 45 percent came from Madagascar. Census data indicate that two male slaves were imported for every female slave, a ratio comparable to that of the transatlantic slave trade at the same time.

The slaves were employed as fishermen, sailors, harbor and dock workers, and household servants, but most worked as agricultural laborers growing foodstuffs for local consumption and small quantities of tropical commodities for export. Like slaveowners elsewhere, Mauritian colonists tended to stereotype the slaves in their midst. Accordingly, Indians and Malays, who were perceived as being less suited to physical labor than other slaves, were often employed as domestic servants and skilled craftsmen while slaves of African and Malagasy origin frequently worked as field hands.

Inclusion in the British Empire ended the legal slave trade for Mauritius. Development of the colony's sugar industry during the early-nineteenth century ensured, however, that demands for servile labor remained high, and the island became the center of a notorious clandestine slave trade that lasted until the mid-1820s. Contemporary observers estimated that 30,000 or more slaves were introduced illegally from Madagascar and the East African coast between 1811 and the mid-1820s. To suppress this trade, British authorities mounted antislave naval patrols and negotiated treaties banning slave exportation from Madagascar. When slavery was formally abolished on February 1, 1835, there were 66,613 slaves on Mauritius, and like emancipated slaves elsewhere in the British Empire, they were required to serve their former masters as "apprentices" for up to six years before they became completely free.

Like other plantation colonies, in the late-eighteenth and early-nineteenth centuries there was a rise of a free population of color on Mauritius composed of free colored immigrants, many of whom came originally from the French possessions in India; manumitted slaves; and their descendants. By 1830, free persons of color made up almost one-fifth of the island's total population and controlled perhaps 20 percent or more of the colony's gross domestic product. Their economic resources subsequently allowed the free colored community to thwart attempts to drive ex-apprentices back onto sugar estates after the apprenticeship system ended on March 31, 1839.

—*Richard B. Allen*

For Further Reading
Allen, Richard B. 1989. "Economic Marginality and the Rise of the Free Population of Colour in Mauritius,

1767–1830." *Slavery and Abolition* 10 (2): 126–150; Allen, Richard B. 1983. "Marronage and the Maintenance of Public Order in Mauritius, 1721–1835." *Slavery and Abolition* 4 (3): 214–231; Filliot, J. M. 1974. *La traite des esclaves vers les Mascareignes aux XVIIIe siecle*. Paris: ORSTROM; Toussaint, Auguste. 1972. *Histoire des iles Mascareignes*. Paris: Berger-Levrault.

MESOPOTAMIA

The primary word for slave in ancient Mesopotamia (the area of the Tigris-Euphrates River valley) was *wardum* (Sumerian, *arad*), an Akkadian word that designated not only a slave but also someone who was in some sense dependent upon another. Thus, all the king's subjects, including his high officials, were considered to a certain extent to be his slaves. There were also temple slaves (Akkadian, *shirkum*), whose status was hereditary. In the first millennium, a number of specialized terms were also used to designate certain types of slaves.

Throughout most of Mesopotamian history (c. 3500–100 B.C.), there existed three types of labor: independent labor of free peasants and craftsmen, labor of the semifree populace *(mushkēnum)*, and slave labor. In Mesopotamia, slavery was a form of personal dependence and an economic necessity, and the slave was deprived the means of production available to other segments of the population.

Slavery as an institution probably appeared in Mesopotamia in the late-fourth millennium B.C. The earliest slave source was probably captured prisoners of war, many of whom labored in the construction of canals, roads, and public buildings. But there were never great masses of slaves in Mesopotamia, even though there was never any shortage of prisoners of war. It appears that the state organization and economy were too underdeveloped to control large numbers of slaves. Most slave labor was thus confined to the domestic sphere, which required less supervision.

Many native peoples were relegated to debt-slavery, a circumstance usually limited by law to a specific period of time (normally three to six years). This practice apparently had become obsolete to some extent by the first millennium B.C. A man's children were also sold into slavery if he could not pay his debts. The Middle Assyrian laws (c. 1200 B.C.) allowed brothers to sell sisters into debt-slavery, and on at least one occasion, some citizens of Nippur, an ancient city of Babylonia, sold their children to moneylenders to pay off the invading army of the Babylonian king Nabopolassar (625 B.C.). In the third and second millennia B.C., some people who could not feed their young children aban-

doned them at city walls or in baskets on the river so that others could take and either adopt them or make them slaves. A monarch could issue an edict releasing those (and their families) who had become debt-slaves. For example, the Babylonian monarch Ammisaduqa in the seventeenth century B.C. released all in his kingdom who had been reduced to debt-slavery.

Free persons could become slaves if they violated the law. In the third millennium B.C. Sumerian civilization, thieves were turned over to their victims to become slaves, and the wives and children of convicted murderers were also enslaved. There appears to have been a difference in the institution of slavery in the first millennium B.C., as slaves then were allowed to remain with their families and reproduce, thus replenishing the slave population.

Temple slavery was a thriving institution throughout Mesopotamian history. By the Old Babylonian period (c. 2000–1600 B.C.), devout masters often would dedicate their slaves for temple service. In the Late Babylonian period (eighth to sixth centuries B.C.), a main source of temple slaves was the dedication of prisoners of war to the temple. There is a text of the same period, during the reign of Nabonidus (r. 556–539 B.C.), which records that a widow dedicated her two children to the Eanna Temple at Uruk so that they might not starve.

Domestic slave labor reached a higher level of complexity in southern Mesopotamia during the first millennium B.C. Wealthy families owned a comparatively greater number of slaves (some as many as 100) than in previous periods, and it was not unusual for a middle-class person to own as many as 5 slaves.

Throughout Mesopotamian history, slaves were considered immovable property. They were thus transferred by inheritance, deposited as security, and included in dowries. Slaves were typically branded, but in Assyria the slaves' ears were often pierced instead. Escape attempts by slaves were not uncommon. The laws of Eshnunna (early second millennium B.C.) stipulated a fine of double the slave's value for someone who stole or concealed a slave (Laws 49–50). The laws of Lipit-Ishtar in the same period made a citizen who harbored a slave return him to his master within a month and pay 25 shekels of silver (Law 12). The average slave's price rose from 10 to 15 shekels in late-third-millennium-B.C. Sumer to about 50–60 shekels in the Late Babylonian period.

Although slaves were considered mere chattel, they appeared to have greater freedom in Babylonia in the first millennium B.C. than in other periods. Slaves at that time were able to rent fields and other items from their masters or from other persons. Many slaves owned their own house and some movable property, engaged in economic activity, ran taverns, and taught various trades. They could appear as witnesses, plaintiffs, and defendants in court; have their own personal seals; purchase their own slaves; and even hire other individuals to work in their households.

A slave could receive manumission only from his master and could be freed by a legal contract, a court edict, or a ritual of purification of the slave. Often the slave received his freedom by being adopted by his master, mostly when the owner was elderly and had no heirs. One text from Assyria (c. 1800 B.C.) states that an adopted former slave was required to support and obey his former masters until their deaths, at which time he received certain movable and immovable properties.

—*Mark W. Chavalas*

For Further Reading
Dandamaev, M. 1984. *Slavery in Babylonia from Nabopolassar to Alexander the Great, 626–331 B.C.* DeKalb: Northern Illinois University Press; Gelb, I. J. 1973. "Prisoners of War in Early Mesopotamia." *Journal of Near Eastern Studies* 32: 70–98; Mendelsohn, I. 1949. *Slavery in the Ancient Near East.* New York: Oxford University Press; Powell, M., ed. 1987. *Labor in the Ancient Near East.* New Haven, CT: American Oriental Society.

MESTIZAJE

Race mixture or miscegenation (*mestizaje* in Spanish) occurred as a result of the cohabitation and sometimes marriage of Europeans, Native Americans, and Africans in the Americas and the Caribbean. Although Europeans in the New World sought to maintain two societies—white and Indian—the introduction of millions of African slaves dramatically altered the two-tier racial system. Increasingly, race mixture resulted in the creation of several racial categories developed in order to maintain white superiority at the top of the race-based pyramid.

Throughout the New World, however, to varying degrees, race mixture undermined social domination by Europeans and their descendants. In Spanish America, interracial liaisons and marriages among Europeans, Native Americans, and Africans produced multiracial societies throughout the New World, most notably in Cuba, Peru, Haiti, Mexico, Panama, and North America. In Brazil, miscegenation led to the extensive blurring of racial lines between Europeans and Africans. *Mestizaje* in English America and the French colonies also caused the emergence of large mulatto and Creole groups, many of which served as buffer zones between whites and slaves. Race mixture was perhaps more common in the Caribbean as European males frequently took female slaves as sexual partners.

Overall, miscegenation led to acculturation by all groups and when combined with economic growth, engendered flexibility. Thus, despite many legal, racial, and cultural restrictions, many biracial persons rose to high levels of respectability.

—*Jackie R. Booker*

For Further Reading
Burkholder, Mark, and Lyman L. Johnson. 1990. *Colonial Latin America.* New York: Oxford University Press; MacLachlan, Colin, and Jaime E. Rodriguez. 1980. *The Forging of the Cosmic Race: A Reinterpretation of Colonial Mexico.* Berkeley: University of California Press; Segal, Ronald. 1995. *The Black Diaspora.* New York: Farrar, Straus and Giroux.

MEXICO, INDIGENOUS SLAVERY

Indigenous African and Amerindian styles of slavery were similar in concept, including, of course, the Indians in Mexico. Both styles shared the notion of "rights in person," which meant that slaves were not mere property and that there were certain family ties and duties between master and slave, like a father-son relationship. The European concept of slavery is based on the idea of the slaves' lack of judgment, inherited by either birth or nature.

In pre-Hispanic Mexico, the words *tequiyotl* and *tlacoyotl* implied a type of compulsory work done for another person but not involving the ownership of the individual. There were two main causes why one could become enslaved: as a social punishment against an offender and as a result of economic necessity when an individual had to sell himself into slavery in order to feed his family. In the first case, delinquent debts or tributes, drunkenness, unredeemed gambling, juvenile disobedience, burglary, and homicide could bring slavery to the transgressor. In the second, only emergency situations, like extreme starvation, compelled an individual to sell himself or another family member to obtain food. The Aztec held a special banquet to legalize one's entrance into slavery, and at that time, the slave's ears were perforated as a perpetual sign of his bondage. The Aztec freed the offspring of slaves, but Mayan descendants continued being slaves until they could pay their price by their own means.

Occasionally, the terms slave and captive overlapped, but there were distinct meanings to each status. War captives were eventually sacrificed to the gods whereas slaves could not be sold without their consent and had the right and the opportunity to redeem themselves in case of bad behavior before being sacrificed. Slaves maintained rights like family, citizenship, property, and the possibility to buy slaves and get married during slavery just as if they were free. Slaves had many avenues available to gain their liberty, including marriage to a free person, the master's death, paying money for himself, substituting himself for another family member, fleeing from the master to the king's palace, or conversion to Christianity. Among the Maya, someone marrying a slave also became a slave, and the same was true for the offspring. The only possibility for obtaining freedom was through paying for themselves. Finally, there was a ceremony in which a slave was recognized as a free person anew, which consisted of a feast at which the slave was naked, took a bath, and dressed in new clothes. He was then presented to a chief governor who explained he had been liberated because of his abilities and good behavior; thus he became a free man.

With Mexico's conquest, Indian slavery underwent some changes, primarily because the Spanish took advantage of misunderstandings about the differences between Indian and European slavery. Slavery and *encomienda* were the two systems of economic and political relationships that dominated Indian life in New Spain during the sixteenth century. Initially, according to Spanish law, only cannibals or those Indians who resisted Christianity were appropriate subjects of slavery, which existed as punishment.

Another device used during the Spanish conquest to get slaves was the *requerimiento*, a juridical statement that asked submission to Christianity and Spanish law. If submission was not forthcoming, which commonly occurred, the conquistadors had the right to enslave the "rebel Indian." But if Indians accepted the *requerimiento*, they were subject to the *encomienda* system, a kind of compulsory servitude. In addition, all individuals considered slaves by Indians remained in that condition under Spanish rule. Indian slaves were the main laborers in mines, on haciendas, as sheepherders, in building, and in *obrajes* ("small factories") between 1521 and 1540.

In the 1530s, Bartolomé de Las Casas, among others, challenged the theological justification of Indian slavery and asked for its abolition and the importation of the stronger black slaves to replace the Indian slaves. In 1542, the Leyes Nuevas, or New Laws, enforced by the Spanish crown prohibited the most common forms of Indian slavery. Yet that form of slavery survived during the process of northern expansion because of the continuous state of war.

—*Nora Reyes Costilla*

See also

Encomienda System; Las Casas, Bartolomé de; New Spain (Mexico), Colonial Experience; The Requirement

MFECANE

The term Mfecane comes from the Xhosa words *ukufaca* ("to be thin from hunger") and *fetcani* ("starving intruders") and is used to refer to the period of great disruption and population dislocation in southern Africa's interior in the 1820s and 1830s. That period is also known by the Sotho word *difaqane*.

Historians have much debated the causes and nature of the Mfecane. Nineteenth-century writers depicted it as a period of chaos and barbarism caused by the aggressive expansion of the Zulu state under its ruler Shaka and the raids of the breakaway Ndebele (Matabele) people under their ruler Mzilikazi across the Drakensberg Mountains, through the high-veld interior, and into modern Zimbabwe. Depictions of African devastation and depopulation gave white settlers a justification for colonizing a region they depicted as empty wasteland.

In the 1960s, historians portrayed the Mfecane more positively as a period of nation building, a "revolution in Bantu Africa" in which Shaka played a central role as founder of Natal's Zulu state while Moshoeshoe created the Sotho kingdom in the high veld as self-defense against the Zulu. Some writers also suggested that Shaka was able to expand his power and resources by controlling the ivory trade to the Natal coast and Delagoa Bay (site of the capital of Mozambique, Maputo).

More recent scholarly work has challenged these Zulu-centered explanations. For instance, archaeological evidence shows that drought and environmental changes in the late-eighteenth century caused increased competition for land and water and encouraged the migration of farmers and cattle herders throughout the region.

The most controversial explanation comes from historian Julian Cobbing. He has proposed that white traders and colonists invented the very notion of the Mfecane to disguise their illegal slave-trading activities and that their demands for forced labor caused much of the disruption. The activities and demands came from several directions: from Portuguese and Brazilian slavers in Mozambique's Delagoa Bay region, whose activities spread southward; from Dutch and British farmers of the expanding Cape Colony's eastern frontier, who required indentured farm workers after the external slave trade ended in 1808; and from the Griqua people (descended from indigenous pastoralist communities), whose interior raids provided "refugee" laborers for the colonists of the northern Cape Colony. In other words, the emergence of the Zulu kingdom and other African states resulted from the disruption but did not cause it.

Cobbing's proposal has been criticized on several

grounds. African nationalists claim that it denies Shaka's active achievements as a nation builder, there is little indication that the demand for slaves from Delagoa Bay was high before the 1820s, and evidence for Griqua and Cape colonist slave raiding has not yet been convincingly linked to the Mfecane in Natal or the high veld. Nonetheless, the debate has made historians much more aware of various forms of indentured and forced labor existing in the southern African interior in the early-nineteenth century.

—Nigel Worden

See also
Cape Colony; Great Trek
For Further Reading
Cobbing, Julian. 1988. "The Mfecane as Alibi: Thoughts on Dithakong and Mbolompo." *Journal of African History* 29 (3): 487–519; Eldredge, Elizabeth, and Fred Morton, eds. 1994. *Slavery in South Africa: Captive Labour on the Dutch Frontier.* Boulder, CO: Westview Press and Pietermaritzburg: University of Natal Press; Hamilton, Carolyn, ed. 1995. *The Mfecane Aftermath: Reconstructive Debates in Southern African History.* Johannesburg: Witwatersrand University Press and Pietermaritzburg: University of Natal Press; Omer-Cooper, John. 1966. *The Zulu Aftermath: A Nineteenth Century Revolution in Bantu Africa.* London: Longman.

MIDDLE ASSYRIAN LAWS

The Middle Assyrian laws are a collection of laws known primarily from 14 cuneiform tablets found at the site of the Assyrian capital Assur or Ashur (modern Qal'at Sherqat). According to most scholars, the collection was compiled during the reign of King Tiglath-pileser I (c. 1114–1076 B.C.), but it was probably based on sources that were several centuries older.

Like other ancient Near Eastern law collections, the Middle Assyrian laws do not constitute a comprehensive legal code. Rather, they are a collection of rules, which may have been a record of previous legislation, a summary of current law, or a jurisprudential treatise, among other possibilities. There are few references to slaves, both in the laws and in contemporary contracts. Although it is most probably incorrect to offer from this paucity of material that slavery was not a major public concern, the dearth of references and the fragmentary state of many of the tablets make any general assessment of slavery in the period difficult.

Nonetheless, the laws do exhibit a preoccupation with rank and status, and a particular stringency with respect to women (a pattern also observable in the contemporary compilation of court rules known as the Middle Assyrian palace decrees). A prostitute *(harimtu)* and a slave woman were to be visibly distinguished from other women so they were prohibited from wearing a veil in public (Tablet A/Law 40), which may have emphasized their marginality or sexual availability. The anomalous *esirtu,* possibly a type of slave-concubine, could wear a veil in public if in the company of her mistress and could be elevated to the status of a wife if her master veiled her before witnesses (A/41). The sons of an *esirtu* inherited if the veiled wife had no sons. The situation of an *esirtu* may thus have been comparable to the general Near Eastern practice of using female slaves to provide heirs if a wife were childless.

The legal status of slaves in this period exhibits the same inconsistencies observed in other ancient legal systems. In some cases, slaves were apparently considered real property: there are brief references in the laws to slaves being part of an inheritance (0/2) and to slaves being pledged as security for debt (C/7), a practice confirmed in several contracts.

Like married women and children, the slave could transact business with the master's property with the master's explicit consent (C/9). Slaves who received property stolen by a wife from her husband were punished, if the husband also chose to punish his wife, and were liable to "make good the theft" (A/4). If this latter provision meant returning the value of the goods, that raises the issue of whether slaves were able to amass property of their own. One contract speaks of a male slave redeeming a female slave in order to marry her (KAJ/7). Also notable in the laws is the removal of the ears or noses of slave miscreants, a type of mutilation found elsewhere in the Near Eastern codes.

Like the Code of Hammurabi and the Hittite Code, the Middle Assyrian laws tell us much about the nature of slavery in some of the world's oldest civilizations.

—Diane Kriger

See also
Hammurabi, Code of; Hittite Code
For Further Reading
Cardellini, I. 1981. *Die biblischen "Sklaven"—Gesetze im Lichte des Keilschriftlichen Sklavenrechts.* Bonn: Verlag Peter Hanstein; Driver, Godfrey R., and John C. Miles. 1935. *The Assyrian Laws.* Oxford: Clarendon Press; Grayson, A. Kirk. 1972. *Assyrian Royal Inscriptions.* Wiesbaden: Otto Harrassowitz; Roth, Martha. 1995. *Law Collections from Mesopotamia and Asia Minor.* Atlanta, GA: Scholars Press.

MIDDLE PASSAGE

The label Middle Passage has long been used to describe the voyage of slaving vessels from African to American ports. Beginning in the sixteenth century, this involuntary voyage was taken by over 11 million people before slave trading ended in the nineteenth century. Voyage lengths could vary considerably. Gambia River slavers made the passage to Barbados in as little as three weeks while those from Angola to Virginia or Cartagena might take several months. Descriptions of the treatment of slaves aboard ship, the terror experienced by the captives, and the high mortality rates on some of the voyages often have been used to demonstrate some of slavery's worst aspects.

Before embarking upon the transatlantic voyage, slaves had already endured significant trauma. Most had been enslaved by fellow Africans, as Europeans rarely ventured into the interior to capture slaves and purchased them from African merchants instead. Some slaves had been sentenced to their status for criminal activity, indebtedness, or religious infractions while others were victims of political disorders or wars of aggression by imperialist African nations. Prior to 1700, over half of all slaves were prisoners of war, but in the eighteenth century, banditry and large-scale kidnapping expeditions were responsible for about two-thirds of the slaves delivered for coastal sale. Exhausted from long treks from the interior and crowded conditions of detention in pens awaiting the arrival of European traders, slaves were often ill because of inadequate diets and fouled water supplies. Adding to their misery was the terror of seeing the ocean and hearing the pounding of the surf for the first time and their fear that the mysterious white men with long hair and strange languages might be cannibals.

After boarding the sailing ships, the slaves faced almost indescribable conditions. Although women and children had some freedom of movement, men were usually shackled in pairs. Slave traders bought primarily men because planters in the tropics preferred them for plantation laborers. Throughout the slave-trading era, men outnumbered women by about two to one, and children under 10 seldom constituted more than 10 percent of the cargo. Whenever possible, captains permitted slaves on deck during the day, but at night and during stormy weather, they faced the horrors of the conditions below deck.

Olaudah Equiano, an eighteenth-century slave from the Niger Delta, published an account of his travail. He related that slaves first noticed an overwhelming smell when forced below deck. There was little breeze through portholes or ventilators, and sanitation facilities rarely were adequate. The resulting foul odor overcame Equiano, as it did countless others, who not only became ill but also found it difficult to eat amid the horrid stench. It became common knowledge that one could smell a slaving vessel five miles downwind.

Some captains preferred packing their slave cargoes more tightly than others. Below deck on most ships there was seldom more than 5 feet of headroom. The "tight packers" installed shelves to halve the headroom and increase the number of slaves transported. Eighteenth-century abolitionists circulated a diagram of a Liverpool slave ship named the *Brookes,* which showed a cargo of slaves barely having enough room to move. The captain had allotted just 2.5 feet of headroom and an area of only 6 feet by 16 inches for each man to lie down in.

Although it is doubtful that the *Brookes* was typical of most of the slave ships, even under ideal circumstances on the "loosely packed" vessels, the space allotted to slaves for the passage was seldom half that provided for indentured servants, soldiers, and convicts. By the eighteenth century, the typical slaving vessel carried about two slaves for every ton of displacement. With slaving vessels averaging 200 tons by 1750, the average slaving voyage had at least 400 slaves, and several exceeded that with some carrying up to 700 slaves. During the years of peace in the eighteenth-century Atlantic, nearly 170 vessels carried slaves to colonial ports in these cramped conditions.

The meals furnished by ship captains usually depended upon the African region where they procured their cargoes. They supplied plantains and manioc for Angolans, yams for slaves from the Bight of Biafra, and rice and cornmeal for those from the windward coast of Africa. Most captains supplemented these meals with boiled horsebeans and, on rare occasions, a small ration of meat. Two meals a day were common, served with water.

The cramped vessels were horrible disease environments in which Europeans and Africans with little immunity to each other's diseases spent much time in close contact. Measles, malaria, leprosy, scurvy, and syphilis were all threats, but smallpox and dysentery were the biggest killers. Smallpox outbreaks could claim half or more of the slaves during a voyage, as could dysentery. Dr. Alexander Falconbridge, testifying to the British Parliament when that body was investigating the slave trade in the late-eighteenth century, explained that a combination of having to keep slaves below deck in bad weather and an outbreak of dysentery created a hell of blood, mucus, and fever that could kill dozens. Even when it did not kill large numbers, the "bloody flux," as contemporaries called the dysentery, often so weakened the slaves that they were unable to handle the harsh work environment of the New World plantations. Crew members also faced great risks, as a higher proportion of crew members

Woodcut made from a daguerreotype of the slave deck of the bark Wildfire, an American ship captured off Key West for participation in the illegal slave trade. A contemporary account noted that the slaves on this ship were considerably healthier than most slaves at this stage of the voyage because 600 slaves had been shipped in a vessel that normally accommodated 1,000.

than the slaves died during the Middle Passage; on English slave ships in the late-eighteenth century, nearly 22 percent of the crew members died, mostly as they obtained cargoes along the African coast.

Most slave ships had at least one doctor on board. The better ones could do little more than urge captains to keep the holds as clean as possible, to provide the slaves with ample opportunities for exercise and fresh air, and to supply adequate rations of food. Some doctors used traditional herbal treatments they encountered along the African coast. Yet, given their limited knowledge of hygiene and medicine, the doctors could do little when there was an outbreak of disease on board.

Perhaps more devastating than physical ailments was the psychological trauma endured by some slaves. Slaving crews often noticed that a few slaves became so unresponsive that they even refused to eat. To combat this "fixed melancholy," a depression caused by shock, fear, or the memory of lost home and family, some crews made the slaves dance on deck each day. If the slaves remained unresponsive, crews used threats, violence, and even forced feeding to keep them alive. Occasionally, nothing could be done, and despondent slaves committed suicide by leaping overboard.

The treatment of slaves on the voyages was invariably harsh. Lashings were routine for minor infractions, and sexual assaults on female slaves were common. Captains hired about twice as many crew members for a slaving voyage as for a normal Atlantic crossing and had about one crewman for every 10 slaves to feed and control the cargo. The crewmen were well armed because of a constant fear of slave mutinies, and there certainly was good reason to be concerned. During the eighteenth and early-nineteenth centuries, there were nearly 60 revolts on slave ships crossing from Africa to the Americas.

As the ships neared American markets, the captains began preparing their cargoes for sale. They gave the slaves extra food rations and plenty of water to drink. Crews bathed and shaved the slaves, coated their skin with palm oil to give it a healthier looking sheen, and dyed the gray hair of older slaves. Some captains even provided tobacco and pipes to raise spirits, but it was too late for some. After surviving the horrors of the passage, perhaps 5 percent died while awaiting sale, and others were so weakened that they died shortly after being sold.

There long has been an effort to determine the mortality rate on the Middle Passage. A few voyages experienced very high death tolls. In 1716, the *Windsor* lost 216 of its 380 slaves before arriving in Brazil. Sixty-five years later, the captain of the *Zong*, a ship from Liverpool, started a voyage with 440 slaves; 60 of them died en route to the West Indies, and 132 others were so sick that the captain ordered them thrown overboard to collect insurance for losses at sea. Such catastrophes were rare. The overall mortality rate was about 15 percent, and the figures improved with time. By the late-eighteenth century, British slave ships seldom lost more than 5 percent of their cargoes.

There are many possible explanations for the improvement. With an ever-closer eye on profit margins, captains slowly moved away from the tight packing of ships. Also, doctors increasingly used citrus juices to combat the ravages of scurvy. Most important, the vessels were better, and captains decided to market slaves in the closest ports, thus shortening the voyages. Repeatedly, scholars have shown that the determining factors in the mortality rate during the Middle Passage were distance and speed.

Despite the ever-greater likelihood that slaves would survive the journey, there is no way to minimize its horror. The ridicule, whippings, sexual exploitation of women, poor rations, disease, disorientation, and terror combined to create a living hell for those forced to sail the Middle Passage.

—*Larry Gragg*

For Further Reading
Allison, Robert, ed. 1995. *The Interesting Narrative of the Life of Olaudah Equiano Written by Himself.* Boston: Bedford Books; Klein, Herbert S. 1978. *The Middle Passage: Comparative Studies in the Atlantic Slave Trade.* Princeton, NJ: Princeton University Press; Mannix, Daniel, and Malcolm Cowley. 1962. *Black Cargoes: A History of the Atlantic Slave Trade, 1518–1865.* New York: Viking Press; Rawley, James. 1981. *The Transatlantic Slave Trade, A History.* New York: W. W. Norton.

MITA

The *mita* was a compulsory rotational labor draft (corvée) system used in the Andes by the Incas that was later adopted for use by the Spanish in the New World. Members of individual *ayllu* were subject to this draft. The *ayllu* was the basic unit of Andean social organization, a kinship group whose members claimed descent from a common ancestor. Each village contained several *ayllu*, each *ayllu* owned lands communally, and each head of household was assigned certain lands. Since the Inca empire was based upon the principal of reciprocity, the *ayllu* owed labor not only to their *curacas* (hereditary village chiefs) but also to the Inca emperor. *Ayllu* members worked as *mita* laborers on a *curaca*'s land and on Inca state and church lands.

Tasks assigned to *mita* laborers included clearing and terracing land, building roads and maintaining them, cleaning irrigation channels, constructing military fortresses, and mining. Each village also produced a specified amount of cloth for the state. For their services, the people received the right to work their communal lands, and in times of shortage or drought, imperial storehouses provided grain and cloth. The Inca, through gifts, also redistributed goods from one region of the empire to another.

Conquering Spaniards adapted the *mita* system for their own use. After the *encomienda* labor system failed in the 1550s, the Spanish adopted the corvée system to give them wider access to a diminishing supply of Indian laborers. Although laborers received token wages for their work, the *mita* was essentially an unfree labor system. Indians avoiding service or *curacas* failing to fill required labor quotas could be imprisoned, fined, or physically punished.

Viceroy Francisco de Toledo devised the system used in Peru in the 1570s. It required all able-bodied Indian males subjected to the *mita* to work for six-month periods, one year in seven, in the Potosí silver mines or the Huancavelica mercury mines. *Mita* laborers could also be assigned to Spanish-owned workshops, haciendas, or public works. Most *mita* laborers worked in the mines under such dangerous and unhealthful conditions that 80 percent died in their first year of service. Mercury, necessary for silver production, poisoned many Indians. Villages near the mines could pay the *tasa*, the giving of agricultural produce as tribute to feed the miners, instead of *mita* service. Meanwhile, great wealth accumulated in the hands of the Spanish mine owners.

To escape the *mita's* harsh requirements, many Indians left their villages and became wage laborers either at the mines, where they hoped to get less dangerous jobs, or on local haciendas. Even though native villages lost able-bodied males, the Spaniards did not reduce a village's *mita* obligations, which meant the remaining villagers spent more time in *mita* service. Hacienda wages were paid mostly in kind, and Indians often were allowed areas for cultivation or grazing within the estate.

In the second half of the seventeenth century, the Spaniards developed a new system designed to extract wealth from the Indians. The *repartimiento de mercancías* ("distribution of merchandise") demanded the compulsory purchase of goods from district governors, placed more stress on Indians remaining in the tribute villages, and made the adoption of wage labor more attractive. But even free wage labor was not free for the Indians. On the haciendas, Indians accepted wage advances and ended up in debt-bondage to the Spanish overlords. Still, this system was often more desirable than being subject to the other tribute burdens placed upon native villages, as the hacienda Indian had job security and a plot of land for his family. Overall,

the *mita* system and its consequences proved very disruptive to the life of the *ayllu* and native villages.

—*Kimberly Henke Breuer*

See also
Encomienda System; *Repartimiento; Yanaconaje*
For Further Reading
Fisher, John Robert. 1977. *Silver Mines and Silver Miners in Colonial Peru, 1776–1824.* Liverpool: Centre for Latin-American Studies, University of Liverpool; Spalding, Karen. 1984. *Huarochiri, an Andean Society under Inca and Spanish Rule.* Stanford, CA: Stanford University Press; Stern, Steve J. 1993. *Peru's Indian People and the Challenge of Spanish Conquest: Huamanga to 1640.* Madison: University of Wisconsin Press; Zulawski, Ann. 1995. *They Eat from Their Labor: Work and Social Change in Colonial Bolivia.* Pittsburgh: University of Pittsburgh Press.

MONTESINOS, ANTONIO DE

Antonio de Montesinos was a Dominican missionary who served in the New World, principally on Hispaniola, during the early-sixteenth century. He was an outspoken critic of the abusive treatment accorded the indigenous population by early Spanish colonizers, and his denunciations led directly to the Spanish crown's first systematic attempt to institute protection for the Indians on legal, moral, and spiritual grounds.

The society of conquest established in the New World led inevitably to the exploitation of the native population, the main vehicle for which, in the aftermath of Columbus's voyages, was an institution known as the *encomienda* system—a grant, or allocation, of labor made to individuals *(encomenderos)* by the crown or its agents. To command such labor was deemed the natural right of the conqueror over the conquered.

Indians under the *encomienda* system were theoretically afforded certain protection as "free" people—they were to be treated with respect, Christianized, taught orderly habits of work, could not be bought or sold, and were to pay tribute only as other subjects of the monarch did. In practice, these protections went unobserved. The *encomenderos,* in the tradition of European contact with Africa, assumed slavery's legitimacy and operated accordingly.

Thus, the early form of *encomienda* employed by the Spanish to mobilize Indian labor could scarcely be distinguished from slavery. It entailed forced labor, exacted under extremely harsh conditions, and tribute in the form of food and goods. By the early 1500s, the entire native population of Hispaniola and the neighboring islands had been made subject to this system.

Nevertheless, the atrocities perpetrated against the Indians did not go unprotested. Indeed, the protests mounted. Their source was generally the church and in particular the missionary friars who were charged with the task of evangelizing the native population and converting it to Christianity. Among the voices raised in opposition to the *encomenderos,* the most powerful—in the early 1500s—belonged to Antonio de Montesinos.

In 1511, Montesinos delivered the first of several sermons in which he condemned the unjust enslavement of the Indians on Hispaniola and their brutal treatment by the Spanish. The sermons provoked strong opposition among the colonists, and Montesinos was summoned to Spain to defend his position. There he elaborated upon the evils of the *encomienda,* as currently practiced, and called for greater protection to be given the Indians. The crown, after convoking a council of jurists to deliberate the issue, became convinced of the need for reform. The result was the promulgation in 1512 of the Laws of Burgos (amended in 1513), a code of Spanish-Indian relations that attempted to ameliorate the condition of the Indians and to curb the excesses of the labor system.

Also instituted in 1512 as part of the reform movement inspired by Montesinos was the *requerimiento,* a document that would-be conquistadors were obliged to carry with them and read to the Indians, calling upon them to acknowledge the pope as their spiritual leader and the king as their temporal head. Following his 1512 visit, Montesinos made three more trips to Spain in defense of the Indians, in 1515, 1522–1524, and 1527.

—*Russ Davidson*

See also

Burgos, Laws of; *Encomienda* System; *Repartimiento;* The Requirement

For Further Reading

Burkholder, Mark A., and Lyman L. Johnson. 1994. *Colonial Latin America.* New York: Oxford University Press; Gibson, Charles. 1966. *Spain in America.* New York: Harper and Row; Parry, J. H. 1974. *The Spanish Seaborne Empire.* New York: Knopf.

MONTESQUIEU, CHARLES LOUIS DE SECONDAT (1689–1755)

The writings of Charles Louis de Secondat, baron de la Brède et de Montesquieu, are foundational to modern political culture, and his ideas on slavery are representative of French

Montesquieu

Enlightenment thought. His ideas—like the doctrine of separation of powers—were basic to the legal order that emerged from the American and French Revolutions. His attempt to derive a set of human laws based on a historical understanding of all civilizations was also an important precursor to the human sciences.

Montesquieu wrote three major works: *Lettres persanes* (1721), *Considérations sur les causes de la grandeur des Romains et de leur décadence* (1734), and *De l'esprit des lois* (1748). The first is presented as several letters written by two Persian visitors to Paris; through their eyes, Montesquieu criticized and described his society and theirs. The work is both a critique of the hypocrisy of Parisian habits and a description of what Montesquieu saw as the ingrained despotism of the Orient. In his second work, he described the rise and fall of the Roman Empire and theorized about the different forms of government possible within human societies.

His most influential work, *De l'esprit des lois* (The spirit of the laws), argues for the separation of powers in government and laid the foundation for the French constitution of 1791. It is this work that contains Montesquieu's most sustained discussion of slavery, which is tied to his larger theory of climatic variation. Montesquieu was an early armchair anthropologist, using the writings of European travelers to Asia, Africa, and the New World to develop a general description of "Laws in Relation to the Nature of the Climate" (Bk. 14).

Montesquieu believed that, physiologically, colder climates breed courageous and hardworking people who lack physical sensitivity; in contrast, warm climates encourage laziness but also heighten the senses and therefore the passions. These differences vary from one extreme—"You must flay a Muscovite alive to make him feel"—to the other, where the heat of the climate creates a society with "no curiosity, no noble enterprize, no generous sentiment," where "indolence constitutes the utmost happiness," and where "slavery is more supportable than the force and vigor of mind necessary for human conduct" (Bk. 14, Chap. 2). For Montesquieu, these differences were not immutable; legislation should struggle against the vices created by climates, and education can transform people for the better.

In Book 15 of *De l'esprit des lois*, Montesquieu was harshly critical of slavery and its defenders, claiming that "the state of slavery is bad of its own nature: it is neither useful to the master nor the slave." The slave is drained of virtue, and the master becomes accustomed to "the want of all moral virtues" and grows "fierce, hasty, severe, choleric, voluptuous and cruel" (Chap. 1). Selling oneself is a breach of natural law as serious as suicide: "The liberty of every citizen constitutes a part of the public liberty; and in a democratic state is even part of the sovereignty. To sell one's citizenship is so repugnant to all reason, as to be scarce supposeable in any man." In a footnote, Montesquieu made it clear that he was referring to "slavery in a strict sense, as formerly among the Romans, and at present in our colonies" (Chap. 2). Harshly critical of the use of conversion to Christianity as a justification for slavery (Chap. 4), he satirized as irrational the arguments presented by eighteenth-century defenders of slavery (Chap. 5).

Montesquieu's polemic on the evils inherent in breaking natural law was less virulent when he related it to the problem of labor in different climates. Here, again, he was clearly referring to the sugar colonies of the Antilles. "There are countries where the excess of heat enervates the body," he noted, "and renders men so slothful and dispirited, that nothing but the fear of chastisement can oblige them to perform any laborious duty: slavery is there more reconcilable to reason" (Chap. 7). He argued, as he did in his general discussion of climatic variation, for the relativity of oppression; slavery is more acceptable in a despotic society where everyone is already subject to tyranny. He remained ambivalent in his philosophy of the problem:

"But as all men are born equal, slavery must be accounted unnatural, tho' in some countries it be founded on natural reason; and a wide difference ought to be made betwixt such countries and those where even natural reason rejects it, as in Europe, where it has been so happily abolished" (Chap. 7).

Although accepting that in some climates "natural reason" could justify slavery against "natural law," Montesquieu finally argued that in most places, and with the proper machines, "even the most laborious works" would be better performed by freemen. He suggested that slavery could cede everywhere to such free labor: "Possibly there is not that climate upon earth, where the most laborious services might not, with proper encouragement, be performed by freemen" (Chap. 7). Again, though, a sense of the difference among people—a difference created by bad legislation—imbues the succeeding paragraph: "Bad laws having made lazy men; they have been reduced to slavery, because of their laziness." In the final chapters of Book 15, Montesquieu described the different forms of slavery, argued for the humane treatment of slaves, and discussed the political dangers posed by slavery.

In his attempt to apply a set of universal laws to the variety of human cultures, Montesquieu helped define the culture of the Enlightenment and the political institutions that emerged from it. His engagement with the problem of slavery was the foundation for the French antislavery movement of the late-eighteenth century and embodies the contradictions the political actors of the French Revolution encountered in including the problem of slavery under the mantle of freedom.

—*Laurent Dubois*

For Further Reading
Althusser, Louis. 1970. *Politics and History*. London: New Left Press; Durkheim, Emile. 1970. *Montesquieu and Rousseau: Forerunners of Sociology*. Ann Arbor: University of Michigan Press; Montesquieu, Charles de Secondat. 1977. *The Spirit of Laws: A Compendium of the First English Edition*. Ed. David Wallace Carrithers. Berkeley: University of California Press; Shklar, Judith. 1987. *Montesquieu*. Oxford: Oxford University Press.

MORAVIAN SLAVES

Moravian slaves were African Americans purchased by missionaries affiliated with the Unitas Fratrum or Moravian Brethren. Although we associate missionaries with abolition and the emancipation movements that swept the Atlantic world, it was not uncommon for missionaries and mission societies to rent laborers and/or to purchase involuntary slave labor. Such was the case with the Moravian Brethren.

The Moravian Brethren were one of the first Protestant denominations to establish colonial missions, founding sites in Greenland, South America, North America, and the West Indies during the early-eighteenth century. The brethren began renting labor power and then purchasing enslaved blacks soon after establishing settlements in North America and the West Indies.

The labor shortage during initial stages of mission-community formation was acute, and Moravians frequently rented labor to perform tasks like clearing fields. The patterns of hiring labor led to purchasing slaves and to the baptism and inclusion of enslaved Africans as members of Moravian communities. Slave purchases were intended to promote self-sufficiency and secure a Moravian community's integrity in the face of expansion and possible inclusion within non-Moravian settlements. Precisely when the transition from hired labor to slave purchases occurred, and whether it reflected official Moravian policy, remains unclear. That it occurred is well documented, and that baptism and enslavement presented a contradiction did not go unnoticed by the brethren and others. The religious reformer and Moravian leader Count Nikolaus Ludwig von Zinzendorf reportedly stated to Moravian slaves that the brethren were concerned with spiritual rather than physical freedom.

If the Moravian Brethren could gloss over such contradictions in North America, they were not as successful in island societies like Jamaica. Although they were invited by local planters, organizing an *oeconomy* ("local economy") of interdependent and gender-specific *choirs*, or households, in Jamaica was a formidable task. Carmel, the Moravian settlement in Jamaica and the counterpart of Bethlehem, Pennsylvania, and Salem, North Carolina, was established in 1754 as both a residence and a functioning cattle ranch. As in North America, single brethren were replaced by married couples, and Carmel became a home away from home for 25 Moravians and 30 enslaved Africans. The brethren raised livestock, cultivated provisions, and sold or jobbed their slaves' labor to support themselves and provide the time to work and proselytize among the blacks.

In this settlement, described as a "dismal beginning" and a "blot" by Moravian historians, the Moravians found that patterns established in North America were not so easily reproduced in Jamaica. Although sympathetic planters had invited the brethren to come, Jamaica was a plantation society in which a European minority dominated an African majority. Fearing that preaching would upset the status quo, most planters denied or limited the brethren's access to their estates. On the other hand, the Moravians' reliance upon slave labor had equally dire consequences. None of Carmel's slaves became congregation members, and fewer than 100 out of several thousand slaves on local estates had been baptized by the turn of the nineteenth century.

The Jamaica mission was deemed a failure until the 1820s when slave labor was disallowed and Carmel was sold. With the aid of native helpers such as Robert Peart and George Lewis, the Moravians in Jamaica then established a series of new and far more successful mission communities.

—*John W. Pulis*

See also
Barbados; Church Missionary Society; Danish West Indies; Dutch Caribbean; Jamaica; Quakers
For Further Reading
Buchner, John H., 1854. *The Moravians in Jamaica*. London: Longman and Brown; Hamilton, K. G. 1967. *A History of the Moravian Church*. Bethlehem, PA: Board of Christian Education; Pulis, John W. 1998. *In The Holy Mountains: Missions, Moravians, and the Making of Afro-Christianity in Jamaica*. New York: Gordon and Breach; Sensbach, Jon. 1991. *A Separate Canaan: The Making of an Afro-Moravian World in North Carolina, 1763–1856*. Ann Arbor, MI: University Microfilms.

MOREAU DE ST. MERY, LOUIS MEDERIC (1750–1819)

A lawyer and judge, Louis Médéric Moreau de St. Mery is best remembered for his *Description of Colonial St. Domingue* (1796), an important source for historians of Saint Domingue. Born in Fort-de-France, Martinique, Moreau studied law in Paris and practiced in Cap-Français, Saint Domingue, where he later became a judge. In 1780, he became a member of the island's Conseil Supérieur, and as such, he had the opportunity to travel throughout the French Antilles, gathering information for his later writings. In the early 1780s, Louis XVI called him to Paris to publish a book on colonial legislation for officials in France and the colonies, published in six volumes as the *Loix et constitutions* (1784–1790 [Laws and constitutions]).

Moreau was active in the early years of the French Revolution; as president of the electors of Paris, he spoke to Louis XVI on behalf of the city. His house was a gathering place for Creole representatives in Paris, and he was a delegate for Martinique in the

National Assembly. In this role, he delivered a speech in December 1789 defending the need for a distinct set of laws for the colonies created by people who understood the climate and the culture—a common claim among whites resistant to the full application of republican ideals in the Antilles. As the French Revolution radicalized, Moreau was attacked and then imprisoned as a counterrevolutionary. He managed to escape with his family and his manuscripts to exile in the United States. There, he settled in Philadelphia, where he established a bookstore and publishing house that became a center for the community of refugees from Saint Domingue in the city.

During his exile, he first published a book on the Spanish part of Saint Domingue in 1793, and in 1797, he published his description of the French part of the island. The latter work presents a general history of the colony, including descriptions of daily life and culture among whites, people of color, and slaves. Notable is a description of the *danse Vaudoux* ("voodoo dance"), one of the earliest descriptions of the Haitian religion, and another passage that ascribes names to 120 different outcomes of miscegenation or mixed marriages. Both passages are commonly quoted and referred to in histories and novels about colonial Saint Domingue. Most of the work contains a detailed description of the colony in the form of a walking tour. Among Moreau's other publications was the 1797 *Traité de la danse* (Traits of the dance), a work that compared the dances of different cultures.

Moreau returned to France in the late 1790s and worked as the official historian in the colonial ministry, which allowed him to collect the documents and maps that now compose the Fonds Moreau de St. Mery in the French Archives Nationales. Until his death in 1819, he worked on various manuscripts about the history of the Americas, which he never published. His legacy is a rich series of writings and archives that are central for the study of colonial Saint Domingue.

—*Laurent Dubois*

See also
Haitian Revolution
For Further Reading
Moreau de St. Mery, Louis Médéric. 1793. *Déscription topographique et politique de la partie Espagnol de l'île de Saint Domingue.* Philadelphia: n.p.; Moreau de St. Mery, Louis Médéric. 1797. *Déscription topographique, physique, civile, politique et historique de la partie Française de l'île St. Domingue.* Philadelphia: n.p.; Moreau de St. Mery, Louis Médéric. 1784–1790. *Loix et constitutions des colonies Françaises de l'Amérique sous le vent, de 1550 à 1785.* 6 vols. Paris: n.p.; Moreau de St. Mery, Louis Médéric. 1797. *Traité de la danse.* Philadelphia: n.p.

MORET LAW
(1870)

Segismundo Moret, a member of the Spanish Abolitionist Society and the minister for colonial affairs in the Spanish government formed after the liberal revolution of 1868, was the sponsor of a law that contemplated the gradual elimination of slavery. The Moret Law, approved by the Spanish Cortes (or Parliament) in 1870, was largely a response on the part of the Spanish government to independence-minded Cubans, as an uneasy alliance of abolitionists and slaveowners in Cuba had promised freedom to black slaves if they helped the rebel cause there.

Article 1 of the Moret Law proclaimed free all children born of slave mothers after the law's publication on June 23, 1870. This was the so-called *vientres libres*, or free wombs, clause. All slaves born after September 1868 would be purchased by the state from their owners at the price of 125 pesos per child, but only after the insurrection ceased. Slaves aged 60 or older would be freed, but their owners would not be compensated. The law gave freedom to all slaves helping the Spanish side in the war, and the state still promised monetary reparations to loyal slaveowners whose slaves joined the Spanish army.

Other provisions included taking a census of the slave populations in Puerto Rico and Cuba. Enslaved persons not inscribed in the census by their masters were declared automatically free. Different legal categories of enslavement were created, such as *coartación,* self-purchase by slaves, which gave some slaves rights to keep part of their earnings, seek work for themselves, and change masters of their own accord. The *emancipados,* enslaved persons found in captured slave ships but still owned by the state, were also promised freedom.

Proslavery plantation owners pressured Cuba's governor into delaying, first, the publication of the law for two months and, then, its implementation until 1872. They argued that the law lacked proper regulations and a reliable slave census. The provision freeing unlisted slaves was largely ignored by owners and authorities alike, and the law's application was generally ineffectual, since the enforcing *juntas protectoras,* committees for the protection of freed and yet-to-be-freed slaves, were dominated by proslavery planters. Freed slaves found their mobility limited and that they were in monetary debt to their former masters. Appeals for mistreatment and other illegal acts committed by owners were met with delays and outright stalling. Of the almost 290,000 slaves listed in 1871, only 32,000 had been freed in compliance with the law by 1877, and it was not until the end of the

Ten Years War (1868–1878) between Cuban insurgents and Spain that many slaves on both sides of the conflict gained their freedom.

Recognizing the failure of the Moret Law very early, Puerto Rican representatives in the Spanish Cortes gained approval in 1873 of a law abolishing slavery in Puerto Rico alone. The coup d'état that ended the first Spanish republic in 1874 placed the application of the Moret Law into legal limbo, and it was replaced in 1880 by the law of Patronato, which proclaimed the gradual abolition of Cuban slavery over an eight-year period. Pressure from abolitionists, generalized slave flight, and the threat of insurrection by black slaves forced the Spanish government to proclaim the total abolition of slavery in 1886. By then, only 25,000 slaves still remained in bondage.

—Baltasar Fra-Molinero

See also
Coartación
For Further Reading
Corwin, Arthur F. 1967. *Spain and the Abolition of Slavery in Cuba, 1817–1886*. Austin: University of Texas Press; Mesa, Roberto. 1990. *El colonialismo en la crisis del XIX español*. Madrid: Ediciones de Cultura Hispánica; Navarro Azcue, Concepcion. 1986. "La esclavitud en Cuba, antes y después de las leyes abolicionistas." In *Estudios sobre la abolición de la esclavitud*. Ed. Francisco de Solano. Madrid: Consejo Superior de Investigaciones Científicas; Scott, Rebecca J. 1985. *Slave Emancipation in Cuba: The Transition to Free Labor, 1860–1899*. Princeton, NJ: Princeton University Press.

MORTALITY OF THE SLAVE TRADE

Perhaps the most grisly aspect of the acknowledged horrors of the slave trade was the high rate of mortality encountered during the Middle Passage, the transatlantic voyage, from the sixteenth to the nineteenth centuries. In the years since the slave trade ceased, the atrocities and abuses aboard ship have been vividly recalled from the accounts penned by repentant slavers and slaves who contributed to the abolitionist press.

Although it can be assumed that transportation of human chattel has always involved considerable casualties, owing to a certain neglect of the cargo that contributes to the profitability of such enterprises, reliable qualitative data are not available for periods prior to relatively recent history. There are data, however, for the Islamic trans-Saharan slave trade, which surely rivaled the transatlantic trade's rates of disease and death. Numerous analyses of existing records from the various sources provide a view of the brutal Middle Passage that is more objective, complete, and comprehensive than was available earlier.

The voyage into bondage was harsh from capture to market, and death was an ever-present factor at each stage in the journey. The overland journey from the interior of Africa was a forced march and claimed the lives of many of the recently subjugated before they even reached the coast; there are several reports of slaves being "buried on the road" by Royal African Company agents in the early-eighteenth century. European forts and factories offered the next grim venue. Slaves would be stored in underground facilities, called "truncks," to reduce the possibility of escape. These festering holes, where the slaves dwelled in their own excrement, were confined, damp, and poorly ventilated. The sick would not be quarantined from the healthy, and many slaves perished even before they were taken aboard ship.

The overcrowded hold offered no improvement for the already debilitated slaves. Crews of slavers had to keep vigilant watch when the cargo was brought on deck for exercise and meals to prevent individuals from casting themselves overboard to escape their dreadful conditions. Historical accounts attest to the poor sanitary conditions of the ships' holds: it was claimed that once a ship had made the Middle Passage, the lingering stench of the hold made it unfit for any other service. During the era of British suppression of the trade, it was further claimed that one could identify a slaver easily by the trail of sharks that followed the vessel awaiting the bodies to be cast over.

Numerous afflictions could claim lives during the weeks or even months that it could take to reach the Americas. Diseases from Europe and Africa affected both cargo and crew alike. Smallpox, malaria, scurvy, dysentery, ophthamalia (conjunctivitis), and various "fevers" are the ailments most commonly reported by ship's surgeons. Other factors that contributed to slave mortality in transit were complications that resulted from physical abuse, overcrowding, and, most commonly, malnutrition.

Slave-trading companies made efforts to improve the quality of the transport of slaves and thereby decrease their capital losses, but the efforts were to little avail. Regulations were enacted that set standards for a ratio of slaves per ton of a given vessel and also to improve ventilation, but no mandates were ever set for minimum requirements of food and drink during the passage. Efforts to improve shipboard sanitation were grossly inadequate, exemplified by such futile measures as rinsing the hold with vinegar or citrus juice to disinfect it. Even when a surgeon was present aboard ship, he was generally helpless to combat any disease that might break out and had no control over the conditions that the slaves were kept in prior to their being put on board ship.

The responsibility for cargo and crew fell upon the captain, and his best chance for a successful voyage depended ultimately on the fastest possible passage, reducing the time for incubation and spread of disease as well as consumption of the meager stores. The docking of the vessel did not always mean safety, however: colonial agents frequently reported high rates of mortality among recently arrived slaves, many of whom died in the interim between unloading and the day of the sale.

Various analyses of documents have produced numerous figures concerning the mortality of the slave trade for several periods. There was an apparent declining trend on British vessels, from a loss of 23.5 percent in 1680–1688 to an average of 4.0 percent during the last decade of the trade's legality, and vessels of other nations had similar declines (Sheridan, 1985). Mortality rates as high as 40 percent have been figured for periods in the nineteenth century, but evidence does not support that deregulation of the trade was at fault. Some statistical analyses have shown that regional variations of the sources of the slaves and also the seasonality of the trade were among the most significant factors in slave mortality.

—*David A. Johnson*

For Further Reading
Klein, Herbert S. 1978. *The Middle Passage: Comparative Studies in the Slave Trade.* Princeton, NJ: Princeton University Press; Palmer, Colin. 1981. *Human Cargoes: The British Slave Trade to Spanish America, 1700–1739.* Urbana: University of Illinois Press; Sheridan, Richard B. 1985. *Doctors and Slaves: A Medical and Demographic History of Slavery in the British West Indies, 1680–1834.* Cambridge: Cambridge University Press.

MOTT, LUCRETIA COFFIN (1793–1880)

Quaker minister, abolitionist, and early feminist, Lucretia Coffin Mott has long been acknowledged as the most universally respected antebellum feminist-abolitionist. Unusually well educated for a woman of her time, Mott's Quaker education supported the development of her intellectual prowess and scholarly reputation. Following a long-standing Quaker tradition of opposition to slavery, Lucretia and her husband James Mott became involved in antislavery activities in the 1820s and supported the antislavery teachings of the Quaker Elias Hicks. Lucretia was chosen to be a Quaker minister in 1821.

Both Lucretia and James were devout supporters of the free-produce movement, a Quaker-instigated reform devoted to promoting goods produced without slave labor. Through her ministering, Mott persuaded women to purchase wool and linen instead of cotton, maple sugar instead of cane sugar, and to make other appropriate substitutions.

In August 1830, abolitionist William Lloyd Garrison visited the Mott home in Philadelphia. He convinced the couple that immediate emancipation, not colonization in Africa, was the only viable solution to the slavery problem and urged them to increase their activism. The Mott residence soon emerged as the hub of Garrisonian abolitionism in Philadelphia. In 1833, Lucretia and several other women were invited to attend the first national antislavery convention in Philadelphia, at which the American Anti-Slavery Society was formed.

Spurred by the national convention's call for the creation of more female antislavery societies, Lucretia founded the Philadelphia Female Anti-Slavery Society in 1833. Besides serving as corresponding clerk for the organization, she was its principal leader and activist throughout her years in the movement. Most of the women members were Quakers, though some were Unitarian and some Presbyterian. The society also included several middle-class black women, and it was unique among women's antislavery organizations in its efforts to provide for the needs of Philadelphia's African American community. The women also petitioned Congress to abolish the domestic slave trade and to eradicate slavery in Washington, D.C., and the territories. They raised funds for the American Anti-Slavery Society and the Pennsylvania Anti-Slavery Society, collected a vast library of abolitionist literature, and popularized free-produce purchasing practices.

Although Lucretia acknowledged the importance of raising money for the abolitionist cause, she resisted the efforts of male abolitionists to define money making as the sole function of the female societies. Nor did Lucretia confine her abolitionist efforts to all-female organizations. She was an outspoken, prolific activist in both the American Anti-Slavery Society and the Pennsylvania Anti-Slavery Society, serving on the latter's executive committee.

Lucretia was a major organizer of the First Anti-Slavery Convention of American Women held in New York City in 1837. In 1838, when the Second Annual Convention convened in Philadelphia, a mob of 17,000, incensed by the role of women in the city's much-despised abolitionist activities, disrupted the proceedings, and those attending were forced to flee when the mob destroyed Pennsylvania Hall by fire. Lucretia and her fellow organizers refused to dissolve the convention, instead moving the site and proceeding with the convention.

In 1840, Lucretia and James attended the World Anti-Slavery Convention in London. Although other women were sent as delegates from various U.S. anti-slavery organizations, Lucretia was the only woman among the five delegates sent by the American Anti-Slavery Society. Despite her considerable stature in U.S. abolitionism, Lucretia (and all other women delegates) were not permitted to participate and were forced to sit in the adjoining gallery.

Although that event is often credited, erroneously, as the impetus that impelled Lucretia and Elizabeth Cady Stanton to organize the Seneca Falls Convention of 1848, the actual motivating force behind Mott's feminist activism was her need to redress the years of obstacles placed in the path of women abolitionists. Lucretia believed that such impediments unjustly restricted the ability of women to eradicate the evils of slavery and seriously limited the potential of the abolitionist movement.

Throughout the 1840s and 1850s, Lucretia lectured widely throughout the eastern United States, speaking against slavery. An eloquent orator, she addressed the legislatures of Delaware, Pennsylvania, and New Jersey. During the Civil War, she was a member of the Women's National Loyal League, which petitioned Congress in support of a thirteenth amendment.

Long distressed by the pervasiveness and intractability of racial prejudice in Philadelphia, she led a committee of the Friends Association for the Aid and Elevation of Freedmen in investigating the practice of barring African Americans from passenger cars in that city. In 1866, she was selected president of the new American Equal Rights Association, which was formed to push for universal suffrage. From the late 1860s until the time of her death in 1880, Lucretia continued her interest and involvement in the women's rights and woman suffrage movements, peace organizations, and the free religion movement.

—*Judith E. Harper*

See also
Philadelphia Female Anti-Slavery Society; Women and the Antislavery Movement
For Further Reading
Bacon, Margaret Hope. 1980. *Valiant Friend: The Life of Lucretia Mott*. New York: Walker; Cromwell, Otelia. 1958. *Lucretia Mott*. Cambridge, MA: Harvard University Press; Hersh, Blanche Glassman. 1978. *The Slavery of Sex: Feminist-Abolitionists in America*. Urbana: University of Illinois Press; Lutz, Alma. 1968. *Crusade for Freedom: Women in the Antislavery Movement*. Boston: Beacon Press.

MUDEJARS

Mudejars were the Muslims who remained in Spain after the Christian conquest of Islamic Iberia (eleventh to fifteenth centuries), and the term has come, for modern historians, to refer to any Muslim living in Christian Spain in that period. The word probably derives from the Arabic *mudajjan* ("tributary"), but it was not coined until the fifteenth century. Earlier sources refer to members of this group as *moros, mauri,* or *sarraceni*. Although of free status, the mudejars were very vulnerable to judicial enslavement and constituted an important slave source until their forced conversion and eventual deportation in the sixteenth and seventeenth centuries.

After Toledo's conquest in 1085, Spain's Christian kingdoms began gaining clear military advantage over their Muslim adversaries. Under the Muslims, who had ruled most of the peninsula since the mid-eighth century, al-Andalus (Islamic Spain) had become a rich and urbanized society. The Christian conquerors, faced with the problem of keeping the land economically productive and aware of their own meager numbers, granted liberal surrender terms to the many Muslims who chose to stay and live under their rule.

Initially, the Muslims received freedom of religion and a great measure of judicial and administrative autonomy. In the thirteenth century, most of the Kingdom of Aragon's population was Muslim, and the same was true in the Kingdom of Valencia through the fourteenth century. But the Muslims did not fare as well in Castile. Many Muslims left Toledo following its conquest, and after the Muslim rebellions in Murcia and Andalusia in the 1260s, there were wholesale deportations. Few Muslims remained in Portugal. Muslims resisting Christian domination were liable to enslavement en masse, and such was the fate of Majorca's inhabitants after their conquest by James I of Aragon in 1229.

Generally, the favorable terms the Muslims secured at their surrender were negotiated directly with their conquerors, so the Spanish Muslims came to have a special status whereby they fell under direct royal jurisdiction. This arrangement afforded them some protection against the church and the nobles but left them vulnerable to caprice. In 1287, Alfonso III of Aragon enslaved nearly the entire population of Muslim Minorca even though they had surrendered almost 60 years earlier.

Kings benefited from the taxes, fines, and fees generated by Islamic communities under their rule and also found them to be a steady slave source. For example, since the Muslims were essentially royal property, when Islamic law prescribed capital or corporal punishment, it was generally commuted to slavery. Muslims were also enslaved for many offenses against Christian law. Besides legitimate paths to enslavement, Muslims lost their freedom through kidnapping, rebellion, capture in war, or simply arbitrarily. Many slaves found themselves taken abroad to France or Italy. So steady was the enslavement rate that Aragon's kings depended on the practice as a revenue source, even to the point of pregranting the "next Moor to be enslaved" to favorites or creditors. The Spanish kings also inherited the thriving Andalusian slave trade and reaped rich profits from it, charging a tax on every slave sold.

By the fourteenth century, slaves were so numerous on the Iberian Peninsula that their ownership was limited by law. Males tended to fetch higher prices than females and were more commonly enslaved, but the latter were particularly vulnerable to enslavement for sexual or moral offenses. Women thus enslaved were without a doubt subject to sexual exploitation at their masters' hands, and many ended up in brothels. It was not uncommon for mudejar slaves to purchase their freedom eventually or, along the military frontier, to be traded in exchange for Christians enslaved in Muslim lands.

In 1501, the Muslims under Castile's rule were ordered to convert or emigrate. Those remaining and becoming nominally Christian were known as moriscos. Throughout the sixteenth century, in the Kingdom of Aragon, promulgations limiting freedom of language and religion were issued sporadically and with little success, most notably in 1556. In 1568, a large morisco uprising erupted in southern Spain and was suppressed only with difficulty and at great expense. Not until 1609 were Spain's Muslims, still numbering at least half a million, finally deported.

—*Brian Catlos*

See also
Portugal; Spain
For Further Reading
Boswell, John. 1977. *The Royal Treasure*. New Haven, CT: Yale University Press; Burns, Robert. 1973. *Islam under the Crusaders*. Princeton, NJ: Princeton University Press; Lourie, Elena. 1990. *Crusade and Colonisation: Muslims, Christians, and Jews in Medieval Aragón*. Brookfield, VT: Variorum; Meyerson, Mark. 1991. *The Muslims of Valencia*. Berkeley: University of California Press.

MUHAMMAD TURAY I (ASKIYA AL-HAJJ MUHAMMAD IBN ABI BAKR TURE) (D. 1538)

The relentless and successful military expansionist efforts of Sonni 'Ali Ber (r. 1464–1492) marked the last of the great western Sudanic empires, the Songhai Empire. Gaining control of the empire via political and military usurpation, one of West Africa's most-celebrated heroes, Askiya Muhammad Turay I (r. 1493–1528), led Songhai to greatness and power. Beginning with the political boundaries established by his predecessors, Muhammad extended Songhai's borders to become the largest of the West African kingdoms. Born Abi Bakr, he took the military title "askiya," signaling rank, instead of the title of royalty "sonni." Arab chroniclers interpret this change to mean official severance of ties with the traditional religious past, or "paganism."

Songhai's supremacy rose during the disintegration of the Empire of Mali. Solidified as a kingdom under the adept military capability of Sonni 'Ali Ber, a keen strategist and an efficient administrator, Songhai's power and glory took shape after the ascendancy of Askiya Muhammad Turay I. Oral historical accounts from West Africa inform us that he was son of Kassey, a sister of Sonni 'Ali Ber, and conspired for leadership after the sonni's questionable death. But the throne was given to 'Ali Baru (Abu Bakr Dau), the son of Sonni 'Ali Ber and Muhammad's cousin. However, not all the military chiefs supported 'Ali Baru, and some of them defected with Muhammad to form an opposition. In 1493, Muhammad defeated his rival and established himself as the ruler of the empire.

A key to Muhammad's rise, besides his political ambitions and intrigues, was the fact that Muslim merchants and tradesmen feared losing control of commerce. They also felt their wealth and power would be further usurped if they did not support Askiya Muhammad, for Sonni 'Ali Baru was following the example of his father, and since their loyalty was based in traditional countryside folk, neither Islam nor Muslims were sacrosanct. The seat of Muslim power, however, lay in urban centers of Timbuktu, Masina, Taghaza, Gao, and Jenné, and it was from those centers that the Muslim merchants and tradesmen conspired to assure Askiya Muhammad's victory. This effort also fostered a sustained Islamic growth in areas of learning, conversions, and an overall Islamization of the empire and its satellites.

Askiya Muhammad was also known as the "pilgrim king," and in 1496, he embarked on a two-year pilgrimage, a trek that indicated his confidence in his reign and the abilities of his brother, 'Umar Komdiagha, who was left in charge of the empire. Askiya Muhammad had established a powerful and efficient political machine built upon Islamic models combined with the efforts of his predecessors. While in Cairo, the Abbasid caliphate gave him the title of caliph of Takrur. The famous Islamic scholar, al-Maghili, consulted with Askiya Muhammad about revitalizing Shia Islam among lapsed and marginal Muslims of the surrounding areas shortly after the latter's triumphant return. He was also encouraged to initiate holy wars, or jihads, primarily to revitalize the faith throughout the western Sudan.

As in the earlier kingdoms of Ghana and Mali, Songhai under the leadership of Askiya Muhammad conspired to control all sources of revenue and commerce, and the city of Gao became the nexus of political, commercial, and financial activity. Slavery was a spoil of war, but the captives were also incorporated into the empire as domestics, military personnel, farmers and agriculturalists, and craftsmen making items for trade as well as being objects of trade themselves.

Military campaigns were conducted to convert the non-Islamic regions to the faith, and in many cases, the captives were compelled to accept Islam. Slavery provided the means to further develop urban areas, build a standing army, and provide domestics and bodyguards for the king and nobility. Often, the slaves served in caravans as helpers and carriers of goods or they cared for the domesticated beasts that transported the goods great distances. Under Askiya Muhammad Turay I, the legacy of endemic slavery continued in western Sudan, and the slave markets continued to thrive throughout his reign. The treatment of captives made slaves was humane despite their condition of servitude—in fact the latter word is more appropriate to describe their condition than the former.

—*Au'Ra Muhammad Abdullah Ilahi*

For Further Reading
Clarke, Peter B. 1982. *West Africa and Islam: A Study of Religious Development from the 8th to the 20th Century*. London: Edward Arnold; Fage, J. D.; Roland Oliver; and Richard Gray. 1975. *The Cambridge History of Africa from c. 1600 to c. 1790*. New York: Cambridge University Press; Glasse, Cyril. 1989. *The Concise Encyclopedia of Islam*. San Francisco: Harper and Row; Hiskett, Mervyn. 1984. *The Development of Islam in West Africa*. New York: Longman.

MULATTOES

*I*n the United States, "mulatto," a word of Spanish and Portuguese origin, technically identifies a progeny of one black and one white parent. Popularly, however, it signifies someone with any mixture of black and white ancestry. Debates over the categorization and status of mulattoes within the racial order in the United States began during the colonial era and continued into the twentieth century.

Interracial bonding began soon after the first blacks landed in the English colony of Virginia in 1619. The first mulattoes were the offspring of white indentured servants and blacks and had an uncertain legal status. Although colonial authorities did not outlaw miscegenation, they discouraged it by enacting a series of laws, beginning with one in 1662 which stipulated that children of mixed parentage inherited the status of their mother; therefore, those born of slave women would likewise be enslaved. This same act also imposed double punishment for any "Christian who shall commit fornication" with a black person.

Growing disdain for free mulattoes born of white women led to a 1691 decision specifying that individuals of such "abominable mixture" would be "bound out" as servants for 30 years and that their mothers would suffer 5 years of servitude or a heavy fine. Furthermore, the Virginia Assembly banished whites who intermarried from the colony. In 1705, a six-month jail sentence was imposed upon the whites in such unions. Although estimations of mulatto populations varied throughout the history of the United States, owing partly to differing and unreliable census-taking practices, it is generally agreed that in spite of these and other laws, the number of people of mixed heritage grew steadily. In 1755, the colony of Maryland counted 108,000 whites and 45,000 blacks, and among the black population were 3,600 mulattoes, 1,500 of whom were free.

Before the U.S. Civil War, there were two Souths, differentiated by the treatment of mulattoes within each region. The upper South included North Carolina and areas to the north and west, and it was characterized by a large mulatto population early in the colonial period. Many were free but relatively poor and rural, similar to their white forebears. Anxiety about free mulattoes passing for whites was prevalent, so the "one-drop rule," which categorized an individual with any black blood as black, dominated in all but the legal sense.

In contrast, mulattoes appeared later in the lower South and grew slowly in number during the eighteenth and nineteenth centuries. Most were born of well-to-do white fathers, and those few who were unfettered dominated the free black community and lived in prosperity. Beginning in the 1790s, their numbers were augmented by a huge influx of West Indian mulattoes who emigrated to Louisiana and South Carolina.

Before the 1850s, successful free mulattoes were valued by whites as "a barrier between our own color and that of the black—and in case of insurrection, are more likely to enlist themselves under the banner of the whites" (Berlin, 1974). Influenced by racial policies practiced under French and Spanish rule, whites valued people of mixed heritage above slaves and free blacks as a third, intermediary group, especially in South Carolina and lower Louisiana where free mulattoes were the most affluent. They rose highest in position in these regions, and 242 were listed as property-holding planters in the 1850 U.S. Census.

According to the census of 1850, mulattoes composed 1.8 percent of the national population and numbered 406,000 out of a black population of 3,639,000. In 1860, they numbered a little over 500,000. In the Old South, those areas settled prior to 1750, approximately half were free. In contrast, only 10.4 percent were not enslaved in the New South. During the antebellum era, miscegenation occurred most frequently between upper-class white planters and mulatto slave women, who suffered from their master's sexual aggression and produced numerous "white children of slavery." Although some of these mixed offspring were freed, most were considered bond servants.

As the sectional conflict between the North and the South grew in the 1850s, so did hostility against free mulattoes. Motivated by fresh fears of abolitionism from abroad and internal insurrection, the lower South, traditionally a haven that esteemed people of mixed lineage, grew increasingly intolerant and joined the upper South in clamoring for "two classes, the Master and the slave [as] no intermediate class can be other than immensely mischievous to our peculiar institution" (Williamson, 1980). In 1856, New Orleans newspaper the *Picayune* urged the removal of all free people of color, a "plague and a pest in our community." Order and stability through a rigid dichotomy of slave or free, black or white, were desired; there was no longer room for a triracial society. Increasingly, the one-drop rule predominated.

Stripped of their privileged position, free mulattoes who had previously identified with white Southerners turned to blacks for alliance. During the Reconstruction era (1865–1877), the mulattoes assumed leadership roles in helping to better freedmen's lives. Miscegenation with whites was minimal, and whites, blacks, and people of mixed parentage all came to accept the one-drop rule. At the same time, however, literary portrayals of the "tragic mulatto" began to appear, thus continuing the discussion of the ambiguous status of people of mixed blood. And the number of mixed offspring, mostly of mulatto and black parents, would grow to over 2 million by 1910.

—*Constance J. S. Chen*

For Further Reading
Berlin, Ira. 1974. *Slaves without Masters: The Free Negro in the Antebellum South*. New York: Pantheon Books; Johnson, Michael P., and Roark, James L. 1984. *Black Masters: A Free Family of Color in the Old South*. New York: W. W. Norton; Mencke, John G. 1979. *Mulattoes and Race Mixture: American Attitudes and Images, 1865–1918*. Ann Arbor, MI: UMI Research Press; Williamson, Joel. 1980. *New People: Miscegenation and Mulattoes in the United States*. New York: Free Press.

MURRAY, WILLIAM, FIRST EARL OF MANSFIELD (1705–1793)

Born in Scotland, William Murray left there at age 13 or 14 and was largely educated in England. His long-standing acquaintance with England prompted Samuel Johnson to say of Murray, "Much may be made of a Scotchman if he be caught young" (Shyllon, 1974).

After receiving his degree from Oxford in 1727, he was called to the bar three years later. Murray quickly became established as a lawyer of note: he became solicitor general and entered the House of Commons in 1742; attorney general in 1754; and finally, at the age of 51, lord chief justice of the Court of King's Bench. When he became chief justice in 1756, Murray also became Baron Mansfield, and in 1776 he was made an earl.

As chief justice, Mansfield heard court arguments during the 1760s and 1770s. He took decisions on several pivotal cases concerning the legal status of blacks and the question of whether or not they were property. During that time, Mansfield frequently crossed swords with Granville Sharp—a self-styled champion for the rights of blacks. In 1765, Mansfield was involved in the Jonathan Strong case. Owing to a series of charges and countercharges concerning the tangential issue of assault rather than the central issue of chattel slavery, the case never went to trial.

In 1771, Mansfield heard the case of Thomas Lewis, who had left his master only to be seized and forcibly put on board a ship bound for Jamaica where he was to be sold as a slave. Although the jury found his master guilty of abduction, Mansfield refused to offer judgment, and subsequently, Lewis's kidnappers fled. Mansfield heard similar cases such as *King v. Inhabitants of Thames Ditton* (1785) and the well-known Somersett case (1772). The latter was decided in favor of the plaintiff—James Somersett—who was saved from being sold into slavery by his former master. The decision asserted that slaves, by virtue of their presence in England, were essentially free and hence not obliged to remain in their former master's service. Because of the decision in favor of the slave, the case was long considered the decisive moment at which all black slaves in eighteenth-century Britain were declared free. In fact, though James Somersett triumphed, slavery persisted in Britain until its abolition in 1833.

Mansfield expressed many opinions, several of which, if not exactly contradictory, were nonetheless inconsistent. He concurred with the 1720 legal opinion of Sir Philip Yorke and Charles Talbot that fugitive slaves had to be delivered to their claimants.

However, he also agreed with Sir William Blackstone that "a slave or a Negro, the moment he lands in England, falls under the protection of the laws, and with regard to all natural rights becomes *eo instanti* a freeman" (Shyllon, 1974). Although Mansfield asserted that the color of a slave did not prove property, he was not necessarily championing the rights of the slave.

In the 1780s, Chief Justice Mansfield eventually rejected the Yorke-Talbot opinion. This reversal notwithstanding, he was skillful in avoiding ruling definitively on the core of an issue before him, thus the law remained uncertain concerning the forcible return of a slave to colonial plantations for many years to come.

—*T. K. Hunter*

See also
Sharp, Granville; Somersett Case; Strong, Jonathan
For Further Reading
Gerzina, Gretchen. 1995. *Black London: Life before Emancipation.* New Brunswick, NJ: Rutgers University Press; Shyllon, F. O. 1974. *Black Slaves in Britain.* London: Oxford University Press; Walvin, James. 1971. *The Black Presence: A Documentary History of the Negro in England, 1555–1860.* London: Orbach and Chambers.

MURRELL, JOHN A. (1806–1844)

*I*n 1835, rumors spread across the U.S. South that a criminal mastermind, a white man named John Murrell, had organized an invisible empire of outlaws. According to the stories, he planned to convince slaves to rise against their masters on the Fourth of July. In the confusion of the ensuing bloodbath, Murrell—"the great land pirate"—and his confederates would steal everything in sight.

A man named Virgil Stewart, who claimed to have infiltrated Murrell's gang, published a book that "exposed" the mastermind and his scheme. Stewart's tale bristled with gory details. He claimed Murrell habitually stole slaves, sold and resold them (they would run away from their new masters and return to him, since he had promised to take them to freedom), and then killed his dupes to keep them quiet. According to Stewart, Murrell usually hid his victims' bodies in rivers and lakes, having first cut open their stomachs so they would not swell and float to the surface. As Stewart's book circulated, fearful slaveowners and other whites looked around them, seeing gamblers, white criminals, and Yankees as Murrellites. Insolent enslaved African Americans became rebels, ready to bathe in the blood of white men and take planter women for their brides.

The reality of John Murrell hardly measured up to the myth. In 1835, he was already locked in a Tennessee prison. Instead of being the "master spirit" of insurrection, he was probably nothing more than a horse thief from middle Tennessee who occasionally dabbled in slave stealing. But Stewart's narrative touched chords deep in the slaveholders' psyche. On the cotton frontier, where society was in constant flux, planters feared the breakdown of their dominance over slaves and hegemony over whites on the fringes of plantation society.

Terrified but not paralyzed, slave masters sprang into action to prevent the horrors of Saint Domingue from appearing in the United States. In Mississippi, mobs tortured and hanged slaves who were allegedly plotting an insurrection. "Vigilance committees" summarily executed several whites suspected of being Murrellites. Gentlemen in Natchez deported gamblers, fearing that a criminal underworld linked these "blacklegs" to Murrell, and some Florida planters ran a "Dr. Borland" out of town, threatening death if he ever returned.

The excitement over the rumored Murrellite conspiracy reveals the uneasiness of nineteenth-century Southern planters, especially those on the plantation frontier. They feared their slaves (especially after Nat Turner's revolt in 1831), poor whites, professional gamblers, and strangers who might try to undermine their system. Most of all, they feared an alliance between blacks and nonplanter whites, and slaveowners blamed "slave-stealing" poor whites for a high percentage of slave runaways. Stewart's exaggerated account of Murrell struck a nerve in whites who were too anxious to distinguish rumor from reality. Dozens of slaves (and perhaps a dozen whites) paid the price.

John Murrell remained in prison until shortly before he died, at the age of 38, in 1844. His legend survived, and many believed that only quick action, torture, and the lyncher's noose had defeated his grand conspiracy for insurrection.

—*Edward E. Baptist*

For Further Reading
Morris, Christopher. 1988. "An Event in Community Organization: The Mississippi Slave Insurrection Scare of 1835." *Journal of Social History* 22 (3): 93–111; Penick, James Lal, Jr. 1981. *The Great Western Land Pirate: John A. Murrell in Legend and History.* Columbia: University of Missouri Press; Walton, Augustus Q. 1835. *A History of the Detection, Conviction, Life, and Designs of John A. Murel, the Great Western Land Pirate.* Athens, TN: G. White.

MUSA, MANSA (KANKAN)
(D. 1337)

Mansa Kankan Musa, who ascended the throne of the Mali empire in 1312, was one of the greatest kings of Mali. Mansa Musa became popular in African history, not only for his contributions to imperial territorial expansion and development, but also for the international recognition he gained for the empire during his pilgrimage to Mecca in 1324–1325—and slaves played a prominent role during that trip.

Mali under Musa drew its power and strength from the control of trading routes, which involved the sale of gold, salt, ivory, kola nuts, and slaves. He incorporated into the empire such important trading, mineral-producing, and Islamic cities as Gao, Jenné, Taghaza, Takedda, Takrur, Timbuktu, and Walata. Through his administrative reorganization and the appointment of provincial governors, or emirs, it was possible for Mali to maximize the benefits from regional trade, especially the trans-Saharan trade with the North African Berbers and Arabs. Some of the provincial administrators were given fiefs, horses, and clothes; others were paid annual salaries. Political stability and economic prosperity were sustained by his establishment of a 100,000-strong standing army, including 10,000 horsemen. Although trade contributed significantly to Mali's wealth, the citizens were also involved in agriculture, fishing, cattle breeding, black-smithing, weaving, and carving.

Musa was a devout Muslim who had an immense love for virtue. Hence, he was committed to purifying, strengthening, and spreading Islam throughout the Mali empire. More important, to demonstrate his commitment to the Islamic faith, he embarked on a pilgrimage to the holy land of Mecca in 1324, a pilgrimage that was organized on a very huge scale. Adu Boahen stated: "According to al-Umari, he left Mali with the fantastic amount of 100 camel-loads of gold [Ibn Khaldun puts the figure at 80]. Five hundred slaves were also said to have gone before the king, each carrying a gold staff weighing 4 lb. He also took with him thousands of his subjects including slaves to carry his personal effects, soldiers to protect the entire caravan and officials and dignitaries, as well as his senior wife who was attended by 500 slaves and maids" (Boahen, 1986).

Another source writes that Mansa Musa's "huge caravan included . . . 12,000 slaves, all dressed in brocade and Persian silk. Mansa himself rode on horseback. . . . Directly preceding him were 500 slaves, each carrying a staff of gold weighing 6 pounds. Then came Mansa Musa's baggage—a train of 80 camels, each carrying 300 pounds weight of gold dust" (Hutchin-

Mansa Musa, detail from an early-fifteenth-century map of Europe and North Africa.

son, 1979). Despite the discrepancy in the number of slaves involved in the pilgrimage, what is significant is that slave labor contributed to its success.

During the pilgrimage, Musa gave alms and gifts to the poor and extended his generosity to rulers, officials, and dignitaries in Cairo and Mecca. Indeed, because of his generosity with gold bars, the value of gold fell in Egypt during his visit. As part of his design to publicize Mali to the outside world, Musa established diplomatic relations with the rulers of Morocco and Egypt and invited Arab scholars and traders to Mali. In Mecca, he came in contact with Abu Ishaq al-Sahili, a poet and architect who designed and built a mosque in Timbuktu and a palace for the emperor. Mali owes its fame and fortune partly to the leadership of Mansa Kankan Musa. His extravagance notwithstanding, Mali witnessed a golden age during his reign.

—*Onaiwu W. Ogbomo*

For Further Reading
Boahen, Adu. 1986. *Topics in West African History.* Burnt Mill, Essex, Eng.: Longman; Hutchinson, Louise

Daniel. 1979. *Out of Africa: From West African King-doms to Colonization.* Washington, DC: Anacostia Neighborhood Museum of the Smithsonian Institution; Levtzion, Nehemia. 1973. *Ancient Ghana and Mali.* London: Methuen; Levtzion, Nehemia. 1963. "The Thirteenth- and Fourteenth-Century Kings of Mali." *Journal of African History* 4 (3): 341–353.

MUSLIM SLAVES IN THE AMERICAS

Portuguese incursions into western Africa during the early-fifteenth century generated increased trade with Arabs, Tauregs, and kings of Africa's Guinea coast, causing the Portuguese to have greater vested interests in Africa's ongoing slave trade. Slaves acquired from the Songhai, for example, represented numerous religious persuasions, including animists, Muslims, and Christians.

The trade increased in the territory of Angola, and the region eventually came under Portuguese control. Although initially interested in gold and other precious metals, the Portuguese soon concentrated on exporting slaves to Brazil, and besides western Africa, Brazil, and Angola, the trade came to include distant areas like Mozambique and Cuba. For the next four centuries, the Portuguese transported an average of 15,000 slaves per year as their usual quota to European colonies and points beyond. After Christopher Columbus's maiden voyage to the New World, many newly acquired slaves, including numerous Muslims, were taken to the Americas, as the trade in Muslim slaves, along with other slaves who were non-Muslim, had been an important feature of the Portuguese economy several decades prior to Columbus's first voyage.

It can be accurately stated that Muslim slaves were some of the earliest settlers of the Americas. The Italian navigator and explorer Amerigo Vespucci took a few slaves, three of whom were Muslim, to the New World on one expedition along the Venezuelan coast. Alonso de Hojeda, one of Queen Isabella's favorites, had been commissioned to travel with Vespucci to the region that later become Suriname, and during the expedition, they discovered for the Europeans the mouth of the Amazon River. Besides the Muslim slaves they took with them, they returned with 168 native slaves, pearls, and gold, which Vespucci hoped would greatly please the queen.

An early Muslim slave in the Americas was Abdual-Rahahman Ibrahima, the son of the ruler of Fouta Djallon in what is today the republic of Guinea in Africa. Having studied humanities at Tim-buktu University, a center of Muslim learning in western Africa, Abdual-Rahahman was captured in battle north of Fouta Djallon in 1788. Only 26 when captured, he held tenaciously to the dream of returning someday to his homeland, and spiritually and morally he was able to withstand the harshness of 39 years of slavery. Acquired by Thomas Foster, a Natchez, Mississippi, farmer, Abdual-Rahahman delved deep into his Islamic faith to deal constructively with his ordeal. He eventually won the admiration of many of his contemporaries, and the success of his master's farm was directly attributed to his hard work and dedication.

In 1826, an incident involving his daughter's affair with Foster's son caused her to be exiled from the farm. In indignation, Abdual-Rahahman wrote a strongly worded letter in Arabic to the king of Morocco demanding that as a Muslim who owed his loyalty only to Allah, he and his family must be set free. The Moroccan king took the matter up with President John Quincy Adams, who later addressed the matter with Thomas Foster, and after some persuasion, Foster granted Abdual-Rahahman and his wife their freedom. Shortly thereafter, Abdual-Rahahman toured the United States to gain donations to help him and his wife purchase the freedom of their children and grandchildren. Failing to gain their immediate release as wished, they departed the United States for Fouta Djallon in 1829, with newly created Liberia serving as a transit station.

Their departure took place just as Thomas Foster was publicly expressing his second thoughts about giving them their freedom and his desire for their return. Additionally, political arguments between proslavery and abolitionist forces, including attempts to exploit Abdual-Rahahman's case in the growing dispute, and Adams's failure to be reelected president were strong incentives for Abdual-Rahahman and his wife to leave the country. They would continue the fight for their children after they returned to Fouta Djallon, but Abdual-Rahahman's death a few short months after arriving in Liberia abruptly closed the chapter on this proud man and his family's struggle. Abdual-Rahahman's circumstances repeated themselves, often in slight and varying contexts, in the hardships and struggles of numerous Muslim slaves who were forcibly settled in the Americas.

Many Muslim slaves' narratives about slavery in North and South America and the Caribbean islands are available, and these narratives have been given equal significance by recent historians to those that originated in Europe earlier. By listening to more Muslim slave voices, and not only the silent voices that were often lost in Europe's past concerning the slave trade, historians of slavery, Africa, and the Americas have expanded the historical canvas of discourse.

With this emerging clearer historical image, meaning can be being applied to actions and developments that linked the interior of Africa's past to that of Europe and by extension, to the Americas.

The Muslim slave stories, like those of many non-Muslim slaves, are sad, ironic, and utterly tragic. The narratives being made available offer clearer insight into this chapter of the slave trade, and readers should now gain a further appreciation of the often heroic individuals who were victimized by the institution.

—*Talaat Shehata*

See also
Ibrahima, Abdual-Rahahman
For Further Reading
Diop, Cheikh Anta. 1987. *Precolonial Black Africa.* Trenton, NJ: Africa World Press; Katz, William L. 1990. *Breaking the Chains: African-American Slave Resistance.* New York: Atheneum; Lovejoy, Paul E. 1990. *Transformations in Slavery: A History of Slavery in Africa.* Cambridge: Cambridge University Press; Miller, Joseph C. 1988. *Way of Death: Merchant Capitalism and the Angolan Slave Trade, 1730–1830.* Madison: University of Wisconsin Press.

NABUCO DE ARAUJO, JOAQUIM (1849–1910)

Joaquim Nabuco de Araujo, the great Brazilian abolitionist, was born into an elite Recife family with close connections to the planter class of the northeastern part of Brazil. His father was a leader of the Liberal Party, a jurist, and a councilor of state of the empire. As a student, the young Joaquim was drawn to both literature and sociopolitical reform. After education in the best schools of Brazil, he wrote, traveled extensively in Europe, and served Brazil in diplomatic capacities in London and New York.

In a decade of travel abroad, Nabuco decided upon the great cause of his life—the abolition of slavery in his native Brazil. That struggle began in earnest in 1879 when he was elected as a Liberal deputy to the Brazilian Parliament. At that time, even after the 1871 passage of the Law of Free Birth, there were still approximately 1.5 million slaves in Brazil, which had a total population of about 10 million.

Nabuco, in common with other well-educated and cosmopolitan Brazilians, had suffered in Europe and the United States from the sting of criticism directed at his country because it was the last bastion of slavery in the Western world. Immediately after he became a deputy, he challenged his own party to stop procrastinating and abolish slavery throughout the empire within 10 years. Leaders of the Liberal Party were caught up in a struggle over the role of the Catholic Church in Brazilian society at the time and also did not wish to alienate slaveholding supporters. They were outraged at the temerity of the young deputy and subsequently withdrew party support from him, which ensured his defeat in a reelection bid in 1881.

Free of any party responsibilities, Nabuco turned his considerable energies to the mobilization of public opinion against slavery. A charismatic orator, he wooed the new urban middle sectors as well as labor. An effective organizer, the creation of the Brazilian Anti-Slavery Society was largely owing to his efforts. In 1883, Nabuco penned his greatest work, *0 abolicionismo*, the Brazilian equivalent of *Uncle Tom's Cabin*. In that appeal he emphasized the retrogressive influence of slavery since social and economic progress for the empire could only be achieved under a free labor system. Nor did he ignore the cruelty of the slave labor system and its moral and religious injustice.

Defenders of slavery were on the defensive by the 1880s. Independent of the national government, several provinces abolished slavery in that decade, and officials found it more difficult to capture escaped slaves because elements of the population aided the fugitives. The earlier Law of Free Birth, while greatly flawed, had itself hastened the cause of emancipation. The imperial family favored abolition, and increasingly, urban elites were won to the cause. Although defenders of the institution argued that the economic well-being of agricultural Brazil depended upon slavery, and that abolition would be a blow to holders of property rights, theirs was clearly a last-ditch stand.

The final triumph of the abolitionist movement came in 1887–1888, and Nabuco played a critical role in the victory. In those years, the emperor's absence required that Princess Isabel act as regent. She was an ardent abolitionist and called for the formation of a government to deal with the slavery issue. At much the same time, Nabuco, then in Europe, personally requested Pope Leo XIII to condemn slavery in Brazil. Conservatives became aware of the pope's favorable view of Nabuco's plea and succeeded in persuading the Vatican not to single out Brazil. Nonetheless, Leo XIII's encyclical in early 1888, which proclaimed support for the enslaved everywhere, was rapidly disseminated throughout Brazil. International condemnation, public pressure, the regent's desires, and the views of the church all culminated in the passage of a law outlawing slavery on May 13, 1888.

Nabuco was just one of many abolitionists in Brazil in the 1880s, although arguably he was the most important. The end of slavery in Brazil certainly would have been eventually achieved even without his undeniable gifts, but his energy, commitment, oratory, organizational gifts, and political acumen accelerated the course of abolition.

A supporter of the empire, Nabuco was disappointed by the creation of the Brazilian Republic in 1889—an event that in no small part was aided by the indifference of the planter class to an empire that, through abolition, had impoverished many of them. For years after the establishment of the republic,

Nabuco still considered himself a monarchist. Eventually he served the republic as a most able and respected diplomat, but for most Brazilians, he will always be remembered as the conscience of his nation in the emancipation struggle of the 1880s.

—Jerry W. Cooney

See also
Abolition, Latin America; Abolitionist Confederation; Brazilian Anti-Slavery Society; Free Birth, Law of
For Further Reading
Conrad, Robert E. 1971. *The Destruction of Brazilian Slavery, 1850–1888*. Berkeley: University of California Press; Nabuco, Carolina. 1950. *The Life of Joaquim Nabuco*. Stanford, CA: Stanford University Press; Nabuco, Joaquim. 1883. *O abolicionismo*. London: Kingdom.

NAGWAMATSE, UMORU AND IBRAHIM

Noted by contemporaries and historically remembered as "the destroyer, the raider, and the conqueror," the name Nagwamatse became synonymous with unbridled forms of slavery and invidious nineteenth-century slave-raiding activities in the central Sudan. A grandson of Usman dan Fodio, the Sokoto Caliphate's founder, Umoru Nagwamatse (1806–1876) grew up during the turbulent and far-reaching sociopolitical transformation that marked the early-nineteenth-century establishment and consolidation of the Sokoto Caliphate. Administering a frontier district, he survived the intrigues of Sokoto royal politics and the punitive measures designed to tame his restless energy. With his effective cavalry, consisting largely of slaves and freebooters, he raided many leaderless, decentralized, and highly heterogeneous peoples and groups beyond the caliphate's southwestern frontier.

Umoru's tactics were brutal but effective; his military measures were cruel and unscrupulous. Overrunning an area with lightning speed, he would send raiding parties to destroy outlying settlements, burning houses and crops at harvesttime. With the misery of famine added to war's horrors, the harried inhabitants would be forced to take refuge in towns, which were then besieged and systematically starved out with the inhabitants butchered or sold into slavery. Towns that sued for peace would be required immediately to surrender hundreds or even thousands of their inhabitants as slaves. They also had to agree to the presence of resident imperial agents and the annual payment of exorbitant taxes in the form of cowry shells, grain,

and slaves. Since the region's inhabitants were predominantly non-Muslim, enslavement was permissible under Islamic law. Besides, no evidence suggests that Umoru or his successors were keen on the conversion of the inhabitants, which would have precluded the nefarious activities of the raiders.

In 1859, acknowledging Umoru's remarkable success in subduing the restive "pagan tribes" beyond the reach of the caliphate proper, Sultan Ahmadu, Umoru's brother, gave him the resounding title of Sarkin Sudan ("lord of the blacks"). In 1863, Umoru founded the city of Kontagora, where he reigned as emir and continued his slave-raiding activities until his death in 1876.

Ibrahim Nagwamatse (1880–1922), who succeeded his grandfather Umoru in 1880, soon established a reputation as an inveterate slave raider, and his activities had a lasting and an unprecedented demographic effect on the region. The Nagwamatse saga reached its symbolic climax in 1901, when Ibrahim's slave-raiding activities brought him into confrontation with the advancing force of European imperialism. Urged by his British captors to renounce slavery in order to regain his throne, Ibrahim responded defiantly and mockingly: "Can you stop a cat from mousing? I will die with a slave in my mouth" (Temple and Temple, 1965). Exiled to Lokoja and then to Yola, he was restored to his throne in 1903, where he chafed and ruled as a harnessed ruler until his death in 1922.

—Funso Afolayan

See also
Africa; The Hausa
For Further Reading
Duff, E. C., and W. Hamilton-Browne. 1972. *Gazetteer of the Kontagora Province*. London: Frank Cass; Temple, C. L., and O. Temple. 1965. *Notes on the Tribes, Emirates, and States of the Northern Provinces of Nigeria*. London: Frank Cass.

NAMES AND NAMING

The idea that all human beings must have a unique social identification seems to be constant for all cultures and all strata in a society. Besides being an identifying tool, names may also have a classifying role. The question here is how have slaves, the lowest human category in the social order, been named and socially identified? For proprietorial identification a normal custom was to mark a slave by piercing the ears, branding with a hot iron, or tattooing the name of the slaveowner on the skin. Another way to "mark" the slave was to give the individual a special kind of slave name—a type of name used only for slaves.

In nearly all cultures, a name is more or less intimately tied to an individual, the persona, but it has been stated that this tendency was not the case for slaves, for the slave had no "personality" and owned neither his body nor his name. The name was bestowed upon him by a master, and hence, it was "owned" by the master. It may be correct that the slave did not own his official name, but when discussing the names of slaves, it is important to make clear that there are at least two vital aspects regarding naming and the use of proper names.

A name is a kind of social identification label, and a name may be a part of one's self-identification, tied to one's persona. These two linguistic labels may not be the same, and it is obvious that slaves often had names of both these two categories: one name or "social identification label" given by the owner and another (or several) name(s) used by the slave and by friends and relatives in a close social context.

A normal custom was to give the slave a new slave name. Such was the case as early as the middle of the first millennium B.C. when slaves had typical Babylonian names (e.g., Nana-ittija, Nergal-nuri, Nana-silim). Some of the slaves had had foreign names, especially of Iranian and Egyptian origin, but it was normal for the master or merchant who sold the slave to change those foreign names to local Babylonian ones.

In ancient Greece, the freemen normally had a personal name followed by a patronymic (in the genitive) and also an adjective indicating either their place of origin (city or people) or else the subgroup to which they belonged. By way of distinction, the Greek slaves only had one proper name or a proper name accompanied by the name (in the genitive) of the owner; another view is that slave names were not a distinct category.

A slave name could be the name of the master himself, one denoting some ethnic people (Lydos, Syros), or a geographical area (Asia, Italia). There are also examples of typical native slave names such as Manes (Lydian), Midas (Phrygian), and Tibios (Phaphian). Some slaves were given eponyms, normally after famous persons—Alexander, Cleopatra—or after gods or divine figures—Satyros, Hermes, Eros—but never Zeus, Apollo, or Poseidon. Slave names could also be formed on the basis of such names (Apollodorus). Another possibility was to give names to slaves that related to situations, qualities, or defects of the subject: Titthe ("the nurse"), Eirene ("peace"), Pistos ("the dependable one"), and Harpax ("the rapacious one"). Some names were reserved for slaves alone, namely, those that clearly referred to barbarian countries such as Thrace, Syria, central Asia Minor, or Calabria—areas and places that were despised for being major suppliers of slaves.

In ancient Rome, the whole society more or less depended on the labor of the huge mass of slaves *(servus)* who worked in farming, in mining, and as servants in families. The Roman slaves originally had no name of their own. They took their master's praenomen (the first of the usual three names) in the genitive with the suffix -por (or, puer), e.g., Marcipor, Publipor, Quintipor. Later, when the number of slaves had increased to the extent that it became necessary to have more distinguishable names, there began to be names showing national origin, physical or moral qualities, or simply foreign ones—especially Greek names, and there Eros was the most common.

The suffix "puer" was later replaced by "servus," thus a slave's name could be Aphrodisius Ploti Gai servus. When a slave changed masters, he adopted a partly new name with his former master's name in an adjectival form using -anus, e.g., Cissus Caesaris servus Maecenatianus, the last meaning "formerly slave of Maecenas." Freed slaves in Rome normally kept their slave name as their new cognomen (the third of the usual three names) and adopted the erstwhile master's praenomen and nomen (the second of the usual three).

The derogatory naming of slaves continued in Europe well into the Middle Ages. As an example, one could focus on the slaves, or thralls, of medieval Scandinavia. In eastern Scandinavia, it is notable that the names for thralls seem to have been the same kind of personal names found in the other social categories. However, there are some scanty indications that perhaps thralls were sometimes given at least nicknames or alternative names of a derogatory kind, e.g., Rävunge ("fox cub"), Mus ("mouse"), Tore havresäck ("Tore oat sack").

In western Scandinavia, thralls are mentioned in the Icelandic sagas and poems, sometimes with their names, often Norse names but sometimes foreign (e.g., Celtic) ones. Many slaves must have, as in eastern Scandinavia, had some kind of derogatory name, such as Gríss ("pig"), Flóki ("[maybe] the one with tangled hair"), Haki (Haki prœll skotzskr ["Haki, the slave from Scotland"]), and Kolr ("The black one"). Svartr ("the black one") seems to have been especially frequent among thralls (e.g., svartr prœll irskr ["Svartr the slave from Ireland"]).

As late as the nineteenth century, black Africans, especially those from Sudan, were taken to Egypt as slaves. From records and documents from the eighteenth century, one can study black slavery in Egypt and also the names of the black African slaves. The most common names for female slaves seem to have been Fatima and Zaynab and for the male, 'Abd Allah, Murjan, Sa'id, and Bakhit. Those names were generally popular among all classes of Egyptians, but some names were reserved for slaves. The name Za'faran ("saffron") was normally given to Ethiopian women because of their light skin, and Khudra ("ashen black"), Nila ("indigo"), Hulkiyya ("pitch black"), and Hibra ("ink") normally were given to darker women.

In the records one find that slaves who just had arrived from Sudan often bore strange "Sudanese" names. A general observation is that the slaves could be named after scents, fruits or flowers, jewels, animals, or Qur'anic personalities, or they could be given names suggesting a happy or pleasing servile disposition or an alluring physical appearance. Since certain names for black slaves appear so often in documents, they must have been given by merchants or owners and are probably synonymous with servitude.

Also in the Muslim world, there was a rather amusing name-giving custom for slaves among the Hausa in northern Nigeria. The slaves often were given a long sentence as a name; when addressing a slave, then, the master spoke out the first part of the sentence, and the slave answered by completing it. For example, a slave could be called Ku(l)um Safia ma Godia ("Every morning I give thanks"), so the master said, Ku(l)um Safia, and the slave replied, ma Godia; another example is Bia Maradi-Allah ("The giver of joy is God"). The slave name could also be turned into a question, such as Mine ya fi dadi?—Dan uwa ("Who is best off?—He who has a mother [to look after him]"). Perhaps this custom was a rather practical way of addressing people—to see if they were alert and paying attention.

Especially the West Africans who were deported to the United States during the eighteenth and nineteenth centuries were given a new single, simple name. The most common of these slave names were John, Henry, George, Sam, Jim, Jack, Tom, Charles, Peter, and Joe for males; Mary, Maria, Nancy, Lucy, Sarah, Harriett, Hannah, Eliza, Martha, and Jane for females. Of course, this practice led to a frequent duplication of names, and to avoid confusion, there was often a descriptive addition—Old, Big, Fat, etc. Other early slave names were Cato, Caesar, Hector, Pompey, Jupiter, and Agamemnon.

It is said that very few slaves in the United States were known by their original African name, such as Juba or Mingo, but there is at least one kind of name that is found in the early records of sales and shipments all over the area that saw an import of African slaves, namely, the so-called West African day names, such as Cuffee, Cudjo, Quashee for male and Phibba, Cubba, Quasheba for female. Of these, the most common in the United States was Cuffee ("male born on Friday"). A few anglicized Fanti and Ibo names are also recorded—for example, Duke (Orek), Cobham (Akabom), and Becky (Beke).

—*Stefan Brink*

For Further Reading
Bruce, F. F. 1936. "Latin Participles as Slave Names." *Glotta* 25: 42–50; Jeffreys, M. D. W. 1948. "Names of American Negro Slaves." *American Anthropologist* 50: 571–573; Puckett, Newbell N. 1938. "American Negro Names." *Journal of Negro History* 23: 35–48; Reilly, Linda Collins. 1978. "The Naming of Slaves in Greece." *Ancient World* 1 (3): 111–113.

NAPOLEON BONAPARTE (1769–1821)

When Napoleon Bonaparte attained power in 1799, he apparently had no strong preconceived notions about either slavery or the slave trade, though his background suggests sympathy with the arguments of French Enlightenment abolitionists. The National Convention abolished slavery in 1794, but Napoleon restored the institution in 1802, only to abolish it again in 1815. Pragmatic economic and political considerations motivated both of his acts.

Napoleon's first official pronouncement on the matter, made soon after his coup d'état, was a promise to the delegates from Saint Domingue that black liberty and equality in the French West Indies would be maintained. That stand probably reflected his true sentiments, but soon he came under the strong influence of the so-called Creole Party, led by Joséphine de Beauharnais. Members of this colonial lobby, mainly shippers and sugar planters, desired a return to the status quo of the ancien régime regarding slavery and heightened Napoleon's awareness of the social disturbances and economic disruption that had occurred in the colonies after the 1794 emancipation decree.

A combination of strategic and practical reasons led Napoleon to reconsider the slavery issue. In the Peace of Amiens (March 27, 1802), the British retroceded Martinique and St. Lucia, where they had maintained slavery, to France. Taking planter interests into consideration, in November 1801 Napoleon had informed the French legislative body that Guadeloupe would remain free while slavery would be retained on Martinique. On April 27, 1802, he submitted a formalized proposal to the French statesman Jean-Jacques-Régis de Cambacérès that was designed to institute a two-tier colonial system (slave and free), but that plan contradicted the legislative body's aim of moving rapidly toward a complete restoration of slavery. The senate also rejected the notion as unconstitutional and sent the bill back to the first consul, who was advised to adopt a uniform slave regime.

On May 12, 1802, Napoleon restored the slave

trade and colonial slavery, and much of the old Code Noir. Mixed marriages between slaves and nonslaves were prohibited, slaves were forbidden to enter the metropolis, and the political inequality of free mulattoes in the colonies was confirmed. True to his military character, Napoleon expressly guaranteed the liberty of freedmen who had served the republic (e.g., as military volunteers). In a highly symbolic act, he gave the governorship of Saint Domingue to the island's former ancien régime administrative official.

The Napoleonic Code (adopted on March 21, 1804), which finished the work begun by the early revolutionaries to harmonize the complex legal system of the ancien régime, made no direct mention of slavery. Although Articles 638 and 686 vouchsafed the abolition of "servitude," that meant the serfdom of the old "feudal system." Yet the code's strong paternalist character, strengthening employer rights and especially the guarantee of property rights (Articles 544, 545), was hardly intellectually inconsistent with the notion of human bondage, especially when, even in the most liberal of nations, John Locke's sanctity of property was being invoked selectively to justify the existence of the institution of slavery.

In 1814, the defeated emperor was coming under intense British abolitionist pressure. As early as the peace negotiations at the Congress of Châtillon during February and March 1814, the allies had presented to Armand-Augustin-Louis de Caulaincourt, Napoleon's emissary, a proposal regarding the abolition of the slave trade, though the touchy French response indicated the issue's sensitivity. In the 1814 Treaty of Paris, through the adroit maneuvering of Charles-Maurice de Talleyrand, the restored Louis XVIII was able to obtain a five-year grace period on abolition of the trade, which in the end, was never really enforced.

Meanwhile, Napoleon returned from Elba. Correctly gauging British public opinion, he abolished the slave trade on March 29, 1815, not only declaring its immediate and complete abolition for French slavers but also banning foreigners from importing slaves into the French colonies. Most scholars agree that this was a transparent political ploy to separate Britain from the anti-Napoleon coalition, though Napoleon may also have been motivated by a desire to punish the French ports, whose attitude had been too Anglophile for his taste. Ironically, once Napoleon had been finally defeated, the again-restored Louis XVIII was pressured by Britain to honor the emperor's abolition decree (though the promise was never really enforced).
—*William L. Chew III*

See also
Code Noir; Second Peace of Paris; Vienna, Congress of
For Further Reading
Code Napoléon. 1810. Paris: Firmin Didot; Daget,

Serge. 1971. "L'Abolition de la traite des Noirs en France de 1814–1831." *Cahiers d'Etudes Africaines* (11)1: 14–58; Putney, Martha. 1975. "The Slave Trade in French Diplomacy from 1814 to 1815." *Journal of Negro History* 60 (3): 411–427; Tulard, Jean, ed. 1987. *Dictionnaire Napoléon.* Paris: Fayard.

NARRATIVES

Slave narratives are first-person autobiographies written by slaves and ex-slaves that describe their lives under slavery and their efforts to become free. In the process, the narrative creates for the speaker both an individual identity and a collective history. Many slave narratives were written versions of speeches given at abolition meetings by escaped or freed slaves, and the narratives often retain an oral flavor.

There are more than 6,000 slave narratives, ranging in length from hundreds of pages—like those of Olaudah Equiano and Frederick Douglass—to one-page interviews conducted with slaves and ex-slaves by abolitionist writers, historians, and the Federal Writers Project of the 1930s. During the struggle for abolition, more than 100 book-length slave narratives were published in Britain, the United States, France, Germany, Cuba, and Brazil, and they often proved commercially successful. For example, between 1845 and 1847, *Narrative of the Life of Frederick Douglass* sold 11,000 copies in the United States, and in Britain, 30,000 copies had been sold by 1860.

Slave narratives served as powerful weapons in the abolition struggle. Some planters justified slavery on the grounds that Africans were subhuman; slave narratives were written to refute the notion that Africans were incapable of reason, socialization, and moral improvement. In that sense, writes Henry Louis Gates, the "slave narrative represents the attempts of blacks to write themselves into being" (Davis and Gates, 1985). Consequently, a significant scene in most slave narratives is the moment when the slave first encounters the power of a book to transmit words and ideas and ultimately becomes literate.

Eighteenth- and early-nineteenth-century philosophers like David Hume, G. W. F. Hegel, and Immanuel Kant viewed Africans as inferior because their people had no written history; the slave narrative responds to this challenge, according to Gates: "Accused of lacking a formal and collective history, blacks published individual histories which, taken together, were intended to narrate, in segments, the larger yet fragmented history of blacks in Africa, then dispersed throughout a cold New World" (Davis and Gates,

1985). This fragmentation became part of the narrative's structure, because the speaker often interrupts the autobiography proper to relate the experiences of other slaves. Consequently, most slave narratives share common scenes and an organization that is more anecdotal than chronological. This structure allows slave narrators to present themselves both as unique individuals and as representatives of slaves generally.

Rhetorically, slave narratives advance two lines of argument. The first appeals for freedom based on the "natural rights" discourse of the philosophers John Locke and Jean-Jacques Rousseau. The second appeal relies on eighteenth-century sentimentalism and stresses the infamy of such practices as publicly flogging women, separating families, and sexual violence and raises religious concerns about the Africans' potential Christian salvation.

Frances Smith Foster groups slave narratives into two categories according to their characterization of slavery and their presentation of the narrator. Those published between 1760 and 1807, when both Great Britain and the United States outlawed the slave trade (though not slavery itself), are often tales of adventure told by African narrators of noble birth who condemn slavery for its brutality and curtailment of physical freedom rather than for its dehumanization.

Typical is *The Interesting Narrative of the Life of Olaudah Equiano, or Gustavus Vassa, the African. Written by Himself*, which was published in 1789. Born an Igbo noble, Equiano was owned by honest and evil masters. During the Seven Years War (1756–1763), he served in Canada and sailed the Mediterranean with Adm. Edward Boscawen. Later, he accompanied the 1773 expedition of Constantine John Phipps to the Arctic and lived in Central America with the Miskito Indians. Other narratives from before 1807 describe idyllic moments in Africa enjoying family and traditional life, then kidnapping, the Middle Passage, the slave auction, and finally, after portraying the daily evils of slave life, freedom.

The emphasis of slave narratives changed between 1831 and 1868, a period that corresponded with the rise of antebellum interest in African American issues after the Missouri Compromise and the Dred Scott decision. In these later texts, the narrator is usually an American-born slave, of common ancestry, who indicts slavery as an institution.

Both categories of slave narratives share common features, such as biblical imagery—in particular, references to Moses leading the Israelites out of slavery—and both use Christianity as a basis for abolition, arguing that blacks have souls and therefore must be saved. Post-1831 narratives begin with the innocence of childhood and contrast that with the moment the child first comprehends the meaning of slavery. Next follows a desire to be free, escape or manumission, and freedom—though in the end, the disillusioned ex-slave is often confronted with racism after arrival in a "free" state or in Canada.

The published narrative customarily included material by white abolitionist intermediaries attesting to the voracity of the narrative and the (usually Christian) character of the narrator. For example, in the second edition of *The History of Mary Prince*, which appeared in London and Scotland in 1831, Prince speaks for herself, but her narrative is "book-ended" by material that goes so far as to use her body as evidence. Opening with a "Supplement" by her abolitionist sponsor and editor, Thomas Pringle, and closing with letters of character reference and a letter from her former master, in many ways the book resembles legal evidence more than an autobiography. The third edition even includes testimony by Pringle's wife, Margaret, verifying that she had inspected Prince's body and seen the scars received from her whippings.

Prince's *History* makes a sentimental appeal as it describes her beatings, ill-treatment, overwork, and emotional trauma, and the supplemental material adds an empirical defense of Prince's claims. For critics and historians, the editorial apparatus that accompanied the slave's narrative illuminates the power inequities between abolitionist publishers and slave narrators, particularly in the roles that religion, violence, and sexuality played in constructing the slave narrator's persona. The former slave felt and responded to pressure to conform to an "improved" image of the black person in order to "deserve" freedom. At the same time, many slave narratives are "double voiced" and, by sophisticated rhetorical strategies, resist this pressure.

The slave narrative profoundly influenced the stylistic and thematic development of the African American novel, as can be seen in such works as Ralph Ellison's *Invisible Man*, Zora Neale Hurston's *Their Eyes Were Watching God*, Richard Wright's *Black Boy*, and the works of Toni Morrison and Alice Walker.

—*Arnold Schmidt*

For Further Reading
Davis, Charles T., and Gates, Henry Louis, Jr., eds. 1985. *The Slave's Narrative*. Oxford: Oxford University Press; Ferguson, Moira. 1992. *Subject to Others: British Women Writers and Colonial Slavery, 1670–1834*. New York: Routledge; Foster, Frances Smith. 1979. *Witnessing Slavery: The Development of Ante-bellum Slave Narratives*. Madison: University of Wisconsin Press; Gates, Henry Louis, Jr. 1987. "Introduction." In *The Classic Slave Narratives*. Ed. Henry Louis Gates, Jr. New York: Penguin Books.

NASHOBA PLANTATION

One of the grandest experiments ever conceived, Tennessee's Nashoba plantation promised to end slavery. Based on cooperative labor and established by the first American woman to act publicly against slavery, this colony hoped to emancipate slaves gradually by demonstrating how they might be responsibly educated and then freed.

Located on 1,940 acres 13 miles from Memphis along both sides of the Wolf River (Nashoba is the Chickasaw word for "wolf"), the project may have been doomed from the start by its poor location. Although cheerfully described by its seller as pleasant woodland, the plantation's land was later described as containing second-rate soil. The property may also have been cheap because it was malarial, as nearby swamps were filled with mosquitoes that rose in huge clouds at dusk.

Blissfully unaware of the inherent barriers to prosperity, Nashoba's founders moved boldly ahead in late 1825. Influenced by the French Marquis de Lafayette's attempt to gradually emancipate bond servants on his New Guinea plantation, his protégé Frances Wright decided to make her own attempt at destroying slavery. Considering both the masters' and the slaves' positions, Wright hoped to make emancipation financially appealing to slaveholders while simultaneously demonstrating the ability of African Americans to prosper.

Wright opposed colonization, but she bowed to political realities and made opposition to the mixing of races a basic part of the Nashoba plan. Wright expected freed slaves to leave the United States, perhaps emigrating to Haiti or into Mexican territory. No recorded African American reaction to the plan appears in any black-published books or newspapers, but the Nashoba plan may have been regarded as just another colonization scheme. Most whites also lacked enthusiasm for the project.

A wealthy woman, Wright bought Nashoba's land with her own money and ultimately lost half of her wealth in the venture. She spent most of the funds buying tools, building cabins, and purchasing slaves. In 1826, newly bought slaves Willis, Jacob, Grandison, Redick, Henry, Nelly, Peggy, and Kitty arrived at Nashoba. The cheapest slave cost $500 and the most expensive $1,500. A pregnant woman with five small children later joined the group. Wright and her sister Camilla, along with an ever-changing number of whites, completed Nashoba's population.

To earn freedom, slaves had to perform enough labor to reimburse the plantation for their purchase price plus 6 percent interest and their food and clothing costs. While working, adult slaves learned a trade

Frances Wright, the first American woman to act publicly against slavery.

and how to read, to figure, and to write, and slave children received a full education. Despite the project's ambitious goals, Nashoba's slaves remained subordinate to the whites. Although no corporal punishment occurred while Wright remained on the premises, this experimental plantation probably did not appear too different from any other to the blacks, particularly since they still were expected to complete the heaviest tasks. Once Wright left the area in 1827 because of ill health, Nashoba's managers abandoned her goal of slowly trying to build a sense of importance and self-respect in people who had earlier been denied those traits. The whites now demanded unconditional obedience and used beating as a punishment.

Wright planned that Nashoba would be much more than an emancipation experiment. She saw it as a prototype of advanced living, with women having equal status with men and free education provided to all children regardless of color. But, worried by her illness, Wright decided to change Nashoba's legal structure, for she feared that the blacks might be returned to slavery if she were to die. In Nashoba's revised deed, Wright shared property ownership with 10 other trustees: Lafayette, Camilla Wright, Robert Owen, Robert Dale Owen, James Richardson, Robert Jennings, George Flower, Richesson Whitby, William Maclure, and Cadwallader Colden.

While Wright was away, Richardson, the plantation

overseer, created a huge scandal by advocating and practicing free love with one of the blacks under his charge. The colony, beset by bad publicity, sickness, and business setbacks, failed in 1830. Wright kept her promise to free the remaining colonists by escorting them to Haiti, paying the expenses out of her own pocket. Although the plantation failed, Nashoba remains an innovative attempt at abolition, the remarkable dream of a most remarkable woman.

—*Caryn E. Neumann*

See also
Wright, Frances
For Further Reading
Eckhardt, Celia Morris. 1984. *Fanny Wright: Rebel in America*. Cambridge, MA: Harvard University Press; Lane, Margaret. 1972. *Frances Wright and the "Great Experiment."* Manchester, Eng.: Manchester University Press; Stiller, Richard. 1972. *Commune on the Frontier: The Story of Frances Wright*. New York: Thomas Y. Crowell.

NASHVILLE CONVENTION (1850)

The mid-nineteenth-century sectional debate in the United States about slavery threatened to drive a permanent wedge between North and South. Although the Missouri Compromise (1820) maintained a shaky balance between free and slave states, new territorial acquisitions led to heated arguments about slavery's expansion into the new areas.

The debate continued throughout the Mexican War (1846–1848) as people wondered about slavery's status in territories that might be gained from Mexico. Pennsylvania representative David Wilmot introduced a proviso prohibiting slavery in any territory ceded from Mexico, which outraged Southerners. The Northern-dominated House of Representatives passed the Wilmot Proviso, but Southerners blocked its passage in the Senate. Angered by attempts to block slavery's expansion, South Carolina statesman John C. Calhoun called for action. In 1849, he called on the slave states to attend a convention in Nashville, Tennessee, the following year to discuss plans to protect slaveholders' rights.

Meanwhile, Kentucky senator Henry Clay proposed a congressional compromise that seemingly offered a solution to the conflict. Clay's plan divided the land ceded from Mexico by admitting California as a free state and allowing residents of the New Mexico and Utah territories to choose their status. Two ele-

ments of the plan favored antislavery supporters, as Clay's bill would end both the Washington, D.C., slave trade and Texas's claims for a wider western border. Additionally, Clay's compromise benefited slaveholders by creating a tough fugitive slave law, which would promise federal support in returning runaway slaves.

By June 1850, enthusiasm for the Nashville Convention had dwindled considerably in light of Clay's proposal. The convention's 175 delegates represented only 9 of 15 slave states, with 102 of the delegates representing Tennessee. As the convention opened, radicals led by the South Carolina delegation called for immediate secession. They were overruled by their more moderate colleagues, who hoped to find a solution while remaining loyal to the Union.

Delegates proposed 28 resolutions stressing their conviction that as U.S. citizens, slaveholders had the constitutional right to take property (slaves) into the territories. Furthermore, the delegates believed that the Constitution gave slaveholders the privilege of federal protection of their property. They stressed that any violation of these rights was unconstitutional. As evidence of goodwill, the convention reluctantly agreed to accept the dividing line established by the Missouri Compromise and urged Congress to settle the matter, either by recognizing slaveholders' rights or by fairly dividing the territories.

After offering these resolutions, the convention adjourned to await the outcome of Clay's proposal. After much debate, Congress passed Clay's bill, which became known as the Compromise of 1850. Although 59 delegates reconvened the Nashville Convention to protest the Compromise of 1850, most Southerners accepted the compromise and remained loyal to the Union, hoping for a permanent solution to the slavery expansion debate.

Ultimately, the Nashville Convention accomplished little, but it gave Americans a preview of the debates that would arise during the following decade. Not only did the Nashville Convention give secessionists a chance to express their ideas, it also indicated the extreme measures that some Southerners were prepared to take to protect their way of life and the institution of slavery.

—*Jason H. Silverman*

For Further Reading
Hamilton, Holman. 1964. *Prologue to Conflict: The Crisis and Compromise of 1850*. Lexington: University of Kentucky Press; Jennings, Thelma. 1980. *The Nashville Convention: Southern Movement for Unity, 1848–1851*. Memphis: Memphis State University Press.

NATIVE AMERICAN PEOPLES, ENSLAVEMENT OF

Enslavement of Native American peoples was a common practice among Native American, French, Spanish, and Anglo-American populations, but the slavery varied greatly, both temporally and regionally, among those groups. When comparing enslavement of Native Americans by other Native Americans with slavery as practiced by Europeans and their descendants, one finds that the two systems had few similarities. The motives behind the enslavement, the scale of the institution, and the treatment of slaves varied greatly depending upon whether the master was a Native American or not.

Prior to the European presence in the New World, slavery was practiced in various forms by many of the indigenous peoples, but these forms did not involve the same scale, market orientation, or social alienation of slavery as practiced by Europeans. The word "slave" as it relates to Native Americans in the captivity of other Native Americans must be considered in the broadest sense. In such a case, a slave was one held captive by another and forced to labor for him against his will. The labor that a captive was expected to perform depended upon his captors' needs. Similarly, the treatment of slaves depended upon the individual owner and upon custom. In slavery as practiced by Native Americans, slaves were generally not considered to be inferior to their masters. The slaves also had the ability to obtain freedom in many ways (e.g., through marriage, adoption, death of the captor, trade, release to settle intertribal difficulties, or earning freedom by performing certain services), and a slave might replace a spouse or child lost to warfare, famine, disease, or some other means.

Europeans practiced slavery in perpetuity, Native Americans did not. In most Native American societies a slave was held in servitude for a limited time and for specific reasons; generally, the slaves were captured in local wars. Skin color was not a determining factor as to whether or not a person became a slave, and often the slaves had rights that the master had to respect. In general, slavery of Native Americans as practiced by other Native Americans was much more humane and far less common than slavery of Native Americans as practiced by Europeans.

The Spanish were the first Europeans to have sustained contact with Native Americans and to effect the practice of slavery in the New World. Spanish enslavement of Native Americans began with Columbus's first voyage in 1492 and continued as Spanish explorers reached the mainland. The primary goal of the early Spanish explorers was to extract wealth from the New World, a goal that required extensive labor.

Building and sustaining New World colonies also required extensive labor, and Native Americans were expected to provide it.

Spanish relations with Native Americans were based on *encomienda* and *repartimiento* economic/social systems that were imported from Spain and adapted to New World conditions. In accordance with the *encomienda* system, the Native Americans who inhabited areas that the Spanish conquered were divided among the Spanish, the distribution being authorized by Ferdinand II of Aragon in 1509. The Native Americans were expected to pay their Spanish masters tribute in the form of goods, such as gold and cotton, but exacting personal service in place of tribute was a common practice. According to the *encomienda* and *repartimiento* systems, the Native Americans became wards of the Spanish, who were to care for them and teach them Catholicism. But the Spaniards who came to the New World were more interested in obtaining a labor supply to procure wealth than in caring for or christianizing the Native Americans. Instead, the Spanish enslaved the Native Americans, and as a result, the number of Native Americans in the colonies decreased rapidly owing to harsh forced labor, work in the mines, cruel treatment, disease, and migration to escape the Spanish.

French enslavement of Native Americans began in 1534 when Jacques Cartier seized several Native Americans on his first expedition to the New World and carried two to France. The French presence in the New World was necessitated primarily by a desire to establish trading partnerships with Native Americans and promote the fur trade rather than to establish colonies. Therefore, relations between the French and the Native Americans were quite different than those involving the Spanish. The former were more egalitarian than relations between Native Americans and any other Europeans in the New World, yet the French originated the practice of purchasing Native American captives taken in intertribal warfare. Other methods of procuring Native American slaves included kidnapping, warfare between the French and Native Americans, and trade.

The method of employment of Native American slaves among the French was largely determined by economics. Some Native Americans taken as slaves were sold to Anglo-Americans for profit. Others were used as replacements for Frenchmen killed in war, to serve as interpreters and guides, or to perform certain labor. Still others were taken to France as objects of curiosity. The French would also trade Native American slaves back to their own tribes in order to form an alliance against the Spanish and English.

The French system of slavery was a patriarchal system in that Native Americans worked alongside their owners and were treated as children who must be guided. The conversion of the Native American was seen as an asset for the growth of trade and an obligation of the French masters. French laws did not permit the holding of any Christian in slavery, so successful conversion should have been synonymous with freedom, but this law was not enforced.

In contrast to the Spanish and the French, the earliest Anglo-Americans in the New World had settlement as their primary purpose. They came to the New World to escape oppression and gain freedom from the British government, so it is ironic that they should have forced oppression on others and taken away the freedom of others, but they did so with slavery. The enslavement of people was a contradiction of English law, founded with the understanding that chattel slavery would not be recognized, but slavery was practiced in England and was transferred to the colonies.

Warfare was the primary way in which the Anglo-Americans procured Native American slaves, but kidnapping, trade, and conversion of servitude into slavery were also means of acquiring them. Native American slaves were recognized as property in all of the English colonies and were bought, sold, and traded like other property. Native American slaves were treated the same as African American slaves by the Anglo-Americans. The method of employment of the Native American slaves in the American colonies varied by region. Hunting and fishing, military service, agricultural labor, cooking, and sewing were common slave occupations.

Prior to the European presence in the New World, the Native Americans practiced slavery, but that slavery was quite different from the slavery imposed upon the Native Americans by Europeans. The latter developed into a full-scale slave trade, and the consequence was the severe decimation of many Native American tribes as a result of cruel treatment, harsh labor, exploitation, disease, migration because of the slave trade, and migration as a form of escape. Enslavement of Native Americans began to decline with the importation of Africans into the colonies, but Native American slavery was not fully abolished in the New World until the institution of slavery in general was eradicated in the mid-nineteenth century.

—*Lori Lee*

See also
Amerindian Slavery (General, Pacific Northwest, Plains, Southeast); Central America; Jamaica; Latin America; North American Indigenous Peoples, Slavery among
For Further Reading
Bailey, L. R. 1973. *Indian Slave Trade in the Southwest.* Los Angeles: Westernlore Press; Barber, Ruth. 1932. *Indian Labor in the Spanish Colonies.* Albuquerque: University of New Mexico Press; Lauber, Almon. 1979. *Indian Slavery in Colonial Times within the Present Limits of the United States.* Williamstown, MA: Corner House Publishers; Sherman, William. 1979. *Forced Native Labor in Sixteenth-Century Central America.* Lincoln: University of Nebraska Press.

NAZISM

On January 30, 1933, the National Socialist German Workers (Nazi) Party came to political power in Germany. The Nazi Party was dedicated to the twin goals of German "racial purity" and the territorial aggrandizement of Germany (Lebensraum). Between the party's coming to political power and Nazi Germany's unconditional surrender on May 5, 1945—thus ending World War II in Europe—the Nazis established an extensive system of slave labor. In that relatively short period, approximately 6 million people worked as slave laborers within Germany and throughout Nazi-occupied Europe.

Almost immediately after the Nazis had assumed power they began creating the infrastructure for this massive slave labor system. Beginning in 1933, the Nazi government started establishing concentration camps (*Konzentrationslager*) throughout Germany, building the first at Dachau near Munich. Existing outside the normal German prison system, concentration camps were created primarily for interning political and other real and perceived enemies of the "new Germany" the Nazis envisioned: a Germany existing only for the benefit of Germany's "racial community" (*Volksgemeinschaft*). By 1945, the Nazis had built dozens of concentration camps and hundreds of satellite forced-labor camps (*Zwangsarbeitslager*) throughout Germany, and each held thousands of prisoners working as slave laborers.

From the start of the concentration camp system, the Nazis forced prisoners to perform heavy labor without compensation, i.e., slave labor. The Nazis initially viewed this forced labor solely as punishment. But beginning in approximately 1938, Nazi authorities began viewing the ever-expanding concentration camp system not only as an instrument for the repression and punishment of enemies but also as a potential economic resource—a source of cheap labor for German industry. As the concentration camp system expanded after 1938, so did the economic exploitation of prisoners' labor.

Between the start of the World War II on September 1, 1939, and the end of 1942, Germany conquered most of Europe. In administering this conquered territory, the Nazis established numerous concentration and forced-labor camps outside of Germany, each based on the model of the internal camps. The SS (Schutzstaffel)—the main military arm of the Nazi

A Russian slave laborer from a concentration camp just liberated by U.S. forces in April 1945 points accusingly at a Nazi guard who had brutally beaten prisoners.

Party—was the principal organization involved in creating and running these camps. The SS built most of the non-German camps in Poland, including the largest and most infamous, Auschwitz-Birkenau, which alone had 30 satellite labor camps. Concentration, forced-labor, or other internment camps were established in every country of Nazi-occupied Europe, and by 1945, over 1,600 such camps existed in areas under German control.

After each major concentration camp, both inside and outside of Germany, had been established, industrial firms opened factories in the immediate vicinity. These companies were some of Germany's largest, including I. G. Farben, Krupp, A.E.G., Siemens, and Rheinmetall, and hundreds of smaller German firms also built factories near concentration and forced-labor camps to exploit their large slave labor supplies. Even the SS established its own economic enterprises to gain the economic advantage of using slave labor. The Nazis usually gave slave laborers only enough food to survive or—as in the case of most Jews, slated

for physical destruction in any event for racial reasons—only enough food to live for a few months of work. Most slave laborers lived under exceedingly brutal conditions.

In addition to concentration and forced-labor camp inmates, the Nazis also utilized other slave labor sources. After World War II began, the Nazis forcibly concentrated the Jewish population of occupied Europe into urban ghettos, primarily in Poland and the Baltic States. As with the concentration camps, German industrial firms soon established factories in or near the larger ghettos to take advantage of a cheap, captive labor force. The Nazis forced ghetto occupants to labor in these factories under appalling conditions. Ultimately, the Nazis liquidated the ghettos and deported the occupants to various concentration camps where they were either murdered immediately upon arrival or forced to perform further slave labor.

The Nazis also exploited as slave laborers the many millions of Russian prisoners of war captured following Germany's attack on the Soviet Union on June 22,

1941. The Nazis forced the Russian prisoners to work under exceedingly brutal conditions. Additionally, the Nazis forced millions of non-Jewish civilians from the occupied countries to work as slave laborers in German factories and on German farms. Daimler Benz, B.M.W., Messerschmidt, Siemens, A.E.G., and Telefunken are among the larger German industrial concerns that exploited these imported slave laborers.

The fact that the Nazis created such a massive slave system within a relatively short time is owing largely to Nazi ideology, the key tenant of which was the concept of "race." According to the Nazis, humankind was divided into races and inherent in each were immutable physical and moral attributes. The Aryan race (of which Germanic peoples were the best representatives) was the superior race, both physically and morally. All other races (Untermenschen) descended in value, and far down in the hierarchy were eastern European Slavic peoples and gypsies—according to Nazi ideology, Jews were not even human beings and constituted a purely evil, nonhuman race.

Nazi ideology also held that the races engaged in a life-or-death struggle for existence. For Germans who accepted this ideology, the merciless treatment of the "lower" races for the benefit of the superior race did not pose an ethical dilemma; even mass murder was acceptable. In addition to sanctioning the brutal exploitation of non-Aryans, Nazi ideology also mandated the brutal treatment of Aryans who did not act in accordance with Nazi dictates regarding the needs of the Aryan race in its life-or-death struggle. In other words, Nazi ideology removed any restraint on the total exploitation of any person considered to be "a racial enemy" or assisting "a racial enemy." This ideology helped produce the psychological and material conditions that made the creation of the Nazi slave empire possible.

—Eric Ehrenreich

See also
Ideology of Wartime Forced Labor
For Further Reading
Ferencz, Benjamin B. 1979. *Less than Slaves: Jewish Forced Labor and the Quest for Compensation.* Cambridge, MA: Harvard University Press; Friedrich, Otto. 1994. *The Kingdom of Auschwitz.* New York: Harper-Perennial; Hilberg, Raul. 1967. *The Destruction of the European Jews.* Chicago: Quadrangle Books; Krausnick, Helmut, et al. 1968. *Anatomy of the SS State.* London: Collins.

NEGRO BURIAL GROUND
See African Burial Ground

NEGRO CONVENTION MOVEMENT (1830–1854)

The Negro convention movement was begun by blacks in 1830 and involved their coming together annually to deliberate and exchange ideas about their problems and determine appropriate solutions. The movement signaled the beginning of organized black abolitionism and originated in response to slavery, discrimination, and the denial to blacks of citizenship rights and privileges. The immediate precipitating force was the Cincinnati antiblack race riots of 1829, which prompted Hezekiah Grice, a free black from Baltimore, to implore blacks to organize in response to the challenges of slavery and discrimination. The movement brought together blacks of diverse social backgrounds.

Delegates at the first convention in Philadelphia in 1831 affirmed their strong antislavery commitments and embraced moral suasion, believing that their material and moral improvement would influence public sentiment in favor of abolishing slavery and discrimination. Moral suasion also nurtured a universalist ethos, inducing blacks to embrace the doctrine of one humanity and to welcome white participants. Blacks held five national conventions from 1831 to 1835, all but one of them in Philadelphia. Convinced of the potency of moral suasion, blacks deemphasized political strategies and demands and emphasized self-effort and moral and material elevation.

By the late 1830s, however, the confidence blacks had reposed in moral suasion had evaporated. The moral and material elevation of blacks had not made any significant dent on slavery and racism, and the conventions of the 1840s, both state and national, assumed a racially exclusive and political character. Delegates condemned slavery and demanded full citizenship rights. Although a few delegates seriously considered violence, the conventions never officially adopted that policy.

The passage of the Fugitive Slave Act in 1850 launched the movement's next phase. The federal government's pledge to assist in apprehending fugitives threatened free blacks with reenslavement. Although threatened, free blacks concentrated on cultivating group unity and institutional development, and the national and state conventions of the 1850s evinced a strong resolve to intensify the struggle against slavery and discrimination.

Ideological cleavage soon developed, as was clear in two of the three national conventions of the decade. The convention of 1853 in Rochester, New York, unequivocally declared black commitment to the pursuit and acquisition of social and political equality within the United States. The emigrationist convention of 1854 in Cleveland, Ohio, perceived racism as invincible and opted for establishing an independent black nationality abroad. Although inspired by separatist consciousness, the Cleveland convention failed to activate any serious emigration momentum.

The state conventions of the time overwhelmingly espoused integrationist aspirations. Black Americans committed themselves to resisting slavery and degradation, and they petitioned state legislatures and published addresses and appeals asserting their claims to meaningful freedom and equality.

The abolition of slavery by the Thirteenth Amendment did not terminate the convention movement. Freedom did not obliterate discrimination and degradation, and blacks continued to meet periodically to discuss modalities for change. The movement galvanized blacks and instilled a sense of responsibility while nurturing group consciousness and identity. It also provided forums in which black values and aspirations could be articulated and their material and intellectual resources harnessed.

—*Tunde Adeleke*

For Further Reading
Bell, Howard H. 1969. *A Survey of the Negro Convention Movement, 1830–1861.* New York: Arno Press; Pease, William H., and Jane H. Pease. 1971. "The Negro Convention Movement." In *Key Issues in the Afro-American Experience.* Ed. Nathan I. Higgins et al. New York: Harcourt Brace Jovanovich.

NEW SPAIN

New Spain (Nueva España) included parts of today's Caribbean, Central America, Mexico, and the United States. The Viceroyalty of New Spain was established after the fall of the Aztec capital, Tenochtitlán, when Hernán Cortés and his troops captured Cuauhtémoc, the last Aztec emperor, in 1521. The first viceroy, Antonio de Mendoza, was appointed in 1535 and resided in Mexico City, which was built on the ruins of the pre-Columbian city. New Spain lasted until early-nineteenth-century revolutions ended colonial rule in Spanish America. The royalists, led by Viceroy Juan Ruíz de Apodaca, were defeated by the followers of Agustín de Iturbide, a Creole military officer, in 1821.

Indian slavery predated Cortés's arrival in 1519 and was subsequently rationalized by "just war," or the notion that recalcitrant natives were legally enslaved by the Spanish. Such practices were common in sixteenth-century New Spain in the "mines and in the personal service of the Spaniards. In the first years there was such haste to make slaves that they poured into Mexico City from all directions, and throughout the Indies they were taken in flocks like sheep to be branded" (Zorita, 1963). The indigenous population had declined from about 25 million to less than 17 million in the Valley of Mexico by the 1520s because of European-introduced diseases and exploitation. The New Laws (1542), which outlawed Indian bondage, and the availability of African chattels had curtailed the enslavement of indigenous peoples by the late-sixteenth century.

The *encomienda* system became the "most aggressively competitive [form of labor] in relation to other Spanish institutions" (Gibson, 1964). *Encomienda* Indians were legally free, but, in practice, they were exploited mercilessly. They were sold by their conquerors, and they worked in slavelike conditions. As a result, high death rates and curtailed life expectancies were common among these unfortunates.

Indian miners, who numbered about 5,000 in the silver-mining district of Zacatecas in the mid-1620s, enjoyed more liberties than their consigned and enslaved colleagues since they were paid in kind (i.e., the *pepena,* or a bag of ore) and in wages (Bakewell, 1971). Moreover, the miners sometimes relocated in search of employment. This "free labor" (repression of different kinds was always present) was limited in number because of low pay and poor-quality ore. *Mita* Indians, or rotational draft laborers, also worked in the excavations, including Huancavelica in Peru. That site supplied Zacatecas with the mercury used in the amalgamation process—and approximately 1,675 individuals each year labored at Huancavelica in "terrible working conditions" (Bakewell, 1971).

Africans, "who came as slaves to fill labor demands not met by the Indian population," were another source of labor in New Spain (Palmer, 1976). The plantations in the Caribbean and Brazil received a disproportionate number of chattels, but they were also present in the Viceroyalty of New Spain. For example, 500 slaves worked in Zacatecas in 1570, and they were employed in *obrajes* ("textile workshops") such as Tomás de Contreras's establishment in Coyoacán, which relied on 101 bondsmen in 1660 (Palmer, 1976). African slavery did not supplant other forms of labor in the viceroyalty, though it was demographically significant. In fact, 80,000 slaves resided in New Spain in 1645.

Numerous "slaves, in spite of the obstacles they confronted, succeeded in claiming their freedom even while the institution continued to exist" (Palmer, 1995). The runaways, known as *cimarrones,* established their own settlements *(palenques)* in the colony. One famous *palenque* near Veracruz in the early-seventeenth century had almost 500 inhabitants in 1608 (Palmer, 1995).

Both African and Indian slavery influenced the economic, political, racial, and religious development of New Spain, and it is necessary to study this colonial institution if we are to understand the kaleidoscope that is modern-day Mexico.

—*Fidel Iglesias*

See also
Central America; *Encomienda* System; Latin America; *Mita*

For Further Reading
Bakewell, P. J. 1971. *Silver Mining and Society in Colonial Mexico: Zacatecas, 1546–1700.* Cambridge: Cambridge University Press; Gibson, Charles. 1964. *The Aztecs under Spanish Rule: A History of the Indians of the Valley of Mexico, 1519–1810.* Stanford, CA: Stanford University Press; Palmer, Colin A. 1995. *The First Passage: Blacks in the Americas, 1502–1617.* New York: Oxford University Press; Palmer, Colin A. 1976. *Slaves of the White God: Blacks in Mexico, 1570–1650.* Cambridge, MA: Harvard University Press; Zorita, Alonso de. 1963. *Life and Labor in Ancient Mexico: The Brief and Summary Relation of the Lords of New Spain.* New Brunswick, NJ: Rutgers University Press.

NEW SPAIN (MEXICO), COLONIAL EXPERIENCE

The decline in the Indian population in New Spain as a result of epidemic diseases and wars was the main cause for importing huge cargoes of African slaves into the area in the sixteenth to the eighteenth centuries. Changes introduced by the Leyes Nuevas, or New Laws, of 1542 compelled the conquerors to alter their goals from quick enrichment to land exploitation. Accordingly, they began planting wheat and sugarcane and establishing vineyards, all of which made African labor increasingly necessary. Colonial sources indicate that the first slaves to arrive in Mexico were the conquerors' domestic servants, and many of them are remembered as being the first to introduce the seed of not only wheat but also smallpox.

As the colonial period began, blacks were employed as foremen in the mines, on haciendas, and in *obrajes* ("loom factories") and *trapiches* ("sugar factories") while Indian labor was the basis of the new economic order. The primary employment of blacks involved collecting tribute in Indian communities or supervising Indian servants' activities. Gradually, with changes introduced by the Leyes Nuevas and the constant petitioning of friars like Bartolomé de Las Casas, the status of the African slaves changed from a means of oppression to one of exploitation because their natural resistance to disease kept them strong.

In 1580, the Spanish crown granted the first *asiento,* or contract, to introduce Africans into Mexico. During the next two centuries many blacks were enslaved, but the practice was never massive as some white slaves were brought into the area as well, like Berbers from Mauritania, Moors from North Africa, and inhabitants of the Canary Islands. Others came from Cerdagne in the Pyrenees, the islands of Majorca and Minorca, and even Greece. For black slaves, the most common places of departure during the sixteenth century were Arguin in West Africa, the Cape Verde Islands, and the region of the Senegal and Gambia Rivers. During the seventeenth and eighteenth centuries, they were brought from the Congo and Angola.

As soon as they were bought after the long sea voyage, slaves were branded with a fire signal *(calimbo de fuego)* that consisted of a Greek letter, star, cross, nail, or monogram. Thereafter, they were employed in either the industrial or the urban branch of the colonial economy. Industrial slavery involved extracting gold and silver from the mines, working as cowboys, marines, or skilled artisans in the coastal sugar mills, or laboring in the *obrajes* ("loom factories" for the production of clothes). Urban slavery included both domestic slaves and part-time workers.

A medieval legal code, Las Siete Partidas, protected slaves from their masters' cruelty and shaped the obligations and duties between master and slave. Regulations strictly prohibited mutilation, castration, or killing any slave unless as part of a legal punishment. Slaves should be properly fed, and they had the right to marry freely without the master's intervention, remaining together as husband and wife. There were different methods of becoming a free person: by fugue, through payment on his own; by manumission, or the master's free will; by the master's death; or by supplying the master with another slave instead of money.

The mixture of Indians, Africans, and Europeans created a new society of *castas* in which *pardos* and mulattoes (all mixed-race peoples) made up the free labor force. These workers were more abundant and cheaper than African slaves because it was not necessary to watch them constantly and medical expenditures were reduced, as were costs for clothes and food, for the free laborers were responsible for providing for their own needs. Until the nineteenth century, things remained the same for Mexico's black slaves, but then the transition from slavery to wage labor occurred. As a result, new arrangements were made, and the change was reflected in the attempts to abolish slavery by Miguel Hidalgo in 1810 and José María Morelos in 1813. Neither attempt was successful because royalist troops defeated both Hidalgo and Morelos.

Finally, in 1829, the Mexican president Vicente Guerrero abolished slavery. Some years later, England and Mexico agreed to prohibit the African slave trade because modern nations that were founded upon notions of freedom and equality could not maintain a race- or caste-based society. Mexico's 1857 constitution stated that any slave would be free upon entering Mexican territory, and between 1857 and 1865, many U.S. slaves fled to Mexico in order to gain their liberty. Even though black slavery was never massive in Mexico, the African presence is today a significant part of Mexican identity.

—*Nora Reyes Costilla*

See also
The *Asiento;* Branding of Slaves, Guerrero, Vincente
For Further Reading
Rodriguez, Frederick M. 1972. "Negro Slavery in New Spain and the Yanga Revolt." M.A. thesis, Department of History, DePaul University, Chicago.

NEW TESTAMENT
See **The Bible**

NEW YORK

Slavery in New York, or New Amsterdam as it was known during Dutch rule, had a long history. The first Africans in the colony were 11 male slaves imported by the Dutch West India Company in 1626. Introduced in response to the city's colonial labor shortage, they were put to work on projects that proved unattractive to free white men. Thereafter the company continued purchasing blacks to satisfy the need for convenient and cheap labor.

When the English seized the colony in 1664, they continued the practice. As new Dutch, English, and French settlers flocked into the city, swelling its population, the slave market increased dramatically. The new colonial proprietor, the Duke of York (later James II of Great Britain), was himself a slave trader. After 1672, as the Royal African Company's governor, he held the English slave trade monopoly with the Gold Coast and used New York to increase the demand for that trade slavery, thereby boosting his own profits. No precise figures survive identifying how many blacks were taken to New York at this time, but fragmentary surviving evidence suggests that the number was very large indeed. In 1698, the merchant Jacobus Van Cortland advised a West Indian client that the city's slave market was saturated and that it was almost impossible to sell any slave over 25 years of age.

New York had a far greater concentration of slaves than any other Northern colony in the seventeenth and

eighteenth centuries. They helped to farm large country estates; growing wheat along the Hudson River and raising dairy cows and race horses on Long Island. One-fifth of all New York City households owned slaves by 1790, employing them as domestic servants or skilled craftsmen. Slaves lived and worked in all areas of the city, in close proximity to their masters, and enjoyed much social contact with one another.

Unfortunately, in the early years of the eighteenth century, New Yorkers became increasingly distrustful of their slaves. It was hard to monitor the fluctuating black population, and runaway slaves presented a very real problem to authorities. Few were ever recaptured, and many headed north to French Canadian territory. White fears of impending slave uprisings, both real and imaginary, continued to cause alarm throughout the century. Laws prevented blacks from buying liquor, leaving their master's house after dark, carrying any kind of weapon, and even from training dogs. After a slave conspiracy in 1712, Governor Robert Hunter suggested that New Yorkers should make every effort to discourage the continued importation of black slaves, arguing that white servants should be introduced to replace them. The 1737 trade depression made matters worse since many people felt that the slave trade put free white workers at a disadvantage.

During the American Revolution (1775–1783), slaves were offered their freedom after serving three years in the Continental army while owners were compensated for their losses with land grants. Other slaves were displaced or forcibly carried off during the war by advancing and retreating armies. Some gained their freedom, but others were simply resold or ended up in the British West Indies.

Decisive action to abolish slavery in the region came from the New York State legislature, which was finally able to act because slaves had come to form only a small proportion of the total population and account for only minor economic interests. In 1799 a law was proposed seeking to abolish slavery in the state, but because the legislature did not wish to antagonize slaveowners, only the gradual elimination of slavery was sought. No one was to be freed immediately, but children born to slave parents were to be released upon reaching adulthood. Males were to be freed at age 29, females at 24. Consequently, abolition was a very slow process, and there were still adult slaves in New York well into the nineteenth century.

—*John Callow*

See also
Dutch West India Company
For Further Reading
Kolchin, Peter. 1995. *American Slavery.* New York: Penguin Books; McManus, Edgar. 1966. *A History of Negro Slavery in New York.* New York: Syracuse.

Selling slaves in colonial New York, an illustration by Howard Pyle.

NICHOLAS V, PAPAL BULLS OF

Responding to a petition from the Portuguese crown, Pope Nicholas V issued the bull titled *Dum Diversas* on June 18, 1452. Addressed to King Alfonso V of Portugal, the bull conceded to the Portuguese the right to attack, conquer, and subjugate Saracens, pagans, and other enemies of Christ wherever they were to be found. It also recognized title over any lands and possessions seized and allowed the Portuguese to render the inhabitants into perpetual slavery.

Although the geographical scope of the bull remained undefined, it is clear from the use of the terms "pagans" and "other enemies of Christ" that the pope intended it to apply to the regions newly made known by the Portuguese voyages of exploration along the west coast of Africa. Indeed, the geographical ambiguity of the bull amounted to an implicit exhortation to the Portuguese crown to push the voyages even further afield.

Consciously borrowing from the crusading tradition of the twelfth century, Nicholas urged Alfonso to embark on a holy war for the defense and increase of religion. For their trouble, the pope offered full remission of sins to the king and all participants, together with those who furnished either money or troops to the expedition. In creating this legal fiction of a holy war, Nicholas effectively allowed the Portuguese to treat the military situation in Africa as an extension of that of the Mediterranean; in other words, Christian-Muslim relations were to serve as the model for interaction with Africans.

Although slave raids had been an integral part of voyages since 1441, after the establishment of a permanent trading fort at Arguin in 1448, the raids were superseded by more-peaceful modes of exchange. Given that *Dum Diversas* had only authorized the Portuguese to enslave Africans through raids and conquest, a new sanction had to be sought to justify this regularized commerce with non-Christians. To this end, the Portuguese petitioned Nicholas for a second dispensation, and the result was the bull *Romanus Pontifex* of January 8, 1455.

After confirming the provisions of *Dum Diversas* and outlining the Portuguese discoveries along the African coast, in this second bull Nicholas noted enthusiastically that through trade and fighting the Portuguese had captured many slaves who had been brought back to Portugal and baptized. Expressing his hope that the entire population of these new-found areas might soon be converted, Nicholas granted Alfonso a commercial monopoly between Morocco and the Indies together with the right to subdue and convert the inhabitants of the region. Taken together, the two bulls gave the Portuguese the right to acquire slaves along the African coast through either trade or violence.

The provisions of both of the bulls were later confirmed by Pope Calixtus III in 1456, Sixtus IV in 1481, and Leo X in 1514. Indeed, *Dum Diversas* and *Romanus Pontifex* were models for future European conquests, for on May 3, 1503, Pope Alexander VI issued two bulls in which he extended identical favors and rights to Spain in the Americas.

—*Richard Raiswell*

See also
Eugene IV, Papal Bulls of; Slavery in Medieval Europe
For Further Reading
De Witte, C. M. 1956. "Les bulles pontificales et l'expansion portugaise au XVe siecle." *Revue d'Histoire Ecclesiastique* 51.

NONSLAVEHOLDERS

The typical resident of the U.S. South before the Civil War was neither a slave nor a slaveholder. In 1860, there were 12.2 million people in the 15 slave states. Nearly 4 million were slaves, a quarter-million were free nonwhites, and over 2 million whites lived in slaveholding families. White nonslaveholders comprised the rest of the population: almost 6 million in all. According to the 1860 U.S. Census, just under three-quarters of the white population were nonslaveholders, and the percentages worked out as follows: white nonslaveholders, 48.6 percent; free nonwhites, 2.1 percent; slaveholders, 17.1 percent; and slaves 32.3 percent. If one defines the South as the 11 states that formed the Confederacy in 1861, slaves constituted 38.7 percent of the population, free nonwhites 1.5 percent, slaveholders 19.0 percent, and nonslaveholders 40.8 percent. Roughly two-thirds of the whites in these states owned no slaves.

Although between one-fourth and one-third of the nonslaveholders owned no land, most of them were independent land-owning yeoman farmers. Unlike the "poor whites" who worked as tenant farmers and laborers, the yeomen practiced a form of agriculture that maximized leisure and personal independence. Nonslaveholders frequently lived outside the staple-crop regions and rather than growing cotton or other cash crops, concentrated on producing foodstuffs. Not only did this form of agriculture eliminate the necessity for year-round labor, it also freed the yeomen from the vicissitudes of the marketplace. Sudden drops in crop prices could only marginally threaten their ability to maintain their land from year to year, and by avoiding cash-crop production, the nonslaveholders ensured that they would not compete with the slaveholders. Those nonslaveholders who did grow staple crops often produced only enough to have cash available to pay taxes, satisfy debts, or buy commodities they could not make themselves or get through barter.

Nonslaveholders had a complex relationship to the slave system. In an economic sense, nonslaveholders were unnecessary to slavery. Some sold food surpluses to plantations, others served as overseers, still others hired out their services as shopkeepers and artisans, but that kind of support was hardly necessary to the slave system. Most New World slave economies managed to operate without a large body of nonslaveholders. Slaveholders outside the United States purchased any needed food from outside the region and trained slaves or hired relatives to fulfill many plantation tasks.

Although peripheral in an economic sense, nonslaveholders in the United States were crucial to the long-term social stability of the slave system. A comparison of the United States with a society like Jamaica reveals the problems that resulted from a lack of nonslaveholders. Roughly 85 percent of Jamaica's population was made up of slaves. There were only a small number of white nonslaveholders and a somewhat larger number of black and mixed-race nonslaveholders. Because there were so few whites, rebellions involving hundreds of slaves erupted every few years. In contrast, slave uprisings in the United States were rare. Nonslaveholders in the United States served on slave patrols to help police the institution; they also served in militia units that were readily available to suppress revolts should the need arise.

Nonslaveholders helped preserve the system's political viability in the South. In most slave societies their support would not have been needed, as only in the United States was there a large body of nonslaveholders with the right to vote. Although in theory nonslaveholders could have abolished slavery in the South, there is little evidence that slaveholders worried much about this possibility. What was more problematic was whether nonslaveholders would support the goals of slaveholders in the national arena. Slavery's expansion quickly became a divisive issue in national politics, and the South had to speak with one voice if it were to withstand the equally expansionistic North.

Historians often explain the alliance between Southern slaveholders and nonslaveholders as being the result of a shared racial identity. Some writers have asserted that a "*herrenvolk* democracy" emerged, meaning that Southern society granted social equality to all white men by insuring black subordination. The only meaningful social distinctions were between white and black. As long as a permanent class of black inferiors existed, all white men enjoyed a comparable degree of status. Therefore, an egalitarian racism ensured that nonslaveholders would defend slavery to safeguard their own position in society.

There is considerable evidence to support the *herrenvolk* thesis. The great mass of white nonslaveholders were racists who viewed African Americans as an inferior people who needed to be kept subordinate. They generally tolerated black people in situations where their own positions were clearly superior, but they were quick to resort to violence to define the black place if their own positions came under attack. Although most nonslaveholders were independent farmers, there were many laborers or artisans who feared economic competition if emancipation were to occur.

Nevertheless, the social realities of Southern society worked against the creation of a true *herrenvolk* democracy. Although nonslaveholders believed that society should consider them personal equals to the elites, they knew all too well that social status and power went hand in hand with wealth. There is little evidence that nonslaveholders resented the slaveholders' wealth per se, but there is abundant evidence that they resented the social prestige and political power accorded men of wealth. The nonslaveholders did not translate this resentment into a class-conscious movement that challenged slaveholders' power, but they did use their collective power to force changes in what they believed was an unfair voting and representation system. By the eve of the Civil War, conflicts had erupted around tax systems that protected slaveholders' interests. In thousands of minor incidents, nonslaveholders expressed their frustration with a system that favored the wealthy.

Nonslaveholders in New World societies outside the United States behaved in ways that were similar to those of their U.S. counterparts. But these nonslaveholders were generally either black or of mixed race. Whether in Brazil or the British West Indies, efforts to suppress colonies of escaped slaves or slave revolts relied on regiments of free black and other nonwhite troops. Likewise, free blacks and other nonwhites assisted in capturing runaway slaves and performed other support services for the regimes. Historians have often cited the willingness of Southern white nonslaveholders to police slavery as evidence of a racial alliance. The willingness of black and mixed-race nonslaveholders in other societies to do the same suggests that alternative explanations may be helpful. The alliance between slaveholder and nonslaveholder was also based on their mutual status as free individuals.

Although nonslaveholders sometimes forged alliances based on race, they in fact developed a variety of alliances. Nonslaveholders also sought out slaves and free nonwhites as friends, lovers, sexual partners, and church members. Slaveholders regularly complained about petty theft schemes in which nonslaveholders allegedly enticed slaves to trade stolen crops for liquor or other forbidden commodities, and nonslaveholder participation on juries made prosecution of this type of "crime" almost impossible. This behavior shows that an interracial alliance based on a shared lower status developed in the United States, and similar arrangements between free blacks and other nonwhites outside the United States suggest that class-based alliances could go in several directions.

Although race was an important element in the alliance between slaveholders and nonslaveholders, other factors were also crucial. The nonslaveholders' understanding of the inappropriate use of wealth and power grew out of experiences in England, Scotland, and Ireland, and slaveholders had learned how to make concessions that maintained the nonslaveholders' sense of honor and egalitarianism. By the early 1800s, most adult Southern white males could vote on an equal footing. Normally, slaveholders did not openly display a sense of social superiority and tried to treat even poor whites with a degree of respect. Only rarely did someone like Hinton Rowan Helper come along and denounce slavery as the cause of nonslaveholders' diminished status.

Nonslaveholders were often part of a common kinship network with their slaveholding neighbors, and the bonds of family and community ensured that neighbors would look out for the needs of other neighbors. Slaveholders lent laborers or provided food; nonslaveholders served on slave patrols and cast proslavery ballots. The nonslaveholders' religion emphasized that joy and satisfaction were not to be found in "this" world but in the next. Their religion gave them a vocabulary to criticize the pretensions of slaveholders, but it did not give them a foundation for a sustained attack on the disparities of wealth. In short, they found little reason not to ally with slaveholders in most instances.

—*Bill Cecil-Fronsman*

See also
Comparative Slavery in the Americas; English Caribbean; Free Persons of Color; Helper, Hinton Rowan

For Further Reading
Cecil-Fronsman, Bill. 1992. *Common Whites: Class and Culture in Antebellum North Carolina*. Lexington: University Press of Kentucky; Hahn, Steven. 1983. *The Roots of Southern Populism: Yeomen Farmers and the Transformation of the Georgia Backcountry*. New York: Oxford University Press; McCurry, Stephanie. 1995. *Masters of Small Worlds: Yeoman Households, Gender Relations, and the Political Culture of the Antebellum South Carolina Low Country*. New York: Oxford University Press; Owsley, Frank L. 1949. *Plain Folk of the Old South*. Baton Rouge: Louisiana State University Press.

NORTH AMERICAN INDIGENOUS PEOPLES, SLAVERY AMONG

The word "slave" or its equivalent in European languages appears sporadically in ethnographic and historical literature on many indigenous North American peoples, but slavery is not generally regarded as a significant trait among Native North Americans. Ethnographers of aboriginal North America have not used the word with much definitional precision or with much regard for the general literature on slavery, and twentieth-century scholars tend to agree that the only region of Native North America where true slavery was found was the northern Pacific coast (Henshaw, 1910).

Warfare was widespread in traditional Native North America, although the intensity and frequency of armed conflict varied greatly among groups and over time. A common outcome of warfare was the taking of captives. In many parts of the continent, especially in the eastern and central regions, captives were frequently tortured, often dying as a result. Those surviving such treatment and who were unable to escape usually had one of two fates: they were either adopted into a family or kinship group of their captors, or they entered a status of permanent servitude. In most indigenous North American societies, adoption or some other form of incorporation into the kinship organization of the captor's community was the most common fate of surviving captives. The major exceptions were on the northern Pacific coast, particularly in the Northwest Coast culture area. There most captives became slaves.

Every traditional Northwest Coast community contained at least a few slaves. (This culture area usually included the Alaska panhandle, the British Columbia and Washington coasts, and sometimes the Oregon coast.) A word translatable as slave appeared in all languages spoken in the culture area, slavery was regarded as shameful and degrading, and slave status was hereditary. Slaves had no rights or privileges, being without kinship-group membership. Masters exercised complete physical control over slaves, killing them if they chose.

Slaves were mostly the result of war. Whatever the motive for a particular instance of intergroup fighting, slaves were a common outcome. Even though children of slaves became slaves, it is probable that the birthrate for female slaves was low, so war captives provided a more regular source of slaves. There was also an active slave trade, however, so many of a group's slaves were not captured by group members but were obtained in trade. War captives could be almost anyone; we know of forced enslavement of members of one's own group, and the enslavement of people from communities speaking the same or a very similar language was widespread. Raids for slaves ranged widely, but close neighbors—people with whom one had a number of other important kinds of relationships—were common victims. In earliest contact times, most attacks occurred relatively close to home.

Anyone was a potential slave. Many war captives were already slaves and merely changed owners, but the free could be enslaved as well. Belonging to the elite class did not protect one. The victim's group sometimes tried to ransom the newly enslaved, and members of prominent elite families probably had a better chance of redemption, but many former elites spent their lives in slavery. During the late-eighteenth- and early-nineteenth-century maritime fur-trade period, Europeans were also readily enslaved if the opportunity arose.

Kinship groups probably owned most of the slaves, although the person exercising control over the unit's slaves was its head. The number of slaves held by a kinship group or an individual varied considerably. Neighboring communities might have different percentages of slaves, although the proportion of slaves tended to increase from south to north in the Pacific Northwest. In some communities, slaves constituted a major segment of the population, sometimes reaching 30 percent, and ranges from 15 to 25 percent were not uncommon. Slaves in other communities made up only 1 or 2 percent of the total.

Slavery's economic importance is controversial among students of the Northwest Coast. The orthodox view is that slaves were of no economic significance, but it can be shown that slaves were of considerable importance to the economy of many communities in the region: they were a significant commodity in intergroup transactions, especially trade, and their labor was important in many subsistence activities and other mundane tasks.

Slaves were also used in rituals. In both precontact and early historic times, they were often killed during important ceremonies, especially in the northern part of the Northwest Coast culture area. The most important of these events were elite funerals. Throughout the region, the funeral of a community's leading figure usually included the killing of one or more slaves. Slaves were killed both to accompany the deceased as servants in the next world and to show the heir's power. Distribution of slaves was often associated with feasts that demonstrated the privileges of the tribal elite. In later historic times, slaves began to be freed as part of a ritual rather than killed, partly in response to European pressures about killing slaves. From the slaveowner's perspective, freeing a slave and killing a slave were both property destruction. In some communities, even as late as the 1870s, slaves were sometimes ritually killed.

Aboriginal slavery flourished and even intensified in the early part of the fur-trade period, but from the 1850s on, as Euro-American settlement increased and the Canadian and U.S. governments established political control, the practice came under increased pressure and gradually declined. Although it has long disappeared as an institution, the shame of slave ancestry still has an impact on the social and political life of many contemporary Northwest Coast native communities (Donald, 1997). The extensive development of slavery among the native peoples of that coast is unusual in that they were small-scale societies with a hunting/gathering/fishing subsistence base, a semi-sedentary settlement pattern, and no multicommunity political units.

Elsewhere, captives met a variety of fates. Some were tortured and killed, many were adopted into families and kinship groups in their captor's community, captive women often became wives, and in some communities a few captives probably never lost their marginal, outsider captive status.

In eastern North America, captives who survived torture were usually adopted and were often intended to replace a specific family or group member who had recently died. These adoptees frequently acquired the deceased's full status rights. Such adoptions are particularly well documented for northern Iroquoian-speaking peoples. Some scholars have recently claimed that most such adoptees among the northern Iroquoians were actually slaves, but their case is not strong. There is ample evidence that many adoptees were accepted as complete members of their new kinship groups and communities and that captive status was not hereditary. Additionally, during the early-colonial period, many Europeans became captives, and significant numbers of them refused rescue from their adoptive communities, preferring their new lives—unlikely behavior for slaves.

Throughout colonial times, especially in the southeastern and southwestern parts of North America, Europeans raided for natives to obtain slaves or purchased captives from their native captors. This enslavement of natives by Europeans contributed to the transformation of the indigenous societies. Especially in the Southeast, some native groups developed slaveholding elites. Such a transformation into slaveholding is especially well documented for the Cherokee (Perdue, 1979).

In the Spanish-controlled southwestern part of North America, an extensive trade in captives and slaves developed (Bailey, 1973), but within indigenous communities, adoption rather than slaveholding was usual. Among the Navajo, even if a captive had not been adopted her (more likely than his) descendants were regarded as fully Navajo in a few generations. In this matrilineal society, several clans are recognized as originating from captive women, but no stigma or disadvantage attaches to members of those clans.

Occasional references to people belonging to various disadvantaged status groups as slaves appear in the literature, but outside the Northwest Coast these are rarely true slaves. The Yurok had what are termed debt-slaves, persons given to a kinship group by their own group in payment of a debt, usually incurred as a result of the death or injury of a member of the receiving group. But such so-called slaves were allowed to return to their home communities for extended visits, and their status entailed few of the disadvantages or dangers of the true slave.

—Leland Donald

For Further Reading
Bailey, L. R. 1973. *Indian Slave Trade in the Southwest.* Los Angeles: Westernlore Press; Donald, Leland. 1997. *Aboriginal Slavery on the Northwest Coast of North America.* Berkeley: University of California Press; Henshaw, Henry W. 1910. "Slavery." In *Handbook of American Indians North of Mexico.* Ed. Frederick W. Hodge. Washington, DC: Bureau of American Ethnology; Perdue, Theda. 1979. *Slavery and the Evolution of Cherokee Society, 1540–1866.* Knoxville: University of Tennessee Press.

NORTH STAR

The *North Star* (1847–1851), later called *Frederick Douglass' Paper* (1851–1860), was a weekly abolitionist newspaper owned and edited by Frederick Douglass, the American abolitionist. The newspaper records Douglass's changing views on slavery's constitutionality, legislation regarding African Americans, the antislavery movement and its leaders, and American and international politics. It also describes Douglass's activities and includes many of his orations.

A large donation from British abolitionists enabled Douglass to start the *North Star* in Rochester, New York, in 1847. Douglass argued that his paper would demonstrate African Americans' abilities and present their point of view, one apparently lacking in other antislavery newspapers, which had few black employees and rarely addressed the interests of Northern blacks. Only four other black newspapers operated at that time.

Several white leaders, most prominently William Lloyd Garrison and Maria Weston Chapman, tried to dissuade Douglass. They worried about competition among antislavery papers, but their arguments revealed the racism that tainted the antislavery movement. Chapman thought Douglass was not intellectually capable of producing a newspaper, and she and

Garrison thought that the fact that he started one against their advice was a betrayal and a sign of impertinence. This conflict, and Douglass's very public movement away from Garrisonian antislavery, precipitated an acrimonious split between Douglass and Garrison, his former mentor and friend.

Like other antislavery newspapers, the *North Star* constantly faced financial crises. The subscription list was never large, and subscribers did not always pay. Although Douglass refused Gerrit Smith's proposal to merge the *North Star* with the *Syracuse Standard*, the Liberty Party organ, Smith assisted Douglass financially for many years. Douglass supported Smith's foray into congressional politics but did not follow any party line; he took his own positions in the paper and offered its columns to other abolitionists, even those who disagreed with him. The paper operated more efficiently when Julia Griffiths, a British abolitionist with good business sense, took over its finances in the 1850s. Still, Douglass found it necessary to conduct lecture tours to raise money. From 1859 to 1863 he also published a magazine, *Douglass' Monthly*.

Douglass believed his newspaper would reach a wide audience, but more people knew of his views through his public speaking. As editor and owner of a newspaper, he held an authoritative position, one that insisted on his equality with other abolitionist leaders, particularly Garrison, and asserted his leadership among black Americans. The paper allowed Douglass to express himself through the written word, a central desire from his days as a slave. In many ways, the newspaper represented his freedom and independence.

—Andrea M. Atkin

See also
Douglass, Frederick; Garrison, William Lloyd
For Further Reading
Fishkin, Shelly Fisher, and Carla L. Peterson. 1990. "'We Hold These Truths to Be Self-Evident': The Rhetoric of Frederick Douglass' Journalism." In *Frederick Douglass: New Literary and Historical Essays.* Ed. Eric J. Sundquist. Cambridge: Cambridge University Press; Foner, Philip S. 1950. *Life and Writings of Frederick Douglass.* 5 vols. New York: International Publishers; McFeely, William S. 1991. *Frederick Douglass.* New York: W. W. Norton.

NORTHWEST ORDINANCE (1787)

The Northwest Ordinance was enacted on July 13, 1787, by the United States Congress under the Articles of Confederation as An Ordinance for the Government of the Territory of the United States, Northwest of the River Ohio. Building on Thomas Jefferson's idea of a territorial system in the Land Ordinance (1785), a committee headed by James Monroe organized a governmental structure for the western lands. This Northwest Ordinance addressed the challenges of westward movement, representative government, federal-state relations, individual rights, and sectionalism and slavery in the Northwest Territory. The preamble and first article established republican principles that foreshadowed the Bill of Rights: trial by jury, proportionate representation, common law courts, prohibition of primogeniture and entail, and guarantees of writ of habeas corpus.

The ordinance also provided a means by which a territory could become a state on the basis of equality with the existing states, laid the foundation for a national system of free public education, and outlawed slavery and involuntary servitude north and west of the Ohio River. According to the ordinance, a governor, secretary, and three judges composed the governmental structure of the territory. When a territory consisted of 5,000 free male inhabitants, they could elect representatives to a general assembly. After the territory claimed 60,000 free inhabitants, it could be admitted to the Union as a state on equal footing with the original states. Under the ordinance, the states of Ohio (1803), Indiana (1816), Illinois (1818), Michigan (1837), and Wisconsin (1848) were created. The Northwest Ordinance thus set the basic pattern of settlement and statehood throughout the United States.

The ordinance also maintained that "Religion, Morality and knowledge being necessary to good government and the happiness of mankind, Schools and the means of education shall forever be encouraged." This article of the Northwest Ordinance reinforced the Land Ordinance (1785), which had set aside funds in each township for the establishment of schools. The Ohio General Assembly established Ohio University (1804) and Miami University (1809) as land-grant colleges, and these became the cornerstone for higher education across the nation. With these provisions, the Northwest Ordinance laid the foundation for the nationwide system of public education.

Nathan Dane and Rufus King of Massachusetts proposed Article 6 of the ordinance, which excluded slavery and involuntary servitude in the territories. It also stated that fugitive slaves, "may be lawfully reclaimed and conveyed to the person claiming" them. The common interpretation of territorial governors and judges was that the article prohibited the introduction of new slaves but did not affect the status of slaves already in the territory or that of their descendants. Those slaves and their children continued to live in servitude and were sold and bequeathed in wills.

An extended controversy over the meaning of Article 6 developed between anti- and proslavery factions and included questions about states' rights, popular sovereignty, and the appropriateness of agricultural regions and their labor systems. Northwesterners also argued over the original intent of the authors of Article 6 and that article's constitutional authority. In 1806, the Ohio legislature stated it would "never permit the foul form of slavery to tread on their sacred soil" (Onuf, 1987), and in 1823, proponents of slavery in Illinois claimed that the economy matured and the population grew most rapidly where slavery was legal.

Indiana proslavery settlers circumvented the Article 6 controversy by passing a system of slavery that was thinly disguised as indentured servitude. An Act Concerning the Introduction of Negroes and Mulattoes into This Territory, passed in 1805, permitted any person who had owned or purchased slaves outside the territory to bring them into Indiana and bind them to service. Records show that slaves were frequently made to sign contracts for periods of service that extended beyond their lifetime—sometimes for as much as 90 years. Many wealthy men in the territory, including Governor William Henry Harrison, held blacks under the indenture law.

In practice, there was little difference in the status and treatment of slaves who had been in the territory prior to 1787 and those serving under indentures after 1787. Territorial laws borrowed from the Southern slave codes regulated their conduct and provided punishments for offenses different from those accorded free persons. Eventually, antislavery delegates dominated at constitutional conventions and all states formed from the Northwest Territory excluded slavery in their state constitutions.

The dilemma over slavery in the Northwest Territory reappeared in the establishment of Oregon and California in 1848 and throughout the country in the 1850s before the Civil War. Men like Senator Thomas Corwin from Ohio and President Abraham Lincoln from Illinois took their "stand upon the Ordinance of 1787" to eventually abolish slavery in the United States.

—*Julieanne Phillips*

For Further Reading
Onuf, Peter. 1987. *Statehood and Union: A History of the Northwest Ordinance*. Bloomington: Indiana University Press; Taylor, Robert M., Jr., ed. 1987. *The Northwest Ordinance 1787: A Bicentennial Handbook*. Indianapolis: Indiana Historical Society.

NOTES ON VIRGINIA, BY THOMAS JEFFERSON

Notes on Virginia (1785) was Thomas Jefferson's only published book. He wrote it in 1781–1782 to answer a French official's queries about certain aspects of society in the United States and the country's natural history. In the *Notes,* Jefferson discussed slavery in two chapters, "Laws" and "Manners."

In "Laws," he described a gradual emancipation plan calling for education of blacks "at the public expense, to tillage, arts or sciences, according to their geniuses." Once freed, blacks would be supplied with arms, tools, seeds, and domestic animals; declared a "free and independent people"; and colonized abroad under U.S. protection. Jefferson discussed black "physical distinctions" like dark skin color, lack of facial expression, less facial and body hair, greater heat tolerance, lower sleep requirements, and greater "adventuresome[ness]."

In "faculties," he said blacks were equal to whites in memory and inferior in both reason and imagination. He stated that "to justify a general conclusion" about blacks would require more scientific study and observation, and such a conclusion "would degrade a whole race of men from the rank in the scale of beings which their Creator may perhaps have given them." Without justification, he offered, "as a suspicion only," the "opinion" that blacks were inferior to whites "in the endowments both of body and mind."

In "Manners," Jefferson wrote that slavery had "an unhappy influence" for it prompted "unremitting despotism" in whites and "degrading submissions" in blacks. Whites became immoral tyrants while blacks were forced to "lock up the faculties" and "live and labour for another." Pointing to slavery's injustice, Jefferson hoped that "a total emancipation" would be achieved "with the consent of the masters, rather than by their extirpation."

Jefferson's comments were both praised and denounced by antislavery and proslavery forces, respectively. Jefferson knew his comments were controversial and delayed publishing them for fear they would polarize and "indispose the people towards . . . the emancipation of slaves."

Opponents of slavery praised Jefferson's condemnation of the institution and his call for emancipation. In 1785, John Adams wrote that the passages about slavery would have more effect than volumes written by philosophers. Following Nat Turner's rebellion, Virginia legislators in 1832 debated a plan of gradual emancipation based upon that in the *Notes.* In Charles Sumner's "Landmark of Freedom" speech (1854), the abolitionist senator used Jefferson's own words from the *Notes* to depict slavery as a corrupting influence. In David Walker's *Appeal* (1829), that black writer declared Jefferson's *Notes* to be "as great a barrier to our emancipation, as any thing."

Proponents of slavery embraced Jefferson's comments about the inferiority of blacks while rejecting both his call for emancipation and his assertion that slavery harms white morals. By middle of the nineteenth century, advocates of scientific racism, like Dr. Josiah C. Nott, continued where Jefferson left off by describing black inferiority in terms of quasi-scientific methods. Thomas R. Dew, in the first Southern proslavery book, *Review* (1832), argued that emancipation was economic suicide and refuted Jefferson's comments that slavery had harmful effects on the morals of Southern whites. Jefferson's comments also initiated a colonization movement that culminated in the founding of the American Colonization Society in 1816.

—*Mary Jo Miles*

See also
American Colonization Society; Dew, Thomas Roderick; Jefferson, Thomas; Nott, Josiah Clark; Turner, Nat; Virginia Slavery Debate; Walker, David
For Further Reading
Jefferson, Thomas. 1955. *Notes on Virginia.* Ed. William Peden. Chapel Hill: University of North Carolina Press; Jordan, Winthrop D. 1968. *White over Black: American Attitudes Toward the Negro, 1550–1812.* Baltimore: Penguin Books; Peterson, Merrill D. 1962. *The Jefferson Image in the American Mind.* New York: Oxford University Press; Randell, Willard Sterne. 1993. *Thomas Jefferson: A Life.* New York: Henry Holt.

NOTT, JOSIAH CLARK (1804–1873)

Josiah Clark Nott was a physician, ethnologist, educator, and influential nineteenth-century racist whose writings provided much of the scientific justification for the establishment of strict racial segregation in the United States. Nott was born in Columbia, South Carolina, on March 31, 1804, to Abraham and Angelica Mitchell Nott. His well-to-do family was socially prominent in the antebellum South.

After graduating from South Carolina College in 1824, Nott continued his medical education at Columbia University and the College of Physicians and Surgeons in New York City and at the University of Pennsylvania in Philadelphia, where he received his medical degree in 1827. After several years of teaching at the University of Pennsylvania and studying in Europe, Nott established a private practice in Mobile, Alabama, where he became one of the South's most prominent surgeons. While in private practice, Nott continued teaching medicine, holding various posts at the University of Louisiana and the Medical College of Alabama.

In 1832, Nott married Sarah Deas of Columbia, South Carolina, and they had eight children; in 1853, a yellow fever epidemic in Mobile, Alabama, claimed the lives of four of them. At the outbreak of the Civil War Nott joined the Confederate army and served as a field surgeon throughout the conflict. Two of Nott's sons died in the service of the Confederacy, one at the Battle of Shiloh the other at the Battle of Chickamauga. After the Civil War Nott lived and practiced medicine in Baltimore and New York City for five years before returning to Mobile where he spent the remainder of his life.

Although Nott was a productive and well-respected contributor to the medical literature of his day, including innovative work on yellow fever and surgical techniques, his most lasting impact on society in the United States was through his published works on ethnology, which helped lay the foundation for nineteenth-century American racism. Nott believed that humankind was divided, ever since the Creation, into several "fixed types," that these fixed types corresponded to what he identified as the five "races" of mankind, and that these five races could be distinguished by a clear and immutable hierarchy of physical, mental, and moral characteristics. In Nott's hierarchy, Caucasians occupied the highest position and Ethiopians the lowest. Nott concluded that Ethiopians, meaning Africans and African Americans, had little potential for roles in modern society beyond those of slaves and menial laborers.

Nott introduced his theories on immutable racial characteristics in a widely read book, *Connection between the Biblical and Physical History of Man* (1849), and his theories became fixed in the popular consciousness with the publication of *Types of Mankind* (1854), which he wrote with George R. Gliddon. Then editions of the latter work were eventually published, and it became a standard textbook in biology and medicine during the late-nineteenth century. Nott wrote *Indigenous Races of the Earth* (1857), also with Gliddon, which expanded upon and reinforced his racial theories.

Nott died in Mobile, probably of throat cancer, on his sixty-ninth birthday, March 31, 1873.

—*Frederick J. Simonelli*

See also
Racism
For Further Reading
Nott, Josiah Clark. 1849. *Connection between the Biblical and Physical History of Man*. New York: Bartlett and Welford; Nott, Josiah Clark, and George R. Gliddon. 1857. *Indigenous Races of the Earth*. Philadelphia: Lippincott; Nott, Josiah Clark, and George R. Gliddon. 1854. *Types of Mankind*. Philadelphia: Lippincott, Grambo, and Company.

OBEAH

Obeah (also Obi, Obia) was a set of spiritual practices derived from a creative synthesis of West African beliefs and used by African Americans throughout the English Caribbean and the Guianas. Although lacking a self-perpetuating institutional structure, Obeah was a crucial element of Afro-Caribbean religions everywhere from Suriname's Maroon societies (communities of runaway slaves) to the Leeward Islands' slave societies.

Practitioners exercised some control over the supernatural forces that shaped peoples' lives and served a variety of purposes including divination, medicine, and protection from malevolent forces. For example, practitioners hung "ripe," or ritually powerful, objects ("charms") in front of houses to prevent theft. Similar objects, in a skilled Obeah practitioner's hands, could determine the truth of a person's words, provide a means for seeing into the future, and identify the human sources of spiritually caused afflictions. As healers, the practitioners used plants and charms to cure or ward off illness.

To European observers, Obeah came to mean "witchcraft," partly because Obeah charms and rituals could be used to manipulate the spiritual world, including ancestors, in ways that advanced one's fortunes or harmed one's enemies. Obeah also had sinister overtones for whites because it could promote violent resistance; in several well-publicized slave rebellions, warriors were inspired to act and emboldened in battle by their belief that Obeah protected them from the white man's bullets. Whites also associated Obeah with poisoning, because its medical aspects required much knowledge of mysterious plants and remedies.

Christian missionaries campaigned ceaselessly against Obeah, seeing its practitioners as sorcerers and rivals. Over time, whites managed to redefine the morally neutral Obeah as "black magic" through law, religion, education, and other instruments of colonial cultural hegemony in order to discredit it throughout the Caribbean. Thus, a system that (among other functions) dealt with evil became associated with dealing in evil.

The cosmological beliefs underlying Obeah remained central to Afro-Caribbean spiritual practices throughout slavery times and even to the present. Four beliefs common to West African societies undergirded Obeah. First, the sharp European distinction between the material and spiritual worlds simply did not exist. Instead, the boundary between the material and spiritual worlds appeared porous, overlapping, and indistinct. Some people, particularly the aged, stood especially close to that boundary and enjoyed particularly close contact with the supernatural. Second, the spiritual realm was crowded with gods, spirits, and ancestors, many of whom took a constant, active, and intimate interest in human affairs. Third, disease and other misfortunes were commonly seen as being social and spiritual matters. Fourth, people used Obeah rituals and objects to influence the ancestors and spirits, who in turn influenced human affairs. The Obeah practitioner was an intermediary—a doctor, philosopher, and priest—who could use his power for good or for evil and was capable of working in all places, times, and societies.

—*James D. Rice*

See also
Conjurers; Voodoo
For Further Reading
Bilby, Kenneth. 1995. "A Separate Identity: The Maroons of Jamaica." *Faces* 11 (8): 29; Brathwaite, Edward Kamau. 1974. "The African Presence in Caribbean Literature." In *Slavery, Colonialism, and Racism*. Ed. Sidney Mintz. New York: W. W. Norton; Mullin, Michael. 1992. *Africa in America: Slave Acculturation and Resistance in the American South and the British Caribbean, 1736–1831*. Urbana: University of Illinois Press; Price, Richard. 1983. *First Time: The Historical Vision of an Afro-American People*. Baltimore: Johns Hopkins University Press.

OCCUPATIONS

Work performed by African slaves in the Western Hemisphere varied according to time, place, age, and gender. A slave's occupation always played a crucial role in determining his or her material well-being, including food, clothing, and shelter allotments. Additionally, the nature of slaves' occupations ultimately affected how hard they worked, their safety on the job, and the stability of relationships with family and friends. The variety of occupations slaves performed tremendously affected the nature of their lives in bondage.

With minor exceptions, slavery in England's North American mainland colonies initially exhibited little occupational diversity. Slaves in early South Carolina worked as sailors and guides for whites desperate for such services in the new frontier colony, but intensive rice and tobacco cultivation in the South and Chesapeake Bay regions meant that most African slaves imported to those areas became agricultural laborers. This early confinement of slaves to agricultural occupations was partly conditioned by the whites' belief that the first non-English-speaking Africans were little more than savage brutes who were incapable of learning anything but the most rudimentary of tasks.

Eighteenth-century developments altered the near-absence of occupational diversity in the South that had characterized the previous decades. Factors including the slaves' acculturation and natural increase, larger slaveholding units, and economic development had created new slave occupations by the late-eighteenth century. From the slaveowner's perspective, American-born slaves seemed less alien and barbaric, largely because they learned English as they matured. This difference altered the slaveowners' attitudes as to the slaves' ability to perform skilled tasks and facilitated the slaves' training in skilled occupations.

The development of larger slaveholding units and a growing demand for skilled artisans both on and off the plantation induced many slaveowners to develop a more extensive division of labor among slaves. Consequently, many slaves became blacksmiths, carpenters, and wheelwrights—slaves whose special skills frequently led their owners to hire them out to others. Training in these and other skilled occupations was unavailable to slave women, primarily because the slaveowners believed that skilled labor was men's work.

In urban and rural areas, economic diversification usually entailed the development of new slave occupations. In the Bahamas, Nassau's growth as a late-eighteenth-century trading port stimulated the development of both skilled and unskilled slave occupations. Although slave women were usually confined to domestic service, Nassau's slave men worked as caulkers, sail makers, sailors, pilots, and in other trades associated with a bustling seaport community.

Agricultural diversification created new occupations for the slaves who lived and worked in the Chesapeake Bay region. When Maryland and Virginia slaveowners began supplementing tobacco production with considerable quantities of wheat and other small-grain crops in the late-eighteenth century, they created a demand for laborers to process and store the wheat

in the region's burgeoning urban centers. Therefore, more slaves labored as flour millers and dock workers in Baltimore and Annapolis, Maryland, and other cities. Finally, the economic diversification that characterized the late-eighteenth-century Chesapeake economy also created a demand for individual slaves who possessed various skills. These jobbers repaired mills and fences, whitewashed outbuildings, dug irrigation and drainage ditches, and worked in the fields.

Slavery in the American colonial North assumed a different form than that which developed in the South, and there were also different patterns of occupational development. Because soil and climatic prerequisites for staple-crop production were lacking in the New England and Mid-Atlantic colonies, most Northern field hands toiled in relatively small slaveholding units of one or two slaves, although some larger holdings did exist, particularly on dairy farms in Rhode Island's Narragansett region and on wheat farms along New York's Hudson River. Many Northern slaves labored as blacksmiths, shipbuilders, and at many other skilled tasks, particularly in the larger cities like Boston, New York, and Philadelphia. Slaves also worked as domestics in these cities, on Long Island, and in other places. Since slavery's roots in the Northern economy were shallow, its eventual abolition there was more easily accomplished.

If the American Revolution initiated an era that witnessed the gradual emancipation of slavery in the North, it also stimulated the development of many new occupations for slaves in the South. In Richmond, Virginia, slaves labored in war-related occupations of rope making, lead mining, and various construction projects. Once Southern industrialists perceived the utility of slave labor in industry, they continued utilizing it after the war. Richmond's iron-manufacturing industry employed many slaves, and rural slaves labored in industries that included iron works, coal and gold mines, and canal, turnpike, and railroad construction and continued doing so through the Civil War. Slaves worked as miners in other parts of the Western Hemisphere, too. In Minas Gerais, Brazil, for example, slaves began mining gold early in the eighteenth century.

Though numerous slaves labored in industry, in the Western Hemisphere the overwhelming majority were field hands. Their work lives varied according to their age, sex, type of crops produced, and size of the slaveholding unit where they were held. Most plantations in the U.S. South used slave children to perform lighter chores alongside elderly or otherwise infirm slaves. Of the adult slaves, both men and women worked as field hands, and different labor requirements associated with particular crops shaped their daily lives.

Sugar and rice production involved the most back-breaking labor of all Western Hemisphere staple crops that slaves produced. Field hands raising sugarcane cultivated and harvested by day and spent evenings processing the plantation's crop. Frequently, slaves already exhausted from a day's labor in Pernambuco, Brazil, lost limbs while operating the cane-processing machinery in the evening. Slaves laboring on rice plantations did not work at night but spent their days stooping over water-filled fields in South Carolina and Georgia.

In drier locales in the Chesapeake Bay region and elsewhere, tobacco cultivation required the field hands' regular attention. By contrast, slaves who produced wheat and other small grains tended those crops on an intermittent basis and, consequently, were more likely to be shifted among different chores on the same farm or hired out to work elsewhere. Field hands also raised livestock. Early Carolina white settlers noted the Africans' proclivity for tending herds, and ultimately, slaves raised cattle and horses across the colonial and U.S. South.

In larger slaveholding units, field hands labored under a slave driver's eyes. This job was perhaps the earliest manifestation of occupational diversification among North American slaves laboring in agriculture. In early South Carolina, slave drivers drove new, unacculturated slaves imported from Africa. Most slave drivers were men, but women, too, served as drivers when superintending gangs of slave children, elderly slaves, and pregnant slave women. Additionally, slave drivers kept crop production data for the overseer or owner. Absentee ownership in some areas and an infrequent use of white overseers in others meant that many slaves in the Southern part of the United States worked under the direct supervision of slave drivers.

Some slaveowners rewarded drivers for their services with fancy clothing, extra food, cash, and the opportunity to raise produce and sell it off the plantation. Perhaps most significantly, the slave drivers stood at the point where the interests of master and slaves diverged. Slave drivers were required to facilitate efficient production and had the whip at their disposal, but many attempted to use whatever discretion they had to mitigate the punishments meted out to other slaves.

Field hands labored outdoors, but other slaves worked in the masters' homes as servants. House servants were most frequent in the larger slaveholding units, which made possible an extensive division of labor. From the colonial through the antebellum eras in the United States, many rural slaveowners sought house servants not only for the performance of domestic duties but also as a status symbol in the community. Southern urban dwellers owned and hired house servants in considerable numbers, particularly during the antebellum period.

Scholarly debate respecting house servants centers around the question of their experiences as compared with those of the field hands. Many house servants avoided field labor, dressed better than the field hands, and ate leftovers from the master's table. Conversely, house servants labored under closer, more constant supervision than many of their counterparts in the fields and had a more circumscribed field of autonomous activity. The same constant scrutiny and close contact sometimes fueled tensions among everyone in the house, increasing the likelihood of violence at the hands of the owners. Field hands typically had Sundays off, but house servants remained on call seven days a week.

—*John J. Zaborney*

See also
Agricultural Slavery; Sugar Cultivation and Trade
For Further Reading
Cardoso, Gerald. 1983. *Negro Slavery in the Sugar Plantations of Veracruz and Pernambuco, 1550–1680: A Comparative Study.* Washington, DC: University Press of America; Johnson, Howard. 1995. "Slave Life and Leisure in Nassau, Bahamas, 1783–1838." *Slavery and Abolition* 16 (1): 45–64; Klein, Herbert S. 1986. *African Slavery in Latin America and the Caribbean.* Oxford: Oxford University Press; Kolchin, Peter. 1993. *American Slavery: 1619–1877.* New York: Hill and Wang.

OGÉ, JACQUES VINCENT (C. 1750–1790)

Jacques Vincent Ogé was one of two leaders of the abortive rebellion by free people of color in Saint Domingue (the modern Haiti) in 1790, the first violent outbreak of the great revolution that would bring independence to Haiti. Along with the rural planter Jean-Baptiste Chavanne, Ogé demanded that the colonial government grant free people of color equal rights with whites. Colonial defense forces defeated his quixotic rebellion and executed Ogé, Chavanne, and their companions.

Ogé did not support the abolition of slavery, and his movement refused to accept runaway slaves as fighters. Free colored political activists were working to include free colored land- and slaveowners in plantation society rather than to overthrow that society. This seemingly paradoxical plan was rooted in the unusual situation of prerevolutionary Haiti's free people of color.

French law did not prohibit free people of color from owning slaves or land. At the same time, polite society's rules required white fathers of mixed-race children to free and care for their offspring. Many fathers were quite liberal, and their offspring often multiplied their gifts through careful investment in a booming economy. As the 1780s ended, there was a considerable group of very wealthy, French-educated, aristocratic free people of color in Haiti. Simultaneously, the 1760s and 1770s had witnessed the arrival of many poor white adventurers in the colony, and they had found society's middle ranks already occupied by free people of color. Tension between these groups marked colonial politics in the prerevolutionary years.

Ogé was a typical member of the wealthy class of free people of color. His father was a white merchant who lived in the colony's commercial center of Cap Français, and his parents were married (interracial marriage was not unusual in the upper reaches of Saint Domingue's free colored society). Ogé was educated in France and had important commercial contacts among the merchants of Nantes in that country. Upon his father's death, he ran the business and became a prominent Cap Français merchant.

Ogé's defeat did not mark the demise of free people of color as a political force in Haiti. Julien Raimond, a wealthy planter's son, argued their case before France's Constituent Assembly and obtained a proclamation of equal rights. This proclamation was relatively moot by the time of its issue, however, because by that time, the slave uprising had started. Yet, many other prewar free people of color were also among the leaders of the revolutionary forces, including Alexandre Pétion and André Rigaud.

—*Stewart King*

See also

Free Persons of Color; French Caribbean; Haitian Revolution

For Further Reading

Garrigus, John. 1988. "A Struggle for Respect: The Free Coloreds of Pre-Revolutionary Saint-Domingue, 1760–69." Ph.D. dissertation, Department of History, Johns Hopkins University, Baltimore, Maryland.

OGLETHORPE, JAMES EDWARD (1696–1785)

*J*ames Edward Oglethorpe was a driving force behind the British colony of Georgia and its prohibition of African slavery. First elected to Parliament in Great Britain in 1722, Oglethorpe quickly became interested in philanthropy. In his pamphlet *The Sailor's Advocate* (1727), he attacked naval impressment as contrary to traditional English liberties. In 1729, after the death of a friend in debtors' prison, he chaired a parliamentary inquiry "into the State of the Gaols" of Great Britain. Other notable philanthropists were on the prison committee, including several members of a charitable group called the Associates of Doctor Bray. These associates wished to promote Christianity in the British Empire, including the American colonies. From his work on the committee and with the Associates of Doctor Bray, Oglethorpe concluded that poor Englishmen and women ought to be sent to America, where they could begin new lives.

Oglethorpe's interest in America evolved into a plan for the Georgia colony. In 1732, a royal charter incorporating the Trustees for Establishing the Colony of Georgia in America made Oglethorpe a prominent member of the board and its executive, the Common Council. Oglethorpe headed both the planning and promotion of the new colony. He wrote a series of pamphlets explaining the need for a new settlement, outlining the trustees' plans, and asking for public contributions.

Oglethorpe accompanied the first settlers to America in 1733 and spent much of the next decade overseeing colonial affairs. He remained convinced that the keystone of the project was "to establish the people free," in other words, without slavery. Oglethorpe opposed slavery in Georgia primarily because he feared its effects on the colony's free inhabitants.

He was not entirely averse to slavery, for he borrowed African slaves from South Carolina during the first months of settlement in 1733. More tellingly, he purchased substantial stock in the Royal African Company and became its deputy governor in early 1732, although he sold his stock and had ended his active participation by the end of the year. Nevertheless, Oglethorpe probably had some moral reservations about slavery. While involved in Georgia's colonial development, he aided a Gambian, Job Jolla, who had been illegally enslaved in Maryland, arranging to take him first to London and then back to Gambia. Late in life, Oglethorpe wholeheartedly supported the abolitionist Granville Sharp.

In Georgia, Oglethorpe was an effective, if overbearing, leader. As colonial proslavery sentiment grew, his firm antislavery stance drew increasing fire, and he was accused of tyranny. After 1739, Oglethorpe turned most of his attention to military affairs; in 1740, he led Georgia and South Carolina troops in an unsuccessful invasion of Spanish Florida. Although he repulsed a Spanish counterattack in 1742, South Carolinians blamed him for the 1740 fiasco and forced him to return to England to face a court-martial in 1743. Oglethorpe was acquitted, but he never returned to Georgia.

—*Gary L. Hewitt*

See also

Georgia; Royal African Company; Sharp, Granville

For Further Reading

Ettinger, Amos. 1936. *James Edward Oglethorpe, Imperial Idealist*. Oxford: Clarendon Press; Oglethorpe, James Edward. 1994. *The Publications of James Edward Oglethorpe*. Ed. Rodney M. Baine. Athens: University of Georgia Press; Spalding, Phinizy. 1977. *Oglethorpe in America*. Chicago: University of Chicago Press; Spalding, Phinizy, and Harvey H. Jackson, eds. 1989. *Oglethorpe in Perspective: Georgia's Founder after Two Hundred Years*. Tuscaloosa: University of Alabama Press.

OGUN CULT

Initiation into the Ogboni cult in southwestern Nigeria.

More than 70 million African and New World peoples either participate in or are very familiar with religious systems that include Ogun as a consequence of the African diaspora (Barnes, 1989). Ogun's popularity transcends the usual boundaries of class, ethnic affiliation, and race, not to mention gender. Moreover, Ogun has undergone many transformations over the years.

Ogun traditionally is one of the many Yoruba gods. Ironically, this god, whose popularity has spread among slaves' descendants, once claimed slaves in his sacrifices, and some African slave villages were even dedicated to supplying sacrifices for his altars. He is noted as the god of iron, hunting, and warfare, but in modern times, his concerns have been expanded to include such things as highway safety and modern technology. Ogun combines opposing qualities: the power to kill and the power to heal. He is an example of a god who is both creator and destroyer, a truly formidable being.

Rituals display the duality associated with Ogun, and they may be either solitary affairs conducted in private or they may be public. The rituals may stress his humanity and compassion, or they may stress his fiery nature with violent emotional displays. As one scholar of Ogun notes, "Character strengths and character flaws are as divine as they are human" (Barnes, 1989).

No clear date for Ogun's emergence as a deity can be given. The best estimate is that there has long been an Ogun complex with associated sacred ideas, perhaps arising from the invention of iron, the beginning of a warrior-hunter society, or a conjunction of those developments. Certainly, Ogun was an established Yoruba god by the 1600s and made his way to the New World soon after with Yoruba-speaking slaves.

Regardless the date of Ogun's origin, his tenacity and adaptability have long astonished scholars who have studied the way Africans used to bring numerous cultural items, many of which survive today, with them to the New World. In their research, syncretic religions have been a major concern. One contemporary scholar notes that "the blending of Christianity and precontact religious orientations is so marked that new forms have emerged that can loosely be described as Africa Christianity." This construct is described as "a generic label that glosses a proliferation of well-developed and institutionalized, independent churches and their overarching governing bodies" (Barnes, 1989). It is also recognized that this syncretism is not limited to African forms and Christianity. There are also blends with Islam and even with Christianity and Islam together.

Given these ideas, questions must arise concerning the connection of Ogun's cult to slavery. Several connections exist as Ogun is, for example, the god of revolution and change. He is also the god of the marginal and appeals to people who have been marginalized. Being highly adaptable, he allows worshipers to combine service to him with service to other gods, even merging with them to combine opposites quite comfortably. It is not surprising that his cult, which originated virtually simultaneously with the Atlantic slave trade's beginnings, proved so popular among slaves and their descendants.

The cult spread and developed throughout the Slave Coast of Africa by means of slave exchange, generally as tribute, from one Yoruba kingdom to another and through intermarriage. It offered its adherents the full range of human possibility. One scholar has noted that Ogun "articulates the possibilities and the dangers of power as it is found in contemporary life. He shows the way to the self-assertion and self-respect necessary for success in the modern world. Yet each of his manifestations keeps the negative side of claiming power clearly in view" (Barnes, 1989).

Interpretations of Ogun in the New World must consider both memory and the conditions of life encountered by Africans forced into slavery. "African religions did not survive in happenstance fragments in the New World. They blended, shifted, and took on new forms in response to the new social conditions, and they continue to do so today" (Barnes, 1989).

—*Frank A. Salamone*

For Further Reading
Barnes, Sandra T., ed. 1989. *Africa's Ogun: Old World and New.* Bloomington: Indiana University Press; Barnes, Sandra T. 1980. *Ogun: An Old God for a New Age.* Philadelphia: Institute for the Study of Human Issues.

OLD TESTAMENT
See The Bible

OROONOKO

The prose narrative *Oroonoko: or, The History of the Royal Slave* (c. 1688) by the English dramatist and novelist Aphra Behn (1640–1689), and the stage adaptation *Oroonoko, A Tragedy* (1695) by the Irish dramatist Thomas Southerne (1660–1746) both offer a pitiable hero destroyed by the evils of European slavery. Accordingly, they are early examples of sympathy with slavery's victims.

In Behn's narrative, Oroonoko is the grandson and heir apparent to the king of Coramantien (Kormantine) in West Africa. Educated by a French tutor in European arts and sciences, Oroonoko develops a high regard for European civilization. He falls in love with Imoinda and marries her without royal consent. The king, who also falls in loves with Imoinda, forces her to join his harem. When she is discovered in Oroonoko's arms, the king secretly sells her into slavery, telling Oroonoko that he killed her in a rage. After months of deep melancholy, Oroonoko forgives the king.

Oroonoko then befriends an English slave ship's captain by supplying him with captured enemy soldiers as slaves. Eventually, the captain tricks Oroonoko himself and takes him into slavery. Transported to the South American colony of Surinam, Oroonoko, renamed Caesar by his master, discovers that Imoinda is alive and is enslaved to the same master. Unable to secure freedom for Imoinda and himself, Oroonoko leads 300 fellow slaves in a revolt, which fails. At Imoinda's request, Oroonoko kills her to avoid torture by the English. Oroonoko's own attempted suicide is thwarted, allowing slave masters the chance to torture him to death.

In his adaptation of the novel, Southerne changed the unalloyed tragedy into a split-plot tragicomedy. Besides adding a comic subplot—in which two London sisters seek husbands of fortune in Surinam—Southerne changed Imoinda's race from black to white; replaced lengthy digressions about Coramantien and Surinamese Indian societies with a single comic subplot; allowed Oroonoko to kill the lieutenant governor, who lusts after Imoinda; and permitted Oroonoko to kill himself at the end.

Southerne's tragicomedy was an instant hit, becoming one of the most popular of all eighteenth-century plays and inspiring at least five variations over 65 years. Although some critics describe both versions of the Oroonoko story as early representations of abolitionist rhetoric, it is more likely that the stories represent defenses of traditional aristocratic values against the rise of new commercial institutions, which are symbolized by chattel slavery.

Oroonoko's participation in the enslavement and sale of conquered enemies, coupled with his arguments for the justness of enslaving the morally inferior, make this legend an imperfect vehicle for abolitionist argument. However, multiple editions of Behn's prose work and frequent production of Southerne's play throughout the eighteenth century may have contributed to popular sympathy for the enslaved Africans' plight and may have helped bring about the eventual abolition of the slave trade and slavery itself in the nineteenth century.

—*Thomas W. Krise*

See also
English Caribbean; Literature; Suriname
For Further Reading
Brown, Laura. 1993. *Ends of Empire: Women and Ideology in Early Eighteenth-Century English Literature.* Ithaca, NY: Cornell University Press; Ferguson, Moira. 1992. *Subject to Others: British Women Writers and Colonial Slavery, 1670–1834.* New York: Routledge; Novak, Maximillian E., and David Stuart Rodes. 1976. "Introduction." In *Oroonoko, by Thomas Southerne.* Lincoln: University of Nebraska Press; Todd, Janet. 1992. "Introduction." In *Oroonoko, The Rover, and Other Works by Aphra Behn,* Janet Todd, ed. London: Penguin.

OTTOMAN EMPIRE

Like its predecessors in the Middle East and the Balkans, the Ottoman Empire employed slaves in various roles. Apart from Balkan and Anatolian *devsirme* recruits (discussed below), slaves came from two principal regions: the Caucasus and eastern Africa. Caucasian slaves were transported by ship through the Black Sea to the slave markets of Istanbul, and many were subsequently resold in other Ottoman provinces. African slaves traveled, often under deplorable conditions, in two enormous slave caravans that arrived annually in Cairo from the Sudan. In Cairo, they were purchased by Egypt's administrative and commercial elites; many were then redistributed in the capital and to other provinces.

Agricultural slavery within the empire remains relatively unexplored. Since it is known that East Africans toiled on the salt and rice plantations of southern Iraq during the Abbasid empire (750–1258) and the sugar plantations of upper Egypt under the Mamluk sultans (1250–1517), it is logical to assume that the Ottomans, who ruled both regions, continued the practice even though they did not engage in plantation agriculture to the same degree. Beginning in the late-sixteenth century, East African slaves were shipped across the Red Sea to Yemen, where they cultivated coffee beans in the northern highlands. The spiraling international demand for Yemeni coffee during the seventeenth and early-eighteenth centuries made a steady supply of slaves indispensable. Agricultural slavery was more likely than elite slavery to be decentralized, and local authorities took the initiative in purchasing and deploying slaves.

More modest forms of slavery were also common throughout the Ottoman Empire. Muslim court records suggest the existence in most sizable towns of household slaves, who might be male or female and of various ethnic backgrounds. Families of modest means often found it most economical to purchase a single African female as a domestic servant. Although religious minorities were technically forbidden to own slaves, quite a number of Jews and Christians, particularly those who were wealthy merchants, did so.

Elite slavery, encompassing both eunuchs and military slaves, or *mamluks,* was the preserve of the ruling elite and the wealthiest religious authorities and merchants. Like their predecessors in the region, the Ottomans employed eunuchs as guardians of the rulers' and the imperial women's private quarters and as military leaders.

Istanbul's Topkapl Palace in the late-sixteenth century housed a corps of several hundred eunuchs; paramount among them were the *Babüssaade Agasi,* who guarded the entrance to the sultan's audience chamber and directed the palace pages' school, and the *Darüs-*

This thirteenth-century illustration depicts African slaves in an area (probably modern-day Syria) that became a part of the Ottoman Empire.

saade Agasi or *Kizlar Agasi,* who guarded the entrance to the imperial women's harem. The eunuchs who held these positions administered the enormous imperial pious foundations that serviced the holy cities of Mecca and Medina and that drew revenues from lands and properties all over the empire. Their connections with the local grandees who administered the foundations' revenues in the provinces gave these chief eunuchs a dense network of provincial influence.

Initially, both positions were filled by Caucasian eunuchs, but by the late-sixteenth century, eastern African eunuchs were monopolizing the post of *Darüssaade Agasi.* Indeed, African eunuchs gradually displaced Caucasian eunuchs as harem guardians throughout the empire and as guardians of the Prophet Muhammad's tomb in Medina. A major reason for this transformation was the relative ease of access to African slaves, for while the Russians were encroaching on the Caucasus, the Ottomans controlled the Sudan. Yet the Africans' greater natural immunity, owing to Africa's dense disease pool, probably also played a part since it rendered Africans better able to survive castration and the secondary infections that followed that procedure.

Military slavery in the Ottoman Empire comprised both the *devsirme*—the institution of enslaving non-Muslim boys from Balkan and Anatolian territories under Ottoman control—and the purchase of *mamluks* from the Caucasus. The *devsirme*, which originated with the late-fourteenth-century exploitation of Byzantine prisoners of war as soldiers, eventually took shape as a regular levy of boys from Balkan and Anatolian villages. *Devsirme* recruits filled the Janissary corps and the corps of palace pages. It was possible for a *devsirme* boy to rise through the ranks of either the Janissaries or the pages to become a high official, perhaps even grand vizier. During the seventeenth century, *devsirme* slaves grew fewer and fewer in number as free Muslims entered the military and bureaucracy in ever-greater numbers; during the eighteenth century, the *devsirme* system was abandoned altogether.

The purchase of *mamluks* from the Caucasus continued in Egypt and Yemen after the Ottoman conquest in 1517; during the seventeenth century, it grew increasingly common in other Ottoman provinces and in the imperial capital. The eighteenth century saw an explosion of Georgian *mamluks* in the Ottoman capital and the Arab provinces, as eastern Georgia fell under Ottoman suzerainty following the collapse of Iran's Safavid empire in 1722. East Africans were also employed as *mamluks*. Muhammad Ali Pasha, the autonomous governor of Egypt from 1805 to 1848, built an army of Sudanese *mamluks*.

Female slaves were also imported from both the Caucasus and eastern Africa. Although the African slaves were more likely to become domestic servants, the Caucasians typically joined the harems of the elite.

By the sixteenth century, when sultans rarely married, Caucasian concubines dominated the imperial harem. As the mother or favorite concubine of a sultan, these women could exercise enormous influence; when a weak or underage sultan came to the throne, his mother became, arguably, the most powerful figure in the palace. Sultans' mothers played a major role in endowing charitable foundations throughout the empire.

During the nineteenth century, Britain, which was steadily encroaching on Ottoman territory, pressured the Ottomans to suppress the slave trade. The trade was formally abolished in 1857, although eastern African slaves continued to be imported to the North African provinces and the Hejaz (the western Arabian peninsula) in particular. Although the slave trade had all but disappeared by the turn of the century, slaves remained in the Ottoman Empire until its collapse. The Saudi government has quietly allowed the tradition of eunuchs guarding the Prophet's tomb to lapse since the 1920s.

—*Jane Hathaway*

See also
Eunuchs; Janissaries; Mamluks
For Further Reading
Hathaway, Jane. 1996. *The Politics of Households in Ottoman Egypt: The Rise of the Qazdaglis*. Cambridge: Cambridge University Press; Lewis, Bernard. 1990. *Race and Slavery in the Middle East*. Oxford: Oxford University Press; Peirce, Leslie P. 1993. *The Imperial Harem: Women and Sovereignty in the Ottoman Empire*. Oxford: Oxford University Press; Toledano, Ehud R. 1982. *The Ottoman Slave Trade and Its Suppression, 1840–1890*. Princeton, NJ: Princeton University Press.

PACIFIC ISLANDER LABOR IN AUSTRALIA

The British colony of Queensland, established in 1859, developed rapidly on the basis of tropical agriculture and cattle raising. Serious labor shortages led to generous assistance for British immigrants, whose numbers reached a peak in the 1880s. But the British were regarded as unsuited for work in the tropics, and the other possible workers, Aborigines and local Chinese, were not actively encouraged, although they were quite numerous.

After a brief expansion of cotton cultivation caused by shortages during the U.S. Civil War, northern Queensland turned toward sugar growing, which remains of considerable importance. A new labor force was sought, one that would be able to work in tropical conditions, be cheap and malleable, and live close enough to be easily recruited and repatriated. Slavery was no longer legal within the British Empire and had never been practiced in Australia where the origins of the labor force lay in transported convicts or assisted immigrants, both predominantly British.

Although a French colony had been established in New Caledonia in 1853 and a British colony in Fiji in 1874, most of the islands of the Pacific were not under colonial control and had no effective modern governments of their own. Many of the islanders, especially in the New Hebrides (now Vanuatu), Samoa, and Tahiti, had been proselytized by Christian missionaries while others, as in Papua New Guinea and the Solomon Islands, had scarcely been touched by Western influences. Australian plantation owners looked especially toward the New Hebrides as a source of labor, as links had already been established with that area through missionaries and traders. A group of islanders had been brought to Australia in 1847 as shepherds, but that experiment had not been a success. Nevertheless, mass recruitment for the Queensland plantations began in 1863.

Between 1863 and 1904, over 62,000 laborers were recruited to Australia, of whom 33,000 were from the New Hebrides, nearly 18,000 from the Solomon Islands, nearly 7,000 from the Banks and Torres Islands, and the rest from elsewhere in the Pacific. Although officially called "Polynesians," they were almost exclusively Melanesians from various language groups and cultures. They did not fall under the jurisdiction of any modern government, and the methods used to recruit them were initially crude and sometimes brutal. Known as "blackbirders," some of the recruiters were little better than pirates. Their methods were increasingly criticized by Christian missionaries, although some of them also encouraged recruitment. Most of the imported laborers worked around the sugar towns of Mackay and Bundaberg, and almost all were located in Queensland.

The Queensland government moved to regulate the labor trade from its early stages with the Polynesian Labourers Act (1868). This act fixed a minimum age of 16, although many recruits would not have known their exact age, and later measures included the founding of a special hospital in an attempt to reduce the very high death rate. These ameliorative measures, however, were offset by illegal and oppressive practices.

Charges of forced kidnapping were common, leading to a Queensland Royal Commission to look into the labor trade in 1885. The Queensland Parliament then passed legislation to prohibit further recruitment of "kanakas" after 1890, but this law was suspended because of strong opposition from plantation owners who influenced conservative legislators. Much of the agitation against the labor trade came from outside Queensland, from the metropolitan area around Brisbane, and from a rapidly growing trade union movement based on the mass immigration of the 1880s.

The Melanesian laborers were indentured for fixed terms under specific conditions regulated by Queensland law, and a few were able to protect their interests through the courts. Some who survived accepted additional terms and began to marry and settle down, although most remained single. But the high death rate, the dubious practices of recruiters, and the growing militancy of the unions combined to doom the trade by the end of the century when the six Australian colonies federated.

The policy of white Australians was to prevent immigration by non-Europeans, especially Chinese and Melanesians. Under the Pacific Island Labourers Act of 1901, the new Commonwealth of Australia not only prohibited immigration but also began forcible repatriation. The latter was completed in 1906, although a small residue of Pacific Islanders remained and formed a continuing community around Mackay and other Queensland towns.

—*James Jupp*

PACIFIC ISLANDS AND QUEENSLAND, INDENTURED LABOR IN

The U.S. Civil War (1861–1865) and the consequent world shortage of cotton were the catalysts for the development of plantation economies in the Pacific basin and colonial Queensland. Although land and capital could be problems, the planters' major concern was the mobilization of labor to work these "factories in the fields." The solution was to import laborers, and the flow of migrant laborers has since become known as the Pacific Islands labor trade.

With slavery a political impossibility, the institutional form of this regional labor trade hinged on indenture with provision for a fixed-term contract (usually ranging between three and five years), criminal penalty for breach of contract, and a fixed remuneration to help stabilize costs. Although the total numbers of laborers imported cannot be accurately determined, they were sizable, amounting to some 1.5 million Pacific islanders up to 1945 and a further 500,000 Asians and their families. Nor was indentured servitude in the Pacific limited to plantation work (cotton, sugar, and copra being the major crops), as it was utilized in other areas of employment such as herding, mining, public works, shipping, and domestic service.

There were four basic stages of the Pacific islands labor trade, with variations from place to place and a considerable degree of overlap. Employers initially relied on local workers. This arrangement, however, proved unsatisfactory because of high levels of absconding and poor discipline and a general unwillingness of islanders to enlist in sufficient numbers to provide a stable labor force. Employers then decided to bear high recruiting costs and import islanders from other parts of the Pacific—what is referred to as the "external labor trade." Removed from the support systems of their own communities, these workers were more easily disciplined and controlled.

But competition for recruits meant that, by the early 1880s, the regional pool of labor was insufficient and employers had to turn to the vast Asian labor market to make good the shortfall, especially in Hawaii, Fiji, and New Caledonia. The final stage was

the creation of "internal labor trade" as newly created colonial governments (the Solomon Islands, for example) increasingly restricted or excluded foreign labor recruiters. In other words, the labor trade had returned to the first stage of reliance on local laborers, the difference being that employers could now rely on the colonial state to help control and discipline the workforce.

The methods of labor mobilization and the motivations for enlisting also varied. The external labor trade was initially characterized by a high degree of outright kidnapping, either through force or misrepresentation, and critics were soon charging that a slave trade war was in the making. With increasing regulation, notably by Great Britain, and a greater awareness on the part of islanders, kidnapping and other irregularities diminished although petty breaches of the regulations persisted. Despite being more orderly, recruiting remained a dangerous business, especially in Melanesia where recruiting crews were often attacked and full-scale attacks against recruiting vessels were occasionally mounted. Nevertheless, by the mid-1870s, the trade had settled down to something resembling a business, albeit a risky and disreputable one.

Young men enlisted with the consent of their communities and returned three years later, if they were lucky, with a box full of European goods, including firearms and ammunition, that could be converted into bride-price payments. In the Melanesian islands, the recruits were overwhelmingly young men. Unmarried women were a future source of bride wealth for their families while married women represented a substantial investment in bride prices, which explain why Melanesian communities repeatedly banned female enlistment. In the other significant recruiting areas—such as the Kiribati Islands—there was no such prohibition, and some 40 percent of the recruits were female.

Apart from the early years of kidnapping and fraud, recruiting was characterized by a high degree of volunteerism on the part of islanders, but with certain qualifications. Many Kiribati Islanders were, in effect, compelled to enlist, however willingly, in order to escape the effects of prolonged drought. Similarly, Asian workers typically enlisted to escape poverty and oppression in their home countries. In Melanesia, enlistment was most commonly a corporate rather than a personal decision, the motivation being that the individual concerned would bring back European goods for the use of his kinsfolk.

The subordination of individual preference is illustrated by the fact that to recruit a "boy" without giving his relatives a compensatory up-front present (a "beach payment") was to "steal" him, no matter how willing he might be to enlist, whereas a present legitimized the transaction regardless of the feelings of the individual concerned. It is also the case that islanders who had already had access to European goods chose the alternative of cash-cropping to the hazards of labor migration. These considerations put a different complexion on too-assiduous an application of the term "voluntary enlistment."

Within limits, islanders who engaged in the internal labor trade enjoyed a degree of freedom over their choice of destination and whether or not they enlisted at all. The establishment of an internal labor trade by the various colonial states' restrictions on foreign recruiters meant that islanders now had no option but to enlist for local enterprises. Moreover, islanders could now be pushed into indentured servitude, whether they liked it or not, by such colonial devices as the head tax and the imposition of labor quotas.

Conditions varied considerably among places of employment, but common to all were the pace of work and the difficulties encountered by the laborers. The laborers were subject to the penal clauses laid down in their contracts, largely ignorant of the channels of redress or else unable to equitably exploit them, forbidden to form trade unions, often unable to comprehend the language spoken around them, and, more often than not, disadvantaged by collusion between their employer and the state. Beginning in the mid-1880s, Queensland became the best place of employment on the regional labor market, partly because of the enforcement of an increasing number of protective regulations and partly because of the changing nature of the workforce itself. Instead of being composed of raw and inexperienced first-time indentured workers, the workforce was increasingly made up of time-expired and reindentured laborers who had the experience to cope with the work, were able to confront the system, and had become acclimatized to the disease environment of their place of employment.

Mortality rates were high, and debate has centered on whether the situation was largely the result of overwork and unsanitary conditions (the treatment hypothesis) or whether the epidemiological hypothesis has greater explanatory power. Comparative studies have conclusively demonstrated the latter as being more significant: the majority of deaths were owing to the susceptibility of workers to gastrointestinal infections and diseases of the respiratory system against which they had little or no immunity. As a result, there was a susceptibility to death in the first year of service, especially in the first six months, but the possibility tapered off as workers acquired immunity to the diseases around them. Workers from hostile disease environments were also less likely to succumb than their counterparts from benign disease environments. In Fiji, for example, Indian workers and imported Pacific islanders died from the same range of diseases, but the Indians experienced a lower death rate as they had previously acquired a degree of immunity.

The abolition of indentured servitude in the Pacific was gradual, localized, and a consequence of political pressures brought to bear on unwilling employers. When Hawaii became a U.S. territory in 1900, indenture was automatically abolished as being repugnant to U.S. law. The next abolition was in Queensland in 1906 when the new Commonwealth of Australia government decreed the expulsion of Pacific islanders in the interests of the "white Australia policy." The final contracts for Indians in Fiji were canceled in 1920. Elsewhere, the institution of indentured labor lingered on, especially in Papua and New Guinea where European penetration tapped a huge labor reserve. Indeed, more people were caught up in indenture in the twentieth century than in the nineteenth, but by the 1950s, indenture had finally been laid to rest in the Pacific islands. By that time, it was considered an anachronism and was frowned on by the international community and considered inimical to the emerging mood of decolonization.

The descendants of the Melanesian workers still form underprivileged minority groups in places such as Queensland, Fiji, and Samoa. Asians have fared better economically, less so politically. There were two military coups in Fiji in 1987 when the Indian-dominated coalition party won an election, and the power of indigenous Fijians became entrenched by virtue of the 1990 constitution, now under review, and the army. At the other extreme, the Asian presence in Hawaii has become dominant within the framework of U.S. statehood. Life after indenture for most Asians, however, has typically involved restrictions and problems in their new homes, whether obstacles to participation in trade and commerce, the denial of civil and legal rights, or political discrimination. Nevertheless, the Asian communities, unlike their Pacific islander counterparts, have succeeded by most measurable indexes of status and prosperity.

—Doug Munro

For Further Reading

Moore, Clive. 1992. "Labour, Indenture, and Historiography in the Pacific." In *Pacific Islands History: Journeys and Transformations*. Ed. Brij V. Lal. Canberra, Australia: Journal of Pacific History; Munro, Doug. 1993. "The Pacific Islands Labour Trade: Approaches, Methodologies, Debates." *Slavery and Abolition* 14 (2): 87–108; Newbury, Colin. 1980. "The Melanesian Labor Reserve: Some Reflections on Pacific Labor Markets in the Nineteenth Century." *Pacific Studies* 4 (1): 1–25; Shlomowitz, Ralph. 1996. *Mortality and Migration in the Modern World*. Aldershot, Eng.: Variorum.

PAINE, THOMAS
(1737–1809)

Thomas Paine was a radical, a political theorist, and the author of *Common Sense* (1776), *The Rights of Man* (1791–1792), and articles against slavery. At the heart of the American independence movement in the 1770s, Paine also became a friend of English radical societies in the 1790s and later a member of the French Revolutionary Convention. Although reviled, ridiculed, and forced into exile by royalist supporters, he was enormously influential, and the scope of his work was truly international. In his books, pamphlets, letters, and essays, he tried to communicate the most complex ideas and issues clearly and simply. He combined political radicalism with the dream of technical and scientific progress and a belief in man's unalienable rights regardless of race, creed, or color.

At age 37, after failing in business and a second marriage, Paine left his home country of England for America. He arrived a few months before the outbreak of the American Revolution and sided firmly with the colonists. He tried teaching at first but made his name in journalism. As editor of the *Pennsylvania Magazine*, he wasted no time in putting pen to paper on the subject of slavery.

In March 1775, Paine wrote the article "African Slavery in America" in which he proposed its total abolition. Although not the first opponent of black slavery in the Americas, he was the first popular writer to denounce the system so thoroughly and unreservedly as being evil. Paine stressed the comparison between the colonists overthrowing English servitude with the far harsher physical slavery of the blacks. There was no middle course for him; either all humanity was free, or it was in bondage. Freedom for white Americans required freedom for black Americans.

Throughout the spirited essay, Paine argued that people were more than mere commodities, not just another form of property to be bought and sold at will. Instead, it was the individuality of all men and women that was of overwhelming importance. Blacks, like any other people, were born free. This innate freedom could not be taken from them regardless of how many times they were sold, and they had the right to reclaim their freedom at any given time.

Paine believed the American colonies should set the pace for the rest of the world and make amends for the mistreatment of former slaves. He believed that newly freed slaves should be offered grants of land, allotments that would provide useful employment and enable the freedmen to support themselves and become property holders. Former masters should provide for old and infirm slaves.

Thomas Paine

Although today there is little that is startling in the essay, at the time it was considered revolutionary as slavery was widely assumed to be an integral part of colonial society. Fearing a backlash, the owner of the *Pennsylvania Magazine* thought the article far too disturbing for that paper and printed it instead in the *Pennsylvania Journal*. Nevertheless, Paine's ideas were readily received, and in just over a month, the first American Anti-Slavery Society was formed in Philadelphia. Paine became Thomas Jefferson's friend and confidant and tried to convince him of the justice of black freedom. Yet both men shrank from including an emancipation clause in the Virginia Declaration of Rights of June 12, 1776, fearing that such a clause would alienate Southern planters and Northern merchants alike.

When the Pennsylvania Assembly met on November 2, 1779, it elected Paine its clerk. Among the barrage of radical bills pushed through and certified by Paine was one for the outlawing of slavery. That bill was the first in the world to propose the abolition of slavery, and for many delegates it was the single most important piece of legislation enacted. It became law on March 1, 1780, though it had been greatly weakened with regard to some of its specific commitments.

Returning to the United States from France in 1802,

Paine busied himself with fresh attacks upon slavery. He resolutely opposed plans to put slaves to work in the Louisiana territory that had recently been purchased from France and instead advocated the establishment of Louisiana as a free and democratic state where blacks could participate as free and equal citizens. But the United States was a very different place from the group of colonies he had known in 1775–1776, and his proposals were ignored.

Social protest had all but died away, and though Jefferson renewed contacts with him, Paine was thought by many propertied men to be dangerous on account of his religious, economic, and antislavery beliefs. Largely rejected by the democracy that he had helped to create, he spent his last years in New York City in what is today Greenwich Village. His ideas, though, would shape the vocabulary of the abolitionist cause and bring many people to consider slavery a violation of social and human rights.

—John Callow

See also
Capitalism; The Enlightenment; Jefferson, Thomas
For Further Reading
Edwards, Samuel. 1974. *Rebel! A Biography of Thomas Paine.* New York: Praeger Press; Foot, Michael, and Isaac Kramnick, eds. 1987. *The Thomas Paine Reader.* London: Penguin; Keane, John. 1995. *Tom Paine: A Political Life.* London: Bloomsbury.

PALMARES

Located in the state of Pernambuco, the Negro Republic of Palmares was the largest and one of the most famous *quilombos* (communities of fugitive slaves) in Brazil. Fugitive slaves founded it in the early-seventeenth century when colonial control passed from the Dutch to the Portuguese and Brazil's political instability afforded the slaves a chance to escape and establish a community independent of slavery. Based on European records, Palmares had been founded by 1630 and was destroyed in 1697.

Although no conclusive census of Palmares exists, numerous scholars have offered estimates of the republic's population. Conservative numbers indicate 500–1500 residents, and more generous figures suggest that at its peak, Palmares supported a population of 30,000 inhabitants. Palmares's population was in a constant state of flux since it consisted of people who had been born there, fugitive slaves who had successfully escaped to it, and slaves who had been abducted from adjacent plantations. Most of the *palmaristas* were men, and women were deliberately kidnapped in order to help increase the population. Loyalty was central to the spirit and success of Palmares. Persons who fled the republic were pursued and killed, and any *palmarista* found to be in collusion with the Dutch or the Portuguese would also be killed.

As a republic, Palmares was not one homogeneous community but a collection of small towns. Each town had its own name and characteristics, but all *palmaristas* would band together for mutual self-defense in the event of internal crisis or external attack. Palmares was a relatively self-sufficient society, and contemporary observers noted its well-kept lands, cereal crops, and an irrigation system. Palmares was not isolated from surrounding plantations and towns in the sense that *palmaristas* staged attacks on nearby plantations and were a real threat to Brazil's slaveowners.

Palmares's residents successfully defended their settlement against Portuguese and Dutch attacks for most of the seventeenth century. When the Portuguese, aided by Portuguese-Amerindian *metis* (mestizos), destroyed Palmares in 1697, 400 *palmaristas* died either at their own hands or at the hands of their attackers. Another 500 were captured and returned to the Brazilian slave population. Ganga-Zumba, the elected king of Palmares, was captured and beheaded, and his severed head was displayed publicly to dispel rumors about his alleged immortality.

The history of Palmares illustrates the constant contest for power between Europeans and Africans in the slave communities of Brazil and the rest of the Americas. Neither were enslaved Africans content with their position, nor did the institution of slavery exact absolute control over African people. If slavery had been a totalitarian system, there would have been no room for the establishment and persistence of rebel slave societies. Although no original writings from Palmares remain, contemporary accounts attest to Palmares's preservation of African culture in its family arrangements, religious practices, government, and means of self-defense.

—Maureen G. Elgersman

See also
Quilombos
For Further Reading
Mattoso, Katia de Queiros. 1986. *To Be a Slave in Brazil, 1550–1888.* New Brunswick, NJ: Rutgers University Press; Price, Richard, ed. 1979. *Maroon Societies: Rebel Slave Communities in the Americas.* Baltimore: Johns Hopkins University Press; Reis, Joao Jose. 1993. *Slave Rebellion in Brazil.* Baltimore: Johns Hopkins University Press; Thompson, Vincent B. 1987. *The Making of the African Diaspora in the Americas, 1441–1900.* New York: Longman.

PALMERSTON ACT
(1839)

Parliament passed the Palmerston Act of 1839 to give Great Britain unilateral rights to arrest and try Portuguese citizens suspected of involvement in the slave trade. The British foreign secretary, Lord Palmerston, sponsored the legislation and urged its passage because Britain's inability to negotiate a treaty with Portugal prohibited the British from stopping and searching slave ships flying the Portuguese flag.

After abolishing the slave trade within the British Empire in 1807, Britain attempted to negotiate treaties that would permit British naval enforcement of antislave measures against other nations' slavers. British and Portuguese officials had signed treaties in 1815 and 1817 prohibiting Portuguese involvement in the slave trade north of the equator, and allowing the British to arrest Portuguese nationals trading slaves in the Northern Hemisphere, but Portugal was still free to engage in slave trade south of the equator. This fact was especially significant since two Portuguese colonies, Angola and Mozambique, were major slave suppliers; Portugal's colony of Brazil was one of the world's major slave importers; and all three colonies were located below the equator. Even after Brazilian independence (1822), Portugal was the principal supplier of slaves to Brazil.

Furthermore, by 1838, only the United States and Portugal had not entered the treaty system Great Britain had established to suppress the slave trade. The treaties not only granted British ships the right to stop vessels actively engaged in the trade but each treaty also included what were called equipment clauses, which allowed the British to capture ships that were outfitted to engage in slave transport even when they had not transported a cargo. British efforts had moved toward suppression of the trade, but while Portugal and the United States remained outside the system, other nations' slavers could hide behind those two nations' flags.

There was little public support in Portugal for suppressing the slave trade. Even when the Portuguese government officially abolished the slave trade within its empire (1836), the government was unable to enforce the decree. That government's inability to enforce its ban on the slave trade, combined with Portuguese recalcitrance toward a treaty with Great Britain, compelled Palmerston to push through Parliament legislation that unilaterally gave the British permission to stop and try Portuguese slavers. Portugal bitterly protested this transgression against its sovereignty, but the Portuguese government was unable and unwilling to resist the British.

British actions forced Portugal back into negotiations, and an Anglo-Portuguese treaty signed in 1842 formally allowed the British to seize Portuguese slave ships and established joint Anglo-Portuguese courts to try suspected slavers. Thus, within three years of its enactment, the unilateral Palmerston Act was superseded by bilateral cooperation between Britain and Portugal.

—Tom Lansford

See also
Closing of the African Slave Trade
For Further Reading
Coupland, Reginald. 1962. *The British Anti-Slavery Movement.* New York: Barnes and Noble; Miers, Suzanne. 1975. *Britain and the Ending of the Slave Trade.* New York: Longman; Temperley, Howard. 1972. *British Anti-Slavery, 1833–1870.* New York: Longman.

PAPAL BULLS
See **Eugene IV; Nicholas V**

PAPIAN-POPPAEAN LAW
(LEX PAPIA-POPPAEA)

Emperor Augustus (r. 27 B.C.–A.D. 14) instituted several laws on marriage, adultery, begetting children, and intermarriage between free persons and slaves. The legislation aimed at encouraging marriage and childbearing among the upper classes and discouraging divorce, which was perceived as a problem in Rome at the time. Discouraging marriage between free persons and freed slaves was the main subject of the Julian Law on the Orders Permitted to Marry of 18 B.C. That law was supplemented by the Papian-Poppaean Law of A.D. 9, which was passed by two consuls (ironically, both were bachelors). In the long run, the laws may not have been very effective; in his *Satires,* Juvenal called them "dormant" (2.37).

The Julian Law on the Orders Permitted to Marry prescribed: First, no marriage was permitted between free persons and freed slaves of either sex (the nonmarriage provision extended to marriages between free persons and prostitutes, pimps male or female, persons manumitted by pimps, convicted adulterers or criminals, and actors male or female). Second, precedence of office between the two yearly consuls went to the consul who had more children than his colleague, unless both were married and father of the same number of children, in which case the older consul would have precedence.

Third, persons who had three children (in Rome; four in Italy; five in the provinces) were exempted from the mandatory guardianship of wards of the state frequently imposed on free Roman men. Fourth, freedmen with two or more children were exempted from the usual obligations of freedmen to their former owners. Fifth, bachelors were forbidden to inherit. A man or wife could inherit (a) one-tenth of the other's estate and bequeath to each other in addition as many tenths as they had (not necessarily common) children; (b) the entire estate if they had a common child or had obtained the "three-children exemption" from the emperor; or (c) nothing if they contracted a marriage contrary to the strictures in the first item.

Sixth, women were exempted from remarriage for one year upon widowhood or six months after divorce (but then they were required to marry again). Seventh, unless there was a good reason not to, parents were required to give their children in marriage and supply a dowry for daughters. Eighth, legacies without a legal inheritor were paid into the public treasury.

The Papian-Poppaean Law added these modifications: First, a man or wife could inherit the other's entire estate if the man was at least 60, and the woman at least 50, at the time of death. All younger childless persons, married or unmarried, lost half of any legacy they were bequeathed, and that half was paid into the public treasury. Ineligible inheritors had their portion distributed to married persons with children named in the same will. Second, women were exempted from remarriage for two years upon widowhood, one year six months upon divorce.

—*Jerise Fogel*

PARAGUAY

The first Spanish to arrive in Paraguay in the early-sixteenth century found a fertile territory well populated by the native Guarani people. Because of isolation, lack of precious metals, and subsequent official neglect, the newcomers essentially relied upon subsistence agriculture, pastoral pursuits, and the gathering of yerba maté (Paraguayan tea). Generally, these European conquerors utilized forced Indian labor, and any large-scale plantation agriculture with imported African slaves was nonexistent.

Slavery was legal throughout Spain's New World empire, and some slaves were taken into the interior of South America during the colonial era, usually by way of the Río de la Plata estuary. Some were employed as artisans—blacksmiths, carpenters, leather workers, and the like—but most were domestic servants. Pos-

sessing slaves lent prestige to members of the provincial elite, and through time, a significant black element was introduced into Paraguayan society.

Manumitting domestic slaves was quite common, generally as a reward of service upon a master's death, but Paraguayan custom and the blacks' lower legal status in the Spanish Empire conspired against these freedmen. Free blacks, like Indians, paid a head tax, or *tributo,* to the state. In Paraguay, manumitted blacks were forbidden to live their lives freely and thus earn that tax on their own. Instead, the state assigned them as *amparados* ("those who are protected") under the "protection" of a religious order.

By the 1700s, three black communities existed in the colony, one each under the supervision of the Franciscans, Dominicans, and Mercedarians. Religious officials gave them lands to cultivate, and from their produce they paid the *tributo* in kind. They also were subject, as Indians, to forced labor demands by the state, but by all accounts, that burden was not particularly onerous. By the late colonial era, there were some 4,200 black slaves and 7,300 *amparados* in a population of approximately 115,000.

Besides black slavery, a little-known custom of Indian slavery also existed in colonial Paraguay. During frontier warfare, settlers seized women and children of nomadic tribes in the nearby Gran Chaco, and these captives were assigned civil masters. Colonial law permitted the enslavement of Indians who warred against the Spanish and rejected Christianity and "civilized life." The province's Native American slavery continued into the mid-1700s, but most Indians east of the Paraguay River accepted Christianity and Spanish authority, and thus could not legally be enslaved.

Independence and the rule of José Gaspar de Francia as dictator of Paraguay (1814–1840) reinforced the institution of slavery in Paraguay. Campaigning against the church's authority, Francia secularized the property of the religious orders, converting their estates into *estancias de la republica* ("dwellings of the republic"). Former *amparados* became state slaves on these *estancias,* laboring as agricultural or pastoral workers. The Paraguayan army consumed most of the food produced and cattle raised on the *estancias.* Francia often assigned state slaves of the central region around Asunción to new cattle *estancias* in the far north or in newly developed pastoral regions south of the Tebicuary River, which led to a new phenomenon, the slave cowboy.

Given the new status of Paraguayan blacks, it appears that slave manumission by private individuals decreased drastically as little reason existed to give them their liberty. Although slavery in the private sector was mostly domestic and artisan in nature, some of the slaves worked as cowboys on lands leased from the government.

The rise to power of Carlo Antonio López after Francia's death in 1840 brought a cautious, gradualist approach to the abolition of Paraguayan slavery. The government decreed a Law of Free Womb in 1842, which freed children born to slaves after that year. Those children, termed *libertos,* owed service to their mothers' masters until age 25 if they were male, 24 for females. Paraguay also abolished the international slave trade.

The Law of Free Womb still left many blacks in bondage. In 1862, perhaps 17,000 slaves remained in Paraguay, and there were about 20,000 *libertos.* State slaves and state *libertos* were a useful labor adjunct to the centrally directed economy that characterized the 1840s and 1850s. Not only did they continue working on state *estancias,* but they worked in state-owned brick factories, arsenals, and an iron foundry and on various construction projects. Their lives were little changed from the days of Francia with one important exception: state slaves now could be, and were, sold to private individuals—and the dictator's family members profited from this new arrangement.

For all practical purposes, the bloody War of the Triple Alliance (1865–1870) between Paraguay and an alliance of Brazil, Argentina, and Uruguay destroyed slavery on the upper Plata. The great number of casualties suffered by Paraguayan blacks (and the entire population), the population displacement, and the wrecked economy all spelled the end of slavery in Paraguay. Nonetheless, when conquering Brazilians fanned over the Paraguayan countryside in 1870, they still found slaves scattered here and there, even though slavery had already been abolished.

In a rather ironic action, the commander of the Brazilian army, who was married to the heir of the throne of the last great slaveholding nation in the New World, persuaded a provisional Paraguayan government to enact abolition, and in October 1869, the government decreed that "slavery is totally extinguished in all the territory of Paraguay." The last Spanish-American republic to recognize slavery finally accepted abolition.

—*Jerry W. Cooney*

See also
Abolition, Latin America; *Encomienda* System; Latin America; Native American Peoples, Enslavement of
For Further Reading
Cooney, Jerry W. 1974. "Abolition in the Republic of Paraguay: 1840–1870." In *Jahrbuch für Geschichte von Staat, Wirtschaft und Gesellschaft Lateinamerika.* Ed. Richard Konetzke and Hermann Kellenbenz. Cologne and Vienna: Böhlau Verlag; Pla, Josefina. 1972. *Hermano negro: La esclavitud en el Paraguay.* Madrid: Paraninfo.

PASSES

Slave passes, also called "certificates" or "tickets," were written notes granting slaves permission to leave the plantation on which they lived. Almost all slave societies in the New World required slaves to have written permission from their owners to leave the plantation, and they could not leave without it. Slave passes contained the slave's name, the destination, the trip's duration, the expiration date of the pass, and the master's signature. Passes were most commonly given to male slaves who ran errands and performed transportation work beyond the plantation. Depending upon the master, slave men might also be given passes to visit their wives on weekends.

Beginning in the 1680s, colonial North American lawmakers enacted legislation to control the behavior of the black slave population, which emerged as the principal labor source, replacing white indentured servants. Control over slave mobility was an essential component of effective supervision of the slave population. Slave absenteeism, religious meetings, and parties posed real threats to the stability of the emergent slave society. While away from their owners' plantations, slaves not only were not working, they congregated with one another, with poor whites, and with free blacks sharing grievances and inspiring unruliness; they encouraged and facilitated escape; and whites feared that they plotted insurrection.

Accordingly, colonial legislators treated slave mobility with gravity. Virginia legislation passed in 1680, implying some equality between the two actions, proclaimed the urgency of controlling not only the access of slaves to lethal weapons but also their ability to move freely away from the plantation. Slaves possessing weapons or caught "out of place" without permission were to receive the same punishment: "twenty lashes on the bare back, well laid on." Between 1680 and the early-eighteenth century, other colonial legislatures followed Virginia's lead and attempted to fix the social and geographical location of slaves by securing them to the plantations where they lived and worked.

Barbados had developed a sophisticated set of laws to govern its slave population by 1661. A failed rebellion in 1649, slaves' persistent selling of stolen goods on the black market, and the problem of fugitive slaves led that colony to initiate a ticket system for the "safety of this place." South Carolina and the Caribbean islands of Antigua and Jamaica also adopted Barbados's ticket system in their slave societies. In most places, curfew laws supplemented legislative control over slave mobility, thus containing the slaves in both time and space.

Because some slaves refused to obey the pass laws and would sneak away from their owners' plantations, colonial legislatures were forced to reinforce the initial statutes by conscripting whites into the policing of slaves. Whites in the Caribbean and in North American colonies were compelled during the late-seventeenth and early-eighteenth centuries, under penalty of fine, to administer whippings to stray slaves and to return them to their owners. During the early-eighteenth century, white citizens organized into patrols and militias to police slaves.

The complications of urban slavery forced modifications to the pass system in North American cities in the eighteenth century. Rising numbers of urban-dwelling slaves, increasing numbers of free blacks, and the relatively more autonomous nature of urban slavery demanded a more comprehensive system for monitoring slaves. Additionally, masters needed a simpler method: writing individual passes for every errand their servants ran was tedious. Consequently, many cities devised a badge system. Slaves, and ultimately free blacks, were required at all times to wear badges that their owners bought from the city. Failure to wear one's badge resulted in corporal punishment, imprisonment, or fines imposed on both master and slave.

Pass laws failed to control the movement and behavior of slaves, as slaves devised strategies to circumvent the law. Because most patrollers were illiterate, slaves sometimes successfully used expired passes. Other slaves learned to read and write and, despite stiff punishments if caught, forged their own passes. Most commonly, slaves simply snuck away, kept a watchful eye out for patrols, and went about worshiping their God, visiting family and friends, courting lovers, or engaging in their own celebrations.

—*Stephanie M. H. Camp*

For Further Reading

Fry, Gladys-Marie. 1975. *Night Riders in Black Folk History*. Knoxville: University of Tennessee Press; Hadden, Sally E. Forthcoming. *Slave Patrols and Law Enforcement in the Old South, 1700–1865*. Cambridge, MA: Harvard University Press; Higginbotham, A. Leon. 1978. *In the Matter of Color: Race and the American Legal Process, the Colonial Period.* New York: Oxford University Press; Joyner, Charles. 1984. *Down by the Riverside: A South Carolina Slave Community*. Urbana: University of Illinois Press.

PATERNALISM

Developed during the colonial period and later modified in response to Northern abolitionist rhetoric critical of Southern slavery in the antebellum period, paternalism in the United States was the result of the quandary produced by the ownership of human property. Based on the English model of a hierarchical social order derived from extended family units, the image of the Old South popularized by historian Ulrich Bonnell Phillips, who relied upon the journals and plantation records of antebellum slaveowners, depended upon conveying gentility and family sympathy, pastoral beauty, elegance, and ease, all of which belied the reality of Southern slavery.

In the American colonial period, the extended family exemplified stability—the wife was subservient to the husband, as were the children and servants; the husband did not take advantage of his power but generously provided for his household. This model stressed the complementary nature of the relationships. Men assumed higher political office as an extension of this role, expanding their duty to the care of the larger community. The result was almost perfect order, and it was believed that assumptions of equal status in society were invitations to disorder, even chaos. Since the people on the very bottom were cared for, there was a benefit for all involved.

The racist assumption inherent in the rationale of the time was that their presumption of superiority allowed whites to approach their black slaves with benevolent "affection"; this attitude was further enhanced by Enlightenment ideals concerning both "natural rights" and a morality dictating protection of society's weak and disadvantaged. Thus, slaveholders practiced what they considered to be "a good and wise despotism." An alternate view suggests that the lives of the slaves were circumscribed by constant white interference. Whites inflicted many detailed rules for slave behavior in a fashion that was clearly arbitrary—not only in the areas of work and religious belief, but also in a slave's choice of mate, child rearing, and use of time when not working. Such rules were enforced by various punishments ranging from subtle threats to whipping or sale.

During the antebellum period, paternalism increasingly came to be seen as a form of benign interference. One form this interference took was concern for the slaves' spiritual lives, and white ministers wrote and sermonized on the Christian responsibility of slaveowners to their slaves. Absentee slaveowners frequently included specific instructions to overseers concerning their slaves' religious activities. The Second Great Awakening, a series of fundamentalist revivals in the antebellum period, resulted in an internal missionary movement to increase slave converts to Protestant Christianity, but literacy continued to be prohibited to slaves and the Christian message to slaves was carefully monitored and emphasized biblical injunctions to work hard work and obey your master.

Paternalism was also seen as a justification for increasing restrictions on slaves and even for physical punishment; since respect, if not veneration, of slave-owners by slaves was desired and slaves would not "respect" an overly lenient master, punishment was expected and required. Thus, to be more truly "benevolent," some slaveowners might limit the practice of allowing slaves private garden patches (which they worked on during "off" hours after a full day's work for the owner), visitor's passes, or approval for marriages off the "home" place. In South Carolina and Georgia, the task system was seen as a paternalistic innovation as it allowed slaves to budget their own time once a particular task was completed.

It is ironic that there was such emphasis on family stability when there was also disruption of slave families and the slaveowners depended upon the threat of that disruption to instill "order." The picture of "our family black and white" that is so often described in plantation journals and correspondence was depicted fictionally in Harriet Beecher Stowe's *Uncle Tom's Cabin, or Life among the Lowly* (1852), which was credited with widely disseminating antislavery views. The novel was groundbreaking in that it was the first widely read publication to treat seriously the idea of a black family, albeit one broken by sale.

The folklore tales of plantation slaves, particularly the "trickster" tales, which highlighted the triumph of an underdog character by wiles and subtlety, are evidence of the recognition by slaves of their unequal status rather than reliance upon territorial control, as has been suggested by certain historians. The tendency of former slaves to report both cruelty and affection on the part of slaveowners also suggests the complexity of this particular slaveholding strategy.

Paternalist slaveowners consistently recorded their confusion as to the motives of rebellious slaves—slaves who refused to work, feigned sickness, or ran away—and saw such behavior as being, at the very least, ungrateful. This purported puzzlement was always based on the firm conviction of black inferiority, so that slaveowners generally were serious when they attributed an insurrection or any other organized activity on the part of slaves to the influence of outside agitators, most often from the North—they truly believed their slaves were neither intelligent nor skilled enough to be capable of planning such a thing.

The laws passed by Southern slaveholders indicate how they themselves defined paternalism. Slave mobility was severely restricted and tied to the prohibition on slave literacy since slaves required written permission to be away from their own home place. Such restrictions increased after the 1831 Nat Turner rebellion, as did the ability of slaves to congregate in groups, especially for the purpose of religious worship. Laws also made it increasingly difficult to manumit slaves or for freed slaves to remain in the state where they were freed.

Laws that made it a criminal act for a white person to kill a slave most often reflected the slave's monetary rather than human value, and laws defining the criminal culpability of slave acts against whites were sometimes moot since, in the heat of the moment, slaves were sometimes summarily executed. Historians interpret the existence of such laws as an attempt to live up to a paternalistic ideal—and to occasional instances when slaves received trial at law for offenses against the slave regime.

—*Dale Edwyna Smith*

For Further Reading
Kolchin, Peter. 1993. *American Slavery, 1619–1877*. New York: Hill and Wang; Oakes, James. 1982. *The Ruling Race*. New York: Knopf; Parish, Peter J. 1989. *Slavery: History and Historians*. New York: Harper and Row.

PATROLS

The existence of runaway slaves in every slave system of the world led directly to the creation of formal slave patrols after 1500. Both professional and amateur slave catchers flourished in all slave-based societies whether the settlements were French, Spanish, Portuguese, or English. The earliest New World antecedents of patrols were slave-hunting groups of owners in the 1530s, the volunteer militia *hermandad* ("brotherhood") that looked for fugitives in Cuba. Gradually, the *hermandad* was displaced by professional slave hunters, *ranchadores*, who were paid for each individual capture.

Free blacks and slaves in Caribbean and South American colonies also chased fugitive slaves, and in Peru, these hunters were called *cuadrilleros* ("squad leaders"). In Barbados, the English militia in the mid-seventeenth century operated like the *hermandad* in many ways, designating a portion of its men to serve as slave patrollers. As English planters migrated to the North American mainland in the seventeenth century, particularly to South Carolina, they carried with them well-established views on the proper steps to take in recapturing fugitive slaves.

On the mainland, colonial legislatures enacted laws creating formal slave patrols after enough slaves had been imported to warrant the effort. The earliest patrol laws—in South Carolina (1704), Virginia (1727), and North Carolina (1753)—were enacted in response to rising slave populations, threatened slave revolts, and white insecurity about personal safety. In South Carolina, the existence of a black majority early in the eighteenth century convinced white lawmakers there that some form of community-based slave control was necessary to supplement individual slaveowners' efforts.

The South Carolina laws were soon emulated in colonial Georgia, and as settlers migrated into the Deep South, copies of South Carolina's and Virginia's slave laws, and slave patrols, migrated with them. Patrols existed in all slave states prior to the U.S. Civil War, created by law and sanctioned by state authority. Only the Civil War formally ended the legal use of slave patrols in the United States, and even after the war, patrol methods of violence and intimidation formerly directed at slaves were copied by the Ku Klux Klan and used against freedmen.

In most colonies, and later states, patrol members were drawn from the local militia, often chosen directly from the membership rolls by captains of militia districts. This method of selection ran into problems in the nineteenth century when militia groups fell into a general decline. In North Carolina, county courts had authority over the patrols from the beginning, and patrollers, or "searchers" as they were first called, were exempt from militia duty for their term of service as a patroller. In Virginia and North Carolina, patrollers eventually received exemptions from jury service, militia duty, and roadwork duty while they served.

Patrollers in North Carolina were paid for their work, usually on a per-night or per-hour basis. Some cities (e.g., Wilmington and Raleigh, North Carolina; Charleston and Columbia, South Carolina) adopted a form of payment for urban patrollers instead of relying solely on exemptions. Paid urban patrollers occasionally substituted for official police forces in Southern cities, whose residents viewed slaves as more troublesome than criminal. After the Civil War, police forces displaced urban patrollers in Southern cities.

Patrollers had three main tasks. First, they were to contain slaves' activities once they left the plantation or residence of their owner. Patrollers did most of their work at night—on the roads, in the fields, and between the farms of neighbors—making sure that slaves went where their masters intended them to go. The patrollers were required to chase and interrogate slaves, and they frequently used violence in these nocturnal encounters. Traveling slaves were supposed to carry passes stating their owner's name, their destination, and when they were to return home. Many planters resisted giving their slaves passes of any kind while others gave them freely. In towns, passes complicated everyday life, since no owner wanted to have to write a new pass for every errand, and many towns had slaves wear metal badges, purchased once a year, which clearly indicated their status.

The second job of patrollers was to disperse illegal slave gatherings wherever they might occur. Such assemblies could be used to plot insurrections, which Southern whites dreaded. In breaking up meetings, patrols routinely disrupted religious gatherings organized by slaves on their own. The patrollers' third main task was to enter slave quarters and search for runaway slaves or any items forbidden to slaves (e.g., guns, papers, and books). Some white slave masters would not allow patrollers to enter their property, even though the law gave patrollers the legal right to enter and search slave quarters.

Unlike slave catchers, patrollers were sanctioned by law, appointed by their neighbors, (sometimes) paid for their work, and did more than just hunt fugitives. Their work was local, while that of the slave catcher might range widely. Patrols always worked in groups and were led by a "captain" who supervised the group's activities.

Many historians claim that patrollers were from the lowest classes, that they were the "poor whites" or "white trash" of a community chosen by their social superiors to perform an unsavory social duty. Patrollers have typically been cast as poor nonslaveowners who were being used by the richer slaveowning class. These assertions are often supported by statements drawn from interviews with ex-slaves conducted under the auspices of the Works Progress Administration in the 1930s, in which the slaves routinely stated that patrollers were poor whites.

Studies by Sally Hadden (1993) and Charles Bolton (1994), however, indicate that patrollers were chosen from the middle strata of Southern society, not exclusively from the poorest class, and that patrol groups usually included at least one affluent slaveowner. This makeup makes sense considering that slaves as property were too valuable to allow propertyless poor whites to injure and perhaps kill. Some sort of supervision by the landed gentry was required to keep the slave patrols from brutalizing slaves too much, and the presence of a slaveowner or slaveowners on the patrols would have provided just such restraint.

—*Sally E. Hadden*

See also
Nonslaveholders; Passes; Slave Catchers
For Further Reading
Bolton, Charles. 1994. *Poor Whites of the Antebellum South: Tenants and Laborers in Central North Carolina and Northeast Mississippi*. Durham, NC: Duke University Press; Fry, Gladys-Marie. 1991. *Night Riders in Black Folk History*. Athens: University of Georgia Press; Hadden, Sally E. 1993. "Law Enforcement in a New Nation: Slave Patrols and Public Authority in the Old South, 1700–1865." Ph.D. dissertation, Department of History, Harvard University, Cambridge, MA; Henry, H. M. 1914. "The Police Control of the Slave in South Carolina." Unpublished paper, Emory University, Atlanta, Georgia; Russ, Williams, E., ed. 1972. "Slave Patrol Ordinances of St. Tammany Parish, Louisiana, 1835–1838." *Louisiana History* 13: 399–412.

PAUL (SAINT)
(A.D. 10?–62?)

The apostle Paul (A.D. 10?–62?) has some-times been called the second founder of Christianity because of his immeasurable impact upon the formation of Christian theology. Although the title may be an exaggeration, one cannot doubt that his missionary activity and the letters he wrote to early Christian congregations decisively shaped Christianity's emergence from its Jewish background into a new religious tradition.

First a persecutor of Christians, Paul later converted to Christianity and devoted his energy to spreading the Christian message. He traveled extensively throughout Asia Minor and Greece establishing Christian congregations, and he developed his theology in letters written to these churches. Paul was arrested while on a trip to Jerusalem to convey an offering to the Christian community there. As a Roman citizen, Paul demanded that the emperor hear his case, and he was taken to Rome. It is probable that he died there around A.D. 62–64.

The New Testament contains 13 letters traditionally ascribed to Paul. Today, it is generally accepted by all but the most conservative of biblical interpreters that of the books of the Bible, only Romans, 1 and 2 Corinthians, Galatians, Philippians, 1 Thessalonians, and Philemon are unquestionably by Paul.

Examining the genuinely Pauline letters reveals that Paul occasionally used the word *slave* in a figurative sense to speak of a total commitment—for example, the apostles are described as slaves of the Christians (2 Cor. 4:5, New Revised Standard Version), and Paul describes himself as a slave of Christ (Rom. 1:1; Gal. 1:10). Apart from this metaphorical use of the word *slave* there are three passages that we may turn to in order to examine Paul's position on slavery.

In Galatians 3:28, Paul wrote: "There is no longer Jew or Greek, there is no longer slave or free, there is no longer male and female; for all of you are one in Christ Jesus." Here he seems to assert that the distinction between slave and freeman was transcended and abolished in the Christian community, but it is not clear how far Paul expected to extend the overthrowing of the distinction between slave and free. The parallel between slave and free on the one hand and male and female on the other suggests that the equality between each pole of these pairs was "in the sight of God" and had no relation whatever to temporal affairs.

Paul's ambivalent position also appears in 1 Corinthians. There he wrote: "Were you a slave when called? Do not be concerned about it. Even if you can gain your freedom, make use of your present condition now more than ever [or, avail yourself of the op-portunity?]. For whoever was called in the Lord as a slave is a freed person belonging to the Lord, just as whoever was free when called is a slave of Christ. You were bought with a price; do not become slaves of human masters. In whatever condition you were called, brothers and sisters, there remain with God" (1 Cor. 7:21–24).

As is indicated by the two possible translations in verse 21, Paul's meaning is unclear. He seems to suggest that those who were slaves when they became Christians should not worry about their status, but in the next sentence is he urging them to remain in that status should an opportunity for freedom arise? Or is he suggesting that they should take advantage of that opportunity to gain their freedom? A common interpretation of this passage is that on the whole, it reflects Paul's belief that the time before the return of the resurrected Christ and the end of the age is so short that all should remain in their present social status. In this interpretation, what Paul has done is to relativize slavery and freedom. What matters is, not socioeconomic freedom, but inner freedom in Christ.

Other contemporary scholars have vigorously challenged that interpretation, with many believing that Paul was *not* advising slaves to remain in that status any more than he advised Jews or Gentiles to remain in the religious situation in which they were when they became Christians. In this reading, Paul is best interpreted as asserting that if a person has no opportunity to gain freedom they should not worry about it but that if the opportunity comes to gain freedom they should certainly take advantage of it. In any case, they should remember that they are now freemen and women "in the Lord."

Paul's letter to Philemon is his only extant letter addressed to an individual, and it is commonly believed that Paul wrote the letter because he wished to return Onesimus—a slave he had converted to Christianity—to his owner, Philemon, in order to obtain Philemon's approval and possibly Onesimus's freedom. The possibility that Onesimus was a runaway who may have also wronged his master or stolen something from him complicates the situation. Paul writes so deferentially and cautiously that his intentions are unclear. He asks Philemon to receive Onesimus as he would receive Paul himself—that is, as an equal, not as an inferior. He also indicates that he expects Philemon to do even more than Paul has explicitly asked, and most interpreters believe that means Paul expected Philemon to grant Onesimus his freedom.

Thus, the evidence of Paul's letters is inconclusive. His failure to encourage explicitly the application of themes found in Galatians has often led to the characterization of his position as a kind of "social conservatism." His letters do lend themselves to such an interpretation, but in the final analysis that is probably unfair because it fails to consider his eschatological concerns and his sense of the imminent end to the age. He was not sanctifying the status quo, including slavery, as divinely ordered but was pointing to his belief that the present order was doomed.

—Jerry D. McCoy

For Further Reading
Beker, J. Christiaan. 1980. *Paul the Apostle: The Triumph of God in Life and Thought.* Philadelphia: Fortress Press; Keck, Leander E. 1988. *Paul and His Letters.* 2d ed., rev. and enl. Philadelphia: Fortress Press.

PAX ROMANA

The phrase Pax Romana ("Roman peace") is a modern one, designating the apparent policy of Augustus and his successors until Severus (first and second centuries A.D.), namely, to keep the peace as much as possible both domestically and abroad (Tacitus, *Annales*). By the first century B.C., Rome had conquered territory from Gaul to the Near East and to Egypt and North Africa. Consequently, centralization and systematization rather than expansion were the tasks of the first emperors. The effect of this "peace" on the slave population was generally a reinforcement of older trends of stratification.

Slaves were imported as before into Italy and the provinces; they were usually purchased on the frontiers of the empire and came chiefly from unconquered areas beyond the Danube, north of the Black Sea, and parts of Germany and Britain. The peace seems to have had little effect on the numbers of slaves imported. Slaves continued to be bred for profit, and society was heavily slave-based throughout the Roman Empire.

Approximately 2 million slaves lived in Italy at the end of the Roman Republic; the number remained as high or higher through late antiquity. Lucius Junius Columella's farming handbook, *De re rustica* (written in the first century A.D.), has more space devoted to slave management than do the earlier treatises of Cato and Varro, which indicates that under Augustus and his successors, the amount of agricultural fieldwork done by slaves (hence the number of slaves in the Italian countryside) had probably increased, or at least not decreased.

An important feature of this period was a tendency toward social stratification: as "classical" Roman law, based in large part on personal status, grew in importance, the hierarchical classification of people became an exact science. The result was a complicated system of status classification that made subtle distinctions between different types of unfree workers.

One new classification, and an indication of the trend toward social stratification, was the burgeoning class of imperial freedmen known as the *familia Caesaris*, or "household of Caesar," consisting of slaves freed by the emperor, many of whom took up managerial and administrative roles in what amounted to the Roman civil service. During the first two centuries A.D., this group became established as an elite group among the slave and freedman classes of imperial society, although within the *familia* there remained much social differentiation.

One attempt at controlling the entry of slaves and freedman into citizenship was made through the laws regarding women. In A.D. 52, under Emperor Claudius I, the Senatus Consultum Claudianum became law (*Institutes of Gaius* 1.84; Tacitus, *Annales*). This policy declared that a freeborn mother cohabiting with a slave would be categorized as a slave *(serva)* herself, with the result that her children would be classified as slaves. This stricture on the attainment of citizenship was not lifted until the time of Emperor Hadrian (r. 117–138).

—Jerise Fogel

See also
Roman Empire
For Further Reading
Finley, M. I. 1985. *The Ancient Economy.* 2d ed. Berkeley: University of California Press; Weaver, P. 1972. *Familia Caesaris.* Cambridge: Cambridge University Press.

PEACE CONVENTION (1860–1861)

Hoping to prevent the destruction of the Union during the 1860–1861 secession crisis, 133 delegates met in Washington, D.C., on February 4–27, 1861, to discuss a compromise that would keep the Union together and avert possible civil war. Representatives from Connecticut, Delaware, Illinois, Indiana, Iowa, Kansas, Kentucky, Maine, Maryland, Massachusetts, Missouri, New Hampshire, New York, North Carolina, Ohio, Pennsylvania, Rhode Island, Virginia, and Wisconsin faced the formidable task of creating a compromise to keep the North and South together. Former president John Tyler of Virginia chaired the proceedings.

Members of the convention stressed the theme of a conciliatory attitude between North and South. The Democratic and Republican parties were urged to lay aside their political differences for the good of the nation, but the political motives of both sides were questioned. By the time the convention began debating the issues dividing the country, some of its members had resorted to making insulting remarks about fellow delegates and their states, and disagreements on how to proceed with the convention led to bitter arguments that threatened to end the peace conference before any concrete proposals could be made. Further difficulties in the convention were caused by the exclusion of the press, and closed-door sessions created tension and suspicion, not only with the press, but also within the political community.

Some of the key points for peace between the North and South were included in the compromise proposed by Kentucky senator John J. Crittenden. His proposal stated that the Missouri Compromise line of 36° 30' would be maintained and extended to the Pacific and slavery would be permitted to the south of the line, although new states would have the option to remain free. Slavery on public lands could not be prohibited, and slavery in the District of Columbia could not be abolished as long as slavery existed in Virginia and Maryland or until a majority of the citizens in those states voted for emancipation. Congress could not interfere with the interstate transportation of slaves, and compensation would be given to slaveowners who could not retrieve their runaway slaves because of the activities of abolitionists. Also, Crittenden's proposals could not be nullified by future legislation.

The Peace Convention formally presented its proposals, a modified version of the Crittenden Compromise, to both houses of Congress on February 27, 1861. The subjects of slave territory and the rights of slaveowners had constantly come up for debate, and the convention finally did propose protection for the slaveowners' right to hold slave property. At the same time, however, it stated its desire to see the slave trade suppressed by all means necessary. Congress took the convention report under advisement, but after a brief review of its proposals, the House and Senate failed to act on any of them. The rejection of the Peace Convention's proposals by Congress was evidence of the severe divisions in the nation. The lack of interest shown by Congress in the work of the convention, disagreements within the convention itself, and Virginia's rejection of its proposals doomed the work of the Peace Convention to failure. Within a matter of months, the United States was plunged into civil war.

—*Ron D. Bryant*

See also
Crittenden Compromise
For Further Reading
Keene, Jesse L. 1961. *The Peace Convention of 1861.* Tuscaloosa, AL: Confederate Publishing; Kirwan, Albert D. 1962. *John J. Crittenden: The Struggle for the Union.* Lexington: University Press of Kentucky.

PECULIUM

Roman law defined *peculium* as "what the slave, with his master's permission, holds separately from the master's accounts" (Ulpian, *Digest* 15.1.5.4). In all periods of Roman history, slaves had legal sanction to own personal property. Roman legal texts discuss extensively the uses and limitations of the *peculium*, and the term appears on inscriptions and in technical and imaginative literature.

Any property might compose a *peculium*: a few cattle in the countryside, a shop in the city, or simply the tips, gifts, and wages a slave might obtain when not attending his or her master. Slaves owned by slaves (*vicarii*) belonged to their master's *peculium*, and *vicarii* possessed their own *peculia*, which, in turn, might include slaves.

Although a *peculium* was revocable by the master as a matter of course, Roman law understood it as belonging in practical matters to the slave. Through it the slave had a limited presence in court, where he or she could make agreements with third parties without the master's knowledge.

Slaves put their *peculia* to various uses. A *peculium* might be essential to a slave's livelihood—like the shepherd who lived far from his home estate and its resources and might need the by-products of animals (milk, eggs, etc.) in his *peculium*. Slaves, especially in the cities, might squander their *peculia* on various luxuries and diversions. Better-off slaves often spent sizable sums of money on monuments, and *peculia* could be the foundations of large businesses.

The *peculium* also nourished social stability in the Roman world: with a *peculium* a slave could buy his or her freedom, and the possibility of purchasing freedom inclined the slave toward patience, submission, and hard work for the master. Another allurement must have been that after manumission, unless specifically exempted by the master, the *peculium* followed the slave into freedom. A *peculium* could thus offer (if it were large enough) the prospect of relative economic independence after manumission. Although the Roman slaveowning classes always retained complete legal control over the *peculium*, the practice did loosen the slave's material and spiritual bonds of dependence.

The *peculium* also indicates a certain amount of economic independence on the part of slaves. Its widespread presence shows that many masters did not completely expropriate their slaves' labor and that purchase and sale by slaves must have amounted to a significant amount in the Roman economy.

—*Alexander Ingle*

See also
Roman Empire; Roman Republic

For Further Reading
Brinkhof, Johannes Jacobus. 1978. *Een studie over het peculium in het Klassieke Romeinse recht.* Meppel, Netherlands: Krips Repro; Kirschenbaum, Aaron. 1987. *Sons, Slaves, and Freedmen in Roman Commerce.* Jerusalem. Magnes Press; Micolier, Gabriel. 1932. *Pécule et capacité patrimoniale: Étude sur le pécule, dit profectice, depuis l'édit "de peculio" jusqu' à la fin de l'époque classique.* Lyon, France: Bosc Frères; Zeber, Ireneusz. 1981. *A Study of the Peculium of a Slave in Pre-Classical and Classical Roman Law.* Wroclaw, Poland: Uniwersytetu Wroclawskiego.

PENNINGTON, JAMES W.
(1809–1870)

James W. Pennington was a former slave who escaped from slavery to become a committed minister, teacher, writer, and dedicated abolitionist whose writings and activities helped generate a worldwide revulsion against slavery. The brutalities of enslavement shaped Pennington's early life.

Born a slave on Maryland's Eastern Shore, at age four Pennington was moved to Washington County, Maryland, and it was there that his work on plantations began. A brilliant and versatile character, Pennington learned and became expert in stone masonry and black-smithing. Having never reconciled himself to slavery and frequently contemplating escape, he did escape to Pennsylvania in 1830. He began his elementary education there and later moved to Long Island, New York, where he continued his education.

In the early 1830s, he taught in black schools in New York and Connecticut, and after studying theology, he assumed the pastorship of churches in Long Island and Connecticut. In 1841, he was appointed president of the Union Missionary Society, an antislavery organization whose members boycotted commodities produced by slave labor and opposed colonization.

Pennington published *A Textbook of the Origin and History of the Colored People* (1841), which discussed the Negro's complexion and history, his intellectual capacity, and prejudice in the United States. Pennington's stated objective was to debunk false ideas, and the book remains his lasting contribution to the Negro's intellectual defense. Proud of his "unadulterated African blood," Pennington rejected notions of Negro inferiority and attributed racial characteristics to environmental factors.

In 1843, he represented Connecticut at the World Anti-Slavery Convention. He also represented the American Peace Convention at the World Peace Society meeting in London, where he delivered several antislavery speeches. He toured Europe, taking his antislavery crusade to Paris and Brussels. Returning to the United States in 1847, he lived in New York City until 1850. His autobiography, *The Fugitive Blacksmith*, published in London in 1849, strongly indicted slavery. Pennington also helped organize antislavery protests in New York and fought against colonization.

With the passage of the Fugitive Slave Act in 1850, Pennington felt insecure and escaped abroad, where he remained until his manumission in June 1851. He exposed slavery in the United States and racism in Europe, particularly in England, France, and Germany, and he received a doctor of divinity degree from the University of Heidelberg. He established links with antislavery movements and organizations in England and Scotland, and the Glasgow Female Anti-Slavery Society sponsored some of his activities in the latter country.

In 1851, Pennington returned to the United States and became actively engaged in vigilante activities against the enforcement of the Fugitive Slave Act. He organized fund-raising events in defense of those arrested for obstructing the law's implementation, and in 1853, he organized the New York Legal Rights Association, which fought against discrimination on public transportation. Antislavery activities preoccupied Pennington for much of the 1850s and 1860s. He greatly admired John Brown, whose capture and execution he deplored. He moved to Jacksonville, Florida, in 1870 and founded a small black Presbyterian Church in which he ministered until his death on October 20, 1870.

—*Tunde Adeleke*

For Further Reading
Pease, Jane H., and William H. Pease. 1990. *They Who Would Be Free: Blacks' Search for Freedom, 1830–1861.* Chicago: University of Chicago Press; Quarles, Benjamin. 1970. *Black Abolitionists.* New York: Oxford University Press; Thorpe, Earl. 1971. *Black Historians: A Critique.* New York: William Morrow.

PERIOECI

Perioeci (those who dwell around about) referred to the subject peoples who lived near a dominant Greek city-state or in the rural areas under its control. Although personally free, *perioeci* lacked the political rights enjoyed by citizens of the ruling *polis* (city-state). They could be found in Argolis, Elis, Thessaly, Crete, and other areas of ancient

Greece, but the term more commonly referred to people in Laconia and Messenia who lived on the fringe of agricultural lands worked by Helots. The *perioeci* inhabited towns, a few of which had been created as "colonies" by Sparta using immigrants from the Argolic towns of Asine and Nauplia, which had been destroyed by the Argives. These "colonies" and other *perioeci* settlements were a defense perimeter for Sparta and a buffer zone to prevent the Helots from interacting with the outside world.

The hundred or so *perioecic* towns had their own semiautonomous governments, which managed local affairs and even sent competitors to the great Hellenic games. However, they remained subordinate to Sparta in matters of war and foreign affairs. They were not subject to the usual Spartan discipline, their only obligations being service in the Spartan military, the payment of taxes, and the cultivation of the special estates (*temenos*) held by the kings of Sparta in *perioeci* lands.

Spartans could not live or property in *perioeci* towns, but *perioeci* could reside in Sparta to conduct business. Since the rigorous regulations on the economic and social activities of Spartans did not apply to *perioeci*, many of them owned land and engaged in farming while others toiled as artisans, conducted commerce, worked in the mines of the Taygetus Mountains, or manufactured dyes for woolens, furniture, and chariots. As metalworkers they achieved distinction as embossers and as craftsmen in brass, and the Spartan state gave them the responsibility, or privilege, of manufacturing arms. The *perioeci* also produced Laconian pottery, which during the Archaic period (1500–500 B.C.) was noted for its high-quality artistry and craftsmanship. Intellectually, there were several *perioeci* poets.

Perioeci did not hold Spartan citizenship, but neither did Sparta regard them as aliens. They seem to have had a second-class or half-citizen status and were included with Spartans as being Laconians, the official designation of the Spartan *polis*. Their civil rights existed only on the sufferance of Sparta. The Spartan ephors, for example, might have any *perioecus* whom they considered subversive or insubordinate arrested and executed without trial. Nevertheless, examples of *perioeci* disaffection with Sparta are rare, and there is no evidence that *perioeci* communities ever struggled to free themselves from Spartan rule.

In general, *perioeci* remained steadfastly loyal to Sparta, composing much of its army (especially as the number of Spartans decreased), serving in inferior commands (although never over Spartans), and contributing significantly to the stability of the state. In Roman times, Titus Quinctius Flaminius (c. 227–174 B.C.) detached several *perioeci* towns from Sparta and put them under the protection of the Achaean League, a confederation of cities on the Gulf of Corinth. The emperor Augustus (r. 27 B.C.–A.D. 14) subsequently freed 24 *perioeci* towns from Spartan control.

—*Charles H. McArver, Jr.*

For Further Reading

Austin, M. M., and P. Vidal-Naquet. 1977. *Economic and Social History of Ancient Greece: An Introduction.* Berkeley: University of California Press; Botsford, George Willis. 1922. *Hellenic History.* New York: Macmillan; Chamoux, Francois. 1965. *The Civilization of Greece.* London: George Allen and Unwin; Fine, John V. A. 1983. *The Ancient Greeks: A Critical History.* Cambridge, MA: Belknap Press.

PERSONAL LIBERTY LAWS

Fourteen Northern states of the United States approved personal liberty laws before the country's Civil War. The first of the laws were statutes passed by many Northern state legislatures between the 1780s and the 1820s in order to protect free blacks from being kidnapped by unscrupulous slave catchers and sold into bondage. Such statutes established an orderly legal process for distinguishing a free black from a fugitive slave, and the laws generally extended certain basic protections—the writ of habeas corpus, the right to a jury trial, and the writ of *de homine replegiando* (a process for the recovery of property)—to people who were accused of being runaway slaves. But these statutes voided the right of recaption (the right to recapture a slave without going to court) that had been claimed by slaveowners under the Fugitive Slave Act of 1793. As a result, the statutes consistently led to questions of comity (the respect of one state for the laws of another) and state sovereignty in the decades prior to the war.

The clearest rejection of Southern slaveowners' claims to the right of recaption came in Pennsylvania when that state passed a new personal liberty law in 1820. This law increased the penalty for kidnapping to up to 21 years in prison at hard labor, and it also limited the role that state officials could play in the recovery of runaway slaves. Slaveowners and officials in Maryland, the state most affected by the act, pressed Pennsylvania to repeal the restriction, and in 1826, the Pennsylvania legislature approved a new personal liberty law. This law softened the restrictions on state officials but kept in place most of the legal protections for anyone accused of being a fugitive slave.

Proslavery interests challenged the personal liberty laws throughout the 1830s and early 1840s in the federal courts. In the case of *Prigg* v. *Pennsylvania* (1842), the U.S. Supreme Court acknowledged a slaveowner's

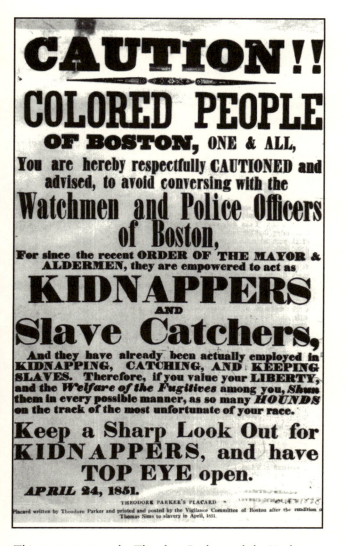

CAUTION!!
COLORED PEOPLE
OF BOSTON, ONE & ALL,
You are hereby respectfully CAUTIONED and advised, to avoid conversing with the
Watchmen and Police Officers of Boston,
For since the recent ORDER OF THE MAYOR & ALDERMEN, they are empowered to act as
KIDNAPPERS
AND
Slave Catchers,
And they have already been actually employed in KIDNAPPING, CATCHING, AND KEEPING SLAVES. Therefore, if you value your LIBERTY, and the *Welfare of the Fugitives* among you, Shun them in every possible manner, as so many *HOUNDS* on the track of the most unfortunate of your race.
Keep a Sharp Look Out for KIDNAPPERS, and have TOP EYE open.
APRIL 24, 1851.

THEODORE PARKER'S PLACARD

Placard written by Theodore Parker and printed and posted by the Vigilance Committee of Boston after the rendition of Thomas Sims to slavery in April, 1851.

This poster put out by Theodore Parker and the Vigilance Committee of Boston warned blacks of the danger to which they were subject following the passage of the Fugitive Slave Act of 1850. In 1855 Massachusetts passed a personal liberty law designed to block enforcement of the act.

right of recaption but held that state or local officials could not be required to assist in the enforcement of the Fugitive Slave Act of 1793. A second wave of personal liberty laws followed, and these ended state assistance in the recovery process and mandated the use of the writ of habeas corpus and jury trials to protect free blacks and obstruct the recovery of fugitive slaves. Between 1843 and 1847, such laws were passed in Vermont, New Hampshire, Massachusetts, Connecticut, Rhode Island, New Jersey, Pennsylvania, and Ohio.

The personal liberty laws of the 1840s were a major reason the South pushed for passage of the Fugitive Slave Act of 1850, which put the federal government in the business of capturing and returning runaway slaves. At first, Northern state legislatures seemed hesitant to challenge the new act, but the notorious rendition (legal return to slavery) of Anthony Burns in 1854, and the reopening of free federal territories to slavery as a result of the Kansas-Nebraska Act in the same year, led to a third wave of personal liberty laws.

One of the strongest of the new laws was passed in 1855 in Massachusetts. It forbade any attorney in the state from acting as counsel for a slave claimant, prevented any officer of the state from issuing an arrest warrant under the Fugitive Slave Act, and appointed special commissioners to defend people who were claimed to be runaway slaves. An antikidnapping section provided for a fine of up to $5,000 and imprisonment for up to five years for parties guilty of fraudulently claiming or seizing anyone as a slave. The law also guaranteed numerous protections for the accused—the writ of habeas corpus, the right to a jury trial, mandated written evidence, required witnesses—and placed the burden of proof on the claimant. Similar laws were passed in Vermont, New Hampshire, Maine, Connecticut, Rhode Island, Ohio, Michigan, and Wisconsin, and combined, these new laws successfully obstructed enforcement of the Fugitive Slave Act throughout much of the North.

In the case of *Ableman* v. *Booth* (1859), the U.S. Supreme Court rejected the constitutionality of the personal liberty laws. Ironically, the Wisconsin and Ohio legislatures announced their intent to practice "positive defiance" of the decision by continuing to enforce the acts as a matter of states' rights. During the secession crisis of 1860–1861, the U.S. Congress appealed to the states to repeal personal liberty laws in the spirit of sectional compromise. But they remained in force until rendered obsolete in 1865 by the ratification of the Thirteenth Amendment.

—*Roy E. Finkenbine*

See also
Ableman v. Booth; Fugitive Slave Act of 1850; *Prigg v. Pennsylvania*
For Further Reading
Morris, Thomas D. 1974. *Free Men All: The Personal Liberty Laws of the North, 1780–1861.* Baltimore: Johns Hopkins University Press.

PERU

Black slavery was introduced by the Spanish into Peru, the former territory of the Incas, in the first part of the sixteenth century. A few slaves were part of the expedition that reached the

Tumbes River in 1528, and the next year, the authorities in Spain authorized Francisco Pizarro to import 50 slaves into the area, including 2 for his personal service. Subsequently, increasing numbers of African slaves were introduced to Peru, totaling an estimated 100,000 between 1529 and 1816. At any given moment, however, the number of slaves was only a small fraction of the population of the viceroyalty. In 1791, for instance, there were only 40,347 slaves in Peru, representing 3.7 percent of the population. Of those slaves, 73.7 percent (29,763) lived in the Lima administrative area, and most of them (13,479) lived and worked in the capital, where they constituted about a quarter of the city's population.

Slave labor was crucial for the development of coastal plantation agriculture, as the production of sugar, wines, and other foodstuffs along the Peruvian coast relied on slave labor. Most slaves worked on medium-sized plantations of 20–50 slaves, but there were also numerous large haciendas, especially in the eighteenth century, that employed between 200 and 400 slaves. The five largest haciendas belonging to the Compañía de Jesús in the 1770s, for instance, averaged 300 slaves each. By the late-eighteenth century, haciendas in the Lima region—including La Molina, San Pedro de Lurín, and Villa—employed up to 400 slaves each.

For plantation slaves in Peru, living and working conditions did not differ much from those of their counterparts in other Latin American regions. Although the conditions were certainly harsh, they were not uniformly so. On the basis of allegiance, hard work, and stable family relations, slaves were selectively given access to provision grounds (chacras de esclavos, gardens that slaves could use to grow their own produce), which gave them greater access to food and other basic needs. Negligent living conditions, low birth rates, high mortality rates, and the frequent use of physical coercion all underline the adverse conditions that agricultural slaves lived under.

Most slaves, however, lived and worked in the urban areas as domestic servants, artisans, and, as jornaleros ("day laborers"), in various other occupations. As part of a multiethnic urban society, they enjoyed both greater degrees of autonomy and more opportunities for manumission than their rural counterparts. Cultural cohesiveness—especially through religious brotherhoods (cofradías)—also helped them cope with their generally adverse conditions.

Although slavery certainly played an important economic and social role in colonial Peru, it was not as central there as it was in places such as Brazil and Cuba. Slavery aided in the amassing of large fortunes and contributed a great deal to the economic and social well-being of the coastal elite. However, it was largely peripheral to the organization and success of the most important sources of profit for the colonial state and elite: mining, commerce, and the extraction of indigenous tribute and labor.

Slaves in Peru responded to their conditions in varied ways. Revolts and rebellions were extremely rare events. The most successful and widespread form of resistance was flight, which led to the formation of numerous—albeit generally small and short-lived—palenques (settlements of runaway slaves). Instead of becoming autonomous black communities, however, most palenques were little more than temporary shelters for runaways and highway robbers.

Many slaves joined the independent armies of the late 1810s and early 1820s, and many more seized the opportunity created by the wars of independence to escape or, at the very least, renegotiate their working and living conditions. After Peru's independence was proclaimed, liberator José de San Martín enacted a free-womb law that created a class of libertos (free children born of slave parents after July 28, 1821) who, nonetheless, were to remain under the control of their mother's master until they reached the age of 21 (later raised to 50). As a result of several factors—the end of the slave trade, changes in slave legislation, and the slaves' own efforts toward autonomy, among others—the number of slaves declined steadily, and slavery gradually disintegrated between 1821 and 1854. By the early 1850s, only about 19,000 slaves remained in Peru, representing 1 percent of the population.

In December 1854, in the middle of a civil war, Gen. Ramón Castilla decreed the abolition of slavery and granted full compensation to slaveowners. Despite fierce opposition, abolition was a very profitable operation for slaveowners, for they not only recovered their investment but also received inflated payments for elderly and dead slaves. For the former slaves, abolition did not convey immediate tangible gains. Several decrees strengthened social and labor control over them while widespread discrimination and exclusion were not significantly altered.

—Carlos Aguirre

See also
Abolition, Latin America; Latin America; Latin American Law

For Further Reading

Aguirre, Carlos. 1993. *Agentes de su propia libertad. Los esclavos de Lima y la desintegración de la esclavitud, 1821–1854.* Lima: Universidad Católica del Perú; Bowser, Frederick. 1974. *The African Slave in Colonial Peru, 1524–1650.* Stanford, CA: Stanford University Press; Hünefeldt, Christine. 1994. *Paying the Price of Freedom: Family and Labor among Lima's Slaves.* Berkeley: University of California Press; Kapsoli, Wilfredo. 1975. *Sublevaciónes de esclavos en el Perú, s. XVIII.* Lima: Universidad Ricardo Palma.

PERUVIAN SLAVE TRADE IN THE PACIFIC ISLANDS

*I*n 1862–1863, some 3,600 Pacific islanders were taken from their homes to work in the South American country of Peru. In all, ships made 38 voyages and called at 51 islands over much of the Pacific Ocean. Although technically an exercise in obtaining contract labor, this brief episode has become known as the Peruvian slave trade because of the extent of the deceit and kidnapping in the recruitment process and the treatment that the islanders received.

Peru's abolition of slavery (1854), the difficulty of maintaining regular supplies of Chinese coolies, and the unwillingness of local Indians to enter the employment market collectively created a labor crisis within the republic. Moreover, the Peruvian economy was becoming more diversified, which meant that the dominant guano industry had to compete with agricultural and urban business sectors for scarce manpower. These enterprises, in turn, were in competition with the high demand for domestic servants.

J. C. Byrne, a French citizen of Irish extraction who had been involved in dubious immigration schemes in places as far apart as Natal, Victoria, and New Caledonia, obtained a license from the beleaguered Peruvian authorities to obtain Pacific Island laborers to work in Peru. He chartered the 151-ton *Adelante* with the intention of recruiting laborers from the New Hebrides (present-day Vanuatu) on the other side of the Pacific. On the voyage out, the *Adelante* called at Tongareva (Penrhyn) in the Northern Cook Islands and discovered that the people there were willing to enlist in order to escape famine and also to raise funds to construct a church. Promising to take them to a nearby

A nineteenth-century view of Easter Island, on the eastern edge of the Pacific islands from which the short-lived Peruvian slave trade drew its victims.

island to engage in light agricultural work for $4 a month, the *Adelante* made two separate voyages to Tongareva and carried 472 people (from a population of 700) to Peru.

Such were the profits that within two weeks of the *Adelante*'s return from its first voyage, another five vessels had departed to recruit Pacific island workers. The success and repercussions of the *Adelante*'s endeavors, as a U.S. consul lamented, "stimulated this infamous business to an appalling extent, parties interested seemingly to be wild in their greed for gold, from this system of slave trade" (Maude, 1981).

Realizing that there was no need to venture as far afield as the New Hebrides, the general pattern was to obtain workers from the Polynesian islands, which were closer to Peru, and move west when their recruiting potential was exhausted. The Peruvians avoided the larger Polynesian islands, where resident European missionaries and consular representatives could report their activities and warn the islanders of their intentions, and adopted whatever recruiting device seemed appropriate to the occasion. Outright force was used occasionally, and another stratagem was to impersonate a missionary ship and carry unsuspecting islanders away to, allegedly, be instructed in the faith. On one occasion, a Peruvian vessel purchased human cargo from a Tasmanian whaler that had kidnapped islanders with the intention of taking them to Peru.

But it did not all go the Peruvians' way. At Mangareva in French Polynesia, a Peruvian vessel entered the lagoon masquerading as a scientific expedition, but suspicions were aroused and the vessel was seized. It was eventually released with a warning never to return. At Rapa, the people captured another Peruvian vessel, the *Cora,* and sailed it to Papeete, the capital of French Polynesia, where they handed it over to the protectorate authorities. The French governor was initially hampered by the absence of an antislave trade convention between France and Peru, but he was able to issue an edict banning Peruvian recruitment within the protectorate. After that, any such vessel entering Papeete was sequestered, including the *Cora*. In Peru itself, a campaign against the trade by a determined French chargé d'affaires and the liberal newspaper *El Commercio* starkly revealed its abuses.

The Peruvian government suppressed the trade on April 28, 1863, less than a year after its commencement. The trade was winding down in any case, but 15 vessels were still at sea. Thereafter, any arriving islanders were transferred to repatriation vessels. Even then they were at risk because smallpox had broken out on the grossly overcrowded ships after Peruvian authorities had prematurely lifted a quarantine ban on a whaling vessel from the United States.

Repatriation was a disaster. The captain of one vessel dumped his 426 smallpox-infected passengers on Cocos Island, a small island in the Pacific off the coast of Costa Rica. It was also rumored that many repatriating captains threw their charges overboard once out of sight of land. Another repatriating vessel landed smallpox-infested islanders on Rapa with disastrous consequences—in a perverse twist of fate, grim retribution was seemingly inflicted on the people of Rapa for the capture of the *Cora*. In the case of many islands, not a single person taken by the Peruvians returned.

Nor did the trade benefit Peru to any extent. Not only did the country suffer from international embarrassment, its labor-starved guano industry received no benefit whatever. All of the islanders who were allocated to employers worked either on haciendas or as domestic servants. Compared to the Atlantic slave trade, the Peruvian excursion in the Pacific islands was minuscule in absolute terms. It was, to be sure, a singular occurrence that would not be repeated.

—*Doug Munro*

For Further Reading
McCall, Grant. 1976. "European Impact on Easter Island: Response, Recruitment, and the Polynesian Experience in Peru." *Journal of Pacific History* 11 (2): 90–105; Maude, H. E. 1981. *Slavers in Paradise: The Peruvian Labour Trade to Polynesia, 1862–1864.* Canberra: Australian National University Press; Munro, Doug. 1990. "The Peruvian Slavers in Tuvalu: How Many Did They Kidnap?" *Journal de la Société des Océanistes* 90: 43–46; Richardson, J. B. 1977. "The Peruvian Barque *Adelante* and the Kanaka Labour Recruitment." *Journal of Pacific History* 11 (4): 212–214.

PETION, ALEXANDRE SABES (1770–1818)

A general and a statesman, Alexandre Sabès Pétion helped to lead an uprising against French colonial power in Saint Domingue. This uprising achieved independence, put an end to slavery for blacks in that colony, and secured civil rights for mulattoes.

Born in Port-au-Prince the son of a French father and a mulatto mother, Pétion trained at the military academy in Paris and became expert in warfare. He admired the French and fervently hoped they would grant mulattoes full civic rights, but after returning to Saint Domingue to serve in the French colonial army, Pétion realized that despite the ideals of the French Revolution, local whites were unwilling to accept mulattoes as equals. He therefore joined Toussaint Louverture's war of liberation. But, as a member of that racially fragmented group, Pétion was always a defender of mulatto interests, and when the mulatto general André Rigaud challenged the black Toussaint Louverture, Pétion defected. He fought heroically in the siege of Jacmel and, when defeated, left for France with Rigaud.

Pétion returned to Saint Domingue in 1802 with the forces sent by Napoleon to reconquer the former colony. When it became clear that Napoleon meant to reinstate slavery, Pétion joined forces with Louverture's successor, Jean-Jacques Dessalines, to overcome the French. Victorious, Dessalines declared the territory independent under its old Arawak name, *Haiti,* and proclaimed himself emperor. He proved to be an arbitrary, cruel ruler, and Louverture's former generals, foremost among them Pétion and Henri Christophe, successfully plotted his assassination in 1806.

Peace was short-lived as the old rivalry between mulattoes and blacks continued unabated. Christophe, a black, ruled northern Haiti while the mulatto Pétion controlled the south. Civil war continued, but neither was strong enough to inflict a decisive defeat on the other.

In 1807, the Senate of the Republic of Haiti, the southern part of the former Saint Domingue, elected Pétion president of the republic. He was reelected in 1811 and made president for life in 1816. He died in 1818, in office.

The brave soldier and brilliant military strategist was a lackadaisical president. As a statesman, he is mostly remembered for instituting a land distribution policy to pay his soldiers and officers. This policy gave rise to a country of small farmers engaged in subsistence agriculture but failed to improve the republic's overall economy. The population was content. Former black slaves cherished their independence and were not interested in working for pay on the large farms, which would have been required to revive Haiti's main international trade product, sugar. They grew what they needed for their families and a little coffee as a cash crop. The mulatto elite was also satisfied: they bought coffee from farmers for a pittance and developed an export market in that commodity, which made them wealthy. Pétion's land policies greatly influenced Haiti's later economic development.

Pétion is celebrated in the rest of Latin America for having given asylum and assistance to Simón Bolívar and his Army of Liberation during the revolution against Spain.

—*L. Natalie Sandomirsky*

See also
Bolívar, Simón; Christophe, Henri; Dessalines, Jean-Jacques; Louverture, Toussaint; Rigaud, André
For Further Reading
Cole, Hubert. 1967. *Christophe: King of Haiti.* New

York: Viking Press; Nicholls, David. 1988. *From Dessalines to Duvalier.* New York: Macmillan; Ott, Thomas. 1973. *The Haitian Revolution.* Knoxville: University of Tennessee Press.

PHILADELPHIA FEMALE ANTI-SLAVERY SOCIETY (1833–1870)

The Philadelphia Female Anti-Slavery Society was the longest lived of all female antislavery societies in the United States; it was also the first biracial antislavery organization in Pennsylvania. The society consciously tried to recruit women of diverse backgrounds and welcomed blacks as members and officers throughout its nearly 40-year existence. Although the society was open to all women, most of its membership consisted of Hicksite Quakers—those who followed the tenets of the antislavery Quaker preacher Elias Hicks.

The American Anti-Slavery Society held its founding convention in Philadelphia on December 4–6, 1833, and invited several women to witness the event silently. Although it was intended that women would be present but nonparticipatory, several of them, especially Lucretia Mott, entered the debate and contributed suggestions for the national society's constitution and its declaration of sentiments. Three days later, Mott and the other women present at the convention invited women interested in the abolitionist cause to a meeting where they founded the Philadelphia Female Anti-Slavery Society. These women pioneered female participation in state and national antislavery societies in addition to founding autonomous female antislavery societies.

The Philadelphia Female Anti-Slavery Society boasted many members besides Lucretia Mott, though she is probably the best-known member. Sarah Pugh was the society's president for most of the 1838–1866 era, and Mary Grew was the society's corresponding secretary from 1834 to 1870. Lydia White, Sydney Ann Lewis, and Alba Alcott (wife of Bronson Alcott and mother of Louisa May Alcott) were all active society members, and there were active members from several prominent families, including the Fortens—Charlotte, Marguerite, Sarah, and Harriet Forten Purvis (wife of Robert Purvis); the Douglasses—Grace and Sarah; and the Grimké sisters—Sarah and Angelina.

Initially, the society's activities included circulating petitions, recruiting new members, and sponsoring public lectures by black and white abolitionists, and its mission was to end slavery and racial discrimination.

Besides its history of racial cooperation, the society hosted the second annual Convention of American Anti-Slavery Women in 1838, during which antiabolitionist mobs burned the newly built Pennsylvania Hall.

As conditions changed within the antislavery movement, owing to dissension over whether women should be allowed to take an active role in the movement and the use of political means to end slavery, the Philadelphia Female Anti-Slavery Society became more focused in both its membership and its activities. Emphasis shifted from various public works to concentrating on the organization of and producing items for the annual fair, and although this change appears to have reduced the society's effectiveness, the women raised substantial funds for the antislavery movement. They also saw their years of work bear fruit toward the end of the society's long life when the state legislature passed laws prohibiting discrimination of blacks on public transportation.

—*Sydney J. Caddel*

See also
Forten, Charlotte; Grimké, Angelina; Grimké, Sarah Moore; Mott, Lucretia Coffin; Quakers; Women and the Antislavery Movement
For Further Reading
Bacon, Margaret Hope. 1986. *Mothers of Feminism: The Story of Quaker Women in America*. San Francisco: Harper and Row; Soderlund, Jean R. 1994. "Priorities and Power: The Philadelphia Female Anti-Slavery Society." In *The Abolitionist Sisterhood: Women's Political Culture in Antebellum America*. Ed. Jean Fagan Yellin and John C. Van Horne. Ithaca, NY: Cornell University Press; Williams, Carolyn. 1994. "The Female Antislavery Movement: Fighting against Racial Prejudice and Promoting Women's Rights in Antebellum America." In *The Abolitionist Sisterhood: Women's Political Culture in Antebellum America*. Ed. Jean Fagan Yellin and John C. Van Horne. Ithaca, NY: Cornell University Press; Williams, Carolyn. 1991. "Religion, Race, and Gender in Antebellum American Radicalism: The Philadelphia Female Anti-Slavery Society, 1833–1870." Ph.D. dissertation, Department of History, University of California at Los Angeles.

PHILIP II OF MACEDON
(382–336 B.C.)

Philip II was a king of Macedonia and the father of Alexander the Great (356–323 B.C.). He turned Macedonia into a powerful, centralized kingdom and brought most of Greece under his control. As king, Philip controlled all the timber and mineral resources of his kingdom, as well as large areas of fertile land, including all lands won by con-

quest, and could exploit them as he saw fit. The most important mining region was Mt. Pangaeus in southern Thrace, which was originally worked by Thracian and Greek concessionaires. It is probable that the operators of these mines employed slave labor, but it is also possible that free labor was used as well.

Philip brought the area under his control in 358–357 and was able to raise productivity to such a level that the mines gave him an annual revenue of 1,000 talents. There was no basis for slavery in Macedonia, except in the Chalcidice (a peninsula in eastern Macedonia), which possessed great mineral wealth. The Macedonian population did not spurn hard physical labor, so many of the large-scale civil works undertaken during Philip's reign, such as road building, swamp drainage, the digging of canals, and the construction of defensive city walls, were all undertaken by the subjects of the king. The free population also engaged in agriculture, stock breeding, and lumbering—the last made them expert in woodworking.

Most of the land in Macedonia was worked by a free peasantry. The agricultural produce of these peasants was necessary for the economic support of nearby cities of "Macedones," i.e., those who provided military service for the king. For this reason, the peasants were forced to stay on the land. The members of the army were recruited from the landed peasantry and were required to be full-time soldiers for extended periods of time. The availability of the labor of the free peasantry placed Philip in a unique position to control the economy of his country, and his policy was followed by his successor, Alexander the Great, who often used the Macedonian army as a free labor pool.

Philip II also followed a policy of transporting communities of Macedonians to help found new cities in areas of economic and military significance. Many of these cities were established in regions recently brought under Macedonian control, and the subject peoples were required to work the land to support the new settlements. Sometimes captured barbarians from outside Macedonia, such as the 20,000 Scythian boys and women or the 10,000 Illyrians captured in 345 B.C., were relocated and settled among the free population of the Macedonian towns and villages to supplement their numbers. Subject peoples could also be moved to another region to found their own communities as compensation for displacement resulting from the founding of a new city of Macedonians. By these policies, Philip was highly successful in uniting the many peoples and tribes of his kingdom into one nation.

—*John F. Shean*

For Further Reading
Hammond, N. G. L. 1994. *Philip of Macedon*. Baltimore: Johns Hopkins University Press.

PHILLIPS, ULRICH BONNELL (1877–1934)

Born in LaGrange, Georgia, in 1877, Ulrich Bonnell Phillips studied history with William A. Dunning at Columbia University (receiving his Ph.D. in 1902) and became the most prolific and influential historian of slavery in the first half of the twentieth century. Phillips's writings combined postbellum proslavery attitudes, conservative racial views, and Progressive Era "scientific" historical methodology. He published nine books and almost 60 articles, most dealing with slavery. Phillips's major works were his in-depth economic and institutional history, *American Negro Slavery* (1918), and his broadly conceived social history, *Life and Labor in the Old South* (1929).

In *American Negro Slavery,* Phillips defined slavery and the plantation regime as part of an organic whole, one that rendered the Old South unique. Drawing heavily on plantation sources (diaries, manuscripts, account books, and letters) and on newspapers, Phillips argued that slavery was a patriarchal system that was beneficial to slaves, whom he considered "inert." He pronounced the plantation "a school constantly training and controlling pupils who were in a backward state of civilization." Paternalistic planters, Phillips contended, fed, clothed, and "civilized" their slaves, often sacrificing economic profits in order to keep their slave families together and to maintain the social and racial order.

After carefully studying slavery's costs and the slaves' productivity, he pronounced the institution an economic burden for white Southerners. To Phillips's mind, slavery "was less a business than a life; it made fewer fortunes than it made men." By this statement, Phillips meant that slavery succeeded less as an economic system than as a social system. It bound master and slave together in a relationship characterized by "propriety, proportion and cooperation." Under slavery, Phillips insisted, the races were interdependent—the blacks "always within the social mind and conscience of the whites, as the whites in turn were within the mind and conscience of the blacks."

In *Life and Labor in the Old South,* Phillips broadened his net to include the Old South's hitherto neglected people—Indians, Latins, yeomen, and mountain folk. Even though Phillips had discovered new plantation sources in the decade since he had published *American Negro Slavery,* his interpretation of slavery in *Life and Labor* remained virtually unchanged. He continued to hammer home his earlier themes—the duality of slavery as unprofitable but its necessity as a vehicle of racial control, slavery's benign and paternalistic qualities, and his belief in the slaves' inherent inferiority. Fewer racial slurs appeared in 1929 than in 1918, but Phillips's essential racism remained unchanged.

Although contemporary black critics, most notably Carter G. Woodson and W. E. B. DuBois, attacked Phillips's racial bias and criticized his one-dimensional view of slavery, most scholars and laymen greeted *American Negro Slavery* and *Life and Labor* enthusiastically. Writing in 1929, Henry Steele Commager praised the latter book as "perhaps the most significant contribution to the history of the Old South in this generation" (review in *New York Herald Tribune,* May 19, 1929). Not surprisingly, white historians from the 1920s until the 1950s applied Phillips's essential method and biases to their research and amassed what scholars call "the Phillips school" of studies on slavery. Phillips reigned as the master of slave historiography until he was ousted by Kenneth M. Stampp and his revisionist book, *The Peculiar Institution* (1956).

On balance, Phillips's works exhibited all the strengths and weaknesses of first-rate white scholars during the age of legally sanctioned social discrimination against blacks. Deeply researched in primary sources, carefully focused on the social and economic aspects of slavery, and gracefully written, his many books and articles set a high scholarly standard for his contemporaries. Phillips also played a major role in locating plantation-generated archival sources, in editing texts, and in delineating the themes and topics that later generations of historians of slavery would address.

Today, Phillips is best remembered for his overt sympathy with the master class and his condescending treatment of blacks as intellectually, culturally, and morally inferior to whites. Phillips's romanticized interpretation of the Old South, where gracious masters succored their grateful slaves, has been thoroughly repudiated by almost a half-century of scholarship.

—*John David Smith*

See also

DuBois, William Edward Burghardt; Stampp, Kenneth M.

For Further Reading

Dillon, Merton L. 1985. *Ulrich Bonnell Phillips: Historian of the Old South.* Baton Rouge: Louisiana State University Press; Roper, John Herbert. 1984. *U. B. Phillips: A Southern Mind.* Macon, GA: Mercer University Press; Smith, John David. 1991. *An Old Creed for the New South: Proslavery Ideology and Historiography, 1865–1918.* Athens: University of Georgia Press; Smith, John David, and John C. Inscoe, eds. 1993. *Ulrich Bonnell Phillips: A Southern Historian and His Critics.* Athens: University of Georgia Press.

PIEZAS DE INDIAS

The *pieza de Indias* was the unit of measurement used in the *asiento* slave trade to Spanish America after 1663 and gradually adopted throughout the Americas. The term did not refer to an individual slave; instead, it constituted a rather theoretical value, equivalent to an adult slave in the prime of his or her life, of a certain height, and without considerable physical defects.

The word *pieza* ("piece") was used irregularly in Spanish America after the early-seventeenth century to denote an adult slave, and the same word was used in the payment of customs duties for black slaves. In Africa, this usage is said to have derived from the custom of selling male adults for a single "piece" of cloth. In the 1630s, officials in several parts of Spanish America began to distinguish between actual slaves and *piezas*, counting young children as fractions of adult companions. At this stage, the standards still varied among ports, but the development eventually resulted in the adoption of a uniform fictitious measure: the *pieza de Indias*.

The term was first used in an *asiento* contract of 1663, and subsequent contracts with the *asiento* holders only mentioned the stipulated supply of *piezas de Indias* rather than actual slaves. (The *asiento* was an agreement between a contractor and the Spanish government that gave the contractor a monopoly on the importation of a certain number of slaves into Spanish America within a specified period of time.) A slave only counted as a full *pieza de Indias* if he or she was at least seven *palmos* (about five feet) in height and was between 15 and 35 years old (age was determined on face value).

Children and adults with physical defects like bad teeth, poor sight, or disease were counted as fractions of the ideal slave and were sometimes referred to as *manquerones* or *macrons*. In practice, the actual number of slaves could therefore outnumber the number of *piezas de Indias* by a large margin. Gender was not relevant to the measurement, although female *piezas de Indias* were cheaper than males. Slaves continued having a market value until about age 45; infants were not counted at all. There were, however, no generally accepted guidelines.

Although originating in Spain's *asiento* slave trade, the term *piezas de Indias* came to be used widely along the African coast. Accordingly, the concepts of *peça de Indias* and *pièce d'Indes* were introduced through the slave trade to Brazil and the French Caribbean colonies, respectively.

—*Wim Klooster*

See also
The *Asiento*

For Further Reading
Palacios Preciado, Jorge. 1973. *La trata de negros por Cartagena de Indias*. Tunja: Universidad Pedagogica y Tecnologica de Colombia; Palmer, Colin A. 1986. "The Company Trade and the Numerical Distribution of Slaves to Spanish America, 1703–1739." In *Africans in Bondage: Studies in Slavery and the Slave Trade*, ed. Paul E. Lovejoy. Madison: African Studies Program, University of Wisconsin-Madison; Vila Vilar, Enriqueta. 1977. *Hispanoamérica y el comercio de esclavos*. Seville: Escuela de Estudios Hispano-Americanos.

PLANTATION ARCHAEOLOGY

Plantation archaeology is the investigation and exploration of former plantation sites located throughout the Southern portion of the United States and the Caribbean. A plantation was an agricultural enterprise in which several subordinate workers produced a crop for someone else's profit to be marketed internationally. The plantation complex was an economic and a social order centering on slave plantations in the New World that significantly shaped the European-dominated part of the world economy. Plantation archaeology seeks to explain plantation history and culture, which are rooted in slaveholding, from plantation residents' material culture remains. Material culture is "that sector of the physical environment people modify through culturally determined behavior" (Deetz, 1993). The role of the plantation archaeologist is to seek the symbolic meanings inherent in the everyday things they find in the ground.

Plantation archaeology is at once a branch of historical archaeology and the parent of African American archaeology. Historical archaeology studies the "spread of European culture throughout the world since the fifteenth century, and its impact on indigenous peoples" (Deetz, 1993). Interdisciplinary in nature, historical archaeology is rooted in both history and anthropology. Written historical documents, ethnography, and the study of material culture all come together to inform the research methods and techniques of historical archaeology. African American, or slave-quarter, archaeology is the investigation of slave sites in an attempt to determine the ways in which Africans adapted to New World situations. Archaeologists attempt to understand how African culture and heritage was displaced, modified, or survived under slavery in the Americas.

Plantation and African American archaeology both emerged in the 1960s amid contemporary debates about the nature of the United States, race relations, and black individual and family character. Charles H. Fairbanks helped create the subfield of plantation ar-

A drab concrete slave cabin with wooden shingles covering the roof stands on the Kingsley Plantation.

chaeology with his pathbreaking work on a Kingsley plantation slave cabin in Florida. Whereas early plantation archaeology focused on recovering artifacts and architectural data in order to interpret and preserve the planters' lifestyle, Fairbanks shaped plantation archaeology into a new discipline that investigated the cultural aspects of all who lived and worked in the plantation complex.

Today, both plantation archaeology and African American archaeology investigate the process of creolization—a multicultural adjustment both slaves and their masters made that involved interaction, exchange, and creativity. The most intensive areas of recent plantation archaeology activity have been in the U.S. South—especially in Georgia, South Carolina, and Virginia. Archaeologists aim to illustrate the behavioral patterns within and relationships among the three main groups of plantation residents: owners, managers, and slave laborers. Since managers (who were sometimes other black slaves) often shared many cultural aspects with slaves because of similar economic circumstances, the biggest cultural separation on the plantation was between the world of the master family and that of its slaves.

Different demographic patterns, historical situa-

tions, and cultural mixtures produced different creolized cultures in various parts of the plantation complex. Therefore, plantation archaeologists attempt to place each plantation or slave-quarter site into its most meaningful socioeconomic context—the region. They ask what the archaeological record of Kingsmill plantation in the tidewater portion of Virginia depicts about life in Virginia and the Chesapeake Bay area. They ask what the artifacts and features found at the Kingsley plantation slave cabin site in coastal Florida highlight about slave life on the Sea Islands or in the lower South.

Trying to make sense out of an incomplete documentary and archaeological record is challenging. Archaeologists have therefore developed a number of theories, methodologies, and techniques to aid their interpretations and analyses of various sites. Invariably, archaeologists use a research design to guide their site excavation. This design, based on written, oral, and ethnographic sources, provides all known information about a site and hypothesizes about the site's former function and its residents' life patterns. The ways in which people settle the land tell archaeologists much about a site's economic purpose and social order. Animal bones and the types of pottery on a site tell them much about the inhabitants' food patterns—the social and political factors that affected diet and nutrition.

Artifact pattern recognition is also used by archaeologists to help identify sites. Artifacts are quantified into functional categories (e.g., kitchen items, architectural items, personal items) to allow comparison with artifacts from other sites. Knowing a particular site's artifact patterns can highlight social class, site function, cultural change, and temporal and regional distinctions. Repeated excavation of documented slave quarters has taught archaeologists that the slave house will leave certain archaeological markings in the ground, certain ceramics will be highly represented, and certain unusual personal items—like buttons, shells, and beads—will appear in large numbers. Simply put, if the next site an archaeologist excavates is not well documented, but the archaeological record is similar to that of known slave quarters, there is strong evidence that the undocumented site might be another slave quarter.

Thus, archaeology's value to colonial, antebellum, and African American history is twofold. First, archaeology provides valuable information about the past because of the ability to identify the commonplace, taken-for-granted, everyday objects that are not described in written documents but nonetheless are meaningful and important in people's daily lives. Second, archaeology provides information on many people in the past who either were excluded from the written record or were unable to speak for themselves. Slaves, indentured servants, tenant farmers, and modest freeholders formed most of the preindustrial population of the United States, but it was the wealthy white elite who left most of the documents. Emphasis on the ordinary and inarticulate—on what was most common in everyday life—has opened the window to new insights concerning larger historical issues.

—*Laura Croghan Kamoie*

See also
Historiography, United States; Housing, United States
For Further Reading
Deetz, James. 1993. *Flowerdew Hundred: The Archaeology of a Virginia Plantation, 1619–1864.* Charlottesville: University Press of Virginia; Ferguson, Leland. 1992. *Uncommon Ground: Archaeology and Early African America, 1650–1800.* Washington, DC: Smithsonian Institution Press; Kelso, William M. 1984. *Kingsmill Plantations, 1619–1800: Archaeology of Country Life in Colonial Virginia.* San Diego, CA: Academic Press; Singleton, Theresa A., ed. 1985. *The Archaeology of Slavery and Plantation Life.* Orlando, FL: Academic Press.

PLATO'S LAWS

Plato (c. 427–c. 347 B.C.) was well acquainted with Socrates, the Athenian philosopher with whose teaching many of Plato's *Dialogues* are concerned. Two of Plato's later works are discussions of the nature and purpose of government, and for Plato, a wisely governed state would allow for the moral and spiritual development of its citizens under the rule of philosophers. Plato's *Laws* discuss in considerable detail the ways in which the conceptual organization of the ideal state was to be implemented. Plato also describes his views of the institution of slavery in these works.

In *The Republic,* he proposed a totalitarian state with no family units, communal living for all, children reared in state nurseries with no knowledge of their parents, and marriages arranged for genetic reasons by the state. In the *Laws,* he modified the system to one in which citizens supported their families on the produce of two units of land, each allowance equal so there were no rich or poor and no personal wealth or profit motive. In this work, Plato produced a hypothetical set of legislative instruments to ensure that his perfect society would function in fact and in theory.

Plato was greatly influenced by the example of Sparta. Born into an aristocratic Athenian family, Plato saw within his city-state the problems that could arise from democratic government and from the growth of commerce and personal wealth. The imperial expansion of Athens led to power struggles that were damaging to Athenian stability, so Athens was no match for Sparta and its allies during the Peloponnesian War (431–404 B.C.). It was against the background of that war and the clash of ideologies between the main protagonists that Plato grew to manhood.

When Plato was about 20 or 30 years of age, his friend and mentor, Socrates, was condemned to death for sacrilege and for misleading the young and Plato was present when Socrates drank the poison that the Athenian democratic assembly had decreed should be his means of execution. Socrates believed that he should be obedient to the authority of the democratic state of which he was proud to be a citizen and accepted his sentence: Plato's doubts about democracy deepened.

Slavery was such a universal institution in Greece that Plato did not conceive of an ideal state without slaves in either *The Republic* or the *Laws*. But, in both works, he did adopt the communistic approach of Sparta and insist that slaves should not be owned by individuals. He followed the example of the agriculturally based serfs who were the strength of the Spartan economy.

The slaves in the *Laws* were to be owned by the state and under the direction of the state could be deployed wherever they were needed for whatever purpose. As in Sparta, all lands, goods, and resources of the state were to be held in common under a council, an assembly, and 37 appointed law-guardians. The modified oligarchy of this system of government gave an elite council, trained in philosophy, power over the 5,040 citizens. The citizens were assigned tasks appropriate to their abilities, which the state-controlled education system was designed to identify and develop. Teaching and trade were to be the responsibility of resident foreigners, whose numbers were to be kept proportional to the citizens to ensure that the citizens were never outnumbered.

Plato's legislation included free sexual association for slaves among themselves and for higher social orders among themselves. However, all marriages were to be state approved. No children of irregular unions could be regarded as legitimate, and among all classes, infanticide and abortion were to be used to keep the population numbers stable. Slaves were to breed only under strict supervision to maintain the supply of labor. They were not to produce more children than the state required, so abortion and infanticide were to be enforced by the state, along with abstinence, to keep the slave population from exceeding the level determined by the law-guardians. Plato had seen Sparta suffer from a decrease in the number of citizens and an increase in the number of Helots, and he was determined to protect his ideal society from becoming unbalanced.

Slaves, like citizens, raised their own children, but the state saw to their education and training. Plato made any change of status from slave to free citizen, or from one class of citizen to another, a punishable offense unless instigated by the law-guardians. In that respect, all adults were restricted to their appointed functions, whether slave or free. Plato also took from the Spartan example the ideas of communal dining and living for men of military age and boys and girls being schooled. Public work, social service, and military preparation all depended upon cooperative effort, and the concept of family was supplemented with that of the state as providing nurture and support.

This ideology combined elements of communistic practice with elements of democratic social institutions. Plato had come to believe that both too much regulation and too much freedom could damage the perfect society. Slaves under the system proposed in the *Laws* fulfilled the prime objective of Plato's vision, which was to enable free citizens to pursue the aims of the law-guardians, who were entrusted with advancing society as a whole to greater wisdom and to a life directed by philosophy.

Like other Greek philosophers, political theorists, and historians, Plato saw slavery as the only means of sustaining a free class that could pursue educational and developmental objectives without being distracted by the demands of physical labor and menial tasks. Only the trade in slaves was forbidden, since private ownership of all goods was replaced by a centralized distribution of necessities by the state administration. The state retained the right to execute or exile slaves who did not comply with their assigned tasks or threatened the peace of their community. As long as they were obedient to the state and accepted the limitations on their procreation, they could live secure on what the state provided to meet their daily needs and serve on the estates of their masters from cradle to grave.

—*Lindy J. Rawling*

See also
Helots; Lycurgus
For Further Reading
Crombie, Ian M. 1962–1963. *An Examination of Plato's Doctrines*. 2 vols. New York: Humanities Press; Guthrie, William K. C. 1975. *A History of Greek Philosophy*. Cambridge: Cambridge University Press; Hare, Richard M. 1982. *Plato*. Oxford: Oxford University Press; Vlastos, Gregory, ed. 1971. *Plato: A Collection of Critical Essays*. Garden City, NY: Doubleday.

POINTE COUPEE CONSPIRACY (1795)

The Pointe Coupee conspiracy, an abortive slave revolt, created such a legacy of paranoia that it was sometimes called an uprising in early histories of Louisiana. In spring 1795, when Louisiana was under Spanish control, the remote Pointe Coupee district located on the Mississippi River about 150 miles upriver from New Orleans was not an unlikely place for slave revolt. Colonial economic troubles had caused reductions in already meager rations, and masters, isolated from each other on plantations stretched along the river, were significantly outnumbered by their slaves. In fact, the district's population included approximately 2,000 whites and 7,000 slaves, a differential that would certainly have given rebelling slaves reason to be optimistic about their chances for success.

The night of April 12–13 was set for the revolt, which was to be initiated on the estate of Julien Poydras, a bachelor who lived alone except for his slaves. Poydras, a prominent Louisiana literary figure, was considered one of the most humane planters in his treatment of slaves. He had planned to visit the United

States in April, which may have been a factor in timing the rebellion. The slaves planned to steal guns and ammunition from Poydras's store and then set fire to a building on the estate. It was hoped that masters from neighboring estates would come to help extinguish the blaze, and when they arrived, they would be killed. Slaves would then march on other estates, killing both the masters and those slaves who refused to participate in the rebellion.

On April 10, two Tunica Indian women betrayed the rebellion when they informed Spanish authorities of a conversation they had overheard. Upon learning that the slaves intended to kill all the whites except for the young women, the Indian women apparently feared for their own safety if the revolt were successful. Patrols were immediately dispatched with orders to arrest all blacks assembling at plantations other than their own and any strangers found in the slave quarters. Authorities found several witnesses who confirmed the story told by the Tunica women. Governor of Louisiana and West Florida Luis Francisco Hector de Carondelet was informed of the plot, and he ordered all commandants of Louisiana to make a simultaneous raid on slave quarters, to confiscate all firearms, and to arrest any strangers found there.

A total of 63 people were implicated in the conspiracy—mostly black slaves, but 3 free men of color and 4 white men were also convicted. Trials began on May 8, 1795, and continued through May 19. More than 20 slaves were sentenced to be hanged while the remainder of the conspirators were sentenced to military duty or simply banished from the colony. During the trial, residents discovered that the conspiracy had not been isolated to Pointe Coupee but that slaves in other parts of the region had known of the conspiracy and had intended to revolt simultaneously. In response to this threat and as a grisly deterrent to rebellion, Spanish authorities placed the severed heads of those who had been executed on posts throughout the region.

There were many reasons why the slaves at Pointe Coupee and elsewhere in Louisiana conspired to revolt, but perhaps the most fundamental was a realistic hope for freedom. Political chaos caused by war between France and Spain and an anticipated French invasion of the colony made the timing ideal, and the French National Convention's abolition of slavery in all its colonies in 1794 made freedom a real possibility. The trial summary also indicated the slaves' awareness of the success of the Saint Domingue revolt in 1791, which certainly provided inspiration.

In response to the conspiracy, Louisiana prohibited all slave imports even though there was an increasing dependency on slave labor in the colony as a result of expanding sugar and cotton production. The slave trade later reopened in November 1800 to satisfy the merchants' interests. Colonial officials made attempts to assert greater control over slaves by restricting their movement between plantations and giving whites the authority to arrest slaves without a pass "or for any other reason." Perhaps the revolt's most significant effect was that it created a legacy of paranoia that plagued Louisiana's plantation economy throughout the antebellum period.

—*Mark Cave*

For Further Reading
Hall, Gwendolyn Midlo. 1992. *Africans in Colonial Louisiana: The Development of Afro-Creole Culture in the Eighteenth Century*. Baton Rouge: Louisiana State University Press; Holmes, Jack D. L. 1970. "The Abortive Slave Revolt at Pointe Coupee, Louisiana, 1795." *Louisiana History* 11: 341–362.

POLICRATICUS, BY JOHN OF SALISBURY

The *Policraticus*, begun in 1156 and completed in 1159, was written by the archbishop of Canterbury's able assistant John of Salisbury, a learned clergyman who would ultimately become bishop of Chartres (1176–1180). Addressed to Thomas à Becket, John's work is a massive treatise on politics and the ethics of sociopolitical life set within the framework of contemporary monarchical government. It contains the earliest comprehensive and systematic exposition of medieval political philosophy extant and sheds light on medieval views concerning the institution of slavery.

In using an organic metaphor to describe the state in *Policraticus*, John of Salisbury attempted to define the relative status and social function of the individuals, classes, and professions that made up the society of Latin Christendom. According to his perspective, each member of the social body was analogous to a member of the human body: the king functioned as the head; the king's councillors, as the heart; his soldiers and officials, as the hands; and laborers, such as peasants and craftsmen, the feet. Thus, the health of the whole hierarchical body politic was seen as depending upon the health of and harmony among each of its constituent members.

John's remarks on slavery and other forms of servitude must be seen within the context of this overarching system of sociopolitical subordination and interdependence. Regarding slavery, John offered a powerful legitimization of the institution by quoting the biblical injunction that commanded slaves to be obedient, even to the most difficult masters, but he urged all masters to treat their slaves well and argued, on the basis of classical authorities like Seneca, that slaves should not be despised or condemned simply because of their low social status.

Generally, John seems to have been less interested in slavery per se than in another form of unfree labor, namely serfdom, which was far more prevalent in the society in which he lived—which is not surprising since John wrote during a period when slavery was all but disappearing from much of Western Europe. But the same basic principles that underlie John's remarks on slavery are clearly fundamental to his discussion of medieval serfdom. He wrote that serfs, like slaves, must be obedient even to malicious superiors, but he advised those superiors to behave in a just and protective manner toward those under their authority.

Invoking the organic metaphor, John maintained that while the feet of the commonwealth (serfs, craftsmen, laborers) supported the entire body, they must be obedient to the head if the body were to avoid stumbling on the rocks in its path. However, just as it was the duty of the feet to obey the head, so it was the head's duty to shield and direct the feet. A monarchy that maltreats its serfs, John stated, could function no better than a person without feet, for such is the natural and divinely instituted order of things.

According to his thesis, each member of the body politic worked in a fixed role toward a common good, and every member was seen as a necessary and integral part of the whole. To John, serfdom and slavery, like government itself, were instruments by which God curbed the excesses of human vice, and so to resist or to question the legitimacy of either institution would be to display sacrilegious presumption.

For the first century after its composition, *Policraticus* remained relatively little known outside the circle of John's immediate friends and admirers. After the mid-thirteenth century, however, its circulation expanded rapidly, and its influence came to be felt in many different fields, from politics and law to rhetoric, education, and theology. Additionally, its ideas became the subject of famous debates and were incorporated into the works of figures as prominent and as diverse as Aegidius Romanus (Giles of Rome), Dante Alighieri, Geoffrey Chaucer, Christine de Pisan, and Coluccio Salutati.

By popularizing the organic metaphor, John had succeeded in providing an easily understood and theologically orthodox legitimization, not only of the medieval monarchy itself, but also of the hierarchical socioeconomic relationships that were so vital to its existence. As a result, his *Policraticus* was to remain a famous and influential work until the end of the Middle Ages.

—David Hay

See also

The Bible; Serfdom in Medieval Europe; Slavery in Medieval Europe; Stoicism

For Further Reading

Dickinson, John, ed. and trans. 1927. *The Statesman's Book of John of Salisbury*. New York: Knopf; Linder, Ammon. 1977. "Knowledge of John of Salisbury in the Late Middle Ages." *Studi Medievali* 18 (2): 315–366; Pike, Joseph B., ed. and trans. 1938. *Frivolities of Courtiers and Footprints of Philosophers*. Minneapolis: University of Minnesota Press; Wilks, Michael, ed. 1984. *The World of John of Salisbury*. Oxford: Basil Blackwell.

POLYBIUS
(C. 200–C. 120 B.C.)

The Greek historian Polybius chronicled Rome's rise to world empire. He is the best source for the history of the first two Punic Wars between Rome and Carthage, which wrought profound economic and demographic transformations in the Mediterranean world, changes that led to Rome's emergence as a slaveowning society.

Polybius was born a member of the Greek aristocracy, and his early political career groomed him for the highest public office in the Achaean confederation of Greek states—until events determined otherwise. After the Roman victory over Macedonia in the Battle of Pydna in 168 B.C., the victors collected nearly 100,000 suspected Macedonian sympathizers in Greece and sent them to Italy where they were detained for 16 years as political hostages. Polybius was among them, and he used this period of exile to write his monumental history of Rome's rise to world empire.

Like most classical authors, Polybius took the institution of slavery for granted. His concern was the workings of power among the narrow elite of the Greek and Roman aristocracies, and he showed little interest in slaves or other nonelite groups. Nevertheless, Polybius did preserve precious pieces of incidental information about ancient Mediterranean slavery.

In his relation of a dispute by two Locrians in southern Italy over possession of a slave, one of the litigants cites a law of Zaleucus, a Greek lawgiver whose laws were considered to be the first codification of Greek law (c. 650 B.C.). Zaleucus's law stated that in cases of disputed slave ownership, the party from whom the slave has been abducted shall retain possession until trial. The disputants then argue over which of them has forcibly abducted the slave, as both at various times have been in possession, whereupon the judge states that undisputed possession for a certain amount of time is the criterion. When neither litigant agrees on this point, the judge appeals to Zaleucus's "law of the thousand." According to this law, litigants appeared with halters around their necks before a thousand citizens. Whichever of the litigants seemed to interpret the law the worst would be hanged before the thousand. At this point, according to Polybius, one of the disputants relinquishes his claims to the slave.

Polybius's account of Scipio Africanus's capture of New Carthage in Spain in 209 B.C. provides insight into Greek aristocratic notions of freedom and slavery. Scipio informed the workingmen that their status would temporarily be that of Roman public slaves, but he promised freedom at the termination of the Carthaginian war if they exhibited goodwill and industry on Rome's behalf. Polybius commented that henceforth, the workmen were most zealous in their duties, driven by the hope of freedom from servitude.

Yet those were freemen in temporary bondage, and elsewhere, Polybius's writings reveal a more powerful aristocratic bias against the servile. In his eyes, the rebellion of the Carthaginian mercenaries after the First Punic War (264–241 B.C.) was an abominable act of treachery, and in order to sway his reader to this interpretation of the event, Polybius stated that the mercenaries were a rabble of different ethnic groups, including slaves.

One of the villains of Polybius's story is Spendius the Campanian, who suspended negotiations with Carthaginian authorities and prolonged the mercenary rebellion. Polybius accentuated his portrait of Spendius's loathsomeness by relating that he was a fugitive Roman slave. The bestial nature of these mercenaries in the final days of the rebellion is revealed when they are forced to eat, first their prisoners, and then their slaves.

Polybius's work exhibits a traditional aristocratic ethos, which in his thought is the monopoly of the socioeconomic elites. Acts of courage, selfless bravery, and the exercise of reason are their preserve. Slaves, among other nonelite groups—like barbarians, women, and mercenaries—help to define the freeborn aristocrat, and impulse and irrational passions characterize those groups. Polybius is typical of classical authors both in his disregard for the institution of slavery and in his evaluative, dichotomous language that defines the free in opposition to the slave.

—*Craige Champion*

See also
Cato; Punic Wars; Roman Republic
For Further Reading
Eckstein, Arthur. 1995. *Moral Vision in the Histories of Polybius*. Berkeley: University of California Press; Polybius. 1969. *Polybius: The Histories*. Trans. William R. Paton. London: Heinemann; Walbank, Frank William. 1972. *Polybius*. Berkeley: University of California Press.

POMBAL, MARQUIS OF
(1699–1782)

Diplomat (to England, 1738–1743, and Austria, 1745–1749) during the reign of King John V (r. 1706–1750) and chief minister during much of the reign of King Joseph I (r. 1750–1777), Sebastião José de Carvalho e Melo, first count of Oeiras (1759) and first marquis of Pombal (1769), is best known by the second of his titles. One of the most famous and controversial figures in Portuguese history, the marquis of Pombal is perhaps best seen as an economic nationalist. During his years in power, he, with the monarch's approval, undertook many administrative, economic, social, and ecclesiastical reforms, and his approach can be seen in the fields of slavery and race relations, where economic and political motives frequently outweighed any humanitarian ones.

In 1754, Pombal's brother, Francisco Xavier de Mendonça Furtado (1700–1769), while captain-general of Grão Para and Maranhão in northern Brazil, argued that an increase in the number of African slaves brought into Portuguese America would help save the Amerindian population from mistreatment and enslavement. A series of edicts in 1755, 1758, and 1761, prompted by Pombal, declared the freedom of the Amerindians in Brazil and outlawed discrimination against them.

In 1755, Pombal had the Jesuits removed from the temporal control of their many missions in Portuguese America, and four years later, the Jesuits were expelled from the entire Portuguese world and their properties expropriated. In April 1761, the king, at Pombal's prompting, lifted the color bar in Portuguese Asia declaring, "His Majesty does not distinguish between his vassals by their color but by their merit" (Boxer, 1969).

A decree of September 19, 1761, prohibited the transportation of slaves from Brazil, Africa, and Asia to Portugal. In 1773, all African slaves in Portugal were given their freedom. However, while Pombal was abolishing slavery in Portugal, he was promoting the African slave trade to Brazil, especially by founding two monopolistic charter companies—one, the Companhia Geral do Grão Pará e Maranhão (1755–1778), for northern Brazil; the other, the Companhia Geral de Pernambuco e Paraíba (1759–1780), for northeastern Brazil. Both of these companies subsidized the African slave trade to help settlers purchase slaves. During the years the two companies were in operation, more than 25,000 slaves were sent from Portuguese Guinea to Pará and Maranhão and more than 30,000—mostly from Angola—were transported to Pernambuco and Paraíba.

—*Francis A. Dutra*

See also
Portuguese Slave Trade
For Further Reading
Azevedo, João Lúcio de. 1909. *O Marquez de Pombal e a sua epoca*. Lisbon: Livraria Classica Editora; Boxer, Charles R. 1969. *The Portuguese Seaborne Empire, 1415–1825*. New York: Knopf; Maxwell, Kenneth. 1995. *Pombal: Paradox of the Enlightenment*. Cambridge: Cambridge University Press; Serrão, Joaquim Veríssimo. 1982. *O Marquês de Pombal: O homen, o diplomata, e o estadista*. Lisbon: n.p.

PORT ROYAL EXPERIMENT

Called the "rehearsal for Reconstruction," the Port Royal Experiment was an effort by federal officials, military officers, abolitionists, teachers, and missionaries in the United States to demonstrate that freedmen could convert from slave labor to free labor. The Port Royal Experiment also was a way to prepare for the upcoming emancipation of the slaves and to deal with the numerous slaves who had attached themselves to advancing Union forces.

On November 7, 1861, the U.S. Navy bombarded the town of Beaufort, South Carolina, located on the island of Port Royal a few miles north of Savannah, Georgia. Most of the island's whites had already fled, leaving behind 10,000 slaves, who were referred to as contraband. The "contrabands," who were technically still slaves, showed a strong reluctance to work the cotton crop, a traditional slave crop. Instead, they concentrated on growing subsistence crops and hunting and fishing in order to live. Both contrabands and freedmen preferred to distance themselves from any contact with whites, Northern or Southern.

Northern entrepreneurs, and U.S. Treasury officials responsible for administering confiscated property, which included slaves, considered the acquisition of Port Royal an economic opportunity for the federal Treasury. But federal officers and the Treasury, under the direction of Secretary Salmon P. Chase, faced the problem of how to manage the thousands of slaves who remained on the plantations. Chase appointed Edward L. Pierce to establish a new labor system on the island, and he implemented a system that resembled the former antebellum plantation, complete with plantation supervisors, the gang system of labor, and restricted movement of laborers. Instead of providing cash wages for work performed on the plantation, workers received basic necessities and free education.

Northern missionaries believed that with guidance and education, freedmen could be transformed into an obedient and effective workforce. Missionaries and teachers also advocated giving land to freedmen, but their impact on the direction of the experiment was minimal. Entrepreneurs like Edward S. Philbrick wanted to convert the former slaves into a large "free labor" workforce that was also tied to a market economy (i.e., to make them both laborers and consumers). Unlike Pierce, Philbrick implemented a wage labor system on his plantation based on the example of Northern labor, replacing the gang system with a labor program based on incentives, giving families their own garden plots, and paying cash wages to field laborers. Federally supervised plantations soon converted to Philbrick's model.

In 1863 and 1864, Treasury officials auctioned Port Royal plantations for nonpayment of taxes, and Northern speculators purchased most of the 60,000 acres of confiscated land. Officials had reserved over 16,000 acres for purchase by freedmen at $1.25 per acre, but only a few freedmen, who pooled their meager resources, were able to purchase land. The island's military governor, Gen. Rufus Saxton, tried to help the freedmen by allowing them to acquire land through preemption, but President Abraham Lincoln overturned Saxton's policy in 1864.

By 1865, Philbrick realized that his experiment to prove that African Americans could be more profitable working as wage laborers than as slaves had failed. Throughout the experiment to establish a new economic system based on wage labor, the freedmen resisted working in the cotton fields, and cotton production never reached pre–Civil War rates. Philbrick divided his plantation into small lots, sold them to former workers, and returned North. On other plantations, military authorities required freedmen to sign labor contracts or leave.

On January 16, 1865, Gen. William Tecumseh Sherman issued Special Field Order No. 15, which entitled freedmen to 40-acre plots of land in an area along the coast from Charleston, South Carolina, to Jacksonville, Florida. Later that year, President Andrew Johnson commanded that all confiscated lands be returned to their owners. Many of the Port Royal freedmen who had acquired land during the experiment thus lost their claims to those plots, and the Port Royal Experiment came to a close.

—*Craig S. Pascoe*

See also
Civil War, United States; Emancipation Proclamation; Sea Islands; Transition from Slave Labor to Free Labor, North America
For Further Reading
Foner, Eric. 1988. *Reconstruction: America's Unfinished Revolution*. New York: Harper and Row; Gerteis, Louis S. 1973. *From Contraband to Freedmen: Federal Policy toward Southern Blacks, 1861–1865*. Westport, CT: Greenwood; Jacoway, Elizabeth. 1980. *Yankee Missionaries in the South: The Penn School Experiment*. Baton

Rouge: Louisiana State University Press; Rose, Willie Lee Nichols. 1976. *Rehearsal for Reconstruction: The Port Royal Experiment*. New York: Oxford University Press.

PORTUGAL

During the wars of the twelfth and thirteenth centuries, as the Christians drove the Muslims from territory that was to become Portugal, captured Muslims were enslaved. The exact number is not known, though it is known that the number of slaves reached a peak in the mid-thirteenth century. During the Middle Ages, the number declined until there were relatively few Muslim slaves in Portugal during the sixteenth and seventeenth centuries.

Beginning in the 1440s, voyages sponsored by Prince Henry the Navigator and his successors brought many black slaves from Africa back to Portugal. The leading authority on African slavery in Portugal for the years 1441–1555 states that "Portugal became the first European society in modern times where black slavery was commonplace" (Saunders, 1982). He estimates that by the mid-sixteenth century, there were 32,370 black African slaves living in Portugal and 2,580 freedmen. By the end of the sixteenth century, however, it seems that the number of African slaves living in Portugal was slowly decreasing while the number of freedmen was increasing either by manumission, miscegenation, or higher birthrates. No reliable statistics are available for the seventeenth and eighteenth centuries for either the number of slaves or the number of freedmen.

Although slaves could be found in most parts of Portugal, most were in the cities, especially Lisbon and Évora, and in the southern third of the country, namely, the Tagus Valley, the Alentejo, and the Algarve. Contemporaries estimated that in the mid-sixteenth and early-seventeenth centuries, approximately 10 percent of Lisbon's population was composed of slaves.

With the demand for African slaves greatly increasing in Brazil, first in the sugar areas (beginning in the second half of the sixteenth century) and later in the mining areas (especially in the first half of the eighteenth century), slaves prices rose, which made any extensive use of African slaves in Portugal uneconomical. Black African slaves in Portugal were used in various occupations—rural as well as urban. By the sixteenth century, however, most were in urban employment or domestic service.

Although people of all classes were slaveowners, most of the African slaves were owned by the nobility, the clergy and religious institutions, and crown officials. Over time, almost all of the African slaves and freedmen became Christianized and acculturated to the Portuguese way of life. Many belonged to religious brotherhoods or confraternities, especially that of Our Lady of the Rosary (Nossa Senhora do Rosário).

A few Amerindians from Brazil were also sent to Portugal as slaves, especially in the sixteenth century. In addition, a relatively small number of Asians in various levels of servitude returned with Portuguese ships from India.

In the third quarter of the eighteenth century, chiefly through the efforts of the Marquis of Pombal, legislation was enacted to eliminate the slave trade to Portugal and do away with slavery there. By a decree of September 19, 1761, the transportation of slaves from Brazil, Africa, and Asia to Portugal was prohibited. As of January 16, 1773, measures were taken to emancipate slaves living in Portugal. Great-grandchildren of slaves and the newly born of slave mothers in Portugal were freed immediately. However, children whose mothers and grandmothers had been slaves would remain slaves for the rest of their lives. Despite the legislation restricting African slavery in Portugal, slavery there continued to exist into the nineteenth century. However, people trying to bring slaves into Portugal for commercial purposes were often prosecuted.

In the nineteenth century, pressure from Great Britain and enlightened Portuguese opinion gradually eliminated Portugal's involvement in the international slave trade. In a decree of December 10, 1836, the viscount of Sá da Bandeira attempted to prohibit the import and export of all slaves in the Portuguese colonies south of the equator, but the decree met with strong opposition. In 1854, slaves belonging to the Portuguese state were emancipated, and two years later, slaves owned by Portuguese town councils, religious brotherhoods, and churches were freed as were all children born of slave mothers. That same year, slaves arriving in Portugal, the Portuguese Atlantic islands of the Madeiras and the Azores, Portuguese India, and Macao were declared free. Finally, a law enacted on February 25, 1869, by a government again headed by Sá da Bandeira (now a marquis), slavery was abolished in all parts of the Portuguese world.

—*Francis A. Dutra*

See also
Pombal, Marquis of; Portuguese Slave Trade
For Further Reading
Marques, A. H. de Oliveira. 1976. *History of Portugal*. 2d ed. New York: Columbia University Press; Saunders, A. C. de C. M. 1982. *A Social History of Black Slaves and Freedmen in Portugal, 1441–1555*. Cambridge: Cambridge University Press; Tinhorão, José Ramos. 1988. *Os negros em Portugal: Uma presença silenciosa*. Lisbon: Caminho.

PORTUGUESE SLAVE TRADE

Southern Europe's long tradition of slavery dated from ancient times. In the twelfth and thirteenth centuries, the number of Muslim slaves captured by the Iberian kingdoms greatly increased as the tempo of the Reconquista—the centuries-long struggle to drive the Muslims out of the peninsula—increased. By 1249, the last Muslim stronghold in what is now Portugal had been captured, and in the following two centuries, Portugal had a relatively small Muslim slave population.

In the fifteenth century, however, first via caravan routes from sub-Saharan Africa to Morocco and after 1441 by the Portuguese by sea, increasing numbers of black Africans were transported to the Mediterranean world and especially to the Iberian Peninsula. The papal bull *Romanus Pontifex* (1455) of Nicholas V provided further justification for Portuguese activities, for it authorized the Portuguese monarch "to invade, search out, capture, vanquish, and subdue all Saracens and pagans whatsoever, and other enemies of Christ wheresoever placed . . . and to reduce their persons to perpetual slavery."

The Portuguese African slave trade quickly evolved from raids along the African coast, which began in 1441 and were on the wane by the end of that decade, to peaceful trade with African chieftains and merchants. Beginning in Mauritania, with the *feitoria* (trading hall and local administrative center) of Arguin frequently handling a thousand slaves annually, the trade soon extended south along the upper Guinea coast and eventually, in the sixteenth and seventeenth centuries, to the Congo and Angola. During most of the fifteenth century, the slaves that were gathered from the African mainland were transported back to Portugal. Upon arriving in Portugal, many of these slaves were re-exported, especially to Spain and, after 1492, to Spanish America.

Slaves sent to the Madeira Islands early on were from the Canary Islands, Morocco, and the African mainland south of the Sahara. By the early 1500s, perhaps as much as one-tenth of Madeira's population was slave. Slaves were also imported, mostly from Guinea, to the Cape Verde Islands, and by the early-sixteenth century, the island of Santiago in the Cape Verde archipelago had become a distribution center for slaves on their way to the Americas. This role was later played by the island of São Tomé, which in addition to becoming a slavery depot, was a major sugar-producing center for much of the sixteenth century. In the upper Guinea region, Portuguese traders, freelancers, and *degredados* ("exiles") penetrated into the interior. Called *lançados* ("outcasts"), they often settled in African villages, served as intermediaries in the

A rendering in bronze of a Portuguese musketeer by an artist in Benin illustrates one aspect of the nefarious influence of the slave trade.

slave trade, and frequently left Euroafrican descendants who served in similar capacities.

For the period 1500–1850, scholars have divided Portuguese slave exports into four waves—none of them mutually exclusive. The first was the so-called Guinea wave of the sixteenth century, in which most of the slaves came from both upper Guinea (Senegal River to Cape Palmas) and lower Guinea (Volta River to Cape Catarina). The second wave, in the seventeenth century, was dominated by slaves from equatorial and central Africa with great emphasis on Angola and the Congo. The third wave, in the eighteenth century, encompassed the Gold Coast (Ghana) and the Bight of Benin as well as Angola, with more than twice as many coming from the latter kingdom. The fourth wave, in the nineteenth century, focused on Angola and Mozambique.

According to the best estimates, Brazil received 38 percent of all the slaves that arrived alive in the Americas from 1492 to 1870. Information is scarce for the sixteenth and seventeenth centuries, though it is estimated that approximately a half-million or so slaves arrived in Portuguese America during that period. During the eighteenth century, another 1,750,000 were landed, and 1,350,000 were transported in the nineteenth century until passage of the Queirós Law (1850) effectively ended the African slave trade to Brazil.

Under good conditions in the sixteenth and seventeenth centuries, the slave voyages from Angola to Pernambuco took 35 days, to Bahia 40 days, and to Rio de Janeiro 50 days. During the eighteenth century, the voyage to Rio de Janeiro was reduced to 40 days, though unfavorable weather and other mishaps could delay voyages for another two to four months. Mortality rates ranged on the average from 15 to 20 percent.

Although there were exceptions, in general the African slave trade was a Portuguese monopoly—at least for the Iberian world—until near the end of the Hapsburg period in Europe. In late 1640, the Portuguese revolted against Spanish rule, which seriously limited slave sales to the Spanish-American world. In 1637 the Dutch captured São Jorge da Mina and in 1642 Axim, thus managing to control an important section of the Guinea coast. The Dutch also briefly held the Angolan ports of Luanda and Benguela (1641–1648) until driven out by Salvador Correia de Sá.

In 1721, the Portuguese established themselves at Whydah (São João Baptista da Ajudá; today, Ouidah), which was a major center for slaves for Bahia until about 1770 when it was replaced for the next half-century by the area around the Bight of Benin. Rio de Janeiro and Minas Gerais continued to be supplied largely by Angola, while northern Brazil, at least in the second half of the eighteenth century, received a considerable number of slaves from what is now Guinea-Bissau. Although Luanda dominated the eighteenth-century Angolan trade, by 1780 approximately a quarter of all the slaves going to Brazil from Angola were exported from Benguela.

—*Francis A. Dutra*

See also
East Africa; Pombal, Marquis of; Portugal; Queirós Law; Slave Coast; Spain

For Further Reading
Boxer, Charles R. 1963. *Race Relations in the Portuguese Colonial Empire, 1415–1825*. Oxford: Clarendon Press; Klein, Herbert S. 1978. *The Middle Passage: Comparative Studies in the Atlantic Slave Trade*. Princeton, NJ: Princeton University Press; Mattoso, Katia M. de Queirós. 1986. *To Be a Slave in Brazil, 1550–1888*. New Brunswick, NJ: Rutgers University Press; Saunders, A. C. de C. M. 1982. *A Social History of Black Slaves and Freedmen in Portugal 1441–1555*. Cambridge: Cambridge University Press.

PORTUGUESE-OMANI WARS IN EAST AFRICA (1652–1730)

The Portuguese-Omani wars in East Africa were significant in the formation of the Swahili culture in that area and in determining the nature of that region's economic development. The wars, which Oman eventually won, laid the foundation for the slave-based clove plantation economy that was centered on Zanzibar and Pemba and the grain-producing plantations of mainland Swahili settlements. Later, the Zanzibar-based Arab state under Said ibn Sultan (Said Sayyid) would be the driving force behind the extension of the slave-trading economy into central Africa during the mid- and late-nineteenth century.

The Portuguese first reached the Swahili coast and the Gulf during their great period of exploration and expansion in the fifteenth and sixteenth centuries. Prior to Portuguese penetration, the Swahili coast was dominated by several independent city-states containing mixed populations of Africans, Arabs, and South Asians who were primarily engaged in long-distance trade in the Gulf and with the Indian subcontinent. The Portuguese first touched on the Swahili coast under Vasco da Gama's leadership in 1498, and during that initial trip, da Gama visited and later bombarded several Swahili and African ports, including Mombasa and Mogadishu. The Portuguese later began to consolidate their control of the Swahili coast through the efforts of Francisco de Almeida and, later, Afonso de Albuquerque, the governor of Goa in India.

Although Portugal was a very lightly populated country, it had major advantages that allowed its navy to dominate the Indian Ocean littoral. The most obvious advantage was technological. After the decline of the Ming dynasty's navy in the fifteenth century, there was no naval power with ships capable of challenging the Portuguese fleet. Although sea travel was very important commercially, none of the African, Middle Eastern, or South Asian rulers along the Indian Ocean littoral had seen much need for developing a heavily armed navy.

The period of Portuguese domination had mixed effects on the people of the Swahili coast. Negative Portuguese attitudes toward Muslims made trade with the old Arab partners of the Gulf and Red Sea problematic, and as a result, some of the older Swahili cities like Malindi never were able to regain the prosperity they had enjoyed earlier. Other cities, like Mombasa, were able to adjust to the new political economy.

Despite initial success, the Portuguese were never able to gain total control of the Red Sea, but it would be the Gulf in particular that would be the source of the eventual Portuguese downfall along the Swahili coast. The Portuguese conquered Muscat, the capital of Oman and gateway to the Gulf in 1507. Despite the efforts of the Ottoman Turks under Admiral Piri Reis, who sacked Muscat in 1551–1552, the Portuguese maintained this strategic location.

By 1650, the Omanis had been able to retake their traditional capital, and they also had captured several Portuguese vessels. These ships allowed the Omanis to develop a navy that could effectively compete with the Portuguese for control of the East African coast. By the mid-seventeenth century, the glory days of the Portuguese as explorers and empire builders were over, and in India, the East Indies, and even Brazil they faced increasing pressure from other Europeans, like the English and Dutch, in addition to the Omani pressure.

Once the Omanis began their offensive against the Portuguese in East Africa, they were able to take advantage of their religious and traditional commercial ties to the Swahili coast for assistance against their foes. The local Swahili merchants blindly followed the Omanis but were more than willing to make peace with the Portuguese when it appeared that they might be winning.

Despite occasional shifts, the general trend throughout the late-seventeenth century was an erosion of Portuguese power along the Swahili coast. By 1652, Omani ships were common off the Swahili coast, and by 1687, the Omanis had permanently captured Pate off the coast of Kenya. In 1698, the Omanis captured Fort Jesus outside of Mombasa after a three-year siege, which effectively meant the end of Portuguese rule in East Africa north of Cape Delgado in Mozambique. Although the Portuguese would temporarily reoccupy Mombasa from 1728 to 1729, they were no longer a major force along the Swahili coast.

—*Anthony Q. Cheeseboro*

For Further Reading
Beachey, R. W. 1996. *A History of East Africa: 1592–1902*. London: Tauris; Boxer, C. R. 1969. *The Portuguese Seaborne Empire: 1415–1825*. New York: Knopf; Risso, Patricia. 1986. *Oman and Muscat and Early Modern History*. New York: St. Martin's; Sheriff, Abdul. 1987. *Slaves, Spices, and Ivory in Zanzibar*. London: James Currey.

POTTAWATOMIE MASSACRE

The Pottawatomie massacre occurred on May 24, 1856, on Pottawatomie Creek, Kansas Territory, and initiated John Brown's rise to national prominence. Brown and seven followers executed five proslavery settlers in retaliation for a proslavery raid on Lawrence, an antislavery center in the territory. The massacre highlighted the controversy over popular sovereignty and revealed the volatile consequences of the Kansas-Nebraska Act (1854).

Brown arrived in Kansas Territory on October 7, 1855, to help several of his sons establish claims under the terms of popular sovereignty. Owing to a prolonged drought, which destroyed their crops, Brown's sons had left Ohio in spring 1855 to start anew in the unorganized territory. Besides their financial motivation, the younger Browns were also eager to rush to Kansas and reinforce antislavery settlers there.

Throughout the first year of settlement, tensions mounted between proslavery and antislavery pioneers, and many people prepared for war. Prior to his move west, Brown solicited funds from sympathetic abolitionists and purchased a shipment of arms in preparation for what he thought would be imminent bloodshed. The crate included a cache of broadswords, medieval weapons symbolic of Brown's self-imposed image as an antislavery crusader ordained by Christ.

During his adult life, Brown called for guerrilla warfare against Southern plantations and the execution of slave catchers. In Kansas, he put his words into action. Shortly he arrived at Brown's Station near Pottawatomie Creek, Kansas turned bloody. In late November 1855, proslavery and antislavery forces mobilized at Lawrence in a prelude to the impending confrontation. Although a treaty averted bloodshed, tensions smoldered during the winter months as both sides issued calls for arms and men. In April 1856, Brown gained regional attention by publicly announcing that he would kill any peace officer who attempted to enforce territorial laws banning abolitionist activity. A month later, after years of agitating for a violent end to slavery, Brown moved toward fulfillment of his destiny.

On May 21, 1856, a proslavery militia force raided Lawrence with impunity. The following morning, Brown and his sons marched with a company known as the Pottawatomie Rifles to help repel the attack. A messenger stopped them and ordered Brown to turn back since the proslavery men had retreated following the arrival of federal troops. After the Pottawatomie company refused to press forward, an exasperated Brown called for volunteers for a secret mission. Further electrified by the news of Preston Brooks's assault upon Charles Sumner on the floor of the U.S. Senate on May 22, Brown led a small squad, including four of his sons, back to Pottawatomie Creek. There, on May 24, 1856, Brown and his men wielded sharpened broadswords and hacked to death five proslavery residents. The slaughter sent proslavery settlers into a frenzy and sparked unbridled guerrilla warfare throughout southeastern Kansas.

Coupled with the raid on Lawrence, the Pottawatomie massacre brought both sides to local civil war. In this unruly environment, known as Bleeding Kansas, Brown and his men avoided persecution for their night of carnage and fought in several small skirmishes. Brown left Kansas in October 1856 and gained national attention as an antislavery guerrilla fighter and speaker. This recognition helped him recruit men and garner financial support for another secret mission waged at Harpers Ferry, Virginia, in October 1859, a mission that ultimately played a major role in plunging the whole nation into civil war.

—*Robert J. Zalimas, Jr.*

See also
Bleeding Kansas; Brown, John; Harpers Ferry Raid
For Further Reading
Malin, James C. 1942. *John Brown and the Legend of Fifty-six*. Philadelphia: American Philosophical Society; Oates, Stephen B. 1984. *To Purge This Land with Blood: A Biography of John Brown*. Amherst: University of Massachusetts Press; Potter, David M. 1976. *The Impending Crisis, 1848–1861*. New York: Harper and Row; Yang, Liwen. 1992. "John Brown's Role in the History of the Emancipation Movement of Black Americans." *Southern Studies* 3: 135–142.

PRESTER JOHN

The legend of the Christian priest-king Prester John exerted a great hold on the European imagination for almost four centuries. Indeed, it was partly a desire on the part of the Portuguese to find and ally themselves with his kingdom that prompted them to make contact with the West African coast in the early-fifteenth century.

The first mention of Prester John comes from the German historian Otto of Freising. Writing around 1145, Otto recorded a report that had reached him of a Nestorian king, a descendant of the Magi, who ruled an enormous kingdom beyond Persia. In the thirteenth century, Alberic of Trois Fontaines noted that a letter allegedly written by Prester John had appeared in Europe in 1165. According to Alberic, in his letter Prester John described himself as the ruler of a kingdom of fabulous wealth and full of wonders that spanned the length of all three Indias (today, the Middle East, India, and China).

At a time when European holdings in the Levant were increasingly hard-pressed by the resurgence of Muslim power, the strategic potential of an alliance forged with a powerful Christian located on the eastern flank of Islam proved an alluring prospect. For the next century and a half, then, all Europeans who crossed the breadth of Asia to Cathay (China) in search of luxury goods also looked for evidence of the elusive potentate's kingdom.

Failing to find any such evidence in Asia, the location of Prester John was transplanted to Ethiopia in the middle of the fourteenth century. Influenced by the presence of Ethiopian pilgrims in Jerusalem, Europeans had become aware of the existence of a Christian kingdom lying south of Egypt, and although the location of the kingdom did not coincide with the Indies proper, Ethiopia was part of the "middle India" defined by Marco Polo.

Prince Henry the Navigator of Portugal hoped, among other things, to find Prester John when he sent missions down the West African coast in the early-fifteenth century. With the Ottoman Turks advancing rapidly in the east of Christendom, the idea of an alliance with this powerful king once again held out the prospect of dealing Islam a final blow. In the attempt to receive word of Prester John, the Portuguese captured Africans and transported them back to Portugal for interrogation. They were converted, taught Portuguese, and then returned to the African coast in the hope that some account of Portugal might reach Prester John.

In 1486, the Portuguese received some encouragement in their quest for Prester John from an ambassador of the king of Benin. This ambassador told the Portuguese about a powerful far-off king who sent newly crowned kings of Benin a cross to be worn around the neck. Although there is no consensus as to who this king may have been, the Portuguese redoubled their efforts down the African coast. King John II immediately sent out two missions, and while the mission sent overland only penetrated as far as Jerusalem, the other, under Bartholomeu Dias, rounded the Cape of Good Hope.

When a Portuguese mission finally penetrated Ethiopia from the Red Sea in 1520 and secured an audience with the emperor, now invariably referred to as Prester John, they were disappointed. Prester John greeted them coolly and seemed decidedly offended by the poor quality of the gifts they had brought for him. By the time they had managed to secure his permission to return home some six years later, the mystique of Prester John had faded.

—*Richard Raiswell*

See also
Dias, Bartholomeu
For Further Reading
Beckingham, C. F. 1995. "The Quest for Prester John." In *The European Opportunity*. Ed. F. Fernandez-Armesto. Aldershot, Eng.: Variorum; Boxer, C. R. 1969. *The Portuguese Seaborne Empire: 1415–1825*. London: Hutchinson; Slessarev, V. 1959. *Prester John: The Letter and the Legend*. Minneapolis: University of Minnesota Press.

PRIGG V. PENNSYLVANIA
(1842)

Perhaps the most famous fugitive slave case decided by the U.S. Supreme Court before the Civil War, *Prigg v. Pennsylvania* (41 U.S. 539 [1842]) concluded that the Fugitive Slave Act of 1793 was constitutional and that states could not add additional requirements to hinder people who captured runaway slaves. An 1826 Pennsylvania statute (one of many such state laws, usually called "personal liberty laws") required that slave catchers obtain a "certificate of removal" before they could take fugitives back to the U.S. South and a life of slavery.

One slave catcher, Edward Prigg, requested a certificate of removal in 1842 from a Pennsylvania official for a fugitive slave, Margaret Morgan, and several of her children, one of whom was born in Pennsylvania and thus considered free by state law. Even though his request was refused, Prigg took Morgan and her children from Pennsylvania back to slavery in Maryland. Prigg was then indicted in Pennsylvania for kidnapping, and convicted; he appealed his conviction to the U.S. Supreme Court.

At issue was whether states had the ability to pass laws that might interfere with or burden the performance of existing federal laws. Justice Joseph Story wrote in the majority opinion that any state law that impeded the Fugitive Slave Act was unconstitutional, and thus Pennsylvania's personal liberty law was null and void. He added that the federal Fugitive Slave Act of 1793 was thoroughly constitutional and that any slaveowner or slave catcher could enforce it privately if recapturing the fugitive could be accomplished without breaking the law. If they complied with the federal Fugitive Slave Act, professional slave catchers could operate freely in the North without having to notify state or local officials about their actions.

In the opinion's stunning conclusion, Story wrote that state judges and all state officials should enforce the federal Fugitive Slave Law but that the national government could not require them to do so. Many Southerners objected to this caveat, since virtually no Northern official would willingly volunteer to help slave catchers in their work and without their assistance, it would be extremely difficult to recapture runaway slaves.

Chief Justice Roger B. Taney wrote a concurring opinion in *Prigg v. Pennsylvania* in which he took issue with Story's conclusion. Taney believed that with the exception in place, slave recapture would become a dead letter since only federal officials would enforce the Fugitive Slave Act and assist slave catchers in returning runaways to the South. Taney was correct in his belief, as many Northern state judges began to refuse to hear fugitive slave cases and state assemblies passed laws barring the use of state facilities (like jails) in the process of slave recapture.

Prigg v. Pennsylvania and *Jones v. Van Zandt* (1847), another fugitive slave case, set the stage for rewriting the 1793 Fugitive Slave Act as part of the Compromise of 1850, which included a much harsher series of penalties for harboring or assisting runaway slaves. These cases, and related slavery cases like *Dred Scott v. Sandford* (1857), significantly heightened sectional tensions in the decades preceding the U.S. Civil War.

—*Sally E. Hadden*

See also
Ableman v. Booth; Abolition, United States; *Dred Scott v. Sandford*; *Jones v. Van Zandt*; Taney, Roger Brooke; U.S. Constitution

For Further Reading
Cover, Robert. 1975. *Justice Accused: Antislavery and the Judicial Process*. New Haven, CT: Yale University Press; Finkelman, Paul. 1981. *An Imperfect Union: Slavery, Federalism, and Comity*. Chapel Hill: University of North Carolina Press; Morris, Thomas. 1974. *Free Men All: The Personal Liberty Laws of the North, 1780–1861*. Baltimore: Johns Hopkins University Press; Wiecek, William E. 1978. "Slavery and Abolition before the United States Supreme Court, 1820–1860." *Journal of American History* 65: 34–59.

PRINCE, MARY

The *History of Mary Prince, a West Indian Slave (Related by Herself)* was the first published slave narrative written by a female slave. It appeared in 1831 in London's *Anti-Slavery Reporter*, a newspaper published by the English Anti-Slavery Society. It is the autobiography of Mary Prince (also called "Molly") who was originally named by her masters, "Mary, Princess of Wales," as it was common for masters to ridicule slaves by giving them outlandish names.

Mary was born in Brackish-Pond, Devonshire Parish, Bermuda; her mother was a house slave and her father a sawyer for a shipbuilder. Their owner, Charles Myners, died when Mary was still an infant, and the family was divided: Mary and her mother were sold to a Captain Darrel and given to his grandchild, Betsey Williams. Mary, raised by her mother and able to play with her siblings, remembers her early childhood happily, for Mrs. Williams was "kindhearted," though her largely absent husband was cruel and tyrannical.

At age 12, Mary's sisters were auctioned off to different masters, and she herself was sold from one master to another, each crueler than the last. Mary tells of Hetty, a kindly fellow slave she called "aunt," who, though pregnant, was stripped naked and beaten severely, causing her miscarriage and death. Mary escaped years of beatings to seek refuge with her mother, only to be returned to her master by her father. She was then sold to a master on Tuck's Island, the center of salt production in Bermuda, where the daily routine of working knee-deep in saltwater caused boils that ate down to the bone. Among the atrocities she witnessed on Tuck's Island was one slave whose regular beatings inflicted wounds that festered and filled with maggots.

Prince desired to escape the island and move to Antigua, where comparatively liberal attitudes toward freed blacks made manumission more likely. She was sold to John Wood of Antigua, but he refused her repeated offers to buy her freedom. There, Prince became involved in the Moravian Church, where she learned to read and write. She married in 1826, though soon afterward she was separated from her husband when the Woods traveled to England. Prince's failing health and ill treatment led her to leave her master and seek aid from Moravian missionaries. Both Prince and the missionaries repeatedly offered to buy her freedom so she could return to Antigua a freedwoman and live with her husband, but their offers were refused. Prince's narrative ends with a plea for abolition and her hope to rejoin her husband someday.

Public response to Prince's story in the *Reporter* was profound. James Macqueen, the plantocratic editor of the Glasgow *Courier,* writing in the magazine *Blackwoods,* painted Prince as a liar and malcontent, attacked her character, and denied that slaves generally shared her opinions. Elsewhere, James Curtin, an Anglican missionary, made similar charges. The result was two libel cases: Prince sued Thomas Cadell, Macqueen's publisher, and John Wood sued Thomas Pringle, Prince's publisher. The court decided in favor of both Prince and Pringle.

—*Arnold Schmidt*

For Further Reading
Andrews, William L. 1987. "Six Women's Slave Narratives, 1831–1909." In *Black Women's Slave Narratives.* Ed. William Andrews. New York: Oxford University Press; Ferguson, Moira. 1992. *Subject to Others: British Women Writers and Colonial Slavery, 1670–1834.* New York: Routledge; Paquet, Sandra Pouchet. 1992. "The Heartbeat of a West Indian Slave: The History of Mary Prince." *African American Review* 26: 131–146; Prince, Mary. 1987. *The History of Mary Prince, a West Indian Slave (Related by Herself).* In *The Classic Slave Narratives.* Ed. Henry Louis Gates, Jr. New York: Penguin Books.

PROSLAVERY ARGUMENT, AFRICA

The proslavery argument for Africa can be stated in two parts: the argument that slavery was an efficient way to bring civilization to otherwise savage Africans and the idea that Africa was insufficiently developed economically to engage labor voluntarily. The concept of slavery as a route to cultural uplift is especially ancient in Africa. Although its use may go back to classical times, slavery as a conveyance of civilization began to be a common belief during the period of Islam.

One of the earliest examples of Islam as a justification for slavery appears in writing of Buzurg ibn Shahriyar, the author of *Al-Kitab Al-Ajaib, Al-Hind* (The book of the south and India) from A.D. 922. The book tells of sailors who trick an African king into coming onto their ship and then enslave him. Years later, the same sailors, after a storm, land at the same kingdom, where to their surprise, they meet the same king. To their great astonishment, the king is most forgiving and hospitable. The reason for the king's behavior is that he found Islam while he was a slave in the Middle East and now he has introduced Islamic practice to his people. Although the king makes it clear to the sailors that he has contempt for them as individuals, he is still grateful for the chance to learn of Islam.

Despite the positive tone of Buzurg's story, the message is clear that that no indigenous people of Africa deserved the level of respect that might be given to other nonbelievers, like the Chinese. Therefore, even the mightiest of Africans might benefit from slavery. Because of this attitude, a rift developed between African societies that embraced Levantine monotheistic religions and those that believed in traditional African religions. Consequently, Muslim societies earlier, and even the Christians of modern-day Ethiopia and Eritrea, used their religion to justify enslaving their neighbors.

The use of religion continued as a justification for slavery into the twentieth century. In those parts of Africa like Senegambia (the region of the Senegal and Gambia Rivers in the west) and the Swahili coast (roughly the eastern coast from Somalia to Mozambique), where Muslim populations bordered significant non-Muslim populations, the spread of religion was often offered as a rationale for the continued acquisition of slaves.

In addition to religion, race was often used as another important justification for slavery in Africa. In South Africa, the Boer community enslaved large numbers of people of African and Asian origin. Although the Boers were strict Calvinists who justified slavery in terms of religion, they also developed a racial component to their slavery very early. Needless to say, the Boer ideology of white supremacy eventually led to apartheid.

There were also racial justifications for slavery among some of the indigenous African peoples. For example, the Moors of Mauritania generally referred to themselves as the Bidan, or whites, to distinguish themselves from the Kwar, or black Africans, who were their victims in the slave trade. Even in Somalia, where the difference in skin color was not noticeable, physical distinctions were made. In southern Somalia, most of the slaves were of Bantu origin and had less straight hair and more rounded facial features.

The last major factor to explain the existence of slavery in Africa are the economic circumstances found within the continent. Specifically, Africa had very few fully developed market economies prior to the twentieth century, and this lack of market economies meant that most people lived in a subsistence economy and traded only for rare or luxury goods. Because of this economic reality, Africans had to be forced to produce economic surpluses in numbers sufficient for commercial market production. Good examples of slaves being used in market production for "legitimate trade" during the nineteenth century can be found in the Niger Delta palm oil trade and on Zanzibar and Pemba, where they produced cloves for the world market. It was for this reason that colonial rulers, even after taking power, failed to change the dynamics of the local economies they found already in place.

—*Anthony Q. Cheeseboro*

For Further Reading
Miers, Suzanne, and Richard Roberts. 1988. *The End of Slavery in Africa.* Madison: University of Wisconsin Press; Omer-Cooper, J. D. 1994. *History of Southern Africa.* London: James Currey; Schwartz, Stuart; Linda Wimmer; and Robert Wolff. 1997; *The Global Experience.* New York: Longman; Webb, James L. A. 1995. *Desert Frontier.* Madison: University of Wisconsin Press.

PROSLAVERY ARGUMENT, BRITISH

Although slavery had existed in the British Empire since the early-seventeenth century, there was little need to justify it in the mother country until there emerged an organized and serious challenge against slavery, which did not occur until the late-eighteenth century. The few justifications for slavery before that time were largely philosophical in nature. They emphasized that slaves were part of a fixed social order, that slavery was sanctioned by God and ancient tradition, and that Africans could be made slaves because of inherent "inferiorities." Hebrew and classical history, the Bible, and Christian theologians like St. Augustine and St. Thomas Aquinas all provided support for this view of "absolute and perpetual slavery," which was last seriously explained and defended in the late-seventeenth century by John Locke (Davis, 1975). With the rise of the antislavery movement in Britain in the 1770s and 1780s, proslavery arguments were put forward more or less constantly until the Emancipation Act (1833). Throughout the 60-year struggle, the main lines of the proslavery defense remained generally the same, with only a shift in emphasis over certain issues.

Many proslavery writers focused simply on addressing the abolitionists, accusing them of misrepresentation, exaggeration, ignorance, or hypocrisy. One of the most common tactics for slavery defenders was to compare the condition of slaves with that of English workers and ask why the humanitarian impulses of their opponents did not extend to their own countrymen. Moreover, slavery advocates claimed that antislavery ideas undermined plantation owners' authority and encouraged slaves to rebel. The Haitian Revolution (1791–1804) became a popular example of the cataclysmic effects of exposing the slaves to ideas like freedom and liberty. Indeed, every slave revolt in this period was blamed to some extent on the antislavery campaign.

Until the abolition of the British slave trade in 1807, many defenses of slavery continued to focus on philosophical justifications for slavery. The Enlightenment had influenced many commentators like Bryan Edwards, who agreed that Africans were not inherently lower beings and consequently could not be permanently fixed at the bottom of some cosmic hierarchy, so they justified slavery on the grounds that it civilized a savage people. The slave system taught the slaves the value of work and other so-called civilized values. It was agreed that the worst abuses of the system should be eliminated, and writers were increasingly anxious to prove that slaves were contented, and—particularly after the government passed measures for general slave registration in 1819 and resolutions on amelioration in 1823—that plantation conditions had improved.

In principle, then, most proslavery advocates from the beginning of the debate agreed that slaves could progress toward civilization and, thus, emancipation. However few writers even bothered to raise this point until the 1820s, when they were faced with a remobilized antislavery campaign and an alarming number of calls for immediate emancipation. Now, clearly on the defensive, proslavery writers insisted that the process toward emancipation would have to be "very gradual." Other philosophical arguments regarding the Bible or the level of African civilization continued to be put forward, but as the 1820s progressed, these abstract positions became less tenable. As early as 1823 most proslavery writers, like John Gladstone, found themselves prefacing their defenses of slavery with claims of being "an opponent of slavery in the abstract."

By conceding important philosophical positions, proslavery polemicists increasingly retreated to economic and legal justifications for slavery, which had all been raised before to a lesser degree. Economically, it was argued, the Caribbean colonies would be ruined without slavery and with them, the navy and, ultimately, the empire. Moreover, the slaves would suffer worst of all from a collapse of the West Indian economy. The most compelling arguments were legal in nature, however. The most obvious point raised was that all slaves had been purchased under the sanction of British law and they were the legal property of their owners. Related to this argument were denunciations of parliamentary interference in colonial affairs and, turning an antislavery argument on its head, an appeal for the rights of British colonists to liberty.

In the last years before emancipation, there were threats of secession or of armed rebellion modeled on the American colonies, though these were recognized as hollow and had little effect. The legal arguments remained the most solid defense and provided the foundation for claims of compensation. In fact, it was a sign of how weak the proslavery position had become by the last decade of the debate that most of its polemicists focused on the compensation issue. On the other hand, it was a sign of how well their legal arguments hit home that the planters were able to secure a compensation grant of £20 million, still the largest government grant in British history.

—*Jeff Pardue*

See also
Augustine (Saint); The Bible; Compensated Emancipation; The Enlightenment; Immediatism; Locke, John

For Further Reading
Davis, David Brion. 1975. *The Problem of Slavery in the Age of Revolution, 1770–1823*. Ithaca, NY: Cornell University Press; Davis, David Brion. 1984. *Slavery and Human Progress*. Oxford: Oxford University Press; Ragatz, Joseph Lowell. 1963. *The Fall of the Planter Class in the British Caribbean, 1763–1833*. New York: Octagon; Williams, Eric. 1944. *Capitalism and Slavery*. New York: Capricorn.

PROSLAVERY ARGUMENT, GENERAL

For centuries, a certain body of arguments to legitimize slavery was used in the debates between defenders of the slave system and their critics and opponents of the slave trade and slavery. Especially from the late-eighteenth century onward, the antislavery debate forced defenders of the slave trade and slavery to formulate their arguments more precisely. Antislavery writers used proslavery arguments predominantly in a rhetorical way to expose the defenders and their line of argumentation.

Proslavery and antislavery arguments were both derived from the Bible and Christian theology, from philosophy and history, from "age old" customs and law systems, and from the natural sciences. Whether defenders of slavery had read their classical, medieval, and contemporary authors or not, they used them as they saw fit, often in an eclectic way. In the eighteenth and nineteenth centuries, when the debates between defenders and abolitionists were at their height, that usage became clear. For some proslavery writers, just one argument sufficed to make a point; for others, a combination was needed to support their claims. A defender of slavery could agree with his opponent on, let us say, biblical grounds but at the same time fiercely defend his case by using historical and legal arguments.

The Bible proved to be a long-lasting source for defenders of slavery. The best-known biblical reference was Genesis 9:18–29, which stated that the Canaanites, the offspring of Ham who was one of the sons of Noah, were cursed to eternal obedience and serfdom. However, the Bible did not mention that Ham's offspring were black. This connection with skin color was a medieval development, but the blackness of the Canaanites became a powerful argument for the enslavement of blacks and other people of color that lasted for centuries.

In the eighteenth century, natural science theories existed alongside or even replaced biblical arguments, and environmental explanations were especially popular. Some scholars were even led to believe that on scientific grounds, the white skin color was the norm whereas the black color an aberration. "This was, in a sense, a secular version of Ham's curse, the climate taking the place of God's judgment" (Davis, 1988).

The theological notion of dualism, in which the physical "body" and the spiritual "mind" were distinguished, led to the argument that it did not matter whether the body was enslaved as long as the mind was free. This argument could be taken to mean that Christianizing was synonymous with freedom of the mind, and since obedience to secular and/or religious leaders as such was part and parcel of most Christian denominations, it seemed that slaves were not in such a bad state as it was often said they were.

The idea that it is inappropriate to enslave a fellow citizen can be found in the writings of Greek philosophers like Plato and Aristotle. According to Plato, foreigners, or the so-called barbarians, were the ones to enslave if necessary. In his *Politics,* Aristotle defended slavery on the grounds that by nature, there are people who rule—they possess reason and better moral faculties—and people who have to obey—they lack reason, are inferior by nature, and have to be guided by their masters. According to Aristotle, slavery was essentially a domestic relationship and good for both master and slave. For the slave, it was the only way to fulfill his function in life.

Another theme in classical writings was the idea that the black skin color was in one way or another different from and even inferior to a white skin color, and it was argued that environmental causes, especially climate, were responsible for the difference. However, slave was not synonymous with a black skin color in Greek and Roman antiquity.

In the modern era, the Greek and Roman argument that you do not enslave your fellow citizens was similar to the notion that one could not enslave people of one's own faith. But as critics of slavery raised their voices more loudly, it was necessary for defenders of the slave system to formulate other, more convincing arguments. Since critics of the slave trade and slavery predominantly used arguments based on natural and human rights, the defenders had to meet this challenge. And as calls for a better, more humane treatment of slaves became an important issue for antislavery pamphleteers, as did in a lesser sense the call for allowing slaves to be Christianized and even taught to read and write, defenders had to react to these humanitarian arguments as well.

In the eighteenth and nineteenth centuries, apologists of the slave trade and slavery were likely to use economics as the main reason for maintaining the slave trade and slavery and argue that private and public economic interests benefited from the slave system. Whatever later historians have written on the alleged profitability of the trade and of slavery itself, contemporaries were convinced that the profits for individual traders, plantation owners, and national treasuries were considerable enough for the system to continue. Or at least they tried to convince their readers of that fact. Slaveowners also used their inalienable property rights as a weapon against antislavery attacks. Some authors held that without slavery, the colonial economy, the backbone of empire, would collapse and that as a consequence, the welfare of the state and even the nation as such would be in danger.

In the seventeenth century and even more in the eighteenth, it was not unusual for proslavery authors to adhere to a natural rights theory. They could agree with statements that every human being is born free and equal, but they held that customs and laws, which had grown historically, had surpassed those natural rights. This kind of reasoning also supported the argument that since slavery allegedly was a normal fact of life in Africa, it was not that improper to engage in the system.

Furthermore, it was believed that most of the captured Africans were either prisoners of war or convicted criminals. And not only people of those two categories but also free Africans would always be better off as slaves in the European colonies—some people even argued they would be better off than European servants. According to this line of reasoning, slave traders were even depicted as saviors. Slaves should be grateful, not only because they were saved from a certain death, but also because they were brought into contact with European civilization.

Another argument was that only black Africans were capable of working the land in a hot climate. Bartolomé de Las Casas had already advanced this argument in the sixteenth century to protect the Indians against the hardships of forced labor and slavery. In general, this notion of physical unfitness was applied to whites in the colonial slave societies and not to American Indians.

Human rights were also incorporated in the defenses of proslavery authors. Ameliorating the conditions under which slaves had to live and even conversion to Christianity were the most important issues. Proposals for better treatment and conversion were presented without attacking the slave system as such, and they mostly served as ways of securing the system. Apologists of the slave system reasoned that better treatment would lead to a more obedient slave force, a lower death rate, and a higher birthrate (as long as the child inherited slave status from its mother). Some of the defenders of slavery were aware that one day the slave system would come to an end, but any future change in the system—amelioration, manumission, even total abolition—was in the hands of God or even "history."

Most participants in the slavery debates, including the defenders of the slave system, had a monogenist position. Monogenism meant that all of mankind was descended from one original pair, Adam and Eve. Polygenism, which meant that mankind consisted of separate races with different origins, was shared by a minority of the participants, certainly before the nineteenth century. The polygenist thinkers could and would argue that blacks were not only different but also inferior to whites. But, monogenist as well as polygenist authors could be pro- or antislavery. And both could share the idea that not only were blacks inferior, on whatever grounds, but that they were more animal-like than other humans.

Partly as a result of scientific debates in the eighteenth century, a consensus was reached that black people were human beings and that they were certainly not animals as such. But the belief that black Africans were to be found on the borderline that separated animals, especially the great apes, and humans was widespread in the eighteenth and nineteenth centuries. Such an image of black people supported proslavery arguments.

—*Angelie Sens*

See also
Ham, Curse of; Las Casas, Bartolomé de
For Further Reading
Davis, David Brion. 1988. *The Problem of Slavery in Western Culture*. Oxford: Oxford University Press.

PROSLAVERY ARGUMENT, UNITED STATES

The proslavery argument in the United States was a philosophical rationale for slavery as the core component of the antebellum Southern culture and worldview. Defense of slavery began in the colonial period, though it intensified in the antebellum period, when it became a wholly Southern ideology espoused by the best theological, political, and scientific thinkers of the time.

Religion led the way, and one historian believes that the Bible was an indispensable tool of the "proslavery mainstream" since, like manifest destiny, proslavery theory was based in Scripture. Slaveholders noted that Jesus had not specifically prohibited slaveholding and that, in the Old Testament, Noah's descendants through Canaan had been "cursed" to labor as slaves. When all else failed, Christianity was presented as a "civilizing" influence for Africans.

Slavery was also seen as a practical method of controlling the population and maintaining social order. Blacks were viewed as inherently disruptive, imposing pagan ways and sexual license upon an otherwise orderly society. After the 1831 Nat Turner insurrection, white attitudes toward blacks, free and slave, hardened. Thomas Roderick Dew published the *Review of the Debate in the Virginia Legislature* (1832), a debate over whether to abolish slavery because of the Turner rebellion, which had served to reinforce proslavery sentiment. Dew concluded that large-scale emancipation was impractical, echoing the Founding Fathers' doubts that blacks could fit into society in the United States.

The most forceful argument in the Southern defense of slavery was based on the assumption of white superiority. Medical arguments by Dr. Samuel Cartwright, who worked in the field of "ethnology," were presented as proof of black inferiority. Likewise, the physician Josiah Nott contributed comparisons of cranial capacity to buttress physiological arguments supporting the theory of the superior intelligence of whites. However, suggestions that blacks actually represented a separate species from whites were generally viewed with skepticism because they clashed with the Christian doctrine of the Creation.

Finally, retaining slavery was portrayed as an economically sound policy, an argument that was tied to the individual's right to private property. Accordingly, Southern slavery was declared to be both more efficient and more humane than free labor in the industrial North; apologist George Fitzhugh echoed those sentiments, arguing that expanding slavery to include white slaves was a logical extension of the patriarchal family model wherein white children and wives were subservient to the husband and father.

One of the critical elements of Southern politics was the position of race-based slavery in their society, especially of the right to establish and maintain internal systems without outside interference. Political arguments favoring slavery also had a racial component, attempting to convince slaveless whites that the presence of black slaves ensured white equality. Indeed, rather than thinking that white liberty founded on black slavery was a "paradox," white Southern politicians pointed to black slavery as indispensable to white liberty.

Occasional opposition to slavery from within the South, such as Hinton Helper's pamphlet *The Impending Crisis of the South* (1857), recognized that slavery was a drain on the Southern economy rather than a boost to it. However, slaveholders insisted that because their slaves freed them from being encumbered by the mundane details of daily life, they were able to elevate their community.

And indeed, Southern politics was dominated by slaveholders until the Civil War. James Henry Hammond, for example, ardently defended the necessity of the role of a "mudsill" class of black slaves for the achievement of political and cultural greatness. In 1835, as a freshman congressman from South Carolina, Hammond defended slavery as a "positive good" requiring defense to the point of civil war. Such politicians and writers eventually defended slavery in secession conventions, as not merely a component part of Southern culture, but rather, as the vice-president of the Confederate States of America, Alexander Stephens, described it, "the cornerstone of the Confederacy" (Oakes, 1982).

Historians' analyses of the development of the proslavery ideology include speculation that it is evidence of antebellum guilt over slavery, although it is

This portrayal of an overseer supervising slaves exemplifies one appeal of the proslavery argument to whites—the idea that slavery buttressed the position and status of all whites.

more likely that these writings were meant for Southerners' own edification, not to persuade Northern abolitionists of the rightness of their views. Feminist analyses have variously speculated upon an identity or sympathy of attitude between white slaveholding women and black slave women, although it is more likely true that, as has been more recently found, white slaveholding women, by their attitudes and actions, contributed to the hegemony of the slave regime. Scholars of American literature perceive the energy exerted by antebellum Southern writers and intellectuals as leading to the paucity of important literary contributions by Southerners during a period of marked literary production in New England.

—*Dale Edwyna Smith*

For Further Reading
Bleser, Carol, ed. 1988. *Secret and Sacred: The Diaries of James Henry Hammond, a Southern Slaveholder.* New York: Oxford University Press; Faust, Drew Gilpin. 1981. *The Ideology of Slavery: Proslavery*

Thought in the Antebellum South, 1830–1860. Baton Rouge: Louisiana State University Press; Fox-Genovese, Elizabeth. 1988. *Within the Plantation Household: Black and White Women of the Old South.* Chapel Hill: University of North Carolina Press; Oakes, James. 1982. *The Ruling Race.* New York: Knopf.

PROSSER, GABRIEL
(C. 1775–1800)

Very little is known of the early life of Gabriel Prosser, but in 1800, he was a slave coachman who belonged to Thomas Prosser of Henrico County, Virginia. Gabriel was a literate and highly skilled blacksmith who was determined to gain freedom for himself and other enslaved Africans in his area. Thus, he planned an uprising of slaves, which was to occur on August 30, 1800.

Gabriel was a deeply religious man and was 6 feet 2 inches tall. In various literary representations, Gabriel has been described as an almost messianic figure who wore his hair long like his idol, Samson, though such representations are more mythical than real. His wife, Nanny, and his brothers, Martin and Solomon, supported him in his plans to organize a massive slave revolt. They all held meetings with other interested Africans at fish fries and barbecues.

Richmond, Virginia, was believed to be an ideal location for instigating a large-scale slave revolt. The area around Richmond contained a population of 32,000 slaves and only 8,000 white residents. Gabriel went to Richmond every Sunday to review the layout of the city. He would also check and bring more clubs, swords, guns, and ammunition to the stockpile of weapons that he was stashing for the planned insurrection.

Gabriel planned to strike the city of Richmond during harvest season so there would be no starvation as a result of the uprising. His group of enslaved Africans, estimated to be in the thousands, had orders not to kill any Quakers, Methodists, French, elderly women, or children. Armed and ready, three columns were to attack Richmond. The right wing was to grab the arsenal and seize the guns. The left wing was to take the powderhouse. The central wing would enter town at both ends simultaneously and cut down every white male except Frenchmen, Methodists, and Quakers, who were believed to be sympathetic to the cause.

After Richmond was secure, Gabriel and the group were to capture other cities. He hoped that Virginia's 300,000 slaves would join his movement in vast numbers. If the entire plan worked, he would become the king of Virginia; if it did not, the group was to go into the woods and wage guerrilla warfare.

A group of approximately 1,000 slaves met at Old Brook Swamp six miles outside of Richmond on August 30, 1800, as scheduled. As they began to march upon the city, a violent thunderstorm hit, and bridges and roads were washed out.

Two house slaves who did not want to see their master killed informed the authorities of the situation. Governor James Monroe called in 600 troops and notified all militia commanders in the state. Eventually, 35 members of the group were caught and executed. Gabriel was captured in late September aboard the schooner *Mary,* which had traveled to Norfolk from Richmond. He was returned to Richmond in chains to stand trial. During his interrogation, he refused to divulge any information regarding his plans or the identities of his associates. Gabriel was executed by hanging on October 7, 1800.

—*Marquetta L. Goodwine*

For Further Reading
Egerton, Douglas R. 1993. *Gabriel's Rebellion: The Vir-* *ginia Slave Conspiracies of 1800 and 1802.* Chapel Hill: University of North Carolina Press.

PROVISION GROUNDS
See **Gardens, Slave**

PUNIC WARS

Much of the subsequent history of Rome as a slave-based society was influenced by the Punic Wars, which derived their name from the Roman word for Carthaginian, *Punici.* The first two Punic Wars between Rome and Carthage were of an unprecedented scale in ancient Mediterranean warfare in terms of the expenditure of manpower and material resources. In the Third Punic War (149–146 B.C.), the Romans besieged and eventually annihilated a much weaker state, but this final destruction of Carthage is of small importance for the history of slavery.

The First Punic War (264–241 B.C.), Rome's first overseas venture, marked the beginning of Roman imperial expansion, which ultimately engulfed the Mediterranean basin and much of its hinterland. This war, whose crucial and decisive tests were naval battles, was for the possession of Sicily. In the aftermath of the final Roman victory near the Aegates Islands (or Egadi Islands, off the coast of Sicily), while Carthage was embroiled in war with its rebellious mercenaries, Rome seized the Carthaginian provinces of Sardinia and Corsica (238 B.C.). A vengeful Carthage, having lost Sicily in war and Sardinia and Corsica by Roman treachery, then built a powerful Punic empire in Spain in the 230s and 220s B.C.

Hannibal Barca, one of the most brilliant generals in history, led a rejuvenated Carthage against Rome in the Second Punic War (218–202 B.C.). The Romans survived Hannibal's first stunning victories in northern Italy and the devastating defeat at Cannae in Apulia in southeastern Italy (216 B.C.). Rome's superior manpower reserves, combined with the able generalship of Scipio Africanus the Elder in the war's last phase, finally prevailed over Carthage. Africanus defeated Hannibal in a battle at Zama in northern Africa, which ended the war.

Rome became undisputed master of the western Mediterranean, and the Romans rapidly moved into the vacuum that Carthage had left in Spain. Roman conquests accumulated inexorably, and the Hellenistic

Slaves making bread in a Roman kitchen. Roman victories in the Punic Wars brought in an influx of slaves to the empire.

known of which was based in southwestern Asia Minor. Ephesus became a noted slave emporium, and the Cycladic island of Delos emerged as a principle transshipment center—the geographer Strabo relates that 10,000 slaves were sold there in a single day.

Slave labor became indispensable to Roman agricultural estates as a result of the level of concentrated wealth among the Roman elite, which in turn was a consequence of Rome's imperial success initiated by the Punic Wars. Slaves figure prominently in Roman agricultural treatises, the earliest extant example of which is Cato the Elder's *De Agricultura* (c. 160 B.C.).

—*Craige Champion*

See also
Cato; Columella's *De re rustica*; Latifundia; Roman Republic; Sicilian Slave Wars; *Vernae*

For Further Reading
Brunt, P. A. 1971. *Italian Manpower, 225 B.C.–A.D. 14.* Oxford: Clarendon; Hopkins, Keith. 1978. *Conquerors and Slaves.* Cambridge: Cambridge University Press; Toynbee, Arnold. 1965. *Hannibal's Legacy.* London: Oxford University Press.

monarchies in the east fell to Rome's power in quick succession. Before the middle of the second century B.C., there was no power left in the Mediterranean world that could seriously challenge Rome.

The Punic Wars and Rome's subsequent imperial successes unleashed new social and economic forces that disrupted the ancient Mediterranean world. One consequence was the evolution of Roman Italy into a slaveowning society. The real victors of the Punic Wars and the beneficiaries of their aftermath were the members of the narrow Roman aristocracy, who grew enormously wealthy through war booty. The Punic Wars established new patterns for the Roman conduct of war, which in turn caused a demographic transformation of Roman Italy.

Rank-and-file soldiers returned to homesteads destroyed by Hannibal's ravages in the Italian phase of the Second Punic War. Legionnaires on extended campaigns abroad during the second-century wars, particularly those pressed into hard and unpopular service in the tedious, drawn-out Roman attempt to subdue Spain, had often lost the taste for returning to the peasant-farmer lifestyle. In any event, they often returned to properties that were so dilapidated as to be beyond their material capacities to restore. These men gravitated to Italian urban centers and particularly to Rome, where they swelled into an impoverished urban proletariat.

The wealthy few of the Roman senatorial elite acquired vast tracts of the abandoned properties, as they possessed the material resources to restore war-devastated lands to productivity. They employed slaves, either war captives or purchased from a burgeoning and lucrative slave market, on a massive scale to work their estates.

By 150 B.C., in order to meet the great Roman landowners' demand for labor, thriving and well-organized slaving systems had arisen, the most well-

PYRAMID CONSTRUCTION

*T*he pyramids of Egypt are the most enduring architectural legacy of the ancient Egyptian peoples, and through the years, people have debated both the means by which they were constructed and whether or not slaves were employed in their construction. Egyptian society in the Old Kingdom (2700–2300 B.C.) was dominated by the pharaoh, a divine monarch who was considered to be the living embodiment of the god Horus, becoming Osiris at death. The pharaoh was also identified with the god of the sun. Directly attached to the pharaoh was a vast bureaucracy of noble officials responsible for the daily workings of the state. These noblemen spent their careers in service to the pharaoh, and the tomb inscriptions left by these individuals show careers marked by a steady progression through numerous offices and an accumulation of titles. The pharaoh was also the center of the Egyptian economy, since everything belonged to him.

The centralized political and economic structure of Egypt made it possible for the pharaohs to organize resources and labor on a scale unheard of in other ancient states. The bulk of Egyptian society was made up of a landed peasantry which, although technically free, was bound to the soil and always attached to the land whenever it changed ownership. However, the peasants did own their own homes. The peasants worked the lands—which belonged to the pharaoh, the temples, or the nobility—on a sharecropping system. The economic surplus they produced helped support the pharaoh, the temples and their priests, and the state bureaucracy.

In theory, all Egyptian citizens were required to provide the state with a certain number of days of labor, a type of work tax known as corvée. The brunt of this conscription fell on the peasants, since others could evade their duty by hiring substitutes or making some form of payment instead. Most of the labor was employed in constructing and maintaining the irrigation canals upon which Egyptian agriculture depended. However, peasant labor was also drafted for use in the construction of the pharaohs' tombs and temples.

The pyramid was used as the chief form of royal tomb during the Old and Middle Kingdoms (2700–2300 B.C. and 2134–1785 B.C., respectively). The most famous pyramids are the ones located at Giza, which were constructed during the reigns of Cheops (Khufu), Chephren (Khafre), and Mycerinus (Menkaure), who all ruled during the fourth dynasty (2680–2565 B.C.). We do not know why the pyramid was the predominate form of royal tomb during this period, but it is possible that it was intended as a ramp for the dead king to reach heaven. There are about 80 known pyramids.

The largest of the pyramids, that of Cheops, is made up of 2,300,000 stone blocks of an average weight of 2.5 tons each with some weighing as much as 15 tons. Stones weighing 2.5 tons could be moved by a gang of 8 men. The Greek historian Herodotus reported that it took 100,000 workers, who were employed for periods of three months each, 20 years to build the pyramid of Cheops.

The Egyptian system of corvée labor obviated the use of slaves in the construction of the pyramids. Farmers could be employed on pyramid construction during the time of year when the Nile was in flood and agricultural work was not possible, usually between the end of July through October. Since the workers were only temporary conscripts, the size of the workforce would vary as individuals' terms of service expired or if they were needed elsewhere. In addition to peasant laborers, there was also a core group of professional craftsmen and architects who were responsible for the detailed workmanship. As many as 4,000 of these full-time artisans may have been used on the pyramid of Cheops.

No evidence on the organization of the workers survives from the Old Kingdom, but there is information surviving from the Middle Kingdom site of Kahun, which was where workmen laboring on the pyramid of Senwosret (Sesostris) II (1897–1878 B.C.) were housed. Evidence from this site shows the presence of a substantial community of foreigners among the construction crew. Some, such as immigrants from the Aegean, may have been traders or itinerant artisans who settled in Egypt while others, such as the Asiatics, may have been brought to Egypt as prisoners of war.

Apart from domestic servants, slavery did not exist on a large scale in Egypt. The greatest influx of slaves occurred during the New Kingdom (1560–1070 B.C.), when Egypt established an empire outside its traditional frontiers. The chief purpose of the military campaigns was to acquire booty and slaves. By that time, the Egyptians had shifted from the construction of pyramids as royal tombs to the rock-cut sepulchres located in the Valley of the Kings outside of Thebes.

—*John F. Shean*

See also
Egypt, Slavery in Ancient; Egypt, Condition of Slaves in
For Further Reading
Bierbrier, Morris. 1982. *The Tomb-Builders of the Pharaohs.* London: British Museum Publications; David, A. R. 1986. *The Pyramid Builders of Ancient Egypt.* London: Routledge; Edwards, I. E. S. 1980. *The Pyramids of Egypt.* Harmondsworth, Eng.: Penguin Books.

QUAKERS

The Society of Friends (Quakers) played a fundamental role in the history of abolition. From the society's founding in England in the 1640s, members promoted a spiritualistic and rigorous Christianity. They radically rejected worldly society and the established church by refusing to take oaths, wage war, or recognize the usual class and sexual distinctions.

The Quaker drive for purity rapidly led them to question the institution of slavery. George Fox was the first to speak out in 1657 when he advised Friends who owned slaves to convert them and treat them as brothers. While visiting Barbados in 1671, he preached to slaves and later suggested that Quakers should limit the service of slaves to 30 years and give them compensation at the end of that period for their time of service. Fox's companion, William Edmundson, went even further in a 1676 tract when he stated that Christian freedom could not coexist with physical slavery.

However, those ideas were sidelined as Quaker leaders in Pennsylvania, London, and Rhode Island became prominent in the transatlantic slave trade and slaveowning. The society's efficient organization in representative monthly, quarterly, and yearly meetings helped create a profitable transatlantic trade and communication network, and by the eighteenth century, Quakerism had entered into a phase in which its strict social rules were more sectarian and more focused on the church.

Yet the Germantown Protest—the first complaint against slavery and the first call for abolition in what became the United States—was merely one example of how slavery remained a dilemma for some Quakers. From 1711 onward, there was continuing controversy in the Philadelphia Yearly Meeting over slavery, mainly from Quaker farmers, but a conservative majority ensured that the meeting went no further than to advise members not to participate in the slave trade. Subsequent decades saw similar debates elsewhere in America, the publication of Quaker tracts on the issue, and radicals like John Farmer and Benjamin Lay being disowned for causing dissension.

Thus, by the 1740s, Quaker testimony against slavery was well defined, but only through the work of John Woolman and Anthony Benezet did it become widely accepted within the Society of Friends. In 1755, the Philadelphia Yearly Meeting ordered that members who traded in slaves should be officially admonished, a step soon followed elsewhere. In 1776, the Philadelphia meeting ruled that Friends should free their slaves and provide them compensation, or risk dismissal, once again setting a trend to be followed even by Southern Quakers. Quaker influence encouraged the state of Pennsylvania to declare slavery to be illegal in 1780, and prompting by American Quakers encouraged the London Yearly Meeting to adopt an active abolitionist stance.

Despite their small numbers, the Quakers provided an essential nucleus of leadership and financial backing for the fledgling abolitionists, and the long tradition of Quaker female activism and separate women's meetings gave women a noticeable role in the effort. Particularly after 1808, when the slave trade had been abolished by Great Britain and the United States, most American Quakers found a gradualist position more in keeping with their sectarian feelings and hatred of public controversy, and they were also distracted by a theological schism in the 1820s. Thus, abolitionist Friends tended to advocate peaceful lobbying, publishing campaigns, boycotts of slave-produced products, plans for educating freed slaves and colonizing them in Africa, and, more radically, the sanctuary offered by the Underground Railroad.

In contrast, in Britain after 1807, abolition was far less contentious, and Quakers became more radical than their American brethren, with Quakers leaders playing a critical role in the total triumph of Britain's abolition of slavery in 1833. It was their example and suggestions that inspired some American Friends to support the American Anti-Slavery Society, which advocated the immediate and unconditional abolition of slavery. To most American Quakers, immediatism seemed divisive and unchristian, and some local meetings banned Friends from joining the society.

The Society of Friends' commitment to gradualism meant that the society remained united, North and South, and it seemed to help its lobbying against the Fugitive Slave Act, but the group forfeited its leadership role. Disputes aroused by immediatism meant some radical Friends, like Angelina and Sarah Grimké, left or were expelled, and in 1842, a local schism occurred and Charles Osborn formed the Indiana Anti-Slavery Friends.

As war approached, most Friends, no matter how committed they were to abolition, remained true to their pacifist principles and refused to support it. Involvement in Reconstruction was more suited to Quaker ideals, and they were conspicuous in philanthropic attempts to help ex-slaves and to transform the South. Friends have continued to be leaders in campaigns against slavery and forced labor in other areas of the world up to the present day.

—*Gwilym Games*

See also
Abolition (British Empire, United States); Coffin, Levi; Grimké, Sarah Moore; Mott, Lucretia Coffin; Woolman, John
For Further Reading
Anstey, Roger. 1975. *The Atlantic Slave Trade and British Abolition, 1760–1810*. Cambridge: Cambridge University Press; Braithwaite, William. 1961. *The Second Period of Quakerism*. Cambridge: Cambridge University Press; Drake, Thomas. 1954. *Quakers and Slavery in America*. New Haven, CT: Yale University Press; Soderlund, Jean R. 1985. *Quakers and Slavery: A Divided Spirit*. Princeton, NJ: Princeton University Press.

part: "Brazilian vessels wherever found, and foreign vessels found in the ports, bays, anchorages, or territorial waters of Brazil, having slaves on board, whose importation is prohibited by the Law of November 7, 1831, or which may have landed them, shall be seized by the authorities, or by Brazilian ships of war, and considered importers of slaves." Article 6 stated: "All the slaves seized shall be re-exported at the cost of the State to the ports from whence they came."

Although several shiploads of slaves were landed after the passage of the Queirós Law, the legislation effectively ended Brazil's external trade in African slaves.

—*Francis A. Dutra*

For Further Reading
Bethell, Leslie. 1970. *The Abolition of the Brazilian Slave Trade: Britain, Brazil, and the Slave Trade Question, 1807–1869*. Cambridge: Cambridge University Press; Burns, E. Bradford. 1966. *A Documentary History of Brazil*. New York: Knopf; Manchester, Alan K. 1933. *British Preeminence in Brazil, Its Rise and Decline: A Study in European Expansion*. Chapel Hill: University of North Carolina Press; Mattos, Ilmar Rohloff de. 1987. *O tempo saquarema*. São Paulo: Editora Hucitec.

QUEIROS LAW
(1850)

The Queirós Law, dated September 4, 1850, abolished the external African slave trade to Brazil and reinforced a similar law of November 7, 1831, that had rarely been fully enforced. It was named after Eusébio de Queirós Coutinho Matoso da Câmara (1812–1868), the Brazilian minister of justice from 1848 to 1852 and Conservative Party leader in the September 1848 cabinet, which was initially headed by Pedro de Araújo Lima, visconde de Olinda. Queirós was born in Luanda in Angola and was chief of police in Rio de Janeiro for most of 1833–1844. He served in the Brazilian Chamber of Deputies, representing the province of Rio de Janeiro, from 1842 to 1844 and again from 1848 to 1852. In 1854, he was elected to the Brazilian Senate, and in 1855, he was made a member of the Council of State.

The Queirós Law was based on an 1837 antislave trade bill of Felisberto Caldeira Brant Pontes, marquês de Barbacena, which had not been enacted into law. The earlier bill was modified and reintroduced into the Brazilian Chamber of Deputies in 1848; this time, the bill passed. Article 1 of the 10-article law stated in

QUILOMBOS

Known also as Maroon societies, *quilombos* (Portuguese term; *cimarrones* in Spanish) were settlements founded by runaway slaves in the sixteenth to nineteenth centuries. Enslaved Africans often took advantage of weaknesses in the plantation system to escape to the surrounding hills and mountains and establish their own communities. The initial escape could involve violence to the planter or overseer, or it could be more passive and simply involve fleeing the slave quarters during the night. The founding of early *quilombos* was inhibited by opposition from Native Americans, but Africans who escaped from Brazil's sugar plantations managed to organize remote, semi-independent communities.

Residents of *quilombos* raised many of their own crops, but they were also known to undermine the slave system by sabotaging nearby sugar plantations, stealing provisions, and abducting others to increase their population. Women were especially targeted for capture since there were comparatively fewer women than men in the *quilombos* and reproduction was essential to the survival of the runaways' settlements.

The most extensive and famous *quilombo* was the Negro Republic of Palmares. Evidence of the Africans' awareness of the political instability and international rivalry that surrounded them, Palmares was founded in the early-seventeenth century when control of Brazil passed from the Dutch to the Portuguese. The Africans of Palmares used the frontier's rough exterior to their advantage and managed to withstand numerous organized attacks by the Dutch and the Portuguese until the settlement was finally captured in 1697.

Other less successful *quilombos* existed throughout Brazil, including in the states of Rio de Janeiro, São Paulo, and Mato Grosso. *Quilombos* were situated in very remote regions or in relatively close proximity to Brazilian cities and towns. Fugitives chose the locations of their settlements strategically and took advantage of elevated, rocky exteriors, which allowed them to survey a community's circumference and reduce the likelihood of a surprise assault.

When not engaged in defensive or offensive actions, fugitives practiced and preserved indigenous African language, religion, government, and ways of child rearing. In those instances where Africans and Amerindians coexisted in Maroon communities, a new, syncretic culture often emerged that reflected both sources of influence. Because Africans resisted the conditions of enslavement and the inferior status that had been forced upon them, *quilombos* of different sizes and durations existed throughout the Americas. Most *quilombos* were temporary, but some have survived to the present. The Maroons in Jamaica, who forced the English government to sign an official military treaty with them, still exist today.

—*Maureen G. Elgersman*

See also
Palmares; Trelawney Town Maroons
For Further Reading
Conniff, Michael L., and Thomas J. Davis, eds. 1994. *Africans in the Americas: A History of the Black Diaspora.* New York: St. Martin's; Mattoso, Katia de Queiros. 1986. *To Be a Slave in Brazil, 1550–1888.* New Brunswick, NJ: Rutgers University Press; Price, Richard, ed. 1979. *Maroon Societies: Rebel Slave Communities in the Americas.* Baltimore: Johns Hopkins University Press; Reis, Joao Jose. 1993. *Slave Rebellion in Brazil.* Baltimore: Johns Hopkins University Press.

QUITMAN, JOHN A. (1798–1858)

A staunch defender of slavery and states' rights, Mississippian John A. Quitman was a Southern nationalist in the pivotal secession era. Quitman was born near Kingston in Rhinebeck, New York, to a Lutheran minister; he was one of eight children. He graduated from Hartwick Seminary in New York in 1816, studied law, and in 1821, was admitted to the Ohio bar. He taught briefly in Pennsylvania but began a legal practice in Natchez, Mississippi, in 1821.

Quitman was a large landowner with several plantations and hundreds of slaves. Although it is difficult to determine just how many slaves he held at any one time, records indicate that his largest plantation, at Palmyra, included 311 slaves in 1848. At Monmouth, his base of operations, he had primarily house servants, but on smaller holdings, Quitman's slaves numbered 30, 45, and 85 at various times.

From 1821 to 1858, Quitman was a significant figure in Mississippi politics as a state representative, senator, governor and, from 1855 to 1858, as a U.S. congressman. During his years of leadership in state politics, he became associated with the nullification movement, was a protégé of John C. Calhoun, and became the most recognized figure in antebellum Mississippi.

When Calhoun and South Carolina advocated nullification of the 1828 and 1832 tariffs, Henry Clay pushed a compromise through Congress to lower tariff rates over a 10-year period, and South Carolina reacted by repealing its tariff nullification. In Mississippi, Quitman nevertheless encouraged support for the principle of nullification and formation of a states' rights party, which culminated in a May 1834 nullification convention in Jackson, Mississippi.

Quitman envisioned himself as a military man. He led an expedition in 1836 to support Texas independence, and although the unit saw no combat, the effort enabled Quitman to pursue his military interests. During the Mexican War (1846–1848), Quitman was commissioned a brigadier-general under Gen. Zachary Taylor. Active at Monterey, Mexico (September 1846), Quitman's troops were the first to enter Mexico City after its surrender in November 1846, and the commanding general, Winfield Scott, appointed the Mississippian military governor of the city. Quitman became a major-general in April 1847.

Quitman was considered for nomination as the presidential candidate at the Democratic convention in 1848 in Baltimore but was elected governor of Mississippi in 1849 instead. Inaugurated in January 1850, Quitman's term in office was brief and, at best, stormy. The governor opposed the Compromise of 1850 and called a state legislative session to protest Henry Clay's latest compromise measures, thus reaffirming his role as the leader of Mississippi's proslavery forces.

After becoming involved with the Cuban leader Narciso Lopez, Quitman was indicted by a New Orleans grand jury for violating neutrality laws. He resigned the governor's office in February 1851 but was later acquitted. Quitman served in Congress from 1855 until he died on July 17, 1858.

The question remains, Was Quitman a secessionist? Evidently he did support secession (as governor in 1850) when he responded to what he deemed an attack on states' rights, but he never became an extreme Southern nationalist.

—*Boyd Childress*

For Further Reading
Claiborne, J. F. H. 1860. *Life and Correspondence of John A. Quitman, Major-General, U.S.A., and Governor of the State of Mississippi.* New York: Harper; May, Robert E. 1985. *John A. Quitman: Old South Crusader.* Baton Rouge: Louisiana State University Press.

THE QUR'AN

*D*efining what is a slave must precede any discussion of slavery as a social institution, and historical consensus regards a slave as a person whose labor is completely owned by another and who is deprived of his or her natural right to freedom. Slaves do not produce for themselves—their labor is the entitlement and at the discretion of their owner. The West views a slave as an inheritable market item procured for private ends and subject to sale, purchase, or transfer with absolutely no control over his or her own destiny or that of any progeny.

Slavery is one of humanity's oldest social institutions, and various forms of servitude have existed throughout the world since ancient times. Defined by law and custom of the dominant society, slavery had various meanings within the social infrastructure that legitimized it, and it has been manifested in varying degrees throughout human history. In premodern times, slaves often had limited rights and some privileges, and they were incorporated into the family or the society that enslaved them. With the commencement of the transatlantic slave trade in the fifteenth century, however, there was a radical departure from earlier forms of human bondage.

The European mode of slavery removed all rights and dignities of the slave and was economically parasitic. Europeans sanctioned bondage based on skin pigmentation as criteria for perpetual servitude after the 1700s, and African captives were systemically dehumanized and were regarded as chattel. By the eighteenth century, "slave" had become synonymous with African.

The institution of slavery operated as an appendage to society, resulting in a class that was distinct from everyday citizenry. The slave was stigmatized as "other" and was marginalized by this position in all social interactions. A few slaves, however, did achieve acceptance once they were manumitted in the society that had enslaved them, and a few freed bond servants throughout the world attained prominence. Islam too, acknowledged this possibility. Bilal ibn Rabah, an Ethiopian slave and one of Islam's earliest adherents, became friend, adviser, and companion of Muhammad of Arabia, Islam's prophet. The slave also became the first mu'adhdhin (muezzin, or "caller of prayers"), an indispensable practice for Muslims.

The Qur'an, Islam's sacred text, accepts slavery on its legal basis because the practice existed before Muhammad's message. For centuries, the slave trade across northern Africa, Egypt, and Arabia was an aspect of commercial exchange, and among Africans and Arabs, it affected social behavior as well. But after the seventh century, when Islam advanced in Africa, Muslim Arabs and Africans over time exported an estimated 5–10 million Africans across the Sahara to the Muslim world and beyond. For the Qur'an to abolish the slave trade outright would have created strong resistance among the principals because of the trade's widespread social foundation. The Qur'an does stress humane treatment of slaves and expressly prohibits the enslavement of Muslims, but that fact was no guarantee that the injunctions received widespread acceptance, for there were African slaves in colonial America who were Muslim.

Islam was not hostile to slavery or to slave traders. Muslims constituted most of the western Sudan's slave traders, and Muslim societies were often the most systematic in the exploitation of slave labor. The slave trade was particularly important to Muslims after Islam's emergence as a world power following its spread over North Africa, Spain, and parts of Christian Europe, and Islam's control of key overland trade routes in Africa and to the Far East, where the slave trade flourished, provided incentive for the continuance of the institution.

The Qur'an, however, encourages freeing slaves or allowing them the possibility to manumit themselves. In effect, the Qur'an condones slavery but insists on kindness for the slave's welfare. "And those of your slaves who wish to enter into freedom purchasing contracts, accept their proposals if [their intentions] are any good and give of the wealth that God has given you. God is forgiving and merciful" (Ali, 1946).

Islamic slavery was more like earlier forms of slavery than the Eurocentric slave system. The Qur'an urges genial treatment of "those whom your right hand possess" and encourages slaveowners to take their slaves as spouses (or members of their extended family) and treat them with dignity as a measure to protect them (the owners) from shameful and undignified acts against their slaves' humanity. The Qur'an

A late-fifteenth-century Persian miniature shows African workmen helping to build Khawarnaq Castle.

also expressly makes provisions for the just treatment of female slaves whose honor should be uncontested. "And marry those who are single among your male slaves and . . . female slaves; . . . compel not slave-girls to prostitution when they desire cha[stity] . . . seeking frail goods of this world's life" (Ali, 1946).

A corpus of formal interpretations, or *fatwas,* based on the Qur'an arose within Islam that reconciled slavery as a "tolerable" condition but one that, over time, would disappear from human history. Hence, the Qur'an responded to slavery by acknowledging its historical context but "mitigated slavery by imposing specific guidelines toward maintenance and manumission" (Glasse, 1989). Qur'anic legal proscriptions regulate slave ownership as captives of war or as part of the preexisting trade before the revelation to Muhammad.

Early religious jurists interpreted sacred texts in a biased way in order to provide ideological parameters for the justification of slavery. This tendency was true for Christianity during the transatlantic slave trade, and Islam, like Christianity, was not antislave. Islam's approach, however, was to advocate legal temperance and tolerance. Thus, principals in both the trans-Saharan and the transatlantic slave trade—especially the latter—were able profit through the exploitation of the human condition with religious sanctions to underscore the forced migration of Africans.

The key to the growth of slavery was the rationale that the slavery system did not cost the state much, so it was justified as an inexpensive form of labor. Slavery's principal function, then, was to serve the needs of the state as large commodity markets expanded, for slavery made large-scale production possible in places where the number of people beyond the family system was low compared to the amount of land that could be cultivated.

Nonetheless, the Qur'an recognizes slavery as being ephemeral in human society and envisions its eclipse as society practices the moral and spiritual tenets of the faith. Although much of the modern world has eradicated the institution of slavery, there is evidence that in remote societies of Africa, the Middle East, India, and South America, some form of human bondage still persists today, despite the laws of the international community and efforts to abrogate its presence. So tenacious was slavery in Muslim Arabia, that it did not end there until Saudi Arabia's King Faisal enacted a decree with legal enforcement provisions in 1970.

—*Au'Ra Muhammad Abdullah Ilahi*

For Further Reading
Ali, A. Yusuf, ed. 1946. *The Holy Qur'an: Text, Translation, and Commentary.* Washington, DC: American National Printing; Glasse, Cyril. 1989. *The Concise Encyclopedia of Islam.* San Francisco: Harper and Row; Inikori, Joseph E., ed. 1982. *Forced Migration: The Impact of the Export Slave Trade on African Societies.* London: Hutchinson; Miers, Suzanne, and Igor Kopytoff, eds. 1977. *Slavery in Africa: Historical and Anthropological Perspective.* Madison: University of Wisconsin Press.

RACISM

The primary scapegoat of racism in the United States has been the peoples of the African diaspora. An orchestrated and methodical process of removal from spheres of economic access, political and social empowerment, and decision making has marginalized the African American experience in that society. Minimizing the direct participation of African Americans in government, the corporate world, education, and all levels of society has persistently made them second-class citizens from emancipation until recent decades.

Racist doctrine evolved in early colonial America to place humanity into compartmentalized groups based on distinctive physical, social, and mental traits, which presumably established a ranking founded upon the "unilinear evolutionist" thinking of the time. "Its practitioners [white supremacists] sought to delineate biocultural boundaries, coinciding with innate and heritable mental and moral differences," as justification for a polarization of the races that led to the subsequent exploitation and oppression of the darker races of the world (Inikori and Engerman, 1992).

The ideology of racism espouses a set of beliefs and practices that views the world as an exclusively cultural realm. Although an acceptable and universal definition of racism is difficult to ascertain among historians of race and slavery, one thing is common to writers on this subject: as a social practice in Europe and the Americas, racism eradicated the political, sociological, and natural rights of the peoples of the African diaspora and, to a lesser degree, other peoples of color.

Racism flourished during the capitalist-industrialist phase of economic development in the nineteenth century. It is an ideology that initially sought to justify slavery's existence as a principal means of cheap labor for the development of the precapitalist economic system and furthered that exploitation on the premise that Africans were the legitimate source of slaves because of heritable traits. The evolution of the doctrine was intricately intertwined with the development of slavery as that "peculiar institution" in the Americas that helped fuel the Industrial Revolution in both Europe and the United States.

The slave system was somewhat color-blind until religious, social, legal, and political legitimation within the infrastructure of the Americas became aligned with the racist doctrine fostered by environmentalist thinking of the nineteenth century (although the scientific fact of its efficacy is questionable). Nevertheless, slaves were a principal source of labor serving societies in the Americas as a particular social and political feature that furthered the development of racism in American society for various "justifiable" reasons.

Slaves also filled specific roles in economic development, market expansion, and the military as well as being public administrators and civil servants. They formed large-scale agrarian production units in the U.S. South and elsewhere in the Americas, and expansion (as in Manifest Destiny) was served by the spread of slave-based societies, which contained a substantial population.

The definition of slavery as practiced in the Western Hemisphere is most of all as a commodity, a piece of chattel, that has no exclusive rights or privileges over its labor, its fruits, or its own person. A slave, in effect, existed solely for the exclusive use of the owner. Nor did the slave have any natural, political, or legal rights to use in defense against an owner; further, the rights to property, marriage, and progeny belonged solely to owner—in effect, the slave had no humanity.

Historians are often at loggerheads when dealing with racism and slavery and slavery's aggregate components. To argue the question of which gave birth to the other may be ludicrous, however. According to historical accounts, racism might be more aptly defined as extreme ethnocentrism or xenophobia as it existed in some form or another in human history. However, the idea of a concerted effort to eradicate the African culture and religion and to exploit and subjugate the African is without historical precedent.

Racism has its roots in the legacy of the transatlantic slave trade, as it was that trade that created the ideology of white supremacy as a justification of or support for the "forced migration" of millions of Africans to the Americas and Europe. Supported by philanthropic venture-capitalists, governments, and the pseudoscientific race ideology of the Enlightenment; sanctioned by the church; and legitimized through the legal and social framework of the broader society, the transatlantic slave trade was by far the most insidious and dehumanizing form of slavery to have existed in history.

The impetus of that trade and the subsequent legitimation of slavery based on color was motivated by the need for an extensive slave labor pool to create the industrial system for the United States and expand the agrarian-based antebellum Southern economy. Thus, the principal motivations for the institution of slavery and its justification based on race lay in the realm of economics and political power. Slavery was the vehicle for the development of white racism, which sought to validate its existence and the right to exploit and subjugate peoples of the African continent through the systemic institutionalization of slavery in American society in the nineteenth century and beyond.

Racism emerged over time in the United States from the theory of the division of humanity into races that can supposedly be ranked according to criteria based on organic, genetically transmitted differences—whether real or imaginary. Focusing on these natural distinctions, racists made postulations that noted the presence or absence of certain socially relevant abilities or characteristics and alleged that these differences

> are a legitimate basis of invidious distinctions between groups socially defined as races . . . the existence of races in a given society presupposes the presence of racism, for without racism physical characteristics are devoid of social significance. It is not the presence of objective physical differences between groups that creates races, but the social recognition of such differences as socially significant or relevant (Van den Berghe, 1967).

Thus, racism is not valid since, historically, we know that groups with different physical distinctions coexisted prior to racist ideology in many parts of the world without a concerted effort to dehumanize based on those distinctions—even when enslaved.

The political reality of racist doctrine is only one aspect of that perception. Racist views are untenable and lack scientific verification. Racism is not an idea but an ideology and to have any social existence, it must have a set of conditions and conclusions that are assumed to have scientific justification. The concept of race as developed in the nineteenth century catapulted into an ideology and methodized criteria and parameters for its existence with supporting mechanisms that directed human behavior to ensure its continuity through internalized behavioral patterns that are instilled in and accepted by superior and inferior "races" in society.

During the years in the history of the United States when slavery became synonymous with Africa, African Americans constituted the largest visible group of nonwhites in society. In the nineteenth century and after the Civil War and emancipation, the scorn of racial exclusiveness was hurled at them and their legal status was yet to be defined. Since the nineteenth century, they have assiduously been targeted by racial policies that seek to control and minimize their contribution to and role in society. Since the ending of slavery, racial policies embedded in the fiber of American life have affected both the oppressor and the oppressed by giving the one a false sense of superiority and the other a false sense of inferiority.

The connection between slavery and racism and why this enigma has remained despite legal abolishment of the institution of slavery throughout the modern world over a century ago may lie in the sociological process. The mechanisms within the framework of society in the United States that have legitimized racism on a nonnative level, buttressed by legal sanctions over time, still remain so that, despite real attempts at legal redress, racism persists as a social plague that continually polarizes the society.

Over time, Western democracies have deliberately followed a continuous pattern of discrimination and separateness to foster societies that are, in effect, two societies. Apparent more in the continental United States than in any other industrialized nation, it can thus be said that "perhaps the most worrying legacy of African slavery in the New World is the persistent oppression of all people of African descent in the Americas [and Europe]" (Van den Berghe, 1967). Social attitudes, mores, and behavior prompted by racist ideology are the legacy of slavery in the Americas, a heritage that gave rise to the ideological framework that "justified" both slavery and racism in the United States.

The internalization of racist ideology—not only in the world of laws and social consensus that serve as signals for racist behavior and response but also in the incorporation of racist behavior within the psychic and thinking process of Americans—is the key to understanding the persistence of that ideology and the avenue to reform. Thus, in order to remedy the effects of racism in the United States, society must reeducate African Americans and European-Americans about the pitfalls of racist thinking.

—*Au'Ra Muhammad Abdullah Ilahi*

For Further Reading
Inikori, Joseph E., ed. 1982. *Forced Migration: The Impact of the Export Slave Trade on African Societies.* London: Hutchinson; Inikori, Joseph E., and Stanley L. Engerman, eds. 1992. *The Atlantic Slave Trade: Effects on Economies, Societies, and Peoples.* Durham, NC: Duke University Press; Miers, Suzanne, and Igor Kopytoff, eds. 1977. *Slavery in Africa: Historical and Anthropological Perspective.* Madison: University of Wisconsin Press; Van den Berghe, Pierre L. 1967. *Race and Racism: A Comparative Perspective.* New York: Wiley.

RAIMOND, JULIEN
(1744–1801)

Perhaps the wealthiest man of color in the eighteenth-century French Caribbean, Julien Raimond led a campaign against colonial racism that helped spark the Haitian Revolution (1792–1804). By the time of his death in 1801, this planter of one-quarter African descent had allied with Toussaint Louverture to make Saint Domingue a self-governing French territory where black, brown, and white planters directed the work of black ex-slaves.

Born in legitimate marriage in 1744 to a French immigrant and a free woman of color, Raimond was one of ten children. Well-read and highly articulate, he became an entrepreneurial planter, not a lawyer as some historians have speculated. In the 1770s, he and his brothers built medium-sized plantations to produce indigo dye for a thriving contraband trade. Widowed after a brief marriage to his first cousin, Raimond married a second time to Julie Dasmard Challe, a wealthy widow and the recognized daughter of a white planter and a slave woman. Raimond and his wife owned at least 100 slaves.

Although early colonial authorities regarded Raimond's mother as white, new racial laws and attitudes removed even wealthy free people of partial African descent from white society after 1763. In 1784, Raimond and his wife left Saint Domingue for France, partly to press the French government at Versailles for racial reforms. In 1789, he moved to Paris. Rejected by white absentee planters, Raimond and Vincent Ogé, another prosperous free man of color from Saint Domingue, became the leading mulatto spokesmen in revolutionary Paris.

Raimond helped make mulatto citizenship the French National Assembly's dominant colonial issue through publishing, speech making, and alliances with French abolitionists. On May 15, 1791, the National Assembly granted citizenship to wealthy men of color born to free parents, but Saint Domingue's whites refused to acknowledge the law. As the colony's white and free colored populations, nearly equal in size, began fighting each other, on August 22, 1791, Saint Domingue's slaves rose in revolt.

Raimond became even more active in Parisian politics. In letters and pamphlets he urged colonial allies to remain faithful to France, refuting accusations that the French had inspired the revolt in Saint Domingue. In April 1792, the National Assembly extended civil rights to all free men, regardless of color.

Imprisoned during the Reign of Terror in France in 1794, Raimond was exonerated of all charges against him, and he returned to Saint Domingue in 1796 as one of four revolutionary commissioners. France,

after years of revolt, had officially abolished slavery, and much of the colony was under Toussaint Louverture's de facto control. Raimond worked under Louverture to restore the colony's plantations with a system of involuntary, but compensated, field labor by ex-slaves. In 1797, he supported Louverture's attempts to remove Félicité Sonthonax, the governing white commissioner. Nevertheless, Raimond's association with the old mulatto planter class attracted much criticism, and in 1798, he returned to France.

Two years later, Napoleon Bonaparte named Raimond to a new colonial commission, again dealing with agricultural policy. French planters attacked Raimond for placing vacant estates under the control of black and brown proprietors, but Louverture named him to a committee charged with drafting an autonomous colonial constitution for Saint Domingue. Raimond died on October 17, 1801, apparently of natural causes.

—*John D. Garrigus*

See also
Haitian Revolution; Louverture, Toussaint; Rigaud, André

RAMSAY, JAMES
(1733–1789)

A prolific and highly influential antislavery propagandist, the Reverend James Ramsay was a pioneer in the late-eighteenth-century British campaign to abolish the Atlantic slave trade. The former West Indian slaveholder published 10 antislavery tracts between 1784 and 1789, and by disclosing the iniquities of colonial slavery, they captured public attention and provoked fierce ripostes from slavery's defenders. In proposing a plan for the amelioration of slavery and the abolition of the slave trade, and in framing the scheme as beneficial to Britain and to Caribbean planters and slaves, Ramsay armed people who had moral objections to slavery with pragmatic arguments and a concrete agenda for reform.

Away from public view, the Scottish-born surgeon and chaplain inspired and counseled the emerging abolitionist leadership, and his friendship with well-placed evangelicals facilitated the inclusion of abolitionism in a broader initiative to reform British morals and manners. Ramsay's calls in 1784 and 1785 for a parliamentary inquiry into the slave trade helped define the strategy adopted by Thomas Clarkson, William Wilberforce, and the Society for Effecting the Abolition of the Slave Trade (formed in 1787).

Ramsay owed much of his influence to an intimate acquaintance with Caribbean slavery. From 1762 to 1781, he served on St. Christopher (St. Kitts), where he attempted unsuccessfully to obtain slaveholder support for converting slaves to Christianity. Disgusted by the way slavery degraded both master and slave, Ramsay drafted a plan to ready slaves for the privileges and responsibilities of citizenship.

Ramsay hoped his manuscript would interest the bishop of London or the archbishop of Canterbury, both of whom he petitioned in 1778 for a post in England so he could prepare his work for publication. But he would not leave St. Christopher for England until 1781, the year his evangelical patrons, Sir Charles and Lady Margaret Middleton, secured for Ramsay a vicarage near their estate in Kent. With their guidance, Ramsay's manuscript, the first and most important of his antislavery tracts, was printed in 1784 as *An Essay on the Treatment and Conversion of African Slaves in the British Sugar Colonies*.

As with most of his writings (including those not on the subject of slavery), the work described religion and the rule of law, both of which Ramsay thought absent from West Indian society, as being necessary to the common good. Slaves, whose humanity and intellect Ramsay passionately defended, could serve neither their masters nor themselves effectively, in his view, without moral instruction and legal protection. Echoing an idea popularized by Adam Smith's *Wealth of Nations*, Ramsay argued that gradual emancipation would benefit planters by transforming slaves into self-motivated free laborers and would benefit Britain by enlarging the pool of consumers for British goods.

Attention to the likely consequences of reform characterized each of Ramsay's antislavery pamphlets. Abolition of the slave trade would not only force attention to the welfare of slaves in the West Indies but also foster trade with Africa in "legitimate" staple crops. This latter point was explained by Ramsay in *An Enquiry into the Effects of Putting a Stop to the African Slave Trade, and of Granting Liberty to the Slaves in the British Sugar Colonies*, which was also published in 1784.

Persistent attacks by slavery's apologists led Ramsay to burden his later tracts with defensive passages of little moment. But no other British campaigner in the early years of the movement possessed the expertise to produce pungent, detailed responses to the proslavery arguments as Ramsay did in his widely distributed *Objections to the Abolition of the Slave Trade with Answers* (1788). When committees of the Privy Council (1788–1789) and the House of Commons (1789) conducted inquiries into the slave trade and colonial slavery, Ramsay stepped forward with oral and written testimony. More pamphleteer and lobbyist than organizer or politician, Ramsay vested British antislavery efforts with rigor, sophistication, and savvy—a contribution that survived his death in 1789.

—*Christopher L. Brown*

See also
Atlantic Abolitionist Movement; Clarkson, Thomas; Wilberforce, William
For Further Reading
Schutz, John A. 1950. "James Ramsay, Essayist: Aggressive Humanitarian." In *British Humanitarianism: Essays Honoring Frank J. Klingberg*. Ed. Samuel Clyde McCulloch. Philadelphia: Church Historical Society; Shyllon, Folarin. 1977. *James Ramsay: The Unknown Abolitionist*. Edinburgh: Canongate; Watt, James. 1995. "James Ramsay, 1733–1789: Naval Surgeon, Naval Chaplain, and Morning Star of the Antislavery Movement." *Mariner's Mirror* 81 (2): 156–170.

RAPIER, JAMES THOMAS (1837–1883)

*J*ames Thomas Rapier was a teacher, newspaperman, planter, and congressman from Alabama and one of the most prominent African American politicians in the United States during the Reconstruction era. He was born in Florence, Alabama, in 1837 to John H. and Sally Rapier, both free blacks. His father was a barber, one of the few occupations legally open to free blacks in antebellum Alabama, and a very successful businessman. He accumulated substantial property, and most of his children received an education—out of the state, for it was illegal for free blacks to be educated in Alabama. At the age of 7, James Rapier was sent to live with his slave grandmother and uncle in Nashville, Tennessee, in order to attend school there. After receiving a basic education in Nashville, Rapier spent a year working on steamboats on the Cumberland, Mississippi, and Tennessee Rivers. At the age of 19, Rapier left the South and moved to Canada to continue his education at the Buxton School.

That school was located in Buxton, Ontario, a prosperous black utopian community of over 2,000 founded by ex-slaves in the late 1840s and home to Rapier's aunt and uncle with whom he lived. At first Rapier seemed preoccupied with acquiring material wealth through various business schemes, but after a religious conversion during a Methodist revival, he applied himself to his studies and determined to return to the South to aid enslaved blacks. Rapier left Buxton in 1860 and enrolled in a normal college in Toronto where he received a teaching certificate in 1863. After a year of teaching school in Buxton, Rapier returned to Nashville in 1864 to begin working among the newly freed blacks.

Rapier leased land for cotton planting and served as a correspondent for a Northern newspaper. With the end of the Civil War, Rapier became active in the fight for civil rights for the former slaves. The failure of the Tennessee state government to enact legislation guaranteeing black equality disgusted Rapier, and in 1866 he returned to Florence, Alabama. Renting several hundred acres of rich land, Rapier quickly became one of the most prosperous cotton planters in northern Alabama, and after the passage of the Congressional Reconstruction Act (1867), he actively recruited and organized black political activists in Alabama.

Rapier attended the first Republican state convention in Alabama and quickly became one of the party's most prominent leaders. In 1870, Rapier was the first black to run for statewide office (secretary of state) in Alabama, and although he was defeated in this first bid for political office, two years later he was elected as one of Alabama's representatives to the Forty-third Congress. While in the U.S. House of Representatives, Rapier became known for his fights for civil rights and educational opportunities for blacks and for efforts to improve transportation and commerce in Alabama. Rapier was defeated in his bid for reelection in 1874 and ran for Congress for the last time, unsuccessfully, in 1876.

Rapier devoted the remainder of his life to black labor organizations, encouraging blacks to migrate west, Republican Party politics, and raising cotton. In 1878, Rapier was appointed by Rutherford B. Hayes as collector of internal revenue for the Second District of Alabama, a position he held for the next four years. In 1883, James Rapier died in Montgomery, Alabama, of tuberculosis. Although he was only 45 years old at the time of his death, Rapier had lived a remarkably full life, not only as one of the South's most prominent Republican politicians, but also as a prominent symbol of African American accomplishments in the mid-nineteenth century.

—*James L. Sledge III*

For Further Reading
Schweninger, Loren. 1979. *James T. Rapier and Reconstruction.* Chicago: University of Chicago Press.

RAYNAL, ABBE GUILLAUME-THOMAS-FRANCOIS (1713–1796)

Credited with writing the most widely read antislavery work of his time, Abbé Guillaume-Thomas-François Raynal is said to have inspired the Haitian Revolution. Although he was an ally of France's colonial planters, his abolitionist reputation stems from his partial authorship of the controversial *Histoire philosophique et politique du commerce et des établissements des Européens dans les deux Indes,* especially the third edition of 1780, which was also published under his name.

Born in southwestern France in 1713, Raynal trained as a Jesuit. In 1747, before taking his final vows, he embarked upon a literary career in Paris. He quickly produced political histories of England and the Netherlands for the French government, and in the 1750s, became editor of the official literary journal *Mercure de France.* A familiar figure in Parisian salons, Raynal brokered literary assignments for Denis Diderot, Friedrich Melchior von Grimm, and other philosophes while writing for the Ministry of Foreign Affairs.

Raynal's *Histoire des deux Indes* developed from his connections with both the French foreign ministry and the Enlightenment. After France ceded Canada to Great Britain in 1763, Versailles began considering reforms to reduce imperial costs and encourage greater colonial loyalty. Simultaneously, colonial elites clamored for more autonomy. This debate inspired Raynal to write a history of European colonization; by 1765, Diderot was pursuing his own research for this project.

Only Jean-Jacques Rousseau's *Nouvelle Héloïse* and François-Marie Arouet Voltaire's *Candide* had a greater influence than the *Histoire des deux Indes* on the political and intellectual world of late-eighteenth-century France. Like Diderot's *Encyclopédie,* it was a multivolume project involving several authors. The Catholic Church condemned the first edition in 1770, which probably discouraged Raynal's co-contributors from revealing their involvement. Nevertheless the third edition, dated 1780, owed even more to Diderot, who may have written one-quarter of the text, and also contained the work of other encyclopedists.

The third edition was the largest, most controversial, and most popular version of the *Histoire*: 4,800 octavo pages surveying the history of European imperialism. Noting the work's ever more radical tone, the Parlement of Paris banned the 1780 edition and forced Raynal into exile. This censure triggered an enormous demand for the work, which soon appeared in as many as 50 different editions, many of them abridgments and translations.

Because of its diverse authorship, the *Histoire des deux Indes* broadcast two highly inconsistent messages. Inspired by colonial planters, Raynal criticized Versailles' trade and foreign policies, but his main concern was promoting French colonization. Additionally, the work attacked imperialism and slavery. Writing under Raynal's name, Diderot predicted that colonies would become independent and that slavery and inequality would give way to universal brotherhood. The prophetic style of these radical passages deepened their political impact, and they formed the core of most of the abridgments of the work. In prerevolutionary France, the abridgments functioned as instant popular oratory and were read aloud to illiterate audiences.

Accustomed to royal censorship, French audiences interpreted criticisms of colonial administrators or predictions of slave rebellion as hidden references to controversies in France itself. Yet the work also injected powerful rhetoric into debates over colonial policy. In the early 1790s, revolutionaries like Abbé Henri Grégoire, Jacques-Pierre Brissot de Warville, and Félicité Sonthonax, in arguing for the civil rights of wealthy free men of color, slipped into the visionary tone of the *Histoire* to predict a great Caribbean slave uprising.

That event did occur in Saint Domingue in August 1791, and it led to the establishment of the independent black nation of Haiti in 1804. By then, Raynal had fallen into revolutionary disfavor, but "his" prose was linked to the image of slave rebellion. Haitian tradition credits Raynal with inspiring Toussaint Louverture, who as a slave is said to have read the *Histoire*'s prediction that a black Spartacus would arise in the colonies. Ironically, Raynal and Diderot had plagiarized that passage from Louis-Sébastien Mercier's utopian novel *L'An 2440*, published in 1770. As governor of Saint Domingue in the late 1790s, Louverture had busts and portraits of Raynal displayed throughout Saint Domingue, and in Paris in 1797, Anne-Louis Girodet painted the Senegal-born Jean-Baptiste Belley, a slave elected to represent Saint Domingue in the French National Convention, leaning against a bust of Raynal.

Raynal died in Chaillot, France, in 1796, after five years of internal exile. Hailed as a hero in 1789 and 1790, he was vilified after a speech to the National Assembly in May 1791 in which he denounced popular sovereignty and called for greater power for the monarchy.

—*John D. Garrigus*

See also
Haitian Revolution; Louverture, Toussaint
For Further Reading
Benot, Yves. 1988. *La Révolution française et la fin des colonies (1789–1794)*. Paris: Editions La Découverte; Duchet, Michèle. 1977. *Antropologie et histoire au siècle des lumières*. Paris: Flammarion; Lüsebrink, Hans-Jürgen, and Manfred Tietz, eds. 1991. *Lectures de Raynal: L'histoire des deux Indes en Europe et en Amérique au XVIIIe siècle*. Oxford: Voltaire Foundation; Pluchon, Pierre. 1991. *Histoire de la colonisation française: Le premier empire colonial, des origines à la restauration*. Paris: Fayard.

REALF, RICHARD
(1834–1878)

A poet and radical abolitionist, Richard Realf became a member of John Brown's band of insurgents that hoped to liberate slaves in the United States by invading the mountainous regions of Virginia and inciting a slave insurrection. Realf abandoned the mission prior to Brown's attack on the federal arsenal at Harpers Ferry in 1859, and after the Civil War, he became a well-known poet who often described in verse the efforts to abolish slavery in the United States.

Realf was born in Sussex County, England, into a poor peasant family. He left home at age 17 to pursue a literary career and became a protégé of Lady Noel Byron, widow of the famous poet, George Gordon (Lord) Byron. Realf arranged through Lady Byron to settle on one of her estates in Leicestershire in order to learn estate management and cultivate his literary ambition.

But shortly after beginning his new career, he became the center of a scandalous event that underscored a central tension throughout his adult life: the romantic struggle between the "real" and the "ideal," between the worldly passions of the flesh and those of the mind and spirit. He fell in love with the eldest daughter of the estate, despite what he realized were "great [social] gulfs between us that could never be bridged." She became pregnant, and he, "desirous of finding some other place in which to dwell" and having "instincts" that "were democratic and republican," fled to the United States (Johnson, 1879).

Realf settled in New York City, worked briefly for the evangelical reformer Louis Pease at the House of Industry, and soon became a self-described "radical abolitionist," meaning that he sought the immediate abolition of slavery and was willing to go to great lengths to effect it. He went to Kansas in 1856 to help defend the territory against slavery, and in the following year he joined John Brown's company of revolutionaries. In 1858, the group met with some expatriate African Americans in Chatham, Canada, to recruit new members and to establish a "provisional constitution" to govern areas in the Southern part of the United States that Brown hoped to liberate from slavery. Realf was appointed secretary of state of Brown's provisional government.

Shortly after the Chatham meeting, however, Realf read Francis Wayland's *Limitations of Human Responsibility*, and that work caused him to abandon his radical abolitionism. The "book taught me," he said (Johnson, 1879), that certain ideals should never be acted upon. Instead of working to abolish the sins of the world, he now decided to escape them. In 1859, therefore, he began training to become a Jesuit priest at the Jesuit College at Spring Hill, Alabama, and the following year he joined a utopian Shaker community at Union Village, Ohio.

In 1862, Realf renewed his fight against slavery by joining the Eighty-Eighth Illinois Volunteer Infantry. He continued to write highly romantic verse, fashioned after that of Byron and Percy Bysshe Shelley, and some of his poems were published in *Atlantic* and *Harpers'* monthlies. His efforts to abolish slavery—whether while serving with John Brown or during his service with the Union army—represented the only sustained periods in which he was able to act on his spiritual and reform ideals and reconcile his struggle between the passions of the flesh and those of the mind and spirit.

In 1865, after his discharge from the Union army, Realf married Sophia Emery Graves. But he abandoned her within months and began making plans to join John Humphrey Noyes's Oneida, New York, utopian community, a community that practiced group marriage and a sacred form of free love. "I wanted always to live in accord with the Invisible Truth," Realf told Noyes, "and very many times it seems to me that the struggle in my nature between the beast and the seraph, the flesh and the spirit, was greater than I could bear." He wanted to escape the "howl of the beast" in a world "so very atheistic" and to "become alive to all righteousness" at Noyes's sacred community in Oneida (Johnson, 1879).

But Realf never made it to Oneida. He got as far as Rochester, New York, before succumbing to what he described as a "prolonged debauch" that included a bigamous marriage to a prostitute named Catherine Cassidy. He tried to abandon her as well, but she followed him wherever he went. After she caught up with him in San Francisco in 1878, Realf took a fatal dose of morphine, "as the only final relief" from her "incessant persecutions" (Johnson, 1879).

—*John Stauffer*

See also
Abolition, United States; Bleeding Kansas; Brown, John; Harpers Ferry Raid; Romanticism and Abolitionism; Second Great Awakening

For Further Reading
Hinton, Richard J., ed. 1898. *Poems by Richard Realf: Poet, Soldier, Workman*. New York: Funk and Wagnalls; Johnson, Rossiter. 1879. "Richard Realf." *Lippincott's Magazine* 3: 293–300; Realf, Richard. 1860. Testimony in "Mason Report." In U.S. Senate Committee, *Reports, 1859–60* (January 11–21), 91–113; Stimson, John Ward. 1903. "An Overlooked American Shelley." *Arena* 7: 15–26.

RECAPTIVES

Recaptives (also called "liberated Africans") were former slaves who had been commodities in the transatlantic slave trade before the slaving vessels they were being carried on were intercepted by the British African Squadron prior to reaching the slave markets in the Americas. Essentially, these slaves were recaptured after others had captured them once. The British Admiralty Court located in Freetown, Sierra Leone, used the term to refer to slave cargoes once it had condemned the slaving vessels and their crews. The term applied only after January 1, 1808, the date marking the legal termination of slave trading between Africa and the Americas for both British and U.S. citizens. The term was also used generically to identify slaves recaptured by U.S. and French squadron vessels.

Upon capturing vessels engaged in illegal slaving, the British, French, and U.S. governments, or their coastal agents, faced a dilemma. Generally, all slaves found onboard slavers were merchandise, and as such, had acquired the stigma of property and the status of slaves. Returning them to their places of origin would mean that they would likely retain that new status and become merchandise in future shipments from the African continent.

Another problem facing the captors was identifying the slaves' places of origin. Shippers generally sought entrepôts or bulking centers along the coast where they could purchase full cargoes of slaves and where they could realize a rapid turnaround of trade goods. In these cases, slaves often spoke the same language, a circumstance that made it easy to return them to embarkation points. But many shippers practiced *coasting*, methodically filling slave complements from many purchases along the coast. The latter method made it nearly impossible to return slaves to their places of origin. Rather than become embroiled in these complex and ethical questions, captors began landing liberated Africans at Freetown (British), Monrovia (United States), and Libreville (French).

Recaptives, especially those landed at Freetown, tended to become ideal subjects for acculturation and transformation attempts. Circumstances of initial capture, coastal sale, transportation, recapture, and landing at Freetown had traumatized these recaptives, which made them pliable for assimilation. Separation from family and known cultural patterns, religions, expectations, and language divisions created additional insecurities.

British officials at Freetown evolved a policy of regulating recaptives by assigning them to sponsors, either through apprenticeships, pawnships, or indentureships, or by bunching those with linguistic affinities in separate villages or suburbs close to Freetown. Often, recaptives remained in a condition of servitude similar to that practiced in early-nineteenth-century Britain.

Officials also encouraged various groups (African Institution, Church Missionary Society, Wesleyan Methodists) to establish schools or institutes for the purpose of transforming recaptives into productive subjects. Over time, the recaptives' mixture of languages, customs, and traditions and the assimilation and transformation efforts of officials and their agents helped create Freetown's Krio (Creole) culture.

—Bruce L. Mouser

See also
The African Institution; African Squadron; American Colonization Society; Apprenticeship; Bulking Centers; Church Missionary Society; Courts of Mixed Commission; Sierra Leone

For Further Reading
Clark, Robert. 1846. *Sierra Leone: A Description of the Manners and Customs of the Liberated Africans*. London: Ridgway; Fyfe, Christopher. 1962. *A History of Sierra Leone*. London: Oxford University Press; Porter, Arthur T. 1963. *Creoledom*. London: Oxford University Press; Wyse, Akintola. 1989. *The Krio of Sierra Leone*. London: Hurst and Company.

REPARTIMIENTO

The word *repartimiento* generally refers to one of the early systems of labor in the Spanish Empire. There has been some confusion as to the definitive meaning of the term, since it denoted different systems of labor in different parts of the empire at different times. In the Americas, the term referred to the allotment of the Indians as a source of forced labor. Generally, in the New World the terms *repartimiento, mita, cuatequil,* and *encomienda* became interchangeable.

The word *repartimiento* literally means "partitioning," and the Spaniards had undertaken the policy of partitioning land during the reconquest of the Iberian Peninsula (722–1492), when the newly conquered lands were divided among the Spanish nobility in reward for their services against the Moors. In the context of world slavery, *repartimiento* actually began with Christopher Columbus when he divided New World land and its native inhabitants among his Spanish comrades.

Although the Indians were not considered slaves by Columbus, his successor, Governor Francisco de Bobadilla, reportedly distributed Amerindians among the Spaniards who treated them as a labor force with very few restrictions. Subsequently, the concept of forced labor became official Spanish policy under Governor Nicolás de Ovando, as stipulated in his instructions from Queen Isabella I (dated December 20, 1503) concerning the native New World inhabitants.

It was at this point that the concepts of *repartimiento* and *encomienda* become intermixed. According to a strict interpretation, *repartimiento* applies to the division of the native American Indians into units, which were then allotted to the various Spanish nobles for use as labor, and *encomienda* refers to the grant by the crown of territory and the services owed by the people of the area involved to a specific individual. In this regard, *repartimiento* can be used to denote the method of establishing the Indian labor force (i.e., apportionment of Indian services) while *encomienda* can be used to refer to the governance of that labor force and its actual operation.

The official Spanish policy of *repartimiento* changed after the 1542 New Laws, which specifically outlawed Indian slavery, forced labor, and the establishment of new *encomiendas*. Although forced servitude legally ended, as a general rule Amerindian servitude did not. From 1542 onward, the meaning of *repartimiento* changed to mean the use of natives as a paid labor force, especially in mines, factories, and public works projects, with each Indian expected to contribute a certain number of days per year on public works.

The general format of the post-1542 *repartimiento* system was that a colonist who desired Indian labor for a particular project (such as agricultural harvesting) would submit his request to either the viceroy or the superior court on the basis that the use of the Indians would benefit the country. In most instances, an Indian village was required to provide 2–4 percent of its workforce for a large part of the year, and up to 25 percent during times of peak activity. Shifts were usually organized weekly so that the individual workers spent three or four weeks a year in the system with breaks of several months between shifts. Over time, the system gave way to new versions of servitude, including the *mita, yanaconaje,* and debt-peonage.

Although not significant in the context of labor or slavery, the word *repartimiento* has also been used to refer to the system of mandatary purchase of goods by the Indians from local Spanish officials, although this practice was eventually outlawed in the late-eighteenth century.

—H. Micheal Tarver

See also
Encomienda System; Latin America; *Mita; Yanaconaje*

For Further Reading
Bannon, John F. 1966. *Indian Labor in the Spanish Indies: Was There Another Solution?* Boston: Heath; Simpson, Lesley B. 1934–1940. *Studies in the Administration of the Indians in New Spain*. 4 vols. Berkeley: University of California Press.

THE REQUIREMENT

The opening paragraphs of "The Requirement," a legal document drafted in 1513 by a royal council of Spanish theologians led by Dr. Juan López de Palacios Rubios, one of the foremost jurors of his time, explain the Christian hierarchy of God, the pope, the Catholic monarchs and the fact that the pope "donated" half of the non-Christian world to Spain in 1493. The document was to be read aloud by a representative of each group of conquistadors when they confronted a new native people. If the natives accepted the Spanish monarch's right to dominate their lands, the representative was to announce:

> We in their name shall receive you in all love and charity, and shall leave you, your wives, and your children, and your lands, free without servitude, that you may do with them and with yourselves freely that which you like and think best, and they shall not compel you to turn Christian, unless you yourselves, when informed of the truth, should wish to be converted to our Holy Catholic Faith, as almost all the inhabitants of the rest of the islands have done. . . . [I]f you do not do this, and maliciously make delay in it, I certify to you that, with the help of God, we . . . shall make war against you in all ways and manners that we can, and shall subject you to the yoke and obedience of the Church and of their Highnesses; we shall take you and your children, and shall make slaves of them . . . and we shall take away your goods, and shall do you all the mischief and damage that we can, as to vassals who do not obey . . . and we protest that the deaths and losses which shall accrue from this are your fault, and not that of their Highnesses, or ours, nor of these cavaliers who come with us. (Parry and Keith, 1984)

The Requirement was read for the first time in the New World on June 14, 1514, by the notary Gonzalo Fernández de Oviedo (later the official chronicler of the Indies), who was marching with 300 troops led by Pedri Arias Dávila near Santa Marta in today's Colombia. Knowing that no Indians they might meet would understand the Castilian language or the complex concepts outlined in the document, Oviedo poked fun at the Requirement throughout his *Historia,* but he dutifully notarized each reading, even when the ritual was carried out in abandoned villages or done in a whisper from behind a tree. Oviedo explained that it worked best when read while plying the Indians with "food, drink, bonnets, cloth, shirts, hoods, and 'other little trifles from Castile'" (Hanke, 1949).

Subsequent scholars have also poked fun at the Spanish Requirement, but Patricia Seed, in a detailed comparison of the document with Islamic practices, makes a strong case for its sincerity and legitimacy as a summons to submission that "was not intended to be internally persuasive (as in a consensual relationship) but only to obtain external compliance" (Seed, 1995). When that external compliance was not forthcoming, the ritualized reading aloud, witnessing, and notarization of the Requirement justified, to the legalistic Spanish mind, war against the Indians and their subsequent enslavement.

—Lynne Guitar

For Further Reading
Hanke, Lewis. 1949. *The Spanish Struggle for Justice in the Conquest of America.* Philadelphia: University of Pennsylvania Press; Oviedo y Valdés, Gonzalo Fernández de. 1959. *Historia general de las Indias.* Madrid: Ediciones Atlas; Parry, John H., and Robert G. Keith, eds. 1984. *New Iberian World: A Documentary History of the Discovery and Settlement of Latin America to the Early Seventeenth Century.* New York: Times Books; Seed, Patricia. 1995. *Ceremonies of Possession.* Cambridge: Cambridge University Press.

RIGAUD, ANDRE (1761–1811)

The most prominent mulatto in the Haitian Revolution, André Rigaud symbolized the ambivalence with which France's colonial class of free people of color regarded the abolition of slavery and independence from Europe. Rigaud was a native of Saint Domingue's isolated South Province. His white father was a minor court official and petty landowner, and his mother was probably a slave. Rigaud apparently trained in Bordeaux, France, as a goldsmith and, according to tradition, served at the Battle of Savannah, Georgia (1779), with other French men of color. Like many free mulattoes in the colonial militia, Rigaud did not have official freedom papers.

After 1789, Rigaud emerged as a leader when wealthier free men of color demanded civil rights from revolutionary France. In July 1790, he was the secretary of one such mulatto group in his province and, later that year, helped lead some 500 men of color in an armed protest. French authorities imprisoned Rigaud and others in the colonial capital, Port-au-Prince, but in July 1791, rioters opened the jail. Rather than returning home, Rigaud joined other mulattoes in resisting white harassment and demanding the application of racial reforms approved in Paris. As violence between white and brown erupted outside Port-au-Prince, slaves in Saint Domingue's North Province rose in revolt.

France sent commissioners who relied on free men of color to fight slave rebels and white counterrevolutionaries. In July 1792, Rigaud helped negotiate peace between whites, mulattoes, and slaves in the southern part of the peninsula. By September 1793, he was the region's ranking revolutionary officer, fighting a British invasion from neighboring Jamaica. Within three years, the South Province was virtually an independent republic under Rigaud's control. Placing other men of color in key positions of authority and establishing a militarized form of field labor on local plantations, Rigaud was strong enough to expel French military officers from the peninsula in 1796. French officials were powerless to challenge this autonomy, since the rest of the colony was controlled either by British troops or by Toussaint Louverture's black soldiers.

Consolidating his power in mid-1799, Louverture accused Rigaud of racism, arrested mulatto landowners, and prepared to invade the South Province. The attack began in late August 1799. Nearly a year later, faced with an army almost three times the size of his own, Rigaud fled the colony. Louverture took Les Cayes, Rigaud's former capital, in August 1800.

Rigaud returned to Saint Domingue in 1801 with the military expedition of Napoleon's brother-in-law Gen. Charles Victor Emmanuel Leclerc but was soon deported by Leclerc. Rigaud was still in Europe when Haitian independence was declared in 1804, and he did not return to the southern peninsula until 1810. He established a republic there, distinct from the one run by Alexandre Pétion in Port-au-Prince and from Henri Christophe's empire in the north. Rigaud died in 1811, and his successor turned the seceded territory back to Pétion.

—*John D. Garrigus*

See also
Dessalines, Jean-Jacques; Haitian Revolution; Louverture, Toussaint

RILLIEUX, NORBERT (1806–1894)

By inventing what many people consider to be the most significant technological advancement in the history of sugar refining, Norbert Rillieux, a free octoroon (a person who is one-eighth black), dramatically changed the nature of labor on nineteenth-century sugar plantations. Having been born the son of a Louisiana sugar planter, Ril-

lieux was familiar with the refining process. Later as a student at L'Ecole Centrale in Paris, he devoted himself to the study of engineering and developed expertise in the emerging steam technology. Returning to Louisiana in 1840, he applied his knowledge of steam technology to sugar refining—gaining patents in 1843 and 1846 for variations of his multiple-effect vacuum pan evaporator.

Before Rillieux's technological breakthrough, plantations employed a wasteful and dangerous sugar-refining system known as "the Jamaica train." In this process, a series of large, open kettles were heated, and a line of slaves stood beside the hot steaming kettles pouring boiling sugarcane juice from one kettle to another. As the juice was passed along, it gradually became thicker and eventually crystallized. It was extremely uncomfortable work, and many slaves received disfiguring scars from the boiling juice. The process was slow, labor intensive, and wasteful of fuel and produced a poor-quality sugar.

Rillieux's invention applied the latent heat in the steam to economize on fuel. Using a partial vacuum, he was able to heat a number of kettles with the steam produced by the first. In addition to the obvious fuel savings, the system produced higher-quality sugar, and since the system was completely enclosed, it could be performed by one workman operating a few valves. The enormous savings made sugar production very profitable. Producers were able to lower prices and thus make fine-quality sugar affordable to a much larger market, which in turn drastically increased demand.

In order to feed this growing market, sugar plantations expanded, and thus the demand for slaves to grow and harvest the sugarcane increased. Although Rillieux's invention ended the unpleasant and wasteful system of the Jamaica train, it caused the sugar industry to expand and resulted in greater economic incentives to defend the plantation economy. As the slavery system became progressively more difficult to maintain, greater restrictions were placed on all people of color, which made life in Louisiana increasingly difficult for Rillieux.

Having profited significantly from his patents in the United States, Rillieux returned to France in 1854 and developed an interest in Egyptology. His interests in evaporation and sugar machinery were rekindled later in life, however, and in 1881 he patented a system for heating juice with vapors in multiple effect, a system that is still used in sugar refineries today.

—*Mark Cave*

For Further Reading
Heitmann, John Alfred. 1987. *The Modernization of the Louisiana Sugar Industry 1830–1910.* Baton Rouge: Louisiana State University Press; Klein, Aaron E. 1971.

The Hidden Contributors: Black Scientists and Inventors in America. New York: Doubleday and Company; Meade, George P. 1946. "A Negro Scientist of Slavery Days." *Scientific Monthly* 62: 317–326.

RIO BRANCO LAW
See Law of Free Birth

ROM (GYPSY) SLAVERY

The Romany people, or Gypsies (Rom; plural, Roma), arrived in Europe about A.D. 1300, having migrated from India three centuries earlier when they were forced westward by Islam's expansion. The enslavement of the Roma in the Balkans is the most extensively documented, but Gypsies have been enslaved at different times in other settings. In Renaissance England, Edward VI passed a law stating that Gypsies be "branded with a V on their breast, and then enslaved for two years," and if they escaped and were recaptured, they were then branded with an S and enslaved for life (Hancock, 1987). According to a 1538 Spanish decree, Gypsies were enslaved to individuals in perpetuity as a punishment for escaping from slavery or servitude.

Spain began shipping Gypsies to the Americas in the fifteenth century, and Columbus transported three to the Caribbean on his third voyage in 1498. Spain's later American solution involved shipping Gypsy slaves to that country's eighteenth-century Louisiana colony. An Afro-Gypsy community survives in St. Martin Parish, Louisiana, and reportedly another exists in central Cuba, both descended from intermarriage between the two enslaved peoples.

Portugal shipped Gypsies as an unwilling labor force to its sixteenth-century colonies in Maranhão (part of present-day Brazil), Angola, and even India, the Roma's native country. They were made slaves of the crown in eighteenth-century Russia during Catherine the Great's reign, and in Scotland, they were employed "in a state of slavery" in the coal mines. Both England and Scotland shipped Roma to Virginia and the Caribbean as slaves during the seventeenth and eighteenth centuries; John Moreton, in his *West India Customs and Manners* (1793), described seeing "many Gypsies [in Jamaica] subject from the age of eleven to thirty to the prostitution and lust of overseers, book-keepers, negroes, &c. [and] taken into keeping by gentlemen who paid exorbitant hire for their use."

The arrival of the Romany people in Western Europe during the Middle Ages resulted from the Ottoman takeover of the Byzantine Empire and subsequent expansion into the Balkans. Carried into southeastern Europe with the Turkish expansion, the Gypsies found an agricultural economy that sorely needed technical skills. In Walachia (now part of Romania) especially, they found employment with feudal landowners as metalworkers and carpenters. With the new regime came a gradual shift to a market-based economy and a correspondingly greater demand for, and reliance upon, artisan labor. As the burden this placed upon the Roma increased, they began moving away from Walachia and Moldavia (also part of modern Romania) into the rest of Europe; the response was to introduce legislation making Roma the property of their employers, and thereby for it to be illegal for them to leave. Thereafter, their slavery became steadily more deeply entrenched in the social system until its abolition over five centuries later.

By the early-fourteenth century, Gypsies were being bought and sold and presented as gifts from one estate or monastery to another; in 1654 the civil code of Vasile (Basil the Wolf) of Moldavia included specific laws defining their status as slaves. These were divided into "field" and "house" slaves belonging to the court, the church, and landowners. Slaves were also divided by the tasks they performed (e.g., blacksmiths, spoon makers, gold washers, and grooms). Each category had its own name, but the general word for "slave" was Tsigan. (In 1995, Tsigan was adopted by the Romanian government as the official word for Roma since, it was argued, "Roma" sounded too much like "Romanian" and the outside world might confuse the country's European population with the nonwhite Gypsies.)

Slaves could not marry without permission, and it was illegal for the church to perform Gypsy marriages. Children resulting from the rape of Gypsy women by their owners were automatically slaves. Punishments included flaying the soles of the feet with whips; cutting off lips, noses, or ears; being forced to wear a spiked collar; and, not uncommonly, being flogged to death. A Gypsy child sold for the equivalent of about 50 cents in the 1500s, and by the early-nineteenth century, slaves were being sold by weight—one gold piece per pound.

Abolition of Rom slavery came in the mid-nineteenth century as a response to the abolition of slavery in the Americas and because mechanization was making slavery impractical. Abolition was instituted briefly by an interim government in 1837, but slavery was reinstituted almost immediately. It began to be abolished in Moldavia in December 1855 and in Walachia in February 1856, the last law being finally rescinded in 1864.

Following abolition, former owners were paid for their loss, but no effort was made to reorient or educate the freed slaves or to bring them into society. The centuries of dehumanization have indelibly colored Romanian attitudes toward the Roma, who today number some 3 million in that country and are subject to virulent and growing racist aggression.

—Ian Hancock

For Further Reading
Hancock, Ian. 1987. *The Pariah Syndrome: An Account of Gypsy Slavery and Persecution.* Ann Arbor, MI: Karoma Publishers.

ROMAN EMPIRE

The Roman Empire (44 B.C.–A.D. 476) included the territory within the bounds of modern Armenia, Iraq, the Red Sea, Egypt, and the Sahara in the east and south to the Atlas Mountains, the Atlantic Ocean, the Danube, the Rhine, and England in the north and west. For most of the period, Italy was the empire's political and economic heartland. After A.D. 395, the empire's eastern half—with its capital at Constantinople (modern Istanbul)—became a separate polity. Conventional population estimates of the Roman Empire in the first century A.D. stand at approximately 60 million people.

Slavery existed in all provinces of the empire; although slave labor coexisted with free labor, slaves worked in nearly every area of production, commerce, administration, and the arts. The period's Greek and Latin literature is replete with the mention of slaves, ranging from offhand remarks to detailed instructions for slave breeding, training, and employment to philosophical reflections on slavery. Slaves are fully represented in inscriptions, and an enormous and influential body of slave law matured during the empire period. These sources not only testify to slavery's importance in Roman imperial life but also provide material for a social and economic history of slavery that is unparalleled for any other ancient society.

Slaves came from inside and outside the Roman Empire's borders. Some evidence suggests a rise in the breeding of slaves, but the empire benefited from a ready supply of prisoners of war. Kidnapping remained another source of slaves as did the sale of children and self-sale. Thus, slaves were drawn from all regions and peoples of the empire; servile status was often regarded as an intellectual and a moral handicap but not as a function of ethnicity or race.

Slaves were still their masters' chattel. Severed from their own communities, slaves were almost completely deprived of legal and public rights, and they were subject to beatings, torture, and sexual abuse. Masses of rural slaves often spent the night in slave pens (*ergastula*).

Perhaps as positive inducement to cooperation, slaves could be freed relatively easily in the empire. Masters emancipated some in wills; others, in front of magistrates. Slaves could also buy their freedom with their *peculium*, which was legally a portion of the master's wealth set aside for the slave's use and, in essence, the slave's own property. Unlike slaveholding societies in ancient Greece, Roman ex-slaves readily became citizens and thereby enjoyed legal equality with their former masters.

Ex-slaves, nevertheless, occupied a social status between slaves and the freeborn and could still be tied to their masters through social or economic obligations. Many occupations that were regarded as improper for slaves were often given to freedmen, for example, that of a Roman firefighter. Some ex-slaves rose to powerful positions in the emperor's court, others obtained great wealth, and many left behind inscriptions and monuments in both the city and the countryside.

As in the Roman Republic, large and middling landowners employed slaves on their farms and estates. Slaves plowed the land, tended vines and olive groves, and engaged in rural industries like wine and olive-oil production. Slaves were frequently shepherds and herdsmen. Roman law regarded agricultural slaves as a farm's *instrumenta vocalia* ("speaking equipment"), and as such, they could be leased to tenants with other farm equipment, although tenants might supply their own slaves.

A *vilicus* or bailiff, himself a slave, oversaw a large, slave-run estate. Ideally the *vilicus* not only worked alongside his staff but also bought farm necessities, sold farm produce, kept accounts, and performed religious duties. Imperial agricultural writers emphasize the proper instruction of the *vilicus* and his wife, the *vilica,* who also played a supervisory role on the farm. The *vilicus* and *vilica* occupied a privileged position among agricultural slaves: they married and often had a *peculium* and the use of their master's resources. Indeed, the *vilicus* of a large private or imperial estate may often have had more access to money and power than a free but poor farmer.

Citizens who held only a small number of slaves probably never disappeared from the Roman countryside, although evidence for Italy itself is scarce. One first-century poem attributed to Vergil, the *Moretum,* which may refer to contemporary Italy, describes a poor farmer with a patch of land and a garden. He owns a single slave, although the poem does not specify her duties.

Also in the countryside, there were slaves who mined precious metals or worked in quarries. Mining

This engraving, after a Pompeian wall painting, shows a slave being flogged in the Forum at Pompeii.

labor forces—usually owned by the state—seem to have differed according to local conditions. Imperial authorities contracted some mines out to free workers while in others they worked prisoners to death. In still others, slaves seem to have lived a tolerable existence.

Slaves naturally worked as menial servants in urban domiciles of the rich. The household of Rome's city prefect in A.D. 61 consisted of 400 slaves. The caricatured ex-slave Trimalchio in Petronius's *Satyricon* has scores of slaves around him to pick up fallen objects, carry him, offer their hair as towels, massage him, and make music. It was common in larger households for the master to entrust slaves with care of the family silver or the mistress's jewelry. Slaves also commonly served as doctors and teachers attached to the great households.

Whether dependents of powerful families or not, slaves thrived in the urban markets and craft shops of Rome and the Italian towns. Slave potters signed their work; some servile sellers of wine, salted fish, and sandals might have worked independently but turned over a portion of their profits to their masters. Some captains of seagoing vessels were slaves, and slave bankers financed some trade. One of the triumphs of

Roman law was the detailed attention given to contracts made with, and to the liability of, slaves in commerce.

One far-reaching development in slavery under the empire was the importance of slaves owned by the emperor. Hundreds of imperial slaves maintained Rome's extensive water-supply system, the state mint had numerous specialized slaves, and the prefect of the grain supply had under his authority slave officials in the markets and *vilici* who oversaw state warehouses in the port of Ostia. Imperial *vilici* managed the emperor's estates, which in some cases had large staffs, including slave doctors, painters, builders, and stewards. Some imperial slaves became wealthy, some of them even owned other slaves *(vicarii),* and some of the wealthy slave men married freewomen.

It is clear from the sources that these varieties of slavery existed in the provinces as well as in Italy itself. Greek writers of the imperial period speak of smaller farmers owning slaves in the traditional manner, and the Greek provincial aristocracy and middle farmers also owned slaves. North Africa had large, slave-run estates, but it is impossible to know their specific importance to the economy any more than that of similar estates in Gaul or Spain. Peasants tied to the land may have farmed parts of Anatolia (part of modern-day Turkey). The situation was similar in much of the rest of the empire, and our knowledge about slavery in the provinces does not increase as the political importance of Italy decreased in the Christian era. Only in Egypt are there hundreds of papyri from the Roman period that demonstrate that slavery played a negligible role in cultivation.

Ancient historians have debated at length the importance of slavery during the late antique period (following Diocletian's reforms after A.D. 284). Some scholars believe that over the course of the empire, the free poor (coloni) were gradually debased to slave (servi) status, seeking protection from and ties of dependence to the wealthy, and that slaves were often settled as quasi-independent farmers on plots of their masters' estates. Fourth-century documents show evidence for these processes, but it is unlikely that agricultural slavery was completely replaced. Some late imperial sources speak of slave labor on the land as the norm.

Domestic slavery is attested to throughout the late empire and after its collapse and replacement by barbarian kingdoms in the west after A.D. 410. Nevertheless, there can be little doubt that the origins of the medieval serf lie in the large, semiservile population of the late Roman Empire.

—*Alexander Ingle*

See also
Columella's *De re rustica*; Roman Republic
For Further Reading
Bradley, Keith. 1994. *Slavery and Society at Rome.* Cambridge: Cambridge University Press; Giardina, A., and A. Schiavone, eds. 1981. *Societe la produzione schiavistica.* Rome and Bari: Laterza and Figli; Vogt, Joseph, et al., eds. 1967–1994. *Forschungen zur antiken Sklaverei.* 12 vols. Weisbaden and Stuttgart: Steiner; Vogt, Joseph, and Brockmeyer, Norbert. 1983. *Bibliographie zur antiken Sklaveri.* Bochum, Germany: Studienverlag Dr. N. Brockmeyer.

ROMAN LAW

Roman influence has been fundamental to the legal history of slavery in much of the Western world. Originating in the Roman Republic and the Roman Empire, the Roman-based law of slavery, in innumerable permutations, was pervasive in parts of Europe until the late medieval period and in the European colonies until the late-nineteenth-century abolition of slavery in Brazil.

Even before the eastern Roman Empire declined, the slave law of Rome had an almost 1,000-year history. The earliest known Roman code relating to slavery is the Twelve Tables, which dates to approximately 450 B.C. During the republic and early empire, magisterial edicts, imperial orders, and occasionally senatorial decrees affected the structure, application, and evolution of Roman slave law. Though a few legal texts exist from the first two centuries A.D., no formal and comprehensive compilation of law, including laws pertaining to slavery, appeared before the Theodosian Code (Codex Theodosianus) was assembled in A.D. 435. Finally, the Byzantine emperor Justinian issued the Corpus Juris Civilis (or, the Justinian Code)—composed of the Code, Digests, Institutes, and Novels—around 540. The Corpus Juris Civilis, which covered the general government of the Byzantine Empire, included significant portions dealing with slavery.

Codification efforts in the eastern Roman Empire were principally a compilation of what was known and practiced of classical law. In the codes, the regulation of slavery was central to the law of property, and slaves were considered simultaneously to be chattel and human beings. Conditions under which manumission could occur or testimony could be given, the status of freed persons, punishments, marriages between individuals of unequal status, and the limited rights of slaves to control property were the principle subjects of legal discourse.

Through the Justinian Code, the impact of earlier Roman law was projected forward into the second millennium. In the European Mediterranean kingdoms, where slavery persisted throughout the early and late medieval periods, the Justinian Code formed the basis of most local slave law. Elements of Roman slave law were even sometimes to be found in Germanic societies—perhaps partially the legacy of Roman scribes employed by the Germanic conquerors of Italy or the legacy of Roman conquests in the Danube region. The distinctive features of Roman slave law retained in Western Europe included adaptability to local conditions and the relative ease of manumission by testament of the owner or self-purchase.

The colonization of the New World by Spain, Portugal, and France led to the institution of slavery on a scale not known to Europeans since the fall of Rome. The enslavement of Africans and Amerindians led to reinventions of European customary law and codifications based on the Justinian Code.

In the Spanish and Portuguese colonies, one key link between the Justinian Code and New World slave law was the Siete Partidas, which originated in mid-thirteenth-century Castile. The Portuguese legal code that was formulated to regulate slavery in Brazil, the Ordenaçoes Filipinas, incorporated several aspects of the Castilian law, and in Spanish North America, a genealogy of law can be traced from colonial law to the

Siete Partidas to the Justinian Code. In contrast, the various forms of the Code Noir established in the French West Indies, Louisiana, and Canada between the late-seventeenth and mid-eighteenth centuries have the fewest intermediary medieval European antecedents and represent the most direct reinvention of slave law based on unmediated Roman codes.

—*William H. Foster III*

See also
Code Noir; Justinian, Laws of; Twelve Tables

For Further Reading
Buckland, W. W. 1969. *The Roman Law of Slavery.* New York: AMS; Grubbs, Judith Evans. 1995. *Law and Family in Late Antiquity.* Oxford: Clarendon; Phillips, William D., Jr. 1985. *Slavery from Roman Times to the Early Transatlantic Trade.* Minneapolis: University of Minnesota Press; Watson, Alan. 1989. *Slave Law in the Americas.* Athens: University of Georgia Press.

ROMAN REPUBLIC

Systematic slavery was fully developed in Rome at least as early as 450 B.C. when the legal code of the Twelve Tables was promulgated. This code includes discussions of slaves as possessions (the word *pecunia*, "money" or "chattel," is used once to refer to a slave); freedmen (freed slaves) and their duties toward their former owners; disputes over "the freedom of a human being"; punishment of criminal citizens by delivery for sale into slavery outside of Rome; the permissible sale of sons into slavery by their fathers; the testamentary freeing of slaves; and varying penalties for assault or theft depending on the victim's status as free or slave.

The earliest form of slavery in the Roman Republic was debt-slavery, in which a male citizen and/or members of his family worked for a creditor. If the debt was not paid within 30 days, the debtor could be sold "across the Tiber" (outside the city). This form of slavery was technically illegal by the fourth century B.C., but it still occurred informally in the late republic.

The second major kind of early slavery involved persons captured in warfare who were considered to belong to their captors. Rome enslaved war prisoners en masse and sold them for the benefit of the public treasury in Rome. Captives who were not ransomed were transported to Rome and sold, or sold immediately to dealers who would subsequently hold an auction in the area of the battle.

Children born to slaves belonged to the slaveowner, marriages between slaves were not legally recognized, and no law prohibited the breakup of slave families. Pirate traders frequently kidnapped travelers in the Mediterranean and sold them as slaves; even upper-class citizens were sometimes victimized (Julius Caesar was once kidnapped by pirates, but ransomed). Long-distance trade with peoples beyond the frontiers of Rome's expansion included a trade in slaves, and Black Sea residents supplied foreign slaves for the Mediterranean from the seventh century on. Infants left near the walls of Rome by parents too poor to support them were often adopted and raised by slave dealers, trained and sold (extant contracts show six- and seven-year-old children being sold on their own). Female children were frequently left in this way, which attracted brothel owners.

The ratio of free people to slaves in the republic was sometimes as low as 2 to 1. At the end of the republic, between 65 and 30 B.C., about 100,000 new slaves were sold or born in Italy each year. Geographic origins of slaves were as varied as the wars the Romans fought in the Mediterranean: in earlier periods and even later, Italian slaves from wars against allies and neighboring cities and regions predominated, but beginning with the First Punic War (264–241 B.C.), slaves from Carthage in North Africa, Greece, and the eastern Mediterranean began to enter Rome in great numbers. The siege of a single city could yield more than 20,000 slaves.

Common geographic origins of slaves during the republic included Gaul (entire Alpine tribes were sold into slavery after military victories); Britain (starting in the first century B.C.); Spain (site of wars throughout the period of the republic); the Danube basin (modern Germany and central Europe); the Black Sea area, Greece, and the Balkans (Corinth was destroyed in 146 B.C., and steady warfare occurred in Macedonia, Epirus, and Illyria—roughly modern-day Macedonia, Albania, and northwestern Greece); and Ionia (today the western coast of Turkey). There was a very small influx of Egyptian slaves into Rome during most of the republican period, but the chief permanent Mediterranean slave markets were Rhodes and Delos, which were said to have moved tens of thousands of slaves daily in the second century B.C. Goods given to dealers in exchange for slaves included salt and grain (in the Black Sea) and Italian wine (Gaul and North Africa).

No occupations were designated as off-limits to slaves. Slaves with occupational specialties (e.g., woodworking, stonecutting, baking, knowledge of Greek philosophy, medicine) were actively sought by owners of slaves. In a treatise on farming by Cato the Elder written in the second century B.C., several classes of slaves on a large farm are distinguished. The field-workers, who were poorly educated, were given daily portions of bread, wine vinegar, fish paste, and olive oil and sometimes worked on a chain gang. Female slaves not working in the fields carded wool, wove,

An African slave waits on a Roman mother and child reclining on a couch.

sewed, mended, and did other tasks associated with textile production (textiles produced were sometimes sold beyond the individual farm); made baskets and farm implements, bread, and cheese; and harvested grain, olives, and grapes. The male overseer and his wife lived in separate quarters from the other slaves and were responsible for bookkeeping, renting out slaves when feasible, sales and purchases of produce, legal management (which eventually included representing the owner in court by proxy), security, and the general productivity of the farm.

In a city home, the slaves' work might be less physically demanding. For instance, slaves worked as personal secretaries, teachers of children and adults, personal attendants and hairdressers, cooks, scribes, gardeners, and in various business capacities. The *paedagogus,* or tutor, was a literate slave assigned to guard from physical danger and monitor the behavior and morals of a young male member of the household as he went to school; often the emotional bond between tutor and charge lasted into the adulthood of the boy.

Both city and country slaves were subject to physical violence and sexual advances from owners and other members of the household, and it was legal for any owner to kill a slave. Slaves (like sons and daugh-

ters of the household) could not legally own money or property. Informally, however, slaves sometimes accumulated personal wealth—a *peculium* ("little flock," a portion of the master's wealth set aside for the slave's use), which might be saved to purchase the slave's freedom at a price set by the owner. Some slaves bought businesses or other slaves with their funds, although by law, all possessions of slaves belonged to the master.

The freeing of a slave within his or her lifetime was always possible. Slaves could be informally manumitted by their owners, but this form of manumission did not give the former slaves citizen rights. Formal manumission, on the other hand, did confer the citizen rights of a freedman *(libertus).* Formal manumission took place by census (the owner of the slave would purposely neglect to list the slave as one of the household), by formal emancipation before a magistrate (through a procedure in which a colluding third party and the owner claimed that the slave was actually a free person wrongfully held as a slave), or by testamentary will of the owner.

If male, a freed slave could vote but was classified in such a way that his vote was not effectual; any freed slave, whether male or female, could make contracts, get married, and leave a will, but the freedmen could not run for public office in Rome. The children of freed slaves had full citizen rights, however, which made the reintegration of ex-slaves into Roman society possible. Most freedmen continued to owe services of various kinds, and sometimes money, to their former owners. Slaves were sometimes freed for the express purpose of marriage to the owner: when this happened, the freed slave was not permitted by law to initiate divorce.

The life of an educated slave might not change drastically with his or her freedom: Cicero's slave bookkeeper and literary assistant, Tiro, continued working after his freedom, and when Cicero died, Tiro edited his letters and speeches. Slaves paid homage to the deity of the father of the household in which they served, but they were not necessarily expected to give up their own deities. Thus, the worship of non-Roman deities began in Rome through their slave and freedmen adherents, as was the case perhaps with the worship of Bacchus, Isis, and the gods of the Syrians and Jews.

Escapes of individuals were frequent, and to prevent them, slaves were often branded or had metal slave collars put on them. Suicides were fairly common. Few large-scale revolts are recorded, the earliest being the Secessions of the Plebs at Rome (a significant event when the plebians left the city to demand rights) in the fourth century B.C., in which debt-slavery was technically abolished.

There were large-scale revolts in Sicily in 139–132 and 104–100 B.C., probably because of the many agricultural slaves there. In 133–129, Aristonicus (d. 128), who claimed to be the son of Eumenes II (d. 160?) of the ancient Greek kingdom of Pergamum, led a popular rising against the new ruler of Pergamum (Rome) and appealed to slaves to join him, supposedly in founding a new utopian state, Heliopolis. The revolt of Spartacus (73–71 B.C.) in southern Italy eventually drew the participation of over 100,000 slaves. The slaves defeated Roman soldiers led by consuls in several battles before they were finally defeated by Crassus. After their defeat, 6,000 captured slaves were crucified along the Appian Way.

—*Jerise Fogel*

See also
Peculium; Spartacus; Twelve Tables
For Further Reading
Bradley, Keith. 1994. *Slavery and Society at Rome.* Cambridge: Cambridge University Press; Wiedemann, Thomas. 1981. *Greek and Roman Slavery.* Baltimore: Johns Hopkins University Press.

ROMAN ROAD CONSTRUCTION

Starting with Appius Claudius Caecus, who built the first leg of the Appian Way (Via Appia) in 312 B.C., the Romans constructed a vast network of hard-surface roads that connected the many cities and towns of the empire with one another. Since land transportation was relatively expensive for the movement of goods (water transport being much preferred), the chief purpose of these roads was to allow for the rapid movement of Roman military forces from one region to another. Most of the existing Roman roads were constructed during the imperial period and were a part of a vast public works program that emperors undertook to meet the needs of the state, enhance their own prestige, and provide employment for the poorer members of Roman society. Since Rome was a society largely based on slave labor, slaves occasionally worked on the construction and the maintenance of these roadways.

In *Silvae,* the Roman poet Publius Papinius Statius left us a description of the work involved in building the Via Domitiana, a Roman road that was a shortcut along the Via Appia between Sinuessa and Pozzuoli. He noted the great numbers of men required for tracing the furrows, digging trenches, cutting down trees, clearing the ground, smoothing the outcrops of rock, and planing great beams. Most of the difficult work involved quarrying the stones and carrying them to where they were needed. In addition to the large number of men needed for digging and carrying, the building of a road required the use of skilled laborers, including woodworkers, quarrymen, carpenters, and stonemasons.

The Roman army generally took responsibility for building and maintaining the main arteries, but there is relatively little information on how the labor force used in Roman road building was organized. The army was the only institution that could provide skilled civil or military engineers who had the knowledge and expertise to plan and supervise construction, and these individuals were often veteran volunteers *(evocati).* Roman army soldiers were generally used for much of the actual physical work as it was considered a regular part of their military duties. However, this type of hard physical labor was not popular among the troops, and there are reports of soldiers mutinying because they had to do roadwork. Whenever possible, the army supplemented its workforce with conscripted civilian labor.

There is no specific information on the amount of slave labor used in the construction of Roman roads, but it is likely that the percentage would vary depending on the availability of local labor and the time period concerned. It is probable that a significant number of the workers used as unskilled laborers and quarrymen were either slaves, condemned criminals, or prisoners of war organized into chain gangs. To maintain a high level of work efficiency, these laborers were treated as well as the soldiers. Many of the slaves were owned either by the state or by wealthy individuals. There is evidence to suggest that artisans in Roman Egypt regularly kept two or three slaves, and if such a practice were universal, it is conceivable that artisans employed in road building would have brought their slaves along.

The Romans acquired large numbers of prisoners of war as a result of the wars of conquest and battles fought against barbarians along the empire's frontiers. During the second and first centuries B.C., large numbers of slaves flowed into Italy as a result of Rome's conquest of the eastern Mediterranean. At that time, slave labor was cheap and relatively plentiful. During the imperial period, when the major wars of conquest had been completed, there were far fewer slaves acquired from military action, and many of the slaves were the result of natural childbirth from persons already enslaved. Eventually the price of slaves became too high for them to be used profitably as unskilled labor, so many of them were then employed in skilled jobs in agriculture or as craftsmen and artisans. This trend was further fueled by the breeding of slaves, which ensured that the sons of skilled slaves would follow them in their trades.

Roman roads were relatively well maintained during the first two centuries of the imperial era, but during the fourth century they fell into a state of disrepair owing to a lack of labor and money to pay for the repairs. Roman law in the later empire placed responsibility for road repair on the local civilian population, including the church—although senators and veterans were exempt from this responsibility. In the later empire, slaves were prevalent in the imperial factories but their use in agriculture survived only as a relic of the past, with slaves working side by side with tenant farmers and being socially and economically indistinguishable from them. Throughout the Roman era, the employment of slaves in chain gangs to carry out unskilled labor occurred only in exceptional circumstances.

—*John F. Shean*

See also
Pax Romana; Roman Empire; Roman Republic
For Further Reading
Chevallier, Raymond. 1976. *Roman Roads*. London: B. T. Batsford; Jones, A. H. M. 1956. "Slavery in the Ancient World." *Economic History Review* 1 (9): 185–199; von Hagen, Victor W. 1967. *The Roads that Led to Rome*. London: Weidenfeld and Nicolson.

ROMANTICISM AND ABOLITIONISM

More than mere coincidence accounted for the concomitant rise of romanticism and abolitionism in the United States and Europe. Romanticism placed its emphasis on the natural world and the natural rights of man and made it possible, for the first time really, to write about and dramatize the life and plight of the common man and to elevate such to the level of art.

This was an important development at a time when there was much civil unrest among the growing underclass in Europe, and it predated the Reform Act of 1832 in England as well as the enfranchisement of the propertyless in other European nations and the United States. In many ways, romantic philosophy gave rise to the democratization of Europe and of the United States and provided much of the foundation for huge social and political eruptions like the French and American revolutions. It is not surprising, then, that abolitionism as an organized movement got under way about the same time that romantic thought was sweeping Europe and the United States. In fact, the language of "natural rights" and the "rights of man"—which romanticism borrowed in part from the Enlightenment and extended—was fused with the moral rhetoric of the Bible to provide the substance of the philosophical, moral, and political positions of early abolitionist rhetoric.

Although much historical attention has been devoted to abolitionism and much literary attention has been given to British and U.S. romanticism, little attention has been given to thinking about the relationships between romanticism and the rise of racial politics in the nineteenth century. Such a discussion should not be limited to considerations of the appearance of traditional romantic themes and tropes in texts by black authors—for example, the "innocence" of childhood versus the "experience" of slave identity consciousness, the use of sentimentalism, the emphasis on "self-reliance," the valorizing of the meek and lowly or the "natural man"—but should also include some speculation about the rise of romanticism in light of the political upheavals surrounding the issue of slavery and the rise of a natural rights philosophy.

In other words, literary romanticism (here the rise of Nature in opposition to the ordered civilization associated with the Enlightenment) is less about escaping the political realities and anxieties of civilization than about choosing in Nature a more uncertain, or less determined, terrain on which to work out those political anxieties. Thinkers and writers found that contemporary issues associated with civilization—most notably the French Revolution and its aftermath, rampant poverty among a growing underclass, and abolition-ism—which so plagued the creative imagination were more easily worked out in the coded poetic language of Nature than in the highly charged and volatile po-litical terms of the public debates of the day. Such cross-cultural readings offer new ways of understand-ing and reading romanticism as well as the romantics.

In *Romanticism and Gender* (1993), Anne Mellor poses a monumental question to romanticists and, more broadly, to students of literature. She asks her readers to reconfigure what they have traditionally known as romanticism by centering women's writings in that period instead of on works by men. We are in-structed that by doing so, new dominant themes emerge and new aesthetic principles become norma-tive. Such an inquiry, then, gets to the heart of the ways in which dominant representations of literary ro-manticism get established and maintained through an emphasis on male-authored texts and the suppression of female-authored texts.

Similarly, any serious consideration of romanti-cism's relationship to abolitionism must focus on the literary production and the concerns of blacks during the romantic period, which would inevitably include a number of slave narrative texts as they were the most common literary form among blacks. Even a cursory perusal of these texts demonstrates the extent to which romantic thought so thoroughly permeated the discourse of the abolitionists. And an equally cursory glance at the canonical romantic writers demonstrates the opposite directional flow of such influences.

—*Dwight A. McBride*

See also
Art, Modern
For Further Reading
Davis, David Brion. 1966. *The Problem of Slavery in Western Culture.* Oxford: Oxford University Press; Gaull, Marilyn. 1988. *English Romanticism: The Human Context.* New York: Norton; Gossett, Thomas. 1965. *Race: The History of an Idea in America.* New York: Shocken; Raimond, Jean, and J. R. Watson, eds. 1992. *A Handbook to British Romanticism.* New York: St. Martin's.

ROUSSEAU, JEAN-JACQUES (1712–1778)

In his *Confessions* (1782), Jean-Jacques Rousseau said his first unhappiness was being born. Born in Geneva, Rousseau and his fa-ther (a clockmaker and dancing master) spent long hours grieving over the death of his mother and read-ing sentimental adventure novels aloud. Rousseau re-ceived his only formal education, which lasted less than two years, at the boarding school of a pastor named Lambercier. His father fled to escape persecu-tion by the Genevan authorities, leaving the young Rousseau entirely on his own. At age 16, he became an apprentice to an engraver who mistreated him, but he soon escaped.

Rousseau met Louise de Warens, who influenced him to renounce Calvinism. Rousseau referred to this woman throughout his life as "dear Mom," and from 1729 to 1740, he lived on her estate. He roamed the countryside but also educated himself in music, astron-omy, chemistry, and medicine. Following a brief period as secretary to the French ambassador to Venice, Rousseau went to Paris to copy music, having previ-ously developed a new system of musical notation.

His life and his work reflected his passion for the freedom of human nature based on natural law and his distaste for conventional institutions that repressed individual liberty. While working as a music copyist, Rousseau met Therese Levasseur, a servant at his mod-est hotel. She gave him five children, whom he aban-doned to an orphanage. That action plagued the au-thor of *Émile* (1762), considered one of the most important books on the education of children, and the book was censured by the Sorbonne and burned by the French Parlement.

Forever wandering the countryside trying to escape persecution for his radical ideas, Rousseau did most of his writing in rustic retreats hidden from the salons and the philosophes of Paris. His temperament was quite the opposite of that of the French writer François-Marie Arouet Voltaire, to whom Rousseau deferred as the great master. Still, he courageously confronted Voltaire in *Letter on Providence* (1756), in which he challenged his fellow philosopher's deism, preferring to admire the goodness of God rather than God's transcendence.

Rousseau insisted on the benevolence of creation and on the choice between good and evil belonging to the realm of human morality and responsibility. He called intolerance the most odious of all dogmas be-cause fanatics change their language to suit their own fortunes. For Rousseau, intolerance was damning peo-ple for not thinking as those in power thought. Voltaire later responded indirectly with *Candide,* in which he destroyed the myth of Rousseau's optimism.

References to slavery appear throughout Rous-seau's works. Rousseau considered three of his books as an inseparable unit: *Discourse on Sciences and Arts* (1749), *Discourse on the Origin of Inequality* (1755), and *Émile* (1762). In the first, Rousseau equated slaves to docile innocents who lived in happy igno-rance. The wisdom of his age corrupted all sense of faith and virtue and destroyed any semblance of inno-cence, man's original natural state. The progress of science and art threatened the morality of the human race.

Rousseau's *Discourse on Inequality* criticizes the social order of his age. Rejecting his own Calvinist roots, Rousseau blamed immorality, not on sinful nature, but on social inequalities that oppose natural law. Rousseau maintained that all human beings are naturally equal at birth, but throughout life one is either perfected or one deteriorates, depending on the acquisition of good or bad qualities. Good and evil are learned, not inbred.

Rousseau noted two types of inequalities: those of nature—like health, age, and soul—and those that rely on convention and are established by society's general consensus. In order to make progress, human nature is oppressed beneath the weight of the law. Rousseau criticized those writers who conclude that humanity is naturally cruel, or sinful, and needs civil institutions to tame it. On the contrary, said Rousseau, no one is more gentle than man in his natural state.

Slavery, according to Rousseau, offers a common security to the masters. The worst that could happen in human relationships is for one person to be at the mercy of another. People need a chief to protect them, but not slavery. Politicians attribute to man a natural propensity toward servitude, because they see slaves as patient and innocent, as Rousseau saw them when he wrote *Discourse on the Sciences and the Arts*.

In that work, Rousseau said that unless one possesses liberty, virtue, and innocence, one cannot know them. He suggested making the effort to remain free rather than judging slavery by examining those states that were then practicing slavery. "When I behold numbers of naked savages, that despise European pleasures, braving hunger, fire, the sword and death, to preserve nothing but their independence, I feel that it is not for slaves to argue about liberty." Rousseau was not criticizing slaves for speaking for their freedom. Rather, he was asking those with power over slaves to open their eyes to the importance of giving liberty to all people.

In *Émile*, Rousseau stressed freedom of movement in the education of a child, from a lack of swaddling clothes in the crib to the free development of natural faculties and happiness in play. Rousseau named four stages of development: infancy, sensation (ages 5–13), reason (ages 13–16), and sentiment (ages 16–20). The duty of the parent, the teacher, and society is to develop the natural goodness of man, which will prevent enslavement and lead to equality and liberty for all according to natural law. The fifth book of *Émile*, which is often published alone, summarizes *The Social Contract*, which was also published in 1762. Both works represent the culmination of his thought, which is best represented by the first line of *The Social Contract*: "Man is born free, and everywhere he is in chains."

In *The Social Contract,* Rousseau attempted to explain how equality might be regained through a society based on the general will of a sovereign people. The general principle of the contract, which should be the foundation for every political institution, is that no one has any natural authority over another and thus no king rules by divine right. Therefore, the contract is made, not between the king or prince and the people, but between the people and themselves.

Borrowing heavily from Plato's *Republic,* Rousseau mentioned three possible forms of government—democracy, aristocracy, and monarchy—but he shared Plato's distrust of total democracy and believed an aristocracy was preferable if freely elected or a monarchy if ruled by a benevolent prince. Despite a lifetime devoted to issues of inequality, Rousseau concluded in the fourth book of *The Social Contract* that all minorities should conform to the general will or be banished from the state.

—*Judith T. Wozniak*

For Further Reading
Fellows, Otis E., and Norman L. Torrey, eds. 1942. *The Age of Enlightenment: An Anthology of Eighteenth Century French Literature*. New York: Appleton-Century-Crofts; Kelly, Christopher. 1987. *Rousseau's Exemplary Life: The "Confessions" as Political Philosophy*. Ithaca, NY: Cornell University Press; Rousseau, Jean-Jacques. 1932. *The Social Contract and Discourses*. London: E. P. Dutton.

ROYAL ADVENTURERS

The Royal Adventurers group—also known as the Company of Royal Adventurers and the Royal Adventurers into Africa—was formed in 1618 to enable England to be a viable participant in the West African slave trade, a market that had been largely monopolized by the Portuguese and the Spanish. In forming the group, the English were, in many ways, following the lead of other European empires.

It was not until the late-sixteenth century that England took to the high seas with a purpose, and its original efforts were aimed at exploring and expanding trade. Men like John Hawkins, during the reign of Queen Elizabeth I, sailed to West Africa primarily as a trading venture, not specifically to purchase slaves but to obtain riches in the form of gold, ivory, and spices. Nevertheless, they soon saw opportunities to obtain Africans by various means—by trade, force, or guile—and took them to Hispaniola in the New World. Once there, the Africans were traded for goods like sugar, hides, pearls, and ginger.

British merchants and captains first ventured into the African trade surreptitiously, as the *asiento* (permission to engage in African trade) was in the hands of the Spanish and they were not eager to share the wealth. The financial success of the initial individual forays, however, were signal events in the history of British involvement in the African slave trade and paved the way for more organized efforts. It was for this reason that the Company of Royal Adventurers was founded.

The growth and development of the Royal Adventurers decelerated during the English Civil War (1642–1648), but after the restoration on the monarchy in 1660, attention was once again directed toward the potential of the West African trade. The Royal Adventurers reorganized in 1660 with a new royal charter, which gave the group a monopoly in the British slave trade and provided it with the entire market for buying, selling, and trading with Africans for slaves and merchandise. With King Charles II as the group's head, along with the king's brother James, duke of York, and backed by former supporters of the king during the Civil War, the Royal Adventurers went forth with alacrity to secure what slaves they could and transport them to the West Indies.

Ongoing hostilities between the British and the Dutch in the fight to gain maritime supremacy drastically drained the Adventurers' monetary resources. The group eventually failed and was forced to surrender its charter. The Royal Adventurers was subsequently replaced by the Royal African Company in 1672, and as a result of that reorganization, the English slave trade grew in earnest.

Throughout the late-seventeenth century, political pressure was brought to bear by independent traders against the Royal African Company's control, and in 1698 its monopoly was partially lifted. By the early-eighteenth century, it had become less prosperous through a combination of loss of funds and continued incursions by free traders into the slave market; the company's monopoly was rescinded entirely in 1712. The company acted as keeper of the British forts along the west coast of Africa, where the slave trade had been organized, and its profits in trade were insufficient to pay for the upkeep and defense of those forts. In 1752, the Royal African Company was disbanded, and a new concern, the Company of Merchants Trading to Africa, succeeded it.

—*T. K. Hunter*

For Further Reading

George, Claude. 1968. *Rise of British West Africa*. London: Houlston; Rediker, Marcus. 1987. *Between the Devil and the Deep Blue Sea*. Cambridge: Cambridge University Press; Walvin, James. 1973. *Black and White: The Negro and English Society, 1555–1945*. London: Oxford University Press.

ROYAL AFRICAN COMPANY

The Royal African Company of England was a joint stock company that held the crown monopoly over African trade for 80 years. Founded in 1672, the company operated several forts and "factories" that served as trading centers along the 2,000 miles of West African coast where it had exclusive trade jurisdiction, including over the slave trade. The company was a principle originator of "the triangle trade": shipping cloth, knives, firearms, iron, and brandy from England and the East Indies for sale in Africa; slaves from Africa to the West Indies; then sugar and rum for sale in England. The company also transported African products like gold, ivory, dyewood, hides, hardwood, and wax directly to England for sale.

In England, the company raised capital, purchased goods, and arranged for shipping and personnel, and in Africa, it maintained trading facilities and negotiated with African and European officials and traders. Although exact figures for the company's entire history are not wholly reliable, K. G. Davies (1975) believes that during the company's first 41 years, it exported to Africa more than £1.5 million worth of goods, shipped more than 100,000 Africans as slaves to the West Indies, imported from the West Indies to Britain more than 30,000 tons of sugar, and constructed or refurbished eight African forts.

During the Middle Ages, traders carried African goods to European markets. By the mid-sixteenth century, English expeditions to Africa were returning with gold, ivory, and Guinea pepper, though their economic success was sporadic. During the 1560s, Sir John Hawkins's attempts to sell African slaves in the Spanish West Indies proved unsuccessful because their sale by foreigners was prohibited.

Since the African trade needed substantial capital to finance shipping, forts, and naval support, Queen Elizabeth I organized the trade into "regulated" companies modeled on the East India Company, Hudson's Bay Company, and the Muscovy Company. These allowed English merchants exclusive access to a specific trading area, and trade charters were offered to such organizations as the Senegal Adventurers (1588), the Company of Adventurers (1618), and the Guinea company (1631).

Still, European trade in African goods remained relatively insignificant until the 1630s, when the success of West Indian sugarcane greatly increased the demand for African slaves. By the seventeenth century, Portugal, the United Provinces, France, and England were actively trading in Africa (as were Germany and the Scandinavian countries, though on a smaller scale).

After the restoration of the monarchy in England (1660), African trade increased, and the company of

Royal Adventurers Trading to Africa was founded in 1662, initially to search for gold but by 1663, to trade in slaves as well. The Royal Adventurers, directed mostly by peers and courtiers instead of merchants, failed because of mismanagement and the Second Anglo-Dutch War (1665). Satisfying the government's desire to reorganize England's trade with Africa, the Royal African Company was formed in 1672, and it bought out the assets of the Royal Adventurers' company. Although the Royal African Company boasted prominent court investors, including Charles II, the duke of York, and many ministers and courtiers, most of the new shareholders were experienced in trade, shipping, or colonial plantations.

Arguing that competition had caused the downfall of the Royal Adventurers, the Royal African Company demanded a monopoly on African trade, though noncompetition lingered as a contentious issue. Merchants excluded from the African trade criticized the monopoly as an abuse of royal prerogative while plantation interests complained that a closed market made slaves more expensive and less plentiful. The Bloodless Revolution (also called the Glorious Revolution) of 1688–1689 drove James II of England from the throne, and the former king's close association with the Royal African Company led Parliament to curtail its monopoly.

An act of 1698 allowed other traders access to the African market as long as they paid the Royal African Company a 10 percent export duty. War with France (1689–1697) and the War of the Spanish Succession (1702–1714) further undermined the company's finances. The 10 percent act lapsed in 1712, ending the company's monopoly and precipitating a boom among independent slave traders.

Despite the Royal African Company's 80-year tenure, it never stood on truly sound financial footing. Although some investors who sold stock early profited, the company often paid dividends, not from profits, but from money borrowed in new stock offerings. In the end, several factors precipitated the company's decline: (1) the trade of the "10 percenters" and foreign and domestic "interlopers" who violated the company's slave trade monopoly; (2) the sugar trade losses, which caused the insolvency of planters to whom company had extended credit; and (3) the rising price of West Indian slaves, a response to the increased cost of slaves in Africa owing to increased demand. The company collapsed in 1752, but unrestricted access to Africa had enabled Britain, by the mid-eighteenth century, to achieve the dubious distinction of being the world's preeminent slave-trading nation.

—*Arnold Schmidt*

For Further Reading
Davies, K. G. 1975. *The Royal African Company.* New York: Octagon Books; Drescher, Seymour. 1987. *Capitalism and Antislavery: British Mobilization in Comparative Perspective.* New York: Oxford University Press; Lovejoy, Paul. 1983. *Transformations in Slavery: A History of Slavery in Africa.* Cambridge: Cambridge University Press.

RUFFIN, EDMUND (1794–1865)

According to popular legend, the Southern slaveholder Edmund Ruffin fired the first and last shots of the U.S. Civil War. In April 1861, at age 67, Ruffin was invited to ignite the cannon that fired on Fort Sumter in Charleston Harbor, South Carolina. On June 18, 1865, two months after the conflict had ended, Ruffin committed suicide. Ruffin's biographer enhanced his legend by describing his final moment, when Ruffin wrapped himself in a Confederate flag before firing the fatal shot. This final irony lacks veracity, but Ruffin's suicide note—that he could not live in a world under Yankee rule—is accurate.

Ruffin is one of the more intriguing figures of the antebellum South. A proslavery advocate, plantation owner, and ardent Southern nationalist, he applied scientific farming methods at an early time. Born in Prince George County, Virginia, in 1794, Ruffin attended the College of William and Mary, served briefly in the War of 1812, and began agricultural experiments at age 25 on his land along the James River. His success focused on using marl, a calcium carbonate, to enrich damaged soils and greatly heighten productivity. Ruffin documented his work in *An Essay on Calcareous Manures* (1832) and in *Farmers' Register,* an agricultural journal he edited from 1833 to 1842.

In 1843, he moved to a new estate named Marlbourne in Hanover County, Virginia. Ruffin's outspoken stance on slavery significantly overshadowed his success and reputation as an agricultural reformer, but historians fully recognize his contributions to Southern agriculture. He was a significant but not necessarily a large slaveholder—at Marlbourne there was a total of 41 slaves.

Politically, Ruffin had little experience at either the state or the federal level, even though he served in the Virginia Senate (1824–1828). In 1831, the moderate Ruffin skillfully defended a slave falsely accused of participating in Nat Turner's revolt, but by 1850, he was increasingly agitated about the constant attacks on slavery, and his proslavery stance only solidified as the nation moved closer to war. Ruffin was counted among the staunchest secessionists, fearful the South could never exist without slavery. Ruffin utilized his extensive personal network to spread proslavery views through conversation, and he used the written word to support disunion. Ruffin could be found wherever a favorable audience might be gathered across the South.

In appearance, Ruffin was an unmistakable character with long, flowing white hair in his later years. He wrote extensively for newspapers in Charleston and Richmond. One major article, "African Colonization Unveiled," was serialized in *DeBow's Review* (1859–1860) and also published as a separate pamphlet. Ruffin aired his views on secession in three other widely circulated pamphlets, and a political novel, *Anticipations of the Future* (1860), pointed to the absolute necessity of secession and Southern independence.

Ruffin was visible, vocal, and prolific, but his efforts probably had little impact on progress toward secession. In 1858, he and Alabamian William Lowndes Yancey formed the League of United Southerners to encourage secession, but the group failed to ignite public opinion. Never one to miss an opportunity for calling attention to his cause, Ruffin joined the Virginia Military Institute Cadet Corps in December 1859 just to watch John Brown's execution. He sent pikes seized from Brown's followers to Southern governors for public display in order to promote secession. Finally, the excitable Ruffin joined South Carolina's Palmetto Guard in 1861 and fired the first rounds aimed at Fort Sumter—the opening shots of the Civil War.

By 1861, Ruffin was not in particularly good health, and he spent the war years as a virtual exile. As his family properties were damaged and subject to raids, he finally moved to Redmoor, some 35 miles west of Richmond. As the Southern cause crumbled and the inevitable became more obvious, Ruffin held steadfast to his views of Southern independence. When the end came, Ruffin began preparation for suicide—a solution he had long considered.

Legend has it that just after noon on June 17, 1865, Ruffin wrapped himself in a Confederate flag and ended his life. Although the legend is undocumented, Ruffin did pen a suicide note. Declaring his hatred for the "perfidious, malignant, and vile Yankee race," Ruffin repudiated Northern rule even to the grave, but he chose not to attack blacks or to mention slavery. For Ruffin, though, his proslavery views survived to the end of his life.

—*Boyd Childress*

For Further Reading

Craven, Avery O. 1932. *Edmund Ruffin, Southerner: A Study in Secession.* New York: D. Appleton; Mathew, William M. 1988. *Edmund Ruffin and the Crisis of Slavery in the Old South: The Failure of Agricultural Reform.* Athens: University of Georgia Press; Mitchell, Betty. 1981. *Edmund Ruffin, a Biography.* Bloomington: Indiana University Press.

RUSSIAN SERFDOM

Serfdom developed in Muscovy, the precursor to the Russian Empire, in a gradual and uneven process that lasted several centuries. In the early-fifteenth century, peasants in Muscovy were free; by the late-seventeenth century, most had fallen under the yoke of serfdom. Russia never promulgated a precise legal definition of serfdom, and the conditions of serfdom varied greatly in different regions and in different historical periods. Generally, Russian serfs were tied either to the land or to the person of a lord, and they were subject to their lord's nearly unlimited authority rather than to the state.

Serfdom developed primarily as a means of helping landowners cope with a shortage of peasant labor. In the fifteenth century, as the princes of Muscovy consolidated their rule, they granted land to their supporters. Yet land was of no value unless peasants were there to farm it, and peasant flight was a common problem, which led nobles and monasteries to press for limitations on the peasants' right to migrate.

Initially, certain monasteries were permitted to restrict the movement of indebted peasants to a two-week period around St. George's Day, a traditional holiday in late November marking the end of the autumn agricultural season. By the late-fifteenth century, it had become customary to limit the movement of all peasants to the period around St. George's Day. This custom was codified in the Sudebnik of 1497, the first major Muscovite law code, and was repeated in the Sudebnik of 1550, but the measure was enforced only sporadically. Peasants continued to move, both legally and illegally, and often they were encouraged to do so by wealthy landlords eager to acquire more peasant labor.

In the late-sixteenth century, economic distress initiated by war and famine caused many peasants to leave central Russia for newly conquered lands to the south and southeast. Responding to the resulting drastic labor shortages, Czar Ivan IV decreed a series of "forbidden years" in the 1580s, during which peasants were forbidden to move even during the St. George's Day holiday. The "forbidden years" originally applied only to certain areas, but by 1592, the policy extended to the entire country. In 1592, the government also attempted to register the population in a series of local cadastres. Peasants who left their

A Russian noble receives petitions from his serfs.

registered residences could be seized and returned within a five-year recovery period. Czar Boris Godunov briefly suspended the "forbidden years" in 1601 and 1602, allowing peasants to move, but reinstated them in 1603. Thereafter, every year was a forbidden year.

From this time on, serfdom gradually became more entrenched and its conditions more onerous. The recovery period, during which landlords could legally reclaim peasants who fled, was lengthened and finally abolished altogether in a new legal code, the Ulozhenie of 1649. This measure effectively bound peasants to the land. Other rights formerly held by peasants were also constricted by 1649: they could no longer own property, sue and be sued in courts, or hold elective office. The Ulozhenie of 1649 is generally regarded as the first legal codification of serfdom, although it never established a legal definition of the position of serf or of landlord-serf relations.

The small population segment legally defined as slaves (*kholopy*) was gradually merged with serfs during the seventeenth century, and in 1723, Czar Peter I transferred all remaining slaves into the ranks of serfs. Serfdom increasingly came to resemble slavery, with the exception that serfs, unlike slaves, paid taxes and could be conscripted into the army. Whereas serfdom began as an institution that tied serfs to the land and prohibited them from moving, by about 1750, serfs were treated as their landowners' personal property and could be bought and sold without land.

Serf owners could not legally execute or torture their serfs, but the owners were punished if they did so only in exceptional circumstances. Landlords could use corporal punishment on their serfs, forbid them to marry, and exile them to Siberia. Although serf owners were enjoined not to let their peasants "suffer ruin," there were no other limits on the dues and services landowners could impose.

By the mid-eighteenth century, the myriad distinctions among forms of agricultural and domestic labor had diminished, leaving two primary groups: private serfs and state peasants. The latter were peasants who escaped being made serfs. They lived on "black lands" (i.e., lands not officially owned by the church or private landowners), which tended to be in areas of poor soil or relatively harsh climate, making them unattractive for landed-estate production. Peasants on black lands had to pay taxes to the state but otherwise enjoyed considerable freedom. In Siberia and the northern region of European Russia, state peasants predominated, and there were virtually no privately held serfs. On central Russia's more fertile land, serfs constituted the majority of the population. Generally, serfdom prevailed in those areas most conducive to agricultural production.

Serfs rendered obligations to their lords either in labor (corvée or *barshchina*) or in cash or crops (quitrent or *obrok*). Under the first arrangement, which predominated in the south and southeast where market production was widespread, serfs spent a certain portion of the week (usually three days) working their lord's land. The second system occurred mainly in northern areas, where land was of poorer quality. With the eighteenth century's growth of industry, serfs became the major labor source for mines and factories.

Most historians believe that the serfs' economic condition deteriorated steadily in the seventeenth and eighteenth centuries as obligations to landlord and state increased while agricultural productivity stagnated. Flight was the most common form of peasant protest against serfdom's conditions, but occasionally serfs resorted to widespread violence. Major peasant rebellions were led by Ivan Bolotnikov (1606), Stenka Razin (1670), and Emelian Pugachev (1773).

Beginning in the late-eighteenth century, the czarist government introduced legislation designed to restrict the growth of serfdom and to make it more humane. Restrictions were placed on the sale of serfs, the minimum quantity of land to which they had to be attached, and the amount of time they could be required to work for their lord. Czar Alexander I (r. 1801–1825) ceased the practice of distributing state peasants into private serfdom, allowed state peasants to buy land, and enacted a statute intended to encourage voluntary manumission. Nicholas I (r. 1825–1855) personally deplored serfdom's existence and established nine secret committees to study the problem of ending it, though the only major reform legislation introduced during his reign affected state peasants rather than private serfs.

On February 19, 1861, Alexander II emancipated the serfs. The reasons for the emancipation were not economic—serfdom remained profitable for landlords—nor was fear of peasant insurrection a compelling motive. The primary reason was political: a sense that Russian backwardness, which had been glaringly exposed by the disastrous defeat in the Crimean War (1853–1856), threatened Russia's status as a great power. Progressive government officials believed that sweeping reforms were necessary to modernize Russia and that a necessary first step was the abolition of serfdom, which was increasingly regarded as morally indefensible. Abolition would, moreover, bring Russia in line with enlightened opinion in Western Europe, where slavery and serfdom had already been abolished.

At the time of emancipation, there were about 23 million serfs, and they constituted nearly 40 percent of the Russian Empire's population. The emancipation terms were both complex and conservative, distinguishing among different categories of serfs and among different geographic areas. Serfs were freed in a gradual, multistage process extending over several years. They were granted about half of the privately owned land, for which they had to repay the former landowners utilizing 49-year mortgages financed by the government.

The land was not given to individual peasant households but to the village commune (*mir*), which then became responsible for collecting state taxes and making redemption payments. The peasants were therefore still tied to the land: they could not leave without the commune's approval, and they retained obligations as members of the commune. They did acquire basic civil rights and the right to own property.

Emancipation did not solve the problems of rural Russia as it satisfied neither the gentry landowners, who went into steady decline, nor the peasants. Peasants resented the emancipation terms, particularly the lack of pastureland and the required redemption payments. Also, the commune's authority inhibited individual initiative, which might have led to increased agricultural productivity, and meant that in many ways, the Russian peasants remained second-class citizens.

—*Barbara J. Keys*

For Further Reading
Blum, Jerome. 1966. *Lord and Peasant in Russia from*

the Ninth to the Nineteenth Century. New York: Athenaeum; Field, Daniel. 1976. *The End of Serfdom.* Cambridge, MA: Harvard University Press; Hellie, Richard. 1971. *Enserfment and Military Change in Muscovy.* Chicago: University of Chicago Press; Kolchin, Peter. 1987. *Unfree Labor: American Slavery and Russian Serfdom.* Cambridge, MA: Harvard University Press.

SAINT DOMINGUE
See Haitian Revolution

SALT TRADE

Trade in salt has always been conducted throughout the world, and slavery has often been intimately associated with this trade, either through salt and slaves being traded simultaneously along similar routes or through slave labor being used in the extraction and production of salt. Unfortunately, sources of information on the salt trade and slavery are sparse, with the exception of information regarding the salt trade on the African continent.

As a dietetic necessity, demand for salt has always been high, and salt can be obtained by several means: mining rock salt, boiling seawater, extracting salt from plant ash, and solar evaporation or seawater. Among the most profitable means of obtaining salt throughout history has been the mining of rock salt, which was sought after because of its great purity. Salt mining is very labor intensive and frequently took place, in Africa at least, in conditions of extreme temperature and harsh environment, which meant that free labor was often not forthcoming.

Within Africa's Sahara and Sahel regions there were numerous salines (salt flats and salt pools) and salt mines, with two of the most infamous mines being at Teghaza and Taodeni in northern Mali. There, slaves cut the rock salt and loaded it onto camel caravans, which were sent south via the great trade centers of West Africa, such as Timbuktu. The process described by Moroccan traveler Ibn Battuta in the mid-fourteenth century has changed little today.

Yet there need be no direct correlation between salt production and trade and slavery. P. E. Lovejoy makes the important point that "the organization of the salt industry depended on whether it was more feasible to own the workers or the salt sites and whether or not labor could be mobilized without the coercion inherent in the institution of slavery" (Lovejoy, 1986). Slaves and free peasants could equally work side by side or in isolation from each other.

In the Sahara, economic necessity precipitated the use of slave labor; elsewhere in Africa, salt could be produced by free specialists, as at the Uvinza salines at the northern end of Lake Tanganyika, where up to 20,000 immigrant salt workers supplemented the permanent community for periods of the year from ancient times. Salt was head loaded (literally carried on the head) from Uvinza and other salt workings in the area by human porters, often together with slaves and consignments of ivory destined for the trade centers of the East African coast and offshore islands like Zanzibar. It can even be suggested that slaves might have been employed in carrying the salt on their journey to the coast, which would have made the passage more lucrative for the slave traders.

Throughout history, salt has also been used as currency and directly exchanged for slaves. In Ethiopia, Red Sea salt or salt mined from the Danakil depression was traded for slaves, who were then sent to Arabia or the Sudan. Prices for these slaves varied, depending on where they were from in the country, as origin was thought to affect temperament. Some Ethiopian slaves who were bought with salt were castrated to serve in harems and as personal servants in the Muslim world.

In the ninth century, slaves of East African origin, known as the Zanj, were employed in huge numbers in the marshes and salt pans of what is, today, southern Iraq. Gangs ranging between 500 and 5,000 slaves were employed at tasks like extracting salt for sale and preparing the ground for the cultivation of sugarcane. Eventually becoming dissatisfied with their condition, they fomented the Zanj rebellion, a serious hindrance to the Abbasid caliphate until the rebellion was suppressed in the late-ninth century.

Outside of Africa and Arabia, little information on the salt trade and slavery is to be found, although a connection between the two appears to have existed in certain areas. S. A. M. Adshead (1992) mentions that Ssu-ma Chien, "the Herodotus of China," recorded in his *Shih-chi* or historical records how merchants profited greatly from using slaves, specifically "cunning and clever" ones, to peddle fish and salt during the reign of Emperor Chang Ti (r. 75–88).

Connection between slavery and the salt trade exists to this day as "clientage" relationships are still found in the Saharan salt workings. What could quite easily constitute contemporary slave labor is frequently used in salt mines around the world in the form of prisoners, political or otherwise.

—Timothy Insoll

See also
East Africa; Timbuktu
For Further Reading
Adshead, S. A. M. 1992. *Salt and Civilisation*. London: Macmillan; Lovejoy, P. E. 1986. *Salt of the Desert Sun*. Cambridge: Cambridge University Press; Lovejoy, P. E. 1983. *Transformations in Slavery*. Cambridge: Cambridge University Press.

SAMBO THESIS

In *Slavery: A Problem in American Institutional and Intellectual Life* (1959), Stanley M. Elkins compared slavery in the U.S. South to Nazi concentration camps and concluded that the institution of slavery in the United States had resulted in the obliteration of the African American personality and the creation of a docile, malleable slave personality—the "Sambo." Elkins's study was motivated by what he claimed was evidence of the slaves' disinterest in resisting the slave regime, particularly the lack of consistent slave rebellions in the United States as compared to the slave regimes of Brazil and the Caribbean.

Historian Ulrich Bonnell Phillips's analysis of the Old South was based largely upon the plantation records and journals of slaveowners, which had produced an enduring image of the Southern plantation as a pastoral paradise where content and obsequious blacks worked under the close supervision of "paternalistic" whites. According to Phillips, slaveowners said a black "was what a white man made him." Thus, black slaves were envisioned and memorialized as being highly sociable, hypersensual, musical, superstitious, subordinate, lazy, humorous, affectionate, and loyal.

Elkins's Sambo model of the slave temperament was one peculiar to the United States because of the "totalitarian" nature of slavery in the antebellum South, which Elkins compared to slavery as it was institutionalized in other countries and at other times. In South America, for example, other institutions (e.g., the Catholic Church) had an almost equal impact upon the lives of the slaves whereas in the United States, nothing mediated the absolute power of the slaveowner over the slave. Ultimately, Elkins found the concentration camps of twentieth-century Nazi Germany closest to the closed society of the U.S. South before the Civil War, referring to the camps as a form of human slavery based on "a perverted patriarchy."

Beginning with the transportation of prisoners to the Nazi camps in closed cattle cars, which Elkins compared to the belowdecks shipboard experience of Africans on the transatlantic voyage, absolute control over the inmates of the camps was implemented. Neither camp inmate nor American slave possessed any certainty about the future. And, according to Elkins, both Nazi concentration camps and the institution of slavery in the U.S. South relied upon strategies of terror: deliberate and consistent punishments were intended in each case to reduce the resistance of the prisoner/slave and to control their attitudes and behavior. Yet, according to Elkins, an "adjustment" to conditions was ultimately obtained, and a kind of status quo ensued.

Relying heavily upon the work of the psychologist Bruno Bettelheim, Elkins proposed his own analysis of the slave personality. The experience of slavery in the United States "infantilized" the African Americans, making them "perpetual children" in need of close supervision and direction. Like the inmates of German camps, who saw their guards as father figures and assumed the demeanor of children, slaves in the U.S. South also assumed "childlike" behaviors in accepting the value system of the owner, seeking to please the owner, and judging fellow slaves by the guidelines used by the owner. Because the American slave identified with his or her owner, who became, according to Elkins, the figure who was most emotionally important for slaves, resistance to slavery on the part of slaves in the United States was rare or nonexistent.

Other historians have pointed to the writings of French colonists in Haiti, who at least suggested that their treatment of their own slaves had produced a similar personality type or behavior—but Haiti was the site of the hemisphere's only successful slave overthrow of a slave regime. Slaveowners in Brazil likewise memorialized their impressions of their slaves' docility. And indeed, historians have noted that slaveowners through the centuries have traditionally described their slaves as loyal but lazy, sly, and sexually promiscuous, which perhaps suggests a unified strategy of slaveholding as necessary for the close supervision or "elevation" of the enslaved group rather than the actual existence of a personality type.

Slaves had space to create full-fledged communities, which had their own value systems, and there were people in those communities who had a significant effect upon them, so slaves were not wholly dependent upon the owner or the owner's value system. One response to being a slave was the development of a theory of Afrocentrism, which placed the slave at the center of the story of slavery as subject and actor rather than as merely an object of white action. At least one historian had questioned the plausibility of reaching reasonable conclusions about an institution built around black slaves without addressing the philosophies, communities, and lives of those black slaves.

Whereas historians of slavery once relied almost exclusively upon written documents as source material, documents that had often been produced by slaveowners, new attention began to focus upon so-called slave sources: slave narratives, slave autobiographies, and especially the transcribed interviews of former slaves conducted by the Works Progress Administration in the United States in the 1930s. Also, a new look at slaveowner sources—slave bills of sale; plantation account books listing births and deaths, work assignments, and punishments; and local newspapers listing runaway notices and slave auctions—provided intriguing background material for the construction of histories of the slaves themselves.

Historians have now found evidence of the existence of a community that survived despite the sale and psychological and physical coercion of its members. An extended kin network tended to include both related and "orphaned" slaves who were not necessarily related by blood. Parents and grandparents educated child slaves in the ways of both blacks (including Africans) and whites. Religious interpretations by slaves were sometimes limited by the prohibition on slave literacy—though slaves did sometimes learn to read—and focused not merely upon the attainment of spiritual freedom but also upon the attainment of temporal freedom.

Despite Elkins's support of the Sambo thesis, it is clear from the record that although spectacular resistance—organized or collective militaristic efforts on the part of slaves in the antebellum U.S. South to overthrow slavery (such as the efforts of Denmark Vesey and Nat Turner)—might have been limited, most slaves engaged in acts of daily resistance. This type of resistance included work slowdowns, feigning illness, intentional injury, temporarily running away (truancy), and successfully running away (escape) beyond the reach of slavery's laws. Communities of Maroons (slave runaways who set up camp along the border of settled areas) also existed up to the antebellum period. House slaves, especially the females, were sometimes in a position to resist in more significant ways by poisoning food or water or committing arson. In addition, some historians have speculated as to whether female slaves might have aborted pregnancies in order to prevent an increase of the slave population.

—*Dale Edwyna Smith*

For Further Reading
Blassingame, John. 1972. *The Slave Community: Plantation Life in the Antebellum South.* New York: Oxford University Press; Raboteau, Albert J. 1978. *Slave Religion: The "Invisible Institution" in the Antebellum South.* New York: Oxford University Press; Weinstein, Allen; Frank Otto Gatell; and David Sarasohn, eds. 1968. *American Negro Slavery: A Modern Reader.* New York: Oxford University Press; White, Deborah Gray. 1985. *Ar'n't I a Woman? Female Slaves in the Plantation South.* New York: Norton.

SAQALIBA

Saqàliba is the Arabic word for "Slavs," but it was applied widely, especially in Islamic Spain, to slaves of European origin. *Šaqàliba* (singular, *šaqlab*) were an important component of the Islamic East's slave populations and a major commodity in the thriving Andalusian slave trade from the ninth to the twelfth centuries. *Šaqàliba*, known for their red hair and fair complexions, were favored as concubines and soldiers. Slavic eunuchs were so popular and widely distributed that they became synonymous with *šaqàliba*, but the term really applied to slaves of various origins, including Turks and captives taken in raids on Christian Spain.

By the seventh century, Frankish merchants were buying slaves from pagan Slavs and Avars, a nomadic people of central Asia. Simultaneously, Muslims encountered slaves as Byzantine mercenaries and settlers and among the Khazars of the lower Volga region. Jews dominated the trade in the ninth century, although Italian city-states also played a major role. Most Slavs were not shipped via Byzantium or direct to the East but were taken overland or by sea to castration centers along Spain's Christian-Islamic border. From there, they were distributed within Islamic Spain or exported to the Islamic world abroad (especially North Africa).

In tenth-century Umayyad Spain, *šaqàliba*, who had first been imported by al-Hakam I (r. 796–822), became increasingly important as military slaves. The caliph 'Abd ar-Rahman III (r. 929–961) owned at least 13,000 slaves, some of whom constituted his personal bodyguard. The vizier Abu 'Amir al-Mansur (d. 1002) sought to limit the growing influence of the Slavs by reducing their importation and using Berber mercenaries instead.

With disintegration of the Umayyad caliphate (c. 1031), a constellation of petty principalities, the Taifa kingdoms, arose. Several of them—Almería, the Balearic Islands, Valencia, Tortosa, Badajoz, and Denia in the Spanish Levant—were ruled by *šaqàliba*. The last kingdom, until conquered in 1075–1076 by the rival Kingdom of Zaragoza, enjoyed 60 years of prosperity as a haven for pirates and a center of Islamic learning, absorbing the Balearics and invading Sardinia. None of the "Slav" Taifa kingdoms were long-lived as the *šaqàliba* did not have a broad enough power base to survive as independent rulers in ethnically fragmented Islamic Spain; they were underassimilated and under-Arabized and did not actively replenish their own ranks, as did Egypt's Mamluks.

Despite the immense popularity of the *šaqàliba* in the tenth century, both in Spain and across the Islamic world, by the eleventh century there are very few references to them. In following centuries, Christendom's expansion affected both supply and market: Eastern pagans converted to Christianity, and Christian Spain's stronger kingdoms were thus less interested in supporting such a trade. Meanwhile, the Umayyad state's decentralization, the general decline of Islamic Spain, and the growing popularity of Turks and blacks as slaves further reduced the demand for *šaqàliba*, both in Muslim Spain and abroad. White slaves, no longer called *šaqàliba*, continued to be traded in the Islamic world, but as luxury items. In the seventeenth and eighteenth centuries, they fetched prices six times those of comparable black slaves.

—Brian Catlos

See also
Eunuchs; Mamluks; Spain
For Further Reading
Chejne, Anwar. 1974. *Muslim Spain, Its History and Culture.* Minneapolis: University of Minnesota Press; Levi-Provençal, Évariste. 1950–1953. *Histoire de l'espagne musulmane.* 3 vols. Leiden: Brill; Lewis, Bernard. 1990. *Race and Slavery in the Middle East.* Oxford: Oxford University Press.

SCANDINAVIA
See Abolition, Scandinavia; Vikings; *individual countries*

SEA ISLANDS

The name Sea Islands generally identifies the Atlantic coastal islands of the South Carolina and Georgia low country and northern Florida. There are thought to be at least 1,000 islands scattered from as far north as Georgetown County, South Carolina, to as far south as Amelia Island, Florida. Not all of these islands are inhabitable. Those that are inhabited range from less

Union troops remove the "hobble" from an escaped slave woman on Otter Island, South Carolina.

than 15 square miles to just over 100 square miles. The inhabitable islands are home to the Gullah and Geechee peoples and their associated language and culture.

The English worked to claim mainland North America before the Spanish or the French, but both of those nations had established colonial spheres and begun settlements in the area prior to English arrival. English Loyalists from the sugar plantations of Barbados began settling the region after England's King Charles II granted a charter in 1663 that opened Carolina to colonial settlement. The English lord proprietors who came wanted to increase their wealth by expanding land ownership and producing crops, and they brought with them the Africans who became the base upon which Gullah culture was built and Geechee culture would grow.

During chattel slavery, many of these marsh-strewn and palmetto-lined islands were a financial base for agricultural operations in the United States. It was in this region that long-staple "Sea Island cotton" was grown, reputed to be the finest cotton in the world. The islands were also a center of indigo production, and many ships were built in the region. Local rice plantations also generated a major cash crop and contributed significantly to the economic structure of the United States.

Today, many of the islands have been bought and converted into resort areas that sport huge golf courses and numerous tennis courts. This is sad and ironic given that Gen. William Tecumseh Sherman's Special Field Order 15, issued on January 16, 1865, specifically set aside for former enslaved Africans "the islands from Charleston south [and] the abandoned rice fields along the rivers for thirty miles back from the sea." Unfortunately, President Andrew Johnson nullified the order in September 1865. However, because of other efforts to help the new freedmen and the tenacity of the African American Sea Islanders, many of them were able to purchase property and bequeath it to their descendants. Those descendants are the Gullah and Geechees that still live in the area.

—*Marquetta L. Goodwine*

See also
Geechee; Gullah; Port Royal Experiment
For Further Reading
Crum, Mason. 1968. *Gullah: Negro Life in the Carolina Sea Islands.* New York: Negro Universities Press; Goodwine, Marquetta L. 1995. *Gullah/Geechee: The Survival of Africa's Seed in the Winds of the Diaspora.* Vol. 1, *St. Helena's Serenity.* New York: Kinship Publications; Jones-Jackson, Patricia. 1987. *When Roots Die: Endangered Traditions on the Sea Islands.* Athens: University of Georgia Press; Rose, Willie Lee. 1976. *Rehearsal for Reconstruction: The Port Royal Experiment.* New York: Oxford University Press.

SEAMEN'S ACTS

In 1822, in the wake of Denmark Vesey's famous slave conspiracy in Charleston, South Carolina, that state's legislature passed an act mandating that free black sailors should be jailed while their vessels were in the state's ports. Employers were made liable for the costs of detention, and any sailor unredeemed by his employer (or the ship's captain) by the time the vessel left port could be sold into slavery. Over the next four decades, this law inspired similar seamen's acts in Georgia (1829), North Carolina (1830–1831), Florida (1832), Alabama (1839, 1841), Louisiana (1842, 1859), and Texas (1859).

Southern legislators were particularly concerned about limiting contact between free black sailors and local slaves, as they were fearful that the former would encourage and assist slave escapes. Although these seamen's acts were intermittently enforced, and often only as a result of public scrutiny and pressure, they raised questions of comity (the respect of one state for the laws of another) and state sovereignty and generated court challenges, protests in Northern states, and diplomatic challenges.

The first challenge came in the federal courts, when the U.S. Supreme Court declared the South Carolina act unconstitutional in the case of *Elkison v. Deliesseline* (1823). But influential Charlestonians, working through a newly organized South Carolina Association, pressed for continued enforcement of the law, and state and local authorities complied. No federal official ever saw fit to enforce the Supreme Court's decision. Long after Vesey had faded from the public mind, white Southerners continued to defend these seamen's laws as a symbol of states' rights.

Northern seaboard states frequently challenged the laws. A significant number of free blacks in cities such as Boston, New York, and Philadelphia worked as sailors in the coastal trade, and the seamen's acts threatened their freedom and deprived their employers of their services while in Southern ports. In 1844, Massachusetts sent attorneys Samuel Hoar and Henry Hubbard to Charleston and New Orleans, respectively, to institute suits on behalf of free black citizens of Massachusetts who were jailed under the South Carolina and Louisiana laws. But threats of violence forced both men to return to Massachusetts before they could challenge the constitutionality of the acts. Officials in each city had informed each man that his life was in danger and that he could not be protected from angry crowds.

Britain, which also used free black sailors on commercial vessels, protested enforcement of the acts to federal officials during the 1820s and 1830s. This was one of the factors behind the challenge in the Elkison case. In the 1850s, through a mixture of lobbying, bribery, and obsequiousness, the British consulate convinced Louisiana (1852), Georgia (1854), and South Carolina (1856) to rescind or modify their acts (such acts had already fallen into disuse in several other states by this time). After the sectional controversy stirred up by John Brown's 1859 raid on Harpers Ferry, Virginia, the laws were seen by many Southerners as being too weak and too ineffective to be revived.

—*Roy E. Finkenbine*

See also
Fugitive Slave Acts, State; Vesey, Denmark
For Further Reading
Hamer, Philip M. 1935. "British Consuls and the Negro Seamen's Acts, 1850–1860." *Journal of Southern History* 1 (2): 138–168; Hamer, Philip M. 1935. "Great Britain, the United States, and the Negro Seamen's Acts, 1822–1848." *Journal of Southern History* 1 (1): 3–28.

SECOND GREAT AWAKENING

The Second Great Awakening, which began in the 1790s and lasted until roughly 1850, influenced slavery in the United States in at least two vital ways. First, the movement's revivals created an atmosphere in which religious salvation became a means for social reform, including the eradication of slavery, and its ideas influenced white Northerners to organize for social reform. Second, Southern slaves adapted religious ideas from the revivals, or "camp meetings," which were prevalent during the Second Great Awakening. Slaves created their own religious beliefs and practices after hearing and witnessing the enthusiastic sermons delivered by white ministers. In terms of religious rituals, the Second Great Awakening had a lasting impact on black Southern slave culture and spirituality.

As a broad movement, the Second Great Awakening was a series of religious revivals that swept through New England, the South, western New York State, and frontier regions of the United States and initiated an era of massive social reform efforts, including the movement to abolish chattel slavery in the U.S. South. The movement lasted approximately 60 years in the form of waves of intermittent religious revivals. The Second Great Awakening is also known as the Great Revival.

The religious revivals began to take hold in the 1790s in the Congregational churches of New England. By 1800, Protestant churches across the new republic were being swept with "revivalist fever." Religious revivals became particularly intense in frontier areas, where few established churches existed.

The Protestant faithful on the frontier relied on "circuit riders," Methodist ministers who traveled by horseback from one frontier community to the next. These Methodist circuit riders gave stinging sermons in the frontier areas in order to attract members of the congregation and convert nonbelievers. Methodists, Presbyterians, and Congregationalists—all Protestant faiths—made up the majority of believers in the Great Awakening. Unitarians and Universalists joined the other denominations during the Second Great Awakening in the 1820s, but Methodism particularly embraced the spirit of revival and reform. Methodists believed in salvation through free will and preached that salvation was available to all who wanted to be saved.

The Second Great Awakening resembled the First Great Awakening earlier in the eighteenth century in that the movement took root among evangelical clergy and their congregations and concerned the question of what individuals needed to do to achieve salvation. There was, however, an important difference between the two revivals. The evangelicals of the First Great Awakening in 1720–1770 focused solely on religious matters and individual salvation, but the leaders of the Second Great Awakening emphasized the need for social, rather than merely individual, reform.

Although the emphasis on social reform was to have an impact on abolishing slavery, the Second Great Awakening began as an religious experience for most people because most of the revival preachers emphasized the conversion experience in attaining personal salvation. Charles Grandison Finney, one of the most prominent of the evangelical preachers, told his congregation in western New York State that the only obstacle to salvation was the failure of the individual to submit to the conversion experience. Finney's ideas directly contradicted earlier Calvinist beliefs that salvation was predetermined by God, not a state of grace brought about by human effort. Finney relied on communal conversion experiences during his sermons because he believed many people feared the isolation of individual conversion. The communal conversion experience, in turn, led believers to try to convert other community members. In time, converting others meant reforming their behavior and attempting to perfect human society through social reform.

In part, the Second Great Awakening developed in response to eighteenth-century Enlightenment ideas, which encouraged rational thinking and championed human reason over and above irrational religious faith. Whatever effect the Enlightenment had in secularizing thought in the United States, however, most Americans refused to abandon their religious beliefs. In the early 1800s, Americans feared that rationality would replace religious faith, and camp meetings reflected their widespread popular dedication to Protestant beliefs about salvation.

The Second Great Awakening represented an attempt by reformers to protect the good of the nation with a renewed commitment to Protestantism. The fusion of secularism, patriotism, and Protestantism distinguished the experience of the First Great Awakening from the second. Reformers sought salvation not only for themselves but for the nation as a whole. Religion changed from being an individual matter of salvation to being a social platform for human perfectibility through the eradication of public sins such as drunkenness, poverty, and slavery.

Several spontaneous, interconnected, and simultaneous reform efforts emerged in the wake of the religious agitation, including the temperance, antipoverty, and women's rights movements. Within the context of religious revival, militant antislavery feelings arose among Northern revivalists and reformers, who saw slavery as a sin against God and an obstacle to creating a perfect social union. Abolitionists argued that slavery flew in the face of Christian teaching and that slavery must be eradicated in order to perfect human society. In this way, religious ideas inspired by the Second Great Awakening influenced slavery in the United States and led some white Northerners to oppose it as an institution, even though these same reformers viewed African slaves as inferior to whites.

Black slaves in the U.S. South interpreted the Second Great Awakening differently. Slaves often attended revivalist camp meetings with their masters and witnessed the enthusiastic sermons of the white preachers. Slaves imitated the style of white preachers after hearing a sermon, but the slaves abandoned the white preacher's message of racial inequality. Slaves developed their own style of preaching the gospel by creating the "ring shout" and transforming the meaning of white Protestant preachers. White preachers emphasized obedience to masters and personal salvation. Slaves were less preoccupied with individual salvation and social reform.

Slaves sought earthly freedom, and many slaves found the promise of freedom in the Bible's teachings. Slave preachers led shouts and engaged in a ritual of call and respond between preacher and congregation that resembled the camp meetings of white preachers. But however closely the shouting and emotional style of the black preacher resembled that of the white evangelist, the content of the sermon held special meaning for slaves who sought divine retribution for the wrongs done to them.

Ideas inspired by the Second Great Awakening led many white Northerners to join the antislavery cause, which helped turn the tide of public opinion against slavery in the North by 1850. In the South, the Great Revival gave slaves an opportunity to adapt elements of the camp meeting to their services while at the same time developing a distinct black religious culture that emphasized human freedom and divine retribution. In this way, the Second Great Awakening profoundly influenced the social and cultural life of the United States before the Civil War in general and the course of slavery in that country in particular.

—*Julie R. Nelson*

See also
Abolition, United States; Slave Preachers
For Further Reading
Abzug, Robert H. 1994. *Cosmos Crumbling: American Reform and the Religious Imagination*. New York: Oxford University Press; Walters, Ronald G. 1978. *American Reformers, 1815–1860*. New York: Hill and Wang.

SECOND MESSENIAN WAR

The Second Messenian War is one whose occurrence is problematic as many writers of antiquity did not distinguish a specific number of Messenian wars but rather an extended struggle. The problem resulted from Sparta's invasion and conquest of Messenia in the late-eighth century B.C., and in the following period the descendants of the conquered race rose periodically in local rebellions. The events of the Messenian conflict are even more obscure because of the efforts of fourth-century-B.C. Messenian poets to provide their countrymen with a suitable history.

Any account of the so-called Second Messenian War must deal with chronological problems. Some traditional histories place it in the early-seventh century B.C. (685–668) while others put it later, c. 650–630 B.C. What seems certain is that there was a long and costly insurrection of the Messenian Helots, which was eventually suppressed and which contributed significantly to a major constitutional and social reorganization of the Spartan state.

After conquering Messenia, Sparta made the inhabitants state "slaves," or Helots, and subjected them to an oppressive and sometimes brutal existence, treatment that, as might be expected, caused considerable resentment. At last, after several generations and perhaps emboldened by Sparta's participation in local conflicts with the states of Árgos, Arcadia, and Elis, the Helots rose in revolt. The catalyst may have been the Argive victory over the Spartans at Hysiai (c. 669), which placed a strain on Spartan manpower. The Helot leader was the semi-legendary, charismatic Aristomenes. The Messenian Helots allied with the Argives, Arcadians, and Pisatans, and joining them were many Messenians who had previously gone into exile.

Initially, the rebels experienced some success. They

held their own at Derai and won a major victory over the Spartans and their allies from Corinth and Lepreos at a place called Boar's Grave in Stenyclarus. Subsequently, Aristomenes attacked and sacked the Laconian city of Pharis (Pharae). As a consequence of these setbacks, the Spartans became disheartened and despaired of winning. However, the great elegiac poet Tyrtaeus emerged, perhaps serving as a general, to write several poems and marching songs that inspired the Spartans to renew the conflict with vigor. Tyrtaeus exhorted them to constancy and bravery and described the honor and glory that derived from fighting courageously for one's state.

The turning point in the war came in its third year (631 B.C.), when the Messenians lost the Battle of the Great Foss (Great Trench) owing to an act of treachery by the Arcadian king, Aristocrates. The Spartans had succeeded in bribing Aristocrates, and in the midst of battle, he ordered his troops to withdraw through the Messenian lines. This maneuver threw the Messenians into disarray and enabled the Spartans to push forward and inflict heavy losses. Aristomenes led the Messenian survivors to the northern stronghold Mount Eira (Ira) on the river Nedon, a site near the border of their Arcadian allies and near Pylos, which was not yet Spartan.

From this fortress and under the resourceful leadership of Aristomenes, the Messenians launched periodic raids and ravaged the land of Laconia, seizing grain, cattle, wine, and their victims' personal property. They achieved a notable success at the town of Amyclaei, which they looted. Aristomenes twice escaped after being captured. But after eleven years, the Spartans, assisted by the Samians, finally prevailed because of superior manpower and the aid of an adulterous woman who betrayed her compatriots. During a violent storm in which the Messenian sentinels abandoned their posts to take cover, the Spartans attacked, using ladders to aid their onslaught. A seer familiar with the oracles told Aristomenes to withdraw with as many Messenians as possible while leaving a few behind to hold up the Spartan pursuit. Aristomenes escaped and fled to Mount Lykaion in Arcadia.

The Arcadians warmly welcomed the fugitives. At this time they learned of the earlier treachery of King Aristocrates and discovered that he was about to betray their allies again. The outraged Arcadians then stoned him. In a last desperate attack on the Spartans, Euegetidas and a small band of Messenians returned to Eira where they found their enemies rummaging through the spoils and inflicted considerable damage before succumbing. After considering a plan to occupy an island near the Laconian coast and conduct raids against the Spartans from there, most of the displaced Messenians decide to emigrate to distant lands.

Some went to Sicily where, with the help of Anaxi-las of Region, they captured Zancle and changed its name to Messene (664 B.C., now Messina). Aristomenes reportedly was taken to Sparta where he was killed, but one legend suggests that he found refuge in Rhodes, where he died in exile. By 620 B.C., the Spartans had firm control of the Messenian plain, and the remaining Messenian Helots were consigned to a life of drudgery on the fertile lands of the Pamisus valley. They continued to resent their treatment and waited for another opportunity to revolt.

The Second Messenian War provoked a major reorganization of the Spartan state. Sparta transformed itself into a permanently militarized society, which was to last for another three centuries. The Second Messenian war also stimulated the development of hoplite warfare, in which armored infantry fought together in regiments in close ranks. This transformation reduced Spartan dependence on the nobility in time of war and increased the importance of the general population. Accompanying the Spartan victory was a growing demand for the redistribution of the newly acquired Messenian lands, which was the probable origin of the practice that gave each Spartan male at birth a minimum parcel of land to be worked by Helots. That practice, in turn, became the basis for the Spartans' considering themselves as equals or peers who could all make their contributions to communal life.

—*Charles H. McArver, Jr.*

See also
Aristomenes; Greece; Helots
For Further Reading
Austin, M. M., and P. Vidal-Naquet. 1977. *Economic and Social History of Ancient Greece: An Introduction.* Berkeley: University of California Press; Forest, W. G. 1980. *A History of Sparta, 950–192.* London: Duckworth; Huxley, G. L. 1962. *Early Sparta.* Cambridge, MA: Harvard University Press; Sealey, Raphael. 1976. *A History of the Greek City States, ca. 700–338* B.C. Berkeley: University of California Press.

SECOND PEACE OF PARIS (NOVEMBER 20, 1815)

The Second Peace of Paris (November 20, 1815) was part of a series of marginally successful British diplomatic efforts to obtain French abolition of the slave trade. The series began with the peace treaty negotiated after Napoleon's first defeat in 1814. The First Peace of Paris (May 30, 1814) contained mild territorial terms and called for no reparations, but it did require that the French abolish the slave trade within five years—the result of intense lobbying by British abolitionists.

Louis XVIII, restored to the throne after Napoleon's defeat, agreed to this provision despite the strong opposition of the French colonial lobby. Indeed, economic and political considerations made the French pledge impossible to enforce. Still, at the Congress of Vienna, France signed a formal declaration (February 4, 1815) in which it again denounced the trade.

In March 1815, Napoleon staged his dramatic return from exile. On March 29, he abolished the slave trade, probably in a vain effort to split Britain off the coalition arrayed against him, but Waterloo sealed his fate. The Second Peace of Paris was much harsher than the first, for it punished France with significant territorial losses (most of Savoy and land on the country's Belgian and eastern borders), payment of an indemnity of 700 million francs, and occupation by 150,000 allied troops for five years. Much greater pressure was also placed on the hapless Louis XVIII, now restored for the second time, to abolish the slave trade.

Indeed, by July 30, 1815, the French statesman Charles-Maurice de Talleyrand had more or less been forced to honor Napoleon's decree and promise the immediate abolition of the trade. In the treaty itself, an additional article, signed by the British and French representatives, foresaw the concerted action of the major powers to abolish the slave trade and referred to the Vienna declaration.

In that article, the contracting parties engaged specifically "to renew conjointly Their efforts, with the view of securing final success to those principles which They proclaimed in the Declaration of the Fourth of February, and of concerting, without loss of time, through their Ministers at the Courts of London and of Paris, the most effectual measures for the entire and definitive abolition of a commerce so odious, and so strongly condemned by the laws of religion and nature" (Parry, 1969). Thus, this modest article stated nothing more, nor less, than the intention to discuss further how to abolish the slave trade, which it condemned in the strongest moral terms.

Eventually, Britain convoked a diplomatic conference at London on August 28, 1816, to consult further on measures to be taken for abolition. This conference failed, for Britain was unable to gain further French concessions on abolition of the trade. The French (clandestine) slave trade continued unabated, as France preferred to honor the five-year grace period of the First Peace of Paris rather than Napoleon's cynical or Louis XVIII's coerced abolition. The French colonial lobby was still very powerful, exercising a great influence on the government, and the French planters, newly restored to their islands, needed a great many slaves in order to restock their plantations. The British intensified their diplomatic efforts for abolition of the trade, notably at the Congress of Verona in 1822.

—*William L. Chew III*

See also

Atlantic Abolitionist Movement; Closing of the African Slave Trade; Illegal Slave Trade; Napoleon Bonaparte; Verona, Congress of; Vienna, Congress of

For Further Reading

Daget, Serge. 1971. "L'Abolition de la traite des Noirs en France de 1814–1831." *Cahiers d'Etudes Africaines* (11)1: 14–58; Parry, Clive, ed. 1969–. *Consolidated Treaty Series.* Dobbs Ferry, NY: Oceana Publications; Putney, Martha. 1975. "The Slave Trade in French Diplomacy from 1814 to 1815." *Journal of Negro History* 60 (3): 411–427; Reich, Jerome. 1968. "The Slave Trade at the Congress of Vienna: A Study in English Public Opinion." *Journal of Negro History* 53: 129–143.

SEMINOLE INDIANS

Slavery played an important role in both the removal and the destruction of the Seminole Indians. The Seminole are a Muskogean tribe whose original home was in Georgia and North Florida, an area first colonized by the Spanish, and they became entangled in the struggle for Florida waged between British, Spanish, and American settlers. Their sympathy for blacks and their leniency toward the slaves they themselves owned caused them many problems after the Americans acquired control of Florida in 1819. Eventually, the Seminole retreated into the Everglades to try to escape removal to Oklahoma.

By the seventeenth century, the Seminole had learned about blacks and black culture from free blacks and slaves who had moved or had been brought into Seminole territory by the Spanish. Before the American Revolution, the Spanish offered freedom to slaves who escaped from the British, and some Seminole eventually bought slaves by paying for them with livestock. Most made little money from the slave labor, although slave ownership increased the prestige of Seminole leaders.

Seminole custom allowed slaves to live in a separate settlement, paying their masters a portion of their produce or livestock. Because the slaves knew more about agriculture than the Seminole, the slaves often became prosperous, eventually clearing large fields and owning livestock herds. The black slaves dressed like their Seminole masters, wearing little clothing when they worked in the fields. On festive occasions, they donned turbans, shawls, beaded moccasins, leggings, and the shiny metal ornaments that the Seminole favored.

Slaves owned by white Americans or Creek and Cherokee Indians often fled into Spanish Florida. When their owners crossed the border to recover them, they met resistance from both the Seminole and

Massacre of whites by blacks and Seminole in the uprising led by Osceola in Florida, December 1835.

the Spanish. Because of their allegiance to Spain, the Seminole were considered fair game by the Americans, who killed or wounded many Seminole in several raids conducted in Spanish territory.

Spain eventually realized it could no longer hold Florida and sold the region to the United States in 1819. The terms of the Adams-Onís Treaty (1819) guaranteed fair treatment for the Seminole, but the United States did not keep its word to the tribe. After Florida became part of the United States, slaveowners in states adjacent to Florida demanded the return of escaped slaves living in the former Spanish territory, many of whom had found refuge with the Seminole, who were noted for their lenient attitude toward slaves. Slave catchers, both white and Native American, were allowed to hunt fugitives in Seminole territory.

During the remainder of James Monroe's presidency (which ended in 1825), the U.S. government embarked on a policy of Indian removal. The Seminole were moved to a smaller reservation in Florida, and the Creek received some of the Seminole land. Consequently, the Seminole had conflicts with the Creek, a larger and more powerful tribe. During this period, blacks who had been free for decades were captured and returned to slavery. There were many conflicts over the return of fugitive slaves, but in such disputes between whites and Indians, the cases were usually settled in favor of the white planters.

Between 1832 and 1833, the U.S. government pressured the Seminole to leave Florida entirely and relocate to Oklahoma. The Seminole feared that if they moved to Indian territory their slaves would be taken by the Creek and that if they stayed in Florida they would lose their slaves to the whites. Although many Seminole did sign the treaties of Payne's Landing and Fort Gibson, agreeing to surrender their lands and relocate within three years, others, under the leadership

of Osceola, refused to leave and started an uprising in 1835. They fled to the Everglades, where they fought the U.S. Army for nearly a decade with the help of runaway black slaves who lived with them.

Although the United States used treachery to capture Osceola, who died in prison, and attempted to conduct a plan of systematic extermination, the Seminole continued to fight. They had mastered the art of guerrilla warfare in the swampy Everglades, and the struggle lasted until 1842, when the government abandoned the war. The conflict had cost the United States $20 million and the lives of 1,500 soldiers, and many Seminole had been killed or had fled to the West. But the United States never succeeded in the total removal of this tribe.

—*Elsa A. Nystrom*

See also
Cherokee Slaveowners
For Further Reading
Covington, James W. 1995. *The Seminoles of Florida.* Gainesville: University Press of Florida; McReynolds, Edwin C. 1988. *The Seminoles.* Norman: University of Oklahoma Press.

SENATUS CONSULTUM CLAUDIANUM
(A.D. 52)

A *senatus consultum* was a document that contained the advice of the Roman Senate on a particular issue after it had been debated. It had no legislative force during the time of the Roman Republic but was de facto binding upon the administration. If vetoed by the presiding magistrates, it remained on record with the authority of the Senate. *Senatus consulta* were usually identified by the name of one of the consuls for the year or, more rarely during the imperial period, by the name of the emperor who proposed the subject for debate.

Senatus Consultum Claudianum was named after Emperor Tiberius Claudius Drusus Nero Germanicus, known as Claudius I, who was proclaimed emperor in A.D. 41. By A.D. 52, the year of this *senatus consultum,* the common practice of manumission had created a large number of former slaves, or freedmen, many of whom had risen to positions of power and influence through commerce or in the imperial civil service. However, Claudius was preoccupied by the problems caused by increasingly frequent marriages between free citizens and freedmen or freedwomen. Even more disturbing were marriages between free citizens and slaves.

The status of slaves who became the legal wives of free citizens had always been unclear: their children were regarded as slaves, and the union was seen as ir-regular. Manumission could be used as a means of el-evating the status of the betrothed woman, but her children would never be more than freedmen them-selves, whatever the social standing of the father. Claudius was particularly concerned about marriage between freewomen and slaves and wanted to punish women who crossed this line between established so-cial strata.

The debate was set against the background of an expanding empire in which cultural, racial, and social diversities were eroding the old fixed hierarchy of slave, freedman, citizen, senator, and patrician—a hi-erarchy that had given each family a secure and un-questioned place in Roman law and custom. Com-merce, manufacturing, extractive industries, and construction had created a wealth that had little con-nection with the patrician and senatorial landowning classes. The taboos that had kept marriage within the class system, so that like married like to protect landed inheritance and privilege, were no longer effective. Claudius pressured the Senate into passing a measure that might serve to stem the progressive and insidious breakdown of class distinctions.

During Claudius's rule, Christians were challenging Roman assumptions about slavery and were banned from the city of Rome, but the tendency to question the underlying philosophy of slavery was evident and threatened social stability. Therefore, Senatus Consul-tum Claudianum decreed that a freewoman who mar-ried a slave with his master's knowledge and consent would be reduced to the rank of a freedwoman, and her children would be born slaves of her husband's owner. A freewoman who married a slave without his master's knowledge or consent would be reduced to

being a slave of her husband's owner, as her children would be from birth. Freewomen who married freed-men would be reduced to their rank, and the children of the union would be barred from attaining free status and denied access to citizenship, as were all freedmen.

—*Lindy J. Rawling*

See also
Roman Empire; Roman Republic
For Further Reading
Barrow, R. H. 1928. *Slavery in the Roman Empire.* London: Macmillan; Charlesworth, M. P., ed. 1939. *Documents Illustrating the Reigns of Claudius and Nero.* Oxford: Oxford University Press; MacMullen, R. 1974. *Roman Social Relations.* New Haven, CT: Yale University Press; Rostovteff, M. 1957. *Social and Eco-nomic History of the Roman Empire.* Oxford: Oxford University Press.

SENECA, LUCIUS ANNAEUS (4 B.C.–A.D. 65)

Born in Cordova, Spain, of a wealthy noble family, Seneca became famous in Stoic phi-losophy, rhetoric, and imperial service as the leading Roman public and literary intellectual in the age of Emperor Nero. As tutor and then adviser to the emperor, he exercised significant political, social, and cultural influence while becoming one of the world's richest men. After falling into disfavor and eventually being implicated in a conspiracy against Nero, Seneca committed suicide by imperial order.

In his many writings, Seneca derived principles for the humane treatment of slaves from a philosophical system that had a considerable following among in-fluential Romans. Nevertheless, Seneca also occasion-ally slipped into echoing some of his society's common prejudices against slaves. A similar inconsistency be-tween the ethical ideals Seneca preached and his own practices emerges in his story about Diogenes. After his only slave ran away, Diogenes did not want him back, saying, "It would be a shame if Diogenes is not able to live without Manes when Manes is able to live without Diogenes." Diogenes was the one who was actually liberated, Seneca explains, since he who is possessionless is happier than a master with many slaves. Still, Seneca kept his slaves and excused himself by saying that we who lack Diogenes' strength of character ought at least to reduce the number of our possessions *(De tranquillitate animi).*

Seneca believed in the Stoic doctrine that "heaven is the one parent of us all" *(De beneficiis)* and that those called slaves sprang from the same stock; share the same sky; breathe, live, and die as their masters do. He remarked that it is as easy for the master to see a freeborn man in his slave as for the slave to see a slave in his master *(Epistolae morales ad Lucilium)*. To his friend Lucilius, Seneca emphasized that slaves are human beings, comrades, humble friends, and our fellow slaves, since fortune has as much power over us as over them *(Epistolae)*.

Seneca denied that slavery's condition penetrates the whole human being. Only the body, he insisted, is at the mercy and disposition of a master while the mind is its own master, so free that not even the body which confines it can restrain it from following its own impulses, setting mighty aims, and escaping into the infinite to consort with the stars *(De beneficiis)*.

Seneca decried the common Roman treatment of slaves as extremely arrogant, cruel, and insulting. He ridiculed those masters who thought it degrading to dine with their slaves *(Epistolae)* and, in contrast, advised his friend to treat his inferiors as he would be treated by his superiors, with kindness and courtesy, and to include them in his discussions, plans, and company *(Epistolae)*. Seneca urged that slaves be pardoned, not whipped or shackled, for laziness, carelessness, loud replies, rebellious looks, and remarks muttered under their breath *(De ira)*. Slaves should be lashed only verbally, since beatings are only for animals *(Epistolae)*.

Seneca praised restraint in ordering slaves around. He recommended treating the free, freeborn, and well-born, not as slaves, but as those of lower rank who have been entrusted to their masters as wards. "Slaves have the right of refuge at a god's statue, and though the law allows you to do anything to a slave, yet there are things which the law common to all living creatures forbids you to do to a human being" *(De clementia)*.

He held that the soul that is upright, good, and great is not under the control of chance. "What else could you call such a soul than a god dwelling as a guest in a human body? A soul like this may descend into a Roman knight just as well as into a freedman's son or a slave. For what is a Roman knight, or a freedman's son, or a slave? They are mere titles, born of ambition or of wrong" *(Epistolae)*. "No one is more noble than another except in so far as the nature of one person is more upright and more capable of good actions" *(De beneficiis)*. "Virtue closes the door to no one; it is open to all, admits all, invites all, the freeborn and the freedman, the slave and the king, and the exile; neither family nor fortune determines its choice, it is satisfied with the naked human being" *(De beneficiis)*.

Therefore, Seneca reasoned, since it is possible for a slave to be just, brave, and magnanimous, it is also possible for a slave to confer benefits on his master *(De beneficiis)*. He challenged the master who scorns receiving benefits from his slave: "Are you to call anyone a slave, slave as you are yourself to lust and gluttony, to a mistress, no, the common possession of numerous mistresses? Are *you* to call anyone a slave?" *(De beneficiis)*.

Few are legal slaves, Seneca observed, but many hold fast to the deeper slavery of vice *(Epistolae)*. "'He is a slave.' But his soul may be that of a free man. 'He is a slave.' But is that to count against him? Show me a man who is not a slave; one is a slave to lust, another to greed, another to ambition; all are slaves to fear. I will show you an ex-consul who is slave to an old hag, a millionaire who is slave to a serving-maid; I will show you youths of the noblest birth who are slaves to pantomime players! No slavery is more disgraceful than one which is self-imposed" *(Epistolae)*.

Seneca's most powerful story about slavery describes a Spartan boy who, after being taken captive, kept crying, "I will not be a slave!" The first time he was ordered to perform the menial task of fetching a chamber pot, the boy dashed his brains out against the wall. "Will you not borrow that boy's courage, and say: 'I am no slave!'? Unhappy man, you are a slave to human beings, you are a slave to your business, you are a slave to life. For life, if courage to die be lacking, is slavery" *(Epistolae)*.

—*William O. Stephens*

See also
Roman Empire; Stoicism

SEPULVEDA, JUAN GINES DE (1490–1573)

A leading figure of the Spanish Renaissance, Juan Ginés de Sepúlveda attained fame during his lifetime as a humanist scholar, translator of Aristotle, and supreme master of Latin style. He was confessor and official chronicler to Charles V and counted among his friends and correspondents sixteenth-century luminaries like Desiderius Erasmus and Hernán Cortés. Apart from his translations of and commentaries upon Aristotle's works, Sepúlveda is perhaps best known for his mid-sixteenth-century efforts to defend and justify the Spanish conquest of America and the resultant enslavement and subjugation of its native population.

Sepúlveda wrote about his ideas concerning Spain's American empire in a tract entitled *Democrates alter* (c. 1547). He believed it was the crown's right and duty to conquer the Indians and to subdue them, if necessary by force of arms. He reached this conclusion by applying Aristotelian concepts of natural aristocracy and just war to Spain's New World venture.

The Indians, he asserted, were patently inferior to Spaniards in their social customs, as was shown by their practice of idolatry, human sacrifice, cannibalism, and other barbaric acts. It was therefore the duty of the Spanish, as a more enlightened people, to lift the Indians from their ignorance and superstition and to teach them the ways of civilized life. Conquest, following Sepúlveda's reasoning, was a legitimate means by which to do so. Moreover, as a people living outside the pale of Christianity, the Indians had to be evangelized and converted, a task—as Sepúlveda emphasized—entrusted by the papacy to the Spanish monarchs.

In that undertaking, the use of force was not only legitimate but also, according to Sepúlveda's interpretation of biblical text, divinely authorized. Although upholding the doctrine of natural aristocracy, Sepúlveda never advocated (as he has often been accused of doing) the enslavement of Indians. This, in his view, was impermissible. What he perceived as their social and cultural inferiority did not, and could not under natural law, make the Indians the slaves of the Spanish.

His unqualified defense of the legitimacy of conquest was strongly opposed by many Spanish jurists and theologians, the most persistent and effective of whom was the Dominican priest and missionary Bartolomé de Las Casas. Las Casas' vehement denunciation of *Democrates alter* persuaded the crown that the issues it raised should be subject to further examination. In 1550, the king ordered all conquests suspended while a panel of jurists, convened in Valladolid, Spain, heard arguments on the question.

The proceedings lasted until 1551 and ultimately proved inconclusive, as no formal report was issued. However, two actions make it clear that the balance of royal favor had tilted toward Las Casas' position: the word "conquest" was to be stricken from the lexicon of Spanish exploration and settlement, which henceforth was known as pacification; and Sepúlveda was denied permission to publish his manuscript. It would be nearly 200 years after its author's death before *Democrates alter* was printed.

—*Russ Davidson*

See also
Las Casas, Bartolomé de; The Requirement
For Further Reading
Dominguez Ortiz, Antonio. 1971. *The Golden Age of Spain: 1516–1659.* New York: Basic Books; Gibson, Charles. 1966. *Spain in America.* New York: Harper and Row; Hanke, Lewis. 1965. *The Spanish Struggle for Justice in the Conquest of America.* Boston: Little, Brown.

SERFDOM IN MEDIEVAL EUROPE

"Serfdom" is a useful, though inaccurate, word to describe peasant conditions in the Middle Ages. A "serf" was a member of the dependent peasantry, and this dependence could arise from personal status or from land tenure. Some serfs were legally unfree, but serfs were not owned as property by a master as slaves were. More often, serfs had some legal rights and some personal freedom, though their lands were held by unfree tenure and subject to burdensome ties of dependence on a lord, such as labor services and restrictions on movement. A spectrum of conditions of semiservitude existed between freedom of person and land tenure, on the one hand, and slavery, on the other. Serfs were often subject to duties and obligations that strongly resembled those imposed on slaves, and the confusion between serfs and slaves is sharpened because the same word, *servus,* was used for both types of status in all medieval Latin sources.

The best way to consider serfdom is to examine it over time. In the early Middle Ages, slavery still existed, and the word *servus* did not mean serf. The overall European movement from the eighth to the twelfth centuries, however, was from clearly differentiated free and slave conditions toward an intermediate status among the dependent peasantry. This trend was first observed by the historian Marc Bloch (1975) and has been confirmed recently by other historians, who attribute the shift toward a mixed status of "serf" (generally around 950–1050) as accompanying the rise of more oppressive forms of local lordship. As lordship became more localized and based upon military force, earlier distinctions between free and unfree people and land were erased. By the high and late Middle Ages, most peasant farmers were considered to be serfs.

In the early Middle Ages, the classical distinctions between different types of peasants working on estates had been largely maintained. Agricultural workers were classified, especially on the great estates of northwestern Europe, in three groups. On the lowest level were slaves. Slaves were owned by and dependent on their lord, who was their master in all ways—landlord, judge, executioner—and who held all judicial and property rights in their person. The second group was made up of *coloni* ("tenant farmers"). *Colonus* was a legal term referring to people who were personally free but whose land belonged to their lord and who were subject to obligations, including rent and labor services. Each lord had some judicial control over his *coloni,* and they could not leave the land without his permission.

The third group was composed of the free peasants, who were both personally free and had their own freehold land, or allod. They relied on public courts for

Medieval serfs at work on a great feudal estate in France.

their rights but were often attached to a lord by some tie of commendation or clientage. These personal ties subjected the peasant to a lord in quasi-legal ways, often including the payment of dues or services, which were called franchises.

High medieval serfdom arose out of a mixture of the status, services, and dues of those three early medieval groups—which were easily confused in practice. For example, the personal dues of free peasants (franchises) resembled the dues *coloni* owed their lord for their land. The dissolution of public power around the year 1000 in most regions, especially the decline of public courts, effectively removed the legal advantages of some free peasants. In particular, free peasants were forced to give up their land to their lord and receive it back as a dependent tenure. At the same time, slavery became increasingly rare. As the strict relations between land and status were mixed up and lords began to take on manorial and judicial authority, the distinctions among different peasant statuses became meaningless.

Over time, the peasantry became a more homogeneous group under the lord, dependent on him economically and also subject to his personal and judicial control. For example, at Villemeux (near Chartres) in 826–829, only about 10 percent of heads of household were listed as *servi* ("slaves") and there were only 82 *coloni* out of a population of 1,639 people. By 1078, the monk Paul of Saint-Père-de-Chartres called all of the inhabitants *agricolae* ("farmers"), though he did distinguish those who owed a head tax. After 1100, the peasants of Villemeux were universally referred to as *servi* in the monastery's charters. Gradually, peasants became indistinguishable to their lords; they all became *servi*, or serfs, and their status and obligations merged.

The merging of free and unfree peasant status into serfdom did not take place evenly over time and place. Some serfs were subject to additional obligations like a head tax or a fee for marriage, lingering remnants of their former servile status. Sometimes there was collective memory about land and status, which preserved the rights of free peasants. Some freemen in the eleventh century, such as the men of the *homines de generali placito* of the monastery of Saint-Vaast-d'Arras, claimed to owe only public obligations and to hold their land freely, as allods.

In the Loire River valley, the *coloni* status disappeared in the tenth to eleventh centuries, though a semifree group, the *colliberti* ("fellow-freedmen"), may have survived. These men, however, were the exception, not the rule. Throughout northern Europe, slaves and free peasants were disappearing. In the south, allodial property holders were still numerous in the early-eleventh century, though they, too, were submerged by more oppressive forms of lordship after

1050. By the twelfth century, the dependent peasantry had largely acquired the status of serfdom, and by the thirteenth century, increasing legalism had formally defined serfdom, usually by unfree land tenure and the obligation to make payments or perform labor service.

In the later Middle Ages, economic crises in the early-fourteenth century, combined with the onset of the Black Death, had a dramatic effect on the peasantry as a whole. Sudden depopulation reduced the available labor supply throughout Europe, and as the number of laborers decreased, their wages (in both monetary and real terms) increased. Many serfs were able to replace burdensome labor services with money payments or abandon the farm altogether for wage-earning jobs. Many lords adopted new strategies to deal with the decline in labor, including repressive legislation affirming serfdom and thereby controlling peasant movement and labor. The result was peasant revolts—in England (1381), the "Jacquerie" in France in the fifteenth century, as well as in Catalonia (1388–1486) and Hungary, to name only the most famous instances. A redistribution of fortunes, of more resources among fewer people, allowed peasants to improve their conditions, which allowed many to throw off the yoke of serfdom.

—*Robert Berkhofer*

See also
Coloni; Domesday Book; Roman Law; Slavery in Medieval Europe; Vikings
For Further Reading
Bloch, Marc. 1975. *Slavery and Serfdom in the Middle Ages*. Berkeley: University of California Press; Duby, Georges. 1980. *The Three Orders: Feudal Society Imagined*. Chicago: University of Chicago Press; Freedman, Paul. 1991. *The Origins of Peasant Servitude in Medieval Catalonia*. Cambridge: Cambridge University Press.

SERVI POENAE

Servitus poenae means literally "slavery of the punishment" and roughly translates as "penal slavery." Declared by a Roman local magistrate, governor, or emperor, the sentence was capital, and upon pronouncement the individual became a slave. It differed from other types of slavery, because it was a second-century-A.D. legal development. Several forms of punishment constituted penal slavery, and although the legal evidence refers to the condition of *servi poenae* ("penal slaves") as permanent and unredeemable, reality was otherwise.

Although first mentioned explicitly in a statement by Emperor Antoninus Pius (86–161; r. 138–161) in the Justinian Digests, the nature of the documentation conceals a more complicated evolution. Udo Zilletti (1968) argued that since the penal slave in effect had no master, the status might have been a tangent of another legal condition, *servos sine domino* ("slave without master"). Although the first occurrence of the status of *servi poenae* is impossible to establish, an abolition date is possible, for in the sixth century, Justinian ruled that men sentenced to the mines were no longer *servi poenae*.

The status is evidence for the changing position of slaves within Roman society and the problems created by the extension of citizenship in A.D. 212. It is also cited to support the theory that punishments became harsher in the later empire. The sentence could only be passed on lower-class citizens *(humiliores)* and slaves. In the late empire, the appearance of two classes of citizens led to gradations of punishments. Officials, priests, veterans, and their descendants could not become *servi poenae*. Most unusually, slaves could be punished by further enslavement.

There is no discernible relationship between the type of crime and the penalty. Although some crimes could be committed only by slaves (e.g., running away), political crimes and false allegations were also dealt with severely. Superficially, the status indicates that certain behavior was considered servile in nature.

The characteristics of *servitus poenae* were threefold. It was a punishment that was lawful, capital, and perpetual. Not every capital sentence resulted in slavery, although until Justinian, people sentenced to death were deemed slaves until execution. The interval enabled the captors to extract evidence by torture, as slaves could only be witnesses if tortured first. Common forms of this type of slavery included condemnation to the mines *(in metallum* or *ad opus metalli)* and *ludum venatorium ad bestias* (hunting wild animals in an arena).

Every sentence included seizure of all goods and chattels by the imperial treasury—prearranged gifts and dowries were honored. Although the status was supposedly perpetual, Antoninus Pius provided for the release of old, frail prisoners after a minimum 10-year sentence. Similarly, a convict who successfully managed to outwit the beasts in the arena might be released after 3 years.

Since a *servus poenae* was not individual property, he could not be manumitted. Release resulted in work befitting *servi publici* ("public slaves"). Complete liberty required an imperial decree, and even then the slave did not recover his former private rights or estate. The new freedman was in an unusual and entirely inequitable position. *Servi poenae* who had formerly been private slaves were restored to that position. Thus, the extraordinary situation of a slave released from slavery, only to become again a slave, existed.

—*Benjamin N. Lawrance*

See also
Cicero; Roman Empire; Roman Law; Roman Republic
For Further Reading
Gamsey, Peter. 1970. *Social Status and Legal Privilege in the Roman Empire*. Oxford: Clarendon Press.

SERVUS VICARIUS

The literal meaning of the Latin term *servus vicarius* is "deputy slave" or "substitute slave." A less formal rendering would be "a slave's slave." In Roman law, from the second century B.C. onward, the *servus vicarius* was either a slave who acted as a substitute or helper of another slave or, more specifically, a slave who was part of the *peculium* of another slave. The *peculium* was a fund of money and other objects, including slaves, that was put at a slave's disposal by his owner. Since Roman slaves could not own property of any kind, the *peculium* belonged to the master, who was legally entitled to resume control of it at any time.

Slaves used their *peculium* to conduct business on behalf of their owners and for their own profit. Slaves who were in another slave's *peculium* acted as his agents. In principle, a *servus vicarius* could be assigned his own *servus vicarius* out of the superior slave's *peculium*. The *servus vicarius* as a slave's slave had a parallel in the *servus peculiaris*, a slave given to an unemancipated son (who lacked full legal capacity) by his father.

Only privileged slaves, who were sometimes referred to as *servi ordinarii*, were given deputy slaves. These included financial administrators and business managers, highly ranked domestic servants, and physicians. Both slaves owned by private citizens and slaves owned by the emperor were provided with deputies. A *servus vicarius* helped to augment the funds in the *peculium* of a *servus ordinarius* and increased his prestige within the Roman slave society, where great attention was paid to subtle hierarchical gradations. Thus, the assignment of deputy slaves served as a means of rewarding and gratifying slaves who held positions of trust, or were otherwise of importance to their owners, and helped to ensure their cooperation and productivity. Virtually all slaves known to have had deputies were male, but the *servus vicarius* could be of either sex.

Slaves of slaves were also known outside Roman society. They are noted as early as Homer's *Odyssey* (eighth century B.C.) and are documented as existing in fourth-century-B.C. Athens.

—*Walter Scheidel*

See also
Peculium
For Further Reading
Reduzzi Merola, Francesca. 1990. *"Servo parere": Studi sulla condizione giuridica degli schiavi vicari e di sottoposti a schiavi nelle esperienze greca e romana.* Camerino, Italy: Jovene; Weaver, P. R. C. 1964. "Vicarius and vicarianus in the familia Caesaris." *Journal of Roman Studies* 54: 117–128.

SEXUAL SLAVERY, JAPANESE MILITARY

Japanese military sexual slavery refers to the system of the so-called comfort women that imperial Japan instituted to cater to soldiers' sexual needs before and during World War II. Slavery, defined as an extreme form of the human relation of domination, can be conceived both as a personal relation and as an institutional process, both rooted in the total power of the master and the total powerlessness of the slave (Patterson, 1982). Sexual slavery, then, can be defined as a relation of domination based on sex. According to Kathleen Barry (1984), female sexual slavery is present in a social condition of sexual exploitation and violence from which a woman or a girl cannot escape. Testimonies of former comfort women reveal that they were forced into a social condition of female sexual slavery.

Since 1992, a precedent-setting international human rights debate has raged over the interpretation of the institution of comfort women (in Japanese, *jugun ianfu,* "military comfort women"). In an effort to deny state responsibility, some Japanese—including veteran politicians—claim the comfort women were autonomous prostitutes. International human rights and feminist organizations argue that the women were sexual slaves recruited by the Japanese military.

At the core of the international dispute over the representation of comfort women as prostitutes or sexual slaves is the issue of state responsibility. On a deeper level, many of the central issues of sexual violence against women in warfare and colonialism, and the cultural constructions of gender and sexuality in all patriarchies, are being called into question. Indeed, the issues involved in the comfort women problem are complex, ranging from the perennial question concerning the proper relationship between prostitution and the state to the unprecedented abuse of power by the state in forcing tens of thousands of women—including premenarche teenage girls and young married women—into sexual labor during the war.

The coerced sexual labor (i.e., sexual slavery) was inflicted primarily upon lower-class young females of colonial Korea by imperial Japan during the Pacific war, but Japanese women and women of other occupied territories (such as Taiwan, the Philippines, Indonesia, Burma, Thailand, and the South Pacific islands) were also used as comfort women. There is no way to determine precisely how many women were forced to serve as comfort women, but estimates range between 70,000 and 200,000—about 80 percent of them were Korean.

From the perspective of imperial Japan, the system of comfort women was an institutionalization of paternalistic *omoiyari* ("consideration") to reward the soldiers with time away from their military duties so they might enjoy brief moments of recreational sex under state supervision. Military "comfort stations" (where the members of the Japanese Imperial Army could engage in recreational sex under the supervisory control of the state) came into being as early 1932 for the benefit of soldiers stationed in China after the Japanese had seized Manchuria the previous year. From 1932 to 1945, comfort stations existed wherever the Japanese troops were stationed in Japan, Korea, China, Southeast Asia, and the South Pacific. The comfort women became essential supplies for the military in order to help keep morale high. In fact, when the comfort women were transported on the military ships, they were simply listed as "military supplies" with no record of their personal identities.

Korea was under Japanese colonial rule from 1910 to 1945, which facilitated the conscription of countless Korean women for the sexual pleasure of the Japanese military. Although the draft of Korean women was made legally possible by 1942, their recruitment was nominally carried out on the basis of "voluntary" participation. That is why the Japanese government persistently denied until 1993 that there was any coercion in the recruitment of Korean women into the Voluntary Labor Service Corps (VLSC). In fact, the Teishintai (pronounced Chôngsindae in Korean), which is the Japanese name for the VLSC, literally means the "voluntarily-submitting-body" *(teishin)* corps *(-tai).* From the Japanese perspective, these women were, as colonial subjects of imperial Japan, performing their patriotic, gendered duty by "comforting" soldiers with their sexuality.

Japan had a state-regulated system of licensed prostitution until 1958, so it is easy to understand how the system of comfort women was considered by both the state and the society in general as nothing more than an extension to the troops of a commercial service available to other Japanese men. In traditional, patriarchal Japan and Korea, having recreational sex outside matrimony was one of the unchallenged prerogatives of the husband while the wife was expected be chaste even after the death of her husband. The Japanese criminal code of 1908, for example, punished wives for committing adultery but not philandering husbands unless their partner was someone else's wife (Garon, 1993). Similarly, most women who had served as comfort women were unable to lead a normal family life, for they had lost their virginity, but the men who had had sex with them had no problem being reintegrated into their family and/or marital life after the war ended.

Given the nature of the masculine sexual culture in the patriarchal states of Japan and Korea, it is not surprising that official silence about the comfort women issue was maintained for more than four decades after the war ended in 1945. In fact, any discussion of sexual exploitation of Korean women by imperial Japan during the war was conspicuous by its complete absence in Korean history books until recently. Perhaps recognition that an indigenous system of professional female entertainers (*kisaeng*) had existed in dynastic Korea to "entertain the soldiers" stationed on the northern border may have helped Koreans accept the system of comfort women as a fact of life (Soh, 1996).

The issue of Japanese military sexual slavery came to the attention of the international community in 1992 when the Korean Council for the Women Drafted for Military Sexual Slavery by Japan took the issue to the United Nations Human Rights Commission after the discovery by a Japanese historian of documentary evidence of the heavy involvement of the Japanese government in the comfort women system. As a consequence, the Korean comfort women movement for redress was transformed from a bilateral compensation dispute over forced labor to an international human rights issue.

The revolutionary concept of women's human rights has redefined the issue of comfort women as that of sexual slavery by the state. One must point out, however, that the categorical definition of comfort women as sex slaves ignores the historical reality of commercial sex in which some comfort women participated. Although the universal concept of women's human rights will undoubtedly contribute to more egalitarian heterosexual power relations in patriarchal state systems, there are some fundamental political economic issues of social stratification and sexual slavery that feminist scholars and human rights activists alike must confront at the family, community, national, and global levels. These issues include power relations at the intersection of gender, class, ethnicity, and nation; the philosophical tensions between universal and ethnic-national values as exemplified by the debate over the concept of international human rights and the principle of cultural relativism; and the economic realities of pervasive commoditization of human sexuality in increasingly consumer-oriented pleasure-seeking societies.

—*Chunghee Sarah Soh*

See also
Comfort Women; Kim Hak-sun; Korean Council; Yun Chông-ok
For Further Reading
Barry, Kathleen. 1984. *Female Sexual Slavery*. New York: New York University Press; Garon, Sheldon. 1993. "The World's Oldest Debate? Prostitution and the State in Imperial Japan, 1900–1945." *American Historical Review* 98(3): 710–732; Patterson, Orlando. 1982. *Slavery and Social Death*. Cambridge, MA: Harvard University Press; Soh, Chunghee Sarah. 1996. "The Korean 'Comfort Women' Movement for Redress: From a Bilateral Compensation to a Human Rights Issue." *Asian Survey* 36 (12): 1226–1240.

SHADD, MARY ANN (1823–1893)

The first female editor of a North American weekly newspaper in Canada, Mary Ann Shadd, a black herself, fought for the integration of blacks into society. Fiery and immensely controversial, she promoted abolition, equal rights, and woman suffrage.

Born on October 9, 1823, in Wilmington, Delaware, to Abraham and Harriet Shadd, she grew up in an activist family. Her childhood home was an Underground Railroad stop, and her father represented Delaware at national conventions for the Improvement of Free People of Color. Like many other activists, Mary Ann Shadd decided to settle in Canada West (present-day Ontario) after passage of the Fugitive Slave Act of 1850 made life hazardous for Northern blacks. As the final destination of the Underground Railroad, Canada already had a sizable black community, and after emigrating in 1851, Shadd opened a school to educate fugitive slaves and other blacks who were unable to obtain schooling. She encouraged others to emigrate and published the instructional pamphlet *Notes of Canada West* (1852) as an aid. An immensely popular guidebook, it helped many fugitives survive the trauma of relocation.

After meeting the antislavery journalist Samuel Ringgold Ward, Shadd pressed him into helping launch one of the best fugitive slave weeklies, the staunchly integrationist *Provincial Freeman,* in 1853. Nonsectarian and apolitical, the newspaper advocated temperance to achieve its primary goal, elevating the black race. Although listed as editor, Ward was merely a figurehead: Shadd was the pivot upon which the paper turned.

Through the *Freeman*, she continued advocating black emigration, a preference that placed her in conflict with many influential African American abolitionists. Never faint of heart, Shadd penned powerful editorials encouraging blacks in Canada West to insist on fair treatment, even if that meant being assaulted. Repelled by the begging of newly freed slaves, Shadd pushed fellow emigrants to reach for financial independence. In the *Freeman* of March 25, 1854, she asserted that the fugitives' progress "would be a triumphant rebuke to those who once held them as chattels, and to those who hold that the slave requires to be prepared for freedom, for [former slaves] would exhibit the spectacle of a people just escaped from a galling yoke competing as free men, successfully and honorably."

By the late 1850s, the newspaper was regarded as the organ of Martin R. Delany's African Civilization Society. Plagued by financial difficulties throughout its existence, the *Freeman* folded about 1858, after the black community's sexism had forced Shadd to turn the editorship of the paper over to her brother Isaac.

Marrying Thomas Cary in 1856, Shadd bore two children before being widowed in 1860. Returning to the United States to recruit Union troops, she retired to Washington, D.C., after the U.S. Civil War to teach, and she died there in 1893. A legendary crusader for justice, Shadd blazed a remarkable trail.

—*Caryn E. Neumann*

See also

Delany, Martin R.; Fugitive Slave Act of 1850; Underground Railroad

For Further Reading

Bearden, Jim, and Linda Jean Butler. 1977. *Shadd: The Life and Times of Mary Shadd Cary.* Toronto: NC Press; Hancock, Harold B. 1973. "Mary Ann Shadd: Negro Editor, Educator, and Lawyer." *Delaware History* 15 (3): 187–194; Rhodes, Jane. 1992. "Breaking the Editorial Ice: Mary Ann Shadd Cary and the Provincial Freeman." Ph.D. dissertation, Department of History, University of North Carolina, Chapel Hill; Silverman, Jason. 1985. *Unwelcome Guests: Canada West's Response to American Fugitive Slaves, 1800–1865.* Millwood, NY: Associated Faculty Press.

SHADRACH FUGITIVE SLAVE CASE

The first successful rescue of a runaway slave held in federal custody under the Fugitive Slave Act of 1850 occurred on February 15, 1851, when local blacks seized Shadrach Minkins from a Boston, Massachusetts, courtroom. Minkins was never recaptured, and no convictions were ever secured against the people who had aided in his escape.

Prior to fleeing bondage, Minkins had been a ser-

vant in the Norfolk, Virginia, household of John Debree, a purser in the U.S. Navy. In May 1850, Minkins escaped to Boston, where he worked until his capture as a waiter in the busy commercial district near the city's wharves. To minimize the risk of recapture, he often adopted the pseudonym Frederick Wilkins. On February 12, 1851, John Caphart, a Norfolk constable hired by Debree to track Minkins, arrived in Boston seeking Minkins's rendition (legal return to slavery). Caphart obtained a warrant for Minkins's arrest from George Ticknor Curtis, the federal fugitive slave commissioner in the city, and three days later, Minkins was arrested by U.S. Marshal Patrick Riley.

Minkins was immediately taken before Commissioner Curtis for a hearing on the question of his rendition. The Boston Vigilance Committee appointed six prominent local attorneys, including the black jurist Robert Morris, to serve as his counsel. After they requested and were granted a three-day delay to prepare a defense, everyone except Morris, Minkins, and several marshals left the courtroom. Suddenly, as if by a prearranged signal, several dozen local blacks pushed open the door, rushed inside, seized a surprised Minkins, and hustled him out of the building and into the street. Within minutes, they had disappeared into the African American neighborhood on Beacon Hill. Through the efforts of Morris, the black abolitionist Lewis Hayden, and their contacts on the Underground Railroad, Minkins reached the safety of Montreal, Canada East (now Quebec), within a few days.

News of the rescue reverberated throughout the nation's capital. Senator Henry Clay of Kentucky demanded a thorough investigation, and President Millard Fillmore ordered the U.S. attorney to try all persons who may have "aided, abetted, or assisted" in Minkins's escape (Collinson, 1997). The ensuing investigation led to the arrest of eight local abolitionists, including Morris and Hayden, for their alleged roles in the rescue. All eight were indicted by a federal grand jury and tried in U.S. district court. The initial trials in May and June 1851 showed the weakness of the government's case. Five of the accused were immediately acquitted owing to insufficient evidence; the other three were bound over for retrial on various technicalities. Although the retrials dragged on for over a year, all of the alleged rescuers were eventually acquitted and released.

The Minkins rescue, and the inability of federal authorities to convict any of his rescuers, proved a major embarrassment to the Fillmore administration and raised sectional tensions between North and South. The affair also heightened the determination of free blacks in the North, and their abolitionist colleagues, to resist enforcement of the Fugitive Slave Act of 1850.

—*Roy E. Finkenbine*

See also
Fugitive Slave Act of 1850; Slave Catchers; Underground Railroad
For Further Reading
Collison, Gary. 1997. *Shadrach Minkins: From Fugitive Slave to Citizen*. Cambridge, MA: Harvard University Press.

SHARP, GRANVILLE (1735–1813)

Of the major eighteenth-century British abolitionists, Granville Sharp was the most prolific writer and the most concerned with legal rights of both individual blacks and blacks in general. In 1772, he brought the James Somersett case before the court, and it was that case that established the principle that any slave who reached British soil would become free.

Born in Durham, England, on November 19, 1735, the youngest son of the archbishop of Northumberland and grandson of the archbishop of York, Sharp received only a grammar-school education and was destined for a trade. While apprenticed to a Quaker linen draper in London, Sharp taught himself Greek and Hebrew so that he could understand the Bible better. His first publications involved biblical scholarship and linguistics. In 1758, he obtained a position in the ordnance department, which he felt compelled to resign in 1776 because he opposed war with America's rebellious colonies.

Sharp's introduction to the slavery question came in the person of Jonathan Strong, a slave aged 16 or 17 whose master, David Lisle, a lawyer and planter, had brought him from Barbados to London. In London, Lisle threw Strong into the street after having severely pistol-whipped him. Sharp met Strong outside the door of Sharp's brother William, who gave the poor free medical help. Two years later, having recovered thanks to the Sharps' medical and financial aid, Strong was seen by his former owner and sold by him to a Jamaican planter, James Kerr, for £30, to be paid upon Strong's delivery to a ship bound for Jamaica.

When Strong was jailed by two slave catchers hired by Lisle, he appealed to Granville Sharp, who gained his release by appealing to the lord mayor of London. Sued by Kerr for property loss and challenged to a duel by Lisle, Sharp's own solicitors told him that Strong was legally a slave and thus property. Sharp bought a complete law library to prepare himself to argue the law, which intimidated the plaintiffs' lawyers into dropping the case.

Sharp had won by default, but the experience made him determined to gain a definitive legal ruling that would overturn the 1729 opinion by Attorney General Sir Philip Yorke and Solicitor General Charles Talbot that slavery was legal in England. While waiting for a suitable case, Sharp published his refutation of Yorke and Talbot: *A Representation of the Injustice and Dangerous Tendency of Tolerating Slavery, or of Admitting the Least Claim of Private Property of Men, in England* (1769). This work includes a denunciation of the American colonists' hypocrisy in practicing slavery while objecting to political oppression.

Sharp's intervention on Strong's behalf quickly became well known in London's Afro-British community, and he was consulted in the cases of the kidnapped former slaves Mary Hylas (1766) and Thomas Lewis (1770), both of whom were physically and legally rescued through Sharp's efforts. Neither case resulted in the definitive ruling he sought.

That ruling was finally achieved in the judgment by William Murray, first earl of Mansfield, on the Somersett case (1772), in which Mansfield, lord chief justice of the King's Bench, ruled that masters could not legally force slaves to return to the colonies and thus they were free on English soil. Mansfield's decision was widely received in England as an emancipation proclamation for all slaves in the country.

Not surprisingly, Olaudah Equiano sought Sharp's aid in an effort to rescue the kidnapped former slave John Annis in 1774, but they were unsuccessful. In 1783, Equiano brought to Sharp's attention the atrocity of mass murder on the slave ship *Zong*—the ship's captain had ordered 133 slaves thrown overboard to collect insurance on cargo that had been lost. Although Sharp failed in attempts to have the murderers prosecuted, he remained close friends with Equiano, whom he attended on his deathbed. In 1786, Afro-Britons Quobna Ottobah Cugoano and William Green gained Sharp's help in rescuing Henry Demane from possible reenslavement.

Demane soon left Britain as a participant in the Sierra Leone settlement, the Province of Freedom, which Sharp was involved with from the beginning. Seeing the proposed settlement in Africa of England's black poor as an opportunity to demonstrate the feasibility of his ideas for radical political reform, Sharp published *A Short Sketch of Temporary Regulations (until Better Shall Be Proposed) for the Intended Settlement on the Grain Coast of Africa, near Sierra Leona* (1786). His contribution to the establishment was acknowledged in the naming of its capital Granville Town. Sharp maintained faith in the experiment despite many disappointments, including Demane's engagement in the slave trade and the desertion and death of many original settlers.

After the Province of Freedom failed as the result of internal and external forces, Sharp was instrumental in founding a second Sierra Leone settlement supported by the St. George's Bay Company (later the Sierra Leone Company), which he had conceived to develop trade with Africa. Sharp lived to see the settlement become a crown colony in 1808.

During his activities on behalf of individuals and blacks in general, Sharp continued publishing tracts against slavery—there were five in 1776 alone, including *The Just Limitation of Slavery in the Laws of God, Compared with the Unbounded Claims of the African Traders and British Slaveholders*—and works on political reform, religion, and the evil of naval press gangs. He was a major participant in the movement to abolish the transatlantic slave trade and helped to found in 1787 the Society for Effecting the Abolition of the Slave Trade, which he chaired. He encouraged Prime Minister William Pitt's efforts to legislate the end of the trade, and after the French Revolution in 1789, Sharp corresponded with leaders of the French abolitionist movement. Sharp's attention turned increasingly to religious subjects and activities in his last years. He died on July 6, 1813.

—*Vincent Carretta*

See also

Abolition, British Empire; Clarkson, Thomas; Cugoano, Quobna Ottobah; Equiano, Olaudah; Murray, William; Sierra Leone; *Zong* Case

For Further Reading

Hoare, Prince. 1820. *Memoirs of Granville Sharp, Esq.* London: Printed for Henry Colburn; Lascelles, Edward. 1969. *Granville Sharp and the Freedom of Slaves in England*. New York: Negro Universities Press.

SHIPBUILDING

When ordering the construction of a ship in 1772, Aaron Lopez of Newport, Rhode Island, requested "a double deck brigantine—with an awning, gratings, and airports" (Chapelle, 1967). The awning suggests that the vessel would be anchored for long periods on the African coast; except for gratings and airports, the brigantine might have been engaged in any trade. The fact that the ship was to be double-decked meant that below the slave deck was a lower hold that could carry both provisions for the slaves and some extra cargo. Essentially, vessels engaged in the slave trade were regular merchant ships with some specialized features and could engage in other trades with little difficulty. That facility changed when the slave trade was declared illegal by several nations in the early-nineteenth century.

Most vessels are designed as compromises in order to serve a variety of purposes. When the British navy was hunting slavers after the Napoleonic Wars in the nineteenth century, vessels engaged in the slave trade had to be crafted with speed as the main requirement. The slavers also had to be simply and cheaply built to minimize the owners' financial loss if captured. These factors led to rapid and dramatic changes in ship design and construction.

Traditionally, the rib or frame of merchant ships consisted of two sets of heavy timbers pegged together as they rose from the keel to the upper deck. The space between these double frames was equal to the width of the timbers. This method consumed much wood and labor but produced a stout hull able to carry any cargo and withstand the pounding of huge waves.

But a slave vessel carried far less weight than a merchant ship of the same size. A cargo of 200 slaves would weigh no more than 14 tons. Food for the slaves would not amount to much weight (about 9 tons), but drinking water needs could add up to 18 tons. A crew of 25 men, with larger rations than those given to the slaves, would add 9 tons to the weight aboard the vessel. In order to carry a burden less than half that of an ordinary merchant ship, the slaver had no need of heavy frames spaced closely together. Builders experimented with widely spaced double frames and with alternating double and single frames—again with more than the traditional gap between timbers. The result was a lighter vessel that required less timber to construct.

Another way of saving weight and reducing construction costs was to eliminate the lower deck. The hull thus became an open area with slaves placed on mats that covered the barrels of water and provisions directly beneath. Although this system reduced the number of slaves a vessel could carry, they and their provisions could be loaded in a much shorter time, and the reduction in loading time on the African coast was important to slavers since that was the period they were most vulnerable to British warships. Construction costs were further reduced by lowering the freeboard of the vessels. Placing the height of the deck just three feet above the waterline, instead of the four or five feet of a general merchant ship, meant that the slaver required still less timber to construct and could load a cargo even more quickly.

The changes in slave ship design and construction practices led to serious problems. By reducing the number and size of timbers in the hull, builders saved weight at the cost of strength. Although the slightly built hulls could support the lower weight requirements of the slave trade, they may have been insufficient to withstand the forces generated by the ships' large sails. The weakening of the hull was only the first of several problems with the newer slave ships.

The elimination of the lower deck on some vessels meant that an ocean wave that came aboard could easily and quickly fill the hull and cause the ship to founder. The chances of this happening were increased by the lower freeboard of the slaver, by the practice of carrying more sail than was customary aboard merchant ships, and by some owners' preference for large hatches. The plans of slavers show two types of hatchways: large ones, which offered more air to the slaves and probably increased their survival rate, and small ones, which protected the vessel from waves entering the hull and increased the control of slaves by limiting their movement from hull to deck. Thus, a simple thing like the size of the hatchways reflected whether the ship's owner gave higher priority to the health requirements of the slaves or the survival of the vessel.

The absence of a lower deck in some slavers also meant that the barrels of provisions could not be wedged in as securely as aboard a ship with a double-deck arrangement. If all went well during the passage and no storms were encountered, the provisions probably remained secure, but violent storm waves could cause the barrels to shift and overturn the vessel. Another problem caused by the lack of a lower deck was the pollution of the water supply by the human waste of the slaves who were forced to lie directly above the water barrels. Some slavers attempted to protect the water barrels by laying sheets of lead over them.

A final problem that can be traced to the abandonment of the lower deck was the practice of trying to provide slaves with a level sleeping surface by filling up the gaps between barrels with firewood. Firewood was always in great demand aboard ships and was usually stowed in any available corner. But placing firewood within reach of the slaves meant that they had a supply of crude but useful clubs to use as weapons against the crew.

Although the changes to slave ships made them more difficult to capture, they also became more vulnerable to the problems described above. Consequently, such vessels were better suited to escape pursuers than to survive the surprises of an unforgiving sea.

—Joseph Goldenberg

For Further Reading
British Parliamentary Papers: Slave Trade. 1969–1971. 95 vols. Shannon: Irish University Press; Chapelle, Howard. 1927. *The Baltimore Clipper.* Salem, MA: Marine Research Society; Chapelle, Howard. 1967. *The Search for Speed under Sail.* New York: Norton.

SHIPS

Successful economic systems of subjugation and enslavement involve a transportation component to transport the enslaved a considerable distance from their homelands, and generally, maritime commerce plays a significant role in transporting slaves. Throughout the slave-trading era, vessels specifically built for slaving were the rarity rather than the norm, although it is likely that some vessels were dedicated to the trade, especially in the Atlantic. Archaeology has thus far yielded the remains of only one true slave ship, *Henrietta Marie* (1699), a West Indiaman of 100 or so tons, to provide tangible evidence about the construction of and life aboard a slaver, but for the ships of the transatlantic system, historical documents provide much information.

Slave systems of antiquity depended upon the subjugation of captured peoples to supply the demand. We know there was maritime commerce in small vessels in the Bronze Age, but the archaeological record does not include tangible evidence of slave trading. A shipwreck dating to about the era of Alexander the Great was found near Kyrenia on Cyprus's northern coast. It represents a type of utility trading vessel capable of sailing the waters of the Aegean and Mediterranean that was constructed shell-first with mortises and tenons fastening the planks. Owing to constraints of size because of the construction method, this type of vessel neared a length of 15 meters (nearly 50 feet), had broad beams, and was square-rigged.

There were many slaves throughout the Roman Empire, and they served in various positions, but most notably on the huge agricultural estates called latifundia. The Romans had a diverse and extensive seafaring tradition, which enabled not only overseas conquest but also widespread maritime commerce in the waters of the Mediterranean and beyond. Returning from conquest, generals would parade their captive slaves through Rome's streets prior to sale, most probably having transported them in round sailing ships, or *corbita*.

Those ships were constructed shell first and had large mortise and tenon joinery fastening the planks and frames carved to fit the planking's shape. Iconography depicts them as square-rigged and open-hulled with a platform in the stern where the helmsman stood. The posts were convex, with the stern being higher and fuller and the raking bow lower. Another ship type, the *ponto,* was more fit for sailing in open water as it had a higher bow with a prominent cutwater, and this type of ship probably would have carried slaves from farther distances like the well-traveled route from Carthage to Rome. Roman vessels could be quite large: one vessel, dating to the first or second century B.C., was approximately 40 meters (nearly 131 feet) in length and had a double-planked hull.

Nineteenth-century lithograph of a Brazilian slave ship.

In the medieval period, slaves were shipped in various types of vessels. Pilgrims to the Holy Land reported the shipping of thousands of slaves in Islamic vessels, giant three-masted, double-ended ships that carried goods and passengers. These vessels were rigged fore and aft with traditional lateen sails and were steered by large steering oars lashed to the quarter. Slaves were put to the oars of the war galleys of the crusading knights and the Muslims, who made raids upon one another's cities for the purpose of carrying away more slaves for ransom.

The luxury trade in domestic servants and slave girls, which comprised most of the chattel trade in the medieval period, was probably conducted in the Mediterranean in comparatively small, privately owned merchant craft that were lateen-rigged and steered with quarter rudders. History also reports the transport of slaves on rivers in large canoes by the Russians to Constantinople; the slaves were expected to portage the vessels en route to market when the rivers were impassable.

A revolution in shipbuilding technology during the Renaissance led to the development of a multimasted, full-rigged ship that mounted a stem rudder and could sail to windward better, which made navigation of the African coast and the Atlantic possible. The ships used in these early voyages of discovery, called caravels, were the first vessels to transport African slaves to the New World in 1502. Little is known of the actual construction details of the caravel, except it was a tiny vessel with a composite rig of square and lateen sails. The sixteenth-century transatlantic slave trade was dominated by Iberian craft like the caravel and the *naos*, a generic term for a large round sailing ship.

Colonization and sugar cultivation in the West Indies led to increased shipping of slaves by European nations in the latter-sixteenth and early-seventeenth centuries, and specific companies for the trade and shipping of slaves developed. Initially, the ships that were used in the Africa trade were a mixed lot: John Hawkins, the first Englishman to make a slaving voyage, sailed to the Guinea coast for the first time in 1562 with three ships that could carry loads of 120, 100, and 40 tons. When he returned for a second voyage, his fleet included the aged, former naval vessel *Jesus of Lubeck*, which displaced 700 tons. At the peak of the slave trade, the West Indiamen for the most part averaged around 200–300 tons. These were full-bodied, deep-hulled sailing ships.

Slave ships of the late-seventeenth and eighteenth centuries could be built for and exploited exclusively by the slave trade, but there is scant evidence to show that slavers differed significantly from other contemporary West Indiamen in fundamental design and construction. Ships were specifically fitted out for the conduct of the trade: deck hatches were smaller than on standard merchantmen, the galley apparatus was more extensive to meet the needs of the cargo, and many ships had separate compartments for the stowage of males and females. The holds of slave ships were intensely crowded with rough pallets fitted between the decks so that slaves were stacked one atop another.

Slavers were well-armed vessels, fitted with several cannon to defend against interlopers and pirates that would steal their cargoes and antipersonnel weapons and deck arms that could be and were used as a final means of cargo control aboard ship. Slavers carried larger crews than other merchant ships for those same reasons. During the peak of the Jamaican trade in the 1780s, a ship of slightly less than 200 tons might have 40 sailors aboard to handle the more than 400 slaves that would be packed into the hold.

When the maritime trade in slaves was outlawed by Britain and suppressed by the Royal Navy in the nineteenth century, the ships employed in the slave trade had to undergo a dramatic transformation if the commerce were to continue. Now operating as smugglers, slavers adopted the swift hull form of the Baltimore Clippers. These sharply built vessels sacrificed substantial hold space in comparison to the European ships that had been used in the trade in the late-eighteenth century, but the rise in prices for new slaves made the trade so lucrative that ships could be built for a single voyage and destroyed upon its completion and still turn a profit on the entire venture.

Several shipbuilders from the Chesapeake Bay area in the United States relocated to Havana and Bermuda during the depression in shipbuilding that came after the War of 1812 ended and began to produce ships that were specifically designed for slaving—balancing hold space and speed. These ships typically had straight sheers with no upperworks or pronounced superstructures, which gave them a sleek appearance. Slavers flew a great deal of sail in order to maximize their speed on the transatlantic voyage, usually favoring a brig rig. The holds of these shallow-draft ships were swept and single-decked, with the slaves often lying atop woven mats placed on top of the casks that held the ship's stores.

The use of steam-driven craft by the Royal Navy's African Squadron did much to suppress the swift and nimble privateer-style slavers, who were able to work their vessels in the slightest winds of the Guinea coast and into the shallowest waters in river mouths. Aging and worn-out clipper ships served as slavers and continued to sail the transatlantic routes until the final abolition of slavery in the Western Hemisphere when it was abolished in Brazil in 1888. There is, however, some evidence to suggest that slave ships still sail today, as many people believe that Arab dhows, a traditional hull form harkening back many centuries, continue to carry human cargoes.

—David A. Johnson

For Further Reading
Chapelle, Howard I. 1969. *The Baltimore Clipper: Its Origin and Development*. Hatboro, PA: Folklore Press; Conneau, Theophilus. 1976. *A Slaver's Log Book, or 20 Year's Residence in Africa*. Englewood Cliffs, NJ: Prentice-Hall; Dow, George Francis. 1969. *Slave Ships and Slaving*. Port Washington, NY: Kennikat Press; Moore, David M. 1989. "Anatomy of a 17th-Century Slave Ship: Historical and Archaeological Investigations of the *Henrietta Marie* 1699." M.A. thesis, Department of History, Eastern Carolina University, Greenville, North Carolina.

SIAM
See Thailand

SICILIAN SLAVE WARS

*T*he Sicilian Slave Wars, full-scale insurrections of the second century B.C. (135–132 and 104–100), resulted from Roman imperial success. Sicily had become Rome's first overseas province after the Roman victory over Carthage in the First Punic War (264–241 B.C.) and was the principal grain producer for Rome and Italy. The wealth of imperial conquest enabled small numbers of the enormously rich to acquire vast tracts of Sicilian land where they employed slaves on a massive scale.

The consequent economic and demographic transformations in Sicily caused acute problems. These included the great magnates' ostentatious displays of wealth and luxury; maltreatment of slaves, including fettering and branding; and rampant brigandage practiced by runaway slaves or, in some cases, by herdsmen-slaves working in collusion with their masters, who refused to support them and encouraged predatory ambushes in the Sicilian countryside.

A charismatic Syrian slave named Eunus, who posed as a visionary and mystic prophesying the slaves' liberation, and Damophilus, a cruel and brutal landowner, were catalysts of the first rebellion (135–132 B.C.). Damophilus's brutality incited 400 slaves to revolt, and they chose Eunus, who styled himself Antiochus, king of the slaves, as their leader. The rebellion quickly spread throughout Sicily, and another slave leader of the Agrigentum region, Cleon, joined forces with Eunus.

The Sicilian historian Diodorus reports that the number of slave rebels reached 200,000, and although this figure is probably exaggerated, the revolt was of the highest magnitude. The rebellion's strongholds were in Enna and Taormina. Aristocratic disdain of servile populations led to a failure on the part of Rome to appreciate the situation's gravity, and Romans only crushed the revolt with considerable difficulty after the defeat of several praetorian commanders.

The second slave uprising (104–100 B.C.) resulted from an ill-advised Roman edict to liberate slaves in order to increase military manpower reserves. Under heavy pressure from aggrieved slaveowners, Rome reneged on liberating the slaves and instigated slave rebellion, particularly around Syracuse, a hotbed of slave discontent. This rebellion also had charismatic leaders posing as kings—Salvius-Tryphon and Athenion—and again, the fighting was prolonged by the defeat of praetorian armies before Roman forces finally prevailed. Although sources do not report the colossal figures of the first uprising, this second rebellion was nonetheless of immense scale. There were 30,000 slave casualties, and the rebellion's leaders were sent to the gladiatorial games in Rome.

—*Craige Champion*

See also
Cato; Columella's *De re rustica*; Latifundia; Punic Wars; Roman Republic; Spartacus

For Further Reading
Bradley, Keith R. 1983. "Slave Kingdoms and Slave Rebellions in Ancient Sicily." *Historical Reflections/Réflexions Historiques* 10: 435–451; Brennan, T. Corey. 1993. "The Commanders in the First Sicilian Slave War." *Rivista di Filologia e di Istruzione Classica* 121: 153–184; Yavetz, Zvi. 1988. *Slaves and Slavery in Ancient Rome*. Oxford: Transaction Books.

SIDONIUS, GAIUS APOLLINARIS
See Apollinaris Sidonius, Gaius

SIERRA LEONE

British slave traders originally founded Sierra Leone as a colony, but it eventually became the center of British efforts to suppress the West African slave trade and a major refuge for former slaves. Britain used the territory to resettle freed slaves and "loyal blacks"—African Americans remaining loyal to Britain after the American Revolution. The colony's relative success helped inspire the back-to-Africa movement and the establishment of Liberia.

Portuguese explorers first reached Sierra Leone's coast in 1460. In 1628, Britain established the first significant trading factory in Sierra Leone on Sherbro Island, and Sierra Leone soon became a principal slave-exporting center. Profits that British merchants earned there led the Crown in 1672 to found the Royal African Company to operate the various British trading posts in Sierra Leone. However, conflict between the British and the natives, and a series of devastating French raids, led the Royal African Company to abandon its outposts in 1728. Numerous privately owned slave factories were established at former crown outposts, and the slave trade continued growing in volume throughout the eighteenth century.

Meanwhile, events in Britain would drastically alter Sierra Leone. In the Somersett case (1772), William Murray, first earl of Mansfield, held that masters could not reclaim former slaves in Britain. This decision, combined with Britain's already increasing number of free blacks, spurred popular fear of an emerging large, poor black population in Britain. The British government also became concerned about the future of two other free black groups: the Maroons, former Jamaican slaves who received freedom in 1739 after a lengthy revolt, and loyal blacks, mainly former slaves freed by the British in exchange for supporting the Crown during the American Revolution. Britain transported both groups to Nova Scotia, but recognized this move as only temporary relocation.

In 1787, Henry Smeathman submitted a plan to Parliament to establish a refuge for former slaves in Sierra Leone, dubbed the Province of Freedom. Parliament accepted this plan and sent some 400 blacks to Freetown, the eventual capital of Sierra Leone. In 1791, the Sierra Leone Company was founded to develop and oversee the colony, and within five years, over 1,000 former slaves had been sent to Freetown. Additionally, Britain began transporting Maroons and loyal blacks to Sierra Leone, and over 900 loyal blacks and over 800 Maroons had been transported to Sierra Leone by 1802. With increasing numbers of former slaves being sent to Sierra Leone, the British government took formal possession of the territory as a crown colony in 1808.

With the slave trade's abolition within the British Empire in 1807, Britain undertook a campaign to suppress the West African slave trade. British troops and naval units destroyed slave factories remaining in Sierra Leone, and the British Navy's antislavery squadron began destroying slave factories all along the coast of West Africa. The British built a naval station in Freetown to support these efforts, and this base became the center of military effort to suppress the slave trade. Slaves freed from slave ships or from slave factories were usually resettled in Sierra Leone. By 1815, some 5,925 former slaves had been freed and resettled in Sierra Leone, and by the 1820s, the British Navy was annually depositing 3,000–4,000 former slaves in Sierra Leone.

Financial problems related to the colony's inability to provide either land or employment for the freed slaves led to attempts to relocate some of these former slaves to other areas of the British Empire. In fact, some 10,000 recaptured slaves were sent to the West Indies as freemen. However, none of these attempts were financially successful, and Britain continued to rely on Sierra Leone as the primary refuge for freed slaves.

A wealthy African American, Paul Cuffe, visited Sierra Leone in 1810 and saw it as a place for African Americans to settle and avoid racial problems present in the United States. In 1812, he organized a party of African Americans who attempted to settle in Sierra Leone, but hostility from entrenched merchants and the colonial establishment led Cuffe to focus his back-to-Africa movement on unclaimed African territory, which led, in turn, to the establishment of Liberia.

—Tom Lansford

See also
Closing of the African Slave Trade; General Abolition Bill
For Further Reading
Fyfe, Christopher. 1962. *A History of Sierra Leone.* London: Oxford University Press; Peterson, John. 1969. *Province of Freedom.* London: Faber; Walker, James. 1976. *The Black Loyalists.* New York: Africana; Wilson, Ellen. 1976. *The Loyal Blacks.* New York: Capricorn.

SIMMS, WILLIAM GILMORE (1806–1870)

Along with Edgar Allen Poe, William Gilmore Simms was the antebellum South's leading man of letters. He was also a notable defender of slavery, and his writings helped to articulate the South's proslavery argument.

Perhaps one of the more overlooked Southern antebellum literary figures, Simms stands just below Poe in reputation among the South's literary figures. Born in Charleston, South Carolina, Simms remained in that city for most of his life. His father, a failed merchant, left young Simms in his grandmother's care and traveled to Mississippi. Simms was educated in Charleston, briefly apprenticed to a druggist, married in 1826, and admitted to the bar in 1827.

His real interest was writing, and Simms had published a book of poetry by 1825. He had published four more books of verse by 1830 and, in 1828, began publishing the *Southern Literary Gazette,* which he edited. Although the journal was short-lived, Simms's intent was to defend and promote Southern literature. He published the *City Gazette* in 1829, a local newspaper that Simms was forced to sell in 1832. In 1830, his father and mother died, and his wife died in February 1832.

Simms traveled north in 1832, meeting several important writers and publishers, and produced his first important work, *Atlantis* (1832). The poem was well received in the United States and England and demonstrated his literary potential. Several works of fiction followed, including *Guy Rivers* (1834) and *The Yemassee* (1835), the latter generally being considered his best work of fiction. During this time, Simms earned up to $6,000 a year in royalties, and although this proved the high point of his literary profits, he was one of the few men in the United States then who was able to earn a respectable living by writing. He continued publishing an impressive list of works of fiction for much of the rest of his life.

The defining moment for Simms as a Southerner came in 1837 when an English traveler, Harriet Martineau, published an attack on slavery entitled *Society in America.* In response, Simms penned "The Morals of Slavery," an essay that was first published in the new *Southern Literary Messenger* (housed in Richmond, Virginia) and later reprinted as a pamphlet. In 1852, Simms revised his response to Martineau for a collective volume of writings titled *The Pro-Slavery Argument, as Maintained by the Most Distinguished Writers of the Southern States* (1852).

For Simms, defending slavery was a moral issue. He contended that God approved of the institution as a means both to rescue and to preserve the savage (i.e., slave) and thus slavery represented a moral contract with God. With this direct argument, Simms and others, like Beverley Tucker, J. D. B. DeBow, Thomas Dew, James Henry Hammond, and Edmund Ruffin, became spokesmen for the South and the institution of slavery.

Simms's stance on slavery is also evident in his fiction where there is natural affection between master and slave, a relationship that is generally beneficial toward the slave. In *The Yemassee,* Simms defended the

South, and in another of his successful fictional works, *The Partisan* (1835), he used a slave as a hero. In *Woodcraft* (1852), Simms responded to Harriet Beecher Stowe's view of slavery and Southerners in *Uncle Tom's Cabin* (published as a serial in 1851–1852).

During his prolific career, Simms used essays, fiction, and history to defend slavery and the Southern way of life. He remained in South Carolina during the U.S. Civil War at Woodlands, his Barnwell County plantation. The war interrupted and virtually ended his writing career, and he died in Charleston in 1870. His moral defense of slavery still marks him as a staunch defender of the South and clouds his successful literary achievements.

—*Boyd Childress*

For Further Reading
Guilds, John C. 1992. *Simms: A Literary Life.* Fayetteville: University of Arkansas Press; Waklyn, Jon L. 1973. *The Politics of a Literary Man: William Gilmore Simms.* Westport, CT: Greenwood; Watson, Charles S. 1993. *From Nationalism to Secessionism: The Changing Fiction of William Gilmore Simms.* Westport, CT: Greenwood.

SLAVE CATCHERS

Slave catchers were persons engaged in locating and capturing slaves who attempted to escape a condition of servitude (as in the United States) or in capturing persons who subsequently became commodities in slave commerce (as in Africa). Slave catchers were important members of all slaveholding societies throughout recorded history. Babylonian laws 17–20 defined responsibilities and expectations of such a profession (searching), as did Hittite laws 22, 23, and 61. Elaborate Roman legislation categorized slave types and processes applicable in retrieving fugitive slaves and attempted to remove opportunities for collusion between fugitive slaves and catchers/entrepreneurs. The Romans commonly used branding as a technique for identifying runaways, and officials regularly detained branded persons for collection by owners, even before owners reported them missing. Muslim-influenced African societies appealed to Islamic law (Sura 47) to define an employer's obligations to slave catchers and to legitimize slave catching. Africa's animistic societies appealed to indigenous law.

In the Americas, various slave-catching (retrieving) traditions applied. In the United States, the Fugitive Slave Act of 1793 permitted slaveowners to apply to federal court officials for an order to return fugitive slaves to the state from which they had fled, but that act did not provide for enforcement of the court's decision within the state of discovery or establish procedures for legally returning fugitive slaves to owners. In 1818, Congress considered a new proposal designed to give force to earlier legislation and to satisfy both slaveowners and antislavery sentiments but failed to reach consensus or a compromise sufficient for passage. Consequently, the 1793 act remained the principal law (however flawed) regarding slave retrieval until Congress passed a new Fugitive Slave Act as part of the Compromise of 1850.

Between 1793 and 1850, sentiments of both slaveowners and antislavery advocates changed dramatically, and the slave-catching/searching/retrieving profession also changed. In 1793, significant numbers of settlers and slaves were under a service obligation/contract, and society respected the professional catcher. After 1793, the number of free-based indentures in the North declined significantly, leaving a preponderance of catchers employed in locating and retrieving fugitive slaves who crossed from slaveholding to nonslaveholding states. Until 1850, federal law complicated slave catching/searching/retrieving in the Northern states since it provided no binding process for enforcement. Additionally, state laws, state courts, and state officials confounded the process by obstructing legitimate slave catchers. Abolitionist opposition and successes in blocking lawful retrievals encouraged an increased willingness on the part of slaveowners to sanction extralegal means to retrieve property. Slave catchers consequently changed their search-and-return methods. Rather than risking opposition and time-consuming procedures in the Northern courts, catchers increasingly avoided the legal process altogether, simply seizing fugitive slaves and secretly transporting them to a place that sanctioned slavery. Contemporary abolitionist literature characterized such persons as bounty hunters or kidnappers and often accused them of kidnapping free African Americans to make up for financial losses suffered by slaveowning employers.

The Fugitive Slave Act of 1850 was part of a larger compromise between Northern and Southern states and was designed to remedy the defects of previous legislation. Unfortunately, this act did not halt the excesses of catchers who were accustomed to working outside legal processes. It effectively legalized and sanctioned slave catching in the North, protecting it by federal law and enabling federal marshals and other federal officials to enforce it. Abolitionists interpreted the law as significantly failing to meet its antislavery objective and a victory for slaveowners who pursued fugitive slaves both by legal means (protected by the federal government) and illegal means (kidnapping).

After the fugitive slave act of 1793, bands of slave catchers were authorized to track down and bring back runaway slaves. This 1847 drawing shows one such group capturing a slave family for return to the South.

Slave catching as it relates to capturing people for the purpose of enslaving them mainly applied to Africa in modern times, although slave catching was practiced by others and in other areas much earlier. Wars have always produced winners and losers, and losers often became booty or compensation for the costs of fighting the war. This was particularly true in Greek and Roman societies and to a lesser degree in Spanish territories during the Reconquista (the reconquering of the Iberian Peninsula from the Muslims, 711–1492) and subsequent conquest of the Americas. In Africa, people became captives in various ways. Some African states (Oyo, Abomey, Ashanti, Congo, Benin) waged wars of expansion, often to obtain captives, which they then sent to coastal purchasers of slaves in exchange for European/American merchandise or for goods that could be obtained only on the coast. In some areas, such as the Fulani empire (Guinea-Conakry), powerful ethnic groups considered others inferior or infidel and subject to periodic culling or harvesting; those harvested persons (perhaps age or gender specific) then became commodities in the transatlantic slave trade. In other areas (the Gambia and Sierra Leone), interior raids by coastal peoples produced captives who became coastal commodities.

Generally, the accepted wisdom along the west coast of Africa specified that European buyers needed to pay a fair price and a tax for each slave exported from the coast. Failure to do so would inevitably result in retaliation against other Europeans visiting the area. As a practice, slave catching became increasingly counterproductive for Europeans and threatened the coastal industry of purchasing slaves and selling manufactured goods, so by 1750, most slaves leaving the west coast of Africa were captives of Africans who sold them to European/American buyers for transport across the Atlantic. The significant decrease in transatlantic slave trading after 1830 did not end the slave-catching profession on the continent. Legal indigenous slavery continued throughout Africa into the twentieth century, as did active slave raiding and wars fought for the purpose of collecting slaves.

—*Bruce L. Mouser*

See also
Fugitive Slave Act of 1850; Fugitive Slave Acts (State)
For Further Reading
Campbell, Stanley W. 1970. *The Slave Catchers*. Chapel Hill: University of North Carolina Press; Daube, David.

1952. "Slave-Catching." *Juridical Review* 64: 12–28; Grace, John. 1975. *Domestic Slavery in West Africa.* New York: Barnes and Noble; Watson, Alan. 1987. *Roman Slave Law.* Baltimore: Johns Hopkins University Press.

SLAVE COAST

West Africa's Slave Coast acquired its notorious name from Europeans trading in the region from the sixteenth to the nineteenth centuries. Derived from one of the area's primary commodities, this name distinguished the region from other reaches of West Africa's coast, like the Grain Coast (named for the "grains of paradise," a spice of the ginger family), the Ivory Coast, and the Gold Coast. The geographic region usually defined by the term Slave Coast corresponds to its late-seventeenth-, eighteenth-, and nineteenth-century usage, which identified the western half of the Bight of Benin, an area roughly extending from the mouth of the Volta River eastward to Lagos. In modern terms, this corresponds to Ghana's easternmost coast, the coasts of Togo and Benin, and Nigeria's westernmost coast. The term also referred to the coastal region's immediate hinterlands.

The earliest references to the Slave Coast appear in sixteenth-century Portuguese sources, where the term is used to indicate the West African coast east of Lagos, in the vicinity of the Benin Kingdom in Nigeria. The expression *rios dos escravos* ("slave rivers") indicated the region's role in terms of its economic importance to the Portuguese. The Benin Kingdom and surrounding regions were sources of slaves, which the Portuguese exchanged on the Gold Coast for supplies of gold.

When slave trading declined in the Benin Kingdom, the source area for slaves relocated westward, encompassing the western half of the Bight of Benin. This region, which became known as the Slave Coast in the eighteenth and nineteenth centuries, was initially identified by the Dutch and other Europeans as "the captives coast." By the 1690s, the term Slave Coast was being used commonly in various European languages.

Geographically, the Slave Coast is a distinctive region coinciding with "the Dahomey Gap," a break in the coastal rain-forest band that allows open savanna vegetation to penetrate to the coast. The fact that it was relatively easy to travel in the savanna encouraged trade and interaction to the north. In the eighteenth and nineteenth centuries, the open country also allowed Oyo cavalry, located to the north, to exercise control over several Slave Coast states, including Dahomey. In addition to northern trade, the presence of a nearly continuous lagoon system from the mouth of the Volta to the rivers of Lagos facilitated the east and west trade.

In African terms, the Slave Coast encompassed several different linguistic and political groups, although warfare, conquest, and population movement in the eighteenth and nineteenth centuries complicate the tracking of these. Along the coast, Ewe, also called Aja and Aja-Ewe, was the predominant language group. However, there were many political and ethnic distinctions among the Ewe—the westernmost polity, Anlo, contained the important trading port of Keta.

Moving eastward, a succession of small states lay along the coast. Popo, or Great Popo, was located at the mouth of the Mono River, where a break in the coastal sandbar existed. Popo remained autonomous into the eighteenth century, when the growing hegemony of Dahomey eclipsed its significance in trade.

Another major polity to the east was Hueda, which grew to prominence as a major player in the slave trade in the late-seventeenth and early-eighteenth centuries. European traders from many nations were based in Savi, the capital of the Hueda state. Opportunities for wealth and power presented by the slave trade permitted the Hueda to achieve autonomy from Allada, the state located directly to the interior. Trading success ultimately precipitated the Hueda state's decline, as that success attracted the attention of Dahomey, which conquered Hueda in 1727.

Allada had been a major trading state during the earliest years, but the rise of Hueda in the 1670s eclipsed it and it was engulfed by Dahomey in 1724. Dahomey, further inland, was not a player in the slave trade's early period. With its conquest of seaports, beginning with the Hueda port of Whydah, Dahomey grew to be a potent trading force exporting thousands of slaves annually through the middle of the nineteenth century. The small kingdom of Porto Novo, established by refugees from Allada, was east of Hueda, and refugees fleeing Dahomean conquests also founded Badagry. Inland from Porto Novo and Badagry were the Yoruba, who were forest dwellers, and further north, on the savanna's edge, was the Oyo Kingdom. Despite regional political fragmentation, a remarkable degree of homogeneity existed, both linguistically and culturally.

The Slave Coast earned its name during 400 years of the slave trade. Beginning with the Portuguese, east of Lagos, to the end of the legal slave trade in the first decade of the nineteenth century, massive numbers of enslaved people were exported from the region. Patrick Manning (1982), compiler of the most complete overall figures, estimates that over 1,850,000 Africans were exported from the Bight of Benin from the 1640s to the 1890s. Others believe that this estimate overemphasizes the volume of the Portuguese trade; although, as Manning does not supply figures for the sixteenth and early seventeenth centuries, the overall estimate may be relatively accurate.

European and Western peoples participating in the regional trade included the French, English, Portuguese, Dutch, Danish, Brandenburgers, Brazilians, and Americans. Trade centers of primary importance were Keta, Great Popo, Whydah (Ouidah), and Porto Novo, and Jakin, Offra, and Badagry were also of significance.

With the end of the legal European slave trade, only the Brazilians and Americans still actively acquired slaves from the coastal ports. Brazilians, and especially returned Afro-Brazilians, contributed culturally to the region and to a distinctive architecture that appears in several coastal towns, including Lagos, Porto Novo, and Ouidah. Furthermore, the Afro-Brazilian population frequently achieved high status in coastal societies, as traders in slaves and other commodities and as advisers and administrative officials for the coastal kingdoms.

—*Kenneth G. Kelly*

See also
Benin; Dahomey
For Further Reading
Kelly, Kenneth G. 1997. "The Archaeology of African-European Interaction: Investigating the Social Roles of Trade, Traders, and the Use of Space in the Seventeenth and Eighteenth Century Hueda Kingdom, Republic of Bénin." *World Archaeology* 28 (3): 351–369; Law, Robin. 1991. *The Slave Coast of West Africa, 1550–1750: The Impact of the Atlantic Slave Trade on an African Society*. Oxford: Clarendon Press; Manning, Patrick. 1982. *Slavery, Colonialism, and Economic Growth in Dahomey, 1640–1960*. Cambridge: Cambridge University Press.

SLAVE PREACHERS

African American slave preachers often occupied an uncomfortable middle position between white and black worlds in the U.S. South before the Civil War. Distrusted by white slaveholding society, which suspected them as fomenters of slave rebellion, slave preachers had to rely on their masters' protection to maintain their positions. In return, the preachers were expected to indoctrinate their black flock that heaven awaited slaves who faithfully served their white rulers. Within the slave community, slave clergy preserved African cultural practices while disseminating the Christian gospel. Revered as bold leaders and reviled in slave folklore as craven sellouts, black preachers constructed a worldview that largely preserved black cultural autonomy while accommodating to the reality of antebellum power relations.

The slave preacher filled a spiritual vacuum left by many white masters who feared that Christianity, with its message that slaves possessed souls worth saving and were as human as whites, undermined the slave economy's racist tenets. Many slaveowners even long resisted attempts to Christianize their property, and when white preachers were sent to evangelize slaves, their obvious political mission to encourage black acceptance of servitude undermined their credibility with black congregations. In this atmosphere, slaves often learned an Africanized version of Christianity from other slaves—slave preachers, both licensed and unlicensed; exhorters, individuals who spontaneously "got the spirit" and began preaching with or without training; and conjurers, who often maintained traditional African magic practices and beliefs in earthly ghosts and divinations.

Many slave preachers were ridiculed by white elites because they were illiterate and had no formal theological training. Historians Eugene D. Genovese and Albert J. Raboteau both argue, however, that slave preachers were no more likely to be illiterate than poor white preachers in the South. In any case, Bible tales had become part of the slave oral tradition, and certain slave preachers gained fame for their command of scripture, fiery eloquence, and multilingual fluency.

Some preachers enjoyed a freedom of movement unknown by other slaves, being exempted from manual labor by approving masters and invited to lead white congregations and preside over white funerals. Before white or racially mixed audiences, slave preachers at times bowed to reality and ignored slavery or delivered accommodationist sermons. Such preachers suffered harsh lampooning in slave folklore, but others delivered subtle, highly symbolic antislavery messages.

Historian Sterling Stuckey believes that an essential element of the slave preacher's oratory incorporated an ostensibly Christian message with an African performance style with "the rhythms of [the slave preacher] stirring some to jump and clap their hands and others to shriek" (Stuckey, 1987). Such sermonizing followed West African norms of the ring shout, a style of religious celebration incorporating a call-and-response interplay between an exhorter and the gathered faithful, a clapping of hands, and African dances. Also according to Stuckey, the ring shout was performed in a circle during weddings, funerals, and other religious rituals throughout western and central Africa and served as a method of achieving union with God. Slave preachers incorporated the ring shout into black Protestant practices as well.

Black worship styles heavily influenced Southern white Christianity, even when critics condemned the religious practices of slaves as barely disguised hea-

This portrayal of family worship on a Southern plantation appeared in the Illustrated London News *of December 5, 1863.*

thenism. Slave preachers differed from their white counterparts not only in style but also in substance. While white preachers emphasized the slave's duty to obey his or her master, slave preachers frequently noted that all people are descended from Adam and Eve, in subtle rebuke of white supremacist thinking. Others used tales of Moses and the Israelites as promise of the eventual deliverance of black slaves from white domination.

Southern slaveholders were fully aware of the black church's insurrectionary potential and, while blacks were given relative freedom to preach in the eigh-

teenth century, nineteenth-century Southern state and local governments sought to limit slave preaching. Black preachers were implicated in several actual or threatened slave revolts, such as those led by Gabriel Prosser (1800), Denmark Vesey (1822), and Nat Turner (1831), and each abortive insurrection led to a suppression of slave preaching.

Laws were passed throughout the South that prohibited free blacks from preaching to slaves, required slave preachers to register with local authorities, and/or mandated that whites be present when any black preacher presided over a meeting. Some independent black churches, which had developed in the 1700s, were required to merge with white churches. Yet, the black church had become too entrenched in the slave community to be repressed legally, and slave preaching thrived until the Civil War.

Regardless of some slaveowners' fears, slave preachers have often been painted by many leftist critics as collaborators. As Genovese (1976) argues, traditional African religions had a distinctly nonmessianic, nonmillenarian cast, emphasized community and fidelity to tradition as a means of fulfillment, and promoted the long view on immediate issues of social justice. Time was cyclical in the African view, Genovese argues, which encouraged slave clergy to preach an eventual reversal of fortune, to convey the message that, with time, the last shall be first and the first shall be last. Imbued with African sensibility, these preachers constructed a universe that was morally self-correcting, one in which justice would be restored and imbalances of power reversed over the vast stretch of time.

Rather than being accommodationists, in Genovese's view, slave preachers were hard realists, recognizing the vastly unequal power relations between the African American and white communities. The preachers responded accordingly, providing the slave community with psychological defenses against slavery's assault while bearing in mind the African long view that justice awaits the virtuous and that time, inevitably, is on the African American community's side. What has been typically interpreted by leftists as accommodation was not a lapse into passivity, but a strategy for survival.

—*Michael Phillips*

See also
Prosser, Gabriel; Turner, Nat; Vesey, Denmark
For Further Reading
Blassingame, John W. 1979. *The Slave Community: Plantation Life in the Antebellum South*. New York: Oxford University Press; Genovese, Eugene D. 1976. *Roll, Jordan, Roll: The World the Slaves Made*. New York: Vintage Books; Raboteau, Albert J. 1978. *Slave Religion: The "Invisible Institution" in the Antebellum South*. New York: Oxford University Press; Stuckey, Sterling. 1987. *Slave Culture: Nationalist Theory and the Foundations of Black America*. New York: Oxford University Press.

SLAVE VILLAGES

Slave villages, with regard to Africa, were occupied primarily or solely by slaves. These villages are mentioned in the earliest records and continued into the twentieth century. Although no single definition or description of an African slave village is possible, literature indicates such villages existed in most African slaveholding societies. Before 1800, these villages generally contained persons who were considered subject peoples or the property of another.

The first type of slave village corresponded closely to the feudal relationship of landlord/lord to serf in medieval European society. Landlords/lords obtained land through inheritance or wars or cleared land for the production of goods, receiving title to the land for their investment or labor. Once the land was theirs, the lords staffed their property with subject peoples or laborers who owed them rent or custom, obligations such as labor or military service, and obedience. Accordingly, the subject persons received protection and perhaps certain property rights, including the security that the lord would not alienate them from the land, except for just cause. Feudal relationships (with ambiguous definitions of freedom and tenancy) were an active ingredient in many African societies.

The second type of slave village was similar to the first except that the slaves (as property) worked the land and occupied the village. These slaves often acquired their status through wars in which the winners obtained the losers as property that could be bought and sold as the owners saw fit. Such villages were common among the Susu, Mandingo, and Fula peoples of Guinea-Conakry before 1800. Important political officials owned large estates on which they maintained a central town with satellite slave villages. Each village became self-contained and had strict rules of behavior, customs and labor expected by the lord, and obligations. Slaves could not move freely from village to village. Numerous reports of late-eighteenth-century slave insurrections exist that indicate some villages built defenses and waged wars against landlords, and of a corresponding rallying among the landlords and their allies against such insurrections.

During the height of the slave trade (before 1830), security existed in the first type of village, and there was a lesser degree of security in the latter. Generally, landlords maintained the villages and expected them to generate surplus market products. During war, however, the lords might wish to purchase firearms from the coast and might be willing to exchange some slave property for these more desirable goods. In such instances, the slave villagers were most vulnerable to the landlords' whims and immediate needs. The relative value of products and slaves also affected the slave villagers' marketability.

After 1830, when European and American shippers increasingly visited the coast of Africa searching for commodities such as groundnuts, coffee, and timber, the landlords discovered the economic advantages of maintaining large, active slave villages. Consequently, slave villages grew after 1830 and often took on the appearance of plantations. Such villages continued into the twentieth century.

—Bruce L. Mouser

See also
Africa; Agricultural Slavery; Transition from Slave Labor to Free Labor, Africa

For Further Reading
Dockes, Pierre. 1982. *Medieval Slavery and Liberation.* Chicago: University of Chicago Press; Fisher, Allan, and Humphrey Fisher. 1971. *Slavery and Muslim Society in Africa.* New York: Doubleday; Lovejoy, Paul E. 1981. *The Ideology of Slavery in Africa.* London: Sage Publications; Miers, Suzanne, and Igor Kopytoff. 1977. *Slavery in Africa.* Madison: University of Wisconsin Press.

SLAVERY IN MEDIEVAL EUROPE

The institution of slavery was inherited from the late Roman world. Slaves in the west in the Middle Ages were known by various names, like *mancipia*, *servi*, and *ancillae*. The primary difficulty in defining medieval slavery is to determine how the social and legal meaning of these terms changed from the ancient world.

The most common Roman word for slave, *servus*, was used the during the high and late Middle Ages to refer to dependent peasants, the serfs, who were unfree persons with some legal rights, not slaves. The classical definition in Aristotle's *Politics* was that a slave was the "tool with a voice," and a commonly accepted notion by both Aristotle and Plato was that this tool might also be regarded as an animal. One can see some survivals of this attitude about slaves in some barbarian law codes of the sixth to eighth centuries, in which slaves were ranked with livestock and clauses about theft applied equally to *mancipia*. To the ancient and early-medieval jurist, the slave was owned as property and was not a person with legal rights.

However, it is easy to press such classical and legal distinctions too far when discussing medieval slavery, which could often be much harsher than its ancient equivalent. The most obvious indicators of the subhuman nature of the slave were punishments and sexual relations. Although historians are only beginning to understand the range of punishments that could be inflicted on slaves, according to various early barbarian law codes, they included beating (up to hundreds of blows, exceeding the number for animals), mutilation (including amputation and facial scarring), and death. In most cases, unions between free and slave were considered to be against nature, even analogous to bestiality. As a result of such views, slaves could not own any-

thing or have rights over their children. Like their ancient and modern counterparts, medieval slaves controlled neither their production nor their reproduction.

The most striking feature of medieval slavery was its decline and disappearance by the eleventh century. The chronology of medieval slavery has been a subject of debate ever since the historian Marc Bloch (1975) wrote that slavery had disappeared in the west by the tenth century. Recent scholarship, by Pierre Bonnassie (1991) and others, has shown that several long-term factors contributed to the decline of slavery in the medieval world. These factors included religion, a diminishing supply of slaves, and both agricultural and economic growth.

Church doctrine approved slavery in principle, derived as it was from Paul's injunction that slaves should obey their earthly masters (Cor. 1) and statements by church fathers like Augustine (*City of God*) that slavery was punishment for sin. In practice, the church also was one of the largest holders of slaves, who were ideally used to cultivate great estates. But early Christianity also helped to establish indirectly the humanity of the slave. Church teachings and saints' lives considered manumission of slaves (especially by the laity) a pious act, but, more important, the clergy of the sixth to eighth centuries considered slaves to have souls: they could be baptized, attend mass, and be admitted to other sacraments. These everyday practices gradually eroded the view of slaves as mere property.

As in the ancient world, medieval warfare remained a prime supplier of slaves. From the fifth to eighth centuries, Anglo-Saxon conquests were accompanied by enslavement of Celts, and Merovingian Frankish battles with Germans and Bretons and internal warfare also produced captive slaves. But with the rise of the Carolingians in the eighth century, war was primarily confined to the frontiers, in Spain and Saxony. Taking slave captives was the privilege of the victor, and that privilege declined in western continental Europe when rulers there were thrown on the defensive by Viking and Magyar raids. Of course, there were always other means of enslavement, including voluntary enslavement for debt or in return for protection and involuntary enslavement by judicial condemnation. All of these means continued to be used until the ninth century and were accepted under Carolingian law.

The revival of public order under the Carolingians actually strengthened the slave system. Economically, a gradual growth after 650 as the result of labor-saving technical advances (e.g., new methods of harnessing animals and water mills) and increased yields of small producers in comparison with great estates may have made slavery economically less efficient.

The chronology and geography of the practice of slavery in the medieval period are now better understood. Slavery was destroyed by a combination of long-term trends and a series of crises. The first crisis was when the structures of the state, which supported slavery, were considerably weakened in the third to fifth centuries by civil wars, barbarian migration, and disease. Ancient slavery did not disappear, however, and was reinforced more solidly by the severe legislation of the barbarian kings. Such legislation was most plentiful in Italy and Spain, where slavery was solidly established, but it also existed in Salic law, Anglo-Saxon law, Burgundian law, and the laws of other northern countries. Church doctrine upholding slavery was solidified at this time in the writings of church fathers such as Gregory the Great and Isidore of Seville. These laws provide evidence of the wide diffusion of slavery in Europe generally, perhaps reaching its height in the sixth to seventh centuries.

A new phase began in the second half of the seventh century and in the eighth century, when Christian practices raised the question of the humanity of the slave, and economic conditions began to favor emancipation. Slaves were increasingly able to desert large estates and find employment as free workers, which led to much repressive legislation in Spain and Italy and other Mediterranean regions, which seem to have been chiefly affected. The last revival of the slave labor system occurred with the resurgence of public order from the north, with the rise of the Carolingian empire. But overall, conditions for slavery were no longer as favorable.

The final crisis occurred in the late-tenth and early-eleventh centuries. At that time, all counterslavery trends converged. Christian belief, originally confined to the elite, was more widely spread among the rural population. Technical and agrarian advances were increasingly applied, requiring a greater fluidity of the rural workforce, which emancipation could provide. Public order broke down with the new invasions, and the whole repressive apparatus of the law collapsed.

The disappearance of slavery can be traced region by region: in Latium, 950–1000; in Catalonia, 1000–1035; in the Auvergne, 1000–1050; in northern France soon after 1030; in England, soon after the Norman Conquest (1066). Ultimately, in southern Europe, there was a sharp break between slavery and the new institution, serfdom, that came to replace slavery in 1060–1080. In northern Europe, where slavery was established later, it also disappeared more gradually. About 25,000 slaves (between 1 and 16 percent of any given county) were still recorded in England's Domesday Book of 1086, for example. Nevertheless, in northern Europe, slavery disappeared as the new form of servitude spread in the wake of the feudal revolution.

—Robert Berkhofer

See also

Aristotle's *Politics*; Augustine (Saint); Celts; Christianity; Isidore of Seville; Serfdom in Medieval Europe; Roman Empire; Roman Law; Stoicism; Vikings

For Further Reading

Bloch, Marc. 1975. *Slavery and Serfdom in the Middle Ages*. Berkeley: University of California Press; Bonnassie, Pierre. 1991. *From Slavery to Feudalism in South-Western Europe*. Cambridge: Cambridge University Press; Duby, Georges. 1974. *The Early Growth of the European Economy: Warriors and Peasants from the Seventh to the Twelfth Centuries*. Ithaca, NY: Cornell University Press; Verlinden, Charles. 1955. *L'esclavage dans l'Europe médiévale*. Bruges, Belgium: De Tempel.

SMALLS, ROBERT
(1839–1915)

Robert Smalls made a unique transition from slavery to freedom, becoming a pilot in the Union navy during the U.S. Civil War, a politician, and a businessman. During Reconstruction, Smalls served in South Carolina's legislature as a state representative and state senator before being elected to the U.S. Congress.

Born into slavery in Beaufort, South Carolina, in 1839, he moved with his master to Charleston, South Carolina, in 1851. Having little education, Smalls hired himself out for odd jobs. His owner only required him to pay $15 per month from his total wages. Smalls eventually became adept at piloting boats and sailing along the Georgia and South Carolina coastlines.

When the Civil War began, the Confederacy forced Smalls to become a crew member on the transport steamship *Planter*. On May 13, 1862, while white crew members were ashore, Smalls and other black crew members commandeered the ship in Charleston harbor. Smuggling his family and a small group of slaves aboard, he sailed the vessel out of the harbor and into the hands of the Union fleet, which was blockading the coastline. Responsible for freeing all the passengers, Smalls's action was noted across the country as not only an act of heroism, but also a military success by a group of servants.

This deed led President Lincoln to name Smalls an official pilot in the Union navy. He also received $1,500 for delivering an armed boat and was commissioned a second lieutenant in the U.S. Colored Troops. In 1863, during the siege of Charleston, Smalls again sailed the *Planter* to safe waters. This action earned him a captain's rank and distinguished him as the only black to hold that rank during the Civil War.

Robert Smalls

The ship was refitted as a gunboat, and Smalls played an important part in many battles, including providing food and supplies to black refugees during Gen. William Tecumseh Sherman's invasion of Georgia and South Carolina. Smalls later helped convince Lincoln to allow many South Carolina blacks to enlist in the Union army.

When the *Planter* was decommissioned in 1866, Smalls returned to Beaufort. Black Southerners were allowed many political opportunities during Reconstruction, and Smalls served in South Carolina's House of Representatives from 1868 to 1870 and in the state senate from 1870 to 1874. Smalls later was elected to the U.S. House of Representatives, where he served 1875–1879 and 1881–1887. He became an advocate for freed slaves, health care, and public education. After his political career ended, Smalls served as Beaufort's customs collector from 1889 to 1913. He died on February 22, 1915.

—*Anthony Todman*

For Further Reading
Estell, Kenneth, ed. 1994. *The African-American Almanac*. Detroit: Gale Research; Miller, Edward A. 1995.

Gullah Statesman: Robert Smalls from Slavery to Congress, 1839–1915. Columbia: University of South Carolina Press; Miller, Randall M., and John David Smith, eds. 1988. *Dictionary of Afro-American Slavery*. Westport, CT: Greenwood; Salzman, Jack; David Lionel Smith; and Cornel West, eds. 1996. *Encyclopedia of African-American Culture and History*. New York: Macmillan Library Reference.

SMITH, GERRIT
(1797–1874)

Among the most renowned of the abolitionists in the United States, Gerrit Smith devoted his life and most of his great wealth to the cause of equal rights for all men and women; the immediate abolition of every sin was his most passionate desire, and he went to great lengths to effect it. Smith was born into one of the wealthiest families in the country and grew up in the rural village of Peterboro, Madison County, in western New York State.

The young patriarch had visions of becoming a man of letters, an eminent lawyer, a respected minister, or a statesman, but immediately after graduating as valedictorian from Hamilton College in 1818, a series of incidents occurred that precipitated his turn to reform work; these included the death of his mother, the death of his new bride, and the retirement of his father, who requested that Gerrit manage his vast property concerns. In little more than a year after reaching "manhood," Gerrit found himself back in the family "mansion house" overlooking the village green of Peterboro, bound to his ledger books and land office, his dreams shattered, and the two most important people in his life dead.

In 1823, he married Ann Carroll Fitzhugh Smith, a cousin of George Fitzhugh and a fervent evangelical. She was instrumental in converting Smith to evangelicalism, fueling his religious zeal, and spawning his vision of a broad sacralization of the world. He soon became an avid temperance reformer, and in 1827 joined the respected American Colonization Society, whose efforts to colonize blacks in Africa represented, for Smith, the most effective way to bring about gradual emancipation and an end to degradation among free blacks. In the early 1830s, when many radicals became "fanatics" by turning to immediate abolition and attacking colonization as inherently racist and unrighteous, Smith continued endorsing colonization while also flirting with immediatism.

From 1834 to 1837, Smith was unique among abolitionists in his efforts to reconcile the principles of colonization with those of the American Anti-Slavery

Society. He viewed the efforts of each organization as complementary versions of the same war on slavery and racial prejudice, despite cries from immediatists that the colonizers wanted to preserve slavery and rid the country of free blacks.

Smith's final and complete repudiation of colonization occurred in 1837, two years after he formally resigned from the American Colonization Society, and the break corresponded with an important and fundamental shift in his identity as a patriarch and a reorientation in the source of his values: he became a self-described social "outsider," turned inward, and affirmed the spiritual instincts and passions of the "heart" rather than the sin-infested conventions of social order and existing authority. His belief in the preservation of order, stability, and distinct hierarchies—values on which the principles of colonization were based—had crumbled. The change was owing in part to the panic of 1837, which brought him to the brink of bankruptcy, and to the deaths of two children, one in 1835 and the other in 1836. In conjunction with his shift in values and identity, he became "born again," free from the fetters of original sin, and applied his passions to the immediate abolition of every sin.

One of the most important applications of Smith's religious vision was his reinterpretation of the Golden Rule, which he saw as a fulfillment of the ideal of empathy. He continually sought to participate in the feelings and sufferings of his black brethren and to see himself as a black man. "To recognize in every man my brother—ay, another self" was his wish, and he often described his efforts to "make myself a colored man" (Harlow, 1939).

His empathic awareness had profound results. He worked to transform his own village of Peterboro into an antebellum model of interracial harmony, and in 1846 he gave to each of some 3,000 poor blacks from New York roughly 50 acres of land in the Adirondacks so they could attain the franchise and become self-sufficient and isolated from the virulent racism in the cities. Black leaders throughout the North hailed his efforts to effect equality: Frederick Douglass, James McCune Smith, Henry Highland Garnet, and Samuel Ringgold Ward all became respected friends and allies, and the black abolitionist paper, *Ram's Horn,* went so far as to say: "Gerrit Smith is a colored man!"

From the 1840s through the Civil War, Smith's reform work mirrored in many respects the efforts of the black abolitionist community in New York. He helped found the Liberty Party in 1840, which interpreted the U.S. Constitution as an antislavery document, and he became one of the party's staunchest supporters. He was elected to the U.S. Congress in 1852 but resigned after one term out of disgust with the culture of Washington, D.C., and the existing government, which had just passed the Kansas-Nebraska Act and repealed the Missouri Compromise.

Smith also abandoned nonresistance and advocated violence as a last resort for ending slavery. In an effort to incite a massive slave insurrection, he became a major underwriter of the guerrilla warfare in Kansas and was one of the six leading conspirators in John Brown's raid on Harpers Ferry in 1859. New York black leaders overwhelmingly endorsed political intervention, and by the 1850s, they, too, had little patience with the principles of nonresistance.

Until his death in 1874, Smith continually championed equal rights for all and the end of exploitation, whether for blacks, women, or laborers. In 1873, Henry Highland Garnet summed up the feelings of many radicals by saying, "Among the hosts of great defenders of man's fights who in years past fought so gallantly for equal rights for all men," Smith was "the most affectionately remembered and loved" (Harlow, 1939).

—*John Stauffer*

See also
Abolition, United States; American Colonization Society; Brown, John; Immediatism; Racism; Second Great Awakening

For Further Reading
Friedman, Lawrence J. 1982. *Gregarious Saints: Self and Community in American Abolitionism, 1830–1870.* New York: Cambridge University Press; Frothingham, Octavius Brooks. 1969. *Gerrit Smith: A Biography.* New York: Negro Universities Press; Harlow, Ralph Volney. 1939. *Gerrit Smith: Philanthropist and Reformer.* New York: Henry Holt.

SMITH, VENTURE
(1729–1805)

Author of the autobiography *A Narrative of the Life and Adventures of Venture, a Native of Africa: But Resident above Sixty years in the United States of America, Related by Himself* (1798), Venture Smith was born in Guinea, and his enslavement occurred around 1737 when one Robert Mumford purchased him for "four gallons of rum and a piece of calico." Smith's narrative gives important details on how the transition from freedom to slavery occurred as well as a clear picture of African village life.

Smith recollected that his father, a wealthy prince, tried appeasing the slave traders in his region by giving them goats and cattle, but this tactic ultimately failed and he paid for it with a tortured death at their hands and the destruction of his village. As an adult, Smith recalled, "The shocking scene is to this day fresh in my mind, and I have often been overcome while thinking on it." He remembered his father as "a man of remarkable strength and resolution, affable, kind and gentle, ruling with equity and moderation."

Before the horror of enslavement and destruction, Smith described African village life as being sedentary and concentrated on the production of crops and the raising of cattle, sheep, and goats. Polygamy was the norm, but wives had a veto over whether or not their husband acquired a new one. When Smith's father attempted to take a third wife without the consent of Venture's mother, she left her husband for a brief period for consolation.

Smith's narrative was published in 1798 in New London, Connecticut, and republished by his descendants in 1835. His narrative sought to "exhibit a pattern of honesty, prudence, and industry to people of his own colour; and perhaps some white people would not find themselves degraded by imitating such an example." In the Preface, Smith argued that slavery could inhibit even the genius of George Washington and Benjamin Franklin, but his own sense of being African could not be broken and he "still exhibit striking traces of native ingenuity and good sense."

Smith's good sense led him to help one of his masters pay for his services because Venture saw him as benign. This master, a Colonel Smith, allowed Venture to be hired out so the slave could earn some extra money. With this money, Venture eventually paid for his freedom, after which, during the next several years, Venture purchased his two sons, Solomon and Cuff; his wife, Meg; and eventually his daughter, Hannah.

His hard work and frugality led to a degree of prosperity as he was able to obtain a 76-acre farm and purchase several slaves himself. Smith's labor relations were of a reciprocal nature: black workers and slaves sought him out because of his generous character, and he sought them because he needed their labor and wanted to uplift them from the degradation he had once experienced. Venture Smith died in 1805 at the age of 77 and left an inheritance of a 100-acre farm and three houses.

—*Malik Simba*

For Further Reading
Costanzo, Angelo. 1987. *Surprizing Narrative*. Westport, CT: Greenwood; Smith, Venture. 1971. *A Narrative of the Life and Adventures of Venture Smith*. Boston: Beacon Press; Starling, Marion Wilson. 1981. *The Slave Narrative*. Boston: G. K. Hall.

SOCIETE DES AMIS DES NOIRS

The Société des Amis des Noirs was the first French abolitionist society, active from 1788 to 1793 and sporadically from 1796 to 1798. It promoted equal rights for free persons of color and the abolition of the French slave trade but viewed the abolition of slavery itself as a long-term goal. Successful in gaining recognition of mulatto rights, the society failed to attain its main goal, abolition of the slave trade.

Inspired by pioneers of French abolitionist discourse like Charles Louis Montesquieu and Jean-Jacques Rousseau, Jacques-Pierre Brissot de Warville, a leading revolutionary in close contact with the Society for Effecting the Abolition of the Slave Trade in England, founded the Société des Amis des Noirs in Paris on February 19, 1788. A secular organization, the society was socially egalitarian, cosmopolitan in outlook, and admitted foreigners—even women.

The first members were largely Parisian aristocrats, financiers, professionals, and men of letters. The membership fee was high, participation was low, and the society never attained the popular base of English and American societies. Politically, the French society was widely identified with the Girondist faction, a group of moderate republicans in the French Revolution.

Like its English counterpart, the Société des Amis des Noirs focused on banning the slave trade. Intense planter opposition, the perceived political immaturity of the black population, and the rapid growth of English abolitionism all contributed to this prioritization. Abolition of the trade appeared relatively simple, the members thought, for all that would be needed was an end to the bounty system. Members also reasoned that ending the trade would indirectly improve plantation conditions, because masters would have to rely on natural population growth.

The society was dominated by ideology rather than pragmatism, and most members were quite ignorant of slavery's realities. They made no effort to support their position with original research, like their English colleagues, nor did they make good use of economic arguments. The society was infused with a naive optimism. In the National Assembly, members repeatedly appealed to the principles of 1789 and stated that applying them to black slaves would make France a shining example of humanitarianism. Regarding slaves, members rather romanticized black mentality, for they did not expect black slaves to attempt to emancipate themselves.

Early activities included informing the public about the horrors of slavery, disseminating noted English texts on the subject, and making the case that engaging in slavery and the slave trade was bad economics. When the French Revolution began, the society's work changed. Political upheaval brought extensive freedom of the press, and contemporary newspapers provided welcome channels for influencing public opinion. More important, the society had deputies in the National Assembly.

In 1790, members repeatedly addressed that body concerning abolition of the trade, but the assembly's political preoccupations prevented concrete action. Colonial slave revolts rendered debate difficult, and crucial decisions were impossible to make because the well-organized colonial opposition, the Club Massiac, blocked all problack legislation. Compared to the society's weak economic arguments, the club's assertions that slavery and the slave trade were inseparable, and that abolition would ruin the national economy, appeared more convincing.

Two minor victories were achieved. By 1792, the Girondists had attained power, and on August 22, a decree was passed that confirmed the political rights of mulattoes and organized a delegation to the National Assembly of representatives from the West Indies. On July 27, 1793, the bounty system was abolished.

No progress was made toward abolition of the slave trade, however, for France's internal crisis and the Haitian slave revolt ended any hope of attaining that goal. With the fall of the Girondists in 1793, the society splintered. Thus, when the National Convention finally abolished slavery on February 4, 1794, the act could hardly be attributed to the society's activities, but was rather an ex post facto recognition of an accomplished fact. Still, the practice of slavery became reestablished in the French colonies after 1802, and it was not finally abolished until 1848.

Briefly revived during the rule of the French Directory, the society's meetings were poorly attended and unproductive. Its last recorded meeting was held in 1798. In 1802, Napoleon reintroduced slavery, but his authoritarian regime made a rebirth of the society impossible.

—*William L. Chew III*

See also
Atlantic Abolitionist Movement; Clarkson, Thomas; The Enlightenment; French Caribbean; French Declaration of the Rights of Man and Citizen; Montesquieu, Charles Louis de Secondat; Rousseau, Jean-Jacques; Wilberforce, William

For Further Reading
Daget, Serge. 1980. "A Model of the French Abolitionist Movement and Its Variations." In *Anti-Slavery, Religion, and Reform: Essays in Memory of Roger Anstey.* Ed. Christine Bolt and Seymour Drescher. Folkestone, Eng.: Dawson; Dorigny, Marcel. 1993. "La Société des Amis des Noirs et les projets de colonisation en Afrique." *Annales Historiques de la Révolution Française* 293–294: 421–429; Resnick, Daniel P. 1972. "The Société des Amis des Noirs and the Abolition of Slavery." *French Historical Studies* 7 (4): 558–569; *La Révolution française et l'abolition de l'esclavage: Textes et documents.* 1969. 12 vols. Paris: Editions d'histoire sociale.

SOLON
(C. 630–560 B.C.)

Appointed as lawgiver in Athens after a chaotic period, Solon is accredited with establishing laws that regulated public discourse, laws upon which the Athenian democracy of the fifth and fourth centuries B.C. was founded. He wrote many works of elegaic poetry, which enable the reconstruction of his life and achievements, the most famous being the "disburdening from debt" (or *seisachtheia*), which Aristotle's *Constitution of Athens* claims "freed the people once and for all" from enslavement for debt.

Solon was an Athenian statesman and a poet of noble descent. The traditions forming the basis of our knowledge stem from Plutarch's *Lives*, reconstructed fragments of Solon's poetry, and occasional references to him in other Greek and Latin writers. It is generally accepted that he was a merchant and well traveled. A general in the Athenian-Megarian struggle for control of the island of Salamis, he was made chief archon (magistrate) for 594–593 B.C., but it seems unlikely that he took this opportunity to instigate his wide-ranging reforms as his legislative program is usually dated 20 years later. He traveled for a decade, during which time he may have met Ahmose II, the Egyptian pharaoh. Solon returned to Athens to find his country torn by internecine strife, which ended only with the tyranny of Peisistratus in 560 B.C.

Solon's poetry provides insight into the distribution of wealth and landownership in sixth-century-B.C. Attica. Clearly, there were grave economic and social inequalities. Several leading families, among them the Eupatridai, controlled most branches of the government and succeeded in reducing many of the poorer farmers to servitude or serfdom. The exact nature of this servitude remains unclear, and the fragments of Solon's work shed no certain light on this issue. Most probably the poorest farmers and any other unpropertied countrymen who, becoming indebted and having no collateral to offer for their debts but their person, were compelled to sell themselves into slavery within Attica or even abroad. This phenomenon seems to have grown rapidly and fueled a dangerous class rivalry.

As archon Solon initially canceled all debts where land or liberty was the security, and by doing so, he released all Athenians from serfdom. He purportedly returned the farms to the dispossessed and redeemed from slavery those sold abroad. To entrench this monumental change, he forbade all borrowing on the security of the person.

This *seisachtheia* was accompanied by other protectionist maneuvers and the introduction of Athens' own coinage. Solon also transformed the constitution by dividing the population into four groups based on the relative value of property and land productivity. He created a timocratic constitution, which meant that a certain amount of property was necessary for office. His entire program satisfied no one group completely, and civil unrest returned, but his lasting contributions to the birth of Athenian democracy and the institution of slavery are unquestionable.

—Benjamin N. Lawrance

See also
Aristotle's *Politics*; Greece

For Further Reading
Andrewes, Antony. 1956. *The Greek Tyrants*. London: Hutchinson's University Library; De Ste Croix, Geoffrey E. M. 1981. *The Class Struggle in the Ancient Greek World*. Ithaca, NY: Cornell University Press; Ehrenberg, Victor. 1973. *From Solon to Socrates*. London: Methuen; Freeman, Kathleen. 1976. *The Work and Life of Solon*. New York: Arno Press.

SOMERSETT CASE (KNOWLES V. SOMERSETT) (1772)

The eighteenth-century British case *Knowles v. Somersett* concerned the status of black slaves: could they claim freedom upon their arrival in England or not? The episode centered around James Somersett, a slave who had been brought to England by his master, Charles Stewart. Although the case has historically been discussed as one that concerned a master and slave from Virginia, Charles Stewart was a Scottish paymaster and cashier of customs in the American colonies, where he had resided for several years in Boston. Both Stewart and Somersett were known in Boston, from which both departed for London in November 1769.

In 1771, Somersett ran away from Stewart. He was subsequently captured and taken on board the *Ann and Mary*, a ship bound for Jamaica, where he was to be sold. He was kept in irons on board by a Captain Knowles. Through the action of his friends—who had been present at the kidnapping but unable to prevent it—William Murray, first earl of Mansfield and chief justice of the Court of King's Bench, granted a writ of habeas corpus against the ship's captain. Somersett was returned to the mainland to stand before Lord Mansfield before the end of the court's 1771 Michaelmas term in November.

Granville Sharp appeared as advocate for the rights of blacks in England, though how Sharp became acquainted with Somersett's case is unclear. However, as Sharp had developed a reputation for challenging the courts with respect to black slaves in Britain, Somersett's friends would have known to apply to him. By the time Somersett's case became an issue, Sharp had argued several cases before Chief Justice Mansfield concerning blacks and freedom in Britain. Each case had proved a success both for Sharp and for the slave whose freedom was at stake.

Nevertheless, Sharp's victories had not endeared him to Mansfield, whose views on the rights of blacks in Britain were inconsistent and unsettled, and the two men had developed an adversarial relationship. In an attempt to secure the best conditions of impartiality for Somersett, Sharp absented himself from the courtroom during the trial, fearing that his presence would agitate Mansfield's acrimony toward him. Instead, five others were briefed to represent Somersett while Sharp remained in the background.

The complex trial lasted nearly five months, from its first full hearing in February 1772 until Mansfield's judgment was delivered on June 22, 1772. Knowles argued that Negro slavery thrived in his majesty's colonies and that Somersett had been a slave before Knowles ever met him. Knowles further argued that not only had Negro slaves always been bought and sold as chattel but Somersett had not at any time been freed by Stewart.

Francis Hargreave, arguing for Somersett, claimed that though Somersett was a slave before he came to England, his detention on that basis jeopardized public liberty. If slavery that existed elsewhere were to be acknowledged and upheld in England, then England would soon find itself inundated with foreign slaves imported not only from its own colonies but also from such places as Turkey, Spain, Poland, Russia, and the Barbary Coast.

Hargreave structured his argument around what he saw as two different types of slavery: that of sovereign over subject and that of one subject over another. The former was perfectly acceptable; the latter, not. Hargreave further argued that the only form of domestic slavery England had ever countenanced was that of villeage (an unfree peasant standing as the slave of a feudal lord but free in legal relations with respect to all others); therefore no slavery other than villeage could be lawful in England. After discoursing at length on English laws and history, Hargreave concluded that the law of England bestowed liberty fully—in name and substance—upon blacks brought into the country.

Further, Stewart had no right over Somersett, either in the obvious relationship of master to slave or in the disguised one of master to servant.

After hearing various arguments for and against Somersett, Lord Mansfield offered his decision, based, he asserted, not on compassion, but on the law. On the question of authority, Mansfield ruled that contracts conferred authority and that Stewart's claims did not rest on the existence of a contract. Furthermore, the chief justice declared that the character of slavery was, in effect, so idiosyncratic and so odious that it could be introduced only by specific law, not by moral or political reasons, and that law remained long after reasons ceased to be viable. Mansfield therefore judged that only "positive law" could support slavery. English law did not approve slavery, and Somersett was set free.

In ruling as he did, Mansfield abandoned a 1729 opinion by Attorney General Sir Philip Yorke and Solicitor General Charles Talbot, which held that slaves could be forcibly returned to their masters and removed from the country. Mansfield ruled that masters had no authority and slaves could not be forcibly returned to them or removed from England. But that is all he ruled. The decision did not herald the end of slavery in Britain.

—*T. K. Hunter*

See also
Murray, William, First Earl of Mansfield; Sharp, Granville
For Further Reading
Gerzina, Gretchen. 1995. *Black London: Life before Emancipation.* New Brunswick, NJ: Rutgers University Press; Hoare, Prince. 1828. *Memoirs of Granville Sharp, Esq.* London: Henry Colburn; Scobie, Edward. 1972. *Black Britannia: A History of Blacks in Britain.* Chicago: Johnson Publishing; Shyllon, F. O. 1974. *Black Slaves in Britain.* London: Oxford University Press.

SONGHAI EMPIRE

The Songhai Empire, which flourished from 1464 to 1591, was Africa's third great Sudanese kingdom after Ghana and Mali. It incorporated a large area of western Africa and blended Islam with indigenous animist cultures. Its complete domination extended over the middle Niger region from Kano to Satadougou and from a much wider belt of the Sahel from the Senegal River to the Aïr (Azbine) massif and northern Hausaland. Although a Songhai state existed as early as the eighth century, little is known of its institutions and history before imperial expansion.

During the period of imperial expansion, Songhai developed a civil service to supplement the king's authority. Rather than depending on feudal alliances with local leaders, Songhai kings centralized their power by raising armies that owed their primary allegiance to the king. Some of the soldiers serving during periods of expansive conquest were slaves and were regarded as the king's personal possessions. Slavery existed in the region long before the fifteenth century and continued to exist long after the Songhai Empire collapsed owing to internal rebellion and destruction by the Saidian sultan al-Mansur's Moroccan forces.

The period of Muslim rule under the Askias family (from 1493 onward) differed slightly from the earlier, highly organized African state they had inherited. The earlier state's tradition of institutional slavery remained largely intact. One minor change was that the Askias did not enslave natives who had converted to Islam. Additionally, many of the Askias's military campaigns resulted in the seizure of hundreds, if not thousands, of captives who were brought back to the empire's interior and to the royal city of Gao to be enslaved.

Numerous female captives became mothers of future Askias. Such was the case with Maryam Dabo who was acquired in a raid on Dialan in Mali during the early-sixteenth century and later became the mother of Askia Isma'il (r. 1537–1539). Another woman, captured in a similar raid on Borgu in Benin during that period, was the mother of Askia Musa (r. 1528–1531).

Being a Muslim did not always protect the empire's inhabitants from enslavement. The empire's founder, Sunni Ali (r. 1464–1492), conquered vast territories with largely Muslim inhabitants. Other Songhai rulers, like Askia Muhammad Turay I (r. 1493–1528), legitimized their rule and seizure of power among the Muslim community by denouncing Sunni Ali's "pagan" rule and freeing all Muslims enslaved by the former ruler. The Timbuktu chronicles of Songhai's Askia dynasty include notes and legends of earlier dynasties and end shortly after the Moroccan conquest in 1599.

Both Mahmoud Kati (and three generations of his family) in *Ta'rikh el-Fettach* and Abderrahman as-Sa'di in *Ta'rikh as-Sudan* revealed an awareness of a social hierarchy in opposition to the existing political structure. Where the two conflicted, as in the case of Sunni Ali, or agreed, as with Askia Muhammad, the record of events reflected an African-Islamic worldview. The system described survived in large part because it permeated Songhai society.

On the eve of European colonization, about half of Songhai's population consisted of slaves, a group that included both trade and domestic slaves. From the chronicles, it appears that some people of low origin became wealthy, obtained advanced education, and earned high positions in the imperial administration, but the rise of the slave class created tensions. For instance, it created competition in Songhai, which set the old noble families against the merchants.

As invaluable as the chronicles and compiled records have been to historians of the Songhai Empire, they also are suspect and often seem disconnected in nature. The sources indiscriminately incorporated legends and traditions and contain flowering eulogies for the reigning dynasties and vehement denigration of their enemies. Biographies and obituaries of the 'ulama class (educated clerics), to which most of the compilers belonged, became the evident pattern of unsystematic record keeping.

The short-lived expeditionary Moroccan occupying force effectively destroyed the Songhai social order. The Moroccans sought access to the gold mines near Jenné in south-central Mali, which they hoped would finance the chronic struggles against their Hispanic and Turkish enemies. Lacking a powerful protector, Songhai's inhabitants were themselves raided and enslaved. The wider social history and history of slavery during this era remain rich but, sadly, often underresearched elements of African history.

—Talaat Shehata

For Further Reading
As-Sa'di, Abderrahman ben Abdallah ben 'Imran ben 'Amir. 1964. *Ta'rikh as-Sudan.* Trans. Octave Houdas. Paris: Adrien-Maisonneuve; Hogben, Sidney John. 1967. *An Introduction to the History of the Islamic States of Northern Nigeria.* Ibadan, Nigeria: Oxford University Press; Kati, Mahmoud. 1913. *Ta'rikh el-Fettach.* Trans. Octave Houdas and M. Delafosse. Paris: n.p.; Trimingham, John Spencer. 1980. *The Influence of Islam upon Africa.* New York: Longman.

SOUTH AFRICA
See Boers; Cape Colony; Transition from Slave Labor to Free Labor, South Africa

SOUTHERN COMMERCIAL CONVENTIONS (1852–1859)

Until 1852, commercial conventions in the U.S. South were loosely organized gatherings of economic and political elites who met to discuss ways to strengthen the region's eco-

nomic infrastructure and to show solidarity for the institution of slavery. Beginning in 1852, the commercial conventions became more organized, and from 1852 to 1859, conventions were held in New Orleans, Baltimore, Memphis, Charleston, Richmond, Savannah, Knoxville, Montgomery, and finally Vicksburg. Convention participants discussed ways to improve the Southern economy by promoting the introduction of nonslave industry into the region while still maintaining the slave-based economy.

Early supporters, like James Dunwoody Brownson DeBow, intended to keep the conventions focused primarily on the development of the South's commercial and economic infrastructure and attempted to avoid political debates and sectional rivalries. But with the growing sectionalism between the North and South in the 1850s, and a growing antislavery sentiment in the North, these meetings of the South's economic and political elites increasingly focused on protecting the South's slave economy. The conventions also became the vehicle for a debate over reopening the African slave trade, a debate that grew in intensity as Northern antislavery forces and sectional rivalries increased.

At the 1857 convention in Knoxville, delegates focused almost exclusively on discussing the importance of preserving the slave economy and defending the institution from what they believed was a dangerous threat to its existence from Northern interests. Radical proslavery interests at the conventions insisted that slavery ensured domestic order, provided a satisfactory economic system, and, most important, was the South's right to maintain.

By the 1859 convention in Vicksburg, all pretense of keeping political questions off the convention floor had disappeared. Delegates passed resolutions to repeal federal laws that prohibited the slave trade, to negotiate a treaty with Canada that would provide slaveowners with a way to retrieve runaway slaves, and to promote the protection of slavery in Cuba and Central America. Members of this convention also passed resolutions that emphasized the rights of slaveholders to settle in western territories and, in a move to support the growth of slavery in the new territories, called for slaveholders to move to Kansas to aid slaveholding interests there. The development of the extreme proslavery position of the Southern commercial conventions demonstrates how Southerners increasingly supported efforts in the 1850s to defend slavery from Northern antislavery forces.

—Craig S. Pascoe

See also
Abolition, United States; Capitalism; DeBow, James Dunwoody Brownson; Proslavery Argument, United States

For Further Reading
Johnson, Vicki Vaughn. 1992. *The Men and the Vision of the Southern Commercial Conventions, 1845–1871.* Columbia: University of Missouri Press; Jordon, Weymouth T. 1958. *Rebels in the Making: Planters' Conventions and Southern Propaganda.* Tuscaloosa, AL: Confederate Publishing; Shore, Laurence. 1986. *Southern Capitalists: The Ideological Leadership of an Elite, 1832–1885.* Chapel Hill: University of North Carolina Press; Wender, Herbert. 1930. *Southern Commercial Conventions, 1837–1859.* Baltimore: Johns Hopkins Press.

SPAIN

Beginning in 410, when the Visigothic kingdom was formed, slavery in Spain was a customary institution regulated by Roman law. It coexisted with indentured servitude, from which it was not very different. After Arabs and Berbers (Moors) occupied the Iberian Peninsula in 711, al-Andalus (southern Spain) adopted Islamic customs of incorporating slave populations into the mainstream. Military service, recognition of a Muslim man's child by a slave woman, and conversion to Islam guaranteed progressive assimilation.

North Africa and eastern Europe were the main slave-trading sources during the Califate of Córdoba (929–1035) and later during the period of independent, small emirates. Slavery was regulated in great detail by Castilian monarch Alfonso X (r. 1252–1284), whose code Las Siete Partidas defined slavery as an institution based, not in natural law, but in custom among the nations.

The Christian kingdom of Aragon, which included Catalonia and Valencia, started practicing slavery in significant proportions during the fifteenth century. In Barcelona, Valencia, and Majorca, merchants established insurance policies against slave flight, and the church sponsored special religious guilds for the black slaves' social welfare, a practice that would soon be copied in southern Castilian cities like Seville and Jaén—the *cofradías de negros* ("confraternities of the blacks"). Slave ownership became an exclusive Christian privilege, one not allowed to Jews and Muslims, including Granada's morisco minority. Owners employing female slaves as prostitutes could be penalized with a fine and forfeiture of the slave.

Castile's conquest of the Canary Islands and Portugal's initiation of the West African slave trade after 1441 brought the slave trade to Castile, and slavery became a reality with Spanish and Portuguese participation in the conquest and colonization of large parts of the Americas. The port city of Seville was, after Lisbon, the main Atlantic slave-trading center for over a century. The archbishopric of Seville's census for the 1590s reveals the existence of 14,000 slaves in a population of 150,000 for the city and its surrounding region, and estimates indicate that Spain had 100,000 slaves at the end of the sixteenth century, out of a total population of 8 million.

As the sixteenth century advanced, West African slaves quickly outnumbered slaves of different ethnic origins—like Muslims, Indians, or Guanches (inhabitants of the Canary Islands)—and the Atlantic slave trade became increasingly more important than the trans-Saharan. After Granada's Muslims rebelled in 1568, Philip II ordered the enslavement of much of the morisco minority, and those slaves were sent to different parts of Castile. All sectors of Spanish society participated as slaveowners. Aristocrats and clergy owned most of the slaves, but many artisans, including famous printers in Seville, also employed them in their service. Slaves also labored as agricultural sugarcane workers, as miners, and in soap manufacturing.

According to the Siete Partidas, slaves could be bought, sold, or loaned. They were sometimes allowed to save money to purchase their freedom, and wills manumitted others, especially children of slave women and their owners. Often, slaves found themselves one-quarter, one-third, or half free depending on the amount paid to their owners or their heirs for self-purchase.

After 1510, when Muslims were forced to convert to Christianity en masse, masters were supposed to give their non-Christian slaves religious instruction. The church officially recognized slave marriages, but children of slave women remained the owner's property. Slave flight was a common occurrence, which authorities tried to prevent with a series of measures. Slaves trying to escape toward North Africa, if captured, had the added burden of being accused of apostasy. Black slaves, unlike morisco or North African ones, were subject to special restrictions and penalties. The most notorious was the *pringado,* pouring hot lard over open wounds after administering many lashes. Black slaves concentrated in some urban neighborhoods, where they lived with free black people.

Spanish slavery had declined by the mid-seventeenth century because the demand for African slaves in the American colonies had increased so that the price of those slaves was beyond the reach of most sectors of what had become an impoverished Spanish society. Spain never officially abolished slavery. In the 1830s, the government declared the automatic freedom of slaves brought by their owners from the Caribbean colonies of Cuba and Puerto Rico, hoping to suppress a labor competition in which a potential Spanish slave population would take work from native

Spaniards. In the Spanish colonies, slavery was abolished in Puerto Rico in 1873 and in Cuba in 1886.

—*Baltasar Fra-Molinero*

For Further Reading

Cortés López, José Luis. 1989. *La esclavitud negra en la España peninsular del siglo XVI.* Salamanca: Ediciones Universidad de Salamanca; Domínguez Ortiz, Antonio. 1952. "La esclavitud en Castilla durante la Edad Moderna." In *Estudios de historia social de España.* Ed. Carmelo Viñas y Mey. Madrid: CSIC; Ndamba Kabongo, Albert. 1976. *Les esclaves à Séville au début du XVIIe siècle: Approche de leurs origines et de leur condition.* Microfiche. Paris: Micro Editions Hachette; Verlinden, Charles. 1955. *L'esclavage dans l'Europe médiévale.* Vol. 1, *Péninsule ibérique.* France. Bruges, Belgium: De Tempel.

SPANISH BORDERLANDS

Although there was a great amount of African slavery present in U.S. territory that bordered Spanish territory, it was, in the main, limited to the southeastern part of the United States and Texas. The 1860 U.S. census noted that New Mexico Territory contained eight "chattel servants," the property of white citizens who had emigrated from Texas. Clearly, most African chattel slavery along the Spanish borderlands in the southwestern part of the United States was to be found in Texas, where it was limited by economics and geography. If one includes portions of the Louisiana Purchase in an extended definition of the Spanish borderlands, slaves in Missouri and Kansas can also be counted in this region. Except for Texas and, to a much lower extent, Missouri and Kansas, slavery was unprofitable in the borderlands. Since independence in 1823, the Mexican constitutions had banned African slavery, and the fact that Texas belonged to Mexico until 1836 and remained an independent republic until 1845 because the slavery problem helped cause the "Texas question" as Americans moved into Texas, bringing their slaves with them.

If one uses a broad definition of Spanish borderlands, then the various Indian tribes in Florida and later in Oklahoma (Indian Territory) that owned slaves should be included in any discussion of slavery in the area. Also, the question of using Indians as slaves was considered almost as soon as the Spanish touched the shores of the New World, but while the Spanish seemed to accept African slavery, they worked very hard to keep Indians out of slavery. Father Bartolomé de Las Casas first proposed introducing African slaves into the Caribbean Islands to spare the Indians there the heavy labor that was destroying them, but he later changed his mind and opposed black slavery as well, and for similar reasons.

The Spanish never fought as hard or as consistently against black slavery as they did on behalf of the Indians. Even though Las Casas eventually rejected black slavery, he owned several African slaves as late as 1544. The Spanish did not offer any concerted opposition to African slavery during the sixteenth century, perhaps because the Iberians had become accustomed to having Muslim slaves. There are several examples of slaves being a part of the Spanish conquest in the New World (e.g., a slave by the name of Estevanico accompanied the Spanish explorer Álvar Núñez Cabeza de Vaca and, later, the Coronado expedition). The work to emancipate African slaves in the Spanish New World was led by the Jesuits Alonso de Sandoval and Peter Claver during the seventeenth century. The "great debate" at Valladolid, Spain (1550–1551), was conducted as an inquiry into the nature of the Indian: Was he the "natural slave" described in Aristotle's *Politics?* The debate concluded that Indians were not the people discussed by Aristotle.

Although slavery was expressly prohibited by law in the Spanish dominions, the Indians were subjected to the *encomienda* system and the mission laws of California. The *encomienda* system was devised to provide landowners with an adequate labor supply. The earliest laws on the treatment of Indians in the New World, the Laws of Burgos, went into force in 1513, but these laws, while humane, were unenforceable. Las Casas, in his *History of the Indies* (1520), attacked the system, writing: "The greatest evil which has caused the total destruction of those lands and which will continue . . . is the encomienda of the Indians as it now exists . . . also it is against God and his will and his Church" (Hanke, 1949). The Law of Inheritance for Two Generations (1536) permitted the *encomenderos* (whose who held *encomienda* rights) to pass on their *encomiendas* as inheritance (and the Indians with them) to their legitimate descendants or to their widow for her lifetime.

The other far-reaching example of Indian slavery was in the mission system as established in California. The system, devised by the Franciscan fathers, held the Indians in virtual slavery. The theory was that the fathers were holding the lands in trust for the Indians until they became mature enough to handle the complexities of property and govern themselves. The Indians were tied to the mission lands, were denied free access, and had every aspect of their lives controlled by the priests—much as the *encomenderos* had controlled Indians nearly 200 years earlier. Even after the California was ceded by Mexico to the United States in 1848, California's mission Indians tended to remain on former mission lands. Some tribes even took their current name from the specific mission they lived near.

One other aspect of slavery along the Spanish border-lands was that of Indians who took other tribes as slaves during war and conquest. The Navajo of the American Southwest had a reputation for doing just that, and Spanish chronicles stressed the fear of Navajo slaves for the tribe that held them.

—*Henry H. Goldman*

For Further Reading
Abel, Annie Heloise. 1992. *The American Indian as Slaveholder and Secessionist.* Lincoln: University of Nebraska Press; Bailey, L. R. 1973.*The Indian Slave Trade in the Southwest.* Los Angeles: Westernlore Press; Hanke, Lewis. 1949. *The Spanish Struggle for Justice in the Conquest of America.* Philadelphia: University of Pennsylvania Press; McNitt, Frank. 1972. *Navajo Wars: Military Campaigns, Slave Raids, and Reprisals.* Albuquerque: University of New Mexico Press.

SPANISH CARIBBEAN

The first African slaves imported into the Americas were the personal servants of the conquering Spaniards who went to Hispaniola and Cuba in the two decades following Columbus's voyages. The Spanish conquerors also enslaved native peoples that they found there, but enslavement of the Indians was short-lived. Growing opposition by such luminaries as Bishop Bartolomé de Las Casas and the rapid decline of native populations as a result of European diseases and overwork led to the legal prohibition of Indian slavery under most circumstances.

Following the Spanish conquest of Mexico and the Andean highlands, Spain refocused its imperial attention on the mainland and left the Caribbean colonies pretty much to themselves. Spanish colonists on the Caribbean islands of Cuba, Hispaniola, and Puerto Rico imported small numbers of African slaves and pursued plantation agriculture on a minimal scale, but without access to credit or a steady supply of slaves such as their Portuguese, English, and French competitors enjoyed, their efforts were unsuccessful.

The Spanish Caribbean colonies were also quite spacious and contained large reserves of uninhabited territory into which persons of African descent, either free or slave, could move. This situation contributed to a labor shortage, which further hindered the growth of plantation agriculture. Most of the agricultural land in these colonies, especially in Puerto Rico and the Spanish portion of Hispaniola (now the Dominican Republic), was held by small farmers, many or most of them Creoles of mixed African and Euro-pean ancestry. There were small numbers of slaves who were sometimes employed as plantation laborers but more often as servants or tenant farmers. The farmers, free and slave, produced principally for their own consumption, although they did supply the Spanish garrisons in the cities and resupply the Spanish fleets that protected the shipments of precious metals from the Spanish New World to Europe. It was only after 1790 that this picture changed.

France's plantation industries virtually disappeared after the success of the Haitian revolution in 1804, the success of the Industrial Revolution and abolitionist political pressure brought an end to slavery in the British Caribbean in 1834 and a consequent devastation of the sugar industry in the British colonies, and Spain lost its mainland New World colonies between 1809 and 1825. All of these developments led to an enormous increase in the sugar industry in all the Spanish Caribbean colonies. In addition to sugar, the production of other plantation crops such as coffee and tobacco, which had been produced by small-scale enterprises in the Spanish Caribbean since the sixteenth century, rapidly expanded as large-scale plantation production developed between 1770 and 1850.

Spain had agreed in 1815 to end the slave trade, but it did not make abolition fully effective until 1866. In fact, imports of slaves, especially to Cuba, increased dramatically in the years after the end of the Napoleonic Wars, and as late as 1860, African-born persons made up the majority of the slaves sold in the Havana slave market.

One notable feature of slave life in the Spanish Empire was the institution of *coartación,* or self-purchase. Slaves could petition their master to set a price for their freedom, and the slave was then guaranteed the right to purchase himself or herself at that price at any point in the future. Slaves had a variety of ways to accumulate the wealth necessary to make the purchase, ranging from work for hire outside their normal work hours to theft to gifts from free relatives or white patrons.

Some observers, notably Frank Tannenbaum (1963), have suggested that the Spanish (or Iberian, including the Portuguese) mode of slavery was less harsh than that of the northern Europeans for cultural and religious reasons. It is also said that Spanish law and culture had included a place for the slave since the Middle Ages; a limited and subordinate place, but nevertheless one that accepted the essential personhood of the slave and granted him or her certain legal rights. In addition, the Catholic Church, claiming universality and seeking to address the spiritual needs of all persons, had a moderating effect on the treatment of slaves in the very Catholic Spanish Empire. All of these statements, however, have been disputed and are controversial.

—*Stewart R. King*

Engraving of slaveholder negotiating the sale of one of his slaves on a Caribbean island.

See also

Burgos, Laws of; *Coartación*; Las Casas, Bartolomé de; Tannenbaum, Frank

For Further Reading

Bergad, Laird, Fe Iglesias Garcia, and Maria del Carmen Barcia. 1995. *The Cuban Slave Market, 1790–1880*. Cambridge: Cambridge University Press; Knight, Franklin W. 1970. *Slave Society in Cuba during the Nineteenth Century*. Madison: University of Wisconsin Press; Mintz, Sidney W. 1974. *Caribbean Transformations*. Chicago: Aldine Publishing Company; Tannenbaum, Frank. 1963. *Slave and Citizen: The Negro in the Americas*. New York: Random House.

SPARTACUS
(D. 71 B.C.)

Commander of the largest armed slave rebellion in world history, the gladiator Spartacus led a fugitive army that raided Roman Italy in a series of initially successful campaigns (73–71 B.C.). He reportedly was a veteran of the Roman auxiliaries in his homeland of Thrace, but this description may have been the result of an attempt by ancient writers to account for his tactical proficiency.

The best primary sources are the continuous but not wholly reliable narratives of the Greek biographer Plutarch and the Greek historian Appianos. There are no accounts from the slaves themselves. The sources attribute the rebellion solely to the abusive behavior of one master, Lentulus Batiatus, who had trained Spartacus and other slave blood-fighters at his gladiatorial school in Capua in southern Italy. Thus, the sources reflect a Roman slaveholder ideology which presumes that slaves treated properly would never desire rebellion. The actual causes prove more complex.

The Spartacan war came at a critical period in Roman history and followed two Sicilian Slave Wars (135–132 and 104–101 B.C.), the Italian Social War (91–88 B.C.), and the civil war of Lucius Cornelius Sulla (83–81 B.C.). Continual warfare abroad and military expansion of Rome's borders during the late republic had introduced over a million war captives to slave markets in Italy and Sicily so that Rome had high concentrations of uprooted, dishonored outsiders in its own society. The climate was volatile and ripe for open military rebellion by slaves, especially when many were skilled in the most advanced weaponry of the day.

The revolt began in the summer of 73 B.C. when 70 gladiators escaped the training compound in Capua. Spartacus was not their only leader; two others emerged, the Gauls Crixus and Oenomaus. Other runaway slaves joined the fugitive army, which by 72 B.C. numbered over 70,000 (including herdsmen and other rustics) and had vanquished four Roman armies.

The Roman Senate granted the wealthy Marcus Licinius Crassus, one of Rome's greatest slaveowners, the extraordinary military command of 10 legions, 6 of them newly recruited—the largest number of legions in Rome's history—to battle the slaves. Crassus pursued the fugitive forces south to the toe of Italy. Spartacus bargained with pirates for transport to Sicily, but they sailed off after being paid and left him stranded. Evading Crassus's forces, the fugitive slave army turned east toward the port of Brindisi in another bid to leave Italy altogether.

Pompey the Great was recalled from his Spanish campaign and another general, M. Terentius Varro Lucullus, returned abruptly from fighting in Macedonia. Lucullus landed his forces at Brindisi to block Spartacus, and Pompey moved his veterans into central Italy to prevent retreat. Crassus's legions slaughtered the fugitive army. Spartacus reportedly died in battle, and 6,000 captives were crucified along the Appian Way from Capua to Rome as an example to other slaves of how Rome would respond to servile rebellion.

Despite modern legends, Spartacus neither started nor intended a movement to abolish the institution of slavery: he and his soldiers enslaved many of their former masters. Urban slaves apparently found no solidarity with his war and never joined the rebellion. The circuitous wandering up and down peninsular Italy reveals the lack of an overarching military strategy or revolutionary goal. Reportedly, leadership was divided, with Crixus wanting spoils and Spartacus only wanting to go to his Thracian homeland. The revolt, therefore, is best understood as an outgrowth of Roman military expansion abroad, internal struggles at home, and outright civil war, all of which contributed to the social and political disorder that precipitated the downfall of the late Roman Republic.

—*J. Albert Harrill*

See also

Cicero; Crassus, Marcus Licinius; Latifundia; Roman Republic; *Servi poenae*; Stoicism; *Vernae*

For Further Reading

Bradley, Keith R. 1989. *Slavery and Rebellion in the Roman World, 140 B.C.–70 B.C.* Bloomington: Indiana University Press and London: B. T. Batsford; Scarborough, John. 1978. "Reflections on Spartacus." *Ancient World* 1 (2): 75–81; Ward, Allen Mason. 1977. *Marcus Crassus and the Late Roman Republic*. Columbia: University of Missouri Press; Wiedemann, Thomas. 1981. *Greek and Roman Slavery*. London: Routledge.

STAMPP, KENNETH M. (1912–)

Kenneth M. Stampp, a native of Milwaukee, Wisconsin, earned his Ph.D. at the University of Wisconsin in 1942 and emerged quickly as a leading historian of the Civil War era in the United States. His *Indiana Politics during the Civil War* (1949) and *And the War Came* (1950) marked him as an emerging scholar in the post–World War II years. Stampp's most influential work, however, remains his revisionist interpretation of North American slavery.

In a seminal article in the *American Historical Review* (1952) and in *The Peculiar Institution: Slavery in the Ante-Bellum South* (1956), Stampp thoroughly revised the pioneer writings of the Southern historian Ulrich Bonnell Phillips. Although respectful of Phillips's earlier contributions, Stampp nonetheless attacked him for ignoring slave life on small plantations and farms, for "loose and glib generalizing" about slave life, and for failing to view slavery "through the eyes of the Negro." In describing slavery, Stampp said, Phillips overvalued the "mild and humorous side and minimized its grosser aspects." In his opinion, Phillips was incapable of taking blacks seriously.

Reflecting the anthropological findings of his day, not Phillips's, Stampp remarked that "no historian . . . can be taken seriously any longer unless he begins with the knowledge that there is no valid evidence that the Negro race is innately inferior to the white, and there is growing evidence that both races have approximately the same potentialities." Writing during the opening stages of the civil rights movement, Stampp informed readers of *The Peculiar Institution,* "I have assumed that the slaves were ordinary human beings, that innately Negroes are, after all, only white men with black skins, nothing more, nothing less."

The Peculiar Institution remained the standard work on black slavery until the 1970s. After careful research using plantation sources, Stampp described "the peculiar institution" as a dehumanizing, exploitative, but highly profitable labor system. Slaves toiled from dawn to dusk. "In terms of its broad social consequences for the South as a whole, however," he said, "slavery must be adjudged a failure." Although cognizant that not all masters overworked their bondsmen and women, Stampp nevertheless insisted that the blacks perceived slavery "as a system of labor extortion."

It was above all else a labor system, one predicated on rigid discipline. To function, slavery depended on rigid discipline and demanded unconditional submission by the black slaves to the wishes of their white masters. It also was a social system that repeatedly impressed upon the bondsmen and women their inferiority, a "closed" system determined to inculcate in them "a paralyzing fear of white men."

Whereas Phillips had defined slavery as a "school" for the allegedly heathen African Americans, Stampp interpreted it more like a prison where the slaves gained "a sense of complete dependence" and learned the whites' "code of behavior." According to Stampp, under slave law, "the slave was less a person than a thing." Whites, employing whipping as a symbol of racial control, worked hard to make the slaves "stand in fear." Challenging Phillips's notion of planter paternalism, Stampp charged that "the predominant and overpowering emotion that whites aroused in the majority of slaves was neither love nor hate but fear."

Stampp recognized that masters provided incentives to the slaves—patches of land for truck gardens, passes to visit other farms and plantations, cash payments—as ancillary modes of racial control. Unlike Phillips, Stampp argued that the slave consistently "longed for liberty and resisted bondage as much as any people could have done in their circumstances." Subjected to all manner of brutal and barbaric treatment by their captors, the slaves nevertheless remained "a troublesome property," capable of withstanding and resisting their captivity. In the end, Stampp judged that "slavery had no philosophical defense worthy of the name . . . it had nothing to commend it to posterity, except that it paid."

Stampp's view of slavery—as morally oppressive but economically profitable—generally continues to dominate theoretical approaches to the study of slavery. According to historian Peter J. Parish (1989), "Most authorities now agree that [the slaveholders] received a return on their investment which was in line with, if not superior to, that available elsewhere." But, as Stampp's critics have argued, master-slave relations were more complex, more nuanced, than the author of *The Peculiar Institution* suggested.

Stampp also did not recognize change over time. He envisioned slavery, according to Carl N. Degler (1976), as "a changeless snapshot." Also, whereas Stampp, like Phillips, focused mostly on the masters and their behavior, modern scholars pay considerably more attention to the slaves' perspective of and reaction to their bondage. Few scholars today agree with Stampp's description of slaves as a "culturally rootless people."

In its day, however, *The Peculiar Institution* ranked as a major corrective to the type of writing of Phillips's era, and it thus remains one of the most influential works on the history of slavery. It influenced generations of scholars determined to understand the long history of racism in the United States.

—*John David Smith*

See also
Paternalism; Phillips, Ulrich Bonnell
For Further Reading
Degler, Carl N. 1978. "Experiencing Slavery." *Reviews in American History* 6: 277–282; Degler, Carl N. 1976. "Why Historians Change Their Minds." *Pacific Historical Review* 45: 167–184; Parish, Peter J. 1989. *Slavery: History and Historians.* New York: Harper and Row; Smith, John David. 1991. *An Old Creed for the New South: Proslavery Ideology and Historiography, 1865–1918.* Athens: University of Georgia Press.

STEWART, MARIA W. (1803–1879)

Hailed as America's first black female political writer, Maria W. Stewart was an intensely active abolitionist writer and speaker. She was the first African American woman to speak before a mixed-gender audience and to leave texts of her speeches. Stewart was much more than an abolitionist, as she addressed varied subjects like religion, anticolonization, political and economic exploitation, black self-determination, and women's rights.

A free black born in Hartford, Connecticut, and orphaned at an early age, Stewart lived with a clergyman's family until age 15 when she began working as a domestic servant. Although she did not have the privilege of a formal education, her attendance at local Sunday schools and residence in the clergyman's home offered access to books and knowledge that formed her intellectual views. Following a religious conversion, Stewart believed that born-again Christians were obligated to condemn all forms of injustice and oppression. She began writing antislavery tracts after the mysterious death of her friend and mentor, David Walker, whose famous *Appeal to the Colored Citizens of the World* (1829) called for black militancy to oppose slavery and racial injustice.

Her first tract, *Religion and the Pure Principles of Morality, the Sure Foundation on Which We Must Build* (1831), was printed by William Lloyd Garrison and Isaac Knapp, and excerpts appeared in Garrison's abolitionist weekly, the *Liberator*. Stewart also began speaking before Boston audiences at Franklin Hall and the Afric-American Female Intelligence Society. Using biblical references and the values espoused in the U.S. Constitution, she denounced slavery and asserted African Americans' rights to freedom and full participation in U.S. democracy.

Stewart questioned the American Colonization Society's intentions and recognized the racism of many of its members who believed blacks were inferior and unable to survive successfully on their own in the United States. Stewart challenged colonizationists to support their claims of charity. Speaking before an audience at the African Masonic Hall in Boston, she charged, "If the colonizationists are the real friends to Africa, let them expend the money which they collect in erecting a college to educate her injured sons in this land of gospel, light, and liberty; for it would be most thankfully received on our part, and convince us of the truth of their professions, and save time, expense, and anxiety" (Richardson, 1987). Like many nineteenth-century African American abolitionists, Stewart's discourse displayed a fundamental concern with black civil rights and self-determination.

Unfortunately, Stewart's career as a public speaker was short-lived. Because social constraints impeded women's activities in the public sphere and there was insufficient responsiveness to her addresses, Stewart chose to end her speaking career in 1833 but continued working for freedom and opportunities for African Americans. Stewart published her speeches and writings in *Meditations from the Pen of Mrs. Maria W. Stewart* (1835), which was reprinted as *Productions of Mrs. Maria Stewart, Presented to the First African-Baptist Church and Society, in the City of Boston* (1879). She taught school in New York, Baltimore, and later, in Washington, D.C., during the Civil War. She was appointed matron of Washington's Freedman's Hospital in the early 1870s and supervised the hospital's service to many ill, destitute, and dispossessed former slaves until her death in 1879.

—*DoVeanna S. Fulton*

For Further Reading
Logan, Shirley Wilson. 1995. *With Pen and Voice: A Critical Anthology of Nineteenth-Century African-American Women.* Carbondale: Southern Illinois University Press; Richardson, Marilyn, ed. 1987. *Maria W. Stewart, America's First Black Woman Political Writer.* Bloomington: Indiana University Press.

STILL, WILLIAM (1821–1902)

An abolitionist, writer, and Underground Railroad activist, William Still was a free African American whose mother ran away from slavery and whose father purchased his own freedom. Still began working for the Pennsylvania Anti-Slavery Society in 1847. Three years later, the society made him chairman of its Vigilance Committee to assist fugitives going through Philadelphia. During the eight years he spent in that job, he had contact with about 800 fugitive slaves, including about 60 children.

In Still's largely routine work there were some exciting moments, such as the day a man who had purchased his own freedom contacted Still for family information. The two discovered that they were brothers, the younger having been left behind when their mother escaped from slavery. Still was able to find temporary shelter for fugitives among other African Americans in Philadelphia, and he witnessed the arrival of such famous fugitives as Henry "Box" Brown and William and Ellen Craft. The Vigilance Committee also worked closely with abolitionists Thomas Garrett, Robert Purvis, and Lucretia and James Mott.

One of Still's duties was to interview newly arrived slaves concerning their masters' names, their treatment, and escape experiences. He carefully preserved these records, which years later provided source material for his book on the Underground Railroad. In 1855, Still visited former slaves in Canada and wrote a strong defense of their conduct and status, answering those people who insisted that African Americans could not survive in freedom. His efforts to improve the status of African Americans continued after abolition, when, among other efforts, he led a successful eight-year struggle to desegregate Pennsylvania's streetcars.

William Still's book, *The Underground Railroad* (1872), fills an important place in the history of that escape route. One of a very few such works by African Americans, it is a significant supplement to white abolitionists' memoirs. Although he included sketches of the abolitionists, his emphasis was on the daring and ingenuity of the fugitives themselves—he did not depict them as passive passengers on an abolitionist-run railroad. Besides fugitives' accounts, his book includes newspaper articles, legal documents, letters from abolitionists and former slaves, and biographical sketches. The many illustrations call attention to the role of absconding slaves in the struggle for their own freedom.

Still's book is a powerful testimony against slavery. The story of the fugitives' "heroism and desperate struggles," wrote Still, and "the terrible oppression that they were under," must be preserved for future generations. Moreover, Still argued that books by African Americans would prove their intellectual ability and demolish ideas of racial inferiority. "We very much need works on various topics from the pens of colored men to represent the race intellectually," he wrote.

William Still published his book himself and sold it through his own agents. When the first edition sold out, he printed another, and in 1883, a third edition appeared. It became the most widely circulated of such accounts, and copies are still found in many African American homes. Despite its large circulation, however, it had little influence on the way white Americans viewed the Underground Railroad, for Still's spotlight on the fugitives was often overshadowed by the well-publicized work of their abolitionist collaborators.

—Larry Gara

See also
Craft, William and Ellen; Garrett, Thomas; Underground Railroad

For Further Reading
Blockson, Charles L. 1987. *The Underground Railroad.* New York: Prentice Hall; Boyd, James R. 1883. "William Still: His Life and Work to This Time." In William Still. *The Underground Railroad.* 3d ed. Philadelphia: William Still; Gara, Larry. 1961. "William Still and the Underground Railroad." *Pennsylvania History* (1): 33–44.

STOICISM

Stoicism was a philosophical school of the Hellenistic and Roman periods founded around 300 B.C. by Zeno of Citium on the island of Cyprus. The school lasted into the third century A.D. It was a materialistic philosophy that considered nature as rational and human behavior as informed by ratio *(logos)*. According to the Stoics, the whole universe is permeated by divine *logos* ("reason") or *pneuma* ("spirit"), the only active principle of Stoicism, that orders all motions in the best possible way. It is the individual's duty to conform to this divine will, i.e., nature. No systematic treatment of slavery by the Stoics survives, and only a few fragments and passages make specific reference to the institution. In general, since the Stoics were preoccupied with individual morality and emphasized the role of nature in regulating human behavior, slavery as a legal condition received little attention.

Although the early (Zeno, Cleanthes, and Chrysippus) and middle (Panaetius and Posidonius) Stoics from the third through the first century B.C. showed only limited interest in slavery, the theme resurfaced among the late Stoic authors of the Roman Empire (especially Seneca, Musonius Rufus, and Epictetus) in the first and second centuries A.D. The substance of the Stoic view appears to have been: Slavery according to the law is an external, beyond our control, and therefore not worth close attention. By contrast, slavery as a condition of the soul is both within our control and important, as expressed in the Stoic epigram "every good man is free, every bad man a slave."

According to Zeno, people who are not virtuous

are enemies, slaves, and estranged from one another. Stoics did not explicitly confront Aristotle's theory of natural slavery. Although submission of inferior humans to superior individuals was in principle acceptable, any such inferiority was not considered irredeemable. Slavery according to law was a condition of the body, not of the mind, and slaves could transcend their physical bondage by exercising their freedom of spirit. Thus, in Seneca's view, a slave was capable of conferring a benefit on his owner that goes beyond servile obligation, and in doing so, the slave can assume the status of a man as distinct from that of a slave. One's legal status is unrelated to one's mental or spiritual condition.

Stoics developed a doctrine of common kinship of all living creatures that is expressed through *oikeiosis* ("making something my own"), which includes affinity to and concern for one's fellow beings. Slaves and free people are thought to share the same origin. Seneca stressed that "the man whom you call your slave sprang from the same stock, is smiled upon by the same skies, and on equal terms with yourself breathes, lives and dies" (Bradley, 1986). This plea was meant to dissuade masters from cruelly abusing their slaves, but not to encourage manumission. To Chrysippus, the slave is a hireling for life; his master would extract his labor but should provide him with what is due. Restraint would ultimately benefit the owner, since the Stoic wise man would avoid all forms of excess for the sake of his own moral well-being.

Accidents of fate, such as slavery, have to be borne with equanimity. This doctrine tends to induce acceptance of the existing social order. No high value was placed on legal status; common kinship and affinity in the moral sphere could coexist with recognized social hierarchies. From that perspective, abolition never became an issue. Moreover, Stoicism had no tangible impact on attitudes toward slavery as an institution or on slave-specific legislation. Although it has been argued that individual owners were drawn to a more humane treatment of their slaves on the grounds that there is no natural distinction between master and slave, this view is not supported by empirical evidence.

—*Walter Scheidel*

See also
Aristotle's *Politics;* Epictetus; Plato's *Laws;* Seneca, Lucius Annaeus

For Further Reading
Bradley, Keith R. 1986. "Seneca and Slavery." *Classica et mediaevalia* 37: 161–172; Garnsey, Peter. 1996. *Ideas of Slavery from Aristotle to Augustine.* Cambridge: Cambridge University Press; Manning, C. E. 1989. "Stoicism and Slavery in the Roman Empire." In *Aufstieg und Niedergang der römischen Welt.* Ed. Wolfgang Haase. Berlin and New York: De Gruyter.

STONE, LUCY
(1818–1893)

Despite Lucy Stone's significant contribution to abolitionism, her involvement in the women's rights and woman suffrage movements has overshadowed her years of labor for the antislavery cause. Born in central Massachusetts, Stone was greatly influenced by the outspoken early feminist-abolitionists Angelina and Sarah Grimké and Abigail (Abby) Kelley Foster.

Stone earned her way through Oberlin College, becoming in 1847 the first Massachusetts woman to obtain a college degree. Although abolitionism was rampant at Oberlin in the mid-1840s, it shunned the radical message of the followers of William Lloyd Garrison, upon which Stone modeled her ideology and her antislavery fervor. While at Oberlin, Stone was in charge of disseminating the *Anti-Slavery Bugle*, a journal for western Garrisonians, and though women students were not permitted to speak publicly, she worked to prepare herself for a career as a women's rights and antislavery lecturer.

Shortly after Stone graduated from Oberlin, Samuel May, Jr., general agent of the American Anti-Slavery Society, hired her as an agent of the society to go on antislavery lecture tours. When May chastised Stone for mingling women's rights issues with her antislavery message, the two solved the conflict by agreeing that Stone would address the two concerns in separate lectures. Like her fellow Garrisonian feminist-abolitionists Lucretia Mott, Abby Kelley Foster, and Susan B. Anthony, Stone found it nearly impossible to separate the issues of political and social domination that enslaved African Americans from those that rendered women powerless.

In her first year of touring, Stone earned a solid reputation for converting people to the antislavery cause. Her success was based on a dynamic oratorical strategy—without written notes or text, she focused on relating heartrending, true stories of families tyrannized and destroyed by slavery. Critics especially noted the persuasive effect of her mellifluous voice on belligerent audiences. By the end of 1848, Stone was sharing near-equal billing with William Lloyd Garrison and Wendell Phillips. Until the late 1850s, she lectured throughout all of New England, New York, New Jersey, Ohio, Michigan, Illinois, Wisconsin, and parts of Canada.

Late in the 1850s, several years after her marriage to Cincinnati abolitionist Henry Blackwell, Stone sharply curtailed her speaking engagements to remain at home with her young daughter. In the midst of the U.S. Civil War in 1863, she joined Susan B. Anthony and Elizabeth Cady Stanton in forming the Women's

National Loyal League. Stone was elected president at the league's opening convention, which determined to organize Northern women to petition Congress to secure a thirteenth amendment guaranteeing the freedom of African Americans.

In 1866, she participated with Anthony, Stanton, and others in organizing the American Equal Rights Association and lobbied legislators to make sure the Fourteenth Amendment, and later the Fifteenth Amendment, ensured universal suffrage. In 1869, following a major political and ideological rift with Anthony and Stanton, Stone abandoned this struggle and aligned herself with Wendell Phillips and most of the male abolitionists, who insisted that obtaining the franchise for African American males must take precedence over all other concerns, particularly woman suffrage. Stone dedicated the remainder of her life to women's rights and woman suffrage as a major leader of the American Woman Suffrage Association and as editor of the weekly newspaper *Woman's Journal*.

—*Judith E. Harper*

See also
Anthony, Susan Brownell; Foster, Abigail Kelley; Mott, Lucretia Coffin; Women and the Antislavery Movement

For Further Reading
Blackwell, Alice Stone. 1930. *Lucy Stone: Pioneer of Women's Rights*. Boston: Little, Brown; DuBois, Ellen Carol. 1978. *Feminism and Suffrage: The Emergence of an Independent Women's Movement in America 1848–1869*. Ithaca, NY: Cornell University Press; Hays, Elinor Rice. 1961. *Morning Star: A Biography of Lucy Stone, 1818–1893*. New York: Harcourt, Brace, and World; Kerr, Andrea Moore. 1992. *Lucy Stone: Speaking Out for Equality*. New Brunswick, NJ: Rutgers University Press.

STONO REBELLION (1739)

A slave rebellion broke out near the Stono River in South Carolina in 1739. Known as the Stono Rebellion, it was the largest uprising of its kind to occur during the period of the American colonies. The Spanish Empire in the New World had enticed the slaves of English colonies to escape to Spanish territory, and in 1733, the Spanish monarch issued an edict to free all runaway slaves from British territory who had made their way into Spanish possessions. Five years later, the Spanish in St. Augustine, Florida, earnestly pursued the policy and publicized this news. Information about the policy reached South Carolina's slaves through seamen who landed at Charleston, South Carolina, and throughout 1739,

that colony's government had problems with an increasing number of slaves escaping to Florida. As they promised, the Spanish offered refuge to the runaways, but occasionally, they sold them to other owners.

On Sunday, September 9, 1739, about 20 slaves, most of whom were from Angola, gathered under the leadership of a slave called Jemmy near the Stono River, 20 miles away from Charleston. They massacred several white families and looted their guns and ammunition. The next day they marched south, following the Pongpong River, which ran through Georgia to St. Augustine. While they marched, the rebels cried for liberty, raised flags, and beat drums. On the road, more slaves joined the rebels, whose number reached more than 60—some scholars estimate it was about 100.

In high spirits, the reinforced rebels stopped their march for a while. They began singing and dancing and tried to enlist more people by beating drums; some of them were drunk. Although they had marched more than 10 miles, the rebels had met with no obstacle and were free to burn everything they saw.

In the meantime, the militia was gathering, and when the whites pursued, the rebel ranks were soon broken, and several were killed in battle. For the following month, colonial officials arrested and executed the rebels, hanging their heads on the landmark posts along the road. In total, 44 blacks and 21 whites lost their lives during the rebellion and its aftermath.

Because the leaders of the rebellion were mostly from Angola, whites later avoided purchasing Angolan slaves because they feared their rebellious nature. The Stono Rebellion shocked white South Carolinians so strongly that their assembly passed laws to place import duties on the slaves from abroad to curtail the high black population rate in the colony. Of all the British colonies in North America, South Carolina had the largest majority African population. Blacks began outnumbering white residents in 1730, and in the colony's coastal area, blacks constituted two-thirds of the population.

In 1740, the colony collected all the Negro codes that were in use in order to rearrange them into a comprehensive new law. The new legislation fortified the whites' control of blacks, both free and unfree, by strengthening patrol duties and militia training and by recommending the master's benign treatment of slaves. South Carolina's 1740 Negro Code, along with Virginia and Maryland laws, provided models for the laws governing slaves in the expanding slave territory to the west.

—*Hyong-In Kim*

For Further Reading
Huggins, Nathan Irvin. 1977. *Black Odyssey: The Afro-American Ordeal in Slavery*. New York: Pantheon

Books; Thornton, John K. 1991. "African Dimensions of the Stono Rebellion." *American Historical Review* 96 (October): 1101–1113; Wood, Peter. 1974. *Black Majority: Negroes in Colonial South Carolina from 1670 through the Stono Rebellion*. New York: Norton.

STOWE, HARRIET BEECHER (1811–1896)

Harriet Beecher Stowe, the author of *Uncle Tom's Cabin*, was born in Litchfield, Connecticut. She was the seventh of nine children born to Lyman Beecher, a leading clergyman, and his first wife, Roxana Foote. In 1816, Roxana died, but other than this early encounter with grief, Stowe's childhood seems to have been a happy one.

She first attended Dame School and was later sent to the Litchfield Academy. In 1824, she moved to Hartford where she studied and assisted her sister Catherine, who was a student teacher at Hartford Female Seminary. In 1832, the family moved to Cincinnati, Ohio, as her father had been appointed president of Lane Theological Seminary. Harriet started to teach shortly thereafter, but in Cincinnati she gained firsthand experience of the great moral and religious disturbances surrounding slavery. Her father, finding himself unable to take the radical stand demanded by some of the seminary students, saw many of them withdrawing 1833, under Theodore Weld's leadership, and become the nucleus of Oberlin College in Ohio. Harriet later made use of the incident in her writing.

While in Cincinnati she began writing and published her first fiction work, *The Mayflower: Sketches and Scenes and Characters among the Descendants of the Puritans* (1843). Her life was difficult, and she worked hard, and her situation did not become any easier when she became the second wife of Calvin E. Stowe in 1836, a distinguished biblical scholar who was hopelessly ill-equipped for married life. The family was poor, and while still in Cincinnati, Stowe lived through the births of six of her seven children, the death of one, race riots, and a cholera epidemic before finally leaving in 1850 to move to Brunswick, Maine. Her husband had received a professorship at Bowdoin College there, and the family spent two years in Brunswick before Calvin Stowe joined the faculty of the theological seminary at Andover, Massachusetts, which remained their home until 1864 when they retired to Hartford, Connecticut. Calvin Stowe died in 1886.

For Stowe, there was no "room of one's own" in which to write, but while in Brunswick, the passage of the Fugitive Slave Act (1850) reinforced her abhor-rence of slavery and led to the writing of *Uncle Tom's Cabin* (1852). The work captured the emotions and imagination of the world as no other antislavery literature had managed to do. It brought her fame and, if not fortune, at least freedom from incessant money worries. The work may have sold 3 million copies in the United States alone, and in addition to being translated into many languages, it was the first American book to become a best-seller in Europe. It was admired by the Russian writers Tolstoy and Dostoyevsky, and both Charlotte Brontë and George Eliot wrote admiringly of Stowe's courageous entry into the "political sphere" with a subject deemed unsuitable for women at that time.

Inevitably, the book was challenged, particularly in the journals and papers of the U.S. South, so Stowe accumulated material from laws, court records, newspapers, and slave narratives and wrote *The Key to Uncle Tom's Cabin* (1853) and "Uncle Sam's Emancipation," which later appeared in a book with that title. Her only firsthand experience of slavery occurred while visiting relatives in Kentucky in 1836, and she was never an active member of any abolitionist organization, although her work brought her into contact with Frederick Douglass and others who were. She found the horrors of slavery more dreadful than she had imagined and continued her attack on "the peculiar institution" in *Dred: A Tale of the Great Dismal Swamp* (1856). That work developed a theme of *Uncle Tom's Cabin* to demonstrate that slaveholding demoralized the white population.

At the height of her fame, in 1853, Stowe traveled to Britain and was welcomed by liberals everywhere. On a second visit in 1856, she was honored by Queen Victoria, but on her third visit, in 1869, she was introduced to Lady Byron, and her subsequent book, *Lady Byron Vindicated* (1870), which accused the English poet George Gordon (Lord) Byron of an incestuous relationship with his stepsister, turned many people in Britain against her.

She suffered personal grief, including the loss of two sons, and her talented favorite brother, Henry Ward, accused of adultery, created a scandal involving ecclesiastical and civil trials, which caused incalculable grief to all concerned. Nevertheless, during the 1870s, Stowe embarked on a highly successful public-speaking career, reading from *Uncle Tom's Cabin* and other works. She continued writing, contributing throughout her life to numerous magazines and journals, but her fiction after *Dred: A Tale of the Great Dismal Swamp* consisted largely of New England novels, including *The Minister's Wooing* (1859), which James Russell Lowell saw as her masterpiece.

An inveterate public commentator on personal and public questions, she included in that work an attack on Calvinism, a religion she eventually deserted, and in 1871, she wrote a fictional essay, "My Wife and I," in which she defended a woman's right to a career. Her own career was both long and arduous, and during the 1880s, her critical reputation, together with her health, declined. The woman who, as Abraham Lincoln supposedly remarked, "started the Civil War," died on July 1, 1896, with only her nurse present.

—*Jan Pilditch*

For Further Reading
Adams, J. R. 1989. *Harriet Beecher Stowe.* Updated ed. Boston: Twayne; Crozier, A. 1969. *The Novels of Harriet Beecher Stowe.* New York: Oxford University Press; Moers, E. 1996. *Literary Women.* London: Women's Press; Wagenknecht, Edward. 1965. *Harriet Beecher Stowe: The Known and the Unknown.* New York: Oxford University Press.

STRINGFELLOW, THORNTON (1788–1869)

Thornton Stringfellow was perhaps the leading proslavery spokesman in the Old South to base his arguments on the Bible. He was born in Fauquier County in Virginia's northern piedmont and lived there or in neighboring Culpeper County most of his life. His part of Virginia was majority slave—Culpeper County's population in 1850 was 42 percent white, 54 percent slave, and 4 percent free black. Stringfellow himself, the son of a slaveowning family, owned about 60 slaves. He was also a Baptist minister. He resembled his Northern counterparts in many respects, but in the defense of slavery, he resembled George Fitzhugh, another eastern Virginian.

In essence a Southern model of a Jacksonian reformer, Stringfellow involved himself in temperance activities, domestic and foreign missions, and the proslavery crusade. In the 1840s, when Northern churches determined to exclude slaveowners from Baptist missionary activities, he convinced his fellow Baptists in the South to separate themselves and organize a Southern Baptist Convention.

As a proslavery spokesman, minister, and planter, Stringfellow contributed a scriptural variant to the proslavery writings of the South in the 1840s and 1850s. In Stringfellow's world, the Bible offered a sure guide to "the true principles of humanity," as he wrote in *A Brief Examination of Scripture Testimony on the Institution of Slavery* (1841). He demonstrated how God in the Old Testament ordained slavery and how Christ and the apostles in the New Testament, never challenging the institution, directed all Christians to accept their station in life, whether as servant or as master. How could it be, Stringfellow demanded of abolitionists, that "God has ordained slavery, and yet slavery is the greatest of sins?"

Jacksonian though he was, Stringfellow contested any belief or behavior that would, in general, "level all inequalities in human condition" or, in particular, hold that "the gain of freedom to the slave, is the only proof of godliness in the master." Neither corporal punishment nor the breakup of slave families gave him pause—these were supported in Scripture. It mattered not that some translations of the Bible used the word "servants" instead of "slaves," he said, for we are talking of "not a name, but a thing." Nor did it trouble him that Abraham relied on an army of 300 of his own slaves—that so many "servants" might "bear arms"—though the antebellum variant of slavery displayed no such possible reliance.

The "essential particulars" of slavery in the Old Testament and in the Old South, that it was "involuntary" and "hereditary," were what mattered—but then there was race. "The guardianship and control of the black race, by the white," he argued in *Scriptural and Statistical Views in Favor of Slavery* (1841), "is an indispensable Christian duty, to which we must yet look if we would secure the well-being of both races." One of Stringfellow's works, "The Bible Argument: or, Slavery in the Light of Divine Revelation," was included in an anthology of proslavery writings: E. N. Elliott, ed., *Cotton Is King, and Pro-Slavery Arguments* (1860).

—*Peter Wallenstein*

See also
The Bible; Fitzhugh, George
For Further Reading
Faust, Drew Gilpin. 1977. "Evangelicalism and the Meaning of the Proslavery Argument: The Reverend Thornton Stringfellow of Virginia." *Virginia Magazine of History and Biography* 85 (January): 3–17; Maddex, Jack P., Jr. 1979. "'The Southern Apostasy' Revisited: The Significance of Proslavery Christianity." *Marxist Perspectives* 2 (Fall): 132–141; Snay, Mitchell. 1993. *Gospel of Disunion: Religion and Separatism in the Antebellum South.* Cambridge: Cambridge University Press.

STRONG, JONATHAN (c. 1748–1773)

Little is known of Jonathan Strong's early life. He may have been born in either the West Indies or Africa, and he emerged from obscurity in 1765 when his life intersected that of Granville Sharp. The concerted efforts of the slave

Strong and the abolitionist Sharp would challenge the legitimacy of slavery in England.

Strong was about 16 or 17 when he was taken to England from Barbados by his master, David Lisle, a lawyer. While in England, Strong was severely beaten by Lisle on several occasions, the last one culminating in a pistol-whipping. Severely injuring Strong by his brutal treatment, Lisle believed Strong to be useless and on the verge of death, and he turned the slave out into the street in an unfamiliar country.

When Sharp first saw Strong, he was half-blind and barely conscious. Sharp was struck by Strong's debilitated state and insisted that the young man receive immediate medical care. With the aid of Dr. William Sharp, Granville's brother and a physician who frequently cared for the poor, Strong was admitted to St. Bartholomew's Hospital where it took him three or four months to convalesce.

Once Strong had recovered, the Sharp brothers secured a job for him as an apothecary's messenger in a shop near William's surgery. Strong worked for two years without incident until Lisle saw him by chance and noted that he was alive and reasonably well. With Strong's usefulness no longer in dispute, Lisle made arrangements to sell him to a Jamaican planter, James Kerr, who was preparing to return to the Caribbean. Although the transaction was complete, Kerr refused payment until Strong was safely on board ship, so Lisle had Strong kidnapped and placed in prison while the final preparations were being made.

From prison, Strong was able to send a message to Granville Sharp apprising him of the situation. Once again, Sharp offered his assistance. By appealing to the lord mayor that Strong was being held without an offense having been alleged against him, Sharp managed to secure his release. Although the captain of the Jamaican vessel, David Laird—who was present when the lord mayor's determination was made—attempted to prevent Strong's departure on behalf of Kerr, Jonathan Strong left prison a freeman on September 18, 1767.

The lord mayor's declaration had delivered Strong from imprisonment, but no court case ensued and, hence, no court decision on the larger issue of Strong's freedom. That freedom was short-lived; Jonathan Strong died, still a young man, in 1773.

Although an assertion by Chief Justice Sir John Holt that slaves became free once in England was well known, and Sir William Blackstone, in his *Commentaries,* referred to Holt's reasoning of the law, the status of slaves brought to England remained uncertain until the abolition of British slavery in the early-nineteenth century. Strong is important in the history of slavery and abolition as he represents a principal moment in the articulation of British rights and freedoms and the nascent abolitionist impulse. In Jonathan Strong's case, Granville Sharp asserted the unconditional humanity of blacks and claimed the protection of British laws for Strong. The continued revisiting of the central themes of the dispute helped establish a precedent that led to a reexamination of both the letter and the spirit of British laws regarding human property and freedom.

—*T. K. Hunter*

See also
Sharp, Granville
For Further Reading
Gerzina, Gretchen. 1995. *Black London: Life before Emancipation.* New Brunswick, NJ: Rutgers University Press; Hoare, Prince. 1820. *Memoirs of Granville Sharp, Esq.* London: Henry Colburn; Scobie, Edward. 1972. *Black Britannia: A History of Blacks in Britain.* Chicago: Johnson Publishing; Shyllon, F. O. 1977. *Black People in Britain: 1555–1833.* London: Oxford University Press.

SUDAN

Slavery, in one form or another, has been a feature of society in the Nile region of the Sudan from earliest recorded times, and the region was a source of slaves for successive civilizations from the ancient Egyptians to the Ottoman Turks. Slavery as an aspect of statecraft began with the rise of the sultanates of Sinnar and Darfur in the sixteenth and seventeenth centuries. Profiting from the development of long-distance trade with Egypt and other territories, these states came to rely heavily on the services of professional slave soldiers, who often served in various capacities.

The most common source of slaves for Sinnar and Darfur were the non-Muslim stateless peoples who had settled on the states' peripheries, particularly in the upper Blue Nile, Nuba Mountains, and Bahr el Ghazal regions. Some slave raids were large, well-organized affairs, such as when Darfur exported slaves over the Forty Days Road *(darb al-arba'in)* to Egypt, and as the status of Muslim merchants rose, the trade of Sinnar formed part of a larger East African and Indian Ocean trade. On the whole, however, slave trading remained inefficient and small-scale until the Turco-Egyptian conquest of Sudan (1820–1822).

The Egyptians had as their primary goal the acquisition of slaves to serve as soldiers *(jihadiyya)*, and in methodically organized raids, they captured large numbers of men, who were impressed into the army, and women and children, who were sold—on both domestic and foreign markets—as servants and concubines. The expansion of Egyptian control, in addition to an ongoing exploration of the White Nile, opened up a valuable trade in ivory. This trade, in turn, prompted slave raiding in the southern Sudan among the people of the Nile and the equator, and these raids, combining as they did the interests of government officials, private merchants, and Christian missionaries, became a huge enterprise. Meanwhile, Egyptian tax policies and changes in land tenure in northern Sudan encouraged an increase in domestic slavery, which expanded slaveowning beyond the economic elite.

Procuring slaves for both the government and the marketplace soon became the monopoly of large trading companies, which provided lucrative opportunities to the displaced Nubian population from the north. Large slaving stations (*zara'ib*) were established in the south and southwest of the Sudan, and these contained settled and itinerant Nubian merchants, huge private slave armies, and even-larger dependent populations of free and unfree workers.

The stations often were named for their leaders; for instance, Daym Zubayr was founded by the freebooter Zubayr Rahma Mansur, who settled in Bahr el Ghazal in 1856 and became a virtually independent ruler. In 1873, the Turco-Egyptian government was forced to recognize him as governor of Bahr el Ghazal; one year later, he conquered what remained of the state of Darfur. Given the firepower these stations could muster, resistance by the victimized populations was exceedingly difficult. So, too, was resistance to the slave trade by later Egyptian regimes in Khartoum who, under pressure from abroad, employed several European administrators in the 1870s to suppress it. These men, including Samuel Baker and Charles Gordon, enjoyed only moderate and temporary success.

The Mahdist period in Sudan (1881–1898) had the effect of diminishing the slave trade, since the fate of the slave companies was tied to that of the Egyptian regime. *Jihadiyya* of the Turco-Egyptians were eagerly sought and highly valued, but the Mahdist state had difficulty replenishing their ranks as it was preoccupied with threats to its authority and was largely ineffective in the south.

The Anglo-Egyptian conquest of Sudan (1896–1898) was launched on behalf of eradicating slavery, and the Condominium Agreement (1899), a system of joint rule developed by the British and the Egyptians, officially abolished the slave trade. Nonetheless, the Anglo-Egyptian rulers were loathe to disrupt the Sudanese economy and mindful of their fragile hold on power. Worried by the social and political implications of emancipation, they tended to ignore the continuation of slave practices—and even employed government personnel to recover "runaway servants." The occasional exposure of slavery's continuation in the Sudan caused the Anglo-Egyptians considerable embarrassment.

Independence for Sudan, achieved in 1956, carried with it the promise of social and economic progress. However, the resurgence of civil war in 1983 led to a revival of acts of enslavement, largely by western Arab pastoralists against their non-Muslim neighbors to the south. Underlying the economic and political competition between the groups is a deep-seated antipathy by many northern Sudanese toward southerners, whom they regard as racially inferior.

—Robert S. Kramer

See also
Darfur-Egypt Slave Trade; *Jihadiyya*
For Further Reading
Collins, Robert. 1992. "The Nilotic Slave Trade: Past and Present." In *The Human Commodity: Perspectives on the Trans-Saharan Slave Trade*. Ed. Elizabeth Savage. London: Frank Cass; Holt, P. M., and M. W. Daly. 1988. *A History of the Sudan*. London: Longman; Johnson, Douglas. 1992. "Recruitment and Entrapment in Private Slave Armies." In *The Human Commodity: Perspectives on the Trans-Saharan Slave Trade*. Ed. Elizabeth Savage. London: Frank Cass; Spaulding, Jay. 1982. "Slavery, Land Tenure, and Social Class in the Northern Turkish Sudan." *International Journal of African Historical Studies* 15 (1): 1–20.

SUDRAS

Sudras (or shudras) are one of the four major *varnas* described in the Indian literary classic *Rig Veda*. Scholars debate the meaning of *varna* itself, and it translates variously as caste, division, and class. Generally, Sudras were regarded as the laboring population. Although some scholars argue that the words "slave" and "Sudra" were interchangeable, most agree that not all Sudra were slaves but that the Sudra *varna* provided most of the slave labor. The conditions of Sudras varied by region.

Commonly, Sudras had no right to possess property; all property belonged to the master. Early Brahmanic law attached very little importance to a Sudra's life. Penalties for killing a Sudra, a flamingo, a dog, or any other animal were identical. Unlike untouchables, pure Sudras, which constituted about one-third of India's population, could participate in religious activities to some degree and had more rights than either untouchables or slaves. Like all castes, Sudras were encouraged to marry within their *varna,* and this preference was practiced almost without exception among men. Sudra women who married higher-caste Hindus were frequently concubines.

According to the *Rig Veda,* Sudras were created from the feet of the cosmic being Purusha while the other three *varnas* were created from the mouth, arms, and thighs. Ancient Hindu lawgivers, like Manu, interpreted this distinction to mean that the Sudras' occupation in life was to be servants to members of the other three *varnas*. Sudras were considered too unclean to be twice-born, like people of the other three *varnas*, and therefore Sudras were meant to be walked upon by the rest of society. Yet, another part of the same text offers alternative possibilities concerning the Sudras' emergence. If *varna* is translated as complexion, as some scholars insist, then Sudras were perceived as the people with the darkest-colored skin. Many scholars, however, reject this interpretation of *varna*.

Scriptural evidence recognizes a tribe of people known as Sudras as early as the tenth century B.C. They were probably conquered by Aryans, who eventually referred to all abjected elements of the population as *sudras*. Although the *Law Book of Manu* provides evidence of Sudra rulers, the description probably referred to rulers who did not consult the Brahmans, not to rulers who came from the Sudra *varna*. During the Mogul rule (1526–1858), many lower-caste Hindus converted to Islam to escape the caste system's discrimination.

Although the Indian government no longer sanctions the caste system, like color-based discrimination in the United States, caste-based discrimination is still a problem. Brahmans still dominate India socially and economically. Education has replaced lineage as the means to acquire power, but a higher-birth status usually makes higher education more possible.

—*Eric Martin*

See also
Asian/Buddhist Monastic Slavery; Caste
For Further Reading
Dumont, Louis. 1980. *Homo Hierarchicus: The Caste System and Its Implications*. Chicago: University of Chicago Press; Klass, Morton. 1988. *Caste: The Emergence of the South Asian Social System*. Philadelphia: Institute for the Study of Human Issues; Patnaik, Utsa, and Manjari Dingwaney. 1985. *Chains of Servitude: Bondage and Slavery in India*. Madras, India: Sangam Books; Sharma, Ram Sharan. 1980. *Sudras in Ancient India: A Social History of the Lower Order down to circa A.D. 600*. Delhi, India: Montilal Banarsidass.

SUGAR CULTIVATION AND TRADE

Sugar was first cultivated in Asia about two centuries before the Christian era. Sugarcane from China, Java, India, and Persia began to be cultivated in Egypt after the seventh century A.D., was taken by Arabs to northern Africa, and from there eventually arrived in Spain, France, and Italy. Sugar was also introduced into Syria and the Byzantine Empire. Sugar was first produced in small quantities and was considered a luxury item, but during the fourteenth and fifteenth centuries, the appreciation of its food value emerged, and sugar became a substitute for honey—the principal sweetener in the Western world at that time.

In the newly discovered Atlantic islands and Americas, the introduction of sugar cultivation transformed this expensive luxury item into a principal food product with larger consumption in every location. In 1500, the Portuguese islands of Madeira produced about 2,000 tons of sugar each year, and at that time, sugar was the only western product that competed profitably with eastern spices in European markets.

Colonists in the province of Pernambuco, Brazil, experimented with sugarcane cultivation as early as 1516. In 1532, Martim Afonso de Sousa established the first sugar mill there, and in 1549, under Tomé de Sousa, the first royal governor and captain-general, sugar growers received a 10-year tax exemption. The climate and the white, chalky, claylike soil along the Brazilian coast provided excellent conditions for growing cane. Sugar quickly became the basis of Brazilian prosperity, and the colony was the world's first large-scale sugar producer.

The king presented the first governor with a difficult order: he was both to extend Portuguese authority and to make Brazil a profitable commercial venture. By 1573, Brazil was shipping over 2,500 tons of sugar to Europe each year, and according to conservative estimates, Brazilian production reached 30,000 tons in 1600. The labor requirements for the increasing sugar production promoted the development of a slave system.

Brazil's colonization really began with sugar production—when the conqueror gradually abandoned trading to administer a plantation and sugar mill. Cane planting required large land tracts and an increasing supply of cheap labor. Landowners looked to Native Americans as a natural labor force, but when voluntary labor was no longer adequate, colonists began acquiring slaves. The plantations prospered, but increases in enslavement led to hostilities from Native Americans. Because the Jesuits protected the Indians, they incurred the wrath of both the slave raiders and the *fazendeiros* (those who owned/operated the large- and medium-sized estates in Brazil that produced food for consumption).

After 1550, there was a rapid expansion of sugar plantations while, simultaneously, drought, famine, and smallpox decimated the Indian population. From that time on, black Africans increasingly replaced Indian slaves. The former proved a more economical labor force because of their greater physical strength and their ability to survive hard work under tropical conditions. Also, their fear of the nearby Indian population helped deter runaways. After 1580, the number of African slaves increased rapidly, with the sugar industry providing the wealth needed for their importation.

The religious orders in colonial Latin America began cultivating cane and producing sugar for profit because they did not receive the funds they had been promised to finance their missionary efforts. In 1594, the head of the Jesuit order, Claudio Aquaviva, ruled that Jesuit colleges could produce their own sugar without violating the order's governing rules or invalidating individual poverty vows taken by its members. Religious orders from then on struggled to maintain an adequate workforce to produce the sugar.

Until Brazil abolished the slave trade in 1850, Africans were the most numerous immigrants, and many of them possessed greater skills and energies than their masters. In Brazil, manumission was common, and slaves were usually allowed certain days to work for their own interests. They had legal rights—to own property, to marry without fear of being separated from their families, and to defend themselves—but actual practice at times belied the generous nature of the law.

Sugar plantations were almost self-sufficient socioeconomic units; consequently, no strong cities were established in colonial Brazil. Even after the British and French developed sugar plantations in the Caribbean, Brazil continued to lead the American importation of African slaves. Since the working life of a sugar plantation slave was calculated at seven years, the growth and continuance of the slave trade was assured. Sugar planters made a maximum profit by working the slaves hard, feeding them meager rations, and then replacing those who died or were disabled each year. Some masters even freed nonproductive slaves so that they themselves would no longer have to provide for them.

When the Dutch, who had captured the whole northeastern region in 1633, were expelled from Brazil in 1656, they took with them Africans who were familiar with all phases of sugar production and introduced the sugar culture on French and English islands in the Caribbean. Overproduction caused Brazil to lose its former commercial advantage, and the discovery of great quantities of gold in Minas Gerais changed the economic situation and began an exodus of *fazendeiros* and slaves from the sugar-producing northeastern region. The English reform movement that sought the end of slave trading provoked strong opposition in areas that depended upon slave labor for sugar production. A March 1827 treaty between England and Brazil contained a clause promising the end of the slave trade by 1830, but it, too, met with strong opposition among Brazilians.

During the eighteenth century, slave labor developed an intensive sugar economy that was unique in history. The plantation system became all-important in the British colony of Jamaica and in the French colony of Saint Domingue (present-day Haiti). Sugar became the dominant crop in Cuba, but coffee and tobacco were also important there—as they were also on Puerto Rico. Saint Domingue became the most productive of all the Caribbean sugar colonies and a model for the colonial slaveholding society. By 1785, there were over 500,000 slaves in the French colony, and a large portion of them had been born in Africa. The mortality rate of the imported slaves was high because of the hard labor in a tropical climate, poor sanitation, and inadequate housing, but mainly it was high because of inhumane treatment. The supply of slaves had to be replenished continuously.

—*Sharon Landers*

See also
Bandeiras; *Capitães do mato*; Latin America; Portuguese Slave Trade; Vieira, António; West Indies

For Further Reading
Azevedo, Fernando de. 1950. *Brazilian Culture: An Introduction to the Study of Culture in Brazil*. New York: Macmillan; Poppino, Rollie E. 1968. *Brazil: The Land and the People*. New York: Oxford University Press; Rawley, James A. 1981. *The Transatlantic Slave Trade: A History*. New York: Norton; Schwartz, Stuart. 1985. *Sugar Plantations in the Formation of Brazilian Society: Bahia, 1550–1835*. Cambridge: Cambridge University Press.

SUMER

Sumer is the most ancient of the world's civilizations and represents the first society in which some form of slavery appeared. Sumer refers to the region in southern Mesopotamia where the first urban civilization appeared and flourished from 3500 to 2000 B.C. All available information about this culture derives from archaeology, especially the thousands of cuneiform clay tablets found at the various archaeological sites. The language spoken by these people, Sumerian, is unrelated to any other known language, and scholars are still not certain as to the original homeland of the Sumerian people or when they migrated into southern Mesopotamia. The cuneiform tablets encompass a wide range of documents and different genres of literature, and these reveal many details about Sumerian civilization.

Politically, Sumer was divided up into separate city-states. By 2500 B.C., there were 18 major cities, each one controlling a large area of the surrounding countryside, which provided the city with the economic support necessary for its survival. Each of these cities was under the protection of its own deity, who was also believed to own the city-state. Every member of the community was considered the servant of the city's god and responsible for the god's maintenance. To ensure economic support of its protecting deity and temple, each city assigned a certain portion of its territory to the control of the temple, usually about a third.

Sumerian society consisted of four basic classes. The first was a nobility consisting of members of the city administration, priests, and the royal household. These people owned their own private estates and controlled the land owned by the temples, and the nobility used the labor of both clients and slaves to work these lands. The second class, which made up at least half the total population, was made up of free peasants who worked community land held in the possession of their families.

The third class consisted of clients of both the temple and the nobility. These individuals received land or rations in return for services, and this category included administrators and artisans of the temple as well as a larger group of farmers who received a plot of land in return for some of their produce. In later times, many of these farmers received only food and wool rations for their labor, which practically reduced them to the status of slaves. The fourth class consisted of chattel slaves, owned both by the temple and by private individuals. Records from Lagash suggest that slaves made up as much as 40 percent of the total temple workforce.

During the early dynastic period (2900–2600 B.C.), all agricultural work (including the digging of irrigation canals) was done by freemen while slaves, despite their large numbers, were used in craft industries like weaving. Most slaves came to their status as a result of being captured in war. Warfare was frequent in Mesopotamia, which meant that the number of slaves gradually increased over time. Since slaves came from the same ethnic background as their captors, slavery was not considered a disgrace but merely the result of bad fortune in war; no particular stigma was attached to it. At times, slavery was a temporary status, since freemen could be condemned to slavery for certain offenses and slaves were able to purchase their freedom. Another form of slavery was debt-slavery. Sometimes a father would simply hand over to his creditor one or more of his children (or even his wife) in order to settle a debt. Such servitude could last only three years.

Laws surviving from Sumer give us some information as to the conditions of slavery during the period when that civilization flourished. Since a slave was regarded as his master's possession, like any other piece of property, an unruly slave was liable to branding or flogging and was severely punished if he tried to escape. Anyone who maimed or killed a slave had to pay a fine to the owner, not to the slave. The penalty for helping a slave run away was either restitution in kind or a 25-shekel fine. A slave who disputed his master's control over him could be sold.

However, a master's ownership of his slave was not absolute, as Sumerian law recognized certain rights for slaves. A master was not allowed to kill his slave. A slave could go to court to contest his own sale and was also allowed to give evidence in court. Slaves were permitted to marry free persons, and the children of such a union were considered free. Slaves could borrow money, engage in business, and own their own slaves. Many of the Sumerian laws regarding slavery reappear in the Hammurabi Code (1792–1750 B.C.), but in that code, there is a notable increase in the level of judicial savagery as the penalties for many offenses became much more severe.

—*John F. Shean*

See also
Babylonian *Mushkēnum*; Hammurabi, Code of; Mesopotamia
For Further Reading
Diakonov, Igor M. 1974. "Structure of Society and State in Early Dynastic Sumer." In *Sources and Monographs: Monographs of the Ancient Near East. Vol. 1.* Los Angeles: Undena Publications; Mendelsohn, Isaac. 1949. *Slavery in the Ancient Near East.* New York: Oxford University Press; Woolley, C. Leonard. 1965. *The Sumerians.* New York: Norton.

SURINAME

Prior to European settlement, Suriname (formerly Surinam) was occupied by Arawak and Carib Indians. In 1651, Francis Willoughby, governor of Barbados, sent 300 men to found an English colony on the mainland. The group's leader, Anthony Rowse, made a treaty with the Indians, which provided for settlement. The English settlers brought slaves with them and began plantation agriculture in Suriname. By 1667, the colony included 23 plantations and 560 slaves.

In that year, the Second Anglo-Dutch war ended with the Treaty of Breda, and in that treaty, the English ceded the Suriname colony to the Dutch. With the advent of Dutch rule, the Dutch West India Company began importing slaves in large numbers. Plantation agriculture and slavery grew rapidly. In 1684, the colony had 4,200 slaves, and by the middle of the

A group of slaves just imported into Suriname, an illustration in J. S. Stadman, Narrative of a Five Years Expedition against the Revolted Negroes of Surinam *(London, 1976).*

eighteenth century, the number of plantations had grown to 430 and there were more than 50,000 slaves.

A unique feature of plantation slavery in Suriname was the presence of a large minority of Jews as plantation owners. Although Jews were involved in slavery in places like Brazil and Curaçao, only in Suriname did many become planters. English Jews were among the first settlers, having come to the colony with Lord Willoughby. In 1658, a Jewish colony had settled in Cayenne to the east. In 1664, however, the French drove the Jews from Cayenne, and many of them fled to Suriname. By 1700, the Jews in Suriname owned 40 sugar estates and a total of 9,000 slaves. Jewish colonists established their own village, Joden Savanne, in the area near most of the Jewish sugar estates, three hours rowing from the capital, Paramaribo.

Another notable feature of slavery in Suriname was the success of the Maroons (communities of runaway slaves). Slaves have run away from captivity wherever slavery has existed, but in Suriname, the geographical circumstances helped the runaways remain free. The plantations were all located on rivers and were bordered by swamps and forests that were difficult to penetrate, so slaves who escaped could flee into the forested, swampy area with little fear of being chased and taken back to the plantation. In the early years, many Maroons even felt safe enough to return to the plantations at night to get food. The actual number of runaways was not high, amounting to about 250 per year. Furthermore, the rigors of living in the swamp and the ties to friends and relatives who remained on the plantation led many to eventually return voluntarily. Yet, those who remained in the forest had a great impact on the colony.

Beginning around 1730, the Maroons formed tribes and raided plantations—seeking weapons, ammunition, provisions, and women—and sometimes they destroyed plantations. The Maroon raids led to planter expeditions against the Maroons. The so-called Maroon wars continued until the government signed a treaty with some of the major Maroon tribes in 1760. Among other provisions, the Dutch government recognized the Maroons as free people and agreed to send the tribes tribute in compensation for the goods they usually took from the plantations. Other indigenous tribes, however, continued to raid plantations.

Despite the Maroon wars, the eighteenth century was a period of prosperity for Suriname. Sugar exports varied between 4,000 and 12,000 metric tons per year throughout the century; coffee exports exceeded a million pounds per year and reached more than 10 million pounds per year during the last quarter of the century. Other major exports included cotton and cacao. Most of this trade was produced by slave labor, and the mortality rate among the slaves was very high. From 1668 to 1823, therefore, between 300,000 and 325,000 slaves were imported into the colony while the slave population remained at a level of about 50,000.

During the years 1796–1802 and 1804–1816, the English occupied Suriname, and in 1806, the British Parliament abolished the slave trade in its newly acquired Dutch West Indies possessions. In a treaty with the English in 1814, the Dutch made the slave trade illegal, and Paramaribo was made the seat of a mixed Anglo-Dutch court for the suppression of the illegal slave trade. The Dutch trade had dwindled in the late-eighteenth century, and after 1814, it stopped completely. Still, ships with neither Dutch nor English registry continued to supply slaves illegally. But even the illegal trade ended in 1826 after the introduction of slave registry laws in the colony. Furthermore, by that time, the economy of the Suriname planters had been so weakened by competition from Brazil and Cuba that planters could ill afford to purchase new slaves.

Slavery was abolished in British Guiana (Guyana) in 1834, and in 1848 the French abolished slavery in Cayenne. Both events produced slave unrest in Suriname. In 1853, a state commission was established to study abolition in Suriname, and a plan was finally adopted in 1862 that provided for the abolition of slavery on July 1, 1863. The freed slaves were required to remain on the plantations, however, and work for wages for another 10 years. In 1873, the former slaves were finally free to leave the plantations to seek their own fortunes, and the first of a long series of immigrations began with the arrival of Hindustani as cheap labor to work the fields.

—David M. Cobin

For Further Reading
Goslinga, Cornelis. 1979. *A Short History of the Netherlands Antilles and Surinam*. The Hague: Martinus Nijhoff; Hoogbergen, Wim. 1990. "The History of the Suriname Maroons." In *Resistance and Rebellion in Suriname: Old and New*. Ed. Gary Brana-Shute. Williamsburg, VA: Department of Anthropology, College of William and Mary; Van Lier, Rudolf A. J. 1971. *Frontier Society*. The Hague: Martinus Nijhoff.

SWAHILI

Swahili means "people of the coast" or "coast dwellers," and they are a Muslim ethnic group occupying the East African coast from the Lamu Archipelago in northern Kenya down to northern Mozambique and the offshore Indian Ocean islands of Zanzibar, Pemba, and Mafia. Origins of the Swahili are still much debated, but it is now certain that they are not people of foreign inception, as was once thought, but indigenous in origin, resulting from the fusion of Indian Ocean and African elements. Their cosmopolitan nature is reflected in the Swahili language, which belongs to the Bantu family but contains many words of Arabic derivation.

Foreign Muslim merchants began visiting the East African or Swahili coast regularly for trading purposes in the mid-eighth century. Slaves were among the commodities sought; as the Zanj slave revolts in southern Iraq from about A.D. 689 to 883 attest, the slave trade was then of some importance. Following the suppression of those revolts, the slave trade declined, but the Swahili prospered, especially in the fourteenth and fifteenth centuries.

They traded in other commodities such as gold taken from southern Africa, ivory, and various other commodities, including mangrove poles used for building in the wood-starved areas of the Gulf and Arabia. In return, they imported manufactured goods, often of the luxury category: glazed Chinese, Persian, and Arab pottery, glass vessels and beads, cloth, and metalwork. The Swahili built stone towns along the coast, many of which have been investigated archaeologically, and there were houses and mosques built of coral surrounded by extensive areas of less permanent structures inhabited by slaves and other miscellaneous peoples attracted by trade.

The Portuguese disrupted the Swahili and Indian Ocean commerce when they entered the region at the end of the fifteenth century. The Portuguese established fortified posts—Fort Jesus on Mombasa, for example—and their own trade routes—like the one from Mozambique to Goa—for channeling slaves to India from the Zambezi area. Portuguese dominance of the coast north of Mozambique ended in 1698, 200 years after they entered the Indian Ocean, and the coasts of Kenya and Tanzania and the islands of Zanzibar and Pemba fell under the control of the rulers of Oman. The change would give a new boost to the Swahili coast and to Indian Ocean commerce, slavery included.

The height of the Swahili slave trade occurred in the nineteenth century when both local demand for plantation slaves and international demand in general grew. Figures record the exporting of 718,000 slaves from the Swahili coast during the nineteenth century, and the retention of 769,000 on the coast. These slaves were obtained from East Africa's interior by Swahili and Arab traders and sold in the great coastal markets, as at Zanzibar, so vividly described by early European explorers like Richard Burton.

Notions of class and ancestry were, and to a certain extent still are, greatly important in Swahili society. Society was rigidly demarcated into five categories: the *Wa-ungwana* (freeborn men and women), a term the Swahili use to refer to themselves; *Madada* (female domestic slaves); *Wa-zalia* (locally born slaves); *Wa-tumwa* (plantation slaves); and *Wa-shenzi* (all other Africans, who were regarded as barbarous). Slaves served a variety of functions and were differentiated according to gender. Non-*Wa-ungwana* men were excluded from the process of upward mobility, but it was possible for daughters of a slave girl taken as a concubine to be accepted within the upper echelons of Swahili society after a couple of generations. This process of replication has further added to the diversity that makes up Swahili society.

The Swahili are still the dominant coastal people, though slavery was abolished at the beginning of the twentieth century. Indeed, the slave trade's legacy was felt in the early 1960s during the Zanzibar insurrection or revolution. Many descendants of former slaves rose with much bloodshed against the island's Arab and Arabized rulers, as represented by the Zanzibar Nationalist Party, to create the union with Tanganyika and thus form Tanzania.

—*Timothy Insoll*

See also
East Africa
For Further Reading
Burton, Sir Richard. 1872. *Zanzibar: City, Island, and Coast.* London: Tinsley Brothers; Donley-Reid, L. 1990. "A Structuring Structure: The Swahili House." In *Domestic Architecture and the Use of Space.* Ed. S. Kent. Cambridge: Cambridge University Press; Iliffe, J. 1995. *Africans: The History of a Continent.* Cambridge: Cambridge University Press; Sutton, J. E. G. 1990. *A Thousand Years of East Africa.* Nairobi: British Institute in Eastern Africa.

SWEDISH AFRICA COMPANY

Chartered in 1649, the Swedish Africa Company (*Svenska Afrikakompaniet*) was almost totally controlled until 1654 by the great Swedish industrialist and trader Louis de Geer, of Flemish origin. A small group of Swedish investors were allowed to participate in the company to assure the Swedish crown's support. These businessmen were responsible for Swedish involvement, albeit on a limited scale, in the African slave trade.

The German city of Stade on the Elbe River was chosen as the company's staple city. It was then under Swedish control (in the territory of Bremen-Verden) and had easy access to Dutch and German markets. Stade's city council was also ordered by Queen Christina to grant freedom to all company officers. During the company's initial years, Fort Carolusburg was established at Cape Coast (Cabo Corso) on the

Guinea coast, and operations were extended to other locations along the coast.

The company was small and could not use ordinary strategies, like violence or threats, to improve its terms of trade, so it was highly dependent on local political and military support when threatened, for instance, by the Dutch. It also recruited former Dutch and German employees. Thus, the first representative of the company was Henrich Carlof, the former financial officer of the Dutch West India Company.

Trade was in gold, ivory, and sugar from the island of São Tomé, and the goods were transported to Hamburg and Amsterdam. Slaves were traded only when in demand at São Tomé, and the company participated only marginally in the transatlantic slave trade. Of the 12 ships sent to Cape Coast during the first charter period, 10 reached Guinea. Approximately 650–700 marks of gold and 10,000–12,000 pounds of ivory and sugar worth around 77,000–90,000 Dutch guilders per year were exported from Guinea.

To better suit Swedish state interests and to guarantee the safety of the company's ships on the high seas, the state reorganized the company and gave it a new charter in 1655. Swedish shareholders were encouraged to invest, and de Geer's family was paid off. Four directors, led by a supreme director, took over. The Swedish Africa Company was transformed from a merchant's company to a crown company, but the charter expressed no colonial ambitions.

In 1654, Jost Craemer, who later took over the Danish Africa Company in Glückstadt on the Elbe River, succeeded Isaac Mivilla, who had succeeded Carlof in 1652, as head of the Swedish company. During this second period, Swedish personnel were recruited, and the nobleman Johan Philip von Kruusenstiern became commandant of Fort Carolusburg. He arrived at Cape Coast in 1656, strengthened company forts and trading stations, and extended the trade to the west side of the Ankobra River near Axim in present-day Ghana. During the second charter period, the company was somewhat smaller. A total of nine ships sailed from Stade to Guinea, but only seven arrived. Yet the volume of trade was equal to that during the first charter period.

In January 1658, Carlof arrived on a Danish ship at Cape Coast and attacked Swedish Africa Company forts and stations—Sweden and Denmark were fighting in Europe at the time. Two company ships attempted to retake Fort Carolusburg in 1659, but the captains were unsuccessful. In that same year, Carlof's representatives sold the fort to the Dutch West Indian Company.

Peace negotiations in 1658 and 1660 restored the company's assets to Sweden, but no compensation for losses was obtained. Subsequently, the Swedish state lost interest, and the company was transformed into a company of shareholders. Meanwhile, the Dutch were expelled from Carolusburg by local chiefs, and the fort was offered again to the Swedish Africa Company. Ships were prepared in Hamburg, and on the second ship a new commandant, Johan Neumann, and other employees were sent to Cape Coast. The second ship, *Christina,* was attacked by the Dutch, and Cape Coast was blockaded. No support came from the Swedish crown, and in 1663, local warriors removed Swedish personnel from the fort, which brought an end to Swedish trade in West Africa.

—*Bertil Haggman*

SWEDISH SLAVE TRADE

The history of the Swedish slave trade is somewhat elusive, and it is impossible at this time to estimate accurately the number of slaves exported on Swedish ships. Swedish ships on their homeward journey from West Africa transported slaves from there to the island of São Tomé, which had many sugarcane plantations, but this trade was conducted only when demand for slaves was great on the island. For example, recent sources indicate that in 1655, the ship *Stockholms Slott* carried 36 slaves to São Tomé.

In 1658, two ships, *Johannesburg* and *de Liefde,* were to take 500–600 West African slaves to Curaçao—the slaves had probably been purchased in Benin. There are no records of the voyages, but it is likely that the slave delivery contracts were fulfilled.

Sweden purchased the West Indian island of St. Barthélemy (St. Bart's, now part of Guadeloupe) in 1784, and since slavery was an institution on the island, there were plans for trading in slaves. An expedition was prepared but had to be interrupted because of a war between Sweden and Russia (1788–1790). Later, Sweden's 1844–1845 parliamentary session decreed that slaves in the colony were to be freed by purchase.

—*Bertil Haggman*

TACKY'S REBELLION (1760–1761)

One of the two largest slave rebellions in Jamaican history was a revolt led by the Coromantee (i.e., Akan, from West Africa's Gold Coast) slave known as Tacky that began in St. Mary's Parish in 1760 and eventually spread across the island. Tacky organized the rebellion along ethnic lines, reportedly involving almost every Akan slave in Jamaica but not mobilizing slaves from other African ethnic groups.

The revolt began on Easter Day, April 7, 1760, with an attack on the fort at Port Maria where 150 slaves seized gunpowder and muskets before marching south, gathering new recruits as they went. Although Tacky was captured and executed within days and the rebel band he led disintegrated shortly after, guerrilla war involving thousands of slaves continued for months afterward across Jamaica. The rebellion's total suppression was not announced until October 1761.

The rebellion occurred at a moment of massive expansion in the Jamaican sugar industry. At least 120,000 African slaves had been imported in the previous 20 years—compared to 90,000 in the years 1721–1740 and 53,500 in the 20 years prior to that (Curtin, 1969). In 1760, Britain was involved in the Seven Years War with France and Spain, which both distracted planters from maintaining plantation discipline and reduced the slaves' food supply.

St. Mary's Parish, where the rebellion began, had the highest concentration of Akan slaves and the lowest concentration of whites in Jamaica. The rebels wanted to expel all whites from Jamaica and establish a society that was independent of European powers. The rebels received spiritual guidance and courage from an obeahman, who was captured in the early stages of the rebellion. This African slave prepared the rebels by giving them protective amulets, and the belief that Tacky could not be killed by white bullets was also apparently very common among the rebels.

The rebellion spread beyond St. Mary's, with conspiracies and uprisings reported in Kingston, Spanish Town, Clarendon, St. Elizabeth, St. James, and Westmoreland. Although Tacky's band of rebels was dissipated relatively quickly, ongoing disturbances continued for months in the western part of the island. By the time the rebellion was completely suppressed, nearly 400 slave rebels had been killed in fighting, another 100 executed, and around 500 transported, mainly to British Honduras (now Belize). About 60 whites and another 60 free blacks and people of color had been killed by rebels.

The rebellion caused significant changes in the slave system on Jamaica. Authorities passed several new repressive laws in its wake, Obeah was suppressed more vigorously, greater controls were imposed on slave meetings and on slave access to weapons, and the island's military resources were increased, as was funding for fortifications. Tacky's rebellion was one of the last African-organized rebellions in the West Indies; future unrest there tended to be organized by Creole slaves.

—Diana Paton

See also
Obeah
For Further Reading
Craton, Michael. 1982. *Testing the Chains: Resistance to Slavery in the British West Indies*. Ithaca, NY: Cornell University Press; Curtin, Philip D. 1969. *The Atlantic Slave Trade: A Census*. Madison: University of Wisconsin Press; Schuler, Monica. 1970. "Ethnic Slave Rebellions in the Caribbean and the Guianas." *Journal of Social History* 3 (4): 374–385.

THE TAINO

The Taino were an Arawak-speaking people who settled the Caribbean's Greater Antilles islands of Jamaica, Puerto Rico, Hispaniola (Haiti and Dominican Republic), and Cuba as well as the Bahamas. They had formed a network of interrelated *cazicazgos* ("chiefdoms") centered on Hispaniola by the time the Spaniards arrived there in 1492. *Taino* is derived from *nitaíno*, an adjective meaning "good" or "noble" that the Taino used to distinguish themselves from their enemies, the *Caribes*.

Excellent navigators in dugout canoes, the Taino most likely arrived in several migratory waves over a 5,000-year period. They island-hopped their way from the coast of northeastern South America through the

Lesser Antilles to the Greater Antilles as population and resource pressures pushed them out of the Amazon and Orinoco River basins. There were several thousand to 8 million Taino by 1492; demographers have not established a definitive population estimate.

The Taino were an agricultural people whose primary crop was the tuber they called *yucubia* (yucca or manioc in English). They ate yucca boiled or roasted, or they grated the tubers and dried the flour to make cakes of bread called cassava, which they cooked on a *buren* (stone griddle). They also cultivated corn, beans, sweet potatoes, peanuts, squash, peppers, and pineapple. They developed sophisticated methods for procuring *hutías* (a rodentlike animal), snakes, iguanas, turtles, fish, and other aquatic protein. Scholars believe that the vast amounts of yucca grown by the Taino "liberated" them "from the sporadic foraging of hunters and gatherers, which permitted them to develop newly specialized forms of economic and social organization" (Stevens-Arroyo, 1988).

The class structure of the Taino consisted of nobles, headed by *caciques* ("chiefs"); *behiques* ("religious leaders/healers"); and *naborías* ("workers"). Taino society has been portrayed as less patriarchal than European society at the time because the women—apparently only those of the noble class—could and did inherit as much power as their male counterparts. The Taino had an elaborate ceramic tradition and were expert sculptors.

Histories of their gods and *caciques* were sung and danced at festive communal celebrations called *areitos,* and they had annual rituals connected to the planting/harvesting cycle and regional, interregional, and even inter-island ball games called *bateys*. The last were used to solidify socioeconomic relations and for divination purposes, and the importance of the *bateys* to Taino society is one proof of the active trading networks the Taino had with Mesoamerican peoples.

Left alone, the Taino might have developed an empire as "civilized" as the Maya, Aztec, and Inca did; but in 1492, the Taino were in what has been called a transitional stage, or middle stage, of societal and cultural development. Too settled to evade the Spaniards as nomadic tribes did, people at this stage of development fared the worst in the New World/Old World "encounter," and the Taino were especially hard hit because their tropical environment was such a breeding ground for European-introduced diseases.

Today, no full-blooded Taino remain, but their cultural legacy is strong, especially in linguistics. Many Taino words entered the Spanish language (and later, English) such as canoe, hurricane, tobacco, hammock, papaya, iguana, and manatee.

—*Lynne Guitar*

For Further Reading
Keegan, William F. 1992. *The People Who Discovered Columbus: The Prehistory of the Bahamas.* Gainesville: University of Florida Press; Rouse, Irving. 1992. *The Taínos: The People Who Discovered Columbus.* New Haven, CT: Yale University Press; Stevens-Arroyo, Antonio M. 1988. *Cave of the Jagua: The Mythological World of the Taínos.* Albuquerque: University of New Mexico Press; Wilson, Samuel M. 1990. *Hispaniola: Caribbean Chiefdoms in the Age of Columbus.* Tuscaloosa: University of Alabama Press.

TANEY, ROGER BROOKE (1777–1864)

Roger Brooke Taney, author of the U.S. Supreme Court's opinion in the case *Dred Scott v. Sandford,* was one of the foremost judicial advocates of slavery in the United States in the nineteenth century. Born on a southern Maryland tobacco plantation, Taney grew up in a wealthy planter family and never traveled far beyond Maryland's boundaries. A Jacksonian Democrat, he became the U.S. attorney general in 1831 and expressed early in his career the sentiments that marked his Supreme Court tenure.

In an unpublished opinion on the constitutionality of a North Carolina law regulating the immigration of free blacks, Taney foreshadowed his ruling in the Dred Scott case by referring to blacks as "a separate and degraded people" who "were not looked upon as citizens by the contracting parties who formed the Constitution" (Swisher, 1936). After President Andrew Jackson appointed Taney as chief justice in 1836, Taney began a 28-year judicial career during which he consistently defended slavery and Old South values.

During the 1840s, Taney began his judicial defense of slavery. In *Groves v. Slaughter* (1841), a case involving the sale of slaves in Mississippi, Taney wrote a separate, concurring opinion affirming his commitment to protecting the peculiar institution of slavery. Although the majority opinion addressed only the narrow issue of the validity of the commercial transaction in question, Taney went beyond the scope of the matter and argued that power to regulate interstate slave trading lay exclusively with the states. By doing so, Taney hoped to ensure that the national government would not interfere with slaveholders' rights.

In *Prigg v. Pennsylvania* (1842), he reiterated his position in another separate opinion. This case involved the constitutionality of Pennsylvania's personal liberty law of 1826, which required slave catchers to obtain a proper writ from a state judge before removing any

African Americans from the state. Writing for the majority, Justice Joseph Story invalidated this state restriction on the rendition of fugitives, holding that the power to enforce the slaveholder's right of recovery lay exclusively with the U.S. Congress. Taney, who concurred in overturning the Pennsylvania law, dissented on the issue of congressional control over slavery. The U.S. Constitution, he insisted, restrained states only from *interfering* with slaveholders' property rights; states, in his view, possessed the power—even the obligation—to assist in *protecting* those rights.

As the national debate over slavery and its extension erupted during the 1850s, so too did Taney's partisan commitment to the South. In *Strader v. Graham* (1850), he dismissed a suit for damages involving several slaves who were taken briefly into Ohio and later fled from Kentucky into Canada. When the slaveowner sued several men who allegedly aided their escape, defense counsel argued that the Northwest Ordinance of 1787, which banned slavery in the Old Northwest, freed the slaves as soon as they stepped on Ohio (free) soil. The Kentucky Court of Appeals rejected this argument, and the case went to the U.S. Supreme Court. Writing for a unanimous majority, Taney dismissed the case for lack of jurisdiction, claiming that Kentucky's laws superseded the Northwest Ordinance. Again, the chief justice hoped to preserve slaveholders' rights by upholding the states' power to protect slavery.

The pinnacle of Taney's proslavery constitutionalism came in *Dred Scott v. Sandford* (1857). Scott, a Missouri slave, accompanied his owner, an Army surgeon named John Emerson, to Illinois and later to Wisconsin Territory during the 1830s. Several years later, after Emerson's death, Scott initiated a suit against Emerson's wife claiming that by virtue of his residence in free territory, he had gained his freedom. The Missouri Supreme Court ruled against Scott, and even when he renewed his suit in federal court against his new owner, John F. A. Sanford (the name was misspelled in the official record), Scott was denied his liberty. Ultimately, he appealed to the U.S. Supreme Court.

Instead of confining himself to the specific question of Scott's status and standing to sue, Taney delivered a proslavery diatribe that revealed his deep devotion to slavery and Southern values. Taney held that the lower federal court should have dismissed the case for lack of jurisdiction. Because Scott was black, according to Taney, he was not a citizen and had no right to sue. Even if he were a free black man, he was not a citizen under the U.S. Constitution. Blacks had long been considered, according to Taney, "so far inferior that they had no rights which the white man was bound to respect" (*Scott v. Sandford*, 19 Howard 393 [1857]). Thus, Taney not only ruled that Scott lacked standing to sue but also held, based on his interpretation of the Founders' intentions, that no African American could claim citizenship privileges under the Constitution.

The second part of Taney's opinion attacked congressional authority over slavery. Although the Supreme Court had no grounds for deciding this issue, Taney attempted to steer the discussion of Scott's status to the larger question of slavery in the territories. According to Taney, Scott's sojourn in Wisconsin Territory did not make him a freeman because Congress lacked the power to exclude slavery from the territories. Taney suggested that the Fifth Amendment's due process clause prohibited Congress from interfering with slavery in these areas, because to do so would violate the property rights of slaveholders who settled there.

In arguing that the right to hold slave property was grounded in the Constitution, Taney proved his unflagging support for slaveholders' rights. Northerners feared that Taney's proslavery rhetoric portended the nationalization of slavery—the right to take slaves anywhere in the Union—and the opinion exacerbated the sectional conflict that culminated in the U.S. Civil War.

Taney remained committed to proslavery principles until his career ended. Having positioned the Supreme Court squarely on the side of slaveowners in the Dred Scott case, Taney asserted the unqualified power of the national government to protect slaveholders' rights in *Ableman v. Booth* (1859). This case involved a Wisconsin abolitionist who had helped a fugitive escape, in violation of the Fugitive Slave Law of 1850. Waging a battle with the U.S. Supreme Court over jurisdiction, Wisconsin judges challenged federal authority to prosecute the alleged criminal. In response, Taney issued a sweeping statement of judicial authority, upheld the controversial law, and fanned the growing fears of those who viewed the national government as the captive of slaveholding interests.

Throughout his career, Taney was a staunch judicial advocate of slaveowners. His opinions, though occasionally flawed in their reading of history and inconsistent in their understanding of the relationship between the national government and the states, proved a powerful weapon for Southern whites in their effort to perpetuate slavery. Only a bloody civil war and the subsequent reconstruction of constitutional order would reverse Taney's consistently proslavery interpretation of the U.S. Constitution.

—*Timothy S. Huebner*

See also
Ableman v. Booth; Dred Scott v. Sandford; Prigg v. Pennsylvania; U.S. Constitution
For Further Reading
Fehrenbacher, Don. 1978. *The Dred Scott Case: Its Significance in American Law and Politics.* New York: Ox-

ford University Press; Finkelman, Paul. 1994. "'Hooted Down the Page of History': Reconsidering the Greatness of Chief Justice Taney." *Journal of Supreme Court History* 1994: 83–102; Swisher, Carl. 1936. *Roger B. Taney*. New York: Macmillan.

TANNENBAUM, FRANK (1893–1969)

One of the most significant comparative studies of slavery in the Western Hemisphere, Latin American historian Frank Tannenbaum's *Slave and Citizen: The Negro in the Americas* (1946) launched a fierce scholarly debate over differences in race relations in the United States and Latin America.

Heavily influenced by the Brazilian writer Gilberto Freyre, Tannenbaum argued that Catholic theologians viewed slavery as an earthly misfortune that had no bearing on the slave's humanity. Freyre argued that in the Catholic colonial countries of Spain and Portugal, slavery had a long precedent in Roman law. Since slaves were traditionally prisoners of war or religious heretics, their servitude status was not racially based and was not inheritable. This tradition made slavery in Latin America less harsh, he argued, for there was a greater degree of miscegenation, manumission was achieved with more ease, and free blacks experienced more social mobility.

Meanwhile, slavery had virtually disappeared in Protestant northern Europe by the time of Christopher Columbus, Tannenbaum said, and when it reappeared with the European conquest of the Western Hemisphere, the slaves were invariably black. Slavery became associated with black inferiority in mostly Protestant nations such as the United States, spawning a more virulent race prejudice there. Even a Tannenbaum critic, Carl Degler (1971), concedes that before *Slave and Citizen* was published, it was assumed that slavery was much the same whatever its setting. Slavery's obvious evil aside, Tannenbaum suggested that the moral economy of different slave societies created subtle variations in how slavery was experienced.

In any case, according to Tannenbaum, the African slave's status was enviable compared to the fate suffered by the Western Hemisphere's native populations. Clinging to their cultures and languages, the Indians gradually suffered isolation and extermination. In contrast, African slaves absorbed European culture and thereby achieved a surprising degree of success throughout the Western Hemisphere—the result, in Tannenbaum's view, of cultural deracination. The African slave was stripped of his or her beliefs and past in return for limited access to status and power.

Tannenbaum described the African descendant in the Western Hemisphere as "culturally a European, or, if you will, an American, a white man with a black face" (Tannenbaum, 1946). This condescending portrait of African American culture had a major impact on later scholarship, particularly Stanley Elkins's *Slavery: A Portrait in American Institutional and Intellectual Life* (1959). Elkins depicted American slaves as childish Sambos who, after emancipation, proved incapable of creating stable families and were crippled in their struggle for economic success.

Degler's *Neither Black nor White: Slavery and Race Relations in Brazil and the United States* (1971) sharply critiqued Tannenbaum. Degler argued that the Catholic Church, regardless of theology, was too undermanned and too financially and politically dependent on the planter class to mitigate effectively against the harshness of slave life. He also stated that Tannenbaum overlooked the mortality rate of Brazilian slaves, the inability of the Brazilian slave population to reproduce itself as the American slaves did, the oppressiveness of life on the Brazilian coffee and sugar plantations, and the persistence of slave rebellions in Brazilian history in his comparison of American and Brazilian slavery.

Tannenbaum further ignored the high rate of American miscegenation and the strong presence of African slaves in Southern Protestant churches. Furthermore, according to Degler, antebellum Southern law indicates the American slave was not simply property, as Tannenbaum suggested, but occupied an ambiguous position as both person and chattel.

Leslie B. Rout, in *The African Experience in Spanish America* (1976), also seriously questioned Tannenbaum's interpretation of the slaves' status vis-à-vis the Indians. The Catholic Church, Rout argued, drew a distinction between "innocent" Indian pagans and Africans suspected of carrying the Islamic heresy to the New World. The Spanish crown was also concerned about the uncertain slave status of children born of Indian and black parents. Rout pointed to a series of royal cedulas (decrees) that were aimed at preventing miscegenation between black slaves and Indians and one law that demanded the castration of slaves having sex with Indian women as evidence that Catholic Spanish America valued the native population over African chattel.

Despite criticism, Tannenbaum is still credited with launching a productive debate about the differences among slave systems and the variation of race construction in slave societies. Since Tannenbaum, historians have given closer scrutiny to the moral economy of slavery and have placed the African diaspora in a hemispheric context.

—*Michael Phillips*

See also
Elkins, Stanley M.; Freyre, Gilberto de Mello
For Further Reading
Degler, Carl N. 1971. *Neither Black nor White: Slavery and Race Relations in Brazil and the United States.* New York: Macmillan; Elkins, Stanley M. 1959. *Slavery: A Problem in American Institutional and Intellectual Life.* Chicago: University of Chicago Press; Rout, Leslie B.. Jr. 1976. *The African Experience in Spanish America: 1502 to the Present Day.* Cambridge: Cambridge University Press; Tannenbaum, Frank. 1946. *Slave and Citizen: The Negro in the Americas.* New York: Vintage Books.

TATTOOING

Tattooing is the practice of making a permanent mark on the human body by puncturing the skin with needles and inserting pigment. It is an ancient practice and a universal one, especially when used for decorative and religious functions. When forcibly applied, the tattoo is generally an indication of status, ownership, or punishment, and the tattoo has served as a badge of slavery in many societies since antiquity. The most common site for placing an involuntary tattoo has been the face, especially the forehead, where the stigma of disgrace and the advertisement of power is most noticeable.

According to the Greek historian Herodotus, the ancient Persians tattooed slaves to indicate both ownership and status. From frequent mentions in Greek comedy and elsewhere, the Greeks clearly borrowed the practice from the Persians, though only to designate a delinquent or runaway slave. The Romans borrowed the penal tattoo from the Greeks, using it for the same purpose, and the penal tattoo began to be used as a sign of degradation—to mark the lowering of status that occurred as the result of conviction for certain crimes.

During the Roman Empire some criminals—including Christians—were reduced to slave status and sentenced to hard labor, usually permanently and in state-owned mines or quarries. They were tattooed, beaten with clubs, and chained (often their heads were shaved as well) before being sent on their way. In the later empire, beginning in the fourth century, soldiers and people employed in arms manufacturing, both groups being practically indentured to the state, were tattooed on the arm or hand.

During the Han dynasty in China (206 B.C.–A.D. 220), penal tattooing was associated with the infamy of slavery and forced labor. The same was true in Japan of roughly the same period (where such tattooing was called *irezumi*). Slaves, and criminals and prisoners of war reduced to slave status, were usually tattooed on the face to indicate ownership. Shaved heads, hard labor, and other forms of maltreatment made treatment in this part of the world remarkably similar to contemporaneous practices in the ancient Mediterranean world.

Irezumi was finally abolished in 1870, but the penal tattooing of slaves continued in the West through late antiquity and the Byzantine Empire into the Middle Ages and into the modern period. A European mainstay, it extended from Siberia to Africa and North America. Tattooing was not so prevalent a practice in the United States, where skin color was the primary mark of slave status and when any further indication was needed, the brand was preferred. The imposition of tattooed identification numbers on the forearms of Jews and others in Nazi concentration camps—people who were degraded so much as to be virtually enslaved—is the most notorious example of tattooing in more recent times.

—*Mark T. Gustafson*

See also
Branding of Slaves
For Further Reading
Gustafson, M. 1997. *"Inscripta in fronte*: Penal Tattooing in Late Antiquity." *Classical Antiquity* 16(1): 79–105; Jones, C. P. 1987. *"Stigma*: Tattooing and Branding in Graeco-Roman Antiquity." *Journal of Roman Studies* 77: 139–155; Sellin, J. T. 1976. *Slavery and the Penal System.* New York: Elsevier.

TENTH AMENDMENT

The Tenth Amendment to the U.S. Constitution states: "The powers not delegated to the United States by the Constitution, nor prohibited by it to the States, are reserved to the States respectively, or to the people." This amendment, ratified in 1791 as part of the Bill of Rights, was first used to support states' rights in resolutions passed in Virginia and Kentucky in 1798 and 1799, and Thomas Jefferson cited it in his debate with Alexander Hamilton over the First Bank of the United States. Robert Hayne and John Calhoun, in turn, used the Virginia and Kentucky resolutions in the nullification controversy of the 1830s, which concerned the right of states to declare null and void any federal law they deemed unconstitutional. The states' rights doctrine obviously related to slavery and was used as one of the main arguments as to why the national government could not interfere with the institution. Even in the nullification controversy though, states' rights took center stage and the amendment itself was relegated to secondary status, even though it was the intellectual backing for the doctrine.

Early in the history of the United States, the courts weakened the Tenth Amendment. In *McCulloch v. Maryland* (1819), the U.S. Supreme Court under John Marshall made several significant moves that allowed the federal government to gain more power and thus reduced the importance of the Tenth Amendment. First, the Court denied Maryland's right to tax the Second Bank of the United States and generally prohibited states from taxing any "legitimate" federal function. Second, it expanded the government's allowed powers far beyond those enumerated in the Constitution. Third, in this case Marshall crafted the term, and to some degree the idea, of the "living constitution," and a Constitution that can grow with the times is clearly one that usurps power from the states, which limits the Tenth Amendment.

Fourth, and most important for the discussion here, the Court noted that the Tenth Amendment did not have the word "expressly" in it, which means that any power not specifically mentioned in the Constitution as being prohibited to the federal government could be used by the federal government as long as the power was "necessary and proper" to the carrying out of a legitimate function. This interpretation clearly limited the scope of the Tenth Amendment, even though it was not noted by either Hayne or Calhoun in their speeches concerning nullification.

Congress, which drew up the Bill of Rights, had rejected an attempt to insert "expressly" into the Tenth Amendment (the corresponding provision in the earlier Articles of Confederation discussed the "expressly delegated" powers of the national government), so this amendment, through actions of Congress and the Supreme Court, was soon much more limited in scope that some people had hoped it would be. Judge Spencer Roane of Virginia tried to answer *McCulloch v. Maryland* in a series of essays, arguing that the Supreme Court could not take away the reserved powers, but over time, *McCulloch* and Marshall carried the day.

Related to the slavery issue was the idea that if Congress became accustomed to a wide use of a clause in the Constitution that allowed it to regulate commerce, it might then try to regulate slavery as a part of commerce. Another Supreme Court case, the *Passenger Cases* (1849), removed the possibility that the transportation of persons would not be called commerce, so the issue was fully a concern for the nation in the 1850s. Of course, as long as the balance of power between the North and the South in the Senate remained, the political guarantee of slavery was fairly certain, but the whole issue of Congress's power to regulate commerce added another part to the slavery debate. The Tenth Amendment was cited by both the majority and the dissent in *Dred Scott v. Sandford* (1857) and played a part in that ruling, a ruling that further inflamed the nation.

The amendment has not been cited to any great extent in recent years. With regard to the power of Congress to regulate commerce, the Supreme Court seemed to lay that issue to rest, for the most part, when it held for the government in *Wickard v. Filburn* in 1941. The whole issue of whether or not there were "traditional government functions" for the states to perform—free from federal interference—has been decided several times by the Supreme Court, from *National League of Cities* (1976) to *Garcia* (1985). Finally, the Tenth Amendment was cited by both the majority and the dissent in a 1995 decision that struck down term limits for Alabama's representatives to the U.S. Congress *(U.S. Term Limits)*. Thus, the issue of the bounds of federal power is still pertinent, and the Tenth Amendment is not totally forgotten.

—*Scott A. Merriman*

See also
Dred Scott v. Sandford; Hayne-Webster Debate; U.S. Constitution
For Further Reading
Gunther, Gerald, ed. 1969. *John Marshall's Defense of McCulloch v. Maryland.* Stanford, CA: Stanford University Press; Moore, Wayne D. 1996. *Constitutional Rights and Powers of the People.* Princeton, NJ: Princeton University Press.

THAILAND (SIAM)

Thailand is located on Southeast Asia's Indochinese and Malayan peninsulas. In the first centuries A.D., the Thai peoples developed a *muang* ("town") as the primary unit of social and political organization above the simple village. *Muangs* constituted an efficient means of managing the land and labor problems since land was plentiful but labor was scarce. Society in the *muangs* was hierarchic and paternalistic. By the ninth century, slaves were found in many Thai states, primarily the result of war and natural disasters, and in the first Thai kingdom, the Sukhothai (c. 1240–1438), slaves were part of the inherited property of the ruling family and the bondage labor of the Buddhist monastery was usually made up of free subjects who had been donated by the king, wealthy government officials, or other people to gain merit for themselves.

The basic form of servitude among Thai people after the Sukhothai kingdom was servant *(kha)* in nature, and it emphasized more of the paternal relations than labor exploitation. Even when slavery was widely practiced in Siam later, it was thought to be ameliorated by Thai paternalism and Theravada Buddhism. Such a view toward slavery is still prevalent in Thai society and among Thai historians. The invention of a "gentle slavery," Prince Damrong—the father of modern Thai history—asserted, was to prove one of the unique characteristics of the Thai race, a people who also believed in a love of national independence, toleration, and the power to assimilate.

Slavery developed and expanded during the Ayudhya (1351–1767) period, declined in the early Bangkok period (nineteenth century), and was abolished in 1905. In the Ayudhya kingdom, the Khmer ethnic group's system of kingship with rigid class structures among the population was adopted. The formation of the landed classes led to the development of the *sakdina* ("power of the rice fields"), or seignorialism, in Thai society. In this ordering of society, all subjects were divided into various categories and social statuses.

Most of the population were peasants, or *phrai*, and were subjected to an involuntary labor for a period of time. At the bottom of the *sakdina* system was *thaat*, or slavery, which, theoretically, was a fixed and even a lifetime bondage. Both forms were the basis of servitude in Siam, and slavery functioned as a social alternative for *phrai* who wanted to get free of state obligations or individual financial and living difficulties. In practice, both *phrai* and *thaat* were peasants and slaves came under the control and power of the state, but there were also several other forms of peasantry that were outside the state's purview.

For commoners, *phrai*, and slaves, duties and rights were stipulated by laws and customs. Unlike Western slave codes, which dealt exclusively with slaves, the Thai slave codes were part of the *thammasat*, a legal code derived from the Hindu dharma-sastras (treatises on ethical and social philosophy), that governs all subjects of the land. According to the Thai *thammasat*, or Three Seals Law, there were seven traditional classes of slaves: redeemable, born, acquired by inheritance, acquired by gift, acquired by legal penalties, acquired by famine, and war captives.

The slaves were not outsiders, nor were they an alienated or a "peculiar" element of the community, as was the case of slaves in the United States. There were no sharp color or racial distinctions between slaves and free persons. Thai slavery shared many of the general characteristics or theoretical ideas of slavery: slaves were a form of property and could be bought and sold according to the master's wishes.

Another significant aspect of Thai slavery was a recognition of the slave's personal value, which was articulated mainly by the state in a legal notion of the value of a person. According to social rank in the *sak-dina* system, together with consideration of age and sex, the entire population was given such a monetary value. This practice, which sounds very capitalistic, was influenced by the old Thai Buddhist cosmography in which merit and status positions were quantified. However, the stigma of the slave was that he or she was at the bottom of the hierarchy, implying that the slave status received no respect or trust from other people. In other words, slavery was a dishonor to self.

The abolition of slavery in Siam came with the administrative reform of the kingdom undertaken by Rama V, better known as King Chulalongkorn (r. 1868–1910), in response to the presence and impact of Western colonialism in Asia. Initiated by the king, the gradual legal abolition of slavery began in 1874 and was achieved in 1905.

—*Thanet Aphornsuvan*

For Further Reading
Feeny, David. 1993. "The Demise of Corvee and Slavery in Thailand." In *Breaking the Chains: Slavery, Bondage, and Emancipation in Modern Africa and Asia*. Ed. Martin A. Klein. Madison: University of Wisconsin Press; Panananon, Chatchai. 1982. "Siamese 'Slavery': Institution and Its Abolition." Ph.D. dissertation, Department of History, University of Michigan; Terwiel, B. 1983. "Bondage and Slavery in Early Nineteenth Century Siam." In *Slavery, Bondage, and Dependency in Southeast Asia*. Ed. Anthony Reid. St. Lucia, Australia: University of Queensland Press; Turton, Andrew. 1980. "Thai Institution of Slavery." In *Asian and African Systems of Slavery*. Ed. James L. Watson. Berkeley: University of California Press.

THEOGNIS OF MEGARA'S THEOGNIDEA

A theognid (plural, *theognidea*) was a short Greek lyric poem, usually composed in hexameters, expressing personal emotions and commenting upon the sorrows of mankind and contemporary social issues. The name Theognis may be only a literary pseudonym, derived from this poetic form, and many of the 1,389 lines attributed to Theognis are in elegiac couplets, a hexameter linked to a pentameter.

Theognis, a contemporary of the philosopher Pythagoras and the fabulist Aesop, lived in Athens during the late-sixth century B.C. The internal textual evidence suggests that he came from the city of Megara. His poems reveal him as being greatly disillusioned with the world around him, a mood shared by many Athenian aristocrats for whose symposia his lyrics were probably composed. These gatherings were intended to provide opportunities for like-minded men to meet and discuss serious topics, although some entertainment, including the singing of *skolia* ("drinking songs") like the *Theognidea*, often became part of the proceedings.

Theognis was a member of the landowning, well-established, and wealthy elite and shared the attitudes of his time and class. He regarded slavery as justified for non-Greeks—in his day, mostly Thracians, Scythians, and Asiatics who were enslaved as captives of war or as the result of piracy. *Theognidea* is the first literary expression of the argument that slavery was essential so that free Greek citizens would be able to serve their city-state in more significant capacities than as manual laborers. The service rendered by freemen was to the administrative, military, political, artistic, and educational life of their city-state, and Theognis considered such service of proportionately greater value than their manual toil could be.

From his references to slaves and their activities, we can identify three distinct categories of slaves in late-sixth-century Athens: domestic, industrial, and civic. The first were owned by private citizens and were trained in domestic and agricultural skills, working in the homes and on the farms of their masters. The second type worked in mines, factories, workshops, and construction and were owned by entrepreneurial groups of citizens who were rising in social importance by means of commercial activities. Slaves in the third category were the property of the state and were used in public works, road building, shipbuilding, and the raising of walls for security of the city. Theognis was highly critical of owners who hired out their slaves for cash, regardless of the conditions of their outside work. He emphasized that the master was supposed to treat his slaves as a father would treat his children, not to exploit them for profit with no concern for their welfare.

In accepted Greek tradition, paternalistic authority brought with it paternal responsibility, but Theognis recognized that people who were unused to position and privilege—i.e., members of the emerging mercantile class—did not respect the traditional relationship of owner to slave. Some apparently inserted passages refer to the laws of Solon, which were codified between 593 and 586 B.C. and created the basis of the Athenian legal system for the next four centuries. These insertions concern the reforms made by Solon forbidding any citizen to be taken into slavery for debt by or on behalf of his creditors and making illegal the practice of enslaving the children of a citizen for debt. From these specific points, found in the first book of the *Theognidea,* we can be reasonably certain that the lyrics were in circulation in late-sixth-century Athens.

The surviving texts are fragmentary and difficult, corrupted by frequent copying, but because these col-lected elegiacs were popular enough to be widely copied, there is enough material for us to form a clear impression of the opinions expressed in them about the uses and abuses of slavery at the time. It is significant that most of the poems contain some mention of slaves and their contributions to the proper functioning of free society, to trade, and to domestic production and security.

The emphasis placed upon the exclusion of Greek citizens from the threat of bondage, and upon the freeman as being a vital factor in the intellectual and cultural development of his society, implies that the issue of slavery was under serious discussion in Athens as other institutions in the city-state became more democratic. Even at this early stage, the benefits of slave labor to the well-being of the community were being weighed against the ethical and practical problems presented by an increasing slave population and the consequent economic dependence of free citizens upon it.

—*Lindy J. Rawling*

See also
Solon
For Further Reading
Bowra, C. M. 1961. *Greek Lyric Poetry.* Oxford: Oxford University Press; Finley, Moses I., ed. 1984. *The Legacy of Greece.* Oxford: Oxford University Press; Jay, P., ed. 1973. *The Greek Anthology.* London: London University Press; Lesky, A. 1966. *A History of Greek Literature.* London: London University Press.

THIRTEENTH AMENDMENT

*T*he Thirteenth Amendment was a direct result of the U.S. Civil War, and when it was ratified on December 18, 1865, by 26 of the existing 36 states, the abolition of slavery became a fundamental part of U.S. law. Section 1 provides: "Neither slavery nor involuntary servitude, except as a punishment for crime whereof the party shall have been duly convicted, shall exist within the United States, or in any place subject to their jurisdiction." Section 2 provides: "Congress shall have power to enforce this article by appropriate legislation." As a result of this amendment, both slavery and peonage were absolutely forbidden in the United States, since there is no "state action" requirement. Contemporaries differed as to whether the Thirteenth Amendment was intended to do more than end the master-slave relationship, and this debate led to the passage of the Fourteenth and Fifteenth Amendments as the Reconstruction era progressed.

Although the Thirteenth Amendment, especially when taken together with the Fourteenth and Fifteenth

Amendments, codified a dramatic advance in the legal protection of African Americans and signified the triumph of the abolitionist movement to eliminate slavery, the Thirteenth Amendment never received support from President Andrew Johnson or most Southern Democrats. Radical Republican views of natural law that supported the Thirteenth Amendment as a vehicle of social equality were probably shared by only a minority of mid-nineteenth-century Americans, and the amendment was a monument to the legacy of President Abraham Lincoln that never achieved its full potential.

Therefore, despite its noble intentions, the Thirteenth Amendment proved difficult to implement. The defeated Southern states passed black codes designed to make sure that blacks remained in the functional equivalent of slavery with limited rights to contract, own property, or participate in public life. In response, Congress passed the Civil Rights Act of 1866, and the Fourteenth and Fifteenth Amendments were proposed and ratified in order to assure radical Republicans in Congress that the Civil War gains would not be rendered hollow by determined resistance from the defeated Southern states.

The Supreme Court used the Thirteenth Amendment to suppress attacks on black civil rights in two 1866 cases, *U.S. v. Rhodes* and *In re Turner*. In *U.S. v. Rhodes,* the Thirteenth Amendment was used to uphold the constitutionality of the Civil Rights Act of 1866; in *Turner,* it was used to protect African American children against extremely harsh apprenticeship laws.

As the passions of the Civil War cooled, the impact of the Thirteenth Amendment was narrowed by Supreme Court decisions that limited its scope and assured that African Americans, although free, would not be able to use the amendment as a tool to assure widespread social recognition as the functional social equals of white Americans. Although Justice Samuel F. Miller's 1873 decision in the *Slaughterhouse Cases* spoke of the Thirteenth Amendment in glowing terms and carefully overturned no existing case law, it construed the amendment narrowly. Miller held that the Thirteenth and Fourteenth Amendments supported only very limited rights of federal citizenship, and he stated that these amendments could not be used to break a butcher-shop monopoly in New Orleans that was adverse to blacks.

Despite the setback represented by the *Slaughterhouse Cases,* the Thirteenth Amendment served as the basis for federal authority in passing the sweeping Civil Rights Act of 1875. That act guaranteed African Americans equal access to all forms of public accommodation under terms that were as generous as those provided by the Civil Rights Act of 1964.

In response, the Supreme Court dramatically limited the scope of potential congressional enforcement power under the Thirteenth Amendment in the *Civil Rights Cases* decided in 1883. Although Justice Joseph Bradley's opinion recognized that Congress had broad power to enforce the abolition of slavery against states as well as against individuals, he did not see the Thirteenth Amendment as a basis for enforcing social equality in public accommodations in order to eliminate alleged badges of slavery.

Those decisions meant that the Thirteenth Amendment would be narrowly construed for the remainder of the nineteenth century, but the amendment acquired new life and meaning as the twentieth century progressed. Some significant civil rights decisions used the Thirteenth Amendment as a basis for expanding the civil rights of African Americans. *Jones v. Alfred Mayer Co.* (1968), for example, used the Thirteenth Amendment as a tool to ban housing discrimination by a private developer, and later decisions used the amendment to ban discrimination in leased property and mobile homes. In *Sullivan v. Little Hunting Park* (1982), the *Jones v. Alfred Mayer* decision was expanded to cover membership in community facilities owned by homeowner groups.

Thus, the Supreme Court's interpretation of the Thirteenth Amendment had come full circle. An amendment once frequently described as a relic of the Civil War era assumed new modern significance.

—*Susan A. Stussy*

For Further Reading
Hall, Kermit L., William M. Wicek, and Paul Finkelman. 1996. *American Legal History: Cases and Materials.* New York: Oxford University Press; Lively, Donald E. 1992. *The Constitution and Race.* New York: Praeger; Maltz, Earl M. 1990. *Civil Rights, the Constitution, and Congress, 1863–1869.* Lawrence: University Press of Kansas; Novak, John E., and Ronald D. Rotunda. 1991. *Constitutional Law.* St. Paul, MN: West Publishing.

THOREAU, HENRY DAVID (1817–1862)

*A*lthough originally a reluctant reformer, Henry David Thoreau gradually became an ardent supporter of the antislavery cause and employed his talent as a writer to persuade others of the moral imperative of abolition. Thoreau never joined an antislavery organization, primarily because he spurned organized movements in any form, but his lectures and essays helped convince thousands in the North that slavery was immoral. In the 1830s he primarily directed his energies toward his fledgling career as a writer, but he was sympathetic to the antislavery cause, and over the next 30 years, the national controversy surrounding slavery impelled him to become more active and more militant in his opposition to it.

In the early 1840s, Thoreau's essays on slavery ("Reform and the Reformers" and "Herald of Freedom") were cautious and advocated reform on an individual level. He made his own stand against slavery in 1846 by refusing to pay a poll tax. He would not support the federal government in its efforts to expand slave territory through a war with Mexico, and consequently he spent a night in the Concord, Massachusetts, jail. After his release, he wrote the philosophical piece "Resistance to Civil Government," in which he advocated passive resistance to a government that defied the moral will of the people. His adherence to pacifism rather than violence is a central tenet of the essay. Other than his classic work *Walden* (1854), Thoreau is best remembered for his "Resistance" essay, and it has been reprinted countless times and has inspired Mahatma Gandhi, John F. Kennedy, and Martin Luther King, Jr.

During the 1850s, events on both local and national levels caused Thoreau to revise his position that noncompliance was the only morally justifiable way to oppose slavery. He began to break the law actively by becoming a part of the Underground Railroad, and he fostered friendships with abolitionists like Wendell Phillips, Horace Greeley, and Franklin Sanborn. The passage of the Fugitive Slave Act of 1850 and the subsequent captures of Shadrach, Thomas Sims, and Anthony Burns, all in nearby Boston, ignited Thoreau's rage. In 1854, he wrote a scathing piece entitled "Slavery in Massachusetts," in which he lambasted the governor of Massachusetts for complying with the immoral Fugitive Slave Act and called on the state's citizens to defy it openly. Although he stopped short of advocating violence, he accepted that force should be met with force when moral authority was at stake.

In 1859, John Brown's failed attempt to spark a slave insurrection at Harpers Ferry, Virginia, prompted an even-stronger response from Thoreau. He was appalled at how quickly New England's admiration for Brown's efforts in Kansas had turned to condemnation for his action at Harpers Ferry, and Thoreau wrote three essays in support of Brown, praising both his ideals and his willingness to act on them. All three essays—"A Plea for Captain John Brown," "Martyrdom of John Brown," and "The Last Days of John Brown"—emphasized Brown's high moral stature rather than his actions. In these works, Thoreau made it clear that he believed moral authority justified violence.

Thoreau exercised much influence in his native New England where his antislavery essays were widely read and discussed. His eloquent prose and the moral force of his arguments made him a powerful proponent of the abolitionist cause.

—*Elizabeth Dubrulle*

See also
Brown, John; Burns, Anthony; Fugitive Slave Act of 1850; Harpers Ferry Raid; Shadrach Fugitive Slave Case; Transcendentalism; Underground Railroad
For Further Reading
Glick, Wendell, ed. 1972. *The Writings of Henry D. Thoreau: Reform Papers*. Princeton, NJ: Princeton University Press; Gougeon, Len. 1995. "Thoreau and Reform." In *The Cambridge Companion to Henry David Thoreau*. Ed. Joel Myerson. Cambridge: Cambridge University Press; Harding, Walter. 1982. *The Days of Henry Thoreau: A Biography*. New York: Dover Publications; Richardson, Robert D. 1986. *Henry Thoreau: A Life of the Mind*. Berkeley: University of California Press.

THREE-FIFTHS COMPROMISE

When the U.S. Supreme Court celebrated its bicentennial in 1987, Justice Thurgood Marshall felt he could not join in the celebration. As an African American, he saw the U.S. Constitution—especially its so-called three-fifths compromise—as a document written to secure slavery and slaveowners' rights in an era when most blacks were slaves and free blacks had little hope of attaining full citizenship.

As ratified in 1788, Article 1, section 2, paragraph 3 of the Constitution began: "Representatives and direct taxes shall be apportioned among the several States which may be included within this Union, according to their respective numbers, which shall be determined by adding to the whole number of free persons, including those bound to service for a term of years, and excluding Indians not taxed, three-fifths of all other persons." Without the so-called three-fifths compromise, Georgia and South Carolina would not have joined the United States and the Union would have been stillborn. However, the framers of the Constitution were clearly uneasy about the nature of slavery, and it is interesting that their language made no direct mention of it.

In determining representation to the Continental Congress in 1776, Virginia offered to exclude slaves in computing that colony's population. Later, the Articles of Confederation gave each state equal representation, and the question of representation based upon population was deferred.

The original draft of the Articles of Confederation apportioned taxation based on the full population of each state, including Negroes and mulattoes. Since the Northern colonies objected to this method of determining taxation, the Articles of Confederation left the matter unresolved and unclear in 1781 by stating that taxation should be based on the value of all land. Later, James Madison inserted a three-fifths clause in the 1783 revision of the Articles of Confederation, counting five slaves as three freemen for the purpose of apportioning taxation among the states.

Acrimonious debate at the Constitutional Convention made it clear that the Southern states would not join the Union unless slaves were counted as three-fifths of a man for purposes of representation. William R. Davie stated that North Carolina would never confederate unless slaves were to be counted on at least a three-fifths basis for representation, and Gouverneur Morris, who represented Pennsylvania at the convention, said: "Upon what basis shall slaves be computed in representation? Are they men? Then make them citizens and let them vote. Are they property? Why then is no other property included?" (Farber and Sherry, 1990).

Although South Carolina's Pierce Butler and Charles Pinckney would have liked blacks to be counted equally with whites in terms of representation to bolster the population of their state, which had a black majority, the Northern states would never have agreed to do so. Northern delegates considered the defense of slave states against possible rebellion a serious obligation, and they did not hesitate to point this fact out to overreaching Southerners. The terms of the three-fifths compromise proved very beneficial to the Southern states in the nineteenth century when the population of the Northern states expanded more rapidly than that of the South. In 1820, the Southern states had 20 representatives in the U.S House of Representatives as a result of the compromise.

In issue number 54 of the *Federalist,* James Madison defended the three-fifths compromise as the framers of the Constitution sought its ratification. He attempted to present a rational Southerner making an argument that slaves were justly considered as both persons and property. The Southerner said: "Would the convention have been impartial or consistent, if they had rejected slaves from the list of inhabitants when the shares of representation were to be calculated, and inserted them on the lists when the tariff of contributions was to be adjusted? Could it be reasonably expected that the Southern states would concur in a system which considered their slaves in some degree as men when burdens were to be imposed, but refused to consider them in the same light when advantages were to be conferred?" In conclusion, Madison, a Virginian, stated his support of the Southern posi-

tion. He felt the compromise should apply to both taxation and representation in order to avoid tempting states into a dishonest count of their population for purposes of the federal census.

In the vigorous debate surrounding the adoption of the Constitution, Madison was not the only writer defending the three-fifths compromise, although he was probably the best known. An anonymous writer calling himself "Mark Anthony" in the January 10, 1788, edition of the Philadelphia *Independent Chronicle* also defended the compromise. Mark Anthony responded to previously published criticisms of the compromise by "Brutus," who also wrote anonymously for the *Independent Chronicle.*

Mark Anthony wrote, "The practice of slavery among our confederates ought to be regretted by us, but it is evidently beyond our control." He also cautioned that the French philosopher Montesquieu had shown that emancipating slaves and making them citizens of the Roman Republic had caused great inconvenience to the state, and Anthony warned that Americans should remember this cautionary example and anticipate possible problems of civil disorder before taking any precipitate action. Although recognizing that the anonymous Brutus was an able writer, Mark Anthony felt that Brutus had deliberately inflamed popular feeling by ignoring the fact that taxation and representation were linked. Anthony stated: "The careful reader will observe, that the article under consideration apportions representatives and taxes according to numbers. But the pretended abridgement fabricated by Brutus, mentions representatives only."

However abhorrent twentieth-century Americans find slavery, they should understand the dilemma faced by the framers of the Constitution in 1787. Although blacks were generally regarded as inferior to whites, few delegates to the Constitutional Convention in Philadelphia regarded slavery as desirable. Even so, they had to recognize the economic imperatives faced by the Southern states, particularly the problems of the developing economies in Georgia and South Carolina. The promises of the Declaration of Independence, which held that "all men are created equal," could not realistically be realized in the eighteenth century, and the United States clearly still has a seriously unfulfilled constitutional agenda in the area of civil rights as the twentieth century ends.

—*Susan A. Stussy*

For Further Reading
Farber, Daniel A., and Suzanna Sherry. 1990. *A History of the American Constitution.* St. Paul, MN: West Publishing; Hamilton, Alexander; James Madison; and John Jay. 1961. *The Federalist Papers.* New York: Mentor Book; Levy, Leonard W., and Dennis J.

Mahoney, eds. 1987. *The Framing of the Constitution.* New York: Macmillan; Novak, John E., and Ronald D. Rotunda. 1991. *Constitutional Law.* St. Paul, MN: West Publishing.

TIMBUKTU

Timbuktu is an important trade center situated seven miles north of the Niger River in the West African state of Mali. The city's origins remain unclear, but Timbuktu rose to prominence in the medieval period both through trade—because of its location at the junction of riverine and trans-Saharan trade routes—and also as a center of Muslim scholarship. The city's "high period" occurred roughly between 1350 and 1600. Major commodities upon which Timbuktu's prosperity was founded included gold, salt, and slaves. The slave trade appears to have taken various forms, both local and long distance, but the preeminent markets were in North Africa, so slaves traveled north across the Sahara to Morocco or Algeria.

In addition to the slaves that were sent directly north, others were kept in Timbuktu to work as household slaves, and still others worked on the surrounding region's agricultural plantations. This latter activity appears to have been of special importance, for Timbuktu, which is situated along desert margins, could never supply its own food requirements. Thus, grain and other foodstuffs were imported in large quantities.

Timbuktu also supplied Saharan salt mines with slave labor. Initially, Teghaza in northern Mali was the paramount salt extraction center, but Taodeni, also in northern Mali, replaced it in the late-sixteenth century. Berbers controlled the salt mines in both places and used slaves to cut salt slabs, which were loaded four each to a camel and sent south to Timbuktu for trade onward in exchange for gold, more slaves, and various other commodities.

Although little is known about the sources of slaves sold in Timbuktu (estimates suggest 1,000–2,000 per year were exported north in the nineteenth century), it is believed most were pagans obtained from regions far to the south of the city. Ahmed Baba, a famous Muslim scholar and an inhabitant of Timbuktu, wrote a book on slavery in 1614 that condemned enslavement of Muslims, "but otherwise accepted enslavement as a legal pursuit for Muslims" (Lovejoy, 1983).

Slaves working in Timbuktu households appear to have been spared some of the privations of their colleagues who labored in Saharan salt mines and endured the worst conditions. Eventually, over the centuries, a client-patron relationship often developed between household slaves and their owners, and distinct slave castes came into being, such as the Bela, vassals to the Tuareg who periodically controlled Timbuktu following the collapse of Moroccan rule of the city in 1780.

During the nineteenth century, Timbuktu was visited by many European explorers including Heinrich Barth who mentioned that many North African traders from Fez (Fès), Marrakech, and Ghadames still had representatives in Timbuktu in the 1850s, which attests to its continued economic importance. Finally, in 1893 the French occupied Timbuktu, and slave trading was officially suppressed though, as Horace Miner (1953) relates, even in the 1940s many slaves preferred a life of slavery to "economically precarious freedom."

—Timothy Insoll

See also
Salt Trade
For Further Reading
Barth, Heinrich. 1965. *Travels and Discoveries in Northern and Central Africa.* London: Frank Cass; Lovejoy, Paul E. 1983. *Transformations in Slavery.* Cambridge: Cambridge University Press; Miner, Horace. 1953. *The Primitive City of Timbuctoo.* Princeton, NJ: Princeton University Press.

TOPEKA CONSTITUTION
See Lecompton Constitution

THE TORAH

There were individuals in ancient Israel who were deprived of at least part of their freedom and who could be bought and sold. The most common term for slave in the Torah was '*ebed* (from '*abad*, to work). This vague term (similar to its Akkadian-language counterpart, *wardu*) was used for anyone subordinate to someone of a higher rank; it was thus a term for general dependence and has often been translated as servant. Even patriarchs and monarchs were Yahweh's servants (Exod. 32:13; Lev. 25:55; 1 Sam. 3:9), and all peoples of both Israel and Judah were the king's subjects, including the royal family (1 Sam. 17:8, 29:3; 2 Sam. 19:5). David was a slave (vassal) to the Philistine king Achish (1 Sam. 28:2), and Ahaz of Judah was servant to the Assyrian king Tiglath-pileser III (2 Kings 16:7).

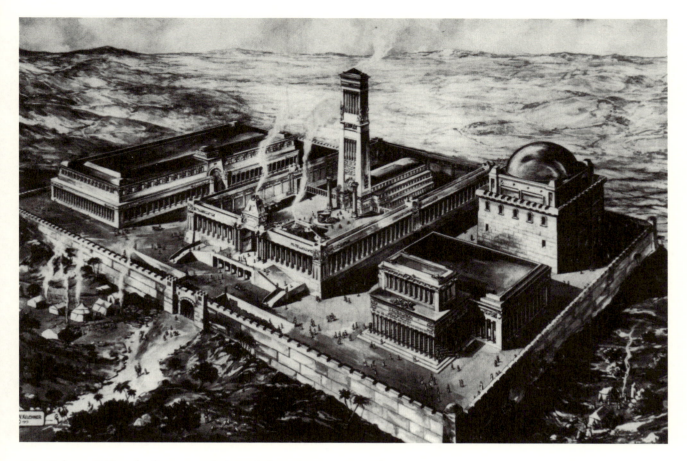

King Solomon's Temple, from an early-twentieth-century reconstruction.

Although the generic term *'ebed* was used in various contexts, it usually is easy to determine its precise meaning. For example, the servants of Abimelech, king of Gerar, were probably his royal officials (Gen. 20:8). The 318 "slaves" that Abraham employed to recover his nephew Lot were probably freeborn members of his extended family (Gen. 14:14), and the servants of the kings of Israel and Judah were either royal soldiers or dignitaries (2 Kings 23:30; 2 Chron. 25:3).

Even nations subject to Israel (e.g., Edomites, Moabites, and Syrians) were considered slaves since they were required to pay tribute (2 Sam. 8:2, 14; 1 Chron. 18:2, 6, 13). Solomon used non-Israelite forced labor to build his temple and royal palace (2 Chron. 2:17–18, 8:7–9), and the Hebrews were slaves in Egypt because they were required to render forced labor. Moreover, the Babylonian captivity of the people of Judah was considered cruel slavery (e.g., 2 Chron. 36:6; Ezra 9:4; Isa. 14:3; Jer. 25:11, 27:7).

A chief labor source was captured prisoners of war who were sold as slaves. Provisions were made for female prisoners who were married by their captors (Deut. 21:10–14), as such women then ceased to be slaves. There are many examples of Israelites who

were sold or threatened with being sold (Judg. 5:30; 1 Sam. 30:2–3; Joel 3:3). Pekah of Israel captured 200,000 citizens of Judah, but they were freed at a prophet's request (2 Chron. 28:8–15). The Torah also allowed Israelites to purchase resident aliens (Lev. 22:11, 25:44–45).

It was a capital crime to abduct an Israelite to make him a slave (Exod. 21:16; Lev. 25:46; Deut 24:7), and although one Israelite could be sold to another as an indentured servant (Lev. 25:39–43), the Israelite could not be forced to do a slave's work. The indentured Israelite could be freed by a close relative or by the Jubilee (which took place every 50 years), but generally slaves were held for only seven years (Exod. 21:11; Lev. 25:40; Deut. 15:12–18). The only way an Israelite could be reduced to servitude was through his own poverty or if he had been used as security for a relative's poverty. This slavery ended once the debt was canceled (2 Kings 4:7; Neh. 5:8, 11). Thieves also were sold to repay the amount of their theft (Exod. 22:2).

Very little is mentioned about the number of domestic servants/slaves in ancient Israel, although a census taken after the Babylonian Captivity (sixth century B.C.) recorded over 7,000 slaves in ancient Israel compared to over 40,000 free persons (Ezra 2:64; Neh. 7:66). An affluent family probably owned at least one or more domestic servants, as is indicated by Gideon (Judg. 6:27), Abigail (1 Sam. 25:19, 42), and Ziba (2 Sam. 9:10). Female slaves made up a special category. They attended to the needs of the mistress of the house (Gen. 16:1; 1 Sam. 25:42), nursed the children (Gen. 25:59; 2 Sam. 4:4; 2 Kings 11:2), and could be taken as concubines, which did not change their status unless their master freed them (Gen. 16:6; Lev. 19:20).

The slave's market value is rarely mentioned. Joseph was sold by his brothers for 20 shekels, which was the average price of a Mesopotamian slave (Gen. 37:28). There is no evidence of any branding of slaves in Israel, although a slave who declined freedom had his ears pierced (Exod. 21:6; Deut. 15:17). The latter was not inflicted upon him but was a sign of his familial attachment. Although a slave was considered property, he or she was also considered human and thus had certain rights. If a slave was gored by another man's ox, the ox's owner had to compensate the slave's master (Exod. 21:32). A man who blinded his slave or broke his tooth had to free him (Exod. 21:26–27). If a slave was beaten to death, the owner was punished (Exod. 21:20), but if the slave survived for a few days, the owner was exempt from punishment, since it was his property (Exod. 21:21).

Slaves at times had money (1 Sam. 9:8), acquired property (2 Kings 5:20–26), owned slaves (2 Sam. 9:10), and could marry the master's daughter (1 Chron. 2:34–35—although it is implied that he would then be emancipated). Many of these more affluent slaves were described by a Hebrew term meaning young men, not 'ebed. The slave was considered a part of the family, as is indicated by the requirement of circumcision for all males (Gen. 17:12–13); rested on the Sabbath (Exod. 20:10, 23:12); and shared in sacrificial meals (Deut. 12:12, 18) and religious feasts (Exod. 12:44, Deut. 16:11, 14). A priest's slave could eat the holy offerings (Lev. 22:10).

One law in the Torah (Deut. 23:15–16) forbade anyone to return to its master a runaway slave who had sought refuge. He was to be welcomed and well treated in the town in which he had chosen to live. Nonetheless, there are examples of runaway slaves (1 Sam. 25:10), some of whom were extradited (1 Sam. 30:15; 1 Kings 2:40).

Although there was no predominance of slave labor in agriculture, the artisan trades, or any branch of the economy, there appears to have been some state slavery during the period of the monarchy (c. 1000–586 B.C.). David set the population to work making bricks (2 Sam. 12:31) while Solomon used "slaves" to work in the mines at Arabah, the factories at Ezion Geber, and, as previously noted, the royal palace and temple

(1 Kings 9:15–21). Most of these were Canaanites, not Israelites (1 Kings 9:21–22). After the exile, descendants of Solomon's slaves performed services for the Levites (Ezra 8:20).

—*Mark W. Chavalas*

For Further Reading
Cardellini, I. 1981. *Die biblischen "Sklaven"-Gesetze im Lichte des keilschriften Sklavenrechts.* Bonn: P. Hanstein; Lemche, N. P. 1975. "The 'Hebrew Slave': Comments on the Slave Law Ex. xxi 2–11." *Vetus Testamentum* 25: 129–144; Van den Ploeg, J. 1972. "Slavery in the Old Testament." *Vetus Testamentum Supplement* 22: 72–87; Westbrook, R. 1988. *Studies in Biblical and Cuneiform Law.* Paris: J. Gabalda.

TORDESILLAS, TREATY OF (1494)

Signed in the early years of American exploration, the Treaty of Tordesillas divided the New World into Spanish and Portuguese dominions and determined to which regions their respective colonists would travel. This division contributed to the future characters of the South American regions. The Portuguese received the area that became Brazil and imported massive numbers of slaves to work on the sugar plantations there; the Spanish held the rest of the continent and extracted labor from the indigenous Indian populations. The Treaty of Tordesillas, with its vague definitions and uncertain geographical clauses, also led to perpetual boundary disputes between the Spanish and the Portuguese in their New World colonies.

After news of Columbus's contact with the Americas reached Spain, the Catholic kings moved quickly to secure papal sanction for Castile's rights to trade and colonization in the unexplored New World. Accordingly, Pope Alexander VI established Spanish dominion in a series of bulls, beginning with Inter Caetera (1493), in which he magnanimously granted "all islands, mainlands, discovered or yet to be discovered, sighted or not yet sighted, to the west and south of a line set and drawn from the Arctic or North Pole to the Antarctic or South Pole, to the line to stand one hundred leagues to the west and south of the so-called Azores or Cape Verde Islands, if they were not actually possessed by another King or Christian prince."

Portugal, a major maritime power with interests along West Africa's coast, immediately perceived this as a new threat to its empire and entered into negotiations with Spain to adjust the line of demarcation to a more reasonable distance farther to the west. Some historians consider this evidence that Portugal knew of Brazil's existence before Pedro Álvars Cabral officially landed there in 1500, but there is no definitive proof.

Nevertheless, Spanish and Portuguese representatives met at Tordesillas in northern Spain in 1494 and agreed to move the boundary a further 270 leagues west of the Cape Verde Islands; Castile had dominion north and west of the line, Portugal to the south and east. This agreement determined that the future territory of Brazil would be Portuguese-speaking and the rest of South America, Spanish-speaking. The Portuguese quickly began growing sugar in their region, a labor-intensive enterprise that stimulated the trade of African slaves to Brazil. The trend was slower and on a much smaller scale in Spain's dominions—with the exception of Cuba—because large Indian populations existed from which labor could be extracted.

The Treaty of Tordesillas was an important diplomatic agreement, yet it contained the seeds of future disputes because its authors were unaware of the geography or extent of the Americas when they developed the document; 1494 was, after all, only two years after Columbus first made contact with the New World. Furthermore, the treaty did not specify from which island the line of demarcation was to be measured or indicate the official length of a league for legal purposes. Accordingly, as exploration opened South America's interior, both sides, but especially the Portuguese, began pushing beyond the imaginary line drawn through the jungle. Even France and England petitioned for portions of the New World in the 1550s, claiming that the Treaty of Tordesillas could not exclude them from commerce and colonies in the New World.

The true boundary was always hazy and ill-defined and became of little practical importance when Spain and Portugal were united under the Hapsburgs from 1580 to 1640. During that time, Portuguese planters expanded Brazilian sugar production and wanted more territory for their lucrative business. They imported more and more African slaves into the region, which gave Brazil a social composition that was markedly different from that of South America's Spanish areas.

Once Portugal's independence from Spain was assured in 1665, the boundary issue took on a new immediacy as the expansionary Portuguese set their sights on the Río de la Plata to the south of Brazil. The Treaty of Utrecht (1713) subsequently modified European proprietary land rights as defined in the Treaty of Tordesillas, but boundary lines in the Amazon basin remain indistinct even to the present time.

—*Karen Racine*

For Further Reading

Catholic Church (Pope Alexander VI). 1927. *The Earliest Diplomatic Documents on America: The Papal Bulls of 1493 and the Treaty of Tordesillas*. Berlin: P. Gottschalk; Harrisse, Henry. 1897. *The Diplomatic History of America: Its First Chapter, 1452–1494*. London: B. F. Stevens; Jornadas, Americanistas. 1973. *El tratado de Tordesillas y su proyeccion*. Valladolid, Spain: Universidad, Seminario de Historia de América; McAlister, Lyle. 1984. *Spain and Portugal in the New World, 1492–1700*. Minneapolis: University of Minnesota Press.

TRADE GOODS

Two desires motivated the Atlantic slave trade: the Europeans' quest for slaves and the African traders' need to obtain items of European manufacture and other exotic origin. It is commonly believed that the predominant European trade articles were beads and firearms and that a desire for these goods precipitated increased conflict and slave-taking. Though true in some respects, the assortment of trade items varied locally, changed over time, and depended on the location where the trade was conducted. One certainty exists: the objects and materials exchanged by Europeans for slaves and other commodities varied in time and place and cannot be simplistically characterized.

Along the Slave Coast, cowries were nearly always the most desired trade items. Europeans obtained these shells in the Indian Ocean and took them to West Africa to exchange for cloth, ivory, gold, food, and slaves. Second in importance were iron and other metals, both as raw stock and as finished objects. Initially, iron was most the important metal, but by the late-seventeenth century, there was more demand for brass. Third was cloth, of both European and Indian manufacture. During the seventeenth century, the items listed fourth and fifth in priority were glass beads and spirits. Firearms were minor trade items during the seventeenth century, and only the occasional presentation of sets of pistols or fowling pieces characterized the weapons trade.

The volume of the slave trade increased during the eighteenth century, and the changing nature of European and colonial output resulted in important changes in the type of trade goods offered. As the Slave Coast's political situation changed, firearms and gunpowder became increasingly desired trade items. New trade goods unrelated to conflict also became popular, with Brazilian tobacco requested to such an extent that it eclipsed cowries in popularity. Brazilian gold was also traded on the Slave Coast, in part for use by local elites for political purposes.

Goods offered by Europeans were exchanged not

only for slaves but also for a host of other items. African-manufactured cloth was a common trade item along the Slave Coast. Palm oil was one of the original commodities Europeans sought, and it grew in importance during the nineteenth century as the slave trade waned. Locally produced food was another common trade item, acquired by Europeans to feed slaves awaiting shipment to the New World and to feed the captives and crews of ships during the long transatlantic voyage.

Trade developed in other areas of the African coast as well, generally for similar imported goods, with Brazilian cane liquor a highly desired trade commodity in Angolan ports. Minor trade items were highly varied, and there are numerous references of European clothing being presented to elites. Historic and archaeological data document the use of Chinese porcelains and European ceramics by Africans involved in trade with Europeans, and fine crystal stemware and other imported drinking vessels were also used by African notables.

—*Kenneth G. Kelly*

See also
Archaeological Record of the Slave Trade
For Further Reading
Connah, Graham. 1975. *The Archaeology of Benin: Excavations and Other Researches in and around Benin City, Nigeria*. Oxford: Clarendon Press; DeCorse, Christopher R. 1992. "Culture Contact, Continuity, and Change on the Gold Coast: A.D. 1400–1900." *African Archaeological Review* 10: 163–196; Law, Robin. 1991. *The Slave Coast of West Africa, 1550–1750: The Impact of the Atlantic Slave Trade on an African Society*. Oxford: Clarendon Press; Miller, Joseph C. 1982. "Commercial Organization of Slaving at Luanda, Angola, 1760–1830." In *The Uncommon Market: Essays in the Economic History of the Atlantic Slave Trade*. Ed. Henry A. Gemery and Jan S. Hogendorn. New York: Academic Press.

TRANSCENDENTALISM

Transcendentalism was an intellectual, religious, and literary movement centered in New England in the mid-nineteenth century that helped to highlight and disseminate the moral imperative of the antislavery cause. The transcendentalist movement originated in the United States in the 1830s and 1840s as a reaction against established religion, particularly Unitarianism. Rejecting the notions that God's will could be interpreted only by ministers and that religious practice must follow guidelines specified by organized churches, transcen-

dentalists believed that God's will was a constant, absolute truth which transcended physical phenomena and resided within everything in the universe, including man. Man could discover this higher law only by listening to his instincts and conscience rather than accepting a truth externally defined by traditional authorities like church and state. Once man discovered absolute truth, he was capable of reforming his behavior and attitudes to achieve perfection.

Reliance on instinct and conscience had two significant impacts on the movement. First, it meant that transcendentalists prized individualism and self-reliance, which produced an eclectic group whose members held varying opinions on almost every topic. The movement's spiritual center was Ralph Waldo Emerson, who relinquished his ministry in the Unitarian Church in 1836 and shortly thereafter, in a commencement address at Harvard University, encouraged his listeners to undertake personal explorations of the soul. This spiritual call to arms, which was also articulated in his published writings, earned Emerson dozens of disciples, each of whom followed the dictates of his own conscience.

Second, elevating individual conscience above society's established institutions resulted in a questioning of traditional notions concerning everything from the nature of the state to hygiene and housekeeping. This questioning coincided with and complemented the growing number of reform movements sweeping New England during the nineteenth century, and most transcendentalists sympathized with one reform cause or another. Although they desired reform, their belief in the integrity of the individual led many to spurn collective action as being too restrictive. Particularly in the movement's early years, reform on an individual basis was the only morally acceptable course of action.

From the beginning of the abolitionist movement, many transcendentalists were sympathetic to the cause, but their involvement varied. Some, like Henry David Thoreau, preferred to focus on reforming themselves before undertaking the reformation of those around them; others, like Amos Bronson Alcott, were involved in too many causes to contribute much time or energy to abolition; still others, Theodore Parker among them, threw themselves wholeheartedly into the antislavery effort.

During the late 1840s and 1850s, national events like the Mexican War and the Fugitive Slave Act produced a unanimity among transcendentalists as the events made the moral imperative of the antislavery cause undeniable. One by one, the transcendentalists concluded that slavery contaminated the moral basis of the whole country and clearly violated God's higher law. The fact that the U.S. government increasingly appeared to sanction the institution particularly infuriated the transcendentalists.

For many transcendentalists, philosophy gave way to action when authorities decided to return the fugitive Anthony Burns to slavery. The crowd that rushed the Boston courthouse to free Burns contained many transcendentalists, including Parker and Alcott. Transcendentalists spoke out publicly against slavery, and some aided in the activities of the Underground Railroad. Several fell under John Brown's influence when he toured New England raising additional funds for his work, and the young Transcendentalist Franklin Sanborn was one of "the secret six" who financially supported Brown's raid on Harpers Ferry. In commemorative addresses, Thoreau and Emerson rushed to Brown's defense after the failed insurrection, lauding Brown's high principles and idealism, although they refrained from mentioning his violent acts.

The antislavery movement gained moral strength from the transcendentalists and their increasing willingness to break man-made decrees that violated God's higher law. In this respect, the impact of transcendentalist thought was far greater than the contributions of the transcendentalists themselves. A younger generation of reformers, like Sanborn and Thomas Wentworth Higginson, believed that obedience to a higher law justified all means, including violence and coercion, that were necessary to abolish slavery. This sense of righteousness contributed to the moral backbone of the antislavery cause during the 1850s as it challenged the government on traditional notions concerning the will of the majority and the rights of the governed.

—*Elizabeth Dubrulle*

See also
Brown, John; Burns, Anthony; Fugitive Slave Act of 1850; Harpers Ferry Raid; Higginson, Thomas Wentworth; Thoreau, Henry David; Underground Railroad
For Further Reading
Boller, Paul F. 1974. *American Transcendentalism, 1830–1860: An Intellectual Inquiry.* New York: G. P. Putnam's Sons; Harding, Walter. 1982. *The Days of Henry Thoreau: A Biography.* New York: Dover; Myerson, Joel, ed. 1984. *The Transcendentalists: A Review of Research and Criticism.* New York: Modern Language Association of America; Rose, Anne C. 1981. *Transcendentalism as a Social Movement, 1830–1850.* New Haven, CT: Yale University Press.

TRANSITION FROM SLAVE LABOR TO FREE LABOR, AFRICA

he most striking reality about the transition from slave labor to free labor in Africa is that it was largely a product of the colonial period. That statement is not meant to suggest any Western moral superiority; it is simply a recognition that the primary goal of the European powers in Africa was to transform African political economies into forms that could be more readily exploited by capitalism, and the most easily exploitable system was one that relied on wage labor. A second important aspect of the colonial drive against slavery was that it was a powerful moral justification of the usurpation of political power from traditional authorities entailed in establishing a colonial state. Most involuntary labor systems in Africa were very flexible and already contained ways in which the status of an unpaid worker or a worker's descendants might be elevated over time.

Emancipation as conducted by colonial authorities was always very limited and designed to minimize any change in the structure of power that Europeans had found in place. For example, in Zanzibar and other areas of the Swahili coast, the British gradually constricted the slave trade throughout the nineteenth century until finally, in 1897, the legal status of slavery was abolished. In Zanzibar, those affluent segments of the population that had previously made money through some combination of clove cultivation and trade then began focusing more exclusively on agricultural production, and the former slaves found themselves essentially the poorly paid employees of the same people who had once legally owned them. The result was a stratified society that existed largely unchanged until the overthrow of Arab rule in Zanzibar in 1965.

Although the violent overthrow of an existing political structure in connection with slavery is fairly rare in Africa, maintaining the general social structure after the end of slavery is extremely common. This tendency was clearly seen in those parts of Africa that were governed under indirect rule. In many of the societies, the colonial authorities did not try to change the essential basis of society; they only modified things to the extent necessary for economic exploitation and some deference to Western scruples. In this light, the continued low social status of groups of servile origin in northern Nigeria can be clearly understood, as can the continued influence of former slaveholding figures, like the marabouts (dervishes believed to have supernatural power) of Senegal, in peanut-producing regions.

Occasionally, the abolition of slavery did lead to significant changes in social structure. For instance, in the city of Rabai outside of Mombasa, numerous slaves were able to escape from their surroundings and claim their freedom under the auspices of a British missionary station. They became known as the WaMisheni, or people of the mission. Since they owed their freedom to the Christian mission, they became a small Christian community within the predominately Muslim coastal region of Kenya.

During the colonial period, the region of Africa that experienced the most complete conversion from slave labor to free labor was the future Republic of South Africa. The Boer communities of the Cape Colony and later the Orange Free State and the Transvaal were based on slave labor, but the discovery of diamonds and later gold introduced massive amounts of British capital and new opportunities for jobs. Under these circumstances, it was virtually impossible for the Boers to maintain absolute compulsion over their labor force, but the movement toward wage labor in South Africa did not lead to equality. Instead, after the South African War (1899–1902), the British and the Boers (soon to be Afrikaners) consolidated a white supremacist system of government.

In some parts of Africa, European intervention apparently failed to make a noticeable difference in the system of unpaid labor. Mauritania in the northern part of West Africa is probably the best example. Although the French ruled Mauritania for nearly six decades, French influence was always restricted because of the country's size and difficult terrain. As a result, traditional slavery practices continued almost unabated. Since independence, Mauritania has abolished slavery on several occasions, but the practice continues and periodically causes a crisis. The last serious one occurred in 1989.

—*Anthony Q. Cheeseboro*

For Further Reading
Abdul, Sheriff, and Ed Ferguson. 1991. *Zanzibar under Colonial Rule*. Athens: University of Ohio Press; Miers, Suzanne, and Richard Roberts. 1988. *The End of Slavery in Africa*. Madison: University of Wisconsin Press; Omer-Cooper, J. D. 1994. *History of Southern Africa*. London: James Currey.

TRANSITION FROM SLAVE LABOR TO FREE LABOR, CARIBBEAN

In the late-eighteenth century, society began questioning the entire slavery system. Certain changes in Britain's industrial and trading life began raising doubts in people's minds as to the soundness of supporting the West Indian slave-based economy, and Europeans' new demands for liberty and the wave of humanitarian reform sweeping Britain at the time led Parliament to abolish the slave trade in all British colonies in 1807. Denmark had abolished the trade in that country's three small possessions of St. Thomas, St. Croix, and St. John four years before Britain did; Cuba continued importing slaves until 1865.

Abolishing the slave trade was regarded as a first step, but emancipation was the main objective of the Anti-Slavery Society founded in Britain in 1823. Some abolitionists believed that planters, if prohibited from importing new slaves, would treat those they had better, gradually grant them greater rights and freedom, and eventually agree to full emancipation.

But the abolition of the slave trade had the opposite effect on most planters, especially in the older British colonies. In Jamaica, for example, white residents had long made their own laws and now bitterly resented Parliament's action in abolishing by law a trade vital to their interests. Indeed, they tended to treat their slaves more cruelly, and the planters' hostility naturally caused daily resistance to outright insurrection among slaves like the Jamaican Montego Rebellion (1831). Moreover, abolition did not bring all trading in slaves to an end. Other nations continued the trade, and even in those countries where it had been made illegal, a certain amount of smuggling continued.

In 1833, Britain managed to abolish slavery throughout its colonies despite planters' anger and protests. All slave children under six years of age and any born after that date were freed. All other slaves were to be apprenticed to their masters for four years before becoming completely free. The apprentices had to work for their masters for 40 and a half hours per week without wages in return for lodging, clothing, food, or provision grounds (areas where the former slaves could grow their own food).

According to the British Parliament, the intermediate period of apprenticeship was necessary to prepare the ex-slaves for freedom and to avoid disorders and the sudden economic ruin of the colonies. Apprenticeship itself, though, was difficult for the ex-slaves to understand. They were told that slavery had ended, but they had to work without wages for three-quarters of every week; besides, they were still considered inferior creatures who were bound to have less than whites.

Although England granted a compensation sum of £20 million to be divided among slaveowners for labor losses, most planters resented abolition and emancipation, obliged apprentices to work longer hours, and did not provide food allowances or started to charge for them by forcing the apprentices to pay in the form of extra labor. Provision grounds, once also a regular allowance during slavery, were now rented to apprentices in return for extra hours of work. Determined to grind the very last ounce of work out of their ex-slaves, planters drove and punished them, in some ways more brutally than they had done while slavery lasted.

No provisions were made either by metropolitan or

local governments for the future of the freed slaves after the apprenticeship period. At least during slavery masters had provided huts and land to slaves; now they needed money for a house and a piece of land. In many cases, even though slavery had ended, the freed slaves had to work harder and longer just to survive. Planters offered wages that were as low as possible, and some of them preferred to employ Asian indentured servants, who started to arrive in the Caribbean after the abolition of slavery.

In some cases, the freed slaves were backward and undisciplined, and they settled in the bush and grew only enough food to survive. Others remained with their former masters, in houses to which they had become attached, and tried to make the best of the situation. Relations between employer and laborer remained unsatisfactory, however, and there was much bitterness over irregularity of work, high rentals, and low wages.

In some British colonies, with the help of nonconformist missionaries—Moravian, Methodist, and Baptist—free villages began to be established where freed slaves were almost self-supporting, earning cash for their needs from the sale of provisions grown on their small allotments. Other blacks moved from rural areas to villages and towns where they found jobs as skilled artisans or servants. The luckier ones who had savings started small businesses like vegetable shops and lodging houses.

With the abolition of slavery, production in most of the West Indies colonies collapsed owing to the disorganized cultivation and production of the plantations. With a lack of unpaid labor, production lessened and costs rose. Planters found themselves in heavy debt, and many had to sell or abandon their property. Sugar, rum, and coffee produced in the British colonies could not compete any longer with similar products from Cuba or Brazil where slavery remained legal.

With the collapse of the plantations, many freed slaves who had depended on them for employment found themselves without work. Those who were still employed had to accept starvation wages. Market prices for peasant-grown produce fell while frequent droughts led to crop failures, which increased the distress and disorder. The black population was neither understood nor accepted; the multiracial future of the Caribbean still needed reform and improvement.

—*Luana Tavernier*

See also
Abolition, British Empire; Atlantic Abolitionist Movement; Closing of the African Slave Trade; English Caribbean; French Caribbean; Spanish Caribbean; Sugar Cultivation and Trade; West Indies
For Further Reading
Black, Clinton. 1958. *History of Jamaica.* Harlow, Eng.: Longman Caribbean; Craton, Michael; James Walvin;

and David Wright. 1976. *Slavery, Abolition, and Emancipation.* New York: Longman; Green, William. 1976. *British Slave Emancipation: The Sugar Colonies and the Great Experiment, 1830–1865.* Oxford: Clarendon Press.

TRANSITION FROM SLAVE LABOR TO FREE LABOR, LATIN AMERICA

When evaluating the transition from slave labor to free labor in Latin America, the first thing to consider is that slaves were a rather limited (small) population, except in Haiti. It is also interesting to consider the slave's location at the moment of liberation. Economics figured largely in the change, but there were some other factors as well.

Most slaves who had served in the armies of independent Latin American countries became incorporated into civilian life as freemen, mostly in the towns they had worked in as slaves, but some of them continued on active duty. Some Brazilian slaves were specifically bought to fight in the Triple Alliance War (1865–1870) and were liberated at the end of that war. Upon returning to the communities in which they had once labored as slaves, they followed an integration process similar to that of the slaves who had obtained their liberty by other legal means. In both cases, even when liberation was legally obtained, skin color was an obstacle to gaining complete acceptance by the general population.

On the sugar plantations in continental Hispanic America (where slavery was abolished no later than the 1830s), integration meant a slow movement toward a free life as peasants. Without exception, no economic compensation was given to slaveowners in Hispanic America, nor were slaves made a part of any of the known manumission programs (except in Cuba). Most of the former slaves living in rural areas remained in those locations and became integrated with the natives, which created ethnically different populations: *campesinos afro-mestizos* ("Afro-mestizo peasants") would be a good description of these groups. Runaway slaves who had settled in remote rural communities (Maroons), followed the commonly used agricultural methods and in those settlements that were legalized, the former slaves remained as peasants and developed commercial relations with nearby haciendas and plantations.

Nowhere in Hispanic America were there restrictions to the liberation of slaves. The opinion of travelers to these countries was that during the last years of

Spanish rule, the government's position favored liberation in specific judicial cases, notably when cruelty was involved, but perhaps the most frequent way slaves obtained their freedom was by buying it. Some skilled slaves (notably merchants) had to surrender their profits to their masters and were able to keep just small amounts for their personal use. Others were "rented out," and their salary was paid to their masters. In the cities, where many of the slaves were artisans, there were procedures that allowed them to be incorporated into the free labor force as skilled laborers, and in this way they were able to continue practicing their profession, which allowed some of them to remain living in the same cities and vicinities after they obtained their freedom.

In cities like Lima, Peru; Quito, Ecuador; and Querétaro, Mexico, where textile manufactures had a certain economic importance—and where many slaves worked during the sixteenth and seventeenth centuries—slaves were considered essential by the end of the eighteenth century as most of them had reached the level of *maestria* ("maestro") in one of the different manufacturing processes. Their ability granted them considerable value, which was reflected in the way they were treated after they were freed.

Slaves who bought their freedom had to have some income and some means of surviving, and it was not uncommon to see them struggling to rebuild their families. In the process, they did not hesitate to move from city to city. In the cities, some masters used to free old or crippled slaves, thereby releasing them of their duties and sending them out into the streets to somehow earn enough to subsist or to die. In some cases, slaves who obtained their freedom chose to continue living as part of the homes where they served, homes that sometimes they had never left since the moment they were born.

The avarice shown by masters and the ways in which the slaves obtained their freedom at the end of the eighteenth century were a result of the severe economic crisis that continental Hispanic America was experiencing. The attitude toward *mestizaje* ("miscegenation") on the part of colonial society came to be one that "accepts but does not give" equality to people of mixed blood. The transition from slave labor to free labor in Brazil and Cuba, which occurred in the late-nineteenth century, was similar to that in continental Hispanic America except that manumission or an apprenticeship period applied in both of those countries.

—*Juan M. de la Serna*

TRANSITION FROM SLAVE LABOR TO FREE LABOR, NORTH AMERICA

The transition from slave labor to free labor was part of a global process of political and industrial capitalism whose central tenet was the shift from slave labor to a rural proletariat. The late-eighteenth century witnessed the emergence of a dual revolution that led to the eventual eclipse of slave regimes throughout the nineteenth century. The political-national forces unleashed by the American and French Revolutions, together with the economic free labor forces of English industrialization, increasingly challenged the ancien régime, which was based upon unfree labor.

Throughout the following decades, unfree societies were progressively dismantled by multiple complex circumstances: by legal acts in the Northern states of the United States (1777–1817); by slave revolution in Haiti (1804); by parliamentary bill in the British West Indies (1833–1838); by decree of the tsar in Russia (1861); by civil war in the Southern part of the United States (1865); and by legal decision in the Spanish Caribbean (1886) and Brazil (1888). Small pockets of slave labor survived in Africa and Asia, but they were temporary.

One of the most dramatic transitions from slave to free labor occurred in North America. During the antebellum period in the United States, slave labor in the South and free labor in the North coexisted uneasily. Slavery was the dominant organization of production in the South: the exploitation of slaves ensured a surplus for a planter ruling class while slavery defined society even for nonslaveholders. Meanwhile, free labor, especially wage labor, was becoming more important in the Northern states, which increasingly removed independent producers from the land into the vortex of competitive market relations. These competing systems clashed over the future status of western territories. The result was civil war.

The U.S. Civil War began under different agendas. The North claimed it was fighting for the preservation of the Union; the South said it fought for the protection of its property under states' rights. In actuality, both were fighting over the position of slavery in society, and it was the actions of the slaves themselves who revealed this social reality during the war. Drawing from the armed struggle for control over their own lives and labor, the slaves transformed the Civil War into a struggle for their own emancipation. In various ways including self-emancipation at federal outposts, embracing Union armies, fighting for the army and navy, work slowdowns, and undermining the psychological security of the slave regime, the slaves placed freedom on the Civil War agenda. As slavery withered, free labor relations germinated according to specific regional and historical conditions.

The Thirteenth Amendment to the U.S. Constitution (1865) legally ratified an imminent social process. Slavery was abolished along with the material basis for the plantocracy's domination, but the central transformation in social relations occurred in the master-slave relationship. Former labor lords were transformed into landlords whose property and power were devastated by emancipation. Former slaves gained personal freedom through the culmination of their successful struggle against slavery, but they were also freed from the minimum material support provided through slave ownership. Once the former slaves were forced to work, they were free to starve.

The freed people had only their labor power to compete in a vicious marketplace, and a myriad of labor arrangements cropped up during the postemancipation period, including wage labor, tenant farming, and sharecropping. In this complex situation, the crucial point was that ex-slaves exchanged their labor for some form of compensation, which rendered them landless, without any other property, and poor. They were originally supported by the federal government in their aspirations, but that support gradually withered. Still, the freed people managed to make invisible slave institutions like the family, school, and church visible, and the building, consolidation, and protection of these institutions became the hallmark of subsequent generations.

If slavery meant more than the master-slave relationship, its abolition did also. With emancipation, subsistence farmers became increasingly drawn into the vortex of the cash-crop economy. The path had been cleared for Northern and foreign capitalist penetration into the prostrate South on its own unimpeded terms. This free market, free labor free-for-all contributed to the advent and consolidation of a prolonged agricultural depression from the early 1870s to the mid-1890s. Rural protest, populist politics, and urban migration were the result. This freeing of labor from the land was the ultimate rung in the emancipation ladder, and it reached across all postemancipation societies.

—*Jeffrey R. Kerr-Ritchie*

See also
Civil War, United States
For Further Reading
Berlin, Ira, et al. 1992. *Slaves No More: Three Essays on Emancipation and the Civil War.* Cambridge: Cambridge University Press; Blackburn, Robin. 1988. *The Overthrow of Colonial Slavery, 1776–1848.* London: Verso; Foner, Eric. 1983. *Nothing but Freedom: Emancipation and Its Legacy.* Baton Rouge: Louisiana State University Press; Reidy, Joseph P. 1992. *From Slavery to*

Agrarian Capitalism in the Cotton South: Central Georgia, 1800–1880. Chapel Hill: University of North Carolina Press.

TRANSITION FROM SLAVE LABOR TO FREE LABOR, POLYNESIA

Slavery as a widespread social institution was associated, not with traditional Polynesian culture, but associated with the integration of Polynesian polities into world economic systems. Since European contact in the sixteenth to eighteenth centuries, the islands have been affected by slavery in several different contexts. Initially, foreign traders forcibly took some Polynesians to serve as sailors or overseas workers and contributed to the coercion of labor by chiefs who entered the sandalwood trade. Slavery in the form of contracted and effectively indentured laborers began on commercial plantations in the nineteenth century. In the early twentieth century, the beginning of organized labor and changing legal contexts began the demise of the most egregious abuses associated with the contract labor system.

Polynesian cultures at the time of European contact in the late-eighteenth century often exhibited a high degree of social complexity and stratification, as was evident in the paramount chiefdoms of Hawaii, Tonga, Tahiti, and other polities. Although these societies often distinguished on a broad level among hereditary chiefs, those with achieved status, and commoners—and designated numerous distinctions along that continuum—it is incorrect to consider terms like the Hawaiian *kauwa* (a landless, untouchable caste confined to living on reservations) to mean slave in the modern sense. Instead, Polynesian words that have been translated as "slave" frequently were used metaphorically to refer to master-servant relationships and as insults.

However, in some Polynesian societies, a hereditary class of so-called slaves did exist, although the concept of slave ownership was poorly developed, if at all. Because of their lack of status, the slaves were vulnerable to being chosen for sacrifice or conscripted to perform difficult or onerous tasks. In other cases, captives of war were forced to serve the victors. However, with a few exceptions, coercion to get labor from commoners was a prerogative exercised only infrequently by chiefs, and often was utilized in the context of constructing public works like irrigation ditches and temples.

In the aftermath of the late-eighteenth-century voyages of discovery, Polynesia was soon populated with traders and opportunists. Although it was more common in Melanesia and Micronesia, the practice of kidnapping islanders for work in the sugarcane fields of Australia (known as "blackbirding") also occurred in western Polynesia from the late 1840s to the 1880s. Rapa Nui (Easter Island) people were also forcibly taken to work in South America. In most of Polynesia, enslavement took a more indirect route. After sandalwood traders and other merchants had maneuvered Polynesian chiefs into debt in the early-nineteenth century, the only escape for the chiefs was to force commoners to harvest sandalwood—even if doing so meant that subsistence staple crops would fail.

It was only in the mid- to late-nineteenth century, however, that the advent of large-scale commercial agriculture on some of the islands of Polynesia led to the rise of a labor system that amounted to indentured, if not always permanent, servitude for the immigrants who were contracted to do the work. Plantation managers maintained ethnically segregated workforces, and the European foremen often had free rein to use physical force on the Asian and Filipino workers. Laborers' contracts could be sold to other plantations, or laborers could be hired out for shorter periods with no recourse. Cooperation of the island governments in the form of legislation and police enforcement meant that attempts to escape met with fines, imprisonment, and sometimes physical violence.

As the first decades of the twentieth century passed, several factors led to the demise of the contract labor system that had previously held workers in de facto bondage. The realization that they would not soon return home caused many workers to send for marriage partners, and they became permanent immigrants. Wives sometimes began small businesses rather than working in the fields and thus brought in income that was not encumbered by the plantation. As their contracts expired, many contract laborers sought their own farmland or went into business, often cooperative ventures that pooled the meager capital of several individuals to increase viability.

Despite segregationist management, the different ethnic groups also eventually realized the value of unified organization, and after mostly unsuccessful strikes staged by one group or another, unified strikes caused management to begin making concessions in the 1920s. Even the practice of bringing in new laborers when the old ones demanded better conditions or more pay eventually proved unsustainable, as governments balked at new waves of immigrants and in some cases enacted legislation to protect workers' rights.

By the time World War II erupted in the Pacific, many plantation operations had moved from being harsh employers who kept workers obligated through total economic control to a somewhat more progressive, if paternalistic, strategy of providing benefits such as recreational facilities. Today, many older plantation workers look back on the past with fondness and consider the modern workforce to be a comparatively insecure and harsh place.

—Maurice Major

See also
Agricultural Labor in the Pacific Islands; Pacific Islands and Queensland, Indentured Labor in; Peruvian Slave Trade in the Pacific Islands
For Further Reading
Malo, David, and Nathaniel Emerson, trans. 1951. *Hawaiian Antiquities (Moolelo Hawaii)*. Honolulu: Bernice Pauahi Bishop Museum; Scarr, Deryck. 1968. *A Cruize in a Queensland Labour Vessel to the South Seas*. Honolulu: University of Hawaii Press; Takaki, Roland. 1983. *Pau Hana: Plantation Life and Labor in Hawaii*. Honolulu: University of Hawaii Press.

TRANSITION FROM SLAVE LABOR TO FREE LABOR, SOUTH AFRICA

Slavery existed almost from the beginning of the Cape Colony in the mid-seventeenth century when the Dutch East India Company tried to entice white freemen into the colony with offers of land and slaves imported from Guinea and Angola. This early experiment failed because of the slaves' recalcitrance, but by the early-eighteenth century, slavery was an acceptable alternative to what was perceived to be expensive free white labor. Indigenous Khoikhoi and San were enslaved, but most slaves at this time came from East African slaving areas—Madagascar and Indonesia—via the East Indian Ocean slave route. Eventually native-born slaves, many with white fathers, gave the Cape a natural slave increase, which created the Cape Coloured population today.

Slave labor in the Cape Colony was diversified because there was no single, dominant crop. Wine and grain growers used slaves in groups of 10 or 20 while other whites used slaves as servants or as skilled or unskilled laborers. Frontier Boers (South Africans of Dutch or Huguenot descent) impressed landless Khoikhoi into their service. Violence between vagabond whites (called knechts), landed burghers, and the Xhosa-Nguni over cattle, land, and women set the stage for the specifics of historical events.

After slavery was abolished in 1833, another practice gained ascendancy. Apprenticeship, first used with children of Khoikhoi and San, was now used in connection with various African peoples by settlers who acquired this labor via raiding expeditions and by intimidating parents to give up their children. The law of apprenticeship led white farmers to acquire laborers and treat them like slaves, but without the legal sanction of slavery.

The slave system was inherited by the British, who assumed control of the colony temporarily in 1795 and permanently in 1815. The British proceeded toward abolition, which was achieved in 1833 throughout the global imperial crown areas. The legal basis of civil rights for the native African revolved around British efforts at such legal forms as the 1809 Calendon code, which regulated the use of African labor.

The earl of Calendon, governor of Cape Colony, insisted that there be equitable labor contracts and that they should include regular pay periods and outlaw debt-peonage. The Black Circuit decision of 1812 recognized white hegemony but indicted various whites for violating the code. Missionaries were able, by 1828, to provide protection for Africans under the Fiftieth Ordinance, which placed limits on forced labor and peonage, and placed time constraints on apprenticeships. Equitable contract procedures were further strengthened by the Master and Servant Acts of 1842 and 1856.

The Boer reaction to British rule was one of massive resistance, especially to labor legislation that elevated the native to a legal level of equality approximate to whites. Eventually, that and other issues led to the Great Trek, which occurred between 1836 and 1843. The trekkers settled in Natal, the Transvaal, and the Orange Free State, which the British recognized in the Sand River Convention of 1852 (South African Republic/Transvaal) and the Bloemfontein Convention of 1854 (Orange Free State). In both conventions, the Boers agreed not to maintain slavery, involuntary labor, or trade in slaves.

The discovery of diamonds in 1867 in Griqualand further solidified African labor's place in the emerging industrialized, capitalist economy, as did the discovery of gold on the Witwatersrand in 1886. The tensions that had led to the Great Trek coupled with this mineral revolution led to the Anglo-Boer War of 1899–1902 and ultimately to the Act of Union in 1910.

The mineral revolution also led to further legal change such as the Glen Grey Act of 1894, which impacted on the black Transkei area. The 1894 act was a purported attempt to smooth the transition from slavery to freedom by establishing "native districts," in which former slaves could become acculturated "whites" by cultivating their private landed property. In reality, the act permitted Cecil Rhodes to obtain workers for the Kimberely mines since land allotments were scarce in the native districts and the landless Africans were forced to seek outside work.

Rhodes's tactics became a model for Afrikaner political and economic interests after the Act of Union in 1910. For instance, the Native Land Act of 1913 accelerated the creation of labor reserves by restricting African land acquisition and thereby African peasant agriculture. The lure of paid work in the mineral industry coupled with the deterioration of native land productivity and the shortage of land forced native African peasants into industrial employment.

—*Malik Simba*

For Further Reading
Cell, John. 1982. *The Highest Stage of White Supremacy*. London: Cambridge University Press; Ross, Robert. 1983. *Cape of Torments*. London: Routledge; Shell, Robert. 1994. *Children of Bondage*. London: Wesleyan University Press; Wilson, Monica, and Leonard Thompson, eds. 1969. *The Oxford History of South Africa*. New York: Oxford University Press.

TRANS-SAHARAN SLAVE TRADE

The Trans-Saharan slave trade was an important aspect of the economy of both northern and central Africa and a major source of slaves for the Islamic world from the tenth to the nineteenth centuries. Slaves captured in sub-Saharan and central Africa were shipped by caravan to points across North Africa and thereafter distributed locally or shipped abroad. Black slaves were called 'abīd (singular 'abd), the generic Arabic word for "slave" and a word that differentiated them from Turkish and Caucasian slaves, šaqàliba or mamàlik (singular mamlūk).

Carthaginians were acquiring slaves from Saharan merchants by the fifth century B.C., but it was not until the domestication and dissemination of the camel (fourth century A.D.) that a large-scale trans-Saharan trade in slaves or any other commodity became viable. The slave trade was brisk by the ninth century, especially to Ifrïqiyya (Tunisia and Algeria), along central Saharan routes. This trade fostered economic development in the bilàd al-Sudàn ("the land of the blacks"), which stretched across central Africa.

There a demand for Turkish and European slaves gradually developed and persisted throughout the eighteenth century, at which time the traffic of black slaves was booming. It did not decline until the second half of the nineteenth century, when it was gradually driven underground owing to the efforts of European states to bring about the abolition of slavery in Muslim lands, which resulted in a general ban on slave trading within the Ottoman Empire in 1857. Despite the ban, the slave trade persisted openly in some areas, including Morocco, as late as 1912. Although the number of slaves shipped across the Sahara is difficult to estimate with any confidence, a yearly average of

8,700 has been suggested for the tenth and eleventh centuries, 5,500 per year during the sixteenth century, and a peak of 14,500 yearly in the nineteenth century.

Three major trade corridors led from south to north: from Timbuktu (in Mali) to Morocco, from Kano (around Lake Chad) to Fezzan (in southern Libya) and on to Ifrïqiyya, and from Darfur and Abyssinia (eastern Sudan) to Egypt. Beginning in the twelfth century, caravans also ran directly between Mali and Egypt. Although trade in gold and luxury items dominated the westernmost route from Timbuktu, the central corridor to Fezzan was given over almost exclusively to the slave trade.

Within the central corridor, there were three main routes: from Aïr to Gadames, from Kano to Fezzan, and from Bornu to Benghazi. By the ninth century, Zawila in Fezzan was established as the main entrepôt. The Egyptian routes from West Africa, or up the Forty Days Road (darb al-arba'in) from Nubia to Cairo, were also important but did not approach the central corridor in terms of trade volume. Egyptians, particularly after the eleventh century, preferred slaves of Turkish or Caucasian extraction.

In the early centuries, Muslim merchants obtained slaves in exchange for staples or salt, the latter an indispensable commodity that was in short supply in central Africa. Later, the emphasis switched to manufactured goods, horses, and in particular, weapons. Finally, in the late-eighteenth and early-nineteenth centuries, East Indian cowries became an important currency in the slave trade.

Sub-Saharan peoples generally favored a nomadic lifestyle, and there existed the usual tensions between mounted pastoralists and sedentary farmers. Nomadic tribes such as the Hausa, aided by superior horses and weapons brought from the north, captured sedentary peoples for export as slaves. Some slaving expeditions penetrated deep into central Africa, but slaves were also taken in clashes or raids between rival mounted peoples or by simple kidnapping.

Among the sub-Saharan tribes, slaves were an important means of exchange, particularly as tribute. There was a strong local market, as slave ownership was common even among the less than wealthy. As was typical in the Islamic world, women and children were preferred for slave export. Women had value as domestic slaves and concubines, and although African women were not as highly prized for beauty as European concubines, they had a reputation for trustworthiness and loyalty.

Male slaves found themselves used in various roles. As in the classical world, slavery in Islam was not necessarily a barrier to career advancement, and some African slaves filled important administrative functions while others were merchants or artisans, but most male African slaves were employed as agricultural workers—as, for example, in Morocco's date palm industry. The Aghlabids of Ifrïqiyya (800–909) and the Egyptian Fatimids (969–1171) used Africans as military slaves, but this practice had all but stopped by the mid-eleventh century.

Black Africans suffered from a general prejudice, which Muslim Arabs inherited from their intellectual predecessors of the classical world, and even after Islam was solidly established in the Sudan, such prejudices persisted. Black Muslims often found themselves captives, despite the Islamic prohibition against enslaving fellow Muslims, in protest of which the Muslim king of Bornu (in northern Nigeria) sent a letter to the Egyptian sultan in 1391.

When Europeans established direct trade links with West Africa (drawn initially by the gold of the Akan forest in Ghana), they established a transatlantic slave trade that dwarfed the Saharan trade in volume. Nevertheless, this new trade, which was to supply new markets created by European colonialism, did not dampen the Saharan trade that supplied North Africa and countries to the east. Through the eighteenth century, caravans still arrived in Tunis and Tripoli carrying no other cargo but slaves, and in the late-nineteenth century, when the slave trade was generally on the decline, slaves were still Bornu's main export. The trans-Saharan trade in slaves and other items was an important factor in drawing central Africa into the Islamic world's cultural and economic orbit and in fostering political and urban development in the Sudan.

—*Brian Catlos*

See also
Africa; Mali; Ottoman Empire; Salt Trade; Sudan
For Further Reading
Austen, Ralph. 1979. "The Trans-Saharan Slave Trade: A Tentative Census." In *The Uncommon Market: Essays in the Economic History of the Atlantic Slave Trade*. Ed. Henry Gemery and Jan S. Hogendorn. New York: Academic Press; Fisher, Allan, and Humphrey Fisher. 1970. *Slavery and Muslim Society in Africa; The Institution in Saharan and Sudanic Africa and the Trans-Saharan Trade*. London: C. Hurst; Lewis, Bernard. 1990. *Race and Slavery in the Middle East*. Oxford: Oxford University Press; Murray, Gordon. 1989. *Slavery in the Arab World*. New York: New Amsterdam.

TRELAWNEY TOWN MAROONS

*T*he Trelawney Town Maroons were the first of Jamaica's Maroon bands to sign a peace treaty with the British after the First Maroon War (1730–1739). Maroons, communities of runaway slaves, were quite common throughout slaveholding regions of the Americas, and the first African slaves to escape and form their own communities were among the earliest slaves brought to the Americas. Spanish slaves on Hispaniola fled into the mountains and intermarried with the native Arawak Indians. Spaniards named these slaves *cimarrones* (from the word *cima*, meaning "mountaintop"). The French called their runaways *marrons*, and the English later corrupted that name to Maroons.

The first *cimarrones* set a precedent for the region. They fought the Spaniards to a standstill until a 1533 treaty gave them a large territory in the interior of Hispaniola where they would not be bothered; the *cimarrones* agreed to return any future runaway slaves. By the late-sixteenth century, all Spanish-held islands and many mainland colonies had such communities. When the English invaded Jamaica in 1655, Spanish ranchers freed their slaves, and they joined a Maroon colony in the island's interior. The English hold on Jamaica was secured only when the Maroon leader, Juan de Bolas, signed a treaty in 1658 in which his group agreed to stop supporting the Spanish guerrilla campaign. In return, the English allowed the Maroons territory in the colony's western interior.

English slaves on Jamaica continued escaping singly, in small groups, and in large rebellions. At least 300 slaves from St. Anne's Parish rebelled and fled to interior mountain settlements in 1673. In 1720, the Jamaican government made an agreement with the Miskito, a mixed Afro-Indian people from the British settlement along Nicaragua's coast, to assist in capturing the Maroons. The Miskito had been quite helpful in protecting English smuggling routes in Nicaragua's highlands, and the Jamaicans hoped their mountain expertise and knowledge of African military tactics would help in penetrating the Maroon strongholds. The Miskito, if successful, could return home with pay and any plunder they took, or they could remain and settle the Maroon lands. This attempt to replace unfriendly Africans with Afro-Indian allies failed.

By the 1730s, four permanent Maroon villages existed on the island: Trelawney Town, Crawford Town, Nanny Town, and Accompong. Conflict developed as pressure to open more land for sugar cultivation brought English planters, intent on clearing new estates, into Maroon territory. The proximity of free Africans proved a powerful incentive for slaves on these new plantations to escape, and the Maroons raided the plantations for supplies. The Jamaican government dispatched troops to remove and capture the Maroons, but this First Maroon War was fought to a standstill as the British troops were unable to flush the independent Africans from their mountain garrisons.

In 1739, the English decided to solve their Maroon problem through diplomacy, and Captain Cudjoe of the Trelawney Town Maroons was the first to agree. In return for reservations on which the Maroons could choose their own governments and make their own laws, the Maroons agreed to stop raiding plantations, return any runaways, and help the militia suppress any future slave revolts. English commissioners lived in the villages to maintain friendly relations.

The peace with the Maroons lasted until 1795 when the Trelawney Town Maroons became displeased after the new English commissioner assigned to their village had two Maroons flogged for stealing pigs from plantations. The local parish government agreed to have the commissioner replaced, but the island's new governor overruled the decision. He feared the large Maroon population and believed that indulging them would encourage a full-scale slave revolt similar to the one that had occurred in Saint Domingue (Haiti). Maroons ambushed British troops sent to capture Trelawney Town, and the British military commander decided on a new strategy, laying siege to Maroon territory by encircling it with military outposts. The Maroons, caught in a war they had no desire to fight, agreed to surrender in return for amnesty.

Those Maroons who surrendered or were captured after the deadline were shipped to Nova Scotia as laborers, and that group eventually migrated to Sierra Leone. Jamaica's remaining Maroon villages agreed to uphold provisions of the 1739 treaty, and peace prevailed between the plantations and villages. But after this untoward British military action, the Maroons turned a blind eye to runaway slaves who entered their territory but lived apart from the Maroon settlements.

—*Kimberly Henke Breuer*

See also
Haitian Revolution; Jamaica; Palmares; *Quilombos*
For Further Reading
Agorsah, E. Kofi, ed. 1994. *Maroon Heritage: Archaeological, Ethnographic, and Historical Perspectives.* Barbados: Canoe Press; Campbell, Mavis Christine. 1988. *The Maroons of Jamaica, 1655–1796: A History of Resistance, Collaboration, and Betrayal.* South Hadley, MA: Bergin and Garvey; Price, Richard, ed. 1979. *Maroon Societies: Rebel Slave Communities in the Americas.* Baltimore: Johns Hopkins University Press.

TRICKSTER

A trickster is one who swindles or plays tricks or a figure who exists to play tricks, swindle, or cheat. In folklore, a trickster lives by his wits and represents conflicting images of good and bad. As a narrative genre, trickster tales include any story involving a trickster and his deeds—a character whose powers both create and destroy, whose role in life is both hero and villain. This character and narrative genre often appear in a subcategory of folklore known as the schwank, an elaborate, relatively long, and well-structured humorous narrative focusing on human frailty.

Arguably one of the most studied of the folklore genres, the trickster narrative remains one of the most problematic areas to define. In an essay on the trickster's nature, Carl Jung defined him as "god, animal, and man all in one, at once subhuman and superhuman, bestial and devine [sic], characterized chiefly by unconsciousness and unreason" (Dorson, 1972). Both creative genius and destructive power identify the trickster figure. A universal character in folk narratives, he has brought humankind not only fire, knowledge, and power but also disease, misery, and despair. Trickster is a study in contrasts, for he plays the roles of both leader/superior and follower/slave. Although he can be creative and benevolent, bringing those items that define culture, he behaves in a manner inconsistent with society's norms.

Almost all folk narrative traditions know trickster by many names. Anansi, the spider-man of West African, Caribbean, and Gulf Coast lore, and characters like Brer Fox and Brer Rabbit are the most generally recognizable. John in American slave tales, and Ti Malice, Nonc' Bouki, Jean Saute, and Jean L'Espirit in Haitian lore are also recognizable tricksters. He also appears in Native American lore as the human Manabozho in the central woodlands, Coyote among the plains and western groups, and Raven in the Pacific Northwest, and he has his place and narrative cycle in every known folk group. Trickster is often a hero. Through wit and power, he brings things to people, such as fire, knowledge, and social order, but he is just as likely to bring chaos, disorder, and pain to people or to himself through attempts at cleverness.

On a basic level, trickster stories explain society's rules through their violation. By showing how not to act, the stories reinforce social order. In the story "Anansi and the Bananas," Anansi returns home with three bananas to feed a family of four. He had dreamed of eating the bananas ever since acquiring them, but he knew he had to take something home to his family. Hatching a clever plan and playing the role of martyr, Anansi encourages his wife and two children to eat their bananas, insisting that he will get satisfaction from knowing they have eaten, even though he has to go hungry. His wife and children take pity on him, and each offers Anansi half of their banana, thus giving Anansi one and a half bananas.

On the surface, the tale can be read to show Anansi's cleverness, and how he can contrive to get what he wants. But a West Indian would explain the story as an admonition not to take advantage of your family and to make sure that you meet family obligations before catering to personal needs and desires. Showing how the rules are violated exemplifies proper behavior and order.

Trickster stories also show the general inequities of a current system or lampoon the prevailing or dominant power structure. In most slave narrative collections, there is typically a trickster figure who inverts societal norms by besting his master, through either cleverness or his master's foolishness. In many of the John tales in the Southern part of the United States, the slave usually gets the better of his master through a combination of his wit and the master's foolishness.

In one of those tales, John asks his master the names of various items around the farm, such as barn, mule, house, fire, and water. Thinking he can trick John, the master gives a litany of nonsensical names for the items, and John goes along with his master by repeating the nonsense names. When the barn catches on fire, endangering the mule and the master's farm, John reports to the master using the nonsensical words for these things. The report makes no sense to the master, and he loses all in the fire. In this tale, underestimation of John causes harm to the master rather than making John look foolish. In this case, the message is a rebuttal of the prevailing ideology, which viewed John and all slaves as ignorant, and demonstrates how the master's poor judgment caused him more harm than it did his slave.

Trickster's meaning and his stories rely upon a recognition of tricksters as liminal characters, which means that the figures operate in a realm that is neither totally good nor totally evil but cross back and forth across the line ascribed by society as separating ethical and unethical behavior. The trickster draws both positive and negative results from his behavior. Figures like Anansi almost always get hurt for their misdeeds, but others like John exemplify the folly of those who would deny the innate intelligence and equality of all.

In that sense, the trickster narrative operates as a steam valve. That is, by expressing discontent with the current social situation in the form of a story or series of stories, teller and audience exchange ideas about how the social situation can be improved. For example, stories in which the trickster and his deeds invert the current order—John tales for example—inequities in the current social order can be discussed in such a way as to avoid direct conflict with the controlling powers. Thus, through a combination of positive and negative actions, tricksters allow narratives to present the proper rules, roles, and perceived norms as defined by the societies in which the tales circulate.

—*Randal S. Allison*

See also
Anansi Stories; Folktales
For Further Reading
Abrahams, Roger D. 1966. "Some Varieties of Heroes in America." *Journal of the Folklore Institute* 3 (3): 341–362; Babcock-Abrahams, Barbara. 1975. "A Tolerated Margin of Mess: The Trickster and His Tales Reconsidered." *Journal of the Folklore Institute* 11 (3): 147–186; Brunvand, Jan Harold. 1986. *The Study of American Folklore: An Introduction.* New York: W. W. Norton; Courlander, Harold. 1985. *The Drum and the Hoe: Life and Lore of the Haitian People.* Berkeley, London, and Los Angeles: University of California Press; Dorson, Richard M., ed. 1972. *African Folklore.* Bloomington: Indiana University Press.

TRUTH, SOJOURNER
(C. 1797–1883)

Abolitionist orator Sojourner Truth was a shrewd campaigner who knew the value of publicity to a worthy cause.

Sojourner Truth was an emancipated slave who became a prominent independent orator for women's rights, antislavery, and freedmen's rights. In 1826, Truth left her New York owner and took refuge with a nearby white family, the Van Wagenens. When she refused to return to her owner, Isaac Van Wagenen purchased her to keep her out of jail. Freed in 1827 under New York's gradual emancipation law, Truth sued later that year to have her son freed from slavery. Most African Americans did not turn to the courts for redress, and those who did rarely succeeded, but Truth won her son's freedom. She had a religious conversion and in 1832 joined the Kingdom of Matthias, a religious cult that collapsed in scandal two years later. Determined to become a traveling evangelist independent of any church, she changed her name from Isabella to Sojourner; by some accounts, she said that God gave her the last name Truth.

She did not actively work against slavery until about 1850. In the years that followed, she was an effective itinerant speaker for abolitionism and women's rights in New England, New York, Pennsylvania, and the Midwest. She spoke extemporaneously and with great power; like other ex-slave orators, she incorporated her own experiences into her speeches, and like other preachers, she drew on parables and lively images. Because Truth was illiterate, her words have come to us through accounts written by other people, accounts that are necessarily shaped by their interpretation of her.

Her best known speech, "Ar'n't I a Woman," is a case in point. Truth spoke at an 1851 women's rights meeting in Akron, Ohio; twelve years later, Francis Gage, an abolitionist and women's rights leader, wrote an account of the speech, which was then included in an 1875 revision of Truth's *Narrative of the Life of Sojourner Truth.* Gage cast the speech in a caricature of slave dialect, which Truth herself did not use. Moreover, some historians argue that Truth may not have given the speech at all. Her autobiography, which she sold to help support herself, was dictated to Olive Gilbert, a white abolitionist. Truth was a shrewd woman, and she understood the value of the stories told about her effectiveness as an orator.

After the U.S. Civil War, Truth continued to work for equal rights for women and especially for African Americans. She helped resettle freedmen and campaigned for western land for them, attempted to desegregate the Washington, D.C., streetcars, and tried to vote in Michigan. "Ar'n't I a Woman" has made her important to the twentieth-century women's rights movement and civil rights activists, but the facts of her life justify seeing her as a strong and independent black woman fighting for justice.

—*Andrea M. Atkin*

For Further Reading
Mabee, Carleton. 1993. *Sojourner Truth: Slave, Prophet, Legend.* New York: New York University Press; Painter, Nell Irvin. 1996. *Sojourner Truth: A Life, a Symbol.* New York: W. W. Norton; Truth, Sojourner. 1991. *Narrative of Sojourner Truth: A Bondswoman of Olden Time.* Ed. Olive Gilbert. New York: Oxford University Press.

TUBMAN, HARRIET
(C. 1821–1913)

Born a slave in Dorchester County, Maryland, Harriet Tubman's parents, Harriet Greene Ross and Benjamin Ross, had 10 other children. As a child, Harriet was assigned simple domestic chores, but she was moved to the fields in her early teens, and there, despite her small stature, Tubman developed legendary physical strength and stamina. When she attempted to prevent the punishment of another slave by the overseer, Tubman was hit on the head with a two-pound weight and often wore a turban in later life to hide the scar. Her marriage to John Tubman, a free black, did not survive her escape to freedom in Pennsylvania in 1849, for when she returned for him, he had already remarried and refused to accompany her north. Tubman continued to use his name, however—even after she remarried.

For more than a decade, Tubman made numerous trips back into the slave South to bring slaves to freedom in the North, and her success as a "rescuer" of slaves resulted in the circulation of reward posters bearing her description throughout the South and the border states. She armed herself with a rifle, both to protect herself from slave catchers and to bolster the courage of a slave who might change his or her mind and endanger the others. Tubman's religious faith strengthened her in her weariness, and she often sang spirituals as she accompanied fugitives on their journey. Although she most often worked alone, Tubman was in touch with other workers along the Underground Railroad, including William Still of Pennsylvania, and Charlotte Forten and Frederick Douglass commended her work to undermine slavery.

During the U.S. Civil War, Tubman acted as a scout for Union military operations. Because of her generosity to others, she was often penniless herself. Petitions to the War Department on Tubman's behalf for a pension for services rendered were unsuccessful, though in 1890, she finally received a widow's pension for the service her second husband (Nelson Davis) had rendered to the Union army. After the war, Tubman focused her energies on women's rights and helping the poor, working with the National Association of Colored Women, which later granted Tubman a lifetime pension. Because of her religious convictions, Tubman also worked closely with black churches, soliciting donations of used clothing and food for the poor and elderly in New York State, where she lived.

Tubman used money from her own meager store to buy a small parcel of land adjacent to her house to erect a home for the elderly poor, which was ultimately operated by the African Methodist Episcopal Zion Church. An invalid in her old age, Tubman lived for two years at the Harriet Tubman Home for Aged and Indigent Colored People until her death in 1913. She has been honored by a U.S. postage stamp, and her home in Auburn, New York, is recognized as a national landmark.

Although she was one of a limited number of slave women who successfully escaped, because she was illiterate, Tubman left no memoir. Still, historian George Rawick perhaps said it best: "Why must we always use Nat as the name for the rebellious slave? Why not Harriet?" (Sterling, 1984).

—*Dale Edwyna Smith*

For Further Reading
Quarles, Benjamin. 1969. *Black Abolitionists.* New York: Oxford University Press; Sterling, Dorothy. 1984. *We Are Your Sisters: Black Women in the Nineteenth Century.* New York: Norton.

TUCKER, ST. GEORGE
(1752–1827)

The author of a five-volume U.S. edition of *Blackstone's Commentaries* (1803) and *Dissertation on Slavery* (1796) as well as being a noted jurist, St. George Tucker was the only prominent member of the generation that fought in the American Revolution to publish a plan for abolishing slavery. Tucker was born in Bermuda in 1752, and in 1771, he went to the American colony of Virginia to study law under George Wythe at the College of William and Mary. Tucker became a member of the Virginia Bar in 1774, but his law practice was shortened by the American Revolution. Tucker, who reached the rank of lieutenant colonel, was injured at Yorktown. After the war, Tucker practiced law at the General Court, Chancery Court, and Court of Appeals in Virginia. In 1786, he served as part of Virginia's delegation at the Annapolis Convention, a forerunner of the Constitutional Convention. In 1790, he was appointed professor of law and police at the College of William and Mary, replacing George Wythe.

Tucker considered the introduction of slavery into the American colonies as one of the country's greatest misfortunes and sought advice on how it might be ended in Virginia. He corresponded with prominent figures in Massachusetts—including Jeremy Belknap, James Sullivan, and John Adams—"having observed, with much pleasure, that slavery [had] been wholly exterminated from . . . Massachusetts" (St. George Tucker to Jeremy Belknap, January 24, 1795). Tucker posed a series of 11 questions "respecting the Introduction, Progress, and Abolition of Slavery in Massachusetts." The correspondence continued into summer 1795, and in 1796, Tucker published *A Dissertation on Slavery: With a Proposal for the Gradual Abolition of It, in the State of Virginia*, the only significant antislavery pamphlet to come out of Virginia in the early years of the United States.

Tucker published his edition of *Blackstone's Commentaries* (1803) with annotations and appendixes commenting on the law of the United States and on the law of Virginia—his *Dissertation on Slavery* was one of the appendixes. Tucker clearly recognized the tragic irony of the continuance of slavery in a land that had fought a revolution for freedom. "Whilst we were offering up vows at the shrine of liberty, and sacrificing hecatombs upon her . . . we were imposing upon our fellow men, who differ in complexion from us, *slavery,* ten thousand times more cruel than the utmost extremity of those grievances and oppressions, of which we complained" (Cullen, 1987).

Despite his impassioned sentiments, Tucker was no radical abolitionist. His plan called for a gradual emancipation that would not eliminate all slavery in Virginia for nearly a century. Tucker himself was a substantial slaveholder, having acquired slaves on his marriage in 1778 to Frances Bland, the widow of John Randolph of Matoax. Moreover, when given the opportunity as a jurist to rule that slavery was outlawed by the Virginia constitution, Tucker refused to do so.

In 1803, Tucker resigned from William and Mary, and in 1804, he was appointed to the Virginia Supreme Court of Appeals. *Hudgins v. Wrights* came before that court from a ruling of Chancellor George Wythe, Tucker's teacher and predecessor at William and Mary. Wythe had ruled that the Virginia Constitution's declaration that all men are free and equal abolished slavery. Judge Tucker disagreed, noting that this provision of the Virginia Bill of Rights was "notoriously framed with a cautious eye" and applied only to free persons (1 Hen. and M.[Va.] 134 [1806]). Despite Tucker's limitations as an antislavery advocate, he should be remembered most as the only Vir-

ginian of the revolutionary era to make a genuine attempt to abolish slavery.

—*David M. Cobin*

For Further Reading
Cullen, Charles T. 1987. *St. George Tucker and Law in Virginia, 1772–1804*. New York: Garland; Kurland, Phillip B., and Lerner, Ralph. 1987. *The Founders' Constitution*. Chicago: University of Chicago Press; Tucker, St. George, ed. 1996. *Blackstone's Commentaries.* 5 vols. Trenton, NJ: Law Book Exchange.

TURAY I
See **Muhammad Turay I**

TURKISH CAPTIVITY

The Turkish captivity, or Tyrkjarán as it is called in Icelandic, was a pirate raid that occurred in 1627 and resulted in the enslavement of some 380 Icelanders in North Africa. Most of them never returned home.

At the time of the captivity, Iceland was a subject of the Danish crown. Denmark maintained what little defenses there were on the island, appointed all officials, and also licensed traders. It had long been the custom to send a military ship from Denmark to Iceland each spring to protect Danish interests there, but owing to financial problems and government turmoil in Denmark resulting from the Thirty Years War (1618–1648), the ship was late in 1627.

In that year, four ships from Algeria, which was at that time part of the Ottoman Empire, took advantage of Iceland's remoteness and lack of defenses and raided the island. The main objective must have been captives, either to enslave or to hold for ransom, as Iceland had little else of value. Two ships raided Grindavik on Cape Reykjanes on Iceland's southwestern corner and took captives and a merchant ship.

Then they went around the cape with the intention of raiding Bessastadir, the home of the island's Danish governor. The settlement was fairly well defended, however, so the raiders turned back, leaving one of the raiding ships stranded. Although the weather was calm, the Algerians were permitted to transfer their captives and booty from the stranded ship to the captured merchant ship without interference from the governor or his troops, which caused much bitterness between the Icelanders and their overlords.

The other two ships spent several days raiding the east coast of the island. They took captives at several settlements from Lon on the southeastern corner of the island to Faskrudsfjord, which is about halfway up Iceland's east coast. Then they turned south and met up with the ships that had raided Cape Reykjanes.

The raiders then attacked the Westman Islands (Vestmannaeyjar), a small group of volcanic islands off Iceland's south coast. The raiders burned buildings, robbed, and took captives for two days in the Westman Islands before returning to Algeria. The main booty of the raid was human beings: almost 400 Icelanders, including several leading citizens, were captured to be sold at auction in Algiers.

The main purpose of taking the captives seems to have been to force them to be ransomed, because a year later, one of them, the Reverend Ólafur Egilsson, who had been the priest in the Westman Islands, was released with instructions to go to Denmark and urge the king to ransom his subjects.

Egilsson's pleas fell on deaf ears, however, as the Danish treasury had been drained by the Thirty Years War. Attempts to gather funds through voluntary contributions and even special taxes dragged out, and it was not until 1636 that money was sent to Algeria to ransom the captive Icelanders. Only 35 were released. It is said that about 100 of the Icelandic captives had embraced Islam and did not want to return home, a few had escaped, and the fate of the rest is unknown. It is certain that some did not survive the radical change in climate, and others died of natural causes and the nature of their circumstances. Of the 35 who were released, only 27 survived the journey from Algeria to Denmark.

Hallgrímur Petursson, a young divinity student in Copenhagen, was engaged to "rechristianize" the former captives. When one, Gudridur Simonardottir, became pregnant by him, he was sent home to Iceland. Hallgrímur and Gudridur were fined for "loose living" but afterward were permitted to marry. Hallgrímur wrote a considerable body of religious poetry and today is recognized as one of Iceland's most important poets.

As a result of the Turkish captivity, "Turkish pirates" entered Icelandic folklore as terrifying bogeymen, and as recently as this century, the threat that "the Turks will get you" has been used to frighten children into obedience. The other result was a vastly diminished trust in the Danish government among the Icelanders.

There is virtually no reference to this event in English-language histories, but there are a number of Icelandic sources. The most valuable is *Reisubis* by Ólafur Egilsson, the priest who was captured and then released to seek ransom.

—*Louise Heite*

For Further Reading
Egilsson, Ólafur. 1969. *Reisubók*. Reykjavik, Iceland: Almenna Bókafélag.

TURNER, NAT
(1800–1831)

Nat Turner was a black mystic who led an insurrection against white families in Southampton County, Virginia, on August 22, 1831. Turner's was the most famous of the Southern slave insurrections because of its bloodiness and the fear it instilled in Southern whites.

The son of slave parents, Nat was born on October 2, 1800, on Benjamin Turner's plantation near Jerusalem in Southampton County. He attended prayer services and Sunday chapel at his Methodist master's insistence, and as a youth, he played alongside white children. He demonstrated a superior intelligence, teaching himself to read and write, and even read and studied the Bible with his master's encouragement.

Several events changed his life dramatically. Shortly after his father escaped to the North, Nat and his mother, Nancy, were loaned to master Benjamin's son, Samuel. In 1810, the elder Turner died, leaving Nat and his mother as the property of Samuel Turner, a strict taskmaster who insisted that his slaves obey him. In 1812, Nat was devastated when he was put to work in the fields. No longer could he play, associate with white children, or follow intellectual pursuits.

Nat became increasingly despondent. In 1812, he escaped the plantation but returned on his own after a month of hiding, claiming that "the Spirit" had instructed him to do so. He took a wife, Cherry, shortly thereafter. In 1822, Samuel Turner died, and Nat and Cherry were sold to separate masters in Southampton County. Although Nat was able to visit Cherry and have children by her, he was not able to have the family life he desired. His new master, Thomas Moore, demanded even more labor of him. As he grew unhappier, Nat turned to Scripture for guidance.

In his *Confessions* (1831), Turner stated that religion became the dominant motivating factor in his young adult life. He recalled that as a youth, other slaves deemed him a "prophet" because he described events that had occurred before his birth. His role as a prophet and mystic increased through early adulthood, and in 1825, he had a vision in which "white spirits and black spirits engaged in battle" appeared beneath a darkened sun as "blood flowed in streams." Shortly thereafter, he claimed to see angels in the sky, blood on the corn in the fields, and symbols on tree leaves.

Proclaiming himself a Baptist preacher, Turner described his visions to slave congregations at Sunday prayer meetings that he conducted. He emphasized the approach of Judgment Day, when God would raise the slave above the master. Preparing for his own role on Judgment Day, he gathered a small following of slaves

Rebel leader Nat Turner is taken prisoner; he was hunted down after evading capture for more than a month after the failure of the insurrection he led.

and free blacks to assist him, telling them, "I am commissioned by Jesus Christ and act under his direction."

Turner continued laboring on weekdays and preaching on Sundays. In 1827, a white overseer asked Turner to baptize him. When local churches refused to allow Turner the use of an altar for the ceremony, he used a nearby pond. He did not forget the insult white church leaders had extended him, and his disillusionment grew. In 1828, he had another vision, which he also described in his *Confessions:* "The Spirit instantly appeared to me and said the Serpent was loosened, and Christ had laid down the yoke he had borne for the sins of men, and that I should take it on and fight against the Serpent, for the time was fast approaching when the first shall be last and the last should be first."

This vision, combined with a chain of circumstances in Turner's life, moved him toward insurrection. Upon telling his master, Thomas Moore, that slaves would be free "one day or other," he was thrashed for insubordination. When Moore died later that year, Turner became the property of the deceased's nine-year-old son until Moore's widow remarried in 1829 and Joseph Travis became Turner's new master. Turner did the work expected of him to gain Travis's "greatest confidence" and thereby be permitted to continue preaching and waiting for a sign from God. In February 1831, a solar eclipse was the first sign Turner needed to proceed with plans for insurrection. A second occurred on August 13 when the sun grew dim and a black spot appeared on its surface.

In the early hours of Monday, August 22, Turner and six followers quietly entered Joseph Travis's house. Armed with axes, they killed all five whites in the home, including an infant in its cradle. From the Travis farm, Turner and his followers moved from house to house, killing whites as they went. Attracting followers and weapons on the way, they soon numbered nearly 60 men mounted on horseback and armed with axes, swords, guns, and clubs. They killed a total of 55 white men, women, and children.

News of the insurrection spread quickly. Confrontations with armed bands of whites resulted in the death of many of Turner's men and the dispersal of the rest. By Sunday, August 28, federal troops, militia, and armed bands of whites had killed or captured all but a handful of the insurrectionists, including Turner. He had evaded capture for several weeks by hiding in a dugout under some fence rails. Finally found and captured on October 30, Turner recited his *Confessions,* an explanation of his actions, to attorney Thomas Gray on November 1. He was tried, found guilty, sentenced to death on November 5, 1831, and hanged six days later.

Nat Turner's insurrection shocked and frightened Virginians. Because of the insurrection, Virginia's legislature held its last serious debate on ending slavery in 1832, and Virginia and most Southern states eventually passed strict laws to police their slave populations and prevent insurrections. Believing that abolitionism had somehow caused the uprising, most Southerners also abandoned the cause of emancipation in the aftermath of Turner's insurrection.

—*Mary Jo Miles*

See also
Virginia Slavery Debate
For Further Reading
Greenberg, Kenneth S. 1996. *The Confessions of Nat Turner and Related Documents.* Boston: St. Martin's; Oates, Stephen B. 1990. *The Fires of Jubilee: Nat Turner's Fierce Rebellion.* New York: Harper and Row.

TWELVE TABLES (LEX XII TABULARUM)

Roman law remained customary and unwritten until the middle of the fifth century B.C. when the *Lex XII tabularum,* or the Twelve Tables, was formulated. Although having an unwritten law served the needs of patrician or upper classes in the city-state, the lower, or plebian classes had neither the time nor the resources to learn the laws that governed them. Ignorance of law threatened their growing control of property, including slaves, and invited abuses by dishonest magistrates.

In 462 B.C., the tribune Terentilius Harsa first demanded a written codification of laws, though the enterprise did not begin until a decade later. In 451 B.C., 10 patrician commissioners *(decemviri)* were appointed to perform the task. According to tradition, after a year's labor the work was incomplete and a new panel, which included five plebians, continued the work. The dilatoriness of the codifiers and personal scandals prompted the plebians literally to "walk out" of Rome in protest, leaving the city in their temporary act of secession until reforms were promised. Work on the law code was quickly completed in 449, and 10 tribunes and 2 consuls, or executives, replaced the *decemviri.*

The result was the first written Roman legal code, which was posted in the public forum. Only some of the terms survive, and these only in the form of quotations by later authors. The Twelve Tables code was, in general, a very conservative document that underlined existing rights and practices rather than creating new ones. It reflected interests of the ruling (patrician) class, especially with regard to property and family matters.

Like all ancient societies, the Romans practiced slavery and recognized it in law. Many slaves came from outside of Roman society, but, as the laws make clear, Romans themselves could become slaves. Of the clauses that have survived, eight concern slaves. They constitute no systematic treatment of the institution, but they do give some clues about the treatment and status of slaves.

As laws 1 and 2 of Table 4 make clear, a father could sell his son into (apparently temporary) slavery. After a third sale, the father had the right to emancipate the son (Table 4.1), and the son had the right to be automatically emancipated (4.2). According to Table 2.5, one could fall into slavery if one committed a theft during the daylight hours and was caught: the offender would be scourged, then made his victim's "slave." The term of slavery involved is not made clear, however.

Manumission by testament and freedom by payment of one's price to one's owner are both preserved in Table 6.2:

Where a slave is ordered to be free by a [last] will, upon his compliance with a certain condition, and he complies with the condition; or if, after having paid his price to the purchaser, he claims his liberty, he shall be free.

The first clause protects both the slave's right to be freed and the dead owner's right to dispose of his property as he wills. The male slave who buys his freedom becomes a freedman and has the legal ability to become a Roman citizen. The latter point necessitated the clear statement of the status of one who bought his freedom.

According to Table 7.10, when someone knocks out the tooth of a freedman, the assailant owes the man the monetary sum of 300 asses (coins); when one does the same to a slave, he owes the owner 150 asses. Laws 2–4 of Table 8 provide fines for "bursting" some part of a slave, for breaking a bone, and for "simple harm." The slave was clearly the owner's property, and any such reduction in value was to be compensated; the slave himself had no right to compensation. Table 10.13 provides for the opposite situation: a slave's victory in any contest is to be reckoned a glorification of the owner, just like a victory of his racehorse would be, for example. In fact, in the later Lex Aquilia (287 B.C.), a slave is specifically equated to a "herd animal."

On the other hand, the master was responsible for the slave's criminal behavior if the master knew of it beforehand:

If a slave, with the knowledge of his master, should commit a theft, or cause damage to anyone, his master shall be given up to the other party by way of reparation for the theft, injury, or damage committed by the slave. (Table 12.3 supplemental)

The errant slave/thief is dealt with far more harshly:

If he who perpetrated the [daylight] theft is a slave, he shall be beaten with rods and hurled from the Tarpeian Rock. (Table 2.5)

Finally, any deceased slave was forbidden funeral ceremonial practices, a funeral feast, or anniversary honors (Table 10.10).

Overall, the Twelve Tables established a clear constitutional demarcation between the class of slaves and the class of free persons in Rome, one that remained virtually unchanged for hundreds of years.

—*Joseph P. Byrne*

For Further Reading
Bradley, Keith. 1994. *Slavery and Society at Rome*. New York: Cambridge University Press; Scott, S. P. 1973. *The Civil Law*. Includes the text of the Twelve Tables. New York: AMS Press; Watson, Alan. 1987. *Roman Slave Law*. Baltimore: Johns Hopkins University Press; Watson, Alan. 1975. *Rome of the XII Tables: Persons and Property*. Princeton, NJ: Princeton University Press.

U

UKRAINE

The Ukraine is a quadrangular-shaped country located on the Black Sea's northern and western shores. The Crimean peninsula protrudes into the Black Sea and for centuries has controlled the sea. The peninsula's convenient location between the Black Sea and the Sea of Azov enables it to connect the Ukraine to Caucasia and gives access to large rivers including the Kuban, Don, Dnieper, Dniester, and Danube. Since the thirteenth century, the region had been colonized and inhabited by the descendants of various nomadic peoples who roamed the Ukrainian steppes, especially the Tatars.

Tatars are descendants of the Mongol-Tatar horde that arrived in the mid-thirteenth century in what was then Rus'-Ukraine. Their leader became the khan of Crimea when he united them in 1449, and after Constantinople fell to the Turks in 1453, the khan allied forces with the Ottoman Empire and became the sultan of Turkey's vassal. The drive into Europe then began.

Crimean Tatars conducted raids in the Ukraine on a regular basis to supply men for the Turkish galleys and women and children for the principal slave markets of Kaffa (ancient Theodosia, modern Feodosiya) and Constantinople. There were many invasions of the Ukraine as well as an annual slave-hunt raid. Between 1450 and 1556, the raiders sacked the Ukraine 86 times. Ukrainian slave routes followed the course of the main rivers: the Don, Dnieper, and Dniester, which flow almost parallel into the Black Sea. Along these river routes, there are still remains of castles and fortified churches that were built to protect the population from the Tatar invasions. Kamenets-Podilskyi is a good example of such a castle.

Located along the Smotrych River, a small tributary of the Dniester, the castle and town of Kamenets-Podilskyi was destroyed by the Mongols in 1240, it fell under dominion of Lithuanian princes in 1360, and Poland gained control of the town in 1430. In the fifteenth and sixteenth centuries, the wooden fortress was replaced by a stone citadel, and the city was fortified with walls and towers to protect inhabitants from the Tatars and the Turks. During the Cossack-Polish War (1658–1667), the city was besieged, and it was captured in 1672 by Hetman P. Doroshenko and his Turkish allies. It remained in Turkish hands until 1699.

The Tatar raids may be judged by their brutal results. In 1575, the Tatars captured over 35,000 Ukrainians, and a 1676 raid took almost 40,000 Ukrainians into slavery from the villages of Volyn, Podolia, and Galicia. A record number of 60,000 Ukrainians were captured in 1688; some were ransomed, but most were sold as slaves.

The infamous "black roads" to slavery, which appear on seventeenth-century maps of Ukraine, date to the early-fifteenth century and were used for over three centuries to carry enslaved Ukrainians south toward Crimea and the slave markets at Constantinople and Kaffa. Ships from Arabia, India, Persia, Syria, and Turkey docked at those ports to buy slaves.

Historical chronicles establish that as early as 1492, Ukrainians organized themselves into a protective body to safeguard their land and their people; these were the Ukrainian Cossacks. On the Dnieper River, the Cossacks established a hidden stronghold, the Sich, which had a history of its own until Russia's Catherine the Great ordered its destruction in 1775. That destruction rendered the Ukrainian people defenseless against the other type of slavery that the Russians imposed. Commonly referred to as serfdom, the black roads to Siberia carried Ukrainians to places where they were no longer sold in slave markets but were put to hard labor. The Ukrainian poet, Taras Shevchenko (1814–1861) was born a serf and died a few months before the Russian czar Alexander II proclaimed the abolition of serfdom.

From the Sich in the Dnieper River rapids, Ukrainian Cossacks conducted military actions on water with shallow-draft boats called *dubi, baidaki,* and *kayuki* and with warships called *chaikas* ("seagulls"). In 1601, the Cossack navy entered the Black Sea and destroyed the Turkish fleet off Kilia at the mouth of the Danube River. In 1606, the Cossacks captured Varna; in 1608, Perekop; in 1609, fortified Turkish Izmail; and in 1614, Sinope. The years 1614–1620 were most heroic under the direction of Peter Konashevich Sahaidachny, who became legendary as a Cossack ruler, or hetman.

On December 24, 1624, the Tatar khan concluded an alliance against Turkey with Hetman M. Doroshenko. Unfortunately, Doroshenko died in 1628 near Bakhchisaray, and his Cossacks had to retreat from Crimea. In 1648, Hetman Bohdan Khmelnytsky concluded an alliance with the Crimean khan Islam-Girei (r. 1644–1654), but he was betrayed after a battle in 1653. Tatars then plundered the Ukraine and took many people into captivity on their return home. This event became known as the *yasyr.*

In *De moribus Tartarorum fragmina* (1615), the writer Michalonis Litvani (Michael of Lithuania) left a vivid description of the Crimean slave trade, which lasted over 300 years before finally ending in 1783. A Roman ambassador to Kaffa gave another account of Tatar-Ukrainian military actions in his *Description of the Black Sea and Tartary* (1634). French engineer and geographer Guillaume le Vasseur de Beauplan recorded the slave trade roads on maps in his *Description de l'Ukraine* (1660), and he was the first to describe the Cossack boats of the Ukraine.

Ukrainian oral and classic literature, through a form called the Duma, offers much information about the slave markets. The best known of these concerns Marusia Bohuslavka, the daughter of a priest who freed 700 enslaved Cossacks from a 30-year imprisonment. In 1520, a Ukrainian girl, Nasta Lisovska, was taken into slavery and became the legendary Roxolana. Her beauty captivated the Turkish sultan Süleyman the Magnificent (Süleyman I), and she became his wife. Hetman Peter Konashevich Sahaidachny and Hetman P. Doroshenko are remembered in oral and classic literature as heroes who freed Christians from the slave markets of Perekop, Kaffa, and Constantinople.

—*Hélène N. Turkewicz-Sanko*

UNCLE TOM'S CABIN
(1852)

Harriet Beecher Stowe's most famous work, *Uncle Tom's Cabin,* was intended, like other nineteenth-century abolitionist literature, to turn its readers against the institution of slavery. Its success was remarkable, selling some 3 million copies in the United States alone. Translated into many languages, the work was the first U.S. book to become a European best-seller.

The Compromise of 1850, along with the Fugitive Slave Act, was the primary impetus for Stowe's novel, but letters from friends also played their part. One of those letters was from her sister-in-law, who urged Stowe to write about the major moral issue of the day with the words, "If I could use a pen as you can, I would write something that would make this whole nation feel what an accursed thing slavery is." Stowe had increasingly been driven to public and written comment on the iniquities of slavery, but on March 9,

1851, she wrote to Gamaliel Bailey, editor of the *National Era,* to tell him that the time had come when even women and children should speak out for freedom and humanity and asked him to accept a work that painted a picture of slavery as it was known to herself and her acquaintances. *Uncle Tom's Cabin* began as a serial on June 5, 1851, the first installment occupying most of the front page.

For the facts of slavery Stowe relied mainly on Theodore Weld's *African Slavery as It Is* (1839), and the story of *Uncle Tom's Cabin* is simple enough. Tom, a valued slave of the Shelby household, is sold to pay off debts and is thus separated from his wife, Chloe, and his family. His life forms the basis of the plot. He is sold downriver, first to St. Clare whose daughter, Eva, Tom rescues from drowning, and ultimately to the evil Simon Legree, in whose ownership Tom dies. As the serial continued long past the original projection of four weeks, another story line developed. This one told of the adventures of Eliza who, having overheard Mr. Shelby agree to sell her young son, flees with her son to join her runaway husband, George. Tom's story exposes the reader to the horrors of slavery as he travels deeper and deeper into the South; Eliza's story exposes the reader to the fears of the runaway as she and her family travel north to freedom.

Prior to writing *Uncle Tom's Cabin*, Stowe wrote mainly about domesticity and sentimental love, subject matter that was deemed suitable for a woman. Her achievement in *Uncle Tom's Cabin* was to transfer the techniques of "the lady's novel" to a subject it was not associated with. The text insists that African American slaves should be perceived as fellow humans possessed of a moral dignity that often surpasses that of the white population. Stowe's slaves suffer when their families are disrupted and their women exploited, and they bleed when they are lashed.

The work relocates the moral center of society away from those with power, that is, the white males of the text, and places it firmly in the realm of the weak and defenseless—with the women, children, and slaves. Nor are the rhetorical strategies of the text purely sentimental. It is made clear from the beginning of the novel that the sale of Tom is "God's curse on slavery." Mrs. Shelby's words initiate a providential plot line in which Tom is marked as God's own and all human efforts to save him are doomed to failure.

Stowe reinforced divine authority throughout the work, emphasizing the religious view of U.S. history via a vast array of scriptural imagery, parallels, quotations, sermons, and preaching. Eliza's famous river crossing is thus both actual and symbolic, and Tom and Eva share a simplicity of faith to which all might aspire. The business of chattel slavery demanded a world without God or conscience, but the character of Tom, whose Christ-like demeanor enables his submission to the worst that slavery can offer, ensures that the first concern remains with God and salvation.

The nineteenth-century reader would have been fully aware of what was at stake: it was eternal life and the death, not only of bodies, but of souls. Yet in the twentieth century, Tom's submissiveness has created considerable debate. It has seemed to many incongruous and even objectionable, particularly when measured against the tenets of realism, political or social, rather than in terms of a nineteenth-century Christian ideal. The most famous challenge comes from James Baldwin's "Everybody's Protest Novel" in *Notes of a Native Son* (1955), in which he argued that Eliza and George escape only because they are mulatto and can pass as white; the blacker Uncle Tom is condemned by the text to die a slave. Baldwin concludes that the text is racist.

Through much of the twentieth century, the designation of an "Uncle Tom" has been pejorative and used to indicate an unnecessarily sycophantic stance adopted toward the white population by an African American. It may be that this use came about as much through the innumerable stage and film versions of *Uncle Tom's Cabin*—none of which were authorized by Stowe and from which she received no profit—than from any reading of the text. From 1853 to 1930, the play, especially George L. Aiken's adaptation, was probably never off the boards, and Americans who saw no other play saw that one. There may have been as many as 500 troupes operating in the 1890s with productions, to quote one critic, "surpassing the fantastic and bordering on the insane" (Crozier, 1969).

In 1918, Paramount produced a feature film, with Marguerite Clark playing both Eva and Topsy, Eliza's daughter; Universal filmed an elaborate production in 1927; and a 1932 version by the Moscow Art Theater emphasized the miseries of the slave, had Topsy save Eva's life, and omitted all references to religion.

It has been claimed that *Uncle Tom's Cabin* altered the course of history and that Abraham Lincoln once referred to Harriet Beecher Stowe as the woman who "started the Civil War." In its day, the work was praised by writers as diverse as George Eliot, Fyodor Dostoyevsky, and George Sand, and more recent studies have recognized the revolutionary nature of the text in terms of women's writing. It may be that no other work, before or since, has done so much to alter the thinking of an entire generation about the major question of the day.

—*Jan Pilditch*

For Further Reading

Crozier, A. 1969. *The Novels of Harriet Beecher Stowe.* New York: Oxford University Press; Forster, C. H. 1954. *The Rungless Ladder: Harriet Beecher Stowe and New England Puritanism.* Durham, NC: Duke University Press; Kirkham, Bruce E. 1977. *The Building of Uncle Tom's Cabin,* Knoxville: University of Tennessee Press; Llowance, Mason I., Jr.; Ellen E. Westbrook; and R. C. DeProspo, eds. 1994. *The Stowe Debate: Rhetorical Strategies in Uncle Tom's Cabin.* Amherst: University of Massachusetts Press.

UNDERGROUND RAILROAD

The Underground Railroad refers to the assistance abolitionists provided fugitive slaves going through the Northern states, usually on their way to Canada to find freedom. Loosely organized local activities later formed the basis for a popular legend that included stories of secret hiding places and various railroad terms such as "stations," "passengers," "conductors," and even several "presidents" of the underground line. In the years after the U.S. Civil War, Underground Railroad stories frequently appeared in the Northern press. Not included in the legend was the role of the fugitive slaves themselves, who planned and conducted their own escapes from a hostile Southern environment with little available help.

Legendary accounts distorted historical reality and often exaggerated the number of slave escapes. Yet the accounts had a basis in fact. Some abolitionists, like Levi Coffin of Cincinnati, Ohio, and Thomas Garrett of Wilmington, Delaware, made a personal cause of aiding fugitive slaves. Their efforts to develop efficient networks of activists gave a semblance of effective organization in their own locales, yet most such work was done on a haphazard and makeshift basis. There was no national system.

An important element in the legend was provided by memories of the vigilance committees that were formed in various Northern communities. Those committees assumed a greater importance after the passage of the Fugitive Slave Act of 1850. They provided food, temporary housing, travel directions, and sometimes transportation to fugitive slaves passing through their communities. They also conducted some well-publicized acts of civil disobedience, like the 1851 rescue of one Jerry Henry by the Syracuse, New York, committee. Less successful was the attempt of the Boston committee to free Anthony Burns, whose return to slavery under heavy military guard sparked protest in Boston and throughout the North. Abolitionist free blacks later purchased and freed Burns.

Some rescues, like the Oberlin-Wellington rescue in 1859, were more spontaneous. When a fugitive slave was arrested a few miles from his home in Oberlin, Ohio, an abolitionist crowd literally removed him from his place of confinement and sent him to

This illustration from William Still's important book The Underground Railroad *shows slaves escaping from the Eastern Shore of Maryland.*

Canada. The federal government indicted 37 of the instigators of the rescue. The trials received national attention and prompted numerous demonstrations near the jail where the rescuers were held. At the same time, a county grand jury indicted the federal marshal and others for kidnapping a Negro. That indictment paved the way for a deal in which federal and state authorities dropped all charges against the rescuers.

Slaves who successfully escaped their bondage were not frightened or passive but courageous individuals who had made their own daring and ingenious escape plans. Slaves who were rescued by Harriet Tubman's heroic trips into the South may have been an exception, but most escaping slaves had no such assistance. Many traveled alone by night, hiding during the day. Ellen and William Craft escaped from Georgia with Ellen disguised as an ailing master and William as the loyal servant. Frederick Douglass borrowed the free papers of a black sailor and refused to reveal his escape method in early editions of his autobiography. Henry "Box" Brown had himself literally shipped from Richmond, Virginia, to Philadelphia where sympathizers collected the box.

When fugitives received help from the Underground Railroad, it was only after they had completed the most dangerous part of their journey. Frederick Douglass,

William Wells Brown, Anthony Burns, the Crafts, and thousands of others deserve at least as much recognition as the white abolitionists who risked their own liberty and property to help the slaves escape.

Although secrecy was clearly essential when a fugitive slave was in actual danger of recapture, abolitionists were quite open at times about their fugitive slave work. In 1844, a Chicago antislavery newspaper published a cartoon with the caption "The Liberty Line" that illustrated and accompanied a story describing the Underground Railroad and listing the names of local "conductors" (people who guided the escapees). Although never arrested by the authorities, Levi Coffin made no secret of his abolitionist sympathies or of his work on behalf of fugitive slaves. Each rescue had widespread notice in the press, and the violation of civil liberties of whites who helped escaping slaves served to deepen anti-Southern sentiment in the North. Some fugitive slaves were featured guests at abolitionist gatherings, while others were speakers.

Although abolitionists used the Underground Railroad to spread their message, Southern apologists attacked it as a violation of the constitutional protection of private property. Southern congressmen exaggerated the numbers of escaping slaves and the monetary losses those escapes caused. Fugitive Slave Act trials gave both sides propaganda material. By 1855, the Fugitive Slave Act of 1850 had become largely a dead letter in the North and a major cause for complaint in the South.

It was in the period after the Civil War that the idea of the Underground Railroad became popular in the United States. People who had formerly opposed the extension of slavery into new territories and abolitionist sympathizers gained inflated reputations, for hundreds of newspaper stories frequently associated all who had been against slavery with local tales of the Underground Railroad. Facts for such stories were often gleaned from interviews with family members or acquaintances of the aging activists, and several leading abolitionists wrote memoirs that later became source material for histories of the Underground Railroad. Although such memoirs contained important information, they were never supplemented by the narratives of former slaves or information from William Still's important book on the Underground Railroad.

Still, who chaired the Philadelphia Vigilance Committee, later published his own contemporary record of slave escapes and emphasized the role of the fugitives themselves. Although the Underground Railroad clearly helped some fugitive slaves reach freedom, it was a far more complex institution than the simplest legend would suggest.

—*Larry Gara*

See also
Coffin, Levi; Fugitive Slave Act of 1850; Garrett, Thomas; Still, William
For Further Reading
Blockson, Charles L. 1987. *The Underground Railroad: First-Person Narratives of Escapes to Freedom in the North.* New York: Prentice-Hall; Gara, Larry. 1996. *The Liberty Line: The Legend of the Underground Railroad.* Lexington: University Press of Kentucky; Siebert, Wilbur H. 1898. *The Underground Railroad from Slavery to Freedom.* New York: Macmillan; Still, William. 1883. *The Underground Railroad.* Philadelphia: William Still.

UNITED NATIONS AD HOC COMMITTEE ON SLAVERY (1950–1951)

The United Nations Ad Hoc Committee on Slavery was an early expression of the United Nations' commitment to continuing the pre–World War II efforts of the League of Nations to end slavery worldwide. Since the early-nineteenth century, the international community had recognized that slavery was incompatible with civilized and just human behavior and had moved haltingly toward its elimination worldwide.

The first such expression was a resolution to that effect by the Congress of Vienna in 1814–1815. Subsequently, most notably in Berlin (1884–1885) and Brussels (1889–1890), international congresses ratified that goal. Following World War I, the League of Nations made the elimination of the remnants of slavery one of its major aims. One of the first modern international conferences dealt with this issue and resulted in the Convention of Saint-Germain in 1919, which expressed the victorious Allies' recognition that slavery remained an issue within the community of nations and its opposition to slavery. In 1924 and 1926, committees of the League of Nations drafted resolutions recognizing the continued existence of slavery and committing its members to its eradication. The demise of the League of Nations in the 1940s effectively ended international efforts on the issue.

Following World War II, the United Nations took up the antislavery work of the defunct League of Nations. The United Nations Charter, in its Universal Declaration of Human Rights, contains a forceful condemnation of slavery and expresses the commitment of UN members to the task of ending slavery in all its forms. In 1949, the General Assembly asked the secretary-general to create a committee to investigate the status of slavery and the slave trade. That committee's report resulted in a General Assembly resolution in which the United Nations embraced the functions previously performed by the League of Nations under the Slavery Convention of 1926.

The United Nations Ad Hoc Committee on Slavery of 1950–1951, a joint effort of the Economic and Social Council and the International Labour Organization, issued a report on complaints lodged against two dozen governments regarding the protection of forced labor and formed the basis for subsequent UN action on that issue.

—*Frederick J. Simonelli*

For Further Reading
United Nations. 1951. *The Suppression of Slavery.* Memorandum submitted by the secretary-general. New York: United Nations.

UNITED NATIONS PROTOCOL OF DECEMBER 7, 1953

The United Nations Protocol of December 7, 1953, condemned forced labor as being contrary to the principles of the United Nations Charter and the Universal Declaration of

Human Rights. In the early years of the Cold War, the United Nations' commitment to ending slavery worldwide was complicated by attempts of the United States and the Soviet Union to exploit the issue for political advantage. Various investigative bodies of the United Nations found that slavery, in the form of state-protected forced labor, still existed in many parts of the world although the emphasis was on the use of forced labor as a tool of social and political control rather than on race-based subjugation.

In late summer 1953, the U.S. delegation to the United Nations, prompted by a request from the American Federation of Labor, requested that the United Nations General Assembly examine the use of forced labor as a form of slavery. That request was interpreted by the Soviet Union's delegation as a covert attack on its country, specifically on labor practices within the communist nations allied with the Soviet Union. The Soviet Union lodged countercharges against the United States, citing repressive labor practices in that country, particularly as those practices related to racial suppression.

The UN investigation determined that forced labor for economic and political purposes did exist in the Soviet Union, Spain, and several Soviet satellite nations. Political realities, however, prevented the ensuing protocol from being anything more than a general condemnation of such practices and an appeal to all UN member states to eliminate those practices within their own borders and spheres of influence.

—*Frederick J. Simonelli*

For Further Reading
United Nations. 1953. General Assembly Official Records, Eighth Session; United Nations. 1953. General Assembly Official Records, Eighth Session, Third Committee, 529th Meeting (November 20); United Nations. 1953. United Nations Document A/2438 (August 17); United Nations. 1953. United Nations Document E/2431/Addendum 2 (August 24).

U.S. CONSTITUTION

Despite slavery's pervasive influence on the political, economic, and social life of the United States, the country's Constitution, at ratification, did not explicitly mention the practice and institution of chattel slavery. Only with the post–Civil War amendments (Thirteenth, Fourteenth, and Fifteenth Amendments) did the Constitution expressly acknowledge slavery's existence. The Founders spoke of slavery euphemistically, preferring ambiguous phrasing to an explicit delineation of slavery's place in the country's political order. Nonetheless, the Constitution's authors consciously designed institutions that accommodated, supported, and eventually entrenched slavery within the structures of political power. Consequently, those few euphemistic references in the original Constitution have had a lasting influence on the course of political development in the United States and on constitutional interpretation.

Constitutional references to slavery fall into three classes: those that could have referred only to slavery; those that encompassed slavery and other practices or institutions; and those that did not directly touch on slavery, but had significant indirect, and perhaps unforeseen, consequences for slavery or slaveholding interests.

Five provisions fall within the first category, and they represent key compromises made at the Constitutional Convention in 1787. The first, Article 1, section 2, paragraph 3 (generally called the three-fifths compromise), stipulated that both representation within the House of Representatives and any direct taxes would be apportioned to the states according to their populations, calculated "by adding to the whole number of free persons, including those bound to service for a term of years, and excluding Indians not taxed, three fifths of all other persons." This stipulation increased the representation of slaveholding states in Congress, but it simultaneously decreased any potential direct tax liability.

Similarly, Article 1, section 9, paragraph 4 ensured that all regions of the country would be equally affected by any possible "capitation" tax. This national uniformity of any possible direct taxes meant that slaveholding could not be singled out for taxation, a concern of some slaveowners who thought Northerners would try to tax slavery out of existence.

Also in Article 1, section 9, paragraph 1 stipulated that Congress could not ban the international slave trade until 1808. This 20-year prohibition fostered an even greater reliance on slave labor in the South and allowed for a domestic slave market to develop. Meanwhile, the fugitive slave clause (Article 4, section 2) not only prevented free states from emancipating runaway slaves within their borders but also required them to release any fugitive slave to his or her owner. Additionally, Article 5 rendered unamendable until 1808 both the fugitive slave clause and the ban on prohibiting the international slave trade.

The second class of constitutional provisions reinforced the economic and physical domination slavery required. Article 4, section 4 required that the federal government help suppress domestic insurrections, if a state so requested, which thereby put the federal government in the position of defending slaveholders' property interests if a slave rebellion occurred. Similarly, Article 1, section 8, paragraph 15 allowed Congress to muster state militias to combat insurrections, including slave revolts. Article 1, sections 9 and 10 prevented the federal and state governments from taxing exports, which precluded any effort to tax the products of slave labor.

The third class of provisions generally gave political advantages to slaveholding interests that enabled them to forestall efforts to eliminate slavery. Because of the three-fifths compromise, Southern states had more votes in the House of Representatives and the electoral college than if only free citizens were represented. Also the amendment process (Article 5) required the agreement of three-quarters of all states, enabling the South to veto any constitutional amendment to ban slavery. In addition, congressional powers to admit new states and adopt regulations for the territories (Article 4, section 3) created opportunities for the slave states to ensure that their numbers would not diminish.

In short, the constitutional provisions that touched on slavery, either directly or indirectly, represented a significant victory for Southern interests at the time of the country's Founding. Why was the South able to prevail on virtually all contested issues relating to slavery at the Constitutional Convention? Mark Tushnet (1981) argues that the political concessions to slavery by the Founders resulted from proslavery interests colliding with antislavery sentiment. That is, the political, economic, and social interests of the slaveowning states came into conflict with a more diffuse antislavery attitude, based on moral or religious sentiment, on the part of the Northerners. Consequently, the diffuse attitude could only yield in the face of such well-focused interests. Indeed, one could argue that the interests of the Northern states lay primarily in promoting a political union, and slavery was the price of that union.

The question remains whether the North drove a very hard bargain in its negotiations at the Constitutional Convention. Were concessions on slavery necessary to the Union's formation? The academic debate has yet to resolve the issue, but clearly the distinctive form of the political union of the United States, its thorough-going federalism, emerged primarily because of the centrifugal forces of slavery. In order to form an economic and political union, the framers of the Constitution found it necessary to preserve, in large part, the existing legal arrangements that enabled slavery to flourish in the South after the American Revolution.

At the time of the Founding, the country's legal framework supporting slavery lay exclusively at the state level. The then-emerging natural law position, articulated most forcefully in *Somerset v. Stewart* (98 English Reports 499 [1772]), held slavery to be contrary to natural law; therefore slavery could exist, in a legal sense, only as a creature of positive law (legislative or executive-made law). The slavery-related provisions of the U.S. Constitution recognized and validated the exclusively local law of slavery, as it then existed in the American states. The constitutional priority of federalism, which allowed both legal systems to coexist under a single constitutional order, thus both sought to restrict federal government intrusion on individuals and tolerated a property right in slaves.

In doing so, the Constitution embodied a tension between the "higher law" impulses of the American Revolution and the deeply political compromises over slavery. The high-toned aspirations of "We, the people" were profoundly at odds with slavery's entrenchment, simultaneously revealing within the Constitution an idealism and a complicit pragmatism.

Through the nineteenth century, these countervailing tendencies gave rise to intense political and normative arguments over the legal meaning of the Constitution's view of slavery. Followers of William Lloyd Garrison echoed his denunciation of the Constitution as a "covenant with hell" while other, equally ardent, antislavery activists sought to confine or eliminate slavery through constitutional practices. On the other side, proslavery politicians, in both the North and the South, viewed constitutional provisions like the fugitive slave clause as the touchstone of the American union. From their perspective, defending the principle of union required a defense of slavery. Proslavery forces tried to transform the constitutional place of slavery from a necessary evil to a positive good; it was, they argued, the glue that held the American union together.

These struggles often emerged in the context of federalism because of the differing positive law of free and slave regions. Northern free states and Southern slave states held fundamentally different assumptions about the legal status of blacks within their respective regions. In general, Northern legal systems assumed blacks to be free citizens unless proven otherwise while Southern law viewed blacks as slaves unless proven to be free.

Conflict over the legal status of blacks typically arose when a slave moved from a slave jurisdiction to a free one, either with or without the owner's permission. The legal status of fugitive slaves was clear within free states—the Constitution explicitly prevented Northern states from emancipating them (Article 4, section 2)—but some Northern judges ruled that free states were not required to protect the slave property of Southern masters traveling through their jurisdiction. Further legal conflicts arose over Northern efforts to protect the free black population in the North from bounty hunters and from the North's refusal to cooperate with slaveowners or their agents seeking to reclaim alleged fugitive slaves.

Later, as the Civil War drew to a close, Northern Republicans began laying the foundation for the constitutional abolition of slavery. Although Congress had banned slavery in the territories and the District of Columbia in 1862 and Lincoln's 1863 Emancipation Proclamation had freed slaves held in the rebellious Southern states, a general abolition required more than statutory or executive action. In their efforts to dismantle slavery, Republicans also aimed at the broader Southern "slave power," which they believed had dominated national politics before the war.

The simple language of the Thirteenth Amendment—"Neither slavery nor involuntary servitude . . . shall exist within the United States or any place subject to their jurisdiction"—not only abolished slavery but also implicitly aimed at the South's racial hierarchy. Opponents to the Thirteenth Amendment argued that it profoundly and impermissibly reconfigured the federal relationship, allowing the national polity to restructure the civil and economic life of an entire region. This opposition soon collapsed as the reelection of President Lincoln in 1864 and the installation of a large Republican majority in the House of Representatives assured passage of the Thirteenth Amendment.

The formal end of slavery in the United States came on December 6, 1865, over 240 years after a Dutch ship unloaded the first cargo of Africans in Virginia. Enormous battles lay ahead to secure basic civil and political rights for the emancipated slaves and, more broadly, to disentangle slavery from the fabric of both the Constitution and society.

—*Douglas S. Reed*

See also
Personal Liberty Laws; *Prigg v. Pennsylvania*
For Further Reading
Cover, Robert. 1975. *Justice Accused: Antislavery and the Judicial Process*. New Haven, CT: Yale University Press; Morris, Thomas D. 1974. *Free Men All: The Personal Liberty Laws of the North, 1780–1861*. Baltimore: Johns Hopkins University Press; Tushnet, Mark V. 1981. *The American Law of Slavery, 1810–1860: Considerations of Humanity and Interest*. Princeton, NJ: Princeton University Press; Wiecek, William. 1977. *Sources of Anti-Slavery Constitutionalism*. Ithaca, NY: Cornell University Press.

U.S. LAW

From 1619 to 1865 in the United States, the people responsible for the law wrestled with the problem of slavery. Although the status of blacks was unclear in the early-seventeenth century, slavery was a fixed part of colonial American law before 1700. Thomas Jefferson, who proclaimed that "all men are created equal" in the Declaration of Independence, was a slaveowner, and slavery became an integral part of the U.S. Constitution in 1787. Law

in the United States did not abolish slavery until the Thirteenth Amendment was ratified in 1865, and contemporary U.S. law still wrestles with the lasting consequences of slavery.

In 1619, when the first 20 blacks arrived at Jamestown, Virginia, the future status of these involuntary immigrants and others like them was unclear. Given the need for labor to develop an expanding economy and the problems encountered in utilizing white indentured servants and Indian slaves, colonial law had codified the status of blacks as subject to fixed, heritable, and permanent property by 1700.

The process of black enslavement is best summarized in Judge A. Leon Higginbotham's *In the Matter of Color: Race and the American Legal Process, the Colonial Period* (1978). Higginbotham treats the status of blacks in colonial Georgia, Massachusetts, New York, Pennsylvania, South Carolina, and Virginia at some length, since there were significant regional differences between North and South and unique concerns in each colony. Higginbotham makes it clear that by 1700, blacks could not look forward to the eventual citizenship rights granted white indentured servants once they had served their term of years. Even if they were legally free, blacks were part of a separate and dramatically unequal social status.

Sadly, even Georgia, originally established as a free state, instituted slavery to compete economically with neighboring South Carolina. By 1776, a North-South division on slavery was apparent, since the Northern colonies were moving away from slavery and the Southern colonies were economically dependent on it.

In 1787, slavery became an integral part of the U.S. Constitution. Neither Georgia nor South Carolina would have joined the Union without explicit protection for the rights of slave states to protect them against the interests of the more populous Northern states. Therefore, Article 1, section 2, paragraph 3 of the Constitution counted slaves as three-fifths of a person in determining the number of representatives a state was entitled to in the U.S. House of Representatives. Article 1 section 2, paragraph 3 and section 9, paragraph 4 apportioned direct taxes using the same fractional formula. Taken together, these sections were called the three-fifths compromise, as they made blacks three-fifths of a person for census and taxation purposes.

The Constitution's references to slavery did not stop with the three-fifths compromise. The international slave trade received explicit protection from congressional regulation until 1808 in Article 1, section 9, paragraph 1. Article 4, section 2, paragraph 3 of the Constitution explicitly required the return of fugitive slaves upon demand from their masters, and this constitutional clause helped fuel sectional conflict in the nineteenth century when the abolitionist movement gained strength in the Northern states and the Northern states increasingly refused to honor this constitutional obligation.

In addition, slave owners received protection in Article 1, section 8, paragraph 15 of the Constitution, which gave Congress the power to suppress slave insurrections; Article 1, sections 9 and 10, which protected slave exports along with other export trade from federal and state taxation; Article 4, section 4, which provided protection to states against domestic violence; and Article 5, which protected the right to import slaves against constitutional amendments before the year 1808. These provisions provided strong support to the slaveholding system in the South.

Throughout the early-nineteenth century, a number of court cases attempted to determine which, if any, rights protected a slave against harsh treatment by cruel masters. In *State v. Mann* (1829), a North Carolina decision (2 Dev. N.C. 263), Judge Thomas Ruffin declared, "We can not allow the rights of the master to be brought into discussion in the courts of justice," even though he theoretically recognized that the states might have to intervene to protect slaves in extreme cases. In *Souther v. Commonwealth* (1851) (7 Gratt Virginia 672), a master was jailed in 1851 for murdering his slave.

In 1842, the plight of fugitive slaves reached the U.S. Supreme Court in *Prigg v. Pennsylvania* (16 Pet., 41 U.S. 539), a case decided by Justice Joseph Story. Although Story upheld the constitutionality of the Fugitive Slave Act of 1793, it is interesting that he held that state officials could not be required to use their police power to enforce federal law.

Even though there was sectional conflict throughout the nineteenth century over the expansion of slavery into the territories, slavery was a secure part of U.S. law until the passage of the Thirteenth Amendment in 1865. To the horror of the North, Chief Justice Roger B. Taney summed up this security in *Dred Scott v. Sandford* (19 How., 60 U.S. 693) in 1857. Taney decided that Dred Scott, a black, was not made free simply by being carried into a free state.

In the eyes of the North, Taney's decision discredited the U.S. Supreme Court, and it certainly helped fan sectional conflict. Only the Thirteenth Amendment adopted after the Civil War in 1865 could finally settle the status of slavery in U.S. law.

—*Susan A. Stussy*

For Further Reading
Hall, Kermit L.; William M. Wiecek; and Paul Finkelman. 1996. *American Legal History, Cases and Materials.* New York: Oxford University Press; Higginbotham, A. Leon. 1978. *In the Matter of Color: Race and the American Legal Process, the Colonial Period.* New York: Oxford University Press; Lively, Donald E. 1992.

The Constitution and Race. New York: Praeger; Maltz, Earl M. 1990. *Civil Rights, the Constitution, and Congress, 1863–1869.* Lawrence: University Press of Kansas.

UTRECHT, TREATY OF (1713)

*A*s a result of the Treaty of Utrecht (1713), which ended the War of Spanish Succession (1702–1713), Great Britain emerged as the leading participant in the African slave trade of the eighteenth century. At the end of the sixteenth century, the Spanish Hapsburgs ruled an empire that included Spain, the Spanish Netherlands, Italian possessions, and most of Central and South America. But King Charles II (1661–1700) was a sick and weakly man with no direct heirs, and two principal contenders arose, each claiming the throne by right of descent: Archduke Charles of Hapsburg, a younger son of Holy Roman Emperor Leopold I; and Philip of Anjou, grandson of the French Bourbon monarch Louis XIV. To maintain Europe's balance of power, the Spanish prize needed to be split between the claimants. Louis XIV and England's William III developed a partition treaty, but the Austrian Hapsburgs refused to cooperate.

In 1700, the Spanish king, in one last patriotic act, named Philip as his sole heir, stipulating that if the Bourbons refused to hold the empire intact, it would pass to Archduke Charles. Shortly afterward, Charles II died, and Louis XIV found himself in a difficult position. If he accepted the entire Spanish Empire for his grandson, he faced war with the rest of Europe. Refusing the inheritance would strengthen the Austrian Hapsburgs, tipping the balance of power in their favor. A neutral course, accepting the empire along the lines of the partition treaty drawn up with William III, meant that France faced war with Austria. Confronted with a no-win situation, Louis XIV chose to seize the prize and support his grandson's full inheritance. The War of Spanish Succession began with Bourbon France and Spain allied against England, the Austrian Hapsburgs, and the Dutch Republic.

Although the war primarily involved annual land campaigns in Europe, the Americas did not escape the conflict. Both sides sent fleets to guard against the loss of Caribbean island territories, and both sides commissioned privateers to harry the other's shipping. Caribbean sugar planters mounted their own raids against rival islands. English planters took the French portion of St. Kitts and raided Guadeloupe, burning fields and mills and seizing many French slaves.

French planters raided English plantations on St. Kitts, Nevis, and Montserrat. French and Spanish forces expelled the English from the Bahamas.

The Treaty of Utrecht ended the war. The parties recognized Philip V as the legitimate king of Spain and its overseas empire, on the condition that he never inherit the French throne, while the Austrian Hapsburgs received Spain's continental possessions. Britain received recognition of the Hanoverian line of succession (necessary since all of Queen Anne's children preceded her in death), thus averting another possible source of general conflict over the lack of a direct heir. The British also gained recognition from France of British ownership of all of St. Kitts, Newfoundland, Nova Scotia, and Hudson Bay. The Bahamas reverted to English control, and Spain took the *asiento* (the slave-trading contract) from France and gave it to Great Britain.

—*Kimberly Henke Breuer*

See also
The *Asiento*

For Further Reading
Dickinson, W. Calvin, and Eloise R. Hitchcock, eds. 1996. *The War of the Spanish Succession, 1702–1713: A Selected Bibliography*. Westport, CT: Greenwood Press; Kamen, Henry Arthur Francis. 1991. *Spain, 1469–1714: A Society of Conflict*. London: Longman; Kamen, Henry Arthur Francis. 1969. *The War of Succession in Spain, 1700–15*. London: Weidenfeld and Nicolson.

VALENTINIAN'S EDICT

Valentinian III, emperor of the western half of the Roman Empire from 425 to 455, issued an edict in February 451 forbidding the practice, undertaken by some impoverished families, of selling children and other close kin into slavery to offset the worst effects of famine.

In the middle years of the fifth century, a grim famine wreaked intolerable hardship on Italy's population. In desperation, some starving people were driven to take extreme measures to survive the worst ravages of hunger. Among the most abhorrent of these was the practice of selling one's children and close relatives into slavery. Reports of this practice reached Valentinian, and, clearly appalled, he promptly issued an edict to prevent further such transactions and annul those that had already occurred.

Valentinian did not cast blame on or condemn the individuals who had resorted to selling their loved ones. It was rather pity, and understanding of their plight, that underlay the emperor's words. His horror and dismay at the extent to which famine had reduced his subjects are apparent in his noting of the "pitiable emaciation and the deathly pallor of the perishing." Although having sympathy for hunger's victims, Valentinian nevertheless could not condone their recourse to slave trading. To him, not even the natural human desire to preserve life should jeopardize the privilege of freedom, a privilege he deemed should not be treated lightly by any freeborn individual.

Valentinian recalled that for the unfree, the bestowal of liberty was the highest possible reward, whereas the people who had sold their kin into slavery had acquired money for food but had scorned the privilege. With some poignancy, he declared that "it is wrong that freedom should perish because life does not perish," and in decreeing the level of compensation due in cases where a transaction was to be annulled, he imposed upon vendors what amounted to a monetary fine. Although all buyers were required to return bought slaves to the families who had sold them, it was the families themselves who were obliged to pay compensation, amounting to one-fifth of the original price, to the buyer. A child bought for 10 solidi, for example, would have been returned to his or her family, who would then have given 12 solidi to the purchaser (of which 2 solidi were the penalty).

The final section of the edict addresses a related topic: the transportation overseas, or to barbarian states, of freeborn individuals who were sold into slavery. Valentinian decreed that a heavy fine should be paid the imperial treasury if a slave dealer knowingly shipped a freeborn slave to a foreign nation.

The edict appears to deal with a problem raised by the Italian famine in a fair and rational manner. It is neither unduly sympathetic nor overly punitive, applying instead the basic principle—one of the fundamentals of Roman slavery law—that freedom is a noble privilege and cannot be casually bought or sold at the whim of an individual, however pressing the need.

—*Tim Clarkson*

For Further Reading
Pharr, Clyde. 1952. *The Theodosian Code and Novels.* Princeton, NJ: Princeton University Press.

VARRO, MARCUS TERENTIUS

The outstanding Roman scholar Marcus Terentius Varro (116–27 B.C.) wrote a systematic treatise on agriculture, *De re rustica,* of which three books have come down to us complete. The first book concerns agriculture in general, the second pertains exclusively to animal husbandry, and the third is devoted to specialized livestock breeding. In the first book's sections on the farm and its equipment, Varro wrote: "Now I turn to the means by which land is tilled. Some divide these into two parts: men, and those aids to men without which they cannot cultivate; others into three: the class of instruments which is articulate, the inarticulate, and the mute; the articulate comprising the slaves, the inarticulate comprising the cattle, and the mute comprising the vehicles" (Bk. 1.17.1).

Articulate tools (*instrumentum vocale*) is one of the most quoted and misinterpreted Latin terms from the ancient sources. It may have had a juridical or legal meaning, since Varro's presentation is schematic. "Articulate tools" is not merely a definition of slaves; it is used as an antithesis to animals and tools and covers all types of human laborers.

Varro discussed the qualities and skills of rustic and pastoral slaves in other passages, where the social status of each is described. The herdsmen were normally slaves, and Varro emphasized that the chief herdsman should be literate in order to draw up accurate accounts and be able to utilize written rules on livestock diseases and their cure. He also recommended that the herdsmen and the experienced foremen on the farm, including the bailiff, should have childbearing wives and property in kind or cash so they would feel more attached to the estate. These slave women generally did some kind of domestic work under the supervision of the bailiff's wife, and perhaps they worked in the fields as well.

Varro elaborated on the bailiff's supervision of the slave staff on the farm. The bailiff's room should be near the entrance, so that he could control who came and went. No slave must leave the farm without permission, and the bailiff should not be absent for more than one day without his owner's consent unless business forced him to do so. According to Varro, the foremen should maintain order and the quality of the work, not by brutality, but by respect and performing the jobs themselves. Good and hardworking slaves should have rewards of food or exemption from work.

It is clear that Varro's instructions on slave management were dictated by the economic motive of promoting slave productivity, and it is difficult to distinguish between descriptive and normative elements. But he wrote on the basis of personal experience, and his treatise on agriculture is an outstanding source of information regarding Roman agricultural slavery.

—*Jesper Carlsen*

See also
Agricultural Slavery; Roman Republic
For Further Reading
Hübner, Wolfgang. 1984. *Varros instrumentum vocale im Kontext der antiken Fachwissenschaften.* Stuttgart: Franz Steiner; Perl, Gerhard. 1977. "Zu Varros instrumentum vocale." *Klio* 59: 423–429; Skydsgaard, Jens Erik. 1968. *Varro the Scholar.* Copenhagen: Munksgaard.

VASA, GUSTAVUS
See Equiano, Olaudah

VERNAE

The Latin word *verna* (plural, *vernae*) has several meanings: a (free) resident of the city of Rome; a slave born to a female slave; and a slave born to a slave in the household of his current owner. As slaves born to slaves, the existence of *vernae* raises the question of the natural reproduction of Roman slavery. Under Roman law, the child of a female slave followed the legal status of the mother and was born a slave.

Enslavement in war and the slave trade were important sources of slaves during the Roman Republic (fifth to first centuries B.C.), and natural reproduction gradually came to be the crucial factor in the Roman slave supply. By about 200 B.C. at the latest, *vernae* must have become very important, and during the early empire (first to third centuries A.D.), people who were born slaves were several times as numerous as the newly enslaved unfree. Natural reproduction was the only reliable means of providing a steady source of new slaves over time. The Greek author Appian (second century A.D.) pointed out that "the ownership of slaves brought rich gain from the multitude of their progeny" (*The Civil Wars* 1.7).

There is no evidence of systematic slave breeding or state regulation. Even in the absence of rational calculations on the profitability of slave-rearing, servile reproduction was frequently encouraged by individual owners. In the first century A.D., the Roman agronomist Columella recommended that slave women be rewarded for bearing children: mothers of three should be given time off work, and mothers of four should be manumitted. Because of high infant mortality, about three slave births were necessary to replace one adult slave.

Vernae were prized more highly than purchased slaves and enslaved prisoners, since *vernae*, having grown up in slavery, knew no other condition and appeared easier to control. Slave children born at home were often cared for by wet nurses and child minders hired by their owners. *Vernae* were trained in and performed the same jobs as other slaves. About 1,000 *vernae* are known from Roman inscriptions. The inscriptions of *vernae* of the Roman emperors, who dominated the imperial bureaucracy, emphasize their status and associate them with an elite within the Roman slave population.

In Egypt under Roman rule, the child of a female slave was called *oikogeneis* (ancient Greek for "born at home"). These slaves had to be registered and were barred from being sold outside Egypt. No such restrictions are known from other parts of the Roman Empire.

—*Walter Scheidel*

For Further Reading
Bradley, Keith. 1987. "On the Roman Slave Supply and Slavebreeding." In *Classical Slavery*. Ed. Moses I. Finley. London: Frank Cass; Herrmann-Otto, Elisabeth. 1994. *Ex ancilla natus: Untersuchungen zu den "hausgeborenen" Sklaven und Sklavinnen im Westen des römischen Kaiserreiches*. Stuttgart: Franz Steiner Verlag.

VERONA, CONGRESS OF

Britain, France, Prussia, Russia, and Austria met at Verona from October to December 1822 to discuss issues of strategic interest, and Britain continued its largely fruitless efforts to gain international abolition of the slave trade. After the Congress of Vienna in 1814–1815, Britain realized that a general convention ending the trade was an unrealistic goal and sought abolition through bilateral agreements instead. Success was limited, but conventions signed with Portugal, Spain, the Netherlands, Sweden, and selected South American nations usually included provisions for a joint right-of-search and mixed commissions to condemn offenders. But France remained uncooperative, and Anglo-French tensions over the slave trade issue ran high.

At the First Peace of Paris (May 30, 1814), France had promised to abolish the trade completely within five years but made little progress in that direction. In 1815 Napoleon abolished the trade, and Louis XVIII confirmed abolition on July 30, 1815, under heavy allied pressure. But abolition was not enforced, nor was the trade with third powers abolished. A French naval detachment was ordered to police violators, but the squadron hardly pursued its task with vigor. On April 15, 1818, even the French Parlement passed a law abolishing the trade—to no avail.

French public opinion was against abolition, and major proponents of abolition like Henri Grégoire or Anna Louise Germaine de Staël had little political power or influence. Even the valiant parliamentary efforts of Benjamin Constant and the Duke de Broglie changed little. Additionally, the colonial and slaving lobbies were strong, and bowing to legislation imposed by the victor was considered unpatriotic, so shippers ignored the law. With the end of hostilities and the restoration of Guadeloupe and Martinique, there was a high demand for slaves. In practice, therefore, France did not honor its engagements—as abolitionists like Zachary Macaulay and evidence presented by the English naval squadron demonstrated at Verona. The British ambassador even accused France officially of disinterest "in the execution of mutual undertakings" (Daget, 1971). British expectations for a satisfactory agreement at Verona could hardly have been lower.

So the powers met in congress as they had been doing regularly since 1814. Although Britain wanted discussion to focus on the status of what would happen to lands in the Ottoman Empire as that empire declined in power and on the independence movements in Latin America, Austria, and Russia pressed for French armed intervention to suppress a revolution in Spain. Britain ultimately walked out of the meeting, effectively killing the system of holding congresses to discuss international affairs, because it opposed antiliberal interventionism. Before doing so, however, Britain succeeded in pushing through the adoption, on November 28, 1822, of a document entitled "Declaration Respecting the Abolition of the Slave Trade."

The document began by referring to the earlier antislave trade declaration of February 8, 1815, at the Congress of Vienna, when the powers had proclaimed their "unshakable resolution to put an end to the commerce known by the name of the African Negro trade" (Parry, 1969). It further noted that the powers had "not ceased . . . to view the Negro trade as a scourge that has too long desolated Africa, degraded Europe and afflicted humanity" (Parry, 1969). Yet, the text continued, despite the Congress of Vienna declaration, individual legislative measures, and various bilateral treaties, the trade had continued unabated and had even intensified. The Congress of Verona declaration closed by launching an ardent appeal to the powers to direct all their efforts at enforcing the abolition of the trade and stamping out clandestine trading, thereby expressing the intention of the signatories' cabinets to work with increased ardor toward policing the ban.

The declaration at Verona was little more than a strong moral condemnation of the trade and a statement of intent by the powers, at British urging, to pursue effective abolition of the trade.

—*William L. Chew III*

See also
Atlantic Abolitionist Movement; Closing of the African Slave Trade; Illegal Slave Trade; Second Peace of Paris; Vienna, Congress of

For Further Reading
Daget, Serge. 1971. "L'Abolition de la traite des noirs en France de 1814–1831." *Cahiers d'Etudes Africaines* (11)1: 14–58; Daget, Serge. 1989. "Traites des noirs, relations internationales et humanitarisme, 1815–1850." *Relations internationales* 60 (Winter): 413–427; Parry, Clive, ed. 1969–. *Consolidated Treaty Series*. Dobbs Ferry, NY: Oceana Publications; Putney, Martha. 1975. "The Slave Trade in French Diplomacy from 1814 to 1815." *Journal of Negro History* 60(3): 411–427.

VESEY, DENMARK
(C. 1767–1822)

Denmark Vesey was born into chattel slavery in the United States. He spent his early life at sea traveling with a slave trader named Captain Vesey, and Denmark got his last name because the trader also owned him.

During his worldwide travels, Denmark Vesey learned several different languages. In 1800, having been a slave for more than 30 years, he won $1,500 in the East Bay, South Carolina, lottery and used $600 of it to purchase his freedom. He then settled in Charleston, South Carolina, where he worked as a carpenter and rose to a position of prosperity and prominence in Charleston's free black community. Vesey became a leader in Charleston's African Methodist Episcopal Church, and he also did a great deal of reading. That reading, along with all that he had witnessed during his lifetime, made him decide to organize an uprising against slavery.

Between 1818 and 1822, Vesey visited various plantations for the purpose of conducting religion classes for slaves, but he also used these opportunities to identify slaves who might join his conspiracy. Vesey began to recruit people to assist him in carrying out his plan around Christmas 1821. In his early fifties at the time, he was tired of seeing people of African descent oppressed and felt that the only way the situation would end would be for African Americans to take control of their own lives. Vesey planned how he and his supporters could take over the city of Charleston, collected a stockpile of weapons, and worked to recruit an army of volunteers to aid his cause. He even requested help from Haiti after having read about the successful revolution there led by Toussaint Louverture.

Several people assisted Vesey in recruiting and planning. These included Gullah Jack, Blind Phillip, Tom Russell, Monday Gell, Peter Poyas, and Mingo Harth. He hired a barber to make Caucasian disguises for those who were going to participate in the revolt to wear. He also had blacksmiths make various weapons for the strike, which was to take place on Sunday, July 16, 1822.

Before the group could carry out the plan, it was betrayed. There is much uncertainty as to the actual strength of Vesey's forces, but some estimates suggest that as many as 9,000 slaves may have been aware of the conspiracy. In the aftermath of the failed plot, 130 blacks and 4 whites were arrested and brought to trial. In the end, 34 blacks were banished from South Carolina, and 35 were sentenced to death for their role in the plot. Vesey was caught, put on trial, and hanged on July 2, 1822, along with 5 of the people who had assisted him. Vesey's conspiracy had far-reaching consequences across the U.S. South as many states adopted stricter systems of slave control in the wake of the aborted uprising.

—*Marquetta L. Goodwine*

See also
Gullah Jack
For Further Reading
Starobin, Robert S. 1970. *Denmark Vesey: The Slave Conspiracy of 1822.* Englewood Cliffs, NJ: Prentice-Hall.

VIEIRA, ANTONIO
(1608–1697)

António Vieira was a Jesuit who showed deep concern for the physical and spiritual welfare of both African and Indian slaves in Brazil. His sermons, twelve volumes of which he edited before his death, contain many references to social conditions. Vieira's lifetime coincided with the rapid expansion of slavery in northeastern Brazil. He spent several months of his novitiate at a Jesuit Indian village, and he studied both the Indian and the African dialects of slaves. When he took his first vows in 1625, he secretly vowed to do missionary work among Amerindian and black slaves, but he was assigned to teach theology instead.

From 1652 to 1661, Vieira was a missionary in the Province of Maranhão in Brazil, and during this time he mounted a verbal and a literary campaign with civil authorities to protect Indians from abuse. He wanted them to be free to cultivate their own crops and to receive wages when they worked for others. He played a prominent role in the debate that generated the laws of April 9, 1655. Shortly thereafter, the colonists and other religious orders united in opposition to Jesuit administration of the Indians.

The governor, Dom Pedro de Melo, supported the new laws and Vieira but was unable to prevent the expulsion of the Jesuits from Maranhão in 1661. Two years later they were allowed to return, with the single exception of Vieira, but they no longer had temporal jurisdiction over the Indians and were forced to share spiritual jurisdiction with other orders.

Vieira believed that the Indians in Brazil needed extra care because their culture was very different from the European model and that colonists had forfeited their role as Christian leaders when they let greed and ambition supersede the just treatment of their workers. By placing the Indians under Jesuit protection in Christian villages, they could evangelize them and help them adapt to European ways. Vieira did not trust the colonists to treat their Indian workers according to fair and just principles.

António Vieira assumed a very different approach with regard to the slaves who had been brought from Africa. He described them as strong and resilient people who adapted easily to new situations. He reasoned that they were better off as Christian slaves in Brazil than as pagan free people in Africa, and he believed that they were the logical choice to provide labor for agricultural production. Vieira railed against the Dutch after they occupied parts of Brazil and began attacking Portugal's African colonies. He argued that Portugal's control of Angola protected the economy of Brazil and said, "Brazil has the body of America and the soul of Africa" (Vieira, 1951). The fact that Brazil did not abolish slavery until late in the nineteenth century is evidence that the principles Vieira espoused were accepted as valid for nearly two centuries.

—*Sharon Landers*

See also
Bandeiras; Capitães do mato; Sugar Cultivation and Trade

For Further Reading
Boxer, C. R. 1962. *A Great Luso-Brazilian Figure: Padre Antônio Vieira, S.J., 1608–1697*. Berkeley: University of California Press; Kiemen, Mathias C. 1954. *The Indian Policy of Portugal in the Amazon Region, 1614–1693*. Washington, DC: Catholic University of America Press; Landers, Sharon Bamberry. 1995. "An Exploration of the Theory and Practice of Slavery in Seventeenth-Century Brazil in the Writings of Padre Antônio Vieira." Ph.D. dissertation, Department of History, Texas Christian University, Fort Worth, Texas; Vieira, António. 1951. *Obras escolhidas*. Lisbon: Livraria Sá da Costa.

VIENNA, CONGRESS OF

*T*he Congress of Vienna met from September 1814 to June 1815 and ranks among the great international conferences in European history. Attended by virtually all European states, proceedings were dominated by Britain, France, Prussia, Austria, and Russia and concentrated on forging a stable territorial and political settlement for post-Napoleonic Europe. Although redrawing the continental map constituted Vienna's most tangible legacy, Britain persuaded the attending powers to adopt an eloquent declaration against the slave trade. This declaration, though in no way binding on the signatories, constituted the first international condemnation of the trade on humanitarian grounds.

Britain's quest for abolition of the trade was motivated by both humanitarianism and economic interests. Abolitionist pressure on Britain's representative at the congress, Robert Stewart, viscount Castlereagh, was great and demonstrates an undeniable moral abhorrence of the trade. Britain had already abolished the trade in 1807, so after the Napoleonic Wars the other powers appeared to have gained an economic edge. Since a repeal of abolition was impossible politically, Britain sought universal abolition for commercial reasons. Clearly, France was the key to a successful abolition of the trade, for Spain and Portugal would probably follow the French lead.

The slaving powers were skeptical of British proposals. Portugal and Spain feared losing their colonies and were still heavily involved in the slave trade. France, as well, was hardly in an enviable negotiating position. Napoleon had abolished the trade in 1815, and Louis XVIII, newly restored by the allies, felt obliged to cooperate with Britain. Yet the French colonial lobby was stronger than ever, and shippers feared British naval hegemony, especially if Britain obtained the highly controversial right of search and seizure. The French perceived the continuation of the slave trade a point of national honor.

Arthur Wellesley, the first duke of Wellington, approached the French statesman Charles-Maurice de Talleyrand with the idea of an international league, armed with the right to search and seize, to suppress the Atlantic slave trade. Yet Talleyrand had decided to make no concessions on the issue while still pledging support for British efforts vis-à-vis Spain and Portugal. Since the ambitious British aims proved unattainable, a compromise was arranged, and the Declaration of the Powers Relative to the Universal Abolition of the Slave Trade was signed on February 8, 1815, by Great Britain, Russia, Sweden, France, Spain, Portugal, Austria, and Prussia and annexed to the General Treaty of the Vienna Congress as Act 15.

The moral tone of the declaration was clear. It described the slave trade as a bane of the whole world that "has been perceived by just and enlightened men of all times as repugnant to the principles of humanity and universal morality" (*Actes du Congrès de Vienne*, 1819). Exaggerating somewhat, the declaration contended that "the public voice in all civilized countries has been raised to demand its abolition as soon as possible." References were made to ongoing efforts toward abolition, and it was specifically noted that Britain and France had, in the First Peace of Paris (May 30, 1814), engaged to urge all the Christian powers at Vienna to "declare . . . the universal and definitive abolition of the Negro trade." The authors recognized that economic circumstances had so far prevented the abolition, or "have hidden, up to a point, the odious nature of its perpetuation."

The moral framework having been drawn, the authors aimed to make a "solemn declaration of principles" upon which the signatories would base themselves in working toward complete abolition. To that end, they declared "to all of Europe that, regarding the universal abolition of the Negro Trade . . . in accordance with the spirit of the age and the generous principles of their August Sovereigns, they are animated by a sincere desire to work for the most prompt and efficacious execution of this measure . . . with all the zeal and perseverance due such a great and beautiful cause."

Important qualifications were made pending further negotiations on implementation. Thus, it was stated explicitly that "this general Declaration shall in no way prejudice the timetable considered suitable by each Power for the definitive abolition of the Negro Trade." Despite these pragmatic reservations, included at the behest of the slaving nations, the declaration closed on a hopeful note, announcing that the "ultimate triumph of the abolition of the trade will be one of the most beautiful monuments of the age which has embraced its cause and brought it to a glorious conclusion."

Though the declaration was little more than a strong moral statement, both sides had compromised under immense domestic pressure and gone as far politically as appeared feasible. Still, the declaration raised European consciousness for the issue. It was considered part of the Final Act of the Congress of Vienna; legally *all* signatories of Vienna subscribed to its condemnation of the trade, giving the declaration considerable international weight. Finally, since the slaving states themselves were signatories, their involvement in the trade became increasingly untenable on moral grounds.

In the aftermath of Vienna, Castlereagh convened a major power conference to further pursue his plan. The conference failed, for French slavers had resumed the trade as early as the end of 1814, and the French opposed granting the British search-and-seizure rights. Thus, Britain returned to its policy of seeking abolition through bilateral agreements, of which it signed about 40. Through these, the trade was gradually reduced, even though it was not abolished altogether by a universally accepted legal document.

—*William L. Chew III*

See also

Atlantic Abolitionist Movement; Closing of the African Slave Trade; Illegal Slave Trade; Napoleon Bonaparte; Second Peace of Paris; Verona, Congress of

For Further Reading

Actes du Congrès de Vienne. 1819. Brussels: Chez Weissenbruch; Berding, Helmut. 1974. "Die Ächtung des Sklavenhandels auf dem Wiener Kongress 1814/15." *Historische Zeitschrift* 2192: 265–289; Putney, Martha. 1975. "The Slave Trade in French Diplomacy from 1814 to 1815." *Journal of Negro History* 60(3): 411–427; Reich, Jerome. 1968. "The Slave Trade at the Congress of Vienna: A Study in English Public Opinion." *Journal of Negro History* 53: 129–143.

VIKINGS

Although Norsemen, commonly called Vikings after their sea raids made on coastal Europe from 793 to 1066, are usually not considered as having a slave society, they were avid slave traders and raiders. Slavery was common in early Germanic times, and early Viking raids on Ireland and Scotland resulted in large numbers of captives, which the Vikings sold as slaves to the Byzantine and Muslim empires. The taking of slaves and furs down Russian rivers resulted in significant Norse cultural influence there and in the substitution of the ethnic word *slav* to replace the Latin *servus* for "slave." Also, Russian slaves were taken to Constantinople in such numbers that they influenced the culture of the Byzantine Empire. Norsemen also enslaved each other for debt, and there were hereditary slaves in Scandinavia whose origin is uncertain, although it is speculated that they were some kind of early native people.

Slaves in Scandinavia served as laborers for the most part, although there were no real plantations there because of the climate. Male slaves farmed, attended the master, took messages, and sometimes served as guards, executioners, or human sacrifices. Female slaves cooked, ground grain, spun and wove cloth, and processed dairy foods and fish—the mainstays of the Viking diet. Men had the legal right to purchase women for "carnal pleasure," but few men were so wealthy, since a slave might cost two to four marks of silver, a large sum at the time.

After Scandinavians converted to Christianity in the tenth to eleventh centuries, the era of Viking raids slowly ended. The Battle of Hastings (1066) is sometimes viewed as an endpoint, but at least by 1100 the North was integrated with the rest of Europe. Slowly, Scandinavian slaves purchased their freedom, were freed by their masters or the church, or were freed by law. A 1314 decree freed all slaves in two Swedish provinces, but as slaves by then were few, that decree is not equivalent to later emancipation documents and should not be interpreted as such.

By 1400, the descendants of former slaves had become integrated into Norse society, though placenames such as *Vestmannsgat* ("street of the Westmen," meaning Irishmen or slaves) in Stockholm and *Vestmannayear* ("isles of the Irishmen") in Iceland recall their presence. Ironically, Algerian and Bristol pirates descended on Iceland and carried off Norsemen themselves as forced laborers in the period 1450–1750, and Norwegian church groups redeemed some taken in 1713 from Heimay, the only inhabited island in the Westman Islands off the south coast of Iceland. Some people claim that the Norse Greenland colony was eradicated by slave trading around 1500, but there is no compelling evidence of such an event.

Of the Scandinavian nations, only Denmark participated in the later African slave trade, establishing colonies in the Virgin Islands to produce sugar and cotton starting in 1671. Its slave trade ended in 1802, slavery was abolished in 1848, and the colonies themselves were sold to the United States in 1917.

—*Jim Comer*

For Further Reading
Gregory, Saint. 1916. *History of the Franks*. Translated with notes by Ernest Brehaut. New York: Columbia University Press; Jones, Gwyn. 1984. *A History of the Vikings*. New York: Oxford University Press; Karras, Ruth Mazo. 1988. *Slavery and Society in Medieval Scandinavia*. New Haven, CT: Yale University Press; Williams, Mary Wilhelmine. 1920. *Social Scandinavia in the Viking Age*. New York: Macmillan.

VILLAGES
See Slave Villages

VIRGINIA SLAVERY DEBATE

A far-reaching debate on slavery occurred in the Virginia House of Delegates in 1832. The 1831–1832 legislative session convened not long after Nat Turner's insurrection in Southampton County on August 22–23 and only weeks after Turner's capture, trial, and execution. White Virginians sought security against a recurrence, and many—even some of the leading slaveowners in eastern Virginia—were prepared to consider ending the institution Turner had rebelled against. Governor John Floyd hoped that a program might be launched during his administration that would bring an eventual end to slavery in Virginia and, in the meantime, greater control over all black Virginians and the expulsion of free blacks.

The legislature's lower house appointed a select committee to consider the removal of free blacks from the state and a program of gradual abolition. William O. Goode, however, introduced a resolution that it was "not expedient to legislate" on the subject of emancipation. Thomas Jefferson Randolph countered with another resolution calling for gradual emancipation: all children of slave mothers born after July 4, 1840, would, if still in Virginia, become the property of the state, women when they reached age 18 and men at age 21, and would then be hired out until their labor had raised funds sufficient to pay for their transportation out of the United States. That meant the first black women would not obtain their freedom until 1858; the first black men, 1861.

Half a century earlier, the state of Pennsylvania had taken the first action of any legislature in the New World to undo slavery when it passed a gradual emancipation act in 1780. By the time of Turner's uprising, every Northern state had acted to end slavery, but no state south of Pennsylvania had gone any further than Virginia when that state, in 1782, merely curtailed the ban that had previously kept slaveowners from manumitting their slaves.

Only in its broad outlines did Virginia's 1832 gradual emancipation proposal resemble Pennsylvania's. Pennsylvania's original proposal had used the same ages for freeing existing slaves as the Virginia proposal, though Pennsylvania's 1780 bill had held slaves yet unborn to the age of 28, beginning with children born the year of the measure's enactment. Pennsylvania's law had granted free blacks all the rights that their white neighbors enjoyed, including the right to remain in their home state and political rights, and it sought to protect black Pennsylvanians from being sold out of state. Virginia's proposal did nothing to expand the definition of black freedom, and it anticipated that slaveowners, acting to protect their investment, would seek a market in the Deep South.

Two weeks of intense debate took place in the Virginia legislature's lower house. A western representative, William Ballard Preston, proposed an amendment to easterner Goode's resolution that would have reversed its intent as the amendment would have declared it "expedient" that the legislature enact an emancipation measure at the current session. Proponents of abolition condemned the "evil" of slavery—sometimes because it injured slaves, always because it damaged the prospects of white Virginians. Their opponents attacked as impractical every proposed remedy for slavery, though they did agree on the expulsion of free blacks. Reformers challenged the sanctity of slaves as property; their opponents insisted on their property rights. No one advocated any proposal to end slavery anytime soon or to permit a significant continued free black presence in Virginia.

Virginia's legislators divided into two main groups, roughly similar in size. One group supported some immediate action toward the eventual abolition of slavery. The other stood opposed. A small but crucial swing group favored eventual emancipation but resisted any specific action at the current session. Preston's amendment lost by 58 to 73. The vehemence of the proslavery spokesmen had paralyzed a sufficient number of wavering delegates so that those who refused to take any action against slavery in 1832 received a majority of the votes.

Had the Virginia constitution of 1830 granted the wish of westerners for greater representation—legislative apportionment according to white population, especially if coupled with white male suffrage—the vote would have been closer, though the reformers might still have lost. The next Virginia constitution, in 1851, offered concessions to the western part of the state on voting and apportionment. Still, even though it empowered the legislature to remove free blacks and to curtail the slaveowners' right to free slaves, it expressly denied the legislature the authority to act against slavery. In 1865 slavery ended, suddenly and without deportation, and citizenship and political rights were granted to the emancipated blacks.

—*Peter Wallenstein*

See also
Turner, Nat
For Further Reading
Freehling, Alison Goodyear. 1982. *Drift toward Dissolution: The Virginia Slavery Debate of 1831–1832.* Baton Rouge: Louisiana State University Press; Freehling, William W. 1990. *The Road to Disunion: Secessionists at Bay, 1776–1854.* New York: Oxford University Press; Robert, Joseph Clarke. 1941. *The Road from Monticello: A Study of the Virginia Slavery Debate of 1832.* Durham, NC: Duke University Press.

VOLUME OF THE SLAVE TRADE

Although it is impossible to establish an accurate figure, historians have endeavored to estimate the number of Africans involved in the slave trade. Equally important, they have sought to determine the effects of that trade upon Africa.

Historians have long debated how many African slaves Europeans transported to the Americas. Edward E. Dunbar, who wrote an 1861 essay called "History of the Rise and Decline of Commercial Slavery in America," produced one of the earliest estimates. Believing that his figure was conservative, Dunbar wrote that between 1500 and 1850 almost 14 million slaves were imported into the Americas. Though Dunbar's figure was little more than a guess, historians cited it in discussions of the slave trade for over a century. More recent citations mention Robert

Rene Kuczynski's work *Population Movements* (1939), which argues for a figure of 15 million. Some writers have argued that both estimates were too low and asserted that the figure was closer to 20 million.

Philip Curtin provided the first scholarly treatment of this question as he based *The Atlantic Slave Trade: A Census* (1969) upon an examination of various published sources. He reviewed shipping records, census data, accounts of slave merchants and ship captains, government publications, and records of slave trading companies. From these sources, Curtin concluded that Europeans imported 274,900 slaves into the Americas prior to 1600, 1,341,100 in the seventeenth century, 6,051,700 between 1701 and 1810, and 1,898,400 between 1811 and 1870, for a total of 9,566,100. He further explained that the peak of importation occurred in the third quarter of the eighteenth century when an average of over 60,000 Africans arrived annually. Yet Curtin emphasized that his numbers were approximations and that his total might be 20 percent too low or 20 percent too high.

He also provided an estimate of the geographical distribution of the slaves imported to the Americas, suggesting that about 40 percent went to Brazil; another 40 percent went to the British, French, and Dutch Caribbean islands; and fewer than 10 percent arrived in North America. He intended that his study would prompt other scholars to research the substantial unpublished sources available on both sides of the Atlantic and modify his calculations.

Since Curtin's book was published, many scholars have accepted his challenge, and after examining varied archival materials, several have offered revised estimates of the volume of the slave trade. Historians working on slave importations into Spanish America and North America and the Portuguese, French, Dutch, and British slave trades have argued that Curtin's overall estimate was too low. Joseph Inikori, Curtin's most prominent critic, asserts that Dunbar and Kuczynski were closer to the truth than Curtin and that over 15 million Africans were involved.

Beyond drawing from different source materials, a major reason for the differences between Curtin and the revisionists lies in their different vantage points in observing the slave trade. Curtin largely focused upon the number of slaves imported into the Americas while scholars arguing for a higher figure have tried to determine the number of slaves exported from Africa. Acknowledging that many Africans died resisting capture, while awaiting shipment across the Atlantic, and during the voyage to American ports, most historians now agree that Curtin's overall figure was too low. Although there are some exceptions, most now regard the total number of slaves exported from Africa to be about 11.5 million and believe that about 10 million reached the Americas.

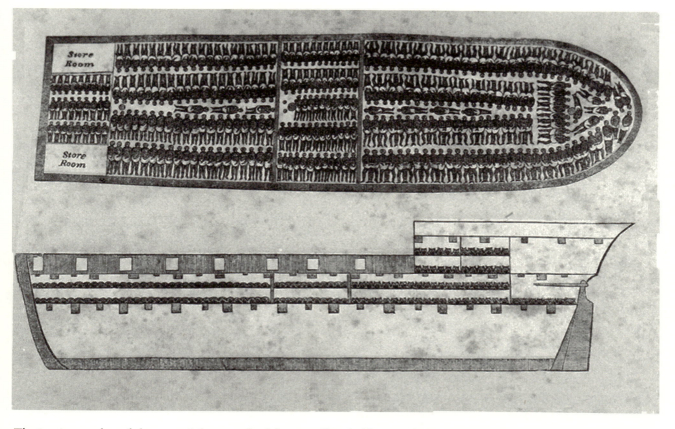

The precise number of slaves carried across the Atlantic will probably never be known, but the unimaginable crowding of human beings required to transport many millions of slaves to the Western Hemisphere is clear from this cross-section of a slave ship.

The impact of the slave trade on Africa is as increasingly important to historians as the number involved in the trade. There is little evidence that profits from the slave trade contributed to economic development in Africa; indeed, some scholars argue that the trade, by taking the healthiest and strongest in the population, retarded development. In some areas, the slave trade had a profound political impact. Along the Gold Coast, a combination of slave trade profits and European firearms contributed to the rise of the powerful kingdom of Dahomey. Most significant was the trade's demographic impact. Although it was not true of all areas, the slave trade contributed to a population decline in West Africa during the eighteenth century. Angola in particular suffered a significant loss of adult males, and by the 1780s, there were twice as many females as males in Angola.

Some scholars caution that factors like disease, drought, and famine better explain Africa's population decline than the slave trade. Still others contend there was no overall decline. Indeed, scholars argue that because of trade with the Americas, new food crops like maize and manioc were introduced into African agriculture and that the successful cultivation of these crops offset the losses to the slave trade by providing a more diverse food supply, one that was capable of sustaining larger and healthier populations.

Complicating matters in determining the impact of the large transatlantic slave trade was the substantial trans-Saharan slave trade. Largely organized by Muslims, nearly 5 million slaves were sold in North Africa and the Middle East prior to 1600, a trade that continued through the nineteenth century and may have involved over 15 million slaves.

Several questions about the volume of the slave trade remain unanswered. Notably, historians have been unable to determine the precise impact of this trade upon all regions where it existed. One scholar, David Henige, asserts there is simply not enough data to ever offer an acceptable global estimate of the slave trade. Nonetheless, there is substantial agreement about the volume of the transatlantic trade. Beginning with the Portuguese trade in the fifteenth century and continuing through the late-nineteenth century, most scholars have concluded that Europeans exported over 11 million Africans to the Americas and that about 10 million of them survived the trip.

—*Larry Gragg*

For Further Reading
Curtin, Philip. 1969. *The Atlantic Slave Trade: A Census*. Madison: University of Wisconsin Press; Ewald, Janet. 1992. "Slavery in Africa and the Slave Trades from Africa." *American Historical Review* 97(1): 465–485; Miller, Joseph. 1988. *Way of Death: Merchant Capitalism and the Angolan Slave Trade, 1730–1830*. Madison: University of Wisconsin Press; Northrup, David, ed. 1994. *The Atlantic Slave Trade*. Lexington, MA: D. C. Heath.

VOODOO

*T*he voodoo religion in Haiti derived as a result of the African slave trade from African beliefs and practices. Today, many Haitians still follow voodoo, and it has spread to parts of the United States, particularly New Orleans. Enslaved Yorubans who were taken from sub-Saharan West Africa and transported to the Caribbean carried their beliefs to the New World. The Yoruba, who originated in western Africa in what now constitutes Nigeria, Benin, and Togo, called their religion *vodoun*, from an African word for "spirit."

When the demand for slaves in the Americas increased in the sixteenth century, many Yorubans were captured by slavers and transported to the Caribbean. In Haiti, they secretly practiced their native religion, gradually adding Roman Catholic beliefs and customs from the religion their French masters forced on them. Voodoo evolved from this mixture of Catholic and Yoruban beliefs.

Some key tenets of the Yoruba religion include a belief in a supreme being, the Grand Master, or Gran Met, who rules over all; several lesser gods; and many lower spirits called *orisa* who are similar to Christian saints. The *orisa* were once human and received immortality from the Gran Met because of their good or heroic lives. The most popular *orisa* is Ogun, the god of hunting, war, and warriors. Through ceremonies and ritual, Yoruba believers contact their gods in an attempt to influence human affairs. They might pray alone or in ceremonial worship with a priest presiding or through ritual sacrifice of animals like dogs, sheep, and goats, depending on the *orisa*'s preference.

Thousands of people travel to the sacred waterfalls of Saut d'Eau in Haiti every year to take part in a voodoo cleansing ceremony during the celebration of the Virgin Mary's feast, also associated with the voodoo goddess of love, Erzulie.

Religious observance was a major part of the Yoruban's life in Africa, but in Haiti, the brutal constraints of slavery made religious observance difficult or impossible.

By 1780, more than 500,000 slaves labored in Haiti (then called Saint Domingue) and were controlled by about 30,000 white planters. The slaves were treated cruelly—whipped if they did not work fast enough, because the commodities they produced were extremely profitable. If they rebelled or tried escaping, they were tortured or killed. Because their lives were so hopeless, the slaves clung to their African memories. A constant influx of new slaves kept the memories alive, and children born in the Caribbean islands learned of Gine, as they called Africa, from their parents. In time, Gine became the undersea home of many voodoo spirits.

Because conditions were so different in Haiti, the Yoruba slaves gradually added to or changed some aspects of their religion. Ogun, once the god of hunting and warriors, became Ogoun, who gave slaves the strength to survive. Because the French Catholic slave-owners believed the slaves' religion was evil, they tried to suppress their slaves' beliefs and forced them to be baptized and instructed in Catholicism.

Although the slaves never relinquished the old beliefs, they came to appreciate some aspects of Catholicism and gradually integrated them into voodoo. Catholic services also provided a cover for voodoo worship. There are some similarities between Yoruba beliefs and Catholicism—particularly the importance of sacrifice and ritual. The Haitians transformed favorite Catholic saints into *loa,* spirit beings who acted as intermediaries between the Gran Met and ordinary humans. St. Patrick, who drove the snakes out of Ireland, became Dambala, a West African god shaped like a snake.

Many people associate voodoo with black magic and zombies, considering it a primitive, barbaric religion, yet contemporary voodoo is a complex and sophisticated religion defining humankind's relationship with God. Followers of voodoo believe in a remote supreme being, the Gran Met, and numerous lesser spirits called *loa* who interact with and help the living. The *loa* have a human need for food, preferring the blood and flesh of freshly killed animals—the sacrificial part of the voodoo service.

Followers of voodoo believe that the soul is separate from the earthly body and has two parts: the *gros bon ange* ("large guardian angel"), which is shared by all, and the *ti bon ange* ("small guardian angel"), which is unique. The *ti bon ange* can leave the body during sleep or a trance. During this time, it is vulnerable to possession by evil spirits, which is why much of voodoo ritual is concerned with the welfare of the soul. Voodoo rituals often coincide with Catholic holidays and are still an integral part of the lives of Haiti's people.

—*Elsa A. Nystrom*

See also
Obeah; Ogun Cult
For Further Reading
Belgium, Erik, and Don Nardo. 1991. *Great Mysteries, Voodoo: Opposing Viewpoints*. San Diego: Greenhaven Press; Davis, Wade. 1986. *The Serpent and the Rainbow*. New York: Warner Books; Miitraux, Alfred. 1959. *Voodoo in Haiti*. New York: Schocken Books.

WAGE SLAVERY

Antebellum workers in the northern part of the United States who were critical of evolving capitalist social relations often claimed they were treated on a par with the South's slaves. This comparison of the emerging wage labor system with chattel slavery was often summarized as "wage slavery." The term originated in Great Britain in the early-nineteenth century and was refined and elevated to the status of a battle cry in the North during the 1830s and 1840s. After the U.S. Civil War, the term was widely used by the Knights of Labor and Marxist writers who continued to link wage work and slavery well into the twentieth century.

The powerful image of "wage slaves," however, had a special meaning in the antebellum North, where the market was rapidly transforming work and social relations in cities like New York, Philadelphia, and the new mill towns like Lowell, Massachusetts. At the same time, a vocal and highly visible group of abolitionists began to call for an immediate end to slavery, which they claimed was both a sin and the antithesis of freedom. During the 1830s, white Northern workers began (hesitantly at first) to compare themselves to enslaved African Americans.

Striking textile millworkers in Lowell were among the first explicitly to make the comparison. Likening their bosses and foremen to Southern planters, women marched through the streets of Lowell in 1836 singing:

Oh! Isn't it a pity, such a pretty girl as I—
Should be sent to the factory to pine away
  and die?
Oh! I cannot be a slave,
I will not be a slave,
For I'm so fond of liberty
That I cannot be a slave. (Laurie, 1989)

For male artisans, who built the nation's first labor movement, the rise of the factory system was an ominous threat to their own independence. The same year as the Lowell strike, supporters of New York City's journeymen tailors published a famous handbill emblazoned with a coffin. The coffin symbolized how the workingman's one-time liberty had been "interred by . . . would-be masters." "Freemen of the North," the handbill warned, "are now on the level with the slaves of the South" (Commons et al., 1910).

Some historians of the antebellum period in the United States have pointed to the use of terms like "wage slavery" (and the popular substitute "white slavery") as evidence that labor reformers cared little about the plight of black slaves. Some have even concluded that the terms embody proslavery leanings among Northern whites. But even if some Northern workers viewed wage slavery as a more serious problem for the republic than chattel slavery, the very idea contained a condemnation of slavery itself. The core values of the early labor movement—which included democracy, independence, and the labor theory of value—were fundamentally at odds with the institution of slavery.

Take, for example, the labor editor and land reformer George Henry Evans, who helped make wage slavery a household term before the Civil War. As early as 1831, Evans called for an end to all forms of slavery and wrote editorials favoring full civil rights for free African Americans. He even went further than the abolitionist William Lloyd Garrison in support of Nat Turner and his rebellion. By the 1840s, Evans had hit upon a plan for universal land reform that, he thought, would end slavery, speculation in land, tenantry, and urban unemployment: free homesteads for actual settlers. For labor leaders and reformers like Evans, slavery of any type was a threat to liberty and progress.

Many of the views of labor radicals like Evans helped constitute the new, free soil ideology, which likewise opposed the expansion of Southern slavery and abolitionist "fanaticism." But the concept of wage slavery was diluted in the politics of both the Free Soil Party and, later, the Republican Party by the more developed ideology of "free labor," which held that with hard work and thrift, any wage earner could someday be an employer or a landowner.

After the Civil War, the broad-based Knights of Labor recycled the concept of wage slavery and railed against it in both print and oratory. By combining unionism and social reform, the Knights of Labor kept the concept before the American public even as a mature capitalist order made the abolition of work for wages an unattainable and radical dream. In the post–Civil War period, labor radicals recycled the term wage slavery to combat the industrial system.

—*Jonathan Earle*

See also
Capitalism; Marxism
For Further Reading
Commons, John R., et al. 1910. *A Documentary History of American Industrial Society*. Cleveland, OH: A. H. Clark; Cunliffe, Marcus. 1979. *Chattel Slavery and Wage Slavery: The Anglo-American Context, 1830–1860*. Athens: University of Georgia Press; Laurie, Bruce. 1989. *Artisans into Workers: Labor in Nineteenth Century America*. New York: Noonday Press; Roediger, David R. 1991. *Wages of Whiteness: Race and the Making of the American Working Class*. London: Verso.

WALKER, DAVID
(1785–1830)

A free black who left the South to settle in Boston, Massachusetts, David Walker was an influential voice in the fight against slavery through his writing. Born the son of a slave father and a free black mother in Wilmington, North Carolina, David Walker was a free black according to North Carolina law. As a youth, Walker was free to travel in the antebellum South, and he observed firsthand both the harsh nature of slavery and the unfair treatment accorded his mother. From an early age, Walker developed an attitude of disgust toward slavery. As a result of the racial unrest and heightened restrictions placed on free blacks caused by the Denmark Vesey conspiracy in 1822, Walker left the Charleston, South Carolina, area. Exactly where he traveled is uncertain, but by 1825, he had settled in Boston.

Once in Boston, Walker learned to read and write and opened a clothing store. He was generous to a fault—Walker never was a business success, but he was well-respected in the black community. Tall and slender with a dark complexion, Walker commanded respect physically as well. Walker continued his self-education and read widely on the institution of slavery, especially its history from Egypt to more contemporary slave societies. His emergence as an outspoken critic of slavery was natural considering his life experiences and his pursuit of a deeper understanding of the status of blacks in the United States.

In 1828, he addressed the General Colored Association of Massachusetts and made a fiery attack on slaveholders, urging blacks to oppose slavery and Southern attempts to recover fugitive slaves. Walker urged the audience to unify in the pursuit of black freedom, but within the limits of the U.S. Constitution. Although his address was later printed in *Freedom's Journal*, Walker's next published work had a far-greater impact on antislavery literature.

In 1829, Walker wrote an ambitious and incendiary tract that attacked slavery and outlined a plan for organized black opposition to the institution—a plan that included violence if necessary. Only a few months before *David Walker's Appeal* appeared, another black, Robert Alexander Young, had published *Ethiopian Manifesto*, a seven-page pamphlet stressing that God had created blacks and whites as equals, but Walker probably knew nothing of its existence.

David Walker's Appeal was published as four "articles" focusing on blacks, their degradation in slavery, and their need to revolt against their white oppressors. The writing is clear and vivid and propounds a well-reasoned argument against slavery. Portraying whites as the enemy, Walker saw racial harmony as unlikely given white attitudes. He did lay the framework for Christian forgiveness, but only if whites admitted their crimes against blacks. Walker adopted a "kill or be killed" philosophy and saw the necessity for insurrection if blacks were to achieve eventual equality.

Walker incorporated most of the major tenets of black nationalism in the *Appeal*. He stated blacks must have a nation of their own, provide for their own defense, and follow black leaders. Many historians view Walker as the earliest of the black nationalists in the United States. He was undoubtedly one of the more significant black ideologists and writers of the antebellum period—given his Southern heritage, Walker was a remarkable figure. White Southerners and slaveholders naturally held Walker in low esteem, but Southern reactions to *David Walker's Appeal* were indicative of their concerns and fears if the book and its ideas were widely circulated in the South.

Walker utilized a series of unofficial agents—black sailors, newspapermen, ministers, and other free blacks—to distribute the *Appeal* in Southern port cities. On December 29, 1829, only three months after the book's initial publication, the police in Savannah, Georgia, seized 60 copies of the *Appeal* that Walker had sent to Rev. Henry Cunningham. The next month, Atlanta officials intercepted 20 copies forwarded to newspaperman Elijah Burritt, a transplanted white New Englander. After it was discovered that Burritt had requested a copy (or more) of the tract, he went back north. Virginia governor William Giles alerted the state assembly that a black had circulated copies in Richmond, and copies were discovered in Walker's birthplace of Wilmington, North Carolina, in August 1830. City officials in Charleston, South Carolina, and New Orleans were alarmed when copies of the *Appeal* reached their cities in March 1830.

Public and legislative reactions were predictable as stricter measures against slave literacy, unsupervised slave religious activity, and the freedom of slaves to interact with free blacks were enforced in some states and passed in others. The circulation of *David*

Walker's Appeal aroused the three central fears of slaveowners: slave literacy was a dangerous skill, black preachers posed a real threat, and literate blacks could read to groups of illiterate slaves.

Rumors surrounding Walker's death in June 1830 were rampant—one spread that he was poisoned, another that several Georgia men had offered a reward of $1,000 (dead) or $10,000 (alive) for Walker. There is, however, no clear evidence that Walker died from anything more than natural causes, most likely consumption. Walker's true legacy focused on the *Appeal*, his active opposition to slavery worldwide, and his role in the evolution of black nationalism.

—*Boyd Childress*

See also
Vesey, Denmark
For Further Reading
Aptheker, Herbert. 1965. *One Continual Cry: David Walker's Appeal to the Colored Citizens of the World, 1829–1830, Its Setting and Its Meaning, together with the Full Text of the Third, and Last, Edition of the Appeal.* New York: Humanities Press; Hinks, Peter P. 1997. *To Awaken My Afflicted Brethren: David Walker and the Problem of Antebellum Slave Resistance.* University Park: Pennsylvania State University Press.

WALKER, WILLIAM
(1824–1860)

*I*n an era when many sought to expand slaveholding territory through the practice of "filibustering" (engaging in expansionist activities in foreign countries), the most notorious adventurer of the antebellum era in the United States, William Walker was born on May 8, 1824, in Nashville, Tennessee. Graduating from the University of Nashville in 1838, he subsequently studied medicine at the University of Pennsylvania and received his M.D. there in 1843. He pursued medical studies in Europe but then abandoned medicine to enter the legal profession. Admitted to the bar in New Orleans, Walker then turned to journalism and by 1848 was editor and proprietor of the New Orleans *Daily Crescent*.

Emigrating to California in 1850, Walker spent three years as an editor and lawyer. However, his restless spirit led him to embrace filibustering as the way to fulfill his longing for fame. In 1853, he sailed from San Francisco to wrest Lower (Baja) California and Sonora from Mexico. With an "army" of only 45 men, Walker's effort was doomed to failure from the start. By early 1854, "President Walker" of the short-lived Republic of Lower California was in full retreat for the U.S. border.

Walker and his chief confederates were tried in San Francisco for violating the neutrality laws. Acquitted by a sympathetic jury, Walker then determined to make Central America his next field of operations, a region that had increasingly become the focus of attention as American and European commercial interests viewed the isthmus as a potential interocean transit route. A prolonged conflict between Nicaragua's liberal and conservative factions offered Walker a second opportunity to fulfill his destiny. Accepting an invitation to organize armed American colonists for the liberal cause, Walker landed near Realejo on June 16, 1855. With his 56 "immortals" he helped the liberals win several important victories, and after the death of several liberal leaders through battle and disease, Walker emerged as the faction's foremost military commander.

Walker's capture of the Nicaraguan conservative stronghold of Granada in late 1855 effectively ended hostilities. The new government, a shaky coalition of both factions with Walker as commander in chief, was recognized by the United States in May 1856. The undisputed power in his adopted country, Walker became president through a controlled election in June of the same year.

However, Walker's position was far from secure. Armed and supplied by the British government, which had its own designs in the region, a coalition of Central American states launched a major invasion of Nicaragua in September 1856. Gradually losing the support of the native population, Walker filled his ranks with North Americans who poured into the country to claim land and other concessions from his administration.

Surrounded by hostile forces, Walker, in a decree dated September 22, restored African slavery in Nicaragua. Although previously regarded as a conservative on the slavery issue, Walker hoped to win support for his cause in the U.S. South. Indeed, historians contend that Southern expansionists, like Pierre Soule of Louisiana who visited Nicaragua in August, were instrumental in convincing Walker that his political survival depended on reinstating slavery. Even though he had opposed slavery's expansion in North America earlier, Walker succeeded in convincing Southerners that he was fighting for the preservation of the institution.

Despite the success of this gamble, Walker's effort was too late to prevent defeat. His rise to power had been partly owing to an alliance with the Accessory Transit Company, a U.S. corporation operating between New York and San Francisco by way of Nicaragua. However, control of the company was bitterly contested, and Walker soon found himself forced to choose between warring U.S. capitalists. When Walker withdrew his support from Cornelius Vanderbilt, one of the most powerful men in the United States, his fate was sealed.

Backed by his millions, Vanderbilt obtained full legal control of the transit company and sent agents to aid the Central American alliance. Led by Vanderbilt's mercenaries, the allies seized Walker's river fleet, thus cutting him off from the coast. At the same time, the British Royal Navy began to blockade the Atlantic coast of Nicaragua. Completely surrounded and with no hope of outside aid, Walker surrendered to the U.S. Navy on May 1, 1857.

Although totally out of favor with the U.S. government, Walker returned to a hero's welcome in the United States. Undaunted, he immediately organized a second expedition to Nicaragua but was thwarted by U.S. naval forces after landing on that country's coast in November 1857. Attempting to use Honduras as a base for another invasion of Nicaragua, Walker was captured by the Royal Navy. Turned over to the Honduran authorities, the greatest of the filibusters was executed by a firing squad on September 12, 1860.

One historian has written, "Walker's experience . . . offers insight into the relationship between filibustering and slavery" (Brown, 1980). Although regarded by Northerners and by many future historians as an agent of proslavery interests in the United States, Walker was not a Southern expansionist. Even at the height of his power he did not consider the annexation of Nicaragua by the United States but rather dreamed of forging the republics of Central America into a "military empire" under his rule. Far from being exploited by the "slave power," Walker apparently sought to exploit the Southern proslavery element in the United States in an effort to preserve his rule over Nicaragua.

—*James M. Prichard*

See also
Filibusters
For Further Reading
Brown, Charles H. 1980. *Agents of Manifest Destiny: The Lives and Times of the Filibusters.* Chapel Hill: University of North Carolina Press; Carr, Albert Z. 1963. *The World and William Walker.* New York: Harper and Row; May, Robert E. 1973. *The Southern Dream of a Caribbean Empire, 1854–1861.* Baton Rouge: Louisiana State University Press; Potter, David M. 1971. *The Impending Crisis, 1848–1861.* New York: Harper and Row.

THE WANDERER

The *Wanderer* was the most infamous slave ship of the period before the U.S. Civil War. Built in 1857 as a sporting schooner, Southern entrepreneurs from the United States, led by Charles A. L. Lamar, commissioned the vessel in 1859 to sail to Africa to obtain a clandestine slave cargo in violation of the U.S. prohibition of the international slave trade. Purporting to sail to St. Helena in the South Atlantic, the *Wanderer*'s crew succeeded in hiding the ship's destination and their nefarious plan. Once in open water, the ship veered east toward West Africa's coast and the Congo River.

Arriving at the Congo, the *Wanderer*'s officers ingratiated themselves with officers of the African Squadron patrolling the West African coast to enforce the abolition of the slave trade. With the British officers' tacit approval, the *Wanderer* boarded over 400 Africans and embarked for Georgia. As the ship dashed for open ocean, a U.S. vessel patrolling the coast as part of the antislavery squadron attempted to stop the *Wanderer*. Unfortunately for the slaves on board, the schooner's sleek design and top speed of nearly 20 knots was too much for the U.S. vessel.

After a six-week voyage, the *Wanderer* arrived off Jekyll Island, 60 miles south of Savannah, Georgia. Fewer than half the stolen African slaves had survived the journey. Those who had were quickly and covertly dispersed among plantations along Georgia's coast.

Federal authorities had learned of Lamar's activities, although too late to prevent the dispersion of the ship's slave cargo. However, the authorities seized the *Wanderer* and arrested three crew members for piracy. Lamar manipulated the crew members' arrests into a spectacle bemoaning abolitionist attacks on Southern society. Although federal judge James M. Wayne recommended conviction, local jurors acquitted the crew members of piracy. When Treasury Secretary Howell Cobb, also a Georgian, ordered the *Wanderer* auctioned, Lamar used intimidation, violence, and his substantial personal wealth to regain control of the ship.

Proponents for reopening the African slave trade saw the *Wanderer* case as a victory. The U.S. Civil War began before the *Wanderer* could make another slave smuggling voyage, and the U.S. Navy seized the ship and impressed it into service as a Union gunboat during the war. In 1871, the *Wanderer* was lost off Cuba.

—*John Grenier*

See also
African Squadron; Closing of the African Slave Trade; Illegal Slave Trade
For Further Reading
Wells, Tom Henderson. 1968. *The Slave Ship Wanderer.* Athens: University of Georgia Press; Wish, Harvey. 1941. "The Revival of the African Slave Trade in the United States, 1856–1860." *Mississippi Valley Historical Review* 27: 569–588.

WASHINGTON, BOOKER T.
(1856–1915)

Booker T. Washington was an educator, a social critic, and a reformer and was nationally and internationally renowned for his efforts at ameliorating the condition of blacks and healing the racial wounds inflicted by the Civil War and Reconstruction in the United States. Born a slave in Franklin County, Virginia, on April 5, 1856, he was the son of a house slave and an unknown white father. Washington spent nine years in slavery, the last four during the Civil War. Though he never quite felt the pinch of slavery as painfully as most other blacks, Washington was mature enough to understand the institution's destructive character.

When he was young, he was hungry, poorly clothed, and denied opportunity for education. His mother moved him and his sister to Malden, West Virginia, to join her husband who had fled during the Civil War, and Washington then worked with his stepfather in the salt mines. Young Washington yearned for knowledge, but his early learning was largely self-taught. Fortunately, Malden's colored population decided to establish a school for their children, the Kanawha Valley School, where Washington received his early formal education. He soon became a houseboy to Gen. Lewis Rufner and his wife, Viola, and having access to their rich library, often took books home to read. At the Rufners', Washington learned to appreciate cleanliness and industry.

He heard of the Hampton Normal Institute (an advanced school for blacks in Hampton, Virginia) founded by Gen. Samuel Armstrong, a Civil War veteran who believed that practical education would more effectively prepare blacks for participation in the emerging New South. Washington left for Hampton in 1872 and arrived tired, penniless, and hungry but filled with an insatiable thirst for knowledge. He gained admission and performed janitorial and cleaning duties to pay for his board and tuition. Hampton exposed him to practical education and manual labor. The curriculum emphasized agriculture, vocational skills, and self-reliance, and Washington learned to appreciate these skills. He graduated in 1875 with a faith in practical education as the key to black elevation.

After teaching briefly in Malden and at Wayland Baptist Seminary in Washington, D.C., he returned to Hampton as an instructor in 1878 and taught there until 1881 when General Armstrong recommended him to Alabama officials to help establish a similar school in that state. By 1881, Reconstruction had ended, and blacks were locked into a vicious cycle of poverty. Their rights and privileges had been sacrificed in the compromise of 1877 (the political compromise

Booker T. Washington

in which Rutherford F. Hayes won the presidency and radical Republicans agreed to end military Reconstruction), and blacks were constantly menaced by the shadow of slavery.

With a paltry $2,000 appropriated by the state of Alabama, Washington methodically built Tuskegee Institute, patterning it after Hampton. Tuskegee emphasized practical education and the inculcation of Christian work ethics and cleanliness. The students built their living quarters and academic buildings, they cultivated the land and produced and cooked their own food, and they studied subjects that instructed them in practical skills. Washington warned of the dire consequences of neglecting a practical education and implored blacks to acquire vocational skills, precisely those that would enable them to function as productive members of society.

He organized periodic fairs to advertise the students' productive efforts, established outreach links with local farmers, and frequently toured the region garnering support for Tuskegee. The fame of the institute spread, and Washington's reputation grew. He endeared himself favorably to whites as someone with vision and prudence, and in 1895, he was invited to address the annual Atlanta Cotton Exposition. That event marked the defining moment of his career.

The speech Washington delivered catapulted him to

the status of a national black leader. He addressed himself to two key audiences—Southern whites and blacks. He recommended agriculture to the blacks as the key to economic elevation and meaningful freedom. Blacks needed practical skills in order to become elevated and respected members of society, and he advised them to remain in the South, where opportunities for elevation abounded. Washington deprecated and discouraged the pursuit of political rights. He even favored suffrage restrictions based on property and education if equitably applied to both races.

He projected progress as a gradual and cumulative process and rejected calls for social equality. He deemed social equality to be of secondary importance. The two races could remain socially separate and yet cooperate on issues pertinent to mutual progress. As he put it, "In all things that are purely social we can be as separate as the fingers, yet one as the hand in all things essential to mutual progress." This statement became the centerpiece of his entire speech, the one that most people remember and quote.

Washington seemingly endorsed segregation. To whites, he gave assurances that their social and political dominance would not be challenged and said that blacks were neither interested in social equality and political rights nor ready for the exercise of such rights. He stressed the importance of economic cooperation between the races and appealed to the whites' moral and economic sensibilities. Whites applauded the speech.

Though Washington publicly counseled compromise and accommodation, clandestinely he sponsored antidiscriminatory activities. His tone of compromise and reconciliation was most reassuring to whites and most discomforting to blacks. His reputation among blacks suffered, even as whites elevated him to stardom. U.S. industrialists and philanthropists responded generously and poured funds into Tuskegee. In 1901, President Theodore Roosevelt invited Washington to dine with him. He became the authority on black affairs and the person whose opinions presidents and philanthropists sought.

Washington used his position to silence blacks who disagreed with him. He envisioned a proliferation of economically self-made blacks, and toward that end, he founded the National Negro Business League in 1900. In 1905, William Monroe Trotter and William E. B. DuBois spearheaded a movement to counter "the Tuskegee machine." This was the birth of the Niagara Movement, which unequivocally rejected compromise and accommodation. In 1909, the Niagara Movement became the National Association for the Advancement of Colored People (NAACP). Neither organization succeeded in effectively undermining Washington's position and power, and he continued to control and dominate the black American struggle until his death in 1915.

—*Tunde Adeleke*

For Further Reading
Harlan, Louis R. 1972. *Booker T. Washington: The Making of a Black Leader*. New York: Oxford University Press; Harlan, Louis R. 1983. *Booker T. Washington: The Wizard of Tuskegee, 1901–1915*. New York: Oxford University Press; Meier, August. 1963. *Negro Thought in America, 1880–1915*. Ann Arbor: University of Michigan Press.

WEBSTER, DANIEL (1782–1852)

Daniel Webster was a leading orator, statesmen, and lawyer of the early-nineteenth century. In the area of slavery, he negotiated the Webster-Ashburton Treaty, which removed the issue of the *Creole* that had been troubling U.S.-British relations; he was the best spokesman for unity during the nullification crisis of the 1830s; and he tried to serve as a voice for union during the period surrounding the Compromise of 1850, but was unsuccessful.

Webster was born in Salisbury, New Hampshire, of a family that had immigrated to America in the 1630s. He was the second youngest of 10 children and went to college at Dartmouth in 1797 when he was 15. He soon excelled in debating and was asked to deliver a Fourth of July address at age 18.

After graduation, he studied law, and was admitted to the Boston bar in 1805. Webster returned to New Hampshire for 11 years, marrying Grace Fletcher in 1808, keeping an office in Portsmouth for most of that time, and following the superior court as it traveled on its circuit. Toward the end of this period, he became more involved with politics, becoming a vocal member of the Federalist Party and opposing the War of 1812. He also made several well-received speeches across New Hampshire. He was elected to the U.S. House of Representatives in 1812 and strongly opposed the war and the embargo, but distanced himself from the Hartford Convention and its talk of disunion.

Webster was reelected in 1814 and promoted the Second Bank of the United States and opposed high tariffs on shipbuilding materials. In 1816, he moved his law office from New Hampshire to Boston and became more involved in legal work. He appeared before the U.S. Supreme Court in *Dartmouth College v. Woodword* (1819) and soon became noted as one of the nation's leading lawyers. A short time later, he reappeared before the Supreme Court to successfully argue for the Bank of the United States in *McCulloch v. Maryland* (1819). He focused on his successful law practice, which earned up to $15,000 a year, and participated in three other constitutionally significant cases: *Gibbons v. Ogden* (1824), *Osborn v. Bank of the United States* (1824), and *Ogden v. Saunders* (1827).

Webster became involved in the battle over nullification, and in 1830 he delivered his famous reply to South Carolina senator Robert Hayne, declaring that he favored "Liberty and Union, now and forever, one and inseparable" (Baxter, 1984). Webster was reelected in 1833, supported the high tariffs of the period in the battle over the "compromise tariff" of 1833, and opposed President Andrew Jackson's attempts to withdraw deposits from the Bank of the United States. Throughout his career, Webster spent heavily and was dependent on loans from friends, associates, and creditors, including the Bank of the United States, so he was a congressional and legal advocate of the bank while also being in debt to it. He increasingly began to overindulge in alcohol, which resulted in weight gain and occasional drunkenness.

Webster was nominated by Massachusetts for president in 1836 but received only the electoral votes of that state in the contest. He was reelected to the Senate in 1839, campaigned for William Henry Harrison in the election of 1840, and was named secretary of state after Harrison's victory. Upon the accession of John Tyler, Webster remained in that office and conducted difficult negotiations regarding the Maine border and several other issues that were solved by the Webster-Ashburton Treaty (1842). The issues raised in the *Creole* case were addressed as the British promised that colonial governors would avoid "officious interference" when U.S. vessels forced by violence or by storm entered their ports, and he also was successful in diplomatic ventures with China, Mexico, and Portugal.

Webster resigned in 1843 under heavy pressure from his party and returned to his legal career, even though he desired an appointment to England. He returned to the Senate in 1845, with financial assistance from his creditors, and opposed the acquisition of Texas and later the Mexican War. In the Mexican War (1846–1848), Webster's second son, Edward, died, and his daughter Julia died not long after.

After the election of 1848, a new sectional crisis loomed, and Webster tried to preserve the nation. In his famous "Seventh of March" speech in 1850, he claimed that keeping the nation together was more important than the issue of slavery. He was widely praised by people in the South but condemned by his own party and Northern abolitionists. Nevertheless, he became secretary of state again in 1850 and performed his duties capably. He was interested in the presidential nomination in 1852 but could not carry the Whig Party. Webster began to decline physically in summer 1852 and died on October 24 of that year, well before the sectional crisis he tried so hard to avoid.

—*Scott A. Merriman*

See also

Adams, John Quincy; Calhoun, John C.; Hayne-Webster Debate; Webster-Ashburton Treaty

For Further Reading

Baxter, Maurice. 1984. *One and Inseparable: Daniel Webster and the Union.* Cambridge, MA: Harvard University Press; Peterson, Merrill. 1987. *The Great Triumvirate: Webster, Clay, and Calhoun.* New York: Oxford University Press; Shewmaker, Kenneth, ed. 1990. *Daniel Webster: The "Completest Man."* Hanover, NH: University Press of New England; Smith, Craig R. 1989. *Defender of the Union: The Oratory of Daniel Webster.* New York: Greenwood.

WEBSTER-ASHBURTON TREATY (1842)

The Webster-Ashburton Treaty of 1842 settled several outstanding issues between the United States and Great Britain, including the handling of U.S. ships carrying slaves forced into British ports and joint U.S.-British efforts to limit the African slave trade. The treaty is named for the two principal negotiators of the pact, Daniel Webster of the United States and Lord Ashburton (Alexander Baring) of Great Britain.

The main issues covered were related to slavery and the northeastern boundary of the United States, the latter having nearly brought the two nations into conflict in 1839 in the Aroostook War. An extradition agreement was one large part of the treaty. This grew out of the *Creole* incident in 1841, in which a slave ship of that name engaged in interstate U.S. trade, was taken over by mutinous slaves, and was sailed by them to Nassau in the British-controlled Bahamas, where the slaves who had not participated in the mutiny were freed. After heated debate, the British finally decided to free the mutineers as well. The whole incident did not please the South, and an extradition agreement covering nonpolitical crimes was inserted in the Webster-Ashburton Treaty to cover a future *Creole* type of case, as the mutinous slaves would now be at least theoretically returned.

In addition, there was also provision for a joint cruising squadron off the African coast to prevent the British from having to interfere with U.S. ships, as the American squadron would do so when needed. This provision was also supposed to prevent slavers trading with Africa from illegally hiding behind the U.S. flag. The United States had banned the slave trade, but without U.S. ships patrolling off the African coast, ships flying the U.S. flag could not be searched. The treaty was supposed to correct this problem.

The treaty also dealt with problems connected with the northeastern boundary. Although the issue seemed to have been solved by the Treaty of Paris (1783), which ended the American Revolution, that agreement had merely established a commission, which never reached a conclusion, and later attempts to arbitrate the boundary had been equally unsuccessful. Another border area that was decided by the Webster-Ashburton Treaty was one involving the area around Lake Superior, which was settled favorably to the United States, including granting that country the Vermilion Range in northeastern Minnesota, which—unknown then—is very rich in mineral deposits. The United States was also granted free navigation of the Saint John River in northeastern Maine and southeastern Canada.

Besides signing the treaty, several important notes were exchanged. One recorded the disagreement of the United States with the former British practice of impressment. A second allowed for the protection of ships by the flag they flew, which theoretically covered incidents like one in the 1830s in which a U.S. ship ferrying supplies to Canadian rebels was attacked and sunk by Canadians, which angered many citizens of the United States. A third note assured that U.S. ships driven into foreign ports would be allowed to continue without interference—this note also dealt with the *Creole* incident.

—*Scott A. Merriman*

See also
Webster, Daniel
For Further Reading
Baxter, Maurice. 1984. *One and Inseparable: Daniel Webster and the Union.* Cambridge, MA: Harvard University Press; Jones, Howard. 1977. *To the Webster-Ashburton Treaty: A Study in Anglo-American Relations, 1783–1843.* Chapel Hill: University of North Carolina Press.

WELD, THEODORE DWIGHT (1803–1895)

Theodore Dwight Weld was a social reformer and one of the most important figures in the antislavery movement in the United States. Through his work at Lane Theological Seminary and later at Oberlin College, both in Ohio, he influenced many people who later became active in the national crusade against slavery. Weld was a tireless worker for the antislavery cause, but his work was virtually forgotten and unknown until the publication of Gilbert H. Barnes's *The Antislavery Impulse,*

1830–1844, in 1933. Barnes was the first historian to recognize Weld's huge contribution at the beginning of the antislavery movement. Writing in the *Dictionary of American Biography,* he said of Weld: "Measured by his influence, Theodore Weld was not only the greatest of the abolitionists; he was also one of the greatest figures of his time."

Weld was born in Connecticut but raised in western New York State. His father was a conservative, small-town pastor. Weld had little formal education, but his "learning [was] prodigious, his powers of reasoning superb." He has been described as "the nerve center of the antislavery movement until the schism of 1840" (Barnes, 1933).

Weld's early career was inextricably connected to the work of Charles Grandison Finney, a clergyman and educator, as both men made antislavery a religious and moral issue, separate from politics and economics. Weld had been an early associate of the abolitionist Charles Stuart, who had interested him in the slavery question. Both Stuart and Weld fell under Finney's influence and were active members of his band of religious revivalists. Finney has long been regarded as the foremost figure of the Second Great Awakening during the early-nineteenth century, and it was through Finney's teachings and Stuart's interest in reform that Finney's followers became interested and, later, heavily involved in the antislavery crusade.

Weld became interested in the slavery issue as early as 1830, and he began to travel, particularly to colleges and universities in northeastern Ohio to "indoctrinate" faculties in opposition to slavery. His association with others in the movement won him respect for his leadership and his oratory. He was a close friend of James G. Birney and the Grimké sisters (he later married Angelina Grimké). Birney's personal knowledge of slavery's sordid aspects developed in Weld an intense, personal patriotism, and he came to view "the peculiar institution" as a "cancerous growth within the body politic." Weld and Birney became active members of the American Colonization Society, and in 1832, Weld became the society's general agent for states lying southwest of the Ohio River.

Weld and his associates gradually moved away from the ideas espoused by the American Colonization Society and toward the idea of general emancipation. The American Anti-Slavery Society was established in 1833 as the result of this change in the movement's direction, and its program was defined as "immediate preparation for future emancipation." This group followed the lead set by Birney and others involved in, what was then, the revolutionary Kentucky Society for the Gradual Relief of the State from Slavery, whose charter proclaimed: "First, that slavery shall cease to exist—absolutely, unconditionally, and irrevocably."

One of Weld's greatest contributions to the anti-slavery crusade came through his work at Lane Theological Seminary in Cincinnati, Ohio. That city had about 2,500 African Americans, more than one-third of all the blacks in Ohio. Many of them were emancipated slaves who had purchased their freedom or who were still paying for themselves or for friends and relatives still in bondage. It was in Cincinnati that emancipated slaves were given the opportunity to test their ability to make economic, cultural, and social advances not otherwise available to them. They threw themselves into the task, and education was their chief goal. They formed Sunday schools, day and evening schools, and a lyceum where lectures were held four evenings a week with local and guest speakers on grammar, geography, arithmetic, philosophy, religion, and politics. In this environment Weld enjoyed his greatest success as the leader of the theological classes.

The students shared their stories of slavery and how they had managed to escape to Ohio. "They had pooled their intimate knowledge of slavery gained by long residence in the slave states, had reasoned and rationalized as became gentlemen [and ladies] trained in the school of the Great Revival, and had concluded that slavery was a sin great enough to justify their undivided attention" (Thomas, 1950). Most of the students and Weld moved from Lane Theological Seminary to Oberlin College where their ideas about slavery were better received and where Finney had become head of the Theology Department.

It was at Oberlin, and after Weld's marriage to Angelina Grimké in 1838, that he wrote and published the first widely distributed book in the United States advocating complete emancipation. *Slavery as It Is: Testimony of a Thousand Witnesses* (1839), a devastating indictment of the institution, was his magnum opus. Nearly all of the episodes mentioned in the book came from the Lane-Oberlin students, and it portrayed the slavery system at its worst by documenting case after case of extreme cruelty. The work was lauded by antislavery and abolitionist groups and was soundly criticized in the South. Few could read it without emotion and without hating slavery. It quickly became abolitionist ammunition since its impact in the North was tremendous.

It was widely distributed and sold for only 37.5 cents a copy or $25 per 100. It was the preeminent book of antislavery literature until 1852 when Harriet Beecher Stowe published *Uncle Tom's Cabin* (Stowe had been one of Weld's Oberlin students, much to the chagrin of her father, Lyman Beecher). *Slavery as It Is* served as one of Charles Dickens's sources for his book *American Notes* (1842), though he gave Weld no credit, and Weld's book also led to British interest in ending slavery in their territories. A book of statistics designed to accompany *Slavery as It Is* was published in London under the title *Slavery and the Internal Slave Trade in the United States* in 1841.

Weld also wrote a companion volume, which argued that God was against slavery. *The Bible against Slavery* (1839) dealt only with the Old Testament, but it led to the publication of still another book, written together with Beriah Green and Elizur Wright, Jr., both eminent theologians, that brought the antislavery argument into the New Testament: *The Chattel Principle, the Abhorrence of Jesus Christ and the Apostles; or, No Refuge for American Slavery in the New Testament* (1839).

Weld's books became instant best-sellers, but his influence peaked in the early 1840s. The antislavery crusade continued on the roller coaster that led, inevitably, to the U.S. Civil War. Weld spent his last years in near seclusion in Massachusetts, occasionally lecturing on literature and religion. He was surrounded by the intellectuals of his day, particularly by the poet John Greenleaf Whittier, who wrote of Weld in 1884, that he had lived "a life of brave unselfishness . . . for Freedom's need" (Thomas, 1950). Weld died on February 3, 1895, at the age of 91 years and two months. His life nearly spanned the entire nineteenth century, and he participated in almost every major reform movement of the age.

—*Henry H. Goldman*

For Further Reading
Barnes, Gilbert Hobbs. 1933. *The Anti-Slavery Impulse, 1830–1844*. Glocester, MA: Peter Smith; Dumond, Dwight Lowell. 1959. *Antislavery Origins of the Civil War in the United States*. Ann Arbor: University of Michigan Press; Lloyd, Arthur Young. 1939. *The Slavery Controversy, 1831–1860*. Chapel Hill: University of North Carolina Press; Thomas, Benjamin P. 1950. *Theodore Dwight Weld, Crusader for Freedom*. New Brunswick, NJ: Rutgers University Press.

WEST AFRICA

When Portuguese navigators first cruised down the West African coast, they found that many of the societies there owned slaves and were willing to sell them. Conditions in West Africa favored the development of slavery. Population densities were low, and the control of people was more important than land. Slavery had been important in the medieval empires of Ghana, Mali, and Songhai, and slave exports had supplemented the export of gold. Slaves were probably the most important export north of the area around Lake Chad, but they were also important in Saharan oases and desert-edge communities where they produced grain for the nomadic peoples.

The Atlantic slave trade encouraged traders to push trade routes deeper into the interior and stimulated the formation of more centralized states, particularly after the development of West Indian sugar plantations increased the demand for African slaves. Between 1650 and 1750, the Oyo, Ashanti, Dahomey, Segu, and Futa Jallon states all appeared. In most of them, and in many of the smaller states, slaves were a major part of the slave-producing machine. They were the best soldiers and the most trusted chiefs; the rich and powerful had slave wives and concubines, and the courts were often fed by slave villages.

Claude Meillassoux (1991) contrasts that aristocratic slavery to that of merchant communities. In West Africa, mercantile communities date back to at least the thirteenth or fourteenth centuries. These communities profited from the slave trade, providing guns and commodities for the slavers and marketing the slaves. They also kept many slaves for themselves and exploited their labor for profit. Demand for slaves by both aristocratic and merchant sectors meant that many of those enslaved, perhaps a majority, were kept within Africa. In particular, women and children were usually kept. Though men were usually more highly valued by European slave traders, the price of women was almost everywhere higher than the price of men.

There were several stages in the absorption of slaves. The newly enslaved were carefully watched and harshly treated, often kept in chains if escape was feared. During the early years of their enslavement, they worked under supervision. After a while, most slaves became what Meillassoux calls allotment slaves. They worked five or six days until about 2:00 P.M. on the master's lands, usually receiving a meal on the days they worked for the master. In the evenings and on their days off, they worked their own plots. In the third stage, which Meillassoux calls settled slaves, slave families had their own plot of land. They still had obligations to the master, but most of the time they worked their lands in exchange for a fixed obligation, usually about what it took to feed an adult male for a year.

Slaves could accumulate wealth but had none of the rights of free persons. Slave women were available as concubines or for casual sex, and slave children were often taken to work in the master's house when old enough and could be given to the master's children when the latter married. Slaves kept any property they accumulated, but when they died, the master could seize it. Some masters allowed slaves to inherit, but it was the master's choice. Slaves "born in the house" were not supposed to be sold, but many were sold during famines or if they misbehaved. Slaves were expected to be deferential and to dress simply. Manu-

mission was recommended as a pious act in the Qur'an. The most common emancipation was for slave women who bore children for their masters, but trusted retainers were also freed. The manumitted slave could marry and bequeath but remained dependent on his or her master.

There was yet another kind of slavery. Many of the egalitarian, less centralized societies did not have slaves. Some got pulled into the slave trade by a desire for commodities or weapons useful for defense, and once involved in selling people, they often kept some of them, but never large numbers, and the offspring of these slaves usually became full members of the families. Slaves in such egalitarian societies generally lived with the family and often ate from the same bowl. In merchant and aristocratic communities, most slaves lived in separate villages or separate quarters. In decentralized societies, slaves worked alongside their masters and did the same kind of work.

Merchant masters watched their slaves work, often reading the Qur'an while they did so, or if they lived in separate villages, had their work supervised. The assimilative model sometimes survived even after development of centralized states. Among the Akan of southern Ghana, it took three generations for slaves to be absorbed into the lineage. There is an Akan proverb that one should never ask a person's origin.

—*Martin A. Klein*

See also
The Ashanti; *Ceddo;* Dahomey; Ghana, Kingdom of; Mali; Slave Villages; Songhai Empire
For Further Reading
Manning, Patrick. 1990. *Slavery and African Life: Occidental, Oriental, and African Slave Trades.* Cambridge: Cambridge University Press; Meillassoux, Claude. 1991. *Anthropology of Slavery.* Chicago: University of Chicago Press; Meillassoux, Claude, ed. 1975. *L'Esclavage en Afrique precoloniale.* Paris, Maspero; Miers, Suzanne, and Igor Kopytoff. 1977. *Slavery in Africa.* Madison: University of Wisconsin Press.

WEST INDIES

Many European nations sought to establish plantation economies in the West Indies in the seventeenth century. Following Columbus's voyages, Spain had claimed all of the West Indies over a century earlier, but they concentrated on the large islands of Cuba, Puerto Rico, Hispaniola, and Jamaica. Beginning in the 1620s, the French, English, and Dutch seized the neglected smaller islands of the Lesser Antilles. Although more than a dozen of these developed plantation economies

Slaves from Charleston, South Carolina, being sent to the West Indies by the British during the American Revolutionary War. British proclamations of freedom for slaves in British-controlled areas were not always honored.

were dependent upon slave labor, the earliest important ones were the English colonies of Barbados, established in 1627, and Jamaica, seized from the Spanish in 1655. Even though Saint Domingue (now Haiti) and Cuba later eclipsed them in significance, the two British islands largely set the pattern of slavery in the West Indies.

Like many islands, Barbados's initial settlers used the labor of white indentured servants from their homeland as they experimented with cash crops like tobacco, indigo, and cotton. After some planters introduced sugarcane to the island in the late 1630s, most shifted to that sweet commodity. Following nearly a decade of learning the techniques of cultivating and processing sugar, planters improved the crop's yield and quality. Because of the remarkable European demand for sugar, it quickly became the highest priced colonial commodity.

Because sugar was a labor-intensive crop, planters needed many workers. Preparing the ground to plant the canes, fertilizing and weeding young plants, cutting mature plants, transporting cane to the mills, grinding the cane, and then boiling and curing the

juice required much hand labor. Compared to tobacco cultivation, planters needed three times as many workers per acre. By the mid-eighteenth century, successful planters on Jamaica and Saint Domingue had about one laborer for every two acres of land in production. Although some planters continued raising tobacco, cotton, or coffee, sugar was the favored commodity. Consequently, planters maintained an insatiable demand for labor, a demand they could never fill with white indentured servants. Instead, they turned to the slave trade. Of the over 10 million slaves imported into the Americas, more than one-third were taken to the West Indies. The largest numbers went to Cuba, Jamaica, and Hispaniola. By 1790, it is likely there were over 1 million slaves in the West Indies—460,000 of them in Saint Domingue alone.

On islands where sugar predominated, nearly 90 percent of all slaves worked on large plantations of 200 acres, which meant a labor force of about 100 slaves. Most were field hands. About one in five (20 percent) was an artisan, carpenter, machinist, cooper, or sugar boiler, and fewer than 5 percent were house slaves. Normally working six days a week from dawn to dusk, during the peak harvesting and milling season the slaves might face a workday of nearly 20 hours. Usually they worked in gangs. The alternative task system, used with other crops and on smaller sugar estates, gave slaves more incentive, and once they had completed their specified tasks, the slaves had control of their time. Yet, large-scale sugar planters believed the gang system was more efficient. Directed by white overseers or black drivers, the most mature slaves, who handled the most arduous tasks, made up the first or primary gang while children or the elderly served in a second or third gang, completing lighter tasks. Because men died at a younger age and performed most of the skilled tasks, women became increasingly important as field hands.

Most slaves in the West Indies suffered from poor health. Upon arrival from Africa they were weak because of poor rations and exposure to various illnesses, notably smallpox and dysentery, during their voyage. Overworked and vulnerable to typhus, tuberculosis, and a range of gastrointestinal ailments, most were sick for much of their remaining years. Nearly a third died within three years, and many more did not survive a decade in the West Indies—particularly the males, who had a shorter life expectancy than females. Consequently, even though planters imported more males, females eventually became a majority in the slave population.

As the ratio of women to men rose, more and more slaves lived as part of a family group. Few were married legally, but most adults had long-term companions. Rarely did they have many children, because disease, overwork, and malnutrition contributed to low birthrates and infant mortality rates were quite high. Homes for these small slave families usually were little more than wattle-and-daub cabins with thatch roofs. The low, dark, and hot structures had scarcely any furniture. The slaves' diet seldom varied. Cassava, potatoes, salt fish, corn, and beans were the staples, and there was only an occasional meat supplement. Infrequently, masters permitted slaves to cultivate their own small garden plots.

Resistance was common among West Indian slaves. Although the temporary desertion of individual slaves posed no significant threat, the development of large communities of runaways, particularly the well-organized Maroon settlements of runaway salves on Cuba, Haiti, and Jamaica, frightened planters. Concern about conspiracy, revolt, and uprising led most planters to support tough slave codes.

The statutes adopted in Barbados in 1661 became a model for the other islands. These codes denied slaves all legal rights and placed complete control over their lives in their master's hands. Other than providing a minimal clothing allotment, planters had scarcely any obligations in caring for their property.

Slaves could not carry weapons or leave their plantation without a pass. Recalcitrant ones could be lashed without restraint, and the punishment for killing one's slaves was only a fine.

Other than the Spanish, few planters showed much interest in their slaves' cultural and religious lives, which enabled most of them to retain some West African traditions and beliefs as they adopted elements of European culture. The resulting cultural mix almost always included traditional folktales, dialects, music, and ancestor worship. This private life was one over which slaves had much control, and while they could not change their servile status, West Indian slaves shaped a culture distinct from that of their European masters.

—*Larry Gragg*

See also
Transition from Slave Labor to Free Labor, Caribbean; Women as Slaves, West Indies
For Further Reading
Bridenbaugh, Carl, and Roberta Bridenbaugh. 1972. *No Peace beyond the Line: The English in the Caribbean, 1624–1690*. New York: Oxford University Press; Dunn, Richard. 1972. *Sugar and Slaves: The Rise of the Planter Class in the English West Indies, 1624–1713*. Chapel Hill: University of North Carolina Press; Klein, Herbert. 1986. *African Slavery in Latin America and the Caribbean*. New York: Oxford University Press; Williams, Eric. 1944. *Capitalism and Slavery*. Chapel Hill: University of North Carolina Press.

WHEATLEY, PHILLIS
(C. 1753–1784)

As the first published black poetess in the American colonies, Phillis Wheatley's life and work contributed to the eighteenth- and nineteenth-century debate about the intellectual capabilities of African Americans. Details about her early life in West Africa remain obscure. She arrived in Boston in July 1761 aboard the slaver *Phillis* and was sold to John Wheatley, a prominent local merchant.

Although the Wheatley family owned several slaves, Phillis appears to have held a privileged position within the household. Initially, she received religious instruction and learned to speak, read, and write in English. Later, her education expanded to include literature, history, Latin, and geography. Wheatley was a bright pupil, and within four years of her arrival, she had begun to write her own poetry, an activity her owner's family encouraged. Wheatley's poems centered around religious themes (particularly

Phillis Wheatley's portrait appears on this page of her book of poems. Testimonials from prominent whites were required to convince a skeptical public that a black woman slave was capable of writing such verse.

Although the success of her volume boded well for Wheatley, upheaval in her personal life during and after the American Revolution put an end to her career as a poet. By 1779, most of the Wheatley family had died, and Phillis herself had married a free black named John Peters. She bore him three children over the next five years, but all of them died young. Financial difficulties plagued the family, and Wheatley's attempts to publish additional volumes of poetry were unsuccessful. Wasted by poverty and disease, she died on December 5, 1784.

Both during her lifetime and after her death, Wheatley's work received attention primarily because she was a woman and a black slave. Serious literary evaluations of her poetry have been overshadowed by efforts to use her as an example in the debate over African American intellectual ability, or lack thereof. Thomas Jefferson, in particular, brought attention to her work when he cited her poetry in his *Notes on Virginia* (1785) as "below the dignity of criticism," a comment that vaulted her to the very center of the controversy about the capacity of African Americans to engage in intellectual pursuits.

In the late-twentieth century, discussions concerning Wheatley have centered around her role in the demise of moral and intellectual justifications for slavery, particularly in New England. Critics condemn her for focusing her poems on the subjects of death, religion, and patriotism rather than on the plight of her fellow Africans in slavery. Supporters counter that Wheatley's concerns about slavery are implicit throughout her work. This debate has led to a reevaluation of her work and additional study into the details of her life.

—*Elizabeth Dubrulle*

For Further Reading

Mason, Julian D., Jr., ed. 1989. *The Poems of Phillis Wheatley*. Chapel Hill: University of North Carolina Press; O'Neale, Sondra A. 1985. "Challenge to Wheatley's Critics: There Was No Other 'Game' in Town." *Journal of Negro Education* 54 (4): 500–511; Robinson, William H. 1981. *Phillis Wheatley: A Bio-Bibliography*. Boston: G. K. Hall; Robinson, William H. 1984. *Phillis Wheatley and Her Writings*. New York: Garland.

death) and the growing tension between Great Britain and the American colonies.

As her talent for writing matured, the Wheatley family became more involved in promoting her work to a wide audience and began a campaign to publish her poems. In December 1767, Wheatley's first poem, "On Messrs Hussey and Coffin," was published in Newport, Rhode Island. In 1770, her poem on the death of Methodist minister George Whitefield brought her considerable attention throughout New England.

Wheatley's first and only book, *Poems on Various Subjects, Religious and Moral* (1773), was published in London. To erase doubts that a black slave, particularly a woman, could write poetry, a letter appeared in the front of the book signed by 18 of Boston's most prestigious citizens, including Governor Thomas Hutchinson and John Hancock, testifying that a close examination of Wheatley and her work had convinced them that she had indeed written the poetry herself. The volume received good reviews and sold well in both England and America.

WHITEFIELD, GEORGE
(1714–1770)

George Whitefield, a pioneering figure in eighteenth-century Christian evangelism in the Anglo-American world, helped lay the abolition movement's foundations but had mixed thoughts on slavery's evils. Ordained an Anglican minister in 1736, Whitefield was a brilliant preacher whose innovative open-air preaching and emotional style won an immense popular following and was part of the British revival that led to Methodism. Visiting the American colonial South in 1739, Whitefield observed plantation society's cruelty, noted with displeasure the lack of religious provision for slaves, and unconventionally decided to address mixed-race meetings.

In 1740, Whitefield began his first major preaching tour in the Northern colonies, helping trigger the revivals that were part of what became known as the Great Awakening. Following this tour, he printed a letter "To the inhabitants of Maryland, Virginia, North and South Carolina concerning their Negroes," which exposed the harsh and unchristian conditions slaves endured. The letter was reprinted in newspapers across the country and aroused intense controversy. Attempts to establish a college to educate freed slaves in Delaware further demonstrated his humanitarian concerns, and that is one reason why the black poet Phillis Wheatley wrote an elegy for Whitefield in which she called him a friend to those in bondage.

Despite Whitefield's concern for the physical well-being of slaves and their spiritual salvation, he never condemned the institution of slavery outright. Whitefield thought slavery was justified by Scripture, that it could bring spiritual benefits because it exposed Africans to the Christian message, and while not approving of the slave trade, he thought it could not be controlled. Whitefield's connection with the struggling colony of Georgia, where he founded an orphanage, influenced his thinking. In 1747, South Carolina planters donated a small plantation to the orphanage, and the plantation's success, run on strict guidelines, supported Whitefield's long-standing belief, voiced in a letter to the Georgia trustees in 1748, that slavery's legalization was necessary for Georgia's success.

Even though Whitefield held proslavery ideas, the active evangelical Christianity he promoted became a seedbed for abolitionism. That fact is obvious from examining the abolitionist tendencies of the movements that Whitefield's work encouraged, like the Methodism of his close friend John Wesley, the Anglican evangelical movement that produced William Wilberforce, and the Great Awakening. A good example is Anthony Benezet, one of those awakened to an intense piety by Whitefield's preaching, who became committed to abolition and condemned Whitefield's views on slavery. Whitefield's emphasis on the need to convert slaves and the spiritual equality between black and white also helped promote black church formation and was the basis of a major argument against slavery. Accordingly, the evangelical and populist ideals behind the abolitionist crusade can be partially seen as Whitefield's legacy.

—*Gwilym Games*

See also
Abolition, United States; Georgia; Stono Rebellion; Wheatley, Phillis
For Further Reading
Heimert, Alan. 1966. *Religion and the American Mind: From the Great Awakening to the Revolution.* Cambridge, MA: Harvard University Press; Lambert, Frank. 1994. *Peddler in Divinity: George Whitefield and the Transatlantic Revivals.* Princeton, NJ: Princeton University Press.

WHITNEY, ELI
(1765–1825)

Eli Whitney invented the cotton gin and developed the assembly line for the mass production of interchangeable parts. Whitney's cotton gin profoundly affected the economy of the United States, revolutionized the cotton industry, and further entrenched slavery in the antebellum South. During his childhood in Westboro, Massachusetts, Whitney demonstrated an exceptional mechanical ingenuity. When he was 16, he established a successful nail-forging business to address the shortage of nails during the American Revolution. He entered Yale College in 1789, despite a friend's remark that "it was a pity that such a fine mechanical genius as his should be wasted" (Olmsted, 1846).

After graduating from Yale in 1792, Whitney went to Savannah, Georgia, to study law and tutor the children of the late Gen. Nathanael Greene. Greene's widow and her friends continually discussed the profitability of growing cotton in the area to satisfy England's heightened demand for the fiber. The growing use of steam power to spin and weave fabric had led to an increased demand for raw cotton in England, and Georgia's inland region was favorable for growing green-seed, short-staple cotton. However, the method of separating the cotton from its seed was so tedious that it was impractical, since one worker could only separate only about one pound of clean green-seed cotton per day.

Whitney devised a machine that would address the problem. During the winter of 1792, he created a model cotton gin (an abbreviation for "engine") that expedited the cotton separation operation. The gin consisted of a roller with comblike teeth that removed the seeds from the fiber and a spinning brush that removed the excess lint from the roller. After perfecting his gin by April 1793, Whitney's machine enabled one worker to process 50 pounds of cotton a day.

Soon, other inventors imitated Whitney's gin, and he depleted his earnings defending his patent rights in court. Heavily in debt in 1798, he contracted with the U.S. government to make 10,000 muskets. Whitney designed a machine that produced a firearm with interchangeable parts, and he created a division of labor whereby each person specialized in making one part of the musket.

The cotton gin transformed the U.S. economy and increased the demand for slave labor. In the South, cotton became the chief crop and the basis of the region's economy. Cotton production in the South increased from about 3,000 bales in 1793 to approximately 178,000 bales by 1800. Cotton was "king" and the greatest export of the country. In 1825, cotton represented $36 billion of an estimated total of $66 billion total domestic exports from the United States. By 1860, cotton production had exploded to 4 million bales per year.

This profound increase in cotton production affected the Northern economy as well. The bountiful cotton crop encouraged New England entrepreneurs to create a native textile industry, and the manufacturing of cotton cloth enabled the North to evolve into an industrialized region.

Coupled with the increased demand for cotton came the need for more slave labor. By the late-eighteenth century, slavery had appeared to be in decline. The Northern states took steps to abolish forced servitude, since it was never vital to their economy, and during the same period, the tobacco market collapsed in the South, and there was a decreased demand for rice and indigo, which used many slaves. By 1800, slavery appeared to be on its way to extinction in the United States.

The invention of the cotton gin revived the institution of slavery. Cotton production required an abundance of unskilled labor—for plowing, planting, ditch digging, weeding, picking, ginning, baling, and shipping. Because of their role in the cotton production process, slaves became more valuable. Slave prices doubled between 1795 and 1804 in conjunction with the great demand for cotton production and the expected closing of the African slave trade. Slaves who had become financial liabilities for their owners in nonproducing cotton states were sold for profit in the Deep South where cotton thrived.

Always seeking more fertile soil, cotton growers migrated west with their slaves from North Carolina and Georgia through the lower South to Alabama, Mississippi, and Louisiana and finally to Texas by the 1840s. Between 1790 and 1860, about 1 million slaves were forced to move west, and most found the experience extremely traumatic. This was the first large-scale dislocation of slaves since their forced immigration to the Americas, and separated from friends and families and far from their homes, slaves experienced heart-wrenching separation ordeals. By 1860, most of the 4.5 million slaves lived in the cotton-producing belt of the U.S. South.

Whitney's invention of the cotton gin expanded the U.S. economy, revitalized the South's dependency on a one-crop system, and transformed the institution of slavery. As the North became more industrialized and the South remained agrarian, slavery became one of the dividing issues between the two regions. Whitney's invention of the cotton gin inadvertently contributed to the coming of the Civil War, and his idea of interchangeable parts for firearms ensured a Union victory. Whitney died in New Haven, Connecticut, on January 8, 1825.

—*Julieanne Phillips*

For Further Reading
Kolchin, Peter. 1993. *American Slavery: 1619–1877.* New York: Hill and Wang; Olmsted, Denison. 1846. *Memoir of Eli Whitney, Esq.* New York: Arno Press.

WILBERFORCE, WILLIAM (1759–1833)

As a member of the British Parliament, Christian philanthropist William Wilberforce devoted himself to the cause of ending the slave trade and slavery. Largely as a result of his parliamentary crusade, Britain prohibited the slave trade in 1807 and abolished slavery across the British Empire in 1833.

The son of a Hull merchant, Wilberforce wrote to a York newspaper, as a boy, denouncing the slave trade and in 1780, persuaded a friend to report information about the condition of Antigua's slaves. Initially moved by the plight of these West Indian slaves, he later he became fascinated by Africa itself and concluded that abolishing the slave trade was the first step toward improving the lives of Africa's millions.

His religious faith primarily motivated his opposition to slavery. Attracted to Methodism in his youth, racked by profound doubts and violent conversion experiences, Wilberforce finally joined the Church of England's evangelical wing. He believed that Christianity should not just be a matter of attending church on Sunday but should resonate into every sphere of day-to-day life. Accordingly, Wilberforce felt impelled to lend support to many causes demanding reform. He founded the Society for the Suppression of Vice and

A well-known symbol of the abolitionist movement in Britain is reproduced in this tribute to William Wilberforce, parliamentary leader of the movement to abolish slavery and the slave trade in the British Empire.

Encouragement of Religion and vigorously supported missionary work in India and Africa.

Yet his tireless work for suppressing the slave trade is most remembered today. Though not an original thinker about slavery, he believed passionately in the abolition cause, seeing it a "sacred charge" given to him by God and holding that all men are God's creatures and should be treated accordingly.

In summer 1787, with Quakers as the nucleus, the Society for the Abolition of the Slave Trade was established. Among the first duties was to secure a parliamentary champion for the movement, and in Wilberforce, the society found the perfect representative. He was wealthy, clever, and charming; a fine orator; and a gifted propagandist. He had influential friends, and his independent position inside Parliament allowed him to be on good terms with Tory allies while enjoying the respect of Whigs and radicals alike. Most important, he possessed an undoubted moral authority that allowed him to speak as the national conscience.

Wilberforce began his work by collecting evidence about the slave trade's nature to put before a Privy Council committee. In winter 1787, he tried inserting several clauses against the trade into a treaty being negotiated in Paris. Although gaining support from the prime minister, William Pitt the younger, this move came to nothing. Wilberforce then embarked upon his struggle to persuade Parliament to pass legislation outlawing slavery. Unfortunately, he was stricken by a serious illness in early 1788, which nearly ended his career.

Returning to the House of Commons in May 1789, he delivered a monumental speech lasting for three hours in which he moved 12 resolutions condemning the slave trade. They carried in the House of Commons without a division but were later postponed as a result of concerted opposition from Liverpool merchants and West Indies plantation owners. Yet Wilberforce remained optimistic about the eventual outcome, for he was convinced that he had public opinion firmly on his side.

He moved further bills against the slave trade in 1791, 1794, and 1796. The debates were acrimonious and often raged into the night. His task was made more difficult by the French Revolution's impact and Haiti's slave revolt. Scared by reports of violence, many members of Parliament, and King George III himself, began associating abolition with political radicalism. The king's opposition effectively kept Pitt's administration from espousing the cause, and Wilberforce was left to continue the parliamentary struggle alone. This situation was particularly ironic as he remained socially conservative throughout his political career. In 1792, and again in 1807, he denied supporting the immediate emancipation of slaves, believing that they were not yet ready for freedom.

Narrowly out-voted on several occasions, and thwarted by the intractability of the House of Lords, he adopted new political agitation methods to keep the campaign alive. His supporters perfected the modern techniques of lobbying Parliament and pressuring its members, and they collected petitions signed by millions, held mass outdoor meetings, and showered the populace constantly with tracts and pamphlets proclaiming their message.

These tactics began paying dividends, and from 1804 onward, the tide of political opinion began turning decisively against the slave trade. Wilberforce intensified the campaign in Parliament, introducing a bill for abolishing the trade in each session. Although defeated in 1804 and 1805, resolutions favoring abolition were carried by overwhelming majorities in the House of Commons in June 1806. During the recess, Wilberforce published a book denouncing the slave trade, and it had a catalyzing effect upon public opinion and converted many new supporters to the idea of black freedom. Success ultimately came in 1807, when the House of Lords, finally bowing to popular pressure, and the House of Commons were able to ratify Wilberforce's bill by 283 votes to 16. Royal assent was granted on March 25, 1807, and effective as of January 1, 1808, it became illegal for any British ship to engage in the slave trade.

The abolition of the slave trade did not mean an end to colonial slavery. Life for most slaves remained every bit as miserable and brutal as it had ever been. Consequently, abolitionists launched a new campaign in 1823. Initially, they aimed at simply improving the slaves' lot, but later they pushed for complete emancipation. Wilberforce was again at the movement's forefront, speaking out against introducing slaves into South Africa and laying the foundation for the Anti-Slavery Society. Ill health forced his retirement in 1825, and he transferred the movement's leadership to Thomas Fowell Buxton.

Wilberforce made one last public appearance at an Anti-Slavery Society meeting in May 1830. He lived long enough to hear the third reading of the bill abolishing slavery in July 1833, legislation that eventually freed slaves throughout the British Empire.

—*John Callow*

See also
Abolition, British Empire; Burke, Edmund; Closing of the African Slave Trade
For Further Reading
Furneaux, Robin. 1974. *William Wilberforce*. London: Hamish Hamilton; Warner, Oliver. 1962. *William Wilberforce and His Times*. London: B. T. Batsford; Wilberforce, Robert Isaac, and Samuel Wilberforce. 1838. *The Life of William Wilberforce*. London: John Murray.

WILMOT PROVISO

The Wilmot Proviso was perhaps the most significant piece of legislation never enacted in U.S. history. Originally proposed as an amendment to the 1846 army appropriations bill, the proviso attempted to prohibit slavery from territories acquired as a result of the Mexican War (1846–1848). A bitterly divided House of Representatives passed the measure, but it was defeated in the Southern-dominated Senate. By focusing the antislavery debate on the institution's potential expansion into new western territories, the proviso set the terms of the national debate over slavery for the 15 years preceding the U.S. Civil War.

The measure's introduction began a new era of sectional politics in the United States: nearly all Northern Democrats and all Northern Whigs voted in favor of the proviso while practically every representative from districts south of the Mason-Dixon line and the Ohio River opposed it. In other words, the expansion of slavery was an issue that split both major political parties into distinct Northern and Southern wings. The initial vote on the Wilmot Proviso (and the dozens that followed it) were an ominous sign that the politics of the second-party system (Democratic and Whig) would be unable to contain the explosive issue of slavery's expansion.

Democratic representative David Wilmot of Pennsylvania introduced the proviso in the House of Representatives on August 8, 1846, just a few months after the Mexican War began. President James K. Polk, a Democrat and a Tennessee slaveholder, had sent Congress an appropriations bill asking for $2 million to negotiate a treaty with Mexico. Wilmot, a first-term lawmaker, offered as an amendment to the bill "that, as an express and fundamental condition of the acquisition of any territory from the Republic of Mexico . . . neither slavery nor involuntary servitude shall ever exist in any part of said territory."

Both the language and the strategy behind the proviso were unremarkable. Its wording, for example, was lifted straight from Thomas Jefferson's Northwest Ordinance (1787), which prohibited slavery in the Old Northwest (lands north and west of the Ohio River). The same legislative device had been used just two days earlier (and with little Southern opposition), when the House of Representatives had voted to provide a territorial government for Oregon.

Several factors marked the proviso as a watershed in antebellum U.S. history. First, it was a turning point between two distinct antislavery eras. Before the measure's introduction, antislavery battles were waged over a range of issues, from the gag rule on abolitionist petitions to the U.S. Constitution's three-fifths clause, which granted Southern states more representation than they would otherwise have had. Afterward, slavery's expansion into the territories absorbed every related issue. The issue of slavery's expansion initially split the major parties into sectional antagonists.

Second, the proviso represented a major shift in the antislavery movement's constituency. The congressmen who hatched the idea for the measure were Northern Democrats, most of whom represented remote, agricultural districts. Democrats like David Wilmot were not usually associated with antislavery politics, which tended to be commercially oriented, evangelical, and aristocratic. But many Northern Jacksonian Democrats had reached the breaking point with Polk's administration by 1846, believing it to be pro-Southern and proslavery.

Some resented Polk's having received the Democratic Party's nomination for president at the expense of New Yorker Martin Van Buren in 1844; others believed the president's acceptance of Oregon's boundary at 49° north latitude was an insult to Northern sentiment and confirmed the administration's Southern bias. Democrats from the Old Northwest were angered by Polk's veto of a popular rivers and harbors bill. A growing number of Northern Democrats had come to believe that a Southern "conspiracy" existed to control the federal government and open the West to slavery. They believed this "slave power" threatened the freedom and future of white Northerners because it advocated replicating the plantation system in the new territories. Taken together, these disgruntled Democrats provided the antislavery movement with the mass political appeal it needed to expand its constituency.

"The time has come," said one Northern Democratic congressman in 1846, "when the Northern Democracy should make a stand. . . . We must satisfy the Northern people . . . that we are not to extend the institution of slavery as a result of this war" (Morrison, 1967). It was precisely this kind of sentiment that turned administration loyalists like David Wilmot against Polk's administration, against Southern members of their own party, and ultimately, against the expansion of slavery.

—*Jonathan Earle*

See also
Free Soil Party
For Further Reading
De Voto, Bernard A. 1989. *The Year of Decision: 1846.* Boston: Houghton Mifflin; Morrison, Chaplain W. 1967. *Democratic Politics and Sectionalism: The Wilmot Proviso Controversy.* Chapel Hill: University of North Carolina Press.

WOMEN AND SLAVERY IN ISLAM

Muslim women were victims of the internal, trans-Saharan, and Atlantic slave trades. In 1862, the missionary Anna Hinderer wrote about a small boy she took in when his mother was taken in the trans-Saharan trade out of Nigeria. The Swahili sometimes desired Somali women as concubines and kidnapped them from their home areas despite prohibitions in the Qur'an against Muslims enslaving Muslims. The same occurred in the case of northern Nigeria's Hausa women, who, as a result of warfare, were marched to southern ports along the Atlantic Slave Coast. Generally, men were preferred over women in the Atlantic trade, and most women were kept in Africa where they were valued for their productive and reproductive capacities.

When traditionalist women were enslaved in African Muslim societies, rudimentary conversion usually followed, even in rural areas where contact between slave and owner was often distant and infrequent. In urban settings, converted slaves had more opportunity for upward mobility, but treatment for both groups depended on the temperament of individual owners and particular social circumstances. Treatment ranged from upward mobility as concubine to masters (or their sons), to intense labor in agricultural pursuits, to domestic drudgery.

Usually a concubine's status was elevated when she gave birth to a child her owner acknowledged as his. Such children were considered free and were attached to their father's lineage, even among the aristocracy. The woman herself remained without family and thus vulnerable, but there were exceptions. Among the Swahili, freed concubines often became part of the family as they aged. Although an urban woman who did not capture her owner's attention was rarely considered an outsider after years of domestic service, rural women tended to remain undefined objects of productivity throughout their lives. In both cases, these Muslim women endowed their slave status to their children, unless acknowledged by the owner and especially if their husbands were also slaves. They also tended to have more freedom of movement than their free Muslim counterparts.

Emancipation for rural and urban women was uncommon, although rural women whose productivity had ceased, and who had no husband, were often allowed to retire on bits of cultivated land that were assigned to them. In the urban setting, older women were often relegated to lesser tasks like caring for the children of able-bodied slaves.

Domestic duties for slave women in Muslim societies were generally onerous and time-consuming. Frequently the slave women fell under the dominance of free wives, who were themselves dominated by the patriarch. Within the confines of the female area in the household, slave and freewomen shared the bond of being subject to the ideology that they were inferior to males. Despite their differences in status, slave and freewomen often engaged in gossip or play and enjoyed bonds of intimacy denied the rural bondwoman. Still, there were instances of women committing cruel and inhumane acts toward their female slaves. Traditionalists and Muslim slave women who practiced spirit possession, divination, or healing and those regarded as witches enjoyed a special status that tended to ensure their well-being.

Slave women were responsible for numerous duties that were necessary to the household's functioning—from carrying water to washing clothes, cleaning, and caring for their owner's children. Domestic slaves literally worked from dawn to dusk and usually seven days a week. Bondwomen in agricultural-based societies worked their own bit of land besides cultivating land for their owners, whereas domestic and urban slaves were dependent on their owners' goodwill for their food and lodging. Rural women worked alongside men: planting, weeding, and harvesting. Additionally, they were responsible for their own households and children.

Like any slaveholding society, there were good and bad owners. Slave women were more subject to rape, beating, and general mistreatment than their free Muslim counterparts. Once purchased, few slave women were ever sold away, and few escaped. In urban settings, and as time allowed, slave women were able to engage in petty trade through cottage industries that they developed within the confines of their owners' homes. For instance, women did sewing and weaving late at night and used their children as street hawkers by day. Rural female slaves were sometimes able to earn extra income by selling excess produce grown on their small private plots.

A few Muslim women trickled into Cape Colony in South Africa as slaves, having been introduced by Dutch East India Company ships from Southeast Asia and later from Madagascar. Despite the influence of Calvinism in the colony, these Muslim slaves perpetuated their religion among themselves and later increased their numbers by converting African slaves. In the Bahia region of Brazil, a few Yoruba and Hausa Muslim women were active in a slave uprising in 1835.

Although Islam did not long survive in Brazil, records indicate that as in South Africa's Cape Colony, conversions occurred among female slaves, extending from the interior to Rio de Janeiro by the late-nineteenth century. Inventories of slaves taken into North America contain garbled references to Muslim names such as Aisha and Fatima, and oral traditions collected from descendants of South Carolina slaveowners suggest that Muslim women were allowed to cease domestic duties in order to face Mecca and offer the requisite prayers. Islam quickly faded in North America, and within a generation or two slaves had been absorbed into the newly created African American culture.

Being subordinate to male domination created bonds in African Muslim societies that breached the divide between slave and freewomen. Although subservient to masters in the Cape Colony, in Brazil, and in North America, the few Muslim women who arrived as slaves on those distant shores kept their faith alive.

—*Patricia W. Romero*

For Further Reading
Gomez, Michael. 1994. "Muslims in Early America." *Journal of Southern History* 60 (4): 671–710; Mack, Beverly. 1992. "Women and Slavery in Nineteenth Century Hausaland." *Slavery and Abolition* 13 (1): 89–110; Reis, Joao. 1993. *Slave Rebellion in Brazil: The Muslim Uprising of 1835 in Bahia*. Baltimore: Johns Hopkins University Press; Romero Curtin, Patricia. 1981. "Laboratory for the Oral History of Slavery: The Island of Lamu on the Kenya Coast." *American Historical Review* 88 (3): 858–882.

WOMEN AND THE ANTISLAVERY MOVEMENT (1832–1870)

Women were active in the antislavery movement, and until 1837, their contributions far outweighed their numbers. Initially in auxiliaries to men's societies and then as members of independent female antislavery societies, women circulated petitions, raised funds, distributed tracts, and organized and attended lectures on slavery and its abolition. A full appreciation of what these women did must be based upon an understanding of the beliefs that influenced their actions and lives. The ideology of the woman's sphere—the Second Great Awakening (1790s–c. 1830), various religious beliefs, and the effects of a pastoral letter—are important elements to an understanding of women's participation in and their withdrawal from the antislavery movement and how the women's rights movement grew out of antislavery.

Women's roles centered around their homes and families as the United States moved toward having a capitalist economy. Women were not only keepers of the home but also guardians of religion and morality. The ideology of the "woman's sphere" gave women moral superiority over men and made them responsible for correcting any ethical wrongs they might see. Women found society corrupt and began exerting their influence in a wider circle, becoming housekeepers of social virtue.

The Second Great Awakening encouraged women to participate in the moral reform of U.S. society. Charles Grandison Finney and his troop of ministers encouraged women to participate publicly in his revivals. Finney also suggested that women might use their piety and moral superiority to reform society. The antislavery movement developed during this reforming surge, and women were drawn to the movement by both their religious beliefs and their ministers' encouragement. Slavery was perceived as a moral and domestic evil affecting women, and antislavery women were determined to end this evil through moral persuasion. Once they began, women were tireless in their efforts, collecting more petition signatures and raising more money than men. Society's house-keepers were hard at work exerting their moral influence on the people of the United States to reform the mess of slavery made by the less-than-moral men.

Women joined the antislavery movement with differing religious beliefs, which reflected their membership in many denominations. Initially, these divergent beliefs did not impede the women's activity, but eventually, the differing beliefs caused trouble. The religious affiliations of the women fell into two basic groups: evangelicals—those belonging to Methodist, Baptist, Presbyterian, and Congregational churches—and liberals—primarily the Quakers and Unitarians. It is important to remember that both groups were motivated by their religious beliefs. The factions differed in that the evangelical abolitionists placed more authority in their ministers while the liberal abolitionists placed little or no authority in theirs.

On July 28, 1837, the Massachusetts General Association of Congregational Ministers issued a pastoral letter that was partly an attempt to discredit the Grimké sisters. It was also a call for men and women to limit their antislavery activity on the advice of their ministers. The conservative Congregational clergy had been under attack for several years for their weak antislavery position, and the letter was meant to reassert the clergy's authority over their congregations. The letter included a veiled threat that ministers would withdraw their guidance and support from those female parishioners who continued their antislavery activities. Evangelical women constituted most of the female antislavery group, and they responded to the pastoral letter dramatically. After 1840, the New York women discontinued their antislavery work completely, and the Boston women's society split and its effectiveness diminished.

The women's rights movement originated in the antislavery movement. As women spoke out for the rights of slaves, they found themselves also defending their own right to speak publicly. As women's antislavery work came under attack, many antislavery women began seeing their own plight reflected in that of the slaves. Many of the most active antislavery women led the movement for women's rights, including Lucretia Mott, Angelina Grimké, Sarah Grimké, and Abby Kelley. Other leaders of the women's rights movement got their start in the antislavery movement, including Susan B. Anthony and Elizabeth Cady Stanton.

Women provided the backbone for the antislavery movement. They collected twice as many signatures as men when they circulated petitions, their fund-raising efforts kept the national organization and its many agents functioning, and their lectures raised the conscience of Northerners to the plight of slaves. Angelina Grimké contributed two powerful antislavery tracts, Angelina and Sarah Grimké fought for the right of women to do antislavery work, Lydia Maria Child edited the *National Anti-Slavery Standard* (an abolitionist newspaper), and Abby Kelley worked tirelessly as a lecturer and fund-raiser. Equally as important in the antislavery movement as the individual contributions of specific women was the entire membership's continuing support and involvement.

—*Sydney J. Caddel*

See also
An Appeal to the Christian Women of the South;
Boston Female Anti-Slavery Society; Ladies' New York City Anti-Slavery Society; Philadelphia Female Anti-Slavery Society

For Further Reading
Hersh, Blanche Glassman. 1978. *The Slavery of Sex: Feminist Abolitionist in America.* Urbana: University of Illinois Press; Kraditor, Aileen. 1989. *Means and Ends in American Abolitionism: Garrison and His Critics on Strategy and Tactics, 1834–1850.* Chicago: Ivan R. Dee; Yellin, Jean Fagan, and John C. Van Horne, eds. 1994. *The Abolitionist Sisterhood: Women's Political Culture in Antebellum America.* Ithaca, NY: Cornell University Press.

WOMEN AS SLAVEOWNERS, AFRICA

The fact that women were the majority of slaves held in Africa was connected to the phenomenon that free African women needed help doing all the work assigned to them by a gender division of labor. This situation characterized the majority of societies that depended on repetitive agricultural work like tilling and weeding, hauling water and fuel, trading, and domestic work.

Except in the relatively few areas where plantation labor dominated, such as Zanzibar, around Malindi in Kenya, and parts of northern and southeastern Nigeria, much African slavery was small-scale with a lineage or a family owning only a few slaves. Those slaves were most likely to be women helping freewomen with their work. So, even if freewomen were not the actual slaveowners in many cases, they were often the ones who benefited the most from the availability of slave labor, especially in societies where small-scale slave ownership predominated.

In some areas that phenomenon contributed in the late-nineteenth century to slavery's perpetuation for women beyond that for men, because the labor of freewomen remained unmechanized while the labor of men began to be skilled wage labor for European missionaries or administrators. Women still maintained the subsistence activities that enabled the society's survival, especially since colonial wages were not intended to support families and women had to assume the work of the men who were drawn off into wage labor.

For some women in certain precolonial societies, the availability of slave labor enabled them to enrich themselves and to partake of the kinds of privileges normally accorded more to men. They became slave-owners, sometimes on a large scale. In many societies women did not have the same right as men to recruit family labor; patriarchy meant that men could call upon women for more help than women could ask from men. Therefore, and especially in commercially developed societies, some women employed slaves to trade for them or to free them from routine agricultural and domestic labor in order to pursue more profitable tasks.

Commanding the labor and loyalty of women slaves not only helped women involved in long-distance trade, it also gave some women political power and the opportunity to establish a lineage. One way to accomplish the latter was through the widespread practice of woman-marriage, an institution in which a woman paid the bride wealth and became the socially recognized "husband" of another woman, usually one of low status. Such a wife then bore children by a lover who was often recruited and controlled by the female husband.

Woman-marriage served different purposes in various societies. Sometimes it merely served to raise sons in a deceased husband's name to perpetuate a patrilineage. But it was just as common for the custom to be a means of empowering a freewoman to establish her own de facto patrilineage and to accumulate wealth through the labor of her wife and children, as men did. Purchasing a slave wife gave these women stronger control over their offspring without competition.

In some societies, slavery was so widespread that even nonelite freewomen owned slaves and some female slaves purchased slaves rather than their own freedom. In situations where wealth and protection came from membership in a lineage, where in many cases assimilation into the lineage was one aspect of slavery and a goal of many slaves, it sometimes made more sense for slaves to purchase other slaves in order to begin their own rise to fame and fortune than to secure a dubious "freedom" by divorcing themselves from the very links that formed their security. Slaves owning slaves was possible because in many societies the only slaves having chattel status were those in the slave trade; slaves who were on their way to partial or full assimilation and effective free status had certain privileges not allowed under chattel slavery: including the rights to own property, move about independently, and earn their own money.

That aspect distinguished the many forms of African slavery from the relatively uniform chattel slavery practiced in North America, and nowhere is that fact more evident than in considering female slaves as slaveowners. Social stratification in many African societies was fluid, and smaller gaps existed between wealthy and poor than in industrializing countries. However, in most of the societies, slaves and those of slave descent bore a social stigma, sometimes expressed in lesser inheritance rights. It is important not to overgeneralize about African forms of slavery and to recognize the variability that allowed many women, some of them slaves themselves, to profit from slavery. In Africa, the marginal utility of slave labor increased in direct proportion to the marginality of those employing it.

—*Claire Robertson*

See also
Women as Slaves, Africa

WOMEN AS SLAVES, AFRICA

Until the mid-1980s, most of Africa's history of slavery was written as if all or most of the slaves were men, and some contemporary works continue that assumption. But, with many regional and cultural variations, approximately two-thirds of the slaves kept in Africa were female. There were also very large regional and cultural variations in forms of servitude in sub-Saharan Africa, ranging from indenture to pawnship to limited term or permanent chattel slavery. Yet whatever form is considered, in most precolonial African societies more women than men held servile status.

The sex ratio in the African slave market varied according to local demand, but female slaves were usually more expensive because of their higher desirability—the reverse of the North American market situation. Why were female slaves usually more highly valued in Africa? Women in precolonial, colonial, and postcolonial Africa did and do more agricultural labor in most societies, and they bear the society's children. Wealth in precolonial Africa depended chiefly on the amount of labor a person, clan, or lineage could mobilize, since land was often plentiful but labor scarce. Thus, women slaves not only supplied labor for their owners and users but also had children, who were added to the community's labor force.

Female slaves were also more useful than male slaves in many societies because much of African slavery was assimilative; that is, the status was not passed to slave children, especially if the father was free and the society patrilineal. Political success in precolonial

African societies often depended on wealth that could be redistributed and the number of clients a person had, both of which could be maximized by adding women slaves to the household. Male slaves, however, could be a liability in a patrilineal situation because if they achieved freedom, they might present a political threat by establishing independent lineages. Therefore, in some cases it was the practice to kill male prisoners of war and enslave the women, a practice that was also common in archaic Greece.

Women slaves were equally or more useful for men in matrilineal societies, whose heirs normally were their sisters' sons. Some men acquired slave wives to set up de facto patrilineages with their children under their own control and so owing no loyalty elsewhere. Yet, in many societies, those of slave descent had inferior inheritance rights and were still stigmatized; therefore, they sometimes edited their genealogy to disguise their slave heritage.

In many societies both free and slave women were disadvantaged, and a freewoman was more vulnerable to enslavement than a freeman. For instance, girls were more likely to be pawned than boys. A debtor would give his daughter or some other junior female relative over which he had authority to creditors thinking that the girl's labor would pay the debt's interest, but she could only be redeemed if the debt were repaid in full.

Frequently, if debts were not repaid, the girl married into the creditor's lineage when she was grown, the debt serving as the bride-price. Or, the creditor (illegally) might cause pawnship to become slavery by selling the girl into the trade to recoup the debt. Abuses became more common in West Africa in the eighteenth century when the rise in the Atlantic slave trade increased the demand for slaves, and it became more common in East Africa during the widespread destruction caused by the nineteenth-century slave trade.

For women, slavery could be a less permanent status than for men because women were effectively freed if they bore a free child. They were, however, less likely to be able to purchase their own freedom because they were less likely to have the kinds of skills that could earn cash. Also, women slaves sometimes did not seize escape opportunities if they had children and had been successfully assimilated into the new society, if they had been enslaved as children, or if they did not know their origins. In many cases, slave women brought new cultural influences to their new homes. But slave women were also likely to have fewer healthy children than freewomen because of higher infant mortality rates and heavier work burdens.

The labor of slave women was usually put at the immediate disposal of freewomen, whether or not the latter were the actual owners of the slaves, because of the many labor obligations of freewomen. Thus, even more female slave labor was needed in Islamic societies as they secluded freewomen while slave women did the outside labor. When slavery was outlawed and/or declined in Africa, women's slavery endured longer than men's because late-nineteenth-century freewomen did not acquire the new skills, such as carpentry and masonry, that enabled men to secure wage jobs, nor did the women have many labor-saving devices.

Still responsible for most of the domestic and field labor (and increasingly so as the men were drawn off into wage labor), freewomen needed the help of slave women, and female slaves were still being sold well after colonialism was imposed in many areas. Recently, there has also been a resurgence of slavery in the wake of wars and in areas where the central government is weak—for instance, the problem is a touchy issue between the governments of Mauritania and Senegal and in the Sudan. Many of the modern slaves are women.

Some female slaves were used as concubines; in some Islamic areas, there was a market for beautiful women, in particular. Concubinage could involve forced sexual relations and abuse, and even women who were purchased mainly for their agricultural labor value were more often than not subject to the owner's sexual desires. But the status of concubine was unlikely to lead to emancipation; indeed, in some cases colonialists, acting on the assumption that all women slaves were concubines, freed them later than other slaves. Even on the Cape of Good Hope, where European-style chattel slavery was practiced in the seventeenth and eighteenth centuries, early Dutch settlers used African women mainly for agricultural labor rather than as concubines.

One reason the colonialists did not act vigorously to free the female slaves upon conquest, despite using the abolition of slavery as a chief justification for conquest, was that many of the slaves were women and they did not want to cause a male revolt by removing women from men's control. The antislavery laws would also have been expensive and impossible to enforce, especially in societies where slavery was pervasive. The colonialists faced labor shortages, in particular because African men were not paid a family wage, and were not overly concerned about freeing a slave population that was predominantly female.

What work did African women slaves do? Not only did they provide the usual agricultural labor on small-scale farms, they also worked as plantation labor on Zanzibar—picking, separating, and drying cloves—and on oil palm plantations in the Niger Delta. Women slaves dyed cloth, mined gold on the Gold Coast, spun thread, traded, carried goods, herded, and sewed; they also did household tasks like hauling water and firewood, cooking, and child minding. They did most of society's low status labor-intensive work. They also served as trusted retainers in elite households.

They were induced to accept their burden by a combination of coercion, rewards, and ideology, but they also resisted or manipulated their lot by versions of sabotage, expressions of gratitude or flattery, slacking on work, avoidance and misinformation, and running away. If African women were more frequently enslaved than men, they were as talented at turning the situation to their advantage, if possible, while enduring a wide range of conditions characteristic of the diversity of Africa's cultures.

—*Claire Robertson*

See also
Women as Slaveowners, Africa

WOMEN AS SLAVES, NORTH AMERICA

Within a relatively stable context, North American slaves built sufficient family ties to become the only self-reproducing slave population in the Western Hemisphere. American slave women experienced a life cycle that was often characterized by gender difference.

Slave children spent their earliest years playing in the care of elderly slave women, sometimes with white children. Gender differentiation at this age was minimal: slave children of both sexes had few clothes, or perhaps only a "shift" (a sliplike garment), and almost none wore shoes. Most children, except the daughters of skilled domestic women who spent their youngest years at their mothers' sides, were separated from both parents while the parents worked.

Gender differentiation began between the ages of 6 and 12 years with the beginning of work. The first difference between boys and girls was that girls began work earlier: more girls than boys began working before the age of 7. Some slave girls, who were more nimble and productive pickers than boys, began their working lives picking cotton. Many children worked with pregnant women and elderly slaves in the "trash gang," whose members performed light agricultural labor: sweeping yards, clearing dying cornstalks from fields, chopping cotton, carrying water to field hands, weeding, picking cotton at a slower pace, feeding work animals, and driving cows to pasture.

Many girls and boys began their working lives doing domestic work. House girls and boys hauled

A female slave newly arrived from Africa. Women slaves played many critical roles in North American slave society, the only self-reproducing slave community in the Americas.

water, carried lunch to field hands, fanned flies from and cleared dinner tables, carried wood to kitchens, and took infants to their mothers in the fields for feedings. While boys acted as valets to their masters and accompanied them on hunting trips, girls churned butter, milked cows, and learned to spin, weave, sew, knit, and cook. Some who belonged to the richest slaveholding families worked as personal maids: they bathed and dressed their mistresses, combed their hair, and ran whatever errands their mistresses wanted—including bringing them water and fanning them. Young girls whose mothers were skilled domestics—seamstresses, weavers, cooks, and nurses—began learning their mother's craft during their young years.

Most children performed domestic and trash gang labor only until they were strong enough for fieldwork. At about age 12, most children began their adult roles as field hands. This shift from child labor to adult labor occurred earlier for girls, about age 14. Mothers initiated their daughters into field labor, but as the girls grew, gaining strength and skill, they slowly moved away from their mother's supervision and assumed harder tasks.

Women and men alike tended crops, but women also spent much of their working lives with other women. Slave labor was largely divided along gender lines—at least on plantations with enough slaves to organize into gangs. On large plantations, women spent the off-season winter months picking out cotton (removing seeds from the fiber to prepare it for spinning) and threshing grain. They hoed, weeded, and grubbed; cleared the land of brush, timber, and dead cornstalks; and repaired and made fences. Women also spent the winters spinning cotton and wool yarn. During the spring and summer, women continued with the same gender-specific labor they performed during winter, and they also anticipated the coming season by preparing seed beds, planting garden vegetables, planting and tending crops, weeding, raking leaves, and stacking hay.

During the fall season, both women and men harvested crops, women harvested their own garden produce, and the women continued their postharvest work of picking out cotton, making and mending fences, and clearing the land. As harvest ended, women spent more time in textile production for their own families, for the plantation, and for the market. Even on smallholdings, where there was less gender stratification of labor, the women spent a large part of their lives in textile production because the small farms were more dependent upon domestic textile production than the wealthier slaveholdings, which purchased some of their textile needs.

On large plantations, many women moved in and out of domestic work throughout their lives, spending their childhood, pregnancies, and old age in the slave-holding household. Some joined a small cadre of full-time skilled and unskilled domestic workers like cooks, nurses, and housekeepers. These workers found themselves almost constantly subjected to their owners' demands. Knitters, weavers, and seamstresses had the same vulnerability to the ever-shifting moods of their owners; all domestics were exposed to sudden and frequent violence like being slapped, stuck with pins, burned, stabbed, and whipped.

Though women living on small slaveholdings did not experience the kind of gender stratification of labor that women on the large holdings did, almost all slave women experienced gender differentiation in their "off time." Women performed a "second shift" after returning from work in the fields or in the slave-holding household. They cooked, cleaned, gardened, and produced household goods like candles, soap, and textiles for their own families. During this second shift and at women's quilting and prayer groups, they had time to socialize and to spend time with their children, who sometimes helped their mothers.

Female networks of extended kin were the backbone of the slave community. Marriage and nuclear families were, for most slaves, the ideal, but this was realized in less than half of all slave families. Separation of families by sale, hiring out, and marriage else-

where combined with survivals of the traditional West African family structure tended to make many slave families extended and focused on the women, who stood at the center of these extended kin networks.

Few slaves lived into old age: between 1830 and 1860, only 10 percent of the slaves in North America were over 50 years old. The women who did live into old age again worked on the trash gang. As women aged, they worked less for their owners and increasingly served their own communities, raising the youngest slave children whose mothers were at work. Black elders were considered repositories of history, knowledge, and advice. Some elderly women had mastered the healing arts, becoming expert in the medicinal manipulation of herbs and roots, and were considered powerful "root doctors," "healers," and "conjurers." Some became midwives, and others became sages who interpreted dreams and strange phenomena and gave spiritual and love advice.

—*Stephanie M. H. Camp*

For Further Reading
Fox-Genovese, Elizabeth. 1988. *Within the Plantation Household: Black and White Women of the Old South.* Chapel Hill: University of North Carolina Press; Morton, Patricia, ed. 1996. *Discovering the Women in Slavery: Emancipating Perspectives on the American Past.* Athens: University of Georgia Press; Stevenson, Brenda. 1996. *Life in Black and White: Family and Community in the Slave South.* New York: Oxford University Press; White, Deborah Gray. 1985. *Ar'n't I a Woman? Female Slaves in the Plantation South.* New York: Norton.

WOMEN AS SLAVES, WEST INDIES

Beginning in the late-seventeenth century, sugar became the most important and lucrative cultivation of the whole West Indies. Indeed, during only a few decades, small sugar plantations were transformed into medium and large factories and black women came to be regarded as an invaluable labor force. West African women used to arrive on a weekly basis in every European colony of the Caribbean and the Americas—to be sold mainly as field-workers and treated worse than cattle.

Female and male slaves shared similar tasks and punishments, but whereas males were valued solely for the economic contributions they made to the plantation, women were expected to perform both sexual and economic functions. In the Caribbean, sexual relationships between black women and white men were widespread, and in most cases, the slave women were forced into those relationships. If they did try to protect their sexual integrity and resist the white men, they risked cruelty and beating. If they accepted the liaison, they were targets of the jealousy of white women and were also excluded from the slave community.

For centuries, misinterpretation or ignorance of West African culture and customs contributed to myths in which African women were viewed mostly as promiscuous prostitutes, passive slaves by nature, or lazy inferiors. Many whites in the West Indies regarded them as evil and as instigators of evildoing.

Despite constant threats of punishment, African women reacted very strongly to slavery through everyday acts of noncooperation like shirking work, damaging crops, and feigning illness as well as through participating in insurrections. Their individual acts of violence also included arson, poisoning, and murder. Many Europeans living in the Caribbean during the colonial period declared female slaves to be more troublesome than male slaves because of the aggressive and uncooperative behavior of the former. Women, moreover, tended to be more persistent offenders than men.

Female slaves were seen as intransigent and negative in their work roles but as energetic and positive in their private lives. They cultivated provision grounds (land given slaves by masters on which they could grow vegetables and wheat), sold surplus crops at slave markets, worked with enthusiasm in their houses, and took part in slave community life. They reacted against and fought slavery and tried with all their means to survive in an unfair and tyrannical society in which white power was exercised through punishment, torture, and control of the slaves' physical needs and environment.

As slavery intensified, plantation conditions deteriorated. With the threat of the abolition of the slave trade in the late-eighteenth century, planters tried to improve the living conditions of female slaves who, owing to the harsh life on the sugar plantations, had a low fertility rate. Despite some ameliorative measures, such as fewer working hours and more food, women slaves consciously avoided having children to save them from slavery. Slavery itself lessened the desire to have children.

Slave women played a vital and indispensable part in the cultural activities of the slave community. They were the principal exponents and protectors of African cultural traditions—religion, medicine, language, song, and music—which were handed down from generation to generation within the slave family and the wider community. Indeed, black women of the Caribbean played a prominent role in religious ceremonies. Old women were valued for their wisdom and knowledge of folklore and medicine: they were priest-

esses, healers, seers, and herbalists. Although they were sometimes persecuted as practitioners of evil witchcraft, whites often turned to them for treatment of tropical diseases since some African-derived treatments were more effective than European medicine.

Female slaves often exhibited an aversion to Christianity because they had little to gain from a doctrine that emphasized female inferiority and subordination, so they stayed with the more egalitarian West African religions. Even when they formally accepted Christianity, the content of their religion remained essentially African.

More than the men, women often expressed their cultural defiance through language and song. Creole languages that were rich in nuances and satire were used effectively against white oppression. Song and music accompanied all the important events in slave life. Slave women sang to render work less burdensome, to console themselves, and to satirize and threaten their masters. Their songs expressed not only sorrow, resistance to slavery, and anger but also joy and hope.

Slave women did not conform to the image created for them by white society. They reacted to enslavement like the males did, if not more so. In order to survive, they adapted superficially to an alien society, avoided despair, and struggled to preserve the right to exercise free will. The greater the human degradation, the more fierce were the desires to survive and to refuse to submit abjectly to the system. Because of their vital role in the struggle to build, maintain, and cohere the slave family and community, they can be considered as the backbone of their family and community. Slave women were fundamental to the black historical process that enabled Africans to survive enslavement with dignity and to create a vigorous culture and society.

—*Luana Tavernier*

See also
Concubinage; Creole Languages; English Caribbean; Family; French Caribbean; Gender; Infanticide; Spanish Caribbean; Sugar Cultivation and Trade; West Indies
For Further Reading
Bush, Barbara. 1989. *Slave Women in Caribbean Society, 1650–1838*. Bloomington: Indiana University Press; Cutrufelli, Maria Rosa. 1983. *Women of Africa: Roots of Oppression*. London: Zed Press; Mair, Lucille Mathurin. 1986. *Women Field Workers in Jamaica during Slavery*. Mona, Jamaica: University of the West Indies; Morrissey, Marrietta. 1989. *Slave Women in the New World: Gender Stratification in the Caribbean*. Lawrence: University Press of Kansas.

WOOLMAN, JOHN
(1720–1772)

John Woolman, Quaker leader and early champion for the abolition of slavery, was born on October 19, 1720, at Ancocas (later Rancocas) in New Jersey and died on October 17, 1772, of smallpox while on a visit to York, England. Woolman's integrity and purity are visible in his writings on slavery and other issues. His true piety was recognized by people of many religions, but Woolman's faith was rooted in the moral and spiritual values of the Quaker faith.

John Woolman was one of 13 children born to Samuel and Elizabeth (Burr) Woolman. The family had some standing in the Northhampton section of the Quaker village now called Rancocas. His grandfather had emigrated to Burlington in West Jersey from Gloucestershire, England, in 1638 and had served as a proprietor of West Jersey while Woolman's father was a candidate for the provincial assembly of that region. Woolman received a modest formal education at the village Quaker school and continued his education through extensive reading.

He later established himself as a tailor and retailer in Mount Holly, New Jersey, after serving his apprenticeship, and married Sarah Ellis of Chesterfield on October 18, 1749. His business was so successful that he was concerned prosperity would distract him from his spiritual concerns, to the point where he directed prospective customers to his competitors. Despite his fears, Woolman had many occupations, including surveying, conveyancing, executing bills of sale, and drawing up wills. He occasionally taught school and published a primer that was reprinted several times. At his death, Woolman left an estate of several hundred acres.

John Woolman's beliefs concerning slavery and other Quaker concerns, including Indian conversion and opposition to conscription and taxation for military supplies, are clearly stated in his autobiographical *Journal* and other writings. Better known in England, he is remembered for his opposition to slavery, the main focus of his adult years. His *Journal* has run through more than 40 editions, not only because of its content, but because of its elegant simplicity.

Woolman's Quaker beliefs were the center of his life from the time he was a small child. When he was 23, he felt called to the Quaker ministry, and for the next 30 years, he traveled as a minister from Carolina to New Hampshire and Pennsylvania and finally to Yorkshire, England, where he caught smallpox while working among the poor.

John Woolman realized as a young man that slavery was counter to the spiritual equality of Quaker society. He was one of the first to preach against and write publicly about the evils of slavery at a time when hardly anyone thought that slavery was unchristian. Woolman was personally acquainted with slavery, as a large number of slaves lived in New Jersey and even Quakers owned slaves if they could afford them.. Recently imported Africans were held at Perth Amboy, and in 1734, the slaves there revolted in an attempt to massacre their masters and gain their freedom. Although his cause was unpopular, Woolman's determined efforts toward the abolition of slavery began a trend that would ultimately awaken the conscience of the Western world to its evils.

Woolman's opposition to slavery was triggered by an event that happened shortly after a series of spiritual "openings" had drawn him to the ministry. As Woolman wrote in his *Journal*, his employer asked him, as a conveyancer, to write a bill of sale for a Negro woman he had sold to another member of the Society of Friends. Woolman wrote the bill of sale, but he was so troubled by the event that he told his master he felt slavery was inconsistent with the Christian religion.

Shortly after that event he set off on a journey to North Carolina where he saw at first hand the evils of plantation slavery. He realized that as he was staying with people who lived well because of the profits of slave labor, he was enjoying the benefits of a system that was morally wrong. Woolman wrote in his *Journal*, "I saw in these Southern Provinces so many Vices and Corruptions increased by this trade and this way of life, that it appeared to me as a dark gloominess hanging over the Land, and in the future the Consequence will be grievous to posterity."

When he returned to New Jersey, Woolman finished a book titled *Some Considerations on the Keeping of Negroes Recommended to the Professors of Christianity of every Description*. Seven years later, in 1753, Part 1 was officially sanctioned and printed by the Philadelphia Yearly Meeting; Part 2 was printed in 1762. Woolman based his arguments on his belief in the brotherhood of all men, stating also that the black people did not voluntarily come to dwell among them. Although Woolman had little success in advancing abolition during his lifetime, his writings influenced many people to realize that slavery was morally wrong.

—*Elsa A. Nystrom*

For Further Reading
Brock, Peter. 1990. *The Quaker Peace Testimony, 1660–1914*. York, Eng.: Ebor Press; Cady, Edwin H. 1965. *John Woolman*. New York: Twayne Publishers; Trueblood, David Elton. 1966. *The People Called Quakers*. Richmond, IN: Friends United Press; Woolman, John. 1922. *The Journal and Essays of John Woolman*. Edited by A. M. Gunmere. New York: Macmillan.

WORKS PROGRESS ADMINISTRATION INTERVIEWS

One of the more intriguing sources of primary material on slave life in the United States is the Slave Narrative Collection compiled by the Works Progress Administration (WPA) of the New Deal domestic reform program of Franklin D. Roosevelt's administration. Between 1937 and 1939, the WPA conducted more than 2,000 interviews of aging ex-slaves, resulting in more than 10,000 pages of typescript. Although free of the methodological defects that attended the creation and use of antebellum interviews, the Slave Narrative Collection was marred by all the problems inherent in a government agency created, not to preserve history, but to dispense relief. Nonetheless, the WPA narratives have garnered increasing respectability with the rise of interest in social history, psychology, and folklore studies.

A host of societal, political, and cultural factors prompted the decision to interview the former slaves who were still alive. Black scholars hoped to refute the rosy image of slavery presented in Ulrich B. Phillips's influential book *American Negro Slavery* (1918), along with his assertion that the reminiscences of ex-slaves were of no scholarly value. Scholarly and popular interest in culture and black folklore added further impetus to collecting firsthand accounts of slavery from the slave perspective. The humanitarian sentiment of the New Deal was important but so was the New Dealers' acute understanding of the significance of blacks within the national Democratic coalition. The narrative project was small enough not to offend the Southern bloc of that coalition yet bold enough to win applause in the black press.

In 1929, unrelated efforts to conduct interviews of former slaves were initiated at Southern University in Baton Rouge, Louisiana, and at Fisk University in Nashville, Tennessee, by John B. Cade and Charles S. Johnson, respectively. In 1934, one of Johnson's assistants, Lawrence D. Reddick, first proposed that the Federal Emergency Relief Administration conduct such interviews to assist black scholars. During the next year, 250 interviews were gathered in Indiana and Kentucky, but the decision to employ interviewers with little training undermined the quality of those transcripts.

The advent of the Works Progress Administration in 1935 provided a powerful impetus for the interviews. A subsidiary unit, the Federal Writers Project, was created to hire unemployed professionals to produce life histories and guidebooks to enhance the quality of life and leisure. Under the leadership of John A. Lomax, a folklore specialist who had moved to the WPA from the Library of Congress, the emphasis of the slave interviews changed from dispensing relief to collecting valuable, intellectually respectable information. Lomax tried to introduce quality control in formulating questions and tolerated no censorship in the compilation or the publication of transcripts. From April 1, 1937, when the first systematic effort to interview former slaves began, to spring 1939, when it ended, freedmen were interrogated in all Southern states, the border states, New York, and Rhode Island.

As with all interviews, there were intrinsic methodological problems with collecting the slave narratives, problems exacerbated by the precarious financial position of the subjects, their advanced age, and white insensitivity to black perspectives in general. Lomax, a white Southerner, saw nothing amiss in sending more white interviewers to interrogate the ex-slaves than black interlocutors, and the results were predictably uneven. Aging subjects often told the interviewers what they thought they wanted to hear, or were guided by the questioner to tell stories of local color that originated more in the interviewer's imagination than in the subject's. More than two-thirds of the ex-slaves had been under 16 at the end of the Civil War, and only 3 percent had been over 30, so the sample was necessarily unrepresentative of the wartime slave population. For all these reasons, historians have agreed that caution must be the watchword in the interpretation and use of the Slave Narrative Collection.

Selections from the narratives appeared in a collection published in 1945 as *Lay My Burden Down: A Folk History of Slavery,* by B. A. Botkin. The complete transcripts were at first available only from microfilm copies of the records, which had been deposited with the Library of Congress following termination of the WPA. In the 1960s there was a renewed interest in black history, and a complete published edition appeared under the editorship of George P. Rawick entitled, *The American Slave: A Composite Autobiography* (1972).

"Beneath all the . . . fantasy and flattery," Botkin had written, the narratives "possess an essential truth and humanity which surpasses as it supplements history and literature" (Botkin, 1941). A generation later, Rawick, believing that the literal content of the narratives was as valuable as their art, stated that they probed "the slaves' daily accommodations to their conditions [and] their resistances and rebellions." Whatever the passage of time did to the memories of the ex-slaves before the Great Depression, it has since scarcely tarnished their luster to the chroniclers of the peculiar institution.

—*Richard A. Reiman*

For Further Reading
Botkin, B. A., ed. 1941. *Slave Narratives: A Folk History of Slavery in the United States from Interviews*

with *Former Slaves.* Washington, DC: U.S. Government Printing Office; Rawick, George P., ed. 1972. *The American Slave: A Composite Autobiography.* Westport, CT: Greenwood; Yetman, Norman R. 1967. "The Background of the Slave Narrative Collection." *American Quarterly* 3: 535–553.

WRIGHT, FRANCES
(1795–1852)

In 1825, writer, lecturer, and reformer Frances (Fanny) Wright became the first woman in the United States to act publicly opposing slavery. A Scottish-born radical who spent much of her life philosophizing, Wright turned her ideas into action briefly in the 1820s by putting her Nashoba plan into effect. This novel method of gradually emancipating slaves involved establishing a plantation to educate blacks and teach them a trade before releasing them and transporting them to another nation.

Born in Dundee, Scotland, Wright traveled to the United States with her sister Camilla in 1818. Returning to Europe, she described her impressions of the visit in *Views of Society and Manners in America* (1821). Through this book, Wright developed a friendship with the Marquis de Lafayette and learned of his attempt, aborted by the French Revolution, to emancipate slaves gradually on his New Guinea plantation.

Perhaps because of ties to Lafayette and her upbringing as a member of the British upper class, Wright never wholeheartedly condemned oppressors. Sympathetic to slaveholders' feelings, she wrote in an 1826 statement to the *New Harmony Gazette,* "We should consider, that what we view, at first sight as a peculiar vice and injustice, is not more so, in fact, than any other vice and injustice stamped by education on the minds and hearts of other men." Wright also decided to imitate Lafayette by supporting the gradual emancipation of slaves rather than abruptly turning them loose to shift for themselves, the method many abolitionists favored.

Initially planned as a black emancipation experiment, Nashoba plantation eventually developed into a exercise in communism, racial integration, and sexual equality. It also turned into a disaster, and Wright lost half her fortune in the venture. Weakened by fever, she left for Europe in 1829, where she later began a family with William Phiquepal D'Arusmont. Except for a brief sojourn to the United States to escort Nashoba's slaves to Haiti in 1830, she remained abroad until 1836. Reports of libertine behavior on the Nashoba plantation, acts that took place while Wright was abroad, effectively destroyed her reputation on both sides of the Atlantic.

Quite inflammatory for her day, Wright continued to stir up controversy after Nashoba's demise. She often lectured publicly, a shocking act for an early-nineteenth-century woman in the United States, and she spoke not only against slavery but also about the repressive nature of marriage and religion. By the 1830s, charges of "Fanny Wrightism" had become a popular way to discredit liberal causes. Never fazed by the scorn directed at her, Wright espoused ever more controversial issues, such as women's legal and social emancipation, until the end of her life. In 1852, she died in Cincinnati following a fall.

An energetic and fiercely determined woman, Frances Wright was easily the most controversial woman in the United States in the antebellum period. Her name a household word after the Nashoba experiment, her name also became synonymous with reformism.

—*Caryn E. Neumann*

See also
Nashoba Plantation
For Further Reading
Eckhardt, Celia Morris. 1984. *Fanny Wright: Rebel in America.* Cambridge, MA: Harvard University Press; Wright, Frances. 1972. *Life, Letters, and Lectures, 1834–1844.* New York: Arno Press.

YANACONAJE

The Incan word *yanaconaje* refers to one of the early systems of labor in the New World. As with most New World institutions, its meaning changed over time to denote different things in different parts of the Americas at different times. Originally, the word referred to a labor system, in Incan Peru, that comprised a hereditary class of servants. These servants, known as *yanaconas,* had been removed from their traditional *ayllus* (Incan kinship groups) and relieved of their *mita* responsibilities to the state (a form of compulsory labor). However, the precise nature of their status and functions remains somewhat unclear, although it is known that they served the both the Incan emperor and the nobility, usually working as agricultural laborers.

Following the Spanish conquest of Peru (1531–1535), the word *yanaconaje* was used to denote a labor system that utilized Indians who had left their communities and attached themselves to individual Spaniards. Similar to the pre-Columbian version of *yanaconaje,* these servants were exempt from paying tribute and from mandatory participation in the various labor services. But because of these exemptions, many of the Indians who were a part of *encomienda* system (another system for extracting labor and tribute in kind from the conquered Indians) sought to better their lives and began to desert into the *yanaconaje* system.

In early Spanish Peru, the *yanaconas* frequently moved about, usually some distance from their birthplace, which created labor shortages for the Spanish mines and *encomiendas.* In reaction, the Peruvian viceroy Francisco de Toledo removed their exemption from tribute in 1572 and ordered them to remain in their current residence. As a consequence, the *yanaconas* turned into a stationary workforce. Thus, from 1572 onward, *yanaconaje* referred to a serflike system of agricultural labor, which was quite different from the original Incan system that bears the same name.

Similar to the European system of serfdom, the *yanaconas* were included with the estate on which they resided when it changed hands. In this regard, the Indians serving as *yanaconas* lost their mobility but continued to be exempt from the *mita.* By 1600, the number of Peruvian Indians serving under the system of *yanaconaje* was almost equal to that of those living in the mountain villages of Peru and Bolivia.

—*H. Micheal Tarver*

See also
Encomienda System; Latin America; *Mita;* Peru; *Repartimiento*

For Further Reading
Castro Pozo, Hildebrando. 1947. *El yanaconaje en las haciendas piuranas.* Lima: Cia. de Impresiones y Publicidad; Matos Mar, Jose. 1976. *Yanaconaje y reforma agraria en el Peru.* Lima: Instituto de Estudios Peruanos; Villar Cordova, Socrates. 1966. *La institucion del yanacona en el incanato.* Lima: Universidad Nacional Mayor de San Marcos.

YANCEY, WILLIAM LOWNDES (1814–1863)

Viewed by many people as a Southern-rights fanatic, William Lowndes Yancey not only was an advocate for Southern secession and a white supremacist, but also was known throughout the South as a fiery and brilliant orator, often called the greatest Southern public speaker since Patrick Henry or John Randolph. Yancey was also noted for his virulent temper and has been compared in that regard to Adolf Hitler. In 1838, his quick temper caused him to commit manslaughter, and he was sentenced to a year in jail and fined $1,500. He served only three months, however, and $1,000 of his fine was returned.

Yancey, born August 10, 1814, in Warren County, Georgia, moved in 1821 with his mother and stepfather to Troy, New York, where he attended the best New York academies and in 1830 enrolled at Williams College in Massachusetts. He dropped out of college in 1833 without obtaining a degree and moved to South Carolina, the home of his father, to study law under the tutelage of Benjamin Perry. In 1835, he married a woman with 35 slaves and was thus immediately catapulted into the planter class. Yancey then stopped his study of law and moved to Alabama where he lived with an uncle, a prominent states' rights advocate who influenced Yancey's politics.

In 1840, Yancey and his brother established a weekly newspaper called *Southern Crisis* in Wetumpka, Alabama, in which Yancey tried to persuade Alabama voters to reelect Martin Van Buren president of the United States. His campaign against William Henry Harrison impressed his fellow Democrats, and he was elected to serve in the Alabama General Assembly. Following his election he passed the bar exam, sold his newspaper, and became a full-time politician. In 1844, he moved from state to national politics when he was elected to fill a vacant seat in the U.S. House of Representatives. Yancey's congressional experience contributed to his disenchantment with the federal government and led to his increased support for states' rights.

In 1847, Yancey returned to Alabama and settled in Montgomery where he established a law firm, Yancey and Elmore. During this time he coauthored several resolutions, known as the Alabama platform, that forbade Congress from obstructing slavery in the territories. The Alabama platform was rejected by the 1848 Democratic Convention in Baltimore by a vote of 216 to 36. Soundly defeated and viewed by many Southern Democrats as extremist, Yancey stormed out of the convention.

Yancey claimed that "African slavery, as it exists in the Southern States of this Union, is both politically and morally right, and that the history of the world furnishes no proof that slavery is either evil or sinful" (Venable, 1945). This statement became part of a successful resolution and appeal for Alabama to secede from the Union, in which Yancey played a leading role. He was elected to the Confederate Senate in 1862 and died on July 27, 1863, blaming Jefferson Davis for Southern military defeats at the hands of the Yankees. A great agitator for change, Yancey was never able to master the art of cooperation, and his time in the Confederate Senate led to a bitter argument with Davis, one that never was resolved.

—*Nagueyalti Warren*

For Further Reading
Venable, Austin L. 1942. "The Conflict between the Douglas and Yancey Forces in the Charleston Convention." *Journal of Southern History* 8 (May): 226–241; Venable, Austin L. 1945. "The Role of William L. Yancey in the Secession Movement." M.A. thesis, Department of History, Vanderbilt University, Nashville, Tennessee; Walther, Eric H. 1992. *The Fire-Eaters.* Baton Rouge: Louisiana State University Press.

YANGA

During New Spain's colonial period, marronage was one possible form of resistance by which African slaves could gain their liberty. The Maroons or runaway slaves escaped alone or in small groups and often took refuge in the mountains. In order to survive, these people revolted regularly, burning haciendas and sometimes killing people. Mexico's best-known runaway slave was Yanga (also known as Nyanga or Ñanga), an African-born leader who claimed to be a Congolese prince from the Bran ethnic group.

Yanga arrived in New Spain in 1579 as part of a huge cargo of African slaves. Jesuit scholars described him as a robust and quite intelligent person. He escaped from his master at the end of the sixteenth century and established a Maroon community—or *palenque*—in the piedmont of the Pico de Orizaba, near present-day Cordoba, Veracruz. For 30 years the Maroons were led by Yanga. The ex-slaves lived by stealing animals and grain from nearby haciendas and towns, robbing travelers on the road from Veracruz to Mexico City, kidnapping African slaves, and seeding fear among area inhabitants.

In January 1609, a widespread rumor circulated stating that Yanga planned to attack the surrounding haciendas and kill all the white men in the area. Fearing this rumor, Viceroy Luis de Velasco organized an expedition, and under the command of Don Pedro González de Herrera, a company of Spaniards, Indians, mestizos, and even mulattoes undertook an anti-Maroon campaign. The Maroons fought against the viceroyal troops but were finally defeated. Since Yanga was then elderly, his lieutenant, Francisco Angola, sent a letter in which Yanga explained that the attacks had been justified because black slaves had the right to "liberate themselves from the ill-treatment and cruelty of Spaniards, who, without any right, pretended to own their liberty" (Rodriguez, 1972).

The Veracruz outbreak did have some successes as well as consequences in Mexico City. Facing the possibility of a combined Maroon attack, the viceroy ordered some black prisoners to be lashed publicly, hanged, and beheaded with their heads exposed in the central plaza. Meanwhile, Spanish troops reached the *palenque*'s center, but Yanga and his followers had managed to flee into the mountains, where they continued fighting. The Maroons surrounded the Spaniards, obliging them to negotiate and imposing several conditions.

Luis de Velasco conceded freedom to slaves who had fled before 1608, provided they remained peaceful and refused to shelter more fugitives. Maroons asked for recognition of an exclusively black town with Yanga as its governor. In return, they accepted the responsibility of paying tribute and recognized the laws of the Spanish monarch, Philip III. Eventually, in 1612, Yanga's *palenque* became a free town named San Lorenzo de los Negros (present-day Yanga, Veracruz).

—*Nora Reyes Costilla*

For Further Reading
Laurencio, Juan B. 1974. *Campana contra Yanga en 1608*. Mexico City: Citlaltepetl; Rodriguez, Frederick M. 1972. "Negro Slavery in New Spain and the Yanga Revolt." M.A. thesis, Department of History, DePaul University, Chicago, Illinois.

THE YORUBA

The Yoruba people comprise several West African groups scattered throughout the western Sudan extending across the Sahara south and west of lower Niger and covering Nigeria and Benin. The Shajia of the Republic of the Sudan, the Wadai of Chad, and the Bagarinus and Kanuri of Bornu all claim descent from the Yoruba who are principally found scattered from northern Nigeria to its middle region and south to Abeokuta, Porto Novo, and Badagry west of Lagos. Some other ethnic groups in West Africa and the Beja and Adandawa of Eritrea and Ethiopia along the Red Sea to the east also claim descent from the cosmopolitan Yoruba.

The origin of the Yoruba people is shrouded in myth, mystery, and the oral tradition of West Africa. However, there are written accounts of their existence after the arrival of Islam and the beginning of Qur'anic scholarship. Sparse records kept by slavers also provide evidence of the Yoruba; much of that information is from the eighteenth and nineteenth centuries during the height and then decline of commercial slavery as a result of the British Empire's declared end to the trade.

According to popular legend, the Yoruba people originated in Saudi Arabia on an isthmus of northeastern Africa. They were said to be part of the Qureshi (Kuraish) tribe of Mecca to which the prophet of Islam, Muhammad (570–632 A.D.), belonged. The same legend indicates that Lamrud (or Namrud), an ardent idol worshiper, was the founder of the Yoruba. When Islam began in the seventh century, the prophet Muhammad was commanded to preach against the pagan idolaters of Mecca. *Yaharba*, a title for the priest that Lamrud used, is an Arabic word meaning "warrior" or "army-general" and, according to this version of Yoruba history, the source of the word Yoruba.

Another account of the origin of the Yoruba name is that the group derived from the great migrations and upheavals of peoples in the western Sudan when they fled from the chaos of war between elements of the old Oyo Kingdom and from the demand of Europeans for slaves to transport to the Americas. According to this account, the origin of the name lay in the context of the impact the Atlantic slave trade had on the region, a horror that prompted millions of homeless, nomadic people to form some kind of defense— real or psychological—in response.

Eventually, a large band of the Yoruba settled in northern region Nigeria and established the Oyo Kingdom. Their beginnings are obscure in history (exact date of founding is not known, and suggestions range from tenth to fourteenth centuries), but nineteenth-century accounts reveal that the rulers of the kingdom established an extensive sovereignty and many satellites in the region paid tribute. The tribute often took the form of slaves and other merchandise. Slavery was also a feature of the kingdom with the ruler sometimes having a large entourage of slaves. Slaves were gathered from subordinate kingdoms, especially during the years when Oyo expanded its borders through military conquests.

In the declining years of the kingdom, conflict between the Alafin (military leaders) and the rulers of Oyo accelerated division throughout the area and caused subject territories to seek their independence through revolt and also eroded the powerful kingdom from within. In addition, the conflict caused chaos in the region, which forced millions of Africans to move. Since the slave trade still persisted, though it had somewhat abated, many of these homeless Africans were captured and sold as slaves to the Europeans. The final eclipse of the Oyo Kingdom signaled the rival state of Dahomey to assert itself and claim territory and slaves for the market that was still active in the Bight of Benin, Badagry, and Porto Novo.

At the height of its power, the Oyo Kingdom and the Yoruba people transported slaves through conquest and as tribute. Although its glory as an African kingdom came late in the period of the Atlantic slave trade, the Yoruba, too, sold and transported slaves for external goods. They also used slaves as soldiers, concubines, domestics, royal guards, and spies.

—*Au'Ra Muhammad Abdullah Ilahi*

For Further Reading
Abiola, E. Ola. 1974. *A Textbook of West African History* (A.D. *1000 to the Present*). Ado-Ekiti, Nigeria: Omolayo Standard Press; Ajayi, J. F. A., and Michael Crowder. 1976. *History of West Africa*. London: Longman; Clarke, Peter B. 1982. *West Africa and Islam: A Study of Religious Development from the 8th to the 20th Century*. London: Edward Arnold; Gailey, Harry A., Jr. 1981. *History of Africa: From 1800 to Present*. Huntington, NY: Robert E. Krieger Publishing.

YUN CHONG-OK
(1926–)

One of the first cochairs of the Korean Council for the Women Drafted for Military Sexual Slavery by Japan, Yun Chông-ok has played a pivotal role in the Korean women's movement for redress of the wartime sexual violence against "comfort women," women who were forced into sexual slavery by the Japanese military from 1937 to 1945.

One of the first Korean scholars to study the comfort women issue, Yun, a professor of English at Ewha Womans University in Seoul, presented a paper on Korean comfort women at the International Conference on Women and Tourism held on Cheju-do Island in Korea in 1988. Her paper brought home to the conference participants the underlying connection between the phenomenon of comfort women during the war and the boom of sex tourism by Japanese men in South Korea since the 1960s. The silenced subject of comfort women soon surfaced as a major issue for the Korean women's movement and Korea-Japan relations (Soh, 1996).

Yun Chông-ok vividly remembers being forcibly fingerprinted at school in 1943. She withdrew from school the following day for fear of being drafted into the so-called Voluntary Labor Service Corps to serve the soldiers sexually. After liberation came in 1945, she wondered what had happened to the comfort women and also noted that the Korean historians remained silent on the topic. Upon reading a Japanese publication in which comfort women were mentioned, Yun started her own research and interviewed former comfort women, including Pae Pong-gi on Okinawa in 1980. (Pae died in 1991.)

After retiring in 1991, Yun devoted her energy to working toward the resolution of the comfort women issue. She helped organize several international conferences on the comfort women issue and led the Research Association on the Women Drafted for Military Sexual Slavery by Japan to publish, among other works, a collection of testimonies given by 19 surviving comfort women (Chôngdaehyôp and Chôngsindae Yôn'guhoe, 1993).

Yun believes that the achievements of the Korean women's movement for redress for the comfort women have surpassed her wildest dreams. Indeed, since the formation of the Korean Council in 1990, the comfort women issue has received much international attention and moral support. The United Nations Human Rights Commission, the International Commission of Jurists, a binational group of Korean and Japanese lawyers, and the Asian Women's Solidarity Forum on Military Sexual Slavery by Japan have all supported the efforts of the Korean Council for the Women Drafted for Military Sexual Slavery by Japan, urging the Japanese government, among other things, to admit its legal responsibility, apologize to the survivors in writing, and compensate the victims.

It is noteworthy that both Yun Chông-ok and Lee Hyo-chae, the first cochairs of the Korean Council, are Christians who have personally challenged the conventional lifestyle of women and successfully withstood the pressures of the traditional gender-role ideology by becoming professionals and remaining single throughout their lives. The Korean National Christian Church recognized their humanitarian efforts by giving both of them a human rights award in December 1994.

—*Chunghee Sarah Soh*

See also
Comfort Women; Kim Hak-sun; Korean Council; Sexual Slavery, Japanese Military

For Further Reading

Chôngdaehyôp and Chôngsindae Yôn'guhoe, eds. 1993. *Kangje-ro kkûllyogan chosônin kunwianpudûl* [Forcibly drafted Korean military comfort women]. Seoul: Hanul; Soh, Chunghee Sarah. 1996. "The Korean 'Comfort Women' Movement for Redress: From a Bilateral Compensation to a Human Rights Issue." *Asian Survey* 36 (12): 1226–1240.

ZANJ SLAVE REVOLTS
(C. 689–883)

A series of revolts, known as Zanj revolts, among slaves of African descent in the Islamic world occurred from the late-seventh century to the late-ninth century and were centered on Baghdad, the nucleus of the Abbasid empire. The uprisings were noted as the bloodiest, most bitter, and most destructive slave revolts in Islamic history.

Commercial relations between the Arab world and the East African littoral date to several centuries before the Christian era and resulted in the presence of many Africans in the Arab world, many of whom were brought there as slaves. The advent of Islam in the seventh century gave added impetus to these interactions because Islamic injunctions forbidding the enslavement of Muslims made non-Muslim sub-Saharan Africa the major source of slaves for the Arab world. Coming from different parts of Africa, the slaves were identified by various names, such as *al-aswad* (blacks from south of the Sahara), Habasha (Ethiopians), *Nuba* (Nubians), and the Zanj, Bantu-speaking peoples from East Africa who constituted the largest group. Employed in various capacities as menial servants, wet nurses, craftsmen, business assistants, civil servants, soldiers, eunuchs, concubines, singers, dancers, and poets, the slaves gratified the pleasures of their masters.

The slave's condition varied with the position occupied. The Zanj, who were used as collective forced labor in large-scale projects, were at the bottom of the social ladder. Grouped into gangs of 500–5,000, these slaves toiled in lower Mesopotamia's extensive salt flats, digging away the top nitrous soil and preparing the ground for cultivation. Evidence shows that life on these plantations of salt flats and marshes was particularly harrowing and dreadful. Underfed, treated harshly by their taskmasters, and perennial victims to recurrent malarial epidemics and other diseases, the slaves harbored a smoldering resentment, which they expressed in frequent revolts.

The first major rebellion occurred in 689, but caliphal forces quickly quelled it and meted out severe penalties to the culprits. Five years later, the Zanj rose again, but this time, they were better organized. Led by the fearsome Riyah, traditionally remembered as the "lion of the Zanj," they terrorized the Euphrates region, attracted many followers, and successfully engaged and defeated government forces before a reinforced caliphal army again suppressed the uprising. A third Zanj revolt was equally brutally suppressed, ending with the massacre of over 10,000 inhabitants of Monsul in northern Mesopotamia, the center of the revolt. Similarly, in 765, black slaves in the Islamic city of Medina revolted, deposed the governor, and seized military posts. It took considerable tact and negotiation before calm and order were restored.

Ali b. Sahid al-Zanj (master of the Zanj), an Arab espousing egalitarian principles, led the most serious revolt, which began in 869. Originating as a class struggle between slaves and masters, it soon became an open and violent sociopolitical struggle against caliphal authorities. In 870, the Zanj army conquered and destroyed the flourishing port city of al-Ubulla. Subsequent successes included the submission of the Persian port of Abbadan, the conquest of the province of Djubba, and the occupation and sacking of Basra, the principal port of Iraq, in 871. When the army acquired the cities of Wasit (877), Nu'mmaniya (878), and Djardjaraya, 70 miles south of Baghdad, the Zanj state reached its peak.

The Abbasid caliphate, the most powerful Islamic empire in the world, took 12 years to recover from the shock and devastating blows of those spectacular losses. Beginning in 881, the caliphate army began an offensive, pushed the invading army south, and eventually blockaded the Zanj in their capital, al-Mukhtara, which fell in 883 after a 3-year siege. The leaders of the short-lived Zanj state were killed.

The Zanj revolt of 869–883 was the greatest protest movement by African slaves in the Islamic world. It lasted for 14 years and, at its peak, involved between 100,000 and 300,000 slaves. It took the caliphate an army of more than 50,000 well-equipped soldiers to restore order. The consequences of the revolt were also profound. The importing of Zanj slaves was officially restricted, and Muslims became more averse to Africa and Africans in general, which led to a widespread diffusion of negative and unfavorable images of blacks in the Islamic world.

—*Funso Afolayan*

See also
East Africa

For Further Reading
Popovic, A. 1976. *La revolte des esclaves en Iraq au IIIe/IXe siecle*. Paris: Geuthner; Talib, Y., and F. Samir. 1988. "The African Diaspora in Asia." In *UNESCO General History of Africa*. Vol. 3, *Africa from the Seventh to the Eleventh Century*. Edited by M. El Fasi. London: Heinemann; van Sertima, I., ed. 1985. *African Presence in Early Asia*. New Brunswick, NJ: Transaction Books; .

ZONG CASE

Gregson v. Gilbert (1781) is the legal reference for the events known as the *Zong* slave ship incident. This maritime case demonstrated that slavery, and specifically the slave trade, was an inhumane system predicated on law and legal relations. The facts of the case are striking. The slave ship *Zong*, under the captaincy of Luke Colling-

wood, embarked with 470 slaves from West Africa, bound for Jamaica, on September 6, 1781. Because of a viral epidemic, sickness spread, and 60 Africans and 17 crew members were dead by November 29. Running low on water and frustrated, Collingwood, over the objections of his chief mate, James Kelsal, decided to throw the weakened and sick slaves overboard. Over a three-day period, 131 Africans were jettisoned into the sea.

Slave resistance to Collingwood's decision took two forms. One group of slaves, who realized what was happening, voluntarily jumped into the sea while still shackled. A second group, consisting of slaves who were thrown overboard, survived by swimming back to the ship and climbing back aboard. Collingwood understood that maritime insurance law would protect his insurers if slaves were lost when thrown into the sea because of a maritime crisis, but he died before the *Zong* returned to London and, thus, did not witness the adversarial litigation between Gregson, the owner of the *Zong,* and Gilbert, the insurance underwriter.

Slaves being thrown overboard in mid-ocean, a tactic sometimes employed by ship captains to garner insurance money. The Zong *case highlighted the horrors of this practice and helped to galvanize the antislavery movement in Britain.*

Gilbert refused to pay the £30 per slave loss that Gregson was claiming, and the case went to court. The first jury found for the plaintiff, Gregson. On appeal, a three-judge panel, including Chief Justice William Murray, first earl of Mansfield, heard Gregson's solicitor John Lee argue that no new trial was needed because the captain had had the legal right to throw the slaves overboard since a crisis created by a lack of water imperiled the entire crew.

Counsel for Gilbert and his business partners argued that no crisis had existed and cited the chief mate's testimony that Atlantic storms had replenished the supply of freshwater on board. They further argued that the real reason Collingwood took such inhumane action was that he did not think he would make a profit on the slaves in the slave markets of Tobago and Barbados. Gilbert's council argued that Collingwood had undertaken to commit insurance fraud. Mansfield observed that the crisis, or "necessity situation," had not occurred either because of a lack of water or because the ship was "foul or leaky." Mansfield and his colleagues recommended a new trial, but the historical record does not reveal what eventually happened with the appeal.

The *Zong* incident, which was widely reported in English newspapers, galvanized an already burgeoning antislavery sentiment in the English consciousness, encouraged by the activity of the free Africans Ottobah Cugoano and Olaudah Equiano and English abolitionists like Granville Sharp. Sharp had urged, unsuccessfully, for the government to bring murder charges against the culprits. Interestingly, during the appellate hearing, abolitionism entered the court record when counsel Lee, noting Granville Sharp's presence, argued there was a person in court who intended to bring murder charges against his clients; however, to do so "would be madness" since the "Blacks were property." Lee's point and the legalism of the case indicate the madness of a world that considered the elimination of humans as a legal issue of commerce, profit, and fault, which ended in the assignment of monetary damages to reestablish civil equilibrium between citizens of the king.

—*Malik Simba*

For Further Reading
Shyllon, F. O. 1974. *Black Slaves in Britain*. London: Institute of Race Relations; Walvin, James. 1994. *Black Ivory*. Washington, DC: Howard University Press.

⚬BIBLIOGRAPHY⚬

General

Adshead, S. A. M. 1992. *Salt and Civilisation*. London: Macmillan.

Althusser, Louis. 1970. *Politics and History*. London: New Left Press.

Asher, R. A., ed. 1994. *The Encyclopedia of Language and Linguistics*. New York: Pergamon Press.

Babcock-Abrahams, Barbara. 1975. "A Tolerated Margin of Mess: The Trickster and His Tales Reconsidered." *Journal of the Folklore Institute* 11 (3): 147–186.

Barry, Kathleen. 1984. *Female Sexual Slavery*. New York: New York University Press.

Beaud, Michel. 1983. *A History of Capitalism, 1500–1980*. Translated by Tom Dickman and Anny Lefebvre. New York: Monthly Review Press.

Beckles, Hilary. 1984. "Capitalism and Slavery: The Debate over Eric Williams." *Social and Economic Studies* 33: 171–185.

Bethell, Leslie. 1966. "The Mixed Commissions for the Suppression of the Transatlantic Slave Trade in the Nineteenth Century." *Journal of African History* 7 (1): 79–93.

Black, Kerrigan. 1996. "Afro-American Personal Naming Traditions." *Names* 44: 105–125.

Carrithers, M., et al., eds. 1985. *The Category of the Person: Anthropology, Philosophy, History*. Cambridge: Cambridge University Press.

Craton, Michael; James Walvin; and David Wright. 1976. *Slavery, Abolition, and Emancipation*. New York: Longman.

Curtin, Philip. 1969. *The Atlantic Slave Trade: A Census*. Madison: University of Wisconsin Press.

Davis, David Brion. 1988. *The Problem of Slavery in Western Culture*. Oxford: Oxford University Press.

———. 1984. *Slavery and Human Progress*. New York: Oxford University Press.

Degler, Carl N. 1976. "Why Historians Change Their Minds." *Pacific Historical Review* 45: 167–84.

Devisse, Jean, and Michael Moliat. 1979. *The Image of the Black in Western Art*. Vol. 2. New York: William Morrow.

Dow, George Francis. 1969. *Slave Ships and Slaving*. Port Washington, NY: Kennikat Press.

Duchet, Michéle. 1977. *Antropologie et histoire au siècle des lumières*. Paris: Flammarion.

Dumont, Louis. 1980. *Homo Hierarchicus: The Caste System and Its Implications*. Chicago: University of Chicago Press.

Eltis, David. 1987. *Economic Growth and the Ending of the Transatlantic Slave Trade*. Oxford: Oxford University Press.

Eltis, David, and James Walvin, eds. 1981. *The Abolition of the Atlantic Slave Trade*. Madison: University of Wisconsin Press.

Engels, Friedrich. 1972. *The Origin of the Family, Private Property, and the State*. New York: International Publishers.

Engerman, Stanley. 1996. "Slavery, Serfdom, and Other Forms of Coerced Labor: Similarities and Differences." In *Serfdom and Slavery: Studies in Legal Bondage*. Edited by M. L. Bush. New York: Longman.

Fanon, Frantz. 1968. *The Wretched of the Earth*. New York: Grove Press.

Fox-Genovese, Elizabeth. 1976. *Origins of Physiocracy*. Ithaca, NY: Cornell University Press.

Fox-Genovese, Elizabeth, and Eugene D. Genovese. 1983. *Fruits of Merchant Capital*. New York: Oxford University Press.

Gilroy, Paul. 1993. *The Black Atlantic*. Cambridge, MA: Harvard University Press.

Gottlieb, Beatrice. 1993. *The Family in the Western World*. Oxford: Oxford University Press.

Guilmartin, John. 1980. *Gunpowder and Galleys: Changing Technology and Mediterranean Warfare at Sea in the Sixteenth Century*. Cambridge: Cambridge University Press.

Herskovits, Melville J. 1958. *The Myth of the Negro Past*. Boston: Beacon Press.

Honour, Hugh. 1989. *The Image of the Black in Western Art*. Vol. 4. Cambridge, MA: Harvard University Press.

Hurston, Zora Neale. 1978. *Mules and Men*. Bloomington: Indiana University Press.

Inikori, Joseph E., ed. 1982. *Forced Migration: The Impact of the Export Slave Trade on African Societies*. London: Hutchinson.

Inikori, Joseph E., and Stanley L. Engerman, eds. 1992. *The Atlantic Slave Trade: Effects on Economies, Societies, and Peoples*. Durham, NC: Duke University Press.

Jakobsson, Stiv. 1972. *Am I Not a Man and a Brother?* Uppsala, Sweden: Almqvist and Wiksells.

Kellet, R. J. 1992. "Infanticide and Child Destruction—The Historical, Legal, and Pathological Aspects." *Forensic Science International* 53: 1–28.

Klein, Herbert S. 1978. *The Middle Passage: Comparative Studies in the Atlantic Slave Trade.* Princeton, NJ: Princeton University Press.

Lovejoy, Paul E. 1986. *Salt of the Desert Sun.* Cambridge: Cambridge University Press.

———. 1983. *Transformations in Slavery.* Cambridge: Cambridge University Press.

Mannix, Daniel, and Malcolm Cowley. 1965. *Black Cargoes: A History of the Atlantic Slave Trade, 1518–1865.* New York: Viking.

Marx, Karl. 1906. *Capital: A Critique of Political Economy.* New York: Modern Library.

———. 1975. "Letter to P. V. Annenkov, December 28, 1846." In *Marx-Engels Selected Correspondence.* Edited by S. W. Ryazanskaya. Moscow: Progress Publishers.

Masani, R. P. 1966. *Folk Culture Reflected in Names.* Bombay: Popular Prakashan.

Mathewson Denny, Frederick. 1987. "Names and Naming." In *Encyclopedia of Religion.* Vol. 10. Edited by M. Eliade et al. London: Macmillan.

Mauss, Marcel. 1985. "A Category of the Human Mind: The Notion of Person; The Notion of Self." In *The Category of the Person: Anthropology, Philosophy, History.* Edited by M. Carrithers et al. Cambridge: Cambridge University Press.

Maxwell, John Francis. 1975. *Slavery and the Catholic Church: The History of Catholic Teaching Concerning the Moral Legitimacy of the Institution of Slavery.* London: Barry Rose Publishers.

Meillassoux, Claude. 1991. *The Anthropology of Slavery: The Womb of Iron and Gold.* Chicago: University of Chicago Press.

Miers, Suzanne, and Igor Kopytoff, eds. 1977. *Slavery in Africa: Historical and Anthropological Perspective.* Madison: University of Wisconsin Press.

Moers, E. 1996. *Literary Women.* London: Women's Press.

Murdock, George P. 1981. *Atlas of World Cultures.* Pittsburgh: University of Pittsburgh Press.

———. 1983. *Outline of World Cultures.* New Haven, CT: Human Relations Area Files.

Murdock, George P., ed. 1931. *The Evolution of Culture.* New York: Macmillan.

Nieboer, H. I. 1910. *Slavery as an Industrial System.* The Hague: M. Nijhoff.

Northrup, David, ed. 1994. *The Atlantic Slave Trade.* Lexington, MA: D. C. Heath.

Padgug, Robert A. 1975. "Problems in the Theory of Slavery and Slave Society." *Science and Society* 40: 3–27.

Parish, Peter J. 1989. *Slavery: History and Historians.* New York: Harper and Row.

Parry, Clive, ed. 1969–. *Consolidated Treaty Series.* 231 vols. to date. Dobbs Ferry, NY: Oceana Publications.

Patterson, Orlando. 1991. *Freedom: Freedom in the Making of Western Culture.* New York: Basic Books.

———. 1979. "On Slavery and Slave Formations." *New Left Review* 117: 31–67.

———. 1982. *Slavery and Social Death.* Cambridge, MA: Harvard University Press.

Pomeroy, Sarah B. 1995. *Goddesses, Whores, Wives, and Slaves.* New York: Schocken Books.

Rawley, James A. 1981. *The Transatlantic Slave Trade.* New York: Norton.

Schwartz, Stuart; Linda Wimmer; and Robert Wolff. 1997. *The Global Experience.* New York: Longman.

Scott, S. P. 1973. *The Civil Law.* New York: AMS Press.

Seed, Patricia. 1995. *Ceremonies of Possession.* Cambridge: Cambridge University Press.

Segal, Ronald. 1995. *The Black Diaspora.* New York: Farrar, Straus and Giroux.

Shell, Robert. 1995. *Children of Bondage.* Johannesburg: Witwatersrand University Press.

Smith, Elsdon C. 1967. *Treasury of Name Lore.* New York: Harper and Row.

Smith, Marion. 1930. "The First Codification of the Substantive Common Law." *Tulane Law Review* 4: 178–189.

Solow, Barbara L. 1991. *Slavery and the Rise of the Atlantic System.* New York: Cambridge University Press.

Stock, Eugene. 1899. *The History of the Church Missionary Society.* London: Church Missionary Society.

Strauss, Leo, and Joseph Cropsey, eds. 1981. *History of Political Philosophy.* Chicago: University of Chicago Press.

Tibbles, Anthony, ed. 1994. *Transatlantic Slavery: Against Human Dignity.* London: Her Majesty's Stationery Office.

Van den Berghe, Pierre L. 1967. *Race and Racism: A Comparative Perspective.* New York: Wiley.

Wallerstein, Immanuel. 1979. *The Capitalist World-Economy.* Cambridge: Cambridge University Press.

Walvin, James. 1984. *Slavery and the Slave Trade: A Short Illustrated History.* Jackson: University of Mississippi Press.

Watson, Alan. 1989. *Slave Law in the Americas.* Athens: University of Georgia Press.

Wesley, Charles H. 1942. "Manifests of Slave Shipments along the Waterways, 1808–1864." *Journal of Negro History* 27 (2): 155–174.

Williams, Eric. 1944. *Capitalism and Slavery.* Chapel Hill: University of North Carolina Press.

Williamson, Laila. 1978. "Infanticide: An Anthropological Analysis." In *Infanticide and the Value of Life*. Edited by Marvin Kohl. New York: Prometheus Books.

Africa

Abdul, Sheriff. 1987. *Slaves, Spices, and Ivory in Zanzibar*. London: James Currey.

Abdul, Sheriff, and Ed Ferguson. 1991. *Zanzibar under Colonial Rule*. Athens: University of Ohio Press.

Abiola, E. Ola. 1974. *A Textbook of West African History (A.D. 1000 to the Present)*. Ado-Ekiti, Nigeria: Omolayo Standard Press.

Adefuye, Ade; Babatunde Agiri; and Jide Osuntokun, eds. 1987. *History of the Peoples of Lagos State*. Ikeja, Nigeria: Lantern Books.

Aderibigbe, A. B., ed. 1975. *Lagos: The Development of an African City*. London: University Press.

Ajayi, J. F. A. 1965. *Christian Missions in Nigeria, 1841–1891: The Making of a New Elite*. London: Longman.

Ajayi, J. F. A., and Michael Crowder. 1985. *Historical Atlas of Africa*. London: Cambridge University Press.

Ajayi, J. F. A., and Michael Crowder, eds. 1971. *History of West Africa*. London: Longman.

Akpan, M. B. 1973. "Black Imperialism: Americo-Liberian Rule over the African Peoples of Liberia, 1841–1964." *Canadian Journal of African Studies*. 7 (2): 217–236.

Alagoa, E. J. 1970. *Jaja of Opobo: The Slave Who Became a King*. London: Longman.

Allen, Richard B. 1989. "Economic Marginality and the Rise of the Free Population of Colour in Mauritius, 1767–1830." *Slavery and Abolition* 10 (2): 126–150.

———. 1983. "Marronage and the Maintenance of Public Order in Mauritius, 1721–1835." *Slavery and Abolition* 4 (3): 214–231.

Allison, Robert, ed. 1995. *The Interesting Narrative of the Life of Olaudah Equiano Written by Himself*. Boston: Bedford Books.

Alpers, E. A. 1975. *Ivory and Slaves in East Central Africa*. London: Heinemann.

Anene, J. C. 1966. *Southern Nigeria in Transition, 1885–1906*. London: Cambridge University Press.

Armstrong, James, and Nigel Worden. 1989. "The Slaves, 1652–1834." In *The Shaping of South African Society, 1652–1840*. Edited by Richard Elphick and Hermann Giliomee. Cape Town: Maskew Miller Longman.

As-Sa'di, Abderrahman ben Abdallah ben 'Imran ben 'Amir. 1964. *Ta'rikh as-Sudan*. Translated by Octave Houdas. Paris: Adrien-Maisonneuve.

Austen, Ralph. 1979. "The Trans-Saharan Slave Trade: A Tentative Census." In *The Uncommon Market: Essays in the Economic History of the Atlantic Slave Trade*. Edited by Henry Gemery and Jan S. Hogendorn. New York: Academic Press.

Ayandele, Emmanuel. 1966. *The Missionary Impact on Modern Nigeria*. London: Longman.

Barboza, Steven. 1988. "The Doorway of No Return—Goree." *American Visions* 3 (3): 6–9.

Barnes, Sandra T. 1980. *Ogun: An Old God for a New Age*. Philadelphia: Institute for the Study of Human Issues.

Barnes, Sandra T., ed. 1989. *Africa's Ogun: Old World and New*. Bloomington: Indiana University Press.

Barry, Boubacar. 1988. *Le Senegambie du XVe au XIXe siecle*. Paris: Harmattan.

Barth, Heinrich. 1965. *Travels and Discoveries in Northern and Central Africa*. London: Frank Cass.

Beachey, R. W. 1996. *A History of East Africa, 1592–1902*. London: Tauris.

———. 1976. *The Slave Trade of Eastern Africa*. New York: Barnes and Noble.

Beckingham, C. F. 1995. "The Quest for Prester John." In *The European Opportunity*. Edited by F. Fernandez-Armesto. Aldershot, Eng.: Variorum.

Birmingham, David. 1966. *Trade and Conflict in Angola: The Mbundu and Their Neighbours under the Influence of the Portuguese, 1483–1790*. Oxford: Clarendon Press.

Boahen, A. Adu. 1987. *African Perspectives on Colonialism*. Baltimore: Johns Hopkins University Press.

———. 1975. *Ghana: Evolution and Change in the Nineteenth and Twentieth Centuries*. London: Longman.

———. 1986. *Topics in West African History*. Burnt Mill, Essex, Eng.: Longman.

Bohannan, Paul, and Philip Curtin. 1971. *Africa and the Africans*. Prospect Heights, IL: Waveland Press.

Bottignole, Silvana. 1984. *Kikuyu Traditional Culture and Christianity: Self Examination of an African Church*. Nairobi: Heinemann.

Bradbury, R. E. 1964. *The Benin Kingdom and the Edo-Speaking Peoples of South-Western Nigeria*. London: International African Institute.

———. 1973. *Benin Studies*. London: International African Institute and Oxford University Press.

Burton, Sir Richard. 1872. *Zanzibar: City, Island, and Coast*. London: Tinsley Brothers.

Clark, Andrew Francis, and Lucie Colvin Phillips. 1994. *Historical Dictionary of Senegal*. Metuchen, NJ: Scarecrow Press.

Clark, Leon E. 1991. *Through African Eyes: The Past, the Road to Independence*. New York: Apex Press.

Clark, Robert. 1846. *Sierra Leone: A Description of the Manners and Customs of the Liberated Africans*. London: Ridgway.

Clarke, Peter B. 1982. *West Africa and Islam: A Study of Religious Development from the 8th to the 20th Century*. London: Edward Arnold.

Cobbing, Julian. 1988. "The Mfecane as Alibi: Thoughts on Dithakong and Mbolompo." *Journal of African History* 29 (3): 487–519.

Collins, Robert. 1992. "The Nilotic Slave Trade: Past and Present." In *The Human Commodity: Perspectives on the Trans-Saharan Slave Trade*. Edited by Elizabeth Savage. London: Frank Cass.

Connah, Graham. 1975. *The Archaeology of Benin: Excavations and Other Researches in and around Benin City, Nigeria*. Oxford: Clarendon Press.

Conneau, Theophilus. 1976. *A Slaver's Log Book, or 20 Year's Residence in Africa*. Englewood Cliffs, NJ: Prentice-Hall.

Cooper, Frederick. 1980. *From Slaves to Squatters: Plantation Labor and Agriculture in Zanzibar and Coastal Kenya, 1890–1925*. New Haven, CT: Yale University Press.

Costanzo, Angelo. 1987. *Surprizing Narrative: Olaudah Equiano and the Beginnings of Black Autobiography*. New York: Greenwood Press.

Crowe, S. E. 1942. *The Berlin West Africa Conference, 1884–1885*. Westport, CT: Negro Universities Press.

Crowther, Samuel. 1970. *Journal of an Expedition up the Niger and Tshadda Rivers*. London: Frank Cass.

Curtin, Philip D. 1968. *Africa Remembered: Narratives by West Africans from the Era of the Slave Trade*. Madison: University of Wisconsin Press.

———. 1969. *The Atlantic Slave Trade: A Census*. Madison: University of Wisconsin Press.

———. 1975. *Economic Change in Pre-Colonial Africa: Senegambia in the Era of the Slave Trade*. Madison: University of Wisconsin Press.

Cutrufelli, Maria Rosa. 1983. *Women of Africa: Roots of Oppression*. London: Zed Press.

Daaku, Kwame Yeboa. 1970. *Trade and Politics on the Gold Coast, 1600–1720: A Study of the African Reaction to European Trade*. Oxford: Oxford University Press.

van Dantzig, Albert. 1980. *Forts and Castles of Ghana*. Accra: Sedco.

———. 1980. *A Short History of the Forts and Castles of Ghana*. Accra: Sedco.

Davidson, Basil. 1991. *Africa in History*. New York: Macmillan.

———. 1969. *A History of East and Central Africa*. London: Longman.

Davies, K. G. 1975. *The Royal African Company*. New York: Octagon Books.

Debbasch, Yvan. 1988. "L'Espace du Sierra-Leone et la politique francaise de traite a la fin de l'Ancien Regime." In *De la traite a l'esclavage*. Edited by Serge Daget. Paris: Harmattan.

DeCorse, Christopher R. 1992. "Culture Contact, Continuity, and Change on the Gold Coast: A.D. 1400–1900." *African Archaeological Review* 10: 163–196.

Dickson, Kwamina B. 1969. *A Historical Geography of Ghana*. Cambridge: Cambridge University Press.

Dike, K. O. 1956. "John Beecroft, 1790–1854." *Journal of the Historical Society of Nigeria* 1 (1): 5–14.

Diop, Cheikh Anta. 1987. *Precolonial Black Africa*. Trenton, NJ: Africa World Press.

Donley-Reid, L. 1990. "A Structuring Structure: The Swahili House." In *Domestic Architecture and the Use of Space*. Edited by S. Kent. Cambridge: Cambridge University Press.

Dorigny, Marcel. 1993. "La Société des Amis des Noirs et les projets de colonisation en Afrique." *Annales Historiques de la Révolution Française*. 293–294, 421–429.

Duff, E. C., and W. Hamilton-Browne. 1972. *Gazetteer of the Kontagora Province*. London: Frank Cass.

Duffy, James. 1959. *Portuguese Africa*. Cambridge, MA: Harvard University Press.

Duke, Marvin L. 1974. "Robert F. Stockton: Early U.S. Naval Activities in Africa." *Shipmate* (December): 22–25.

Eldredge, Elizabeth, and Fred Morton, eds. 1994. *Slavery in South Africa: Captive Labor on the Dutch Frontier*. Boulder, CO: Westview Press and Pietermaritzburg: University of Natal Press.

Equiano, Olaudah. 1995. *Olaudah Equiano: The Interesting Narrative and Other Writings*. New York: Penguin.

Ewald, Janet. 1992. "Slavery in Africa and the Slave Trades from Africa." *American Historical Review* 97 (1): 465–485.

Fage, J. D.; Roland Oliver; and Richard Gray. 1975. *The Cambridge History of Africa from c. 1600 to c. 1790*. New York: Cambridge University Press.

Fanon, Frantz. *The Wretched of the Earth*. New York: Grove Press 1968.

Fisher, Allan, and Humphrey Fisher. 1970. *Slavery and Muslim Society in Africa; The Institution in Saharan and Sudanic Africa and the Trans-Saharan Trade*. London: C. Hurst.

Frederickson, George. 1981. *White Supremacy: A Comparative Study in American and South African History*. New York: Oxford University Press.

Friedman, Ellen G. 1983. *Spanish Captives in North Africa*. Madison: University of Wisconsin Press.

Fyfe, Christopher. 1962. *A History of Sierra Leone*. London: Oxford University Press.

Fynn, John Kofi. 1971. *Asante and Its Neighbours, 1700–1807*. London: Longman.

Gailey, Harry A., Jr. 1981. *History of Africa: From 1800 to Present*. Huntington, NY: Krieger Publishing.

Gates, Henry Louis, Jr. 1996. "Europe, African Art, and the Uncanny." In *Africa: The Art of a Continent*. Edited by Tom Phillips. New York: Guggenheim Museum.

George, Claude. 1968. *Rise of British West Africa*. London: Houlston.

Gershoni, Yekutiel. 1985. *Black Colonialism: The Americo-Liberian Scramble for the Hinterland*. Boulder, CO: Westview Press.

Gilroy, Paul. 1993. *The Black Atlantic*. Cambridge, MA: Harvard University Press.

Glasse, Cyril. 1989. *The Concise Encyclopedia of Islam*. San Francisco: Harper and Row.

Grace, John. 1975. *Domestic Slavery in West Africa*. New York: Barnes and Noble.

Granlund, V. 1879. *En svensk koloni i Afrika eller Svenska Afrika Kompaniets historia*. Stockholm.

Grove, C. P. 1948. *The Planting of Christianity in Africa*. London: Lutterworth.

Hallett, R. 1965. *The Penetration of Africa: European Enterprise and Exploration Principally in Northern and Western Africa University Press to 1830*. London: Routledge.

Hamilton, Carolyn, ed. 1995. *The Mfecane Aftermath: Reconstructive Debates in Southern African History*. Johannesburg: Witwatersrand University Press and Pietermaritzburg: University of Natal Press.

Harris, Joseph, ed. 1993. *Global Dimensions of the African Diaspora*. Washington, DC: Howard University Press.

Hartigan, Royal J. 1986. "Blood Drum Spirit: Drum Languages of West Africa, African-America, Native America, Central Java, and South India." Ph.D. dissertation, Department of History, Wesleyan University, Middletown, Connecticut.

Herskovits, Melville J. 1958. *The Myth of the Negro Past*. Boston: Beacon Press.

Hill, Richard. 1959. *Egypt in the Sudan, 1820–1881*. London: Oxford University Press.

Hilton, Anne. 1985. *The Kingdom of Kongo*. Oxford: Clarendon Press.

Hiskett, Mervyn. 1984. *The Development of Islam in West Africa*. New York: Longman.

Hogben, Sidney John. 1967. *An Introduction to the History of the Islamic States of Northern Nigeria*. Ibadan, Nigeria: Oxford University Press.

Hole, Charles. 1896. *The Early History of the Church Missionary Society for Africa and the East*. London: Church Missionary Society.

Holt, P. M., and M. W. Daly. 1988. *A History of the Sudan*. London: Longman.

Holt, Peter. 1970. *The Mahdist State in the Sudan, 1881–1898*. Oxford: Clarendon Press.

Hutchinson, Louise Daniel. 1979. *Out of Africa: From West African Kingdoms to Colonization*. Washington, DC: Anacostia Neighborhood Museum of the Smithsonian Institution.

Iliffe, J. 1995. *Africans: The History of a Continent*. Cambridge: Cambridge University Press.

James, L. A. Webb. 1995. *Desert Frontier*. Madison: University of Wisconsin Press.

Johnson, Douglas. 1992. "Recruitment and Entrapment in Private Slave Armies." In *The Human Commodity: Perspectives on the Trans-Saharan Slave Trade*. Edited by Elizabeth Savage. London: Frank Cass.

———. 1988. "Sudanese Military Slavery from the 18th to the 20th century." In *Slavery and Other Forms of Unfree Labour*. Edited by Leonie Archer. London: Routledge.

July, Robert W. 1992. *A History of the African People*. Prospect Heights, IL: Waveland Press.

Kelly, Kenneth G. 1997. "The Archaeology of African-European Interaction: Investigating the Social Roles of Trade, Traders, and the Use of Space in the Seventeenth and Eighteenth Century Hueda Kingdom, Republic of Benin." *World Archaeology* 28 (3): 354–364.

Klein, A. Norman. 1994. "Slavery and Akan Origins." *Ethnohistory* 41: 627–656.

Klein, Martin, ed. 1993. *Breaking the Chains: Slavery, Bondage, and Emancipation in Modern Africa and Asia*. Madison: University of Wisconsin Press.

Koslow, Phillip. 1995. *Centuries of Greatness: The West African Kingdoms*. New York: Chelsea House.

Law, Robin. 1977. *The Oyo Empire c. 1600–c. 1836: A West African Imperialism in the Era of the Atlantic Slave Trade*. Oxford: Clarendon Press.

———. 1977. "Royal Monopoly and Private Enterprise in the Atlantic Trade: The Case of Dahomey." *Journal of African History* 18: 555–577.

———. 1991. *The Slave Coast of West Africa, 1550–1750: The Impact of the Atlantic Slave Trade on an African Society*. Oxford: Clarendon Press.

Lawrence, A. W. 1963. *Trade Castles and Forts of West Africa*. London: Jonathan Cape.

Le May, G. H. 1995. *The Afrikaners*. Oxford: Oxford University Press.

Levtzion, Nehemia. 1973. *Ancient Ghana and Mali*. London: Methuen.

———. 1963. "The Thirteenth- and Fourteenth-Century Kings of Mali." *Journal of African History* 4 (3): 341–353.

Lipton, Merle. 1985. *Capitalism and Apartheid*. London: Gower Publishing House.

Littlefield, Daniel C. 1991. *Rice and Slaves*. Urbana: University of Illinois Press.

Lovejoy, Paul E. 1981. *The Ideology of Slavery in Africa*. London: Sage Publications.

———. 1983. *Transformations in Slavery*. Cambridge: Cambridge University Press.

Lovejoy, Paul, and Jan Hogendorn. 1993. *The Slow Death of Slavery: The Course of Abolition in Northern Nigeria, 1897–1936*. Cambridge: Cambridge University Press.

Lugard, Frederick D. 1933. "Slavery in All Its Forms." *Africa* 6: 1–14.

———. 1968. *The Rise of Our East African Empire*. London: Frank Cass.

McEvedy, Colin. 1980. *The Penguin Atlas of African History*. New York: Penguin Books.

Mack, Beverly. 1992. "Women and Slavery in Nineteenth-Century Hausaland." *Slavery and Abolition* 13 (1): 89–110.

Macmillan, William. 1963. *Bantu, Boer, and Briton*. Oxford: Clarendon.

McSheffrey, Gerald M. 1983. "Slavery, Indentured Servitude, Legitimate Trade, and the Impact of Abolition in the Gold Coast, 1874–1901: A Reappraisal." *Journal of African History* 24: 349–368.

Manning, Patrick. 1990. *Slavery and African Life: Occidental, Oriental, and African Slave Trades*. Cambridge: Cambridge University Press.

———. 1982. *Slavery, Colonialism, and Economic Growth in Dahomey, 1640–1960*. Cambridge: Cambridge University Press.

Maxwell, Kevin B. 1983. *Bemba Myth and Ritual: The Impact of Literacy on an Oral Culture*. New York: Peter Lang.

Meillassoux, Claude. 1991. *Anthropology of Slavery*. Chicago: University of Chicago Press.

Meillassoux, Claude, ed. 1975. *L'Esclavage en Afrique precoloniale*. Paris, Maspero.

Miers, Suzanne, and Igor Kopytoff. 1977. *Slavery in Africa*. Madison: University of Wisconsin Press.

Miers, Suzanne, and Richard Roberts, eds. 1989. *The End of Slavery in Africa*. Madison: University of Wisconsin Press.

Miller, Joseph C. 1982. "Commercial Organization of Slaving at Luanda, Angola, 1760–1830." In *The Uncommon Market: Essays in the Economic History of the Atlantic Slave Trade*. Edited by Henry A. Gemery and Jan S. Hogendorn. New York: Academic Press.

———. 1988. *Way of Death: Merchant Capitalism and the Angolan Slave Trade, 1730–1830*. Madison: University of Wisconsin Press.

Miller, Randall, and John David Smith, eds. 1988. *Dictionary of Afro-American Slavery*. Westport, CT: Greenwood.

Miner, Horace. 1953. *The Primitive City of Timbuctoo*. Princeton, NJ: Princeton University Press.

Moore, Shelley. 1986. "Goree." *Crisis* 93 (6): 18–21, 56.

Mouser, Bruce L. 1973. "Trade, Coasters, and Conflict in the Rio Pongo from 1790 to 1808." *Journal of African History* 14 (1): 45–64.

Müller, Wilhelm Johann. 1968. *Die Africanische auf der guneischen Gold Cust gelegene Landschafft Fetu*. Hamburg: Graz.

Mundt, Robert. 1987. *Historical Dictionary of the Ivory Coast*. Metuchen, NJ: Scarecrow Press.

Ndiaye, Joseph. 1989. *The Slave Trade at Goree Island and Its History*. Gorée, Senegal: Ndiaye.

Nicholls, C. S. 1971. *The Swahili Coast*. London: George Allen.

Northrup, David. 1978. "African Mortality in the Suppression of the Slave Trade: The Case of the Bight of Biafra." *Journal of Interdisciplinary History* 9 (Summer): 47–64.

Nurse, Derek. 1980. *Bantu Migration into East Africa*. Nairobi: University of Nairobi Institute of African Studies.

O'Fahey, R. S. 1973. "Slavery and the Slave Trade in Dar Fur." *Journal of African History* 14 (1): 29–43.

O'Fahey, R. S., and J. L. Spaulding. 1974. *Kingdoms of the Sudan*. London: Methuen.

O'Meara, Dan. 1996. *Forty Lost Years: The Apartheid State and the Politics of the National Party, 1948–1994*. Athens: Ohio University Press and Johannesburg: Ravan Press.

Oliver, Roland, and J. D. Fage. 1990. *A Short History of Africa*. New York: Penguin Books.

Oliver, Ronald, and Brian M. Fagan. 1975. *Africa in the Iron Age: c. 500 B.C. to A.D. 1400*. Cambridge: Cambridge University Press.

Omer-Cooper, J. D. 1994. *History of Southern Africa*. London: James Currey.

———. 1966. *The Zulu Aftermath: A Nineteenth-Century Revolution in Bantu Africa*. London: Longman.

Paulme, Denise, ed. 1971. *Women of Tropical Africa*. Berkeley: University of California Press.

Peires, Jeff. 1989. "The British and the Cape, 1814–1834." In *The Shaping of South African Society, 1652–1840*. Edited by Richard Elphick and Hermann Giliomee. Cape Town: Maskew Miller Longman.

Perham, Margery F. 1956. *Lugard*. London: Collins.

Peterson, John. 1969. *Province of Freedom*. London: Faber.

Porter, R. 1968. "The Crispe Family and the African Trade in the Seventeenth Century." *Journal of African History* 9 (1): 57–77.

Posel, Deborah. 1991. *The Making of Apartheid,*

1948–61: Conflict and Compromise. Oxford: Clarendon Press.

Prunier, Gerard. 1992. "Military Slavery in the Sudan during the Turkiyya." In *The Human Commodity: Perspectives on the Trans-Saharan Slave Trade*. Edited by Elizabeth Savage. London: Frank Cass.

Ransford, Oliver. 1972. *The Great Trek*. London: Murray.

Reynolds, Edward. 1974. *Trade and Economic Change on the Gold Coast: 1807–1874*. New York: Longman.

Robertson, Claire, and Martin L. Klein, eds. 1983. *Women and Slavery in Africa*. Bloomington: Indiana University Press.

Rodney, Walter. 1970. *A History of the Upper Guinea Coast, 1545 to 1800*. Oxford: Clarendon Press.

Romero, Patricia. 1981. "Laboratory for the Oral History of Slavery: The Island of Lamu on the Kenya Coast." *American Historical Review* 88 (3): 858–882.

———. 1997. *Lamu: History, Society, and Family in an East African Port City*. Princeton, NJ: Markus Wiener Publishers.

———. 1988. "Slave Children." In *Dictionary of Afro-American Slavery*. Edited by Randall Miller and John David Smith. Westport, CT: Greenwood.

Ross, Robert. 1983. *Cape of Torments*. London: Routledge.

Ryder, A. F. C. 1969. *Benin and the Europeans, 1485–1897*. New York: Humanities Press.

Saumagne, C. 1934. "Ouvriers agricoles ou rôdeurs de celliers? Les circoncellions d'Afrique." *Annals d'histoire économique et sociale* 6: 351–364.

Sempebwa, Joshua Wantate. 1978. *The Ontological and Normative Structures in the Social Reality of a Bantu Society: A Systematic Study of Ganda Ontology and Ethics*. London: Macmillan.

Shell, Robert. 1994. *Children of Bondage: A Social History of the Slave Society at the Cape of Good Hope, 1652–1838*. Hanover, NH: Wesleyan University Press.

Sherlock, Phillip Manderson. *Anansi the Spider Man*. 1954. Binghamton, NY: Vail-Ballou Press.

Shick, Tom W. 1977. *Behold the Promised Land: A History of Afro-American Settler Society in Nineteenth-Century Liberia*. Baltimore: Johns Hopkins University Press.

———. 1971. "A Quantitative Analysis of Liberian Colonization from 1820 to 1843 with Special Reference to Mortality." *Journal of African History* 12: 45–59.

Slessarev, V. 1959. *Prester John: The Letter and the Legend*. Minneapolis: University of Minnesota Press.

Smith, Robert S. 1979. *The Lagos Consulate, 1851–1861*. Berkeley: University of California Press.

Sundiata, I. K. 1980. *Black Scandal: America and the Liberian Labor Crisis, 1929–1936*. Philadelphia: Institute for the Study of Human Issues.

Sutton, J. E. G. 1990. *A Thousand Years of East Africa*. Nairobi: British Institute in Eastern Africa.

Temperley, Howard. 1991. *White Dreams, Black Africa: The Antislavery Expedition to the Niger River, 1841–1842*. New Haven, CT: Yale University Press.

Temple, C. L., and O. Temple. 1965. *Notes on the Tribes, Emirates, and States of the Northern Provinces of Nigeria*. London: Frank Cass.

Thompson, Robert Farris. 1983. *Flash of the Spirit*. New York: Vintage Books.

Thornton, John K. 1992. *Africa and Africans in the Making of the Atlantic World, 1400–1680*. Cambridge: Cambridge University Press.

———. 1983. *The Kingdom of Kongo*. Madison: University of Wisconsin Press.

Toussaint, Auguste. 1972. *Histoire des iles mascareignes*. Paris: Berger-Levrault.

Tremearne, A. J. N. 1913. *Hausa Superstitions and Customs: An Introduction to the Folk-Lore and the Folk*. London: J. Bale, Sons and Danielsson.

Trimingham, John Spencer. 1980. *The Influence of Islam upon Africa*. New York: Longman.

Van der Merwe, Pieter. 1995. *The Migrant Farmer in the History of the Cape Colony, 1657–1842*. Translated from Afrikaans by Roger Beck. Athens: Ohio University Press.

Vansina, Jan. 1966. *Kingdoms of the Savana*. Madison: University of Wisconsin Press.

Venter, C. 1991. "Die Voortrekkers en die ingeboekte Slawe wat die Groot Trek Meegemaak Het." *Historia* 39 (1): 14–29.

Vogt, John. 1979. *Portuguese Rule on the Gold Coast 1469–2*. Athens: University of Georgia Press.

Wallerstein, Immanuel. 1986. *Africa and the Modern World*. Trenton, NJ: Africa World Press.

Walz, Terence. 1985. "Black Slavery in Egypt during the Nineteenth Century as Reflected in the Mahakama Archives of Cairo." In *Slaves and Slavery in Muslim Africa*. Vol. 2, *The Servile Estate*. Edited by John Ralph Willis. London: Frank Cass.

———. 1978. *Trade between Egypt and Bilad As-Sudan, 1700–1820*. Paris: Institut Francais D'Archeologie Orientale Du Caire.

Wilks, Ivor. 1993. *Forests of Gold: Essays on the Akan and the Kingdom of Asante*. Athens: Ohio University Press.

Wilson, Monica, and Leonard Thompson, eds. 1969. *The Oxford History of South Africa*. New York: Oxford University Press.

Worden, Nigel. 1995. *The Making of Modern South Africa: Conquest, Segregation, and Apartheid.* New York: Blackwell.

————. 1985. *Slavery in Dutch South Africa.* Cambridge: Cambridge University Press.

Worden, Nigel, and Clifton Crais, eds. 1994. *Breaking the Chains: Slavery and Its Legacy in the Nineteenth-Century Cape Colony.* Johannesburg: Witwatersrand University Press.

Wyse, Akintola. 1989. *The Krio of Sierra Leone.* London: Hurst.

Zook, George F. 1919. "The Company of the Royal Adventurers Trading to Africa." *Journal of Negro History* 4 (2): 134–231.

Ancient and Classical

Adams, Robert Mc. 1982. "Property Rights and Functional Tenure in Mesopotamian Rural Communities." In *Societies and Languages of the Ancient Near East: Studies in Honour of I. M. Diakonoff.* Edited by J. N. Postgate. Warminster, Eng.: Aris and Phillips.

Adcock, F. E. 1966. *Marcus Crassus Millionaire.* Cambridge: Cambridge University Press.

Altenmuller, Hartwig, and Ahmed M. Moussa. 1991. "Die Inschrift Amenemhets II. aus dem Ptah-Tempel von Memphis: Ein Vorbericht." *Studien zur Altägyptischen Kultur* 18: 1–48.

Andrewes, Antony. 1956. *The Greek Tyrants.* London: Hutchinson's University Library.

Annequin, Jacques. 1972. "Esclaves et affranchis dans la conjuration de Catilina." *Actes du colloque sur l'esclavage.* Paris: Les Belles Lettres.

Astin, Alan E. 1978. *Cato the Censor.* Oxford: Clarendon Press.

Austin, M. M., and P. Vidal-Naquet. 1977. *Economic and Social History of Ancient Greece: An Introduction.* Berkeley: University of California Press.

Badian, Ernst. 1958. *Foreign Clientelae.* Oxford: Clarendon Press.

Bakir, Abd el-Mohsen. 1952. *Slavery in Pharaonic Egypt.* Cairo: Imprimerie de'l IFAOC.

Barrow, R. H. 1928. *Slavery in the Roman Empire.* London: Macmillan.

Bartchy, S. Scott. 1992. "Slavery." In *Anchor Bible Dictionary.* New York: Doubleday.

Beavis, Mary Ann. 1992. "Ancient Slavery as an Interpretive Context for the New Testament Servant Parables with Special Reference to the Unjust Steward (Luke 16:1–8)." *Journal of Biblical Literature* 111 (1): 37–54.

Beker, J. Christiaan. 1980. *Paul the Apostle: The Triumph of God in Life and Thought.* Philadelphia: Fortress Press.

Berlev, Oleg. 1965. Review of William Kelly Simpson.

1963. *Papyrus Reisner I: The Records of a Building Project in the Reign of Sesostris I.* Boston: Museum of Fine Arts. *Bibliotheca Orientalis* 22: 263–268.

————. 1987. "A Social Experiment in Nubia during the Years 9–17 of Sesostris I." In *Labor in the Ancient Near East.* Edited by Marvin A. Powell. New Haven, CT: Yale University Press.

Bierbrier, Morris. 1982. *The Tomb-Builders of the Pharaohs.* London: British Museum Publications.

Bowra, C. M. 1935. *Ancient Greek Literature.* Oxford: Oxford University Press.

————. 1961. *Greek Lyric Poetry.* Oxford: Oxford University Press.

Bradley, Keith R. 1987. "On the Roman Slave Supply and Slavebreeding." In *Classical Slavery.* Edited by Moses I. Finley. London: Frank Cass.

————. 1986. "Seneca and Slavery." *Classica et mediaevalia* 37: 161–172.

————. 1983. "Slave Kingdoms and Slave Rebellions in Ancient Sicily." *Historical Reflections/Reflexions Historiques* 10: 435–451.

————. 1989. *Slavery and Rebellion in the Roman World, 140 B.C.–70 B.C.* Bloomington: Indiana University Press.

————. 1994. *Slavery and Society at Rome.* New York: Cambridge University Press.

————. 1987. *Slaves and Masters in the Roman Empire: A Study in Social Control.* New York: Oxford University Press.

————. 1978. "Slaves and the Conspiracy of Catiline." *Classical Philology* 73: 329–336.

Brennan, T. Corey. 1993. "The Commanders in the First Sicilian Slave War." *Rivista di Filologia e di Istruzione Classica* 121: 153–184.

Brinkhof, Johannes Jacobus. 1978. *Een studie over het peculium in het Klassieke Romeinse recht.* Meppel, Netherlands: Krips Repr.

Brown, Peter. 1967. *Augustine of Hippo.* Berkeley: University of California Press.

Bruce, F. F. 1936. "Latin Participles as Slave Names." *Glotta* 25: 42–50.

Brunt, Peter A. 1971. *Italian Manpower, 225 B.C.–A.D. 14.* Oxford: Clarendon.

————. 1971. *Social Conflicts in the Roman Republic.* London: Chatto and Windus.

Buccellati, G. 1991. "A Note on the Muškēnum as Homesteader." *Maarav* 7: 91–100.

Buckland, W. W. 1970. *The Roman Law of Slavery.* London: Cambridge University Press.

Burn, Andrew R. 1977. *The Pelican History of Greece.* London: Pelican.

Bury, J. B., and Russell Meiggs. 1975. *A History of Greece to the Death of Alexander the Great.* New York: St. Martin's.

Carcopino, Jerome. 1941. *Daily Life in Ancient Rome.* London: Routledge.

Cartledge, P. A. 1979. *Sparta and Lakonia*. London: Routledge.

Casson, L. 1989. *The Periplus Maris Erythraei*. Princeton, NJ: Princeton University Press.

Cato, Marcus Porcius, and Marcus Terentius Varro. 1934. *On Agriculture*. Translated by William Davis Hooper and Harrison Boyd Ash. Cambridge, MA: Harvard University Press.

Chamoux, Francois. 1965. *The Civilization of Greece*. London: George Allen and Unwin.

Charlesworth, M. P., ed. 1939. *Documents Illustrating the Reigns of Claudius and Nero*. Oxford: Oxford University Press.

Chevallier, Raymond. 1976. *Roman Roads*. London: B. T. Batsford.

Chirichigno, Gregory C. 1993. *Debt-Slavery in Israel and the Ancient Near East*. Sheffield, Eng.: Sheffield Academic Press.

Clarke, John. 1996. "Hypersexual Men in Augustan Baths." In *Sexuality in Ancient Art*. Edited by Natalie Boymel Kampen. Cambridge: Cambridge University Press.

Columella, Lucius Junius. 1941. *On Agriculture*. Translated by Harrison Boyd Ash. London: Heinemann.

Copalle, Siegfried. 1908. *De servorum Graecorum nominbus*. Marburg, Germany: Typis Academicis.

Cornell, Tim J. 1995. *The Beginnings of Rome*. London: Routledge.

Crombie, Ian M. 1962–1963. *An Examination of Plato's Doctrines*. 2 vols. New York: Humanities Press.

Crook, J. A.; Andrew Lintott; and Elizabeth Rawson, eds. 1994. *The Cambridge Ancient History*. Vol. 9. New York: Cambridge University Press.

Cruz-Uribe, E. 1982. "Slavery in Egypt during the Saite and Persian Periods." In *Revue Internationale des Droits de l' Antiquite* (Brussels) 29: 47–71.

Dalton, O. M., ed. 1915. *The Letters of Sidonius*. Oxford: Clarendon.

Danadamaev, Muhammad. 1984. *Slavery in Babylonia*. Dekalb: Northern Illinois University Press.

Daressy, Georges. 1915. "Une stèle de l'Ancien Empire maintenant détruite." *Annales du Service des Antiquités de l'Egypte* 15: 207–208.

David, A. R. 1986. *The Pyramid Builders of Ancient Egypt*. London: Routledge.

De Ste. Croix, Geoffrey E. M. 1981. *The Class Struggle in the Ancient Greek World*. Ithaca, NY: Cornell University Press.

Deimel, A. 1930. *Codex Hammurabi*. Rome: Pontifical Biblical Institute.

Diakonov, Igor M. 1987. "Slave-Labour vs. Non-Slave Labour: The Problem of Definition." In *Labor in the Ancient Near East*. Edited by Marvin A. Powell. Ancient Oriental Series 68. New Haven, CT: American Oriental Society.

———. 1974. "Structure of Society and State in Early Dynastic Sumer." In *Sources and Monographs: Monographs of the Ancient Near East*. Vol. 1. Los Angeles: Undena Publications.

Donadoni, S., ed. 1992. *Der Mensch des Alten Agypten*. New York: Campus.

Drinkwater, J. F. 1984. "Peasants and Bagaudae in Roman Gaul." *Classical Views* 3: 349–371.

Driver, Godfrey R., and John C. Miles. 1935. *The Assyrian Laws*. Oxford: Clarendon Press.

———. 1952–1955. *The Babylonian Laws*. 2 vols. Oxford: Clarendon Press.

Du latifundium au latifondo: Un héritage de Rome, une création médievale ou moderne? 1995. Paris: Centre Pierre Paris.

Dumont, J. C. 1987. *Servus: Rome et l'esclavage sous la républic*. Rome: École française de Rome.

Eckstein, Arthur. 1995. *Moral Vision in the Histories of Polybius*. Berkeley: University of California Press.

Edwards, I. E. S. 1980. *The Pyramids of Egypt*. Harmondsworth, Eng.: Penguin Books.

Ehrenberg, Victor. 1973. *From Solon to Socrates*. London: Methuen.

Endesfelder, E., ed. 1991. *Probleme der fruhen Gesellschaftsentwicklung im Alten Agypten*. Berlin: Institut fur Sudanarchaologie und Agyptologie.

Etienne, R. 1972. "Cicéron et l'esclavage." In *Actes du colloque d'histoiré sociale*. Paris: Les Belles Lettres.

Eyre, Christopher. 1987. "Work and the Organisation of Work in the New Kingdom." In *Labor in the Ancient Near East*. Edited by Marvin A. Powell. Ancient Oriental Series 68. New Haven, CT: American Oriental Society.

Fine, John V. A. 1983. *The Ancient Greeks: A Critical History*. Cambridge, MA: Belknap Press.

Finley, Moses I. 1973. *The Ancient Economy*. London: Chatto and Windus.

———. 1980. *Ancient Slavery and Modern Ideology*. New York: Viking.

———. 1981. "Debt-Bondage and the Problem of Slavery." In *Economy and Society in Ancient Greece*. Edited by Brent D. Shaw and Richard P. Saller. London: Chatto and Windus.

———. 1981. *Economy and Society in Ancient Greece*. London: Chatto and Windus.

———. 1984. *Politics in the Ancient World*. Cambridge: Cambridge University Press.

———. 1981. "The Servile Statuses of Ancient Greece." In *Economy and Society in Ancient Greece*. Edited by Brent D. Shaw and Richard P. Saller. London: Chatto and Windus.

———. 1960. *Slavery in Classical Antiquity: Views and Controversies*. Cambridge: Heffer.

Finley, Moses I., ed. 1984. *The Legacy of Greece*. Oxford: Oxford University Press.

Fischer, Henry G. 1958. "An Early Occurrence of *hm* "Servant" in Regulations Referring to a Mortuary Estate," *Mitteilungen des Deutschen Archäologischen Instituts, Abteilung Kairo* 16: 131–137.

Forest, W. G. 1980. *A History of Sparta, 950–192*. London: Duckworth.

Freeman, Kathleen. 1976. *The Work and Life of Solon*. New York: Arno Press.

Frend, W. H. C. 1971. *The Donatist Church*. New York: Oxford University Press.

Freshfield, Edwin, ed. 1926. *A Manual of Roman Law: The Ecloga*. Cambridge: Cambridge University Press.

Friedman, David Noel, ed. 1992. *Anchor Bible Dictionary*. New York: Doubleday.

Gamsey, Peter. 1970. *Social Status and Legal Privilege in the Roman Empire*. Oxford: Clarendon Press.

Gardiner, Alan H. 1940. "Adoption Extraordinary." *Journal of Egyptian Archaeology* 26: 23–29.

Garlan, Yvon. 1988. *Slavery in Ancient Greece*. Ithaca, NY: Cornell University Press.

Garland, A. 1992. "Cicero's Familia Urbana." *Greece and Rome* 39: 163–172.

Garnsey, Peter. 1996. *Ideas of Slavery from Aristotle to Augustine*. Cambridge: Cambridge University Press.

Gelb, I. J. 1973. "Prisoners of War in Early Mesopotamia." *Journal of Near Eastern Studies* 32: 70–98.

Giardina, A., and A. Schiavone, eds. 1981. *Societe la produzione schiavistica*. Rome and Bari: Laterza and Figli.

Gordon, C. 1963. *Hammurabi's Code: Quaint or Forward Looking?* New York: Holt, Rinehart and Winston.

Gragarin, Michael. 1986. *Early Greek Law*. Berkeley: University of California Press.

———. 1995. "The First Law of the Gortyn Code Revisited." *Greek Roman and Byzantine Studies* 36 (Spring): 7–15.

Grant, Frederic C., and H. H. Rowley, eds. 1963. *Dictionary of the Bible*. New York: Scribners.

Grant, Michael, and Rachel Kitzinger, eds. 1988. *Civilization of the Ancient Mediterranean: Greece and Rome*. New York: Charles Scribner's Sons.

Gratien, B. 1995. "La basse Nubie a l' Ancien Empire: Egyptiens et autochtones." In *Journal of Egyptian Archaeology* 81: 43–56.

Grayson, A. Kirk. 1972. *Assyrian Royal Inscriptions*. Wiesbaden, Germany: Otto Harrassowitz.

Griffith. Francis L. 1898. *The Petrie Papyri: Hieratic Papyri from Kahun and Gurob*. London: n.p.

Grote, George. 1951–1957. *History of Greece*. 12 vols. Boston: J. P. Jewett.

Grubbs, Judith Evans. 1995. *Law and Family in Late Antiquity*. Oxford: Clarendon.

Grunert. 1980. "Das demotische Rechtsbuch von Hermopolis-West: Zu den Eigentumsverhaltnissen im ptolemaischen Agypten." *Das Alterum* (Berlin) 12: 96–102.

Gundlach, Rolf. 1994. *Die Zwangsumsiedlung auswärtiger Bevölkerung als Mittel ägyptischer Politik bis zum Ende des Mittleren Reiches*. Forschungen zur Antiken Sklaverei 26. Stuttgart: Franz Steiner Verlag.

Gustafson, M. 1997. "*Inscripta in fronte*: Penal Tattooing in Late Antiquity." *Classical Antiquity* 16 (1): 79–105.

Güterbock, H. G. 1972. "Bermerkungen zu den Ausdrücken ellum, wardum und asirum in hethitischen Texten." In *Gesellschaftklassen im alten Zweistromland und in angrenzenden Gebeiten*. Edited by D. O. Edzard. Munich: Verlag der bayerischen Akademie der Wissenschaften.

Guthrie, William K. C. 1975. *A History of Greek Philosophy*. Cambridge: Cambridge University Press.

Hammond, N. G. L. 1994. *Philip of Macedon*. Baltimore: Johns Hopkins University Press.

Hare, Richard M. 1982. *Plato*. Oxford: Oxford University Press.

Harrill, J. Albert. 1995. *The Manumission of Slaves in Early Christianity*. Tübingen, Germany: J. C. B. Mohr.

Hayes, William C. 1955. *A Papyrus of the Late Middle Kingdom in the Brooklyn Museum (Papyrus Brooklyn 35.1446)*. New York: Brooklyn Museum.

Helck, Wolfgang. 1963. "Materialien zur Wirtschaftsgeschichte des Neuen Reiches III." *Abhandlungen der Akademie der Wissenschaften und der Literatur in Mainz* 2: 135–542.

———. 1984. "Sklaven." In *Lexikon der Ägyptologie*. Vol. 5. Edited by Wolfgang Helck and Wolfhart Westendorf. Wiesbaden, Germany: Otto Harrassowitz.

Hoffner, H. 1995. "Hittite Laws." In *Law Collections from Mesopotamia and Asia Minor*. Edited by M. Roth. Atlanta, GA: Scholars Press.

Holden, A. 1974. *Greek Pastoral Poetry*. London: Penguin.

Hübner, Wolfgang. 1984. *Varros instrumentum vocale im Kontext der antiken Achwissenschaften*. Stuttgart: Franz Steiner.

Huxley, George Leonard. 1962. *Early Sparta*. Cambridge, MA: Harvard University Press.

Janssen, Jacob J. 1967. "Eine Beuteliste von Amenophis II und das Problem der Sklaverei im Altem Aegypten." *Jaarbericht van het Voorazi-*

atisch-Egyptisch Genootschap (Gezelschap) "Ex Oriente Lux" 6: 141–147.

———. 1975. *Commodity Prices from Ramessid Period.* Leiden: Brill.

———. 1975. "Prolegomena to the Study of Egypt's Economic History during the New Kingdom." *Studien zur altagyptischen Kultar* 3: 127–185.

Jay, P., ed. 1973. *The Greek Anthology.* London: London University Press.

Johne, Klaus-Peter; Jens Köhn; and Volker Weber. 1983. *Die Kolonen in Italien und den westlichen Provinzen des römischen Reiches.* Berlin: Akademie-Verlag.

Jones, A. H. M. 1956. "Slavery in the Ancient World." *Economic History Review* 2 (9): 185–199.

———. 1959. "Were Ancient Heresies National or Social Movements in Disguise?" *Journal of Theological Studies,* n.s., 10: 280–298.

Jones, C. P. 1987. "*Stigma:* Tattooing and Branding in Graeco-Roman Antiquity." *Journal of Roman Studies* 77: 139–155.

Jowett, Benjamin, trans. 1885. *The Politics of Aristotle Translated into English with Introduction, Marginal Analysis, Essays, Notes, and Indices.* 3 vols. Oxford: Clarendon Press.

Keck, Leander E. 1988. *Paul and His Letters.* Second edition, revised and enlarged. Philadelphia: Fortress Press.

Kehoe, Dennis P. 1988. *The Economics of Agriculture on Roman Imperial Estates in North Africa.* Göttingen, Germany: Vandenhoeck and Ruprecht.

Kirk, Geoffrey S. 1986. *The Nature of Greek Myths.* London: Pelican.

Kirschenbaum, Aaron. 1987. *Sons, Slaves, and Freedmen in Roman Commerce.* Jerusalem: Magnes Press.

Kuziscin, Vasilij Ivanovic. 1984. *La grande proprietà agraria nell'Italia romana II secolo a.C–I secolo d.C.* Rome: Editori Riuniti.

Lambertz, Max. 1907–1908. *Die griechischen Sklavennamen.* 2 vols. Vienna: Staatsgymnasium.

Lattimore, Richmond, trans. 1967. *The Iliad of Homer.* Chicago: University of Chicago Press.

———. 1991. *The Odyssey of Homer.* New York: Harper Perennial.

Lemche, N. P. 1975. "The 'Hebrew Slave': Comments on the Slave Law Ex. xxi 2–11." *Vetus Testamentum* 25: 129–144.

Lesky, A. 1961. *A History of Greek Literature.* London: London University Press.

Lorton, D. 1977. "The Treatment of Criminals in Ancient Egypt through the New Kingdom." *Journal of the Economic and Social History of the Orient* 20: 2–64.

MacCormack, G. 1973. "The lex Poetelia." *Labeo* 19: 306–317.

MacMullen, R. 1974. *Roman Social Relations.* New Haven, CT: Yale University Press.

Manning, C. E. 1989. "Stoicism and Slavery in the Roman Empire." In *Aufstieg und Niedergang der römischen Welt.* Edited by Wolfgang Haase. Berlin and New York: De Gruyter.

Marshall, B. A. 1976. *Crassus: A Political Biography.* Amsterdam: A. M. Hakkert.

Masson, Olivier. 1973. "Les noms des esclaves dabs la Grece antique." In *Acts du Colloque 1971 sur l'esclavage.* Paris: Belle Lettres.

Meer, Frederick van der. 1961. *Augustine the Bishop.* London: Sheed and Ward.

Mendelsohn, Isaac. 1949. *Slavery in the Ancient Near East.* New York: Oxford University Press.

Micolier, Gabriel. 1932. *Pécule et capacité patrimoniale: Étude sur le pécule, dit profectice, depuis l'édit "de peculio" jusqu' à la fin de l'époque classique.* Lyon: Bosc Frères.

Miller, Fergus. 1984. "Condemnation to Hard Labour in the Roman Empire: From the Julio-Claudians to Constantine." *Papers of the British School at Rome* 39. London: n.p.

Moore, J. M., ed. 1975. *Aristotle and Xenophon on Democracy and Oligarchy.* London: London University Press.

Neeve, Pieter Willem de. 1984. *Colonus: Private Farm-Tenancy in Roman Italy during the Republic and the Early Principate.* Amsterdam: J. C. Gieben.

Neufeld, E. 1951. *The Hittite Laws.* London: Luzac and Company.

Newman, W. L. 1887–1902. *The Politics of Aristotle.* 4 vols. Oxford: Clarendon Press.

Oates, Whitney J., ed. c. 1948. *Basic Writings of St. Augustine.* 2 vols. New York: Random House.

Peet, Thomas E. 1930. *The Great Tomb Robberies of the Twentieth Egyptian Dynasty.* Oxford: n.p.

Perl, Gerhard. 1977. "Zu Varros instrumentum vocale." *Klio* 59: 423–429.

Pharr, Clyde. 1952. *The Theodosian Code and Novels.* Princeton, NJ: Princeton University Press.

Phillips, William D., Jr. 1985. *Slavery from Roman Times to the Early Transatlantic Trade.* Minneapolis: University of Minnesota Press.

Polybius. 1969. *Polybius: The Histories.* Translated by William R. Paton. London: Heinemann.

Powell, M., ed. 1987. *Labor in the Ancient Near East.* New Haven, CT: American Oriental Society.

Reduzzi Merola, Francesca. 1990. *"Servo parere": Studi sulla condizione giuridica degli schiavi vicari e di sottoposti a schiavi nelle esperienze greca e romana.* Camerino, Italy: Jovene.

Reilly, Linda Collins. 1978. "The Naming of Slaves in Greece." *Ancient World* 1 (3): 111–113.

Rose, H. J. 1934. *A Handbook of Greek Literature.* London: London University Press.

Rostovteff, M. 1957. *Social and Economic History of the Roman Empire*. Oxford: Oxford University Press.

Roth, Martha. 1995. *Law Collections from Mesopotamia and Asia Minor*. Atlanta, GA: Scholars Press.

Sasson, J. M., ed. 1995. *Civilizations of the Ancient Near East. Vol. 1*. New York: Simon and Schuster.

Scarborough, John. 1978. "Reflections on Spartacus." *Ancient World* 1 (2): 75–81.

Scheidel, Walter. 1994. *Grundpacht und Lohnarbeit in der Landwirtschaft des römischen Italien*. Frankfurt am Main: Peter Lang.

Scullard, Howard H. 1963. *From the Gracchi to Nero*. London: Methuen.

Sealey, Raphael. 1976. *A History of the Greek City States, ca. 700–338 B.C.* Berkeley: University of California Press.

Sethe, Kurt. 1906. *Urkunden der 18. Dynastie*. Leipzig: Hinrichs.

Skydsgaard, Jens Erik. 1968. *Varro the Scholar*. Copenhagen: Munksgaard.

Speiser, E. A., ed. 1964. *The Anchor Bible*. Garden City, NY: Doubleday.

Stevens, C. E. 1933. *Sidonius Apollinaris and His Age*. Oxford: Clarendon.

Stockton, David. 1979. *The Gracchi*. Oxford: Oxford University Press.

Swartley, Willard M. 1983. *Slavery, Sabbath, War, and Women: Case Issues in Biblical Interpretation*. Scottdale, PA: Herald Press.

Thompson, E. P. 1952. "Peasant Revolts in Late-Roman Gaul and Spain." *Past and Present* 2: 11–23.

Toynbee, Arnold. 1965. *Hannibal's Legacy*. London: Oxford University Press.

Van Dam, Raymond. 1985. *Leadership and Community in Late Antique Gaul*. Berkeley: University of California Press.

Van den Ploeg, J., 1972. "Slavery in the Old Testament." *Vetus Testamentum Supplement* 22: 72–87.

Van Hook, Larue, trans. 1945. *Isocrates*. Cambridge, MA: Harvard University Press.

Varro. *Agriculture*. 1981. Included in Thomas Wiedemann. *Greek and Roman Slavery*. Baltimore: Johns Hopkins University Press.

Vlastos, Gregory, ed. 1971. *Plato: A Collection of Critical Essays*. Garden City, NY: Doubleday.

Vogt, Joseph, and Norbert Brockmeyer. 1983. *Bibliographie zur Antiken Sklaverei*. Bochum, Germany: Studienverlag Dr. N. Brockmeyer.

von Hagen, Victor W. 1967. *The Roads that Led to Rome*. London: Weidenfeld and Nicolson.

Walbank, Frank William. 1972. *Polybius*. Berkeley: University of California Press.

Ward, Allen Mason. 1977. *Marcus Crassus and the Late Roman Republic*. Columbia: University of Missouri Press.

Watson, Alan. 1987. *Roman Slave Law*. Baltimore: Johns Hopkins University Press.

———. 1975. *Rome of the XII Tables: Persons and Property*. Princeton, NJ: Princeton University Press.

Weaver, P. 1972. *Familia Caesaris*. Cambridge: Cambridge University Press.

Weaver, P. R. C. 1964. "Vicarius and Vicarianus in the Familia Caesaris." *Journal of Roman Studies* 54: 117–128.

Westbrook, R. 1988. *Studies in Biblical and Cuneiform Law*. Paris: J. Gabalda.

White, Kenneth Douglas. 1967. "Latifundia." *Bulletin of Institute of Classical Studies* 14: 62–79.

———. 1970. *Roman Farming*. Ithaca, NY: Cornell University Press.

Wiedemann, Thomas, ed. 1981. *Greek and Roman Slavery*. Baltimore: Johns Hopkins Press.

Willetts, Ronald. 1967. *The Law Code of Gortyn*. Berlin: De Gruyter.

Wiseman, D. 1962. "The Laws of Hammurabi Again." *Journal of Semitic Studies* 7: 161–172.

Wolfram, H. 1988. *The History of the Goths*. Berkeley: University of California Press.

Wood, N. 1988. *Cicero's Social and Political Thought*. Berkeley: University of California Press.

Woolley, C. Leonard. 1965. *The Sumerians*. New York: Norton.

Yavetz, Zvi. 1988. *Slaves and Slavery in Ancient Rome*. Oxford: Transaction Books.

Zeber, Ireneusz. 1981. *A Study of the Peculium of a Slave in Pre-Classical and Classical Roman Law*. Wroclaw, Poland: Uniwersytetu Wroclawskiego.

Zilletti, Udo. 1968. "In Tema di *Servitus Poenae*: Note di Diritto Penal Tardoclassico." *Studia et Documenta Historiae et Juris* 34.

Asia

Anderson, Mary M. 1990. *Hidden Power: The Palace Eunuchs of Imperial China*. Buffalo, NY: Prometheus Books.

Biot, M. Edward. 1849. "Memoir on the Condition of Slaves and Hired Servants in China." *Chinese Repository* 18 (7): 347–363.

Ch'u, T'ung-tsu. 1961. *Law and Society in Traditional China*. Paris: Mouton.

Dolgopol, Ustinia, and Snehal Paranjape. N.d. *Comfort Women, an Unfinished Ordeal: Report of a Mission*. Geneva: International Commission of Jurists.

Doolittle, Justus. 1867. *Social Life of the Chinese*. New York: Harper's.

Feeny, David. 1993. "The Demise of Corvee and

Slavery in Thailand." In *Breaking the Chains: Slavery, Bondage, and Emancipation in Modern Africa and Asia.* Edited by Martin A. Klein. Madison: University of Wisconsin Press.

Garon, Sheldon. 1993. "The World's Oldest Debate? Prostitution and the State in Imperial Japan, 1900–1945." *American Historical Review* 98 (3): 710–732.

Gernet, Jacques. 1995. *Buddhism in Chinese Society: An Economic History from the Fifth to the Tenth Centuries.* New York: Columbia University Press.

Grey, John Henry. 1878. *China: A History of Laws, Manners, and Customs of the People.* London: Macmillan.

Hicks, George. 1995. *The Comfort Women: Japan's Brutal Regime of Enforced Prostitution in the Second World War.* New York: Norton.

Hiraki, Minoru. 1982. *Choson huki nobiche yonku* (A study of slavery in the Later Choson). Seoul: Chisik Sanopsa.

Hong, Seung-ki. 1983. *Koryoeui kuijoksahoewa nobi* (Aristocratic society of koyro and slaves). Seoul: Iljokak.

Howard, Keith, ed. 1995. *True Stories of the Korean Comfort Women.* London: Cassell.

Kim, Hak-sun. 1995. "Bitter Memories I Am Loath to Recall." In *True Stories of the Korean Comfort Women.* Edited by Keith Howard. London: Cassell.

Klass, Morton. 1988. *Caste: The Emergence of the South Asian Social System.* Philadelphia: Institute for the Study of Human Issues.

Knaap, Gerrit J. 1996. "Slavery and the Dutch in Southeast Asia." In *Fifty Years Later: Antislavery, Capitalism, and Modernity in the Dutch Orbit.* Edited by Gert Oostindie. Pittsburgh: University of Pittsburgh Press.

Louie, Kam. 1980. *Critiques of Confucius in Contemporary China.* New York: St. Martin's.

Meijer, Marinus J. 1980. "Slavery at the End of the Ch'ing Dynasty." In *Essays on China's Legal Tradition.* Edited by Jerome Alan Cohen, R. Randle Edwards, and Fu-mei Chang Chen. Princeton, NJ: Princeton University Press.

Mitamura, Taisuke. 1970. *Chinese Eunuchs: The Structure of Intimate Politics.* Rutland, VT: C. E. Tuttle Company.

Panananon, Chatchai. 1982. "Siamese 'Slavery': Institution and Its Abolition." Ph.D. dissertation, Department of History, University of Michigan, Ann Arbor, Michigan.

Patnaik, Utsa, and Manjari Dingwaney. 1985. *Chains of Servitude: Bondage and Slavery in India.* Madras, India: Sangam Books.

Reid, Anthony, ed. 1983. *Slavery, Bondage, and Dependency in Southeast Asia.* St. Lucia, Australia: University of Queensland Press.

Salem, Ellen. 1978. "Slavery in Medieval Korea." Ph.D. dissertation, Department of History, Columbia University, New York.

Schopen, Gregory. 1994. "The Monastic Ownership of Servants or Slaves: Local and Legal Factors in the Redactional History of Two Vinayas." *Journal of the International Association of Buddhist Studies* 17: 145–173.

Sharma, Ram Sharan. 1980. *Sudras in Ancient India: A Social History of the Lower Order down to circa A.D. 600.* Delhi, India: Montilal Banarsidass.

Soh, Chunghee Sarah. 1996. "The Korean 'Comfort Women' Movement for Redress: From a Bilateral Compensation to a Human Rights Issue." *Asian Survey* 36 (12): 1226–1240.

Talib, Y., and F. Samir. 1988. "The African Diaspora in Asia." In *UNESCO General History of Africa.* Vol. 3, *Africa from the Seventh to the Eleventh Century.* Edited by M. El Fasi. London: Heinemann.

Terwiel, B. 1983. "Bondage and Slavery in Early Nineteenth-Century Siam." In *Slavery, Bondage, and Dependency in Southeast Asia.* Edited by Anthony Reid. St. Lucia, Australia: University of Queensland Press.

Totsuka, Etsuro. 1995. "Military Sexual Slavery by Japan and Issues in Law." In *True Stories of the Korean Comfort Women.* Edited by Keith Howard. London: Cassell.

Tsai, Shih-shan Henry. 1996. *The Eunuchs in the Ming Dynasty.* New York: State University of New York Press.

Turton, Andrew. 1980. "Thai Institution of Slavery." In *Asian and African Systems of Slavery,* edited by James L. Watson. Berkeley: University of California Press.

Twitchett, Denis C. 1956. "Monastic Estates in T'ang China." *Asia Major* 5 (1): 123–146.

van Sertima, I., ed. 1985. *African Presence in Early Asia.* New Brunswick, NJ: Transaction Books.

Watanabe, Kazuko. 1994. "Militarism, Colonialism, and the Trafficking of Women: 'Comfort Women' Forced into Sexual Labor." *Bulletin of Concerned Asian Scholars* 26 (4): 3–15.

Wilbur, C. Martin. 1943. *Slavery in China during the Former Han Dynasty, 206 B.C.–A.D. 25.* New York: Russell and Russell.

Williams, E. T. 1910. "The Abolition of Slavery in the Chinese Empire." *American Journal of International Law* 4 (4): 794–805.

Yon'guhoe, Chôngdaehyôp, and Chôngsindae Yon'guhoe, eds. 1993. *Kangje-ro kkûllyogan chosônin kunwianpudûl* ([Forcibly drafted Korean military comfort women). Seoul: Hanul.

Australia and the Pacific Islands

Beechert, Edward. 1985. *Working in Hawaii: A Labor History.* Honolulu: University of Hawaii Press.

Journal of Pacific Studies. 1994–1995. Special Issue, *Migration and Labour.* Vol. 20.

McCall, Grant. 1976. "European Impact on Easter Island: Response, Recruitment, and the Polynesian Experience in Peru." *Journal of Pacific History* 11 (2): 90–105.

McCall, Grant; Brij V. Lal; Harold E. Davis; and H. E. Maude. 1983. "Book Review Forum: Slavers in Paradise." *Pacific Studies* 6 (2): 60–71.

Malo, David, and Nathaniel Emerson, trans. 1951. *Hawaiian Antiquities (Moolelo Hawaii).* Honolulu: Bernice Pauahi Bishop Museum.

Maude, H. E. 1981. *Slavers in Paradise: The Peruvian Labour Trade to Polynesia, 1862–1864.* Canberra: Australian National University Press.

Moore, Clive. 1992. "Labour, Indenture, and Historiography in the Pacific." In *Pacific Islands History: Journeys and Transformations.* Edited by Brij V. Lal. Canberra, Australia: Journal of Pacific History.

Moore, Clive; Jacqueline Leckie; and Doug Munro, eds. 1990. *Labour in the South Pacific.* Townsville, Australia: James Cook University.

Munro, Doug. 1993. "The Pacific Islands Labour Trade: Approaches, Methodologies, Debates." *Slavery and Abolition* 14 (2): 87–108.

———. 1990. "The Peruvian Slavers in Tuvalu: How Many Did They Kidnap?" *Journal de la Société des Océanistes* 90: 43–46.

Newbury, Colin. 1980. "The Melanesian Labor Reserve: Some Reflections on Pacific Labor Markets in the Nineteenth Century." *Pacific Studies* 4 (1): 1–25.

Richardson, J. B. 1977. "The Peruvian Barque *Adelante* and the Kanaka Labour Recruitment." *Journal of Pacific History* 12 (4): 212–214.

Scarr, Deryck. 1968. A *Cruize in a Queensland Labour Vessel to the South Seas.* Honolulu: University of Hawaii Press.

Shlomowitz, Ralph. 1996. *Mortality and Migration in the Modern World.* Aldershot, Eng.: Variorum.

Takaki, Roland. 1983. *Pau Hana: Plantation Life and Labor in Hawaii.* Honolulu: University of Hawaii Press.

Europe

Abu-Lughod, Ibrahim. 1963. *Arab Rediscovery of Europe.* Princeton, NJ: Princeton University Press.

Actes du Congrès de Vienne. 1819. Brussels: Chez Weissenbruch.

Albuquerque, Luís de. 1987. *Navegadores, viajantes, e aventureiros Portugueses: Séculos XV e XVI.* Lisbon: Caminho.

———. 1983. *Os descobrimentos Portugueses.* Lisbon: Publicações Alfa.

Albuquerque, Luís de, ed. 1989. *Tratado de Tordesilhas e outros documentos.* Lisbon: Publicações Alfa.

Andrews, Kenneth. 1984. *Trade, Plunder, and Settlement: Maritime Enterprise and the Foundation of the British Empire.* Cambridge: Cambridge University Press.

Anstey, Roger. 1975. *The Atlantic Slave Trade and British Abolition, 1760–1810.* Cambridge: Cambridge University Press.

Anstey, Roger, and P. E. Hair. 1976. *Liverpool, the African Slave Trade, and Abolition.* Liverpool: Historic Society of Lancashire and Cheshire.

Aragão, Augusto C. Teixeira de. 1898. *Vasco da Gama e a vidigueira: Estudo historico.* Lisbon: Imprensa Nacional.

Atchebro, Dogbo Daniel. 1990. *La société des nations et la lutte contre l'esclavage 1922–1938.* Geneva: Memoire of the Institut Universitaire des Hautes Etudes Internationales.

Azevedo, João Lúcio de. 1909. *O Marquez de Pombal e a sua epoca.* Lisbon: Livraria Classica Editora.

Badinter, Elisabeth, and Robert Badinter. 1990. *Condorcet (1743–1794): Un intellectuel en politique.* Paris: Librairie Fayard.

Baker, Keith Michael. 1975. *Condorcet: From Natural Philosophy to Social Mathematics.* Chicago: University of Chicago Press.

Bamford, Paul. 1973. *Fighting Ships and Prisons: The Mediterranean Galleys of France in the Age of King Louis XIV.* St. Paul: University of Minnesota Press.

Barker, A. 1978. *The African Link: British Attitudes to the Negro in the Era of the Atlantic Slave Trade, 1550–1807.* London: Frank Cass.

Behrendt, Stephen D. 1991. "The Captains in the British Slave Trade from 1785 to 1809." *Transactions of the Historic Society for Lancashire and Cheshire* 140: 79–140.

Benot, Yves. 1988. *La Révolution française et la fin des colonies (1789–1794).* Paris: Editions La Découverte.

Berding, Helmut. 1974. "Die Ächtung des Sklavenhandels auf dem Wiener Kongress 1814/15." *Historische Zeitschrift* 219 (2): 265–289.

Blackburn, Robin. 1991. "Anti-Slavery and the French Revolution." *History Today* 41: 19–25.

Blackett, R. J. M. 1978. "Fugitive Slaves in Britain: The Odyssey of William and Ellen Craft." *Journal of American Studies* 12 (1): 41–62.

Blake, J. W. 1949. "The Farm of the Guinea Trade." In *Essays in British and Irish History.* Edited by H. A. Cronne, T. W. Moody, and D. B. Quinn. London: Frederick Muller.

Bloch, Marc. 1975. *Slavery and Serfdom in the Middle Ages.* Berkeley: University of California Press.

Blum, Jerome. 1966. *Lord and Peasant in Russia from the Ninth to the Nineteenth Century.* New York: Atheneum.

Bodin, Jean. 1962. *The Six Bookes of the Commonweale.* Edited by K. D. McRae. Cambridge, MA: Harvard University Press.

Bonnassie, Pierre. 1991. *From Slavery to Feudalism in South-Western Europe.* Cambridge: Cambridge University Press.

Boogaart, Ernst van den, and Pieter C. Emmer. 1979. "The Dutch Participation in the Atlantic Slave Trade, 1596–1650." In *The Uncommon Market: Essays in the Economic History of the Atlantic Slave Trade.* Edited by Henry A. Gemery and Jan S. Hogendorn. New York: Academic Press.

Boswell, John. 1977. *The Royal Treasure.* New Haven, CT: Yale University Press.

Boxer, Charles R. 1969. *The Portuguese Seaborne Empire: 1415–1825.* London: Hutchinson.

———. 1963. *Race Relations in the Portuguese Colonial Empire, 1415–1825.* Oxford: Clarendon Press.

British Parliamentary Papers: Slave Trade. 1969. 95 vols. Shannon, Ire.: Irish University Press.

Bro Jørgensen, and A. A. Rasch. 1969. *Asiatiske, vestindiske, og guinesiske handelskompagnier.* Copenhagen: Rigsarkivet.

Bromberg, E. I. 1942. "Wales and the Medieval Slave Trade." *Speculum* 17: 263–269.

Brooks, George E. 1993. *Landlords and Strangers.* Boulder, CO: Westview Press.

Brown, Laura. 1993. *Ends of Empire: Women and Ideology in Early Eighteenth-Century English Literature.* Ithaca, NY: Cornell University Press.

Brundage, James R. 1987. *Law, Sex, and Christian Society in Medieval Europe.* Chicago: University of Chicago Press.

Bull, Hedley; Benedict Kingsbury; and Adam Roberts, eds. 1992. *Hugo Grotius and International Relations.* Oxford: Clarendon Press.

Canavaggio, J. F. 1990. *Cervantes.* New York: Norton.

Cardellini, I. 1981. *Die biblischen "Sklaven"-Gesetze im Lichte des keilschriften Klavenrechts.* Bonn: P. Hanstein.

Catholic Church (Pope Alexander VI). 1927. *The Earliest Diplomatic Documents on America: The Papal Bulls of 1493 and the Treaty of Tordesillas.* Berlin: P. Gottschalk.

Certeau, Michel de. 1975. *Un politique de la langue: La Révolution française et les patois—L'enquete de Grégoire.* Paris: Gallimard.

Charles, B. G. 1934. *Old Norse Relations with Wales.* Cardiff: University of Wales Press.

Chejne, Anwar. 1974. *Muslim Spain: Its History and Culture.* Minneapolis: University of Minnesota Press.

Clarkson, Thomas. 1808. *The History of the Rise, Progress, and Accomplishment of the Abolition of the African Slave Trade by the British Parliament. Vol.1.* London: Longman, Hurst, Rees, and Orme.

Code Napoléon. 1810. Paris: Firmin Didot.

Colgrave, Bertram. 1968. *The Earliest Life of Gregory the Great by an Anonymous Monk of Whitby.* Lawrence: University of Kansas Press.

Condorcet. 1996. *Politique de Condorcet: Textes choisies et présentés par Charles Coutel.* Paris: Editions Payot et Rivages.

Cone, Carl B. 1964. *Burke and the Nature of Politics: The Age of the French Revolution.* Lexington: University of Kentucky Press.

Cortés López, José Luis. 1989. *Lass esclavitud negra en la España peninsular del siglo XVI.* Salamanca, Spain: Ediciones Universidad de Salamanca.

Coupland, Reginald. 1964. *The British Anti-Slavery Movement.* New York: Barnes and Noble.

Crow, Hugh. 1970. *Memoirs of the Late Captain Hugh Crow of Liverpool.* London: F. Cass.

Crowe, S. E. 1942. *The Berlin West Africa Conference, 1884–1885.* Westport, CT: Negro Universities Press.

Daget, Serge. 1971. "L'Abolition de la traite des Noirs en France de 1814–1831." *Cahiers d'Etudes Africaines* 11 (1): 14–58.

———. 1979. "British Repression of the Illegal French Slave Trade: Some Considerations." In *The Uncommon Market: Essays in the Economic History of the Atlantic Slave Trade.* Edited by Henry A. Gemery and Jan S. Hogendorn. New York: Academic Press.

———. 1980. "A Model of the French Abolitionist Movement and Its Variations." In *Anti-Slavery, Religion, and Reform: Essays in Memory of Roger Anstey.* Edited by Christine Bolt and Seymour Drescher. Folkestone, Eng.: Dawson.

———. 1990. *La traite des noirs: Bastilles négrières et velléités abolitionnistes.* Nantes: Ouest France Université.

———. 1989. "Traites des noirs, relations internationales, et humanitarisme, 1815–1850." *Relations internationales* 60 (Winter): 413–427.

Davis, David Brion. 1966. *The Problem of Slavery in Western Culture.* New York: Oxford University Press.

de la Torre y del Cerro, Antonio, and Luis Suarez Fernandez, eds. 1952. *Documentos referentes a las relaciones con Portugal durante el reinado de los reyes católicos.* Valladolid, Spain: Consejo Superior de Investigaciones Cientificas.

De Witte, C. M. 1953–1954. "Les Bulles Pontificales et l'expansion Portuguese au XVe Siecle." *Revue d'Histoire Ecclesiastique* 48: 683–718 and 49: 438–461.

Defarri, Roy Joseph, et al., eds. 1951–1987. *The Fathers of the Church.* 70 vols. Washington, DC: Catholic University of America Press.

Dickinson, John, ed. and trans. 1927. *The Statesman's Book of John of Salisbury.* New York: Knopf.

Dickinson, W. Calvin, and Eloise R. Hitchcock, eds. 1996. *The War of the Spanish Succession, 1702–1713: A Selected Bibliography.* Westport, CT: Greenwood Press.

Diffie, Bailey W., and George D. Winius. 1977. *Foundations of the Portuguese Empire, 1415–1580.* Minneapolis: University of Minnesota Press.

Dmytryshyn, Basil. 1973. *Medieval Russia: A Sourcebook.* Hinsdale, IL: Dryden.

Dockes, Pierre. 1982. *Medieval Slavery and Liberation.* Chicago: University of Chicago Press.

Domínguez Ortiz, Antonio. 1952. "La esclavitud en Castilla durante la Edad Moderna." In *Estudios de historia social de España.* Edited by Carmelo Viñas y Mey. Madrid: CSIC.

———. 1971. *The Golden Age of Spain: 1516–1659.* New York: Basic Books.

Drescher, Seymour. 1987. *Capitalism and Antislavery: British Mobilization in Comparative Perspective.* New York: Oxford University Press.

———. 1977. *Econocide: British Slavery in the Era of Abolition.* Pittsburgh: University of Pittsburgh Press.

Duby, Georges. 1974. *The Early Growth of the European Economy: Warriors and Peasants from the Seventh to the Twelfth Centuries.* Ithaca, NY: Cornell University Press.

———. 1980. *The Three Orders: Feudal Society Imagined.* Chicago: University of Chicago Press.

Dunlop, O., and R. C. Denman. 1912. *English Apprenticeship and Child Labor.* New York: Macmillan.

Durkheim, Emile. 1970. *Montesquieu and Rousseau: Forerunners of Sociology.* Ann Arbor: University of Michigan Press.

Egilsson, Ólafur. 1969. *Reisubon.* Reykjavík, Iceland: Almenna Ban Press.

Eichler, Eckhard. 1991. "Untersuchungen zu den Königsbriefen des Alten Reiches." *Studien zur Altägyptischen Kultur* 18: 141–171.

———. 1993. "Untersuchungen zum Expeditionswesen des ägyptischen Alten Reiches." Wiesbaden, Germany: Otto Harrassowitz.

Eisenbichler, Konrad, ed. 1991. *Crossing the Boundaries: Christian Piety and the Arts in Italian Medieval and Renaissance Confraternities.* Kalamazoo, MI: Medieval Institute Publications.

Emmer, Pieter. 1981. "Abolition of the Abolished: The Illegal Dutch Slave Trade and the Mixed Courts." In *Abolition of the Atlantic Slave Trade.* Edited by James Walvin and David Eltis. Madison: University of Wisconsin Press.

Ezran, Maurice. 1992. *L'Abbé Grégoire, defenseur des juifs et des noirs: Révolution et tolerance.* Paris: Editions L'Harmittan.

Farrar, F. W. 1907. *Lives of the Fathers: Sketches of Church History in Biography.* London: Adam and Charles Black.

Feldbaek, O. 1981. "The Organisation and Structure of the Danish East India, West India, and Guinea Companies in the 17th and 18th Centuries." In *Companies and Trade: Essays on Overseas Trading Companies during the Ancien Regime.* Edited by Leonard Blussé et al. Leiden: Leiden University Press.

Feldbaek, O., and O. Justesen. 1980. "Kolonierna i Asien og Afrika." In *Politikens Danmarks Historie.* Edited by S. Ellehfj and Kristof Glamann. Copenhagen: Politikens Forlag.

Fellows, Otis E., and Norman L. Torrey, eds. 1942. *The Age of Enlightenment: An Anthology of Eighteenth-Century French Literature.* New York: Appleton-Century-Crofts.

Ferguson, Moira. 1992. *Subject to Others: British Women Writers and Colonial Slavery, 1670–1834.* New York: Routledge.

Fernández-Pérez, Paloma. 1997. *El nuestro familiar de la metrópoli: Redes de parentesco y consolidación de lazos mercantiles en Cádiz, 1700–1812.* Madrid: Siglo XXI de España.

Field, Daniel. 1976. *The End of Serfdom.* Cambridge, MA: Harvard University Press.

Fikes, Robert. 1980. "Black Scholars in Europe during the Renaissance and the Enlightenment." *Negro History Bulletin* 43 (July–September): 58–60.

Filliot, J. M. 1974. *La traite des esclaves vers les Mascareignes aux XVIIIe siecle.* Paris: Office de la Recherche Scientifique et Technique Outre-mer.

Fonseca, Luís Adão da. 1987. *O essencial sôbre Bartolomeu Dias.* Lisbon: Imprensa Nacional-Casa da Moeda.

Franco Silva, A. 1992. *Esclavitud en Andulaucia 1450–1550.* Granada, Spain: Servicio de Publicaciones de la Universidad de Granada.

Freedman, Paul. 1991. *The Origins of Peasant Servitude in Medieval Catalonia.* Cambridge: Cambridge University Press.

Freeman, Michael. 1980. *Edmund Burke and the Critique of Political Radicalism.* Oxford: Basil Blackwell.

Furneaux, Robin. 1974. *William Wilberforce.* London: Hamish Hamilton.

Gaull, Marilyn. 1988. *English Romanticism: The Human Context*. New York: Norton.

Gerzina, Gretchen. 1995. *Black London: Life before Emancipation*. New Brunswick, NJ: Rutgers University Press.

Gibson, Charles. 1971. *The Black Legend: Anti-Spanish Attitudes in the Old World and the New*. New York: Knopf.

Ginnell, Laurence. 1917. *The Brehon Laws*. Dublin: West.

Gregory, Saint. 1916. *History of the Franks*. Translated, with notes, by Ernest Brehaut. New York: Columbia University Press.

Gregory I. 1950. *Pastoral Care*. Translated by Henry Davis. Baltimore: Newman Press.

Grotius, Hugo. 1925. *The Law of War and Peace: De jure belli ac pacis, libri tres*. Indianapolis, IN: Bobbs-Merrill.

Hald, Kristian. 1975. "Traellenavne." In *Kulturhistoriskt lexikon for nordisk medeltid, Vol. 19*. Malmo, Sweden: Allhems.

Hanke, Lewis. 1949. *The Spanish Struggle for Justice in the Conquest of America*. Philadelphia: University of Pennsylvania Press.

Hellie, Richard. 1971. *Enserfment and Military Change in Muscovy*. Chicago: University of Chicago Press.

Hernaes, Per O. 1992. *The Danish Slave Trade from West Africa and Afro-Danish Relations on the 18th-Century Gold Coast*. Trondheim, Norway: Trondheim University.

Herrmann-Otto, Elisabeth. 1994. *Ex ancilla natus: Untersuchungen zu den "hausgeborenen" Sklaven und Sklavinnen im Westen des römischen Kaiserreiches*. Stuttgart: Franz Steiner Verlag.

Hilgarth, J. 1978. *The Spanish Kingdoms, 1250–1516*. Oxford: Clarendon Press.

Hinton, Richard J., ed. 1898. *Poems by Richard Realf: Poet, Soldier, Workman*. New York: Funk and Wagnalls.

Hoare, Prince. 1820. *Memoirs of Granville Sharp, Esq*. London: Henry Colburn.

Hobbes, Thomas. 1985. *Leviathan*. New York: Penguin Classics.

Højlund Knap, Henning. 1983. "Danskerne og slaveriet—negerslavedebatten i Danmark indtil 1792." In *Dansk kolonihistorie—indffring og studier*. Edited by Peter Hoxcer Jensen. Århus, Denmark: Forlaget Historia.

Hollander, Lee M., tr. 1928. *The Poetic Edda*. Austin: University of Texas.

Holm, P. 1986. "The Slave Trade of Dublin: 9th to 12th Centuries." *Peritia* 5: 317–345.

Howell, Raymond C. 1987. *The Royal Navy and the Slave Trade*. New York: St. Martin's.

Hume, David. 1987. "Of National Characters." In *Essays: Moral, Political, and Literary*. Edited by T. H. Green and T. H. Grose. Indianapolis, IN: Liberty Classics.

Hunt, Lynn. 1996. *The French Revolution and Human Rights: A Brief Documentary History*. New York: St. Martin's.

Hurwitz, Edith. 1973. *Politics and the Public Conscience: Slave Emancipation and the Abolitionist Movement in Britain*. London: Allen and Unwin.

Iverson, Tore. 1994. *Trelldommen: Norsk slaveri i middelalderen*. Bergen, Norway: Bergen University.

James, E., ed. 1980. *Visigothic Spain*. Oxford: Oxford University Press.

James, Francis G. 1985. "Irish Colonial Trade in the Eighteenth Century." *William and Mary Quarterly* 19 (3): 329–356.

Jenkins, Dafydd. 1986. *The Law of Hywel Dda*. Llandysul, Wales: Gomer.

Johnson, Merwyn S. 1978. *Locke on Freedom: An Incisive Study of the Thought of John Locke*. Austin, TX: Best Print.

Johnson, Rossiter. 1879. "Richard Realf." *Lippincott's Magazine* 3: 293–300.

Jones, Gwyn. 1984. *A History of the Vikings*. New York: Oxford University Press.

Jornadas, Americanistas. 1973. *El tratado de Tordesillas y su proyeccion*. Valladolid, Spain: Universidad, Seminario de Historia de América.

Kamen, Henry Arthur Francis. 1991. *Spain, 1469–1714: A Society of Conflict*. London: Longman Press.

———. 1969. *The War of Succession in Spain, 1700–15*. London: Weidenfeld and Nicolson.

Karras, Ruth Mazo. 1988. *Slavery and Society in Medieval Scandinavia*. New Haven, CT: Yale University Press.

Kelly, Christopher. 1987. *Rousseau's Exemplary Life: The "Confessions" as Political Philosophy*. Ithaca, NY: Cornell University Press.

Klein, Herbert S. 1978. *The Middle Passage: Comparative Studies in the Atlantic Slave Trade*. Princeton, NJ: Princeton University Press.

Kolchin, Peter. 1987. *Unfree Labor: American Slavery and Russian Serfdom*. Cambridge, MA: Harvard University Press.

Laistner, M. 1957. *Thought and Letters in Western Europe A.D. 500–1000*. London: London University Press.

Lang, David M. 1957. *The Last Years of the Georgian Monarchy, 1658–1832*. New York: Columbia University Press.

Levi-Provençal, Évariste. 1950–1953. *Histoire de l'Espagne Musulmane*. 3 vols. Leiden: Brill.

Levi-Strauss, C. 1962. *La pansee sauvage*. Paris: Plon.

Linder, Ammon. 1977. "Knowledge of John of Salisbury in the Late Middle Ages." *Studi Medievali* 18 (2): 315–366.

Lindsay, Arnett. 1920. "Diplomatic Relations between the United States and Great Britain Bearing on the Return of Negro Slaves, 1788–1828." *Journal of Negro History* 5: 261–278.

Livermore, H. V. 1947. *A History of Portugal*. Cambridge: Cambridge University Press.

———. 1971. *The Origins of Spain and Portugal*. London: Allen and Unwin.

Lobo Cabrera, M. 1990. "La esclavitude en la España Moderna: Su investigación en los últimos cincuenta años." *Hispania* 176.

Lourie, Elena. 1990. *Crusade and Colonisation: Muslims, Christians, and Jews in Medieval Aragón*. Brookfield, VT: Variorum.

Lüsebrink, Hans-Jürgen, and Manfred Tietz, eds. 1991. *Lectures de Raynal: L'histoire des deux Indes en Europe et en Amérique au XVIIIe siècle*. Oxford: Voltaire Foundation.

McNeill, John T., and Helena M. Gamer. 1990. *Medieval Handbooks of Penance*. New York: Columbia University Press.

Marshall, P. J., and G. Williams. 1982. *The Great Map of Mankind: British Perceptions of the World in the Age of Enlightenment*. London: J. M. Dent.

Marti, Evelin. 1929. "The English Slave Trade and the African Settlements." In *The Cambridge History of the British Empire*. Edited by J. Holland Rose, A. P. Newton, and E. A. Benians. Cambridge: Cambridge University Press.

Maso Vazquez, Calixto. 1973. *Juan Latino: Gloria de Espana y su raza*. Chicago: Northeastern Illinois University.

Maxwell, Kenneth. 1995. *Pombal: Paradox of the Enlightenment*. Cambridge: Cambridge University Press.

Mesa, Roberto. 1990. *El colonialismo en la crisis del XIX espanól*. Madrid: Ediciones de Cultura Hispánica.

Miers, Suzanne. 1975. *Britain and the Ending of the Slave Trade*. New York: Longman.

Molina Martínez, Miguel. 1991. *La leyenda negra*. Madrid: NEREA.

Montesquieu, Charles de Secondat. 1977. *The Spirit of Laws: A Compendium of the First English Edition*. Edited by David Wallace Carrithers. Berkeley: University of California Press.

Moore, John S. 1988. "Domesday Slave." *Anglo-Norman Studies* 11: 191–220.

Moreau de St. Mery, Louis Médéric. 1783–1790. *Loix et constitutions des colonies Françaises de l'Amerique sous le vent, de 1550 à 1785*. 6 vols. Paris: Privately printed.

Morris, John. 1976. *Domesday Book*. Chichester, Eng.: Phillimore.

Ndamba Kabongo, Albert. 1976. *Les esclaves à Seville au début du XVIIe siècle: Approche de leurs origines et de leur condition*. Memoir of Mâitrisse. Université de Toulouse le Mirail. Microfiche. Paris: Micro Editions Hachette.

Necheles, Ruth. 1971. *The Abbé Grégoire 1787–1831: Odyssey of an Egalitarian*. Westport CT: Greenwood.

Neveus, Clara. 1974. *Tralarna i landskapslagarnas samhalle: Danmark och Sverige*. Uppsala, Sweden: Uppsala University.

Novaky, György. 1990. *Handelskompanier och kompanihandel: Svenska Afrikakompaniet 1649–1663, en studie i feodal handel*. Uppsala, Sweden: Universitetet.

O'Brien, Connor. 1992. *The Great Melody: A Thematic Biography and Commented Anthology of Edmund Burke*. Chicago: University of Chicago Press.

Oostindie, Gert, ed. 1996. *Fifty Years Later: Antislavery, Capitalism, and Modernity in the Dutch Orbit*. Pittsburgh: University of Pittsburgh Press.

Parry, J. H. 1974. *The Spanish Seaborne Empire*. New York: Knopf.

Peabody, Sue. 1996. *"There Are No Slaves in France": The Political Culture of Race and Slavery in the Ancien Régime*. New York: Oxford University Press.

Pelteret, David. 1995. *Slavery in Early Medieval England*. Woodbridge, Eng.: Boydell.

Peres, Damião. 1983. *História dos descobrimentos Portugueses*. Porto, Portugal: Vertente.

Phillips, W. D., Jr. 1990. *Historia de la esclavitude in España*. Madrid: Siglo XXI de España.

Pieterse, Jan Nederveen. 1992. *White on Black: Images of African and Blacks in Western Popular Culture*. New Haven, CT: Yale University Press.

Pike, Joseph B., ed. and trans. 1938. *Frivolities of Courtiers and Footprints of Philosophers*. Minneapolis: University of Minnesota Press.

Pluchon, Pierre. 1991. *Histoire de la colonisation française: Le premier empire colonial, des origines à la Restauration*. Paris: Fayard.

Postma, Johannes Menne. 1990. *The Dutch in the Atlantic Slave Trade, 1660–1815*. Cambridge: Cambridge University Press.

Priester, L. R. 1987. *De Nederlandse houding ten aanzien van de slavenhandel en slavernij 1596–1863*. Middelburg, Netherlands: Commissie Regionale Geschiedbeoefening Zeeland.

Prytz, Kare. 1991. *Westward before Columbus*. Oslo: Norsk Maritimt Forlag.

Putney, Martha. 1975. "The Slave Trade in French Diplomacy from 1814 to 1815." *Journal of Negro History* 60 (3): 411–427.

Quarta, Pietro Luigi. 1993. "Reflexiones acerca de la leyenda negra en la historia de España. *Rivista de Studi Politici Internazionali* 60 (1): 92–100.

Raimond, Jean, and J. R. Watson, eds. 1992. *A Handbook to British Romanticism*. New York: St. Martin's.

Ravenstein, E. G., ed. 1898. *A Journal of the First Voyage of Vasco da Gama, 1497–1499*. London: Hakluyt Society.

Rediker, Marcus. 1987. *Between the Devil and the Deep Blue Sea*. Cambridge: Cambridge University Press.

Reich, Jerome. 1968. "The Slave Trade at the Congress of Vienna: A Study in English Public Opinion." *Journal of Negro History* 53: 129–143.

Resnick, Daniel P. 1972. "The Société des Amis des Noirs and the Abolition of Slavery." *French Historical Studies* 7 (4): 558–569.

La Révolution française et l'abolition de l'esclavage: Textes et documents. 1969. 12 vols. Paris: Editions d'histoire sociale.

Richardson, David. 1994. "Liverpool and the English Slave Trade." In *Transatlantic Slavery: Against Human Dignity*. Edited by Anthony Tibbles. London: HMSO.

Ripley, C. Peter, ed. 1985. *The Black Abolitionist Papers: The British Isles, 1830–1865*. Chapel Hill: University of North Carolina Press.

Rousseau, Jean-Jacques. 1932. *The Social Contract and Discourses*. London: E. P. Dutton.

Sandoval, Alonso de. 1987. *Un tratado sobre la esclavitud (De instauranda aethiopum salute)*. Madrid: Alianza Editorial.

Saunders, A. C. de C. M. 1982. *A Social History of Black Slaves and Freedmen in Portugal, 1441–1555*. Cambridge: Cambridge University Press.

Schouls, Peter A. 1992. *Reasoned Freedom: John Locke and Enlightenment*. Ithaca, NY: Cornell University Press.

Schutz, John A. 1950. "James Ramsay, Essayist: Aggressive Humanitarian." In *British Humanitarianism: Essays Honoring Frank J. Klingberg*. Edited by Samuel Clyde McCulloch. Philadelphia: Church Historical Society.

Schwartz, Joachim [Condorcet]. 1788. *Réflexions sur l'esclavage des nègres, par M. Schwartz, pasteur du Saint Evangile à Bienne, membre de la Société économique de B****. New edition, revised and corrected. Paris: Froullé.

Schwarz, Suzanne. 1995. *Slave Captain: The Career of James Irving in the Liverpool Slave Trade*. Wrexham, Eng.: Bridge Books.

Scobie, Edward. 1972. *Black Britannia: A History of Blacks in Britain*. Chicago: Johnson Publishing.

Serrão, Joaquim Veríssimo. 1982. *O Marquês de Pombal: O homen, o diplomata, e o estadista*. Lisbon: Camaras Municipias.

Shklar, Judith. 1987. *Montesquieu*. Oxford: Oxford University Press.

Shyllon, F. O. 1974. *Black Slaves in Britain*. London: Oxford University Press.

Sigurdsson, Gisli. 1988. *Gaelic Influence in Iceland: Historical and Literary Contacts*. Studia Islandica 46. Reykjavík: Bokutgafa Menningarsjoos.

Solin, Heikki. 1971. *Beitrage zur Kenntnis der griechischen Personennamen in Rom 1*. Commentationes Humanarum Litterarum 48. Helsinki: Societas Scientiarum Fennica.

———. 1990. *Namenpaare: Eine Studie zur romischen Namengebung*. Commentationes Humanarum Litterarum 90. Helsinki: Societas Scientarum Fennica.

Sommerville, Johann. 1992. *Thomas Hobbes: Political Ideas in Historical Context*. London: Macmillan.

Spratlin, Valaurez. 1938. *Juan Latino: Slave and Humanist*. New York: Spinner Press.

Stein, Robert Louis. 1979. *The French Slave Trade in the Eighteenth Century: An Old Regime Business*. Madison: University of Wisconsin Press.

Stephen, George. 1854. *Antislavery Recollections: In a Series of Letters Addressed to Mrs. Beecher Stowe, Written by Sir George Stephen, at Her Request*. London: Thomas Hatchard.

Tacitus, Cornelius. 1970. *The Agricola and the Germania*. New York: Penguin Books.

Temperley, Howard. 1972. *British Antislavery, 1833–1870*. London: Longman.

Thompson, E. A. 1969. *The Goths in Spain*. Oxford: Oxford University Press.

Thompson, E. P. 1968. *The Making of the English Working Class*. London: Pelican.

Tiainen-Anttila, Kaija. 1994. *The Problem of Humanity: Blacks in the European Enlightenment*. Helsinki: Finnish Historical Society.

Tooley, M. J., ed. and trans. 1955. *Six Books of the Commonwealth by Jean Bodin*. Oxford: Basil Blackwell.

Truxes, Thomas M. 1988. *Irish American Trade, 1660–1783*. Cambridge: Cambridge University Press.

Tucker, St. George, ed. 1996. *Blackstone's Commentaries*. 5 vols. Trenton, NJ: Law Book Exchange.

Tulard, Jean, ed., 1987. *Dictionnaire Napoléon*. Paris: Fayard.

Turley, David. 1991. *The Culture of English Antislavery*. London: Routledge.

Unger, W. S. 1958–1960, 1965. "Bijdragen tot de geschiedenis van de Nederlandse slavenhandel." In *Economisch-Historisch Jaarboek*. Vols. 26, 28. The Hague: n.p.

Verlinden, Charles. 1955. *L'esclavage dans l'Europe médiévale*. Bruges, Belgium: De Tempel.

Vernadsky, George. 1965. *Medieval Russian Laws*. New York: Octagon.

Vieira, António. 1951. *Obras escolhidas*. Lisbon: Livraria sá da Costa.

Vogt, Joseph, et al., eds. 1994. *Forschungen zur An-tiken Sklaverei*. Weisbaden and Stuttgart: Steiner.

Wade-Evans, A. W. 1909. *Welsh Medieval Law*. Oxford: Clarendon.

Wallis, H. 1986. "'Things Hidden from Other Men': The Portuguese Voyages of Discovery." *History Today* 36 (June): 27–33.

Walvin, James. 1973. *Black and White: The Negro and English Society, 1555–1945*. London: Oxford University Press.

———. 1992. *Black Ivory: A History of British Slavery*. London: HarperCollins.

———. 1971. *The Black Presence: A Documentary History of the Negro in England, 1555–1860*. London: Orbach and Chambers.

Ward, William. 1969. *The Royal Navy and the Slavers*. New York: Pantheon.

Warner, Oliver. 1962. *William Wilberforce and His Times*. London: B.T. Batsford.

Warrender, Howard. 1957. *The Political Philosophy of Thomas Hobbes*. London: Oxford University Press.

Watt, William Montgomery. 1967. *A History of Islamic Spain*. Edinburgh: Edinburgh University Press.

Weissman, Ronald F. E. 1982. *Ritual Brotherhood in Renaissance Florence*. New York: Academic Press.

Welchman, Jennifer. 1995. "Locke on Slavery and Inalienable Rights." *Canadian Journal of Philosophy* 25 (1): 67–83.

Wieskel, Timothy. 1980. *French Colonial Rule and the Baule Peoples*. New York: Oxford University Press.

Wilberforce, Robert Isaac, and Samuel Wilberforce. 1838. *The Life of William Wilberforce*. London: John Murray.

Wilks, Michael, ed. 1984. *The World of John of Salisbury*. Oxford: Basil Blackwell.

Williams, Carl O. 1937. *Thraldom in Ancient Iceland*. Chicago: University of Chicago Press.

Williams, G. 1897. *History of the Liverpool Privateers and Letters of Marque with an Account of the Liverpool Slave Trade*. London: Heinemann.

Williams, Mary Wilhelmine. 1920. *Social Scandinavia in the Viking Age*. New York: Macmillan.

Williamson, James A. 1927. *Sir John Hawkins*. Oxford: Oxford University Press.

Wilson, Ellen Gibson. 1990. *Thomas Clarkson: A Biography*. New York: St. Martin's.

Wood, Michael. 1986. *Domesday: A Search for the Roots of England*. New York: BBC Books.

Latin America and the Caribbean

Abrahams, Roger D. 1983. *The Man-of-Words in the West Indies: Performance and the Emergence of Creole Culture*. Baltimore: Johns Hopkins University Press.

Agorsah, E. Kofi, ed. 1994. *Maroon Heritage: Archaeological, Ethnographic, and Historical Perspectives*. Bridgetown, Barbados: Canoe Press.

Aguirre, Carlos. 1993. *Agentes de su propia libertad: Los esclavos de Lima y la desintegración de la esclavitud, 1821–1854*. Lima: Universidad Católica del Perú.

Aguirre Beltrán, Gonzalo. 1972. *La población negra en México: Estudio etnohistórico*. Mexico City: Fondo de Cultura Económica.

Alberro, Solange. 1988. *Inquisición sociedad en México, 1571–1700*. Mexico City: Fondo de Cultura Económica.

Alvarez Argel, Luis Raul. 1964. *Don Diego de Almagro y el descubrimiento de Chile*. Santiago, Chile: Editorial Universitaria.

Anderson, Robert Nelson. 1996. "The Quilombo of Palmares: A New Overview of a Maroon State in Seventeenth-Century Brazil." *Journal of Latin American Studies* 28 (3): 545.

Arranz Márquez, Luis. 1991. *Repartimientos y encomiendas en la isla Española (El repartimiento de Albuquerque de 1514)*. Madrid: Fundación Garcia-Arévalo.

Áviles Fábila, René. 1957. *Vicente Guerrero: El insurgente ciudadano*. Mexico City: Sociedad de Amigos del Libro Mexicano.

Axtell, James. 1992. *Beyond 1492*. New York: Oxford University Press.

Azevedo, Celia M. 1995. *Abolitionism in the United States and Brazil: A Comparative Perspective*. New York: Garland.

Azevedo, Fernando de. 1950. *Brazilian Culture: An Introduction to the Study of Culture in Brazil*. New York: Macmillan.

Bakewell, P. J. 1971. *Silver Mining and Society in Colonial Mexico: Zacatecas, 1546–1700*. Cambridge: Cambridge University Press.

Ballesteros Gaibrois, Manuel. 1987. *Diego de Almagro*. Madrid: Sociedad Estatal para la Ejecucion Programas del Quinto Centenario.

Bannon, John F. 1966. *Indian Labor in the Spanish Indies: Was There Another Solution?* Boston: Heath.

Barber, Ruth. 1932. *Indian Labor in the Spanish Colonies*. Albuquerque: University of New Mexico Press.

Bastide, Roger. 1978. *The African Religions of Brazil: Towards a Sociology of the Interpenetration of Civilizations*. Baltimore: Johns Hopkins University Press.

Beckles, Hilary. 1986. "'Black Men in White Skins': The Formation of a White Proletariat in West Indian Society." *Journal of Imperial and Commonwealth History* 15 (October): 5–21.

———. 1990. *A History of Barbados: From Amerindian Settlement to Nation-State*. Cambridge: Cambridge University Press.

Beckles, Hilary, and Verene Shepherd, eds. 1991. *Caribbean Slave Society and Economy*. New York: New Press.

Belaunde, Victor Andrés. 1938. *Bolívar and the Political Thought of the Spanish American Revolution*. Baltimore: Johns Hopkins University Press.

Belgium, Erik, and Don Nardo. 1991. *Great Mysteries, Voodoo: Opposing Viewpoints*. San Diego, CA: Greenhaven Press.

Bento, Antônio, ed. 1887. *A Redempção*. São Paulo, Brazil: n.p.

Berdan, Frances. 1982. *The Aztecs of Central Mexico: An Imperial Society*. New York: Holt, Rinehart and Winston.

Bergad, Laird W.; Fe Iglesias Garcia; and Maria del Carmen Barcia. 1995. *The Cuban Slave Market, 1790–1880*. New York: Cambridge University Press.

Bethell, Leslie. 1970. *The Abolition of the Brazilian Slave Trade. Britain, Brazil, and the Slave Trade Question, 1807–1869*. Cambridge: Cambridge University Press.

Bettelheim, Judith. 1988. "Jonkonnu and Other Christmas Masquerades." In *Caribbean Festival Arts*. Edited by John W. Nunley and Judith Bettelheim. Seattle: University of Washington Press.

Bilby, Kenneth. 1995. "A Separate Identity: The Maroons of Jamaica." *Faces* 11 (8): 29.

Black, Clinton. 1958. *History of Jamaica*. London: Collins Clear-Type Press.

Blackburn, Robin. 1988. *The Overthrow of Colonial Slavery, 1776–1848*. London: Verso.

Blazquez y Delgado-Aguilera, Antonio. 1898. *El adelantado Diego de Almagro*. Ciudad Real, Spain: Establicimiento Topografico Provincial.

Bolland, O. Nigel. 1988. *Colonialism and Resistance in Belize: Essays in Historical Sociology*. Benque Viejo del Carmen, Belize: Cubola Productions.

———. 1977. *The Formation of a Colonial Society: Belize, from Conquest to Crown Colony*. Baltimore: Johns Hopkins University Press.

Bowser, Frederick. 1974. *The African Slave in Colonial Peru, 1524–1650*. Stanford, CA: Stanford University Press.

Boxer, C. R. 1962. *The Golden Age of Brazil, 1695–1750: Growing Pains of a Colonial Society*. Berkeley: University of California Press.

———. 1962. *A Great Luso-Brazilian Figure: Padre Antônio Vieira, S.J., 1608–1697*. Berkeley: University of California Press.

———. 1952. *Salvador de Sá and the Struggle for Brazil and Angola, 1602–1686*. London: Athlone Press.

Brace, Joan. 1983. "From Chattel to Person: Martinique, 1635–1848." *Plantation Society* 2 (1): 63–80.

Brathwaite, Edward Kamau. 1974. "The African Presence in Caribbean Literature." In *Slavery, Colonialism, and Racism*. Edited by Sidney Mintz. New York: W. W. Norton.

———. 1971. *The Development of Creole Society in Jamaica*. Oxford: Oxford University Press.

Breathett, George. 1988. "Catholicism and the Code Noir in Haiti." *Journal of Negro History* 73 (1): 1–11.

Bridenbaugh, Carl, and Roberta Bridenbaugh. 1972. *No Peace beyond the Line: The English in the Caribbean, 1624–1690*. New York: Oxford University Press.

Brutus, Timoleon C. 1946–1947. *L'homme d'Airain: Étude monographique sur Jean-Jacques Dessalines, fondateur de la nation haïtienne*. Port-au-Prince, Haiti: N. A. Theodore.

Buchner, John H. 1854. *The Moravians in Jamaica*. London: Longman and Brown.

Burdon, John, ed. 1931–1935. *Archives of British Honduras*. 3 vols. London: Sifton Praed.

Burkholder, Mark, and Lyman L. Johnson. 1990. *Colonial Latin America*. New York: Oxford University Press.

Burns, E. Bradford. 1966. *A Documentary History of Brazil*. New York: Knopf.

Bush, Barbara. 1989. *Slave Women in Caribbean Society, 1650–1838*. Bloomington: Indiana University Press.

Bushnell, David. 1970. *The Santander Regime in Gran Colombia*. Westport, CT: Greenwood Press.

Camamis, George. 1977. *Estudios sobre el cautiverio en el Siglo de Oro*. Madrid: Gredos.

Campbell, Mavis Christine. 1988. *The Maroons of Jamaica, 1655–1796: A History of Resistance, Collaboration, and Betrayal*. South Hadley, MA: Bergin and Garvey.

Cardoso, Gerald. 1983. *Negro Slavery in the Sugar Plantations of Veracruz and Pernambuco, 1550–1680: A Comparative Study*. Washington, DC: University Press of America.

Carr, Albert Z. 1963. *The World and William Walker*. New York: Harper and Row.

Cassá, Roberto, and Genaro Rodríguez Morel. 1993. "Consideraciones alternativas acerca de las rebeliones de esclavos en Santo Domingo." *Anuario de la Escuela de Estudios Hispanoamericanos* 50 (1): 103–113.

Castro Pozo, Hildebrando. 1947. *El yanaconaje en las haciendas piuranas*. Lima, Peru: Cia. de Impresiones y Publicidad.

Clementi, Hebe. 1974. *La abolición la esclavitud en América Latina*. Buenos Aires: Pleyade.

Cole, Hubert. 1967. *Christophe King of Haiti*. New York: Viking Press.

Columbus, Christopher. 1960. *The Journal of Christopher Columbus*. Edited by L. A. Vigneras. New York: Bramhall House.

Columbus, Ferdinand. 1959. *The Life of the Admiral Christopher Columbus*. Edited by Benjamin Keen. New Brunswick, NJ: Rutgers University Press.

Conniff, Michael L., and Thomas J. Davis. 1994. *Africans in the Americas*. New York: St. Martin's.

Conrad, Robert E. 1972. *The Destruction of Brazilian Slavery, 1850–1888*. Berkeley: University of California Press.

Cooney, Jerry W. 1974. "Abolition in the Republic of Paraguay: 1840–1870." In *Jahrbuch für Geschichte von Staat, Wirtschaft, und Gesellschaft Lateinamerika*. Edited by Richard Konetzke and Hermann Kellenbenz. Cologne and Vienna: Böhlau Verlag.

Corwin, Arthur F. 1967. *Spain and the Abolition of Slavery in Cuba, 1817–1886*. Austin: University of Texas Press.

Costa, Emilia Viotti da. 1985. *The Brazilian Empire: Myths and Histories*. Chicago: University of Chicago Press.

Courlander, Harold. 1985. *The Drum and the Hoe: Life and Lore of the Haitian People*. Berkeley, London, and Los Angeles: University of California Press.

Cox, Edward. 1982. "Fédon's Rebellion, 1795–96: Causes and Consequences." *Journal of Negro History* 67: 7–20.

Craton, Michael. 1978. *Searching for the Invisible Man: Slaves and Plantation Life in Jamaica*. Cambridge, MA: Harvard University Press.

———. 1982. *Testing the Chains: Resistance to Slavery in the British West Indies*. Ithaca, NY: Cornell University Press.

Crawford, W. Rex. 1961. *A Century of Latin American Thought*. Cambridge, MA: Harvard University Press.

Crosby, Alfred W., Jr. 1972. *The Columbian Exchange: Biological and Cultural Consequences of 1492*. Westport, CT: Greenwood.

Dance, Daryl C. 1985. *Folklore from Contemporary Jamaicans*. Knoxville: University of Tennessee Press.

Davis, Wade. 1986. *The Serpent and the Rainbow*. New York: Warner Books.

Dayan, Joan. 1995. *Haiti, History, and the Gods*. Berkeley: University of California Press.

De Camp, David. 1967. "African Day-Names in Jamaica." *Language* 43: 139–147.

Degler, Carl N. 1971. *Neither Black nor White: Slavery and Race Relations in Brazil and the United States*. New York: Macmillan.

Deive, Carlos Esteban. 1989. *Los guerrilleros negros: Esclavos fugitivos y cimarrones en Santo Domingo*. Santo Domingo, Dominican Republic: Fundación Cultural Dominicana.

Devas, Raymond P. 1974. *A History of the Island of Grenada, 1498–1796*. St. George's, Grenada: Carenage Press.

Dirks, Robert. 1987. *The Black Saturnalia: Conflict and Its Ritual Expression on British West Indian Slave Plantations*. Gainesville: University of Florida Press.

Donoso, Armando. 1913. *Bilbao y su tiempo*. Santiago, Chile: Zig Zag.

Drake, Frederick C. 1970. "Secret History of the Slave Trade to Cuba Written by an American Naval Officer, 1861." *Journal of Negro History* 55: 218–235.

Drescher, Seymour. 1988. "Brazilian Abolition in Comparative Perspective." *Hispanic American Historical Review* 68 (3): 429–460.

Dunn, Richard. 1972. *Sugar and Slaves: The Rise of the Planter Class in the English West Indies, 1624–1713*. Chapel Hill: University of North Carolina Press.

"Edit du Roi, Touchant la Polices des Isles de l'Amérique Française: Du mois de Mars 1685." In *Le Code Noir, ou Recueil des reglemens rendus jusquà présent. Concernant le gouvernement, l'administration de la justice, la police, la discipline et le commerce des negres dans les colonies françoises*. 1980. Basse-Terre, Guadeloupe: Société d'histoire de la Guadelo University Presse.

Edwards, Bryan. 1793. *The History, Civil and Commercial, of the British Colonies in the West Indies*. London: John Stockdale.

Fagan, Brian. 1993. "Brazil's Little Angola." *Archaeology* 46 (July): 14–19.

Falcão, Edgard Cerqueira, ed. 1963. *Obras científicas, políticas, a sociais de José Bonifácio de Andrada e Silva*. São Paulo: Grupo de Trabalho Executivo das Homenagens so Patriarca.

Fausto, Boris. 1995. *História do Brasil*. São Paulo: Editora da Universidade de São Paulo.

Fick, Carolyn. 1990. *The Making of Haiti: The Saint Domingue Revolution from Below*. Knoxville: University of Tennessee Press.

Fisher, John Robert. 1977. *Silver Mines and Silver Miners in Colonial Peru, 1776–1824*. Liverpool: Centre for Latin-American Studies, University of Liverpool.

Freyre, Gilberto. 1966. *The Masters and the Slaves: A Study in the Development of Brazilian Civilization*. 2d English language edition. New York: Alfred A. Knopf.

Fuentes Díaz, Vicente. 1989. *Revaloración del General Vicente Guerrero: Consumador de la indepen-*

dencia. Chilpancingo, Mexico: Gobierno del Estado de Guerrero.

Galván, Manuel de Jesús. 1989. *Enriquillo*. Santo Domingo, Dominican Republic: Ediciones de Taller.

Garrigus, John. 1988. "A Struggle for Respect: The Free Coloreds of Pre-Revolutionary Saint-Domingue, 1760–69." Ph.D. dissertation, Department of History, Johns Hopkins University, Baltimore, Maryland.

Geggus, David P. 1989. "The Haitian Revolution." In *The Modern Caribbean*. Edited by Franklin W. Knight and Colin A. Palmer. Chapel Hill: University of North Carolina Press.

Gibson, Charles. 1964. *The Aztecs under Spanish Rule: A History of the Indians of the Valley of Mexico, 1519–1810*. Stanford, CA: Stanford University Press.

———. 1971. *The Black Legend: Anti-Spanish Attitudes in the Old World and the New*. New York: Knopf.

———. 1966. *Spain in America*. New York: Harper and Row.

Gonzalez, Nancie L. 1988. *Sojourners of the Caribbean: Ethnogenesis and Ethnohistory of the Garifuna*. Urbana: University of Illinois Press.

Goslinga, Cornelis Christiaan. 1985. *The Dutch in the Caribbean and in the Guianas, 1680–1791*. Dover, NH: Van Gorcum.

———. 1979. *A Short History of the Netherlands Antilles and Surinam*. The Hague: Martinus Nijhoff.

Granzotto, Gianni. 1985. *Christopher Columbus, the Dream and the Obsession: A Biography*. Garden City, NY: Doubleday.

Green, William. 1976. *British Slave Emancipation: The Sugar Colonies and the Great Experiment, 1830–1865*. Oxford: Clarendon Press.

Gutierrez A. Ildefonso. 1992. "La Iglesia y los Negros." In *La Historia de la Iglesia en Hispanoamérica y las Filipinas. Siglos XV–XIX*. Edited by Pedro Borges. Madrid: Biblioteca de Autores Cristianos.

Hall, N. A. T. 1992. *Slave Society in the Danish West Indies: St. Thomas, St. John, and St. Croix*. Johns Hopkins Studies in Atlantic History and Culture. Baltimore: Johns Hopkins University Press.

Hamilton, K. G. 1967. *A History of the Moravian Church*. Bethlehem, PA: Board of Christian Education.

Handler, Jerome S., and Frederick W. Lange. 1978. *Plantation Slavery in Barbados: An Archaeological and Historical Investigation*. Cambridge, MA: Harvard University Press.

Hanke, Lewis. 1935. *The First Social Experiments in America: A Study in the Development of Spanish Indian Policy in the Sixteenth Century*. Cambridge: Cambridge University Press.

———. 1949. *The Spanish Struggle for Justice in the Conquest of America*. Philadelphia: University of Pennsylvania Press.

Harrell, Eugene Wilson. 1976. "Vicente Guerrero and the Birth of Modern Mexico." Unpublished thesis, Department of History, Tulane University, New Orleans, Louisiana.

Harrisse, Henry. 1897. *The Diplomatic History of America: Its First Chapter 1452–1494*. London: B. F. Stevens.

Hartsinck, Jan Jacob. 1770. *Beschryving van Guiana, of de Wilde Kust, in Zuid-America*. Amsterdam: G. Tielenbur.

Hemming, John. 1984. "Indians and the Frontier in Colonial Brazil." In *The Cambridge History of Latin America*. Edited by Leslie Bethell. Cambridge: Cambridge University Press.

Henao, Jesús María, and Gerardo Arrubla. 1938. *History of Colombia*. Chapel Hill: University of North Carolina Press.

Hennessey, Alistair. 1989. "Reshaping the Brazilian Past." *Times Literary Supplement*, July 14–20, 763–764.

Higman, Barry W. 1993. "The Slave Population of the British Caribbean: Some Nineteenth-Century Variations." In *Caribbean Slave Society and Economy: A Student Reader*. Edited by Hillary Beckles and Verene Shepherd. New York: New Press.

Higman, Barry W. 1984. *Slave Populations of the British Caribbean, 1807–1834*. Baltimore: Johns Hopkins University Press.

Hoetink, H. 1972. "Surinam and Curaçao." In *Neither Slave nor Free: The Freedman of African Descent in the Slave Societies of the New World*. Edited by David W. Cohen and Jack P. Greene. Baltimore: Johns Hopkins University Press.

Holloway, Thomas H. 1989. "'A Healthy Terror': Police Repression of *Capoeiras* in Nineteenth-Century Rio de Janeiro." *Hispanic American Historical Review* 69: 637–676.

———. 1977. "Immigration and Abolition: The Transition from Slave to Free Labor in the São Paulo Coffee Zone." In *Essays Concerning the Socio-Economic History of Brazil and Portuguese India*. Edited by Dauril Alden and Warren Dean. Gainesville: University Press of Florida.

Holm, John. 1988–1989. *Pidgins and Creoles*. 2 vols. Cambridge: Cambridge University Press.

Hoog, Levina de. 1983. *Van rebellie tot revolutie: Oorzaken en achtergronden van de Curaçaose slavenopstanden in 1750 en 1795*. Leiden: Universiteit van de Nederlandse Antillen.

Hoogbergen, Wim. 1990. "The History of the Suriname Maroons." In *Resistance and Rebellion in Suriname: Old and New*. Edited by Gary Brana-Shute. Williamsburg, VA: Department of Anthropology, College of William and Mary.

Hopkins, Keith. 1978. *Conquerors and Slaves*. Cambridge: Cambridge University Press.

Hünefeldt, Christine. 1994. *Paying the Price of Freedom: Family and Labor among Lima's Slaves*. Berkeley: University of California Press.

James, C. L. R. 1968. *The Black Jacobins: Toussaint L'Ouverture and the San Domingo Revolution*. New York: Random House.

Johnson, Howard. 1995. "Slave Life and Leisure in Nassau, Bahamas, 1783–1838." *Slavery and Abolition* 16 (1): 45–64.

Kapsoli, Wilfredo. 1975. *Sublevaciones de esclavos en el Perú, s. XVIII*. Lima, Peru: Universidad Ricardo Palma.

Karasch, Mary. 1986. *Slave Life in Rio de Janeiro, 1808–1850*. Princeton, NJ: Princeton University Press.

Keegan, William F. 1992. *The People Who Discovered Columbus: The Prehistory of the Bahamas*. Gainesville: University of Florida Press.

Keen, Benjamin. 1966. *A History of Latin America*. Boston: Houghton Mifflin.

Kent, R. K. 1965. "Palmares: An African State in Brazil." *Journal of African History* 6: 161–175.

Kerns, Virginia. 1983. *Women and the Ancestors: Black Carib Kinship and Ritual*. Urbana: University of Illinois Press.

Kiemen, Mathias C. 1954. *The Indian Policy of Portugal in the Amazon Region, 1614–1693*. Washington, DC: Catholic University of America Press.

Klein, Herbert S. 1986. *African Slavery in Latin America and the Caribbean*. New York: Oxford University Press.

———. 1967. *Slavery in the Americas: A Comparative Study of Virginia and Cuba*. Chicago: University of Chicago Press.

Knight, Franklin W. 1970. *Slave Society in Cuba during the Nineteenth Century*. Madison: University of Wisconsin Press.

Landers, Sharon Bamberry. 1995. "An Exploration of the Theory and Practice of Slavery in Seventeenth-Century Brazil in the Writings of Padre Antônio Vieira." Ph.D. dissertation, Department of History, Texas Christian University, Forth Worth, Texas.

Las Casas, Bartolomé de. 1988. *Historia de las Indias*. Madrid: Alianza.

Laurencio, Juan B. 1974. *Campana contra Yanga en 1608*. Mexico City: Citlaltepetl.

Laviña, Javier. "Iglesia y esclavitud en Cuba." *América Negra* 1 (June): 11–29.

Lecuna, Vicente, comp. 1951. *Selected Writings of Bolívar*. Edited by Harold A. Bierck, Jr. New York: Colonial Press.

Lewis, J. Lowell. 1992. *Ring of Liberation: Deception Discourse in Brazilian Capoeira*. Chicago: University of Chicago Press.

Lindo-Fuentes, Héctor. 1995. "The Economy of Central America: From Bourbon Reforms to Liberal Reforms." In *Central America, 1821–1871: Liberalism before Liberal Reform*. Edited by Lowell Gudmundson and Héctor Lindo-Fuentes. Tuscaloosa: University of Alabama Press.

Lipp, Solomon. 1975. *Three Chilean Thinkers*. Waterloo, Canada: Wilfred Laurier University Press.

Lockhart, James, and Stuart B. Schwartz. 1983. *Early Latin America: A History of Colonial Spanish America and Brazil*. Cambridge: Cambridge University Press.

Lombardi, John V. 1971. *The Decline and Abolition of Negro Slavery in Venezuela, 1820–1854*. Westport, CT: Greenwood Press.

Long, Edward. 1972. *The History of Jamaica*. New York: Arno Press.

McAlister, Lyle. 1984. *Spain and Portugal in the New World, 1492–1700*. Minneapolis: University of Minnesota Press.

McClendon, R. Earl. 1933. "The *Amistad* Claims: Inconsistencies of Policy." *Political Science Quarterly* 48: 386–412.

McFarlane, Milton C. 1977. *Cudjoe of Jamaica: Pioneer for Black Freedom in the New World*. Short Hills, NJ: Ridley Enslow.

MacLachlan, Colin, and Jaime E. Rodriguez. 1980. *The Forging of the Cosmic Race: A Reinterpretation of Colonial Mexico*. Berkeley: University of California Press.

MacLeod, Murdo J. 1973. *Spanish Central America: A Socioeconomic History, 1520–1720*. Berkeley: University of California Press.

Madariaga, Salvador de. 1952. *Bolívar*. Coral Gables, FL: University of Miami Press.

Mair, Lucille Mathurin. 1986. *Women Field Workers in Jamaica during Slavery*. Mona, Jamaica: University of the West Indies.

Manchester, Alan K. 1933. *British Preeminence in Brazil, Its Rise and Decline: A Study in European Expansion*. Chapel Hill: University of North Carolina Press.

Masur, Gerhard. 1948. *Simon Bolívar*. Albuquerque: University of New Mexico Press.

Matos Mar, Jose. 1976. *Yanaconaje y reforma agraria en el Peru*. Lima, Peru: Instituto de Estudios Peruanos.

Mattos, Ilmar Rohloff de. 1987. *O tempo saquarema*. São Paulo: Editora Hucitec.

Mattoso, Katia de Queiros. 1986. *To Be a Slave in*

Brazil, 1550–1888. New Brunswick, NJ: Rutgers University Press.

Mavis, Campbell. 1990. *The Maroons of Jamaica.* Trenton, NJ: Africa World Press.

Mencke, John G. 1979. *Mulattoes and Race Mixture: American Attitudes and Images, 1865–1918.* Ann Arbor, MI: UMI Research Press.

Mezière, Henri. 1990. *Le General Leclerc, 1772–1802 et l'expédition de St. Domingue.* Paris: Tallandier.

Miitraux, Alfred. 1959. *Voodoo in Haiti.* New York: Schocken Books.

Mintz, Sidney W. 1974. *Caribbean Transformations.* Chicago: Aldine.

Moore, David M. 1989. "Anatomy of a 17th-Century Slave Ship: Historical and Archaeological Investigations of the *Henrietta Marie 1699.*" M.A. thesis, Department of History, Eastern Carolina University, Greenville, North Carolina.

Moreau de St. Mery, Louis Médéric. 1793. *Description topographique et politique de la partie Espagnol de l'ile de Saint Domingue.* Philadelphia: Privately printed.

———. 1797. *Description topographique, physique, civile, politique, et historique de la partie Française de l'ile St. Domingue.* Philadelphia: Privately printed.

Mörner, Magnus. 1967. *Race Mixture in the History of Latin America.* Boston: Little, Brown.

Mörner, Magnus, ed. 1970. *Race and Class in Latin America.* New York: Columbia University Press.

Morrissey, Marietta. 1989. *Slave Women in the New World: Gender Stratification in the Caribbean.* Lawrence: University Press of Kansas.

Mullin, Michael. 1992. *Africa in America: Slave Acculturation and Resistance in the American South and the British Caribbean, 1736–1831.* Urbana: University of Illinois Press.

Nabuco, Carolina. 1950. *The Life of Joaquim Nabuco.* Stanford, CA: Stanford University Press.

Nabuco, Joaquim de Araújo. 1977. *Abolitionism: The Brazilian Anti-Slavery Struggle.* Chicago: University of Illinois Press.

———. 1883. *O abolicionismo.* London: Kingdom.

———. 1880–1881. *0 Abolicionista: Orgão da Sociedade Brazileira Contra a Escravidão.* Rio de Janeiro: Brazilian Anti-Slavery Society.

———. 1975. *Um estadista do império.* Rio de Janeiro: Editora Nova Aguilar.

Navarro Azcue, Concepcion. 1986. "La esclavitud en Cuba, antes y después de las leyes abolicionistas." In *Estudios sobre la abolición de la esclavitud.* Edited by Francisco de Solano. Madrid: Consejo Superior de Investigaciones Científicas.

Needell, Jeffrey D. 1995. "Identity, Race, Gender, and Modernity in the Origin of Gilberto Freyre's *Oeuvre.*" *American Historical Review* 100 (1) (February): 51–77.

Netscher, P. M. 1888. *Geschiedenis van de koloniën Essequebo, Demerary en Berbice, van de vestiging der Nederlanders aldaar tot op onzen tijd.* The Hague: Martinus Nijhoff.

Nicholls, David. 1988. *From Dessalines to Duvalier.* New York: Macmillan.

Novak, Maximillian E., and David Stuart Rodes. 1976. "Introduction." In *Oroonoko,* by Thomas Southerne. Lincoln: University of Nebraska Press.

Oldendorp, C. G. A. 1987. *A Caribbean Mission.* Edited and translated by Arnold R. Highfield and Vladimir Barac. Ann Arbor, MI: Karoma Publishers.

Olwig, Karen Fog. 1985. *Cultural Adaptation and Resistance on St. John: Three Centuries of Afro-Caribbean Life.* Gainesville: University of Florida Press.

Ott, Thomas. 1973. *The Haitian Revolution, 1789–1804.* Knoxville: University of Tennessee Press.

Oviedo y Valdés, Gonzálo Fernández de. 1959. *Historia general de las Indias.* Madrid: Ediciones Atlas.

Palacios Preciado, Jorge. 1973. *La trata de negros por Cartagena de Indias.* Tunja: Universidad Pedagogica y Tecnologica de Colombia.

Palmer, Colin A. 1986. "The Company Trade and the Numerical Distribution of Slaves to Spanish America, 1703–1739." In *Africans in Bondage: Studies in Slavery and the Slave Trade.* Edited by Paul E. Lovejoy. Madison: African Studies Program, University of Wisconsin-Madison.

———. 1981. *Human Cargoes: The British Slave Trade to Spanish America, 1700–1739.* Urbana: University of Illinois Press.

———. 1976. *Slaves of the White God: Blacks in Mexico, 1570–1650.* Cambridge, MA: Harvard University Press.

Paquet, Sandra Pouchet. 1992. "The Heartbeat of a West Indian Slave: The History of Mary Prince." *African American Review* 26: 131–146.

Parry, John H., and Robert G. Keith, eds. 1984. *New Iberian Worlds: A Documentary History of the Discovery and Settlement of Latin America to the Early Seventeenth Century.* New York: Times Books.

Patrocínio, José do, ed. 1880–1888. *Gazeta da Tarde.* Rio de Janeiro.

Paula, Alejandro F., ed. 1974. *1795. De slavenopstand op Curaçao: Een bronnenuitgave van de originele overheidsdocumenten.* Curaçao: Centraal-Historisch Archief.

Peña Batlle, Manuel Arturo. 1948. *La rebelión de Bahoruco.* Ciudad Trujillo: Impresora Dominicana.

Pla, Josefina. 1972. *Hermano negro: La esclavitud en el Paraguay*. Madrid: Paraninfo.

Pluchon, Pierre. 1989. *Toussaint Louverture: Un révolutionnaire noir d'Ancien Régime*. Paris: Fayard.

Poppino, Rollie E. 1968. *Brazil: The Land and the People*. New York: Oxford University Press.

Porter, Arthur T. 1963. *Creoledom*. London: Oxford University Press.

Price, Richard, ed. 1979. *Maroon Societies: Rebel Slave Communities in the Americas*. Baltimore: Johns Hopkins University Press.

Prince, Mary. 1987. *The History of Mary Prince, a West Indian Slave (Related by Herself)*. In *Classic Slave Narratives*. Edited by Henry Louis Gates, Jr. New York: Penguin Books.

Pulis, John W. 1997. "Bridging Troubled Waters: Moses Baker, George Liele, and the African-American Diaspora to Jamaica." In *Moving On: Black Loyalists in the Afro-Atlantic World*. New York: Garland.

———. 1998. *In the Holy Mountains: Missions, Moravians, and the Making of Afro-Christianity in Jamaica*. New York: Gordon and Breach.

Pulsipher, Lydia Mihelic. 1994. "Landscapes and Ideational Roles of Caribbean Slave Gardens." In *The Archaeology of Garden and Field*. Edited by Naomi Miller. Philadelphia: University of Pennsylvania Press.

Ragatz, Joseph Lowell. 1963. *The Fall of the Planter Class in the British Caribbean, 1763–1833*. New York: Octagon.

Ramos, Donald. 1986. "Community, Control, and Acculturation: A Case Study of Slavery in Eighteenth-Century Brazil." *Americas* (4): 419–451.

Rego, Waldeloir. 1968. *Capoeira Angola, ensaio sócio-etnográfico*. Rio de Janeiro: Graf. Lux.

Reis, Joao Jose. 1993. *Slave Rebellion in Brazil*. Baltimore: Johns Hopkins University Press.

Roberts, Peter A. 1988. *West Indians and Their Language*. Cambridge: Cambridge University Press.

Rodriguez, Frederick M. 1972. "Negro Slavery in New Spain and the Yanga Revolt." M.A. thesis, Department of History, DePaul University, Chicago, Illinois.

Ros, Martin. 1994. *Night of Fire*. New York: Sarpedon.

Rouse, Irving. 1992. *The Taínos: The People Who Discovered Columbus*. New Haven, CT: Yale University Press.

Rout, Leslie B., Jr. 1976. *The African Experience in Spanish America: 1502 to the Present Day*. Cambridge: Cambridge University Press.

Saez, J. Luis. 1994. *La Iglesia y el negro esclavo en Santo Domingo: Una historia de tres siglos*. Santo Domingo, Dominican Republic: Patronato de la Ciudad Colonial.

Sánchez, Joseph P. 1990. *The Spanish Black Legend: Origins of Anti-Hispanic Stereotypes*. Albuquerque, NM: Spanish Colonial Research Center.

Schuler, Monica. 1970. "Ethnic Slave Rebellions in the Caribbean and the Guianas." *Journal of Social History* 3 (4): 374–385.

Schwartz, Stuart B. 1978. "Indian Labor and New World Plantations: European Demands and Indian Responses in Northeastern Brazil." *American Historical Review* 83 (1): 43–79.

———. 1992. *Slaves, Peasants, Rebels: Reconsidering Brazilian Slavery*. Urbana: University of Illinois Press.

———. 1985. *Sugar Plantations in the Formation of Brazilian Society: Bahia, 1550–1835*. Cambridge: Cambridge University Press.

Scott, Rebecca J. 1993. "Explaining Abolition: Contradiction, Adaptation, and Challenge in Cuban Slave Society, 1860–1886." In *Caribbean Slave Society and Economy: A Student Reader*. Edited by Hillary Beckles and Verene Shepherd. New York: New Press.

———. 1985. *Slave Emancipation in Cuba: The Transition to Free Labor, 1860–1899*. Princeton, NJ: Princeton University Press.

Shafer, Robert Jones. 1978. *A History of Latin America*. New York: Heath.

Sharer, Robert J. 1994. *The Ancient Maya*. Stanford, CA: Stanford University Press.

Sheppard, Jill. 1977. *The "Redlegs" of Barbados: Their Origins and History*. Millwood, NY: KTO Press.

Sheridan, Richard B. 1985. *Doctors and Slaves: A Medical and Demographic History of Slavery in the British West Indies, 1680–1834*. Cambridge. Cambridge University Press.

Sherlock, Phillip Manderson. 1954. *Anansi the Spider Man*. Binghamton, NY: Vail-Ballou Press.

Sherman, William. 1979. *Forced Native Labor in Sixteenth-Century Central America*. Lincoln: University of Nebraska Press.

Simpson, Lesley B. 1966. *The Encomienda in New Spain: The Beginning of Spanish Mexico*. Berkeley: University of California Press.

———. 1934–1940. *Studies in the Administration of the Indians in New Spain*. 3 vols. Berkeley: University of California Press.

Skidmore, Thomas E. 1990. "Racial Ideas and Social Policy in Brazil, 1870–1940." In *The Idea of Race in Latin America*. Edited by Richard Graham. Austin: University of Texas Press.

Smith, Theophus. 1994. *Conjuring Culture*. New York: Oxford University Press.

Spalding, Karen. 1984. *Huarochiri, an Andean Society under Inca and Spanish Rule*. Stanford, CA: Stanford University Press.

Sprague, William. 1939. *Vicente Guerrero, Mexican Liberator*. Chicago: R. R. Donnelley.

Stern, Steve J. 1993. *Peru's Indian People and the Challenge of Spanish Conquest: Huamanga to 1640*. Madison: University of Wisconsin Press.

Stevens-Arroyo, Antonio M. 1988. *Cave of the Jagua: The Mythological World of the Taínos*. Albuquerque: University of New Mexico Press.

Stinchcombe, Arthur L. 1995. *Sugar Island Slavery in the Age of Enlightenment: The Political Economy of the Caribbean World*. Princeton, NJ: Princeton University Press.

Stipriaan, Alex van. 1993. *Surinaams contrast: Roofbouw en overleven in een Caraïbische plantagekolonie, 1750–1863*. Leiden: KITLV Uitgeverij.

Stone, Michael C. 1994. "Caribbean Nation, Central American State: Ethnicity, Race, and National Formation in Belize, 1798–1990." Ph.D. dissertation, Department of Anthropology, University of Texas at Austin.

Swahn, Jan-Öjvind, and Ola Jennersten. 1984. *Saint Barthélemy: Sveriges sista koloni*. Hoganas, Sweden: Wiken.

Tannenbaum, Frank. 1946. *Slave and Citizen: The Negro in the Americas*. New York: Vintage Books. Reprinted. 1963. New York: Random House.

Taunay, Alfredo d'Escragnolle. 1930. *O visconde do Rio Branco, gloria do Brasil da humandade*. Second edition. São Paulo: Weiszflog Irmãos.

Thomas, Hugh. 1971. *Cuba: The Pursuit of Freedom*. New York: Harper and Row.

Thompson, Vincent B. 1987. *The Making of the African Diaspora in the Americas 1441–1900*. New York: Longman.

Todd, Janet, ed. 1992. "Introduction." In *Oroonoko, The Rover, and Other Works by Aphra Behn*. London: Penguin.

Toplin, Robert Brent. 1992. *The Abolition of Slavery in Brazil*. New York: Atheneum.

Trouillot, Henock. 1966. *Dessalines, ou, La tragédie post-coloniale*. Port-au-Prince, Haiti: Editions Panorama.

Turner, Mary. 1982. *The Disintegration of Jamaican Slave Society, 1787–1834*. Urbana: University of Illinois Press.

Valtierra, Ángel, SJ. 1980. *Pedro Claver: El santo redentor de los negros. Cuarto centenario de su nacimiento, 1580–24 de junio–1980*. Bogotá: Banco de la República.

Van Lier, Rudolf A. J. 1971. *Frontier Society*. The Hague: Martinus Nijhoff.

Vandercook, John W. 1928. *Black Majesty: The Life of Christophe, King of Haiti*. London: Harper.

Varona, Alberto J. 1973. *Francisco Bilbao: Revolucionario de América*. Panama City: Ediciones Excelsior.

Vila Vilar, Enriqueta. 1977. *Hispanoamérica y el comercio de esclavos*. Seville: Escuela de Estudios Hispano-Americanos.

Villar Cordova, Socrates. 1966. *La institucion del yanacona en el incanato*. Lima, Peru: Universidad Nacional Mayor de San Marcos.

Viotti da Costa, Emilia. 1985. *The Brazilian Empire: Myths and Histories*. Chicago: University of Chicago Press.

Westergaard, Waldemar. 1917. *The Danish West Indies: Under Company Rule*. New York: Macmillan.

White, Jon Manship. 1971. *Cortes and the Downfall of the Aztec Empire*. New York: St. Martin's.

Whitehead, Neil Lancelot. 1990. "Carib Ethnic Soldiering in Venezuela, the Guianas, and the Antilles, 1492–1820." *Ethnohistory* 37 (4): 357–385.

Willams, Eric Eustace. 1971. *From Columbus to Castro: The History of the Caribbean*. New York: Harper and Row.

Wilson, Samuel M. 1990. *Hispaniola: Caribbean Chiefdoms in the Age of Columbus*. Tuscaloosa: University of Alabama Press.

Wood, Russell A. 1984. "Colonial Brazil: The Gold Cycle c. 1690–1750." In *The Cambridge History of Latin America*. Edited by Leslie Bethell. Cambridge: Cambridge University Press.

Zavala, Silvio Arturo. 1973. *La encomienda indiana*. Mexico City: Editorial Porrua.

Zorita, Alonso de. 1963. *Life and Labor in Ancient Mexico: The Brief and Summary Relation of the Lords of New Spain*. New Brunswick, NJ: Rutgers University Press.

Zulawski, Ann. 1995. *They Eat from Their Labor: Work and Social Change in Colonial Bolivia*. Pittsburgh: University of Pittsburgh Press.

Middle East and the Islamic World

Ali, A. Yusuf, ed. 1946. *The Holy Qur'an: Text, Translation, and Commentary*. Washington, DC: American National Printing.

Ayalon, David. 1977. "Eunuchs in the Mamluk Sultanate." In Myriam Rosen-Ayalon, ed., *Studies in Memory of Gaston Wiet*. Jerusalem: Institute of Asian and African Studies, Hebrew University of Jerusalem.

———. 1994. *Islam and the Abode of War: Military Slaves and Islamic Adversaries*. Aldershot, Eng.: Variorum.

———. 1979. *The Mamluk Military Society*. London: Variorum.

———. 1977. "The Muslim City and the *Mamluk* Military Aristocracy." In *Studies on the Mamluks of Egypt*. Edited by David Ayalon. London: Variorum Reprints.

Bates, Ülkü. 1978. "Women as Patrons of Architecture in Turkey." In *Women in the Muslim World*.

Edited by Lois Beck and Nikki R. Keddie. Cambridge, MA: Harvard University Press.

Burns, Robert. 1973. *Islam under the Crusaders.* Princeton, NJ: Princeton University Press.

Cahen, Claude. 1968. *Pre-Ottoman Turkey: A General Survey of the Material and Spiritual Culture and History, c. 1071–1330.* Translated by J. Jones-Williams. New York: Taplinger.

Clarke, Peter B. 1982. *West Africa and Islam: A Study of Religious Development from the 8th to the 20th Century.* London: Edward Arnold.

Clissold, S. 1977. *The Barbary Slaves.* Totowa, NJ: Rowman and Littlefield.

Davison, Roderic. 1963. *Reform in the Ottoman Empire, 1856–76.* Princeton, NJ: Princeton University Press.

Frend, W. H. C. 1969. "Circumcellions and Monks." *Journal of Theological Studies,* n.s., 20: 542–549.

Gibb, H. A. R., and Harold Bowen. 1950–1957. *Islamic Society and the West.* 1 vol. in 2 parts. London: Oxford University Press.

Glasse, Cyril. 1989. *The Concise Encyclopedia of Islam.* San Francisco: Harper and Row.

Hathaway, Jane. 1996. *The Politics of Households in Ottoman Egypt: The Rise of the Qazdaglis.* Cambridge: Cambridge University Press.

———. 1992. "The Role of the Kizlar Agasi in Seventeenth and Eighteenth Century Ottoman Egypt." *Studia Islamica* 75: 141–158.

———. 1994. "The Wealth and Influence of an Exiled Ottoman Eunuch in Egypt: The Waqf Inventory of Abbas Agha." *Journal of the Economic and Social History of the Orient* 37: 293–317.

Hourani, Albert. 1970. *Arabic Thought in the Liberal Age, 1798–1939.* Oxford: Oxford University Press.

Irwin, Robert. 1968. *The Middle East in the Middle Ages: The Early Mamluk Sultanate, 1250–1382.* Carbondale: Southern Illinois University Press.

Kati, Mahmoud. 1913. *Ta'rikh el-Fettach.* Translated by Octave Houdas and M. Delafosse. Paris: n.p.

Lewis, Bernard. 1990. *Race and Slavery in the Middle East.* Oxford: Oxford University Press.

Little, Donald. 1986. *History and Historiography of the Mamluks.* London: Variorum.

Marmon, Shaun E. 1995. *Eunuchs and Sacred Boundaries in Islamic Society.* Oxford: Oxford University Press.

Meyerson, Mark. 1991. *The Muslims of Valencia.* Berkeley: University of California Press.

Murray, Gordon. 1989. *Slavery in the Arab World.* New York: New Amsterdam.

A Narrative of the Adventures of Lewis Marott, Pilot-Royal of the Galleys of France: Giving an Account of His Slavery under the Turks; His Escapes out of It, and Other Strange Occurrences that Ensued Thereafter. 1677. London: Edward Brewster.

Ochsenwald, William. 1980. "Muslim European Conflict in the Hijaz: The Slave Trade Controversy, 1840–1859." *Middle Eastern Studies* 16 (1): 115–126.

Palmer, J. A. B. 1953. "The Origin of the Janissaries." *Bulletin of the John Rylands Library.* 35: 448–481.

Peirce, Leslie P. 1993. *The Imperial Harem: Women and Sovereignty in the Ottoman Empire.* Oxford: Oxford University Press.

Penzer, Norman. 1936. *The Harem.* London: George G. Harrap.

Popovic, A. 1976. *La revolte des esclaves en Iraq au IIIe/IXe siecle.* Paris: Geuthner.

Rahman, Fazlur. 1979. *Islam.* Second edition. Chicago: University of Chicago Press.

Raymond, Andre. 1973–1974. *Artisans et commercants au Caire au XVIIIe siecle.* 2 vols. Damascus: Institut Francais de Damas.

———. 1991. "Soldiers in Trade: The Case of Ottoman Cairo." *British Society for Middle Eastern Studies Bulletin.* 18: 16–37.

Risso, Patricia. 1986. *Oman and Muscat and Early Modern History.* New York: St. Martin's.

Rosenthal, Franz. 1952. *A History of Muslim Historiography.* Leiden: Brill.

Shaw, Stanford J. 1971. *Between Old and New: The Ottoman Empire under Sultan Selim III, 1789–1807.* Cambridge, MA: Harvard University Press.

———. 1976. *History of the Ottoman Empire and Modern Turkey.* Cambridge: Cambridge University Press.

Soden, W. von. 1964. "Muskenum und de Mawali des frühen Islam." *Zeitschrift für Assyriologie* 56: 133–141.

Spaulding, Jay. 1982. "Slavery, Land Tenure, and Social Class in the Northern Turkish Sudan." *International Journal of African Historical Studies* 15 (1): 1–20.

Speiser, E. A. 1958. "The Muskenum." *Orientalia,* n.s., 27: 19–28.

Toledano, Ehud R. 1982. *The Ottoman Slave Trade and Its Suppression, 1840–1890.* Princeton, NJ: Princeton University Press.

Uzuncarsili, I. H. 1943. *Osmanli Devleti Teskilatindan Kapukulu Ocaklari.* 2 vols. Ankara: Turk Tarih Kurumu.

Vryonis, Speros, Jr.. 1971. *The Decline of Medieval Hellenism in Asia Minor and the Process of Islamization from the Eleventh through the Fifteenth Centuries.* Berkeley: University of California Press.

———. 1971. "Isadore Glabas and the Turkish Devshirme." Reprinted in Vryonis, *Byzantium: Its Internal History and Relations with the Muslim World—Collected Studies*. London: Variorum Reprints.

———. 1971. "Seljuk Gulams and Ottoman Devshirmes." Reprinted in Vryonis, *Byzantium* London: Variorum Reprints.

Wittek, Paul. 1958. "*Devshirme* and *Shari'a*." *Bulletin of the School of Oriental and African Studies*. 17: 271–278.

Zygulski, Zdzislaw, Jr. 1992. *Ottoman Art in the Service of the Empire*. New York: New York University Press.

Modern/Contemporary

Ferencz, Benjamin B. 1979. *Less than Slaves: Jewish Forced Labor and the Quest for Compensation*. Cambridge, MA: Harvard University Press.

Friedrich, Otto. 1994. *The Kingdom of Auschwitz*. New York: Harper-Perennial.

Herbert, Ulrich. 1990. A *History of Foreign Labor in Germany, 1880–1980*. Ann Arbor: University of Michigan Press.

Hilberg, Raul. 1967. *The Destruction of the European Jews*. Chicago: Quadrangle Books.

Homze, Edward L. 1967. *Foreign Labor in Nazi Germany*. Princeton, NJ: Princeton University Press.

Krausnick, Helmut, et al. 1968. *Anatomy of the SS State*. London: Collins.

Miers, Suzanne. 1996. "Contemporary Forms of Slavery." *Slavery and Abolition* 17: 238–246.

Milward, Alan S. 1977. *War, Economy, and Society 1939–1945*. Berkeley: University of California Press.

Piszkiewicz, Dennis. 1995. *The Nazi Rocketeers: Dreams of Space and Crimes of War*. Westport, CT: Praeger.

Rone, Jemera. 1995. *Children in Sudan: Slaves, Street Children, and Child Soldiers*. New York: Human Rights Watch.

Silvers, Jonathan. 1996. "Child Labor in Pakistan." *Atlantic Monthly* (February): 79–92.

United Nations. 1953. General Assembly Official Records, Eighth Session, Third Committee, 529th meeting (November 20).

———. 1951. *The Suppression of Slavery*, Memorandum Submitted by the Secretary-General. New York: United Nations.

———. 1953. United Nations Document A/2438 (August 17).

———. 1953. United Nations Document E/2431/Addendum 2 (August 24).

U.S. Congress. House of Representatives. Committee on International Relations. 1996. *Slavery in Mauritania and Sudan*. Joint Hearings. March 13. Washington, DC: Government Printing Office.

North America

Abel, Annie Heloise. 1992. *The American Indian as Slaveholder and Secessionist*. Lincoln: University of Nebraska Press.

Abrahams, Roger D. 1966. "Some Varieties of Heroes in America." *Journal of the Folklore Institute* 3 (3): 341–362.

Abzug, Robert H. 1994. *Cosmos Crumbling: American Reform and the Religious Imagination*. New York: Oxford University Press.

Adams, Charles Francis. 1874. *Memoirs of John Quincy Adams Comprising Portions of His Diary from 1795 to 1848*. Philadelphia: Lippincott.

Adams, John R. 1977. *Edward Everett Hale*. Boston: Twayne.

———. 1989. *Harriet Beecher Stowe*. Updated edition. Boston: Twayne.

Allen, Richard. 1983. *The Life Experience and Gospel Labors of the Right Reverend Richard Allen Written by Himself*. Edited by George A. Singleton. Nashville, TN: Abingdon.

Allen, Will W. 1971. *Banneker: The Afro-American Astronomer*. Freeport, NY: Libraries Press.

Andrews, E. A. 1836. *Slavery and the Domestic Slave-Trade in the United States*. Baltimore: Light and Stearns.

Andrews, William L. 1987. "Six Women's Slave Narratives, 1831–1909." In *Black Women's Slave Narratives*. Edited by William Andrews. New York: Oxford University Press.

———. 1986. *To Tell a Free Story: The First Century of Afro-American Autobiography, 1760–1865*. Urbana: University of Illinois Press.

Anthony, Katharine. 1954. *Susan B. Anthony: Her Personal History and Her Era*. Garden City, NY: Doubleday.

Antieau, Chester James. 1997. *The Intended Significance of the Fourteenth Amendment*. Buffalo, NY: W. S. Hein.

Aphornsuvan, Thanet. 1990. "James D. B. DeBow and the Political Economy of the Old South." Ph.D. dissertation, Department of History, SUNY-Binghamton, New York.

Aptheker, Herbert. 1993. *American Negro Slave Revolts*. 6th edition. New York: International Publishers.

———. 1965. *One Continual Cry*. New York: Humanities Press.

Atkin, Andrea M. 1995. "Converting America: The Rhetoric of Abolitionist Literature." Ph.D. dissertation, Department of English, University of Chicago.

Austin, Allen D., ed. 1996. *African Muslims in Antebellum America: Proud Exiles*. New York: Routledge.

Averkieva, Julia. 1941. *Slavery among the Indians of North America*. Moscow: USSR Academy of Sciences.

Azevedo, Celia M. 1995. *Abolitionism in the United States and Brazil: A Comparative Perspective.* New York: Garland.

Bacon, Margaret Hope. 1986. *Mothers of Feminism: The Story of Quaker Women in America.* San Francisco: Harper and Row.

———. 1980. *Valiant Friend: The Life of Lucretia Mott.* New York: Walker.

Bailey, Hugh C. 1965. *Hinton Rowan Helper, Abolitionist-Racist.* Tuscaloosa: University of Alabama Press.

Bailey, L. R. 1973. *Indian Slave Trade in the Southwest.* Los Angeles: Westernlore Press.

Bailey, N. Louis, and Elizabeth Ivey Cooper, eds. 1981. "John Laurens." In *Biographical Directory of the South Carolina House of Representatives.* Columbia: South Carolina University Press.

Baker, Moses. 1803. "An Account of Moses Baker, a Mulatto Baptist Preacher near Martha Brae." *Evangelical Magazine and Missionary Intelligencer* 11: 365–371.

Bancroft, Frederic. 1928. *Calhoun and the South Carolina Nullification Movement.* Baltimore: Johns Hopkins University Press.

———. 1931. *Slave-Trading in the Old South.* Baltimore: J. H. Furst.

Barber, John W. 1840. *A History of the Amistad Captives.* New Haven, CT: E. L. and J. W. Barber.

Barnes, Gilbert Hobbs. 1933. *The Anti-slavery Impulse, 1830–1844.* Gloucester, MA: Peter Smith.

Barnes, Gilbert Hobbs, and Dwight L. Dumond, eds. 1934. *Letters of Theodore Dwight Weld, Angelina Grimké Weld, and Sarah Grimké, 1822–1844.* New York: D. Appleton.

Barringer, James G. 1987. "The African Methodist Church: 200 Years of Service to the Community." *Crisis* 94 (June/July): 40–43.

Barry, Kathleen. 1988. *Susan B. Anthony: Biography of a Singular Feminist.* New York: New York University Press.

Bartlett, Irving. 1993. *John C. Calhoun: a Biography.* New York: Norton.

Bastide, Roger. 1972. *African Civilization in the New World.* New York: Harper and Row.

Batey, Grant M. 1954. *John Chavis: His Contributions to Education in North Carolina.* Master's thesis, Department of History, North Carolina College, Durham.

Baxter, Maurice. 1984. *One and Inseparable: Daniel Webster and the Union.* Cambridge, MA: Harvard University Press.

Bayliff, William H. 1951. *Boundary Monuments on the Maryland-Pennsylvania and the Maryland-Delaware Boundaries.* Annapolis: Maryland Board of Natural Resources.

Beals, Carleton. 1960. *Brass-Knuckle Crusade: The Great Know-Nothing Conspiracy, 1820–1860.* New York: Hastings House.

Bearden, Jim, and Linda Jean Butler. 1977. *Shadd: The Life and Times of Mary Shadd Cary.* Toronto: NC Press.

Bedini, Silvio A. 1972. *The Life of Benjamin Banneker.* New York: Charles Scribner's Sons.

Belkin, Lisa. 1989. "Freedoms Are Renewed in Recalling Deliverance." *New York Times,* June 19.

Bell, Howard H. 1969. *A Survey of the Negro Convention Movement, 1830–1861.* New York: Arno Press.

Bell, Malcolm. 1987. *Major Butler's Legacy: Five Generations of a Slaveholding Family.* Athens: University of Georgia Press.

Bennett, Robert A. 1974. "Black Episcopalians: A History from the Colonial Period to the Present." *Historical Magazine of the Protestant Episcopal Church* 43 (September 3): 231–245.

Bentley, George. 1955. *A History of the Freedmen's Bureau.* Philadelphia: University of Pennsylvania Press.

Berlin, Ira. 1974. *Slaves without Masters: The Free Negro in the Antebellum South.* New York: Pantheon Books.

Berlin, Ira, and Philip D. Morgan, eds. 1993. *Cultivation and Culture: Labor and the Shaping of Slave Life in the Americas.* Charlottesville: University Press of Virginia.

Berlin, Ira, et al. 1992. *Slaves No More: Three Essays on Emancipation and the Civil War.* Cambridge: Cambridge University Press.

Billington, Ray Allen. 1953. *The Journal of Charlotte L. Forten.* New York: Collier.

Birney, Catherine H. 1885. *The Grimké Sisters.* Boston: Lee and Shepard.

Birney, William. 1969. *James G. Birney and His Times: The Genesis of the Republican Party.* New York: Bergman.

Blackwell, Alice Stone. 1930. *Lucy Stone: Pioneer of Women's Rights.* Boston: Little, Brown.

Blanchard, Jonathan. Papers. Buswell Memorial Library, Wheaton College, Wheaton, Illinois.

Blassingame, John W. 1972. *The Slave Community: Plantation Life in the Antebellum South.* New York: Oxford University Press.

Blassingame, John W., ed. 1977. *Slave Testimony: Two Centuries of Letters, Speeches, Interviews, and Autobiographies.* Baton Rouge: Louisiana State University Press.

Bleser, Carol K. 1987. *The Hammonds of Redcliffe.* Oxford: Oxford University Press.

Bleser, Carol, K., ed. 1988. *Secret and Sacred: The Diaries of James Henry Hammond, a Southern Slaveholder.* New York: Oxford University Press.

Blockson, Charles L. 1987. *The Underground Railroad: First-Person Narratives of Escapes to Freedom in the North*. Englewood Cliffs, NJ: Prentice-Hall.

Blue, Frederick J. 1994. *Charles Sumner and the Conscience of the North*. Arlington Heights, IL: Harlan Davidson.

———. 1973. *The Free Soilers: Third Party Politics, 1848–54*. Urbana: University of Illinois Press.

Boller, Paul F. 1974. *American Transcendentalism, 1830–1860: An Intellectual Inquiry*. New York: G. P. Putnam's Sons.

Boston Slave Riot and Trial of Anthony Burns. 1854. Boston: Fetridge and Company.

Botkin, B. A., ed. 1941. *Slave Narratives: A Folk History of Slavery in the United States from Interviews with Former Slaves*. Washington, DC: U.S. Government Printing Office.

Bowman, Shearer Davis. 1993. *Masters and Lords: Mid-19th Century U.S. Planters and Prussian Junkers*. New York: Oxford University Press.

Boyd, Daniel L. 1974. "Free-Born Negro: The Life of John Chavis." BA thesis, Department of History, Princeton University, Princeton, New Jersey.

Boyd, James R. 1883. "William Still: His Life and Work to This Time." In *William Still: The Underground Railroad*. Philadelphia: William Still.

Boylan, Ann M. 1994. "Benevolence and Antislavery Activity among African American Women in New York and Boston, 1820–1840." In *The Abolitionist Sisterhood: Women's Political Culture in Antebellum America*. Edited by Jean Fagan Yellin and John C. Van Horne. Ithaca, NY: Cornell University Press.

Bracey, John. 1993. "Foreword." In Herbert Aptheker, *American Negro Slave Revolts*. New York: International Publishers.

Braithwaite, William. 1961. *The Second Period of Quakerism*. Cambridge: Cambridge University Press.

Brauer, Kinley. 1967. *Cotton versus Conscience: Massachusetts Whig Politics and Southwestern Expansion, 1843–1848*. Lexington: University of Kentucky Press.

Brawley, Benjamin. 1937. *Negro Builders and Heroes*. Chapel Hill: University of North Carolina Press.

Brewer, W. M. 1928. "Henry Highland Garnet." *Journal of Negro History* 13 (1): 36–52.

Bridges, C. A. 1941. "The Knights of the Golden Circle: A Filibustering Fantasy." *Southwestern Historical Quarterly* 44 (January): 287–302.

Brock, Peter. 1990. *The Quaker Peace Testimony, 1660–1914*. York, Eng.: Ebor Press.

Brock, William. 1979. *Parties and Political American Dilemmas, 1840–1850*. Millwood, NY: KTO Press.

Brodie, Fawn. 1974. *Thomas Jefferson, an Intimate History*. New York: Norton.

Brooks, George E. 1970. *Yankee Traders, Old Coasters, and African Middlemen*. Boston: Boston University Press.

Brown, Charles H. 1980. *Agents of Manifest Destiny: The Lives and Times of the Filibusters*. Chapel Hill: University of North Carolina Press.

Brown, David H. 1990. "Conjure/Doctors: An Exploration of a Black Discourse in America, Antebellum to 1940." *Folklore Forum* 23 (1–2): 3–46.

Brown, Josephine. 1856. *Biography of an American Bondman, by His Daughter*. Boston: R. F. Walcutt.

Brown, William Wells. 1847. *Narrative of William W. Brown, a Fugitive Slave, Written by Himself*. Boston: Anti-Slavery Office.

Brunvand, Jan Harold. 1986. *The Study of American Folklore: An Introduction*. New York: W. W. Norton.

Burke, Edmund, and William Burke. 1835. *An Account of the European Settlements in America*. Boston: J. H. Wilkins.

Burnham, Philip. 1993. "Selling Poor Steven: The Struggles and Torments of a Forgotten Class in Antebellum America: Black Slaveowners." *American Heritage* 44 (1): 90–97.

Byerman, Keith E. 1994. *Seizing the Word: History, Art, and Self in the Work of W. E. B. DuBois*. Athens: University of Georgia Press.

Cable, Mary. 1971. *Black Odyssey: The Case of the Slave Ship* Amistad. New York: Viking Press.

Cady, Edwin H. 1966. *John Woolman: The Mind of the Quaker Saint*. New York: Washington Square Press.

Caldehead, William. 1972. "How Extensive Was the Border State Slave Trade? A New Look." *Civil War History* 18 (1): 42–55.

Calhoun, John C. 1957-. *The Papers of John C. Calhoun*. 23 vols. Edited by Clyde N. Wilson. Columbia: South Carolina University Press.

Campbell, Penelope. 1971. *Maryland in Africa: The Maryland State Colonization Society, 1831–1857*. Urbana: University of Illinois Press.

Campbell, Stanley W. 1968. *The Slave Catchers: Enforcement of the Fugitive Slave Law, 1850–1860*. Chapel Hill: University of North Carolina Press.

Cecil-Fronsman, Bill. 1992. *Common Whites: Class and Culture in Antebellum North Carolina*. Lexington: University Press of Kentucky.

Cell, John. 1982. *The Highest Stage of White Supremacy*. London: Cambridge University Press.

Ceplair, Larry, ed. 1989. *The Public Years of Sarah and Angelina Grimké: Selected Writings, 1835–1839*. New York: Columbia University Press.

Chambers-Schiller, Lee. 1994. "'A Good Work

among the People': The Political Culture of the Boston Antislavery Fair." In *The Abolitionist Sisterhood: Women's Political Culture in Antebellum America*. Edited by Jean Fagan Yellin and John C. Van Horne. Ithaca, NY: Cornell University Press.

Chapell, Naomi C. 1929. "Negro Names." *American Speech* 4: 272–275.

Chapelle, Howard. 1927. *The Baltimore Clipper*. Salem, MA: Marine Research Society.

———. 1967. *The Search for Speed under Sail*. New York: Norton.

Chavis, John. Letters held in the Willia P. Mangum Papers. Library of Congress, Duke University Library, and University of North Carolina, Chapel Hill.

Claiborne, J. F. H. 1860. *Life and Correspondence of John A. Quitman, Major-General, U.S.A., and Governor of the State of Mississippi*. New York: Harper.

Clifford, Deborah Pickman. 1979. *Mine Eyes Have Seen the Glory*. Boston: Little, Brown.

Coffin, Levi. 1876. *Reminiscences of Levi Coffin, Reputed President of the Underground Railroad*. Cincinnati: Western Tract Society.

Cohen, David, and Jack Greene. 1972. *Neither Slave Nor Free*. Baltimore: Johns Hopkins University Press.

Cohen, Hennig. 1962. "Slave Names in Colonial South Carolina." *American Speech* 28: 102–107.

Coit, Margaret L. 1950. *John C. Calhoun, American Portrait*. Boston: Houghton Mifflin.

Coleman, Mrs. Chapman. 1871. *The Life of John J. Crittenden*. Philadelphia: J. B. Lippincott.

Collison, Gary. 1997. *Shadrach Minkins: From Fugitive Slave to Citizen*. Cambridge, MA: Harvard University Press.

Commons, John R., et al. 1910. *A Documentary History of American Industrial Society*. Cleveland: A. H. Clark.

Coniff, Michael L., and Thomas J. Davis. 1994. *Africans in the Americas: A History of the Black Diaspora*. New York: St. Martin's.

Connelley, William E. 1918. *A Standard History of Kansas and Kansans*. Chicago: Lewis.

Cook, James F. 1995. *The Governors of Georgia, 1754–1995*. Macon, GA: Mercer University Press.

Cooley, Timothy Mather. 1837. *Sketches of the Life and Character of the Reverend Lemuel Haynes, A.M., for Many Years Pastor of a Church in Rutland, Vermont, and Late in Granville, New York*. New York: Negro University Press.

Cooper, Richard. 1985. *John Chavis: To Teach a Generation*. Raleigh, NC: Creative Productions.

Cornelius, Janet Duitsman. 1991. *"When I Can Read My Title Clear": Literacy, Slavery, and Religion in the Antebellum South*. Columbia: University of South Carolina Press.

Cover, Robert. 1975. *Justice Accused: Antislavery and the Judicial Process*. New Haven, CT: Yale University Press.

Covington, James W. 1995. *The Seminoles of Florida*. Gainesville: University Press of Florida.

Cox, LaWanda. 1981. *Lincoln and Black Freedom: A Study in Presidential Leadership*. Urbana: University of Illinois Press.

Craft, William, and Ellen Craft. 1860. *Running a Thousand Miles for Freedom, or The Escape of William and Ellen Craft from Slavery*. London: William Tweedie.

Craven, Avery O. 1932. *Edmund Ruffin, Southerner: A Study in Secession*. New York: D. Appleton.

Creel, Margaret Washington. 1988. *A Peculiar People: Slave Religion and Community-Culture among the Gullahs*. New York: New York University Press.

Crenshaw, Ollinger. 1941. "The Knights of the Golden Circle: The Career of George Bickley." *American Historical Review* 47 (October): 23–50.

———. 1942. "The Speakership Contest of 1859–60." *Mississippi Valley Historical Review* 29: 323–338.

Crofts, Daniel W. 1971. "The Black Response to the Blair Education Bill." *Journal of Southern History* 37 (1): 41–65.

Cromwell, Otelia. 1958. *Lucretia Mott*. Cambridge, MA: Harvard University Press.

Crozier, A. 1969. *The Novels of Harriet Beecher Stowe*. New York: Oxford University Press.

Crum, Mason. 1968. *Gullah: Negro Life in the Carolina Sea Islands*. New York: Negro Universities Press.

Cullen, Charles T. 1987. *St. George Tucker and Law in Virginia, 1772–1804*. New York: Garland.

Cunliffe, Marcus. 1979. *Chattel Slavery and Wage Slavery: The Anglo-American Context, 1830–1860*. Athens: University of Georgia Press.

Cunningham, Noble. 1987. *In Pursuit of Reason: The Life of Thomas Jefferson*. Baton Rouge: Louisiana State University Press.

Curry, J. L. M. 1969. *A Brief Sketch of George Peabody, and a History of the Peabody Education Fund through Thirty Years*. New York: Negro Universities Press.

Curtin, Philip D. 1990. *The Rise and Fall of the Plantation Complex: Essays in Atlantic History*. Cambridge: Cambridge University Press.

Cushing, J. D. 1961. "The Cushing Court and the Abolition of Slavery in Massachusetts: More Notes on the Quock Walker Case." *American Journal of Legal History* 5: 118–119.

Dabney, Virginius. 1981. *The Jefferson Scandals: A Rebuttal*. New York: Dodd, Mead.

Daube, David. 1952. "Slave-Catching." *Juridical Review* 64: 12–28.

Davenport, Frances, ed. 1967. *European Treaties Bearing on the History of the United States and Its Dependencies to 1648*. Gloucester, MA: Peter Smith.

David, Paul, et al. 1976. *Reckoning with Slavery: A Critical Study in the Quantitative History of American Negro Slavery*. New York: Oxford University Press.

Davis, Charles T., and Henry Louis Gates, Jr., eds. 1985. *The Slave's Narrative*. New York: Oxford University Press.

Davis, David Brion. 1986. "The Emergence of Immediatism in British and American Antislavery Thought." In *From Homicide to Slavery: Studies in American Culture*. Edited by David Brion Davis. New York: Oxford University Press.

———. 1986. *From Homicide to Slavery: Studies in American Culture*. New York: Oxford University Press.

———. 1975. *The Problem of Slavery in the Age of Revolution, 1770–1823*. Ithaca, NY: Cornell University Press.

———. 1966. *The Problem of Slavery in Western Culture*. Oxford: Oxford University Press.

The Debate on the Constitution: Federalist and Antifederalist Speeches, Articles, and Letters during the Struggle over Ratification, Part One. 1993. Edited by Bernard Bailyn. New York: Library of America.

Debo, Angie. 1970. *A History of the Indians of the United States*. Norman: University of Oklahoma Press.

DeBoer, Clara Merritt. 1994. *Be Jubilant My Feet: African American Abolitionists in the American Missionary Association, 1839–1861*. New York: Garland.

———. 1995. *His Truth Is Marching On: African Americans Who Taught the Freedmen for the American Missionary Association, 1861–1877*. New York: Garland.

———. 1973. *The Role of Afro-Americans in the Origin and Work of the American Missionary Association, 1839–1877. Part 1 and 2*. Ph.D. dissertation, Department of History, Rutgers University. Ann Arbor, MI: University Microfilms.

Deetz, James. 1993. *Flowerdew Hundred: The Archaeology of a Virginia Plantation, 1619–1864*. Charlottesville: University Press of Virginia.

Degler, Carl N. 1978. "Experiencing Slavery." *Reviews in American History* 6: 277–282.

———. 1971. *Neither Black nor White: Slavery and Race Relations in Brazil and the United States*. New York: Macmillan.

Delany, Martin R. 1852. *The Condition, Elevation, Emigration, and Destiny of the Colored People of the United States, Politically Considered*. Philadelphia: Martin R. Delany.

De Voto, Bernard A. 1989. *The Year of Decision: 1846*. Boston: Houghton Mifflin.

Diehl, Lorraine. 1992. "Skeletons in the Closet: Uncovering the Rich History of the Slaves of New York." *New York* 25 (39): 78–86.

Dillard, Joey L. 1971. "The West-African Day-Names in Nova Scotia." *Names* 19 (4): 257–261.

Dillon, Merton L. 1985. *Ulrich Bonnell Phillips: Historian of the Old South*. Baton Rouge: Louisiana State University Press.

Donald, David. 1960. *Charles Sumner and the Coming of the Civil War*. New York: Knopf.

———. 1995. *Lincoln*. New York: Simon and Schuster.

Donald, Leland. 1997. *Aboriginal Slavery on the Northwest Coast of North America*. Berkeley: University of California Press.

Donnan, Elizabeth, ed. 1931. *Documents Illustrative of the History of the Slave Trade to America*. Washington, DC: Carnegie Institution of Washington.

Donovan, Herbert. 1925. *The Barnburners: A Study of the Internal Movements in the Political History of New York and of the Resulting Changes in Political Affiliations, 1830–1852*. New York: New York University Press.

Dormon, John H. 1977. "The Persistent Specter: Slave Rebellion in Territorial Louisiana." *Louisiana History* 18: 389–404.

Dorris, Jonathan T. 1936. *Old Cane Springs*. Louisville, KY: Standard Printing.

Douglass, Frederick. 1855. *My Bondage and My Freedom*. New York: Miller, Orton.

———. 1845. *Narrative of the Life of Frederick Douglass, an American Slave*. Boston: American Anti-Slavery Office.

Douty, Esther M. 1968. *Forten the Sailmaker: Pioneer Champion of Negro Rights*. Chicago: Rand McNally.

Drake, Thomas. 1950. *Quakers and Slavery in America*. New Haven, CT: Yale University Press.

———. 1938. "Thomas Garrett Quaker Abolitionist." In *Friends in Wilmington, 1738–1938*. Edited by Edward P. Bartlett. Wilmington, OH: Clinton County Historical Society.

Driver, Leota S. 1969. *Fanny Kemble*. New York: Negro Universities Press.

DuBois, Ellen Carol. 1978. *Feminism and Suffrage: The Emergence of an Independent Women's Movement in America, 1848–1869*. Ithaca, NY: Cornell University Press.

DuBois, W. E. B. 1909. *John Brown*. Philadelphia: G. W. Jacobs.

Dumond, Dwight Lowell. 1959. *Antislavery Origins of the Civil War in the United States*. Ann Arbor: University of Michigan Press.

Eckhardt, Celia Morris. 1984. *Fanny Wright: Rebel in America*. Cambridge, MA: Harvard University Press.

Edelstein, Tilden G. 1968. *Strange Enthusiasm: A Life of Thomas Wentworth Higginson*. New Haven, CT: Yale University Press.

Edwards, Lillie Johnson. 1996. "Episcopalians." In *Encyclopedia of African-American Culture and History*. Edited by Jack Salzman, David Lionel Smith, and Cornel West. New York: Macmillan.

Edwards, Samuel. 1974. *Rebel! A Biography of Thomas Paine*. New York: Praeger Press.

Egerton, Douglas R. 1993. *Gabriel's Rebellion: The Virginia Slave Conspiracies of 1800 and 1802*. Chapel Hill: University of North Carolina Press.

Ehrlich, Walter. 1979. *They Have No Rights: Dred Scott's Struggle for Freedom*. Westport, CT: Greenwood Press.

Elkins, Stanley M. 1959. *Slavery: A Problem in American Institutional and Intellectual Life*. Chicago: University of Chicago Press.

Ellis, William. 1985. *Madison County: 200 Years in Retrospect*. Richmond, KY: Madison County Historical Society.

Escott, Paul D. 1979. *Slavery Remembered: A Record of Twentieth-Century Slave Narratives*. Chapel Hill: University of North Carolina Press.

Essien-Udom, Essien Udosen. 1969. *Black Nationalism: A Search for Identity in America*. New York: Dell.

Estell, Kenneth., ed. 1994. *The African-American Almanac*. Detroit: Gale Research.

Ettinger, Amos. 1936. *James Edward Oglethorpe, Imperial Idealist*. Oxford: Clarendon Press.

Farber, Daniel A., and Suzanna Sherry. 1990. *A History of the American Constitution*. St. Paul, MN: West Publishing.

Farrison, William Edward. 1969. *William Wells Brown: Author and Reformer*. Chicago: University of Chicago Press.

Faust, Drew Gilpin. 1977. "Evangelicalism and the Meaning of the Proslavery Argument: The Reverend Thornton Stringfellow of Virginia." *Virginia Magazine of History and Biography* 85 (January): 3–17.

———. 1981. *The Ideology of Slavery: Proslavery Thought in the Antebellum South, 1830–1860*. Baton Rouge: Louisiana State University Press.

———. 1986. *A Sacred Circle: The Dilemma of the Intellectual in the Old South, 1840–1860*. Philadelphia: University of Pennsylvania Press.

———. 1979. "A Southern Stewardship: The Intellectual and the Proslavery Argument." *American Quarterly* 31 (Spring): 63–80.

Fehrenbacher, Don E. 1978. *The Dred Scott Case*. New York: Oxford University Press.

Feldman, Lynne B., and John N. Ingham, eds. 1994. *African American Business Leaders: A Biographical Dictionary*. Westport, CT: Greenwood.

Ferguson, Leland. 1992. *Uncommon Ground: Archaeology and Early African America, 1650–1800*. Washington, DC: Smithsonian Institution Press.

Finkelman, Paul. 1994. "'Hooted Down the Page of History': Reconsidering the Greatness of Chief Justice Taney." *Journal of Supreme Court History* 1994: 83–102.

———. 1981. *An Imperfect Union: Slavery, Federalism, and Comity*. Chapel Hill: University of North Carolina Press.

———. 1996. "Legal Ethics and Fugitive Slaves: The Anthony Burns Case, Judge Loring, and Abolitionist Attorneys." *Cardozo Law Review* 17 (May): 1793–1858.

———. 1985. *Slavery in the Courtroom. An Annotated Bibliography of American Cases*. Washington, DC: Library of Congress.

Finkelman, Paul, ed. 1995. *His Soul Goes Marching On: Responses to John Brown and the Harpers Ferry Raid*. Charlottesville: University Press of Virginia.

———. 1988. *Statutes on Slavery: The Pamphlet Literature*. New York: Garland.

Fisher, Ruth Anna. 1942. "Manuscript Materials Bearing on the Negro in British America." *Journal of Negro History* 27 (1): 83–93.

Fishkin, Shelly Fisher, and Carla L. Peterson. 1990. "'We Hold These Truths to Be Self-Evident': The Rhetoric of Frederick Douglass' Journalism." In *Frederick Douglass: New Literary and Historical Essays*. Edited by Eric J. Sundquist. Cambridge: Cambridge University Press.

Fitzhugh, George. 1960. *Cannibals All! or Slaves without Masters*. Cambridge, MA: Belknap Press.

Fladeland, Betty. 1955. *James G. Birney: Slaveholder to Abolitionist*. Ithaca, NY: Cornell University Press.

———. 1972. *Men and Brothers: Anglo-American Antislavery Cooperation*. Urbana: University of Illinois Press.

Fluche, Michael. 1975. "Joel Chandler Harris and the Folklore of Slavery." *Journal of American Studies* 9 (December): 347–363.

Fogel, Robert, and Stanley Engerman. 1974. *Time on the Cross: The Economics of American Negro Slavery*. Boston: Little, Brown.

———. 1974. *Time on the Cross: Evidence and Methods—A Supplement*. Boston: Little, Brown.

Fogel, Robert William. 1989. *Without Consent or*

Contract: The Rise and Fall of American Slavery. New York: Norton.

Foner, Eric. 1995. *Free Soil—Free Labor—Free Men.* New York: Oxford University Press.

———. 1983. *Nothing but Freedom: Emancipation and Its Legacy.* Baton Rouge: Louisiana State University Press.

———. 1988. *Reconstruction: America's Unfinished Revolution.* New York: Harper and Row.

Foner, Philip S. 1964. *Frederick Douglass: A Biography.* New York: Citadel.

———. 1950. *Life and Writings of Frederick Douglass.* 5 vols. New York: International Publishers.

Foner, Philip S., and Josephine F. Pacheco. 1984. *Three Who Dared: Prudence Crandall, Margaret Douglass, Myrtilla Miner—Champions of Antebellum Black Education.* Westport, CT: Greenwood Press.

Foot, Michael, and Isaac Kramnick, eds. 1987. *The Thomas Paine Reader.* London: Penguin.

Forster, C. H. 1954. *The Rungless Ladder: Harriet Beecher Stowe and New England Puritanism.* Durham, NC: Duke University Press.

Foster, Frances Smith. 1979. *Witnessing Slavery: The Development of Ante-bellum Slave Narratives.* Madison: University of Wisconsin Press.

Fox-Genovese, Elizabeth. 1991. *Feminism without Illusions.* Chapel Hill: University of North Carolina Press.

———. 1988. *Within the Plantation Household.* Chapel Hill: University of North Carolina Press.

Franklin, John H. 1943. *The Free Negro in North Carolina, 1790–1863.* Chapel Hill: University of North Carolina Press.

Franklin, John H., and Alfred Moss. 1994. *From Slavery to Freedom: A History of African Americans.* New York: McGraw Hill.

Frederick, Duke. 1966. "The Second Confiscation Act: A Chapter of Civil War Politics." M.A. thesis, Department of History, University of Chicago, Chicago.

Frederickson, George. 1981. *White Supremacy: A Comparative Study in American and South African History.* New York: Oxford University Press.

Freehling, Alison Goodyear. 1982. *Drift toward Dissolution: The Virginia Slavery Debate of 1831–1832.* Baton Rouge: Louisiana State University Press.

Freehling, William W. 1965. *Prelude to Civil War: The Nullification Controversy in South Carolina, 1816–1836.* New York: Oxford University Press.

———. 1990. *The Road to Disunion: Secessionists at Bay, 1776–1854.* New York: Oxford University Press.

Frey, Sylvia. 1991. *Water from the Rock: Black Resistance in a Revolutionary Age.* Princeton, NJ: Princeton University Press.

Fridlington, Robert. 1995. *The Reconstruction Court, 1864–1888.* Danbury, CT: Grolier.

Friedman, Lawrence J. 1982. *Gregarious Saints: Self and Community in American Abolitionism, 1830–1870.* New York: Cambridge University Press.

Friedman, Lawrence M. 1973. *A History of American Law.* New York: Simon and Schuster.

Frothingham, Octavius Brooks. 1969. *Gerrit Smith: A Biography.* New York: Negro Universities Press.

Fry, Gladys-Marie. 1975. *Night Riders in Black Folk History.* Knoxville: University of Tennessee Press.

Fuller, Edmond. 1971. *Prudence Crandall: An Incident of Racism in Nineteenth-Century Connecticut.* Middletown, CT: Wesleyan University Press.

Gara, Larry. 1961. *The Liberty Line: The Legend of the Underground Railroad.* Lexington: University of Kentucky Press.

———. 1961. "William Still and the Underground Railroad." *Pennsylvania History* 1: 33–44.

Gates, Henry L., Jr. 1987. *Figures in Black: Words, Signs, and the "Racial" Self.* New York: Oxford University Press.

Gates, Henry Louis, Jr. 1987. "Introduction." In *The Classic Slave Narratives.* Edited by Henry Louis Gates, Jr. New York: Penguin Books.

Geggus, David P. 1989. "Racial Equality, Slavery, and Colonial Secession during the Constituent Assembly." *American Historical Review* 94 (December): 1290–1309.

Genovese, Eugene. 1980. *From Rebellion to Revolution: Afro-American Slave Revolts in the Making of the Modern World.* Baton Rouge: Louisiana State University Press.

———. 1974. *Roll, Jordan, Roll: The World the Slaves Made.* New York: Pantheon Books.

George, Carol V. R. 1973. *Segregated Sabbaths: Richard Allen and the Emergence of Independent Black Churches, 1760–1840.* New York: Oxford University Press.

Georgia. 1861. *The Code of the State of Georgia.* Prepared by R. H. Clark, T. R. R. Cobb, and D. Irwin. Atlanta: Franklin Steam Publishing House.

———. 1867. *The Code of the State of Georgia.* Revised and corrected by David Irwin. Atlanta: Franklin Steam Publishing House.

Georgia Writers' Project. 1940. "Drums and Shadows." Athens: University of Georgia Press.

Gerteis, Louis S. 1973. *From Contraband to Freedom: Federal Policy toward Southern Blacks, 1861–1865.* Westport, CT: Greenwood Press.

Gilmore, Al-Tony, ed. 1978. *Revisiting Blassingame's "The Slave Community": The Scholars Respond.* Westport, CT: Greenwood Press.

Glatthaar, Joseph. 1990. *Forged in Battle: The Civil War Alliance of Black Soldiers and White Officers*. New York: Free Press.

Glick, Wendell, ed. 1972. *The Writings of Henry D. Thoreau: Reform Papers*. Princeton, NJ: Princeton University Press.

Going, Allen J. 1957. "The South and the Blair Education Bill." *Mississippi Valley Historical Review* 44 (2): 267–290.

Gomez, Michael. 1994. "Muslims in Early America." *Journal of Southern History* 60 (4): 671–710.

Goodwine, Marquetta L. 1995. *Gullah/Geechee: The Survival of Africa's Seed in the Winds of the Diaspora*. Vol. 1, *St. Helena's Serenity*. New York: Kinship Publications.

Gossett, Thomas. 1965. *Race: The History of an Idea in America*. New York: Schocken.

Gougeon, Len. 1995. "Thoreau and Reform." In *The Cambridge Companion to Henry David Thoreau*. Edited by Joel Myerson. Cambridge: Cambridge University Press.

Grant, Mary H. 1994. *Private Woman, Public Person: An Account of the Life of Julia Ward Howe from 1819 to 1868*. Brooklyn, NY: Carlson.

Green, Fletcher M. 1930. *Constitutional Development in the South Atlantic States, 1776–1860: A Study in the Evolution of Democracy*. Chapel Hill: University of North Carolina Press.

Green, Richard L., ed. 1985. *A Salute to Black Scientists and Inventors*. New York: Empak.

Greenberg, Kenneth S. 1996. *The Confessions of Nat Turner and Related Documents*. Boston: St. Martin's.

Greene, Helen Ione. 1946. "Politics in Georgia, 1853–1854: The Ordeal of Howell Cobb." *Georgia Historical Quarterly* 30 (2): 185–211.

Griffith, Cyril F. 1975. *The African Dream: Martin R. Delany and the Emergence of Pan-African Thought*. University Park: Pennsylvania State University Press.

Guilds, John C. 1992. *Simms: A Literary Life*. Fayetteville: University of Arkansas Press.

Guillory, James Denny. 1968. "The Pro-Slavery Arguments of Dr. Samuel A. Cartwright." *Louisiana History* 9 (4): 209–227.

Gummere, Amelia Mott. 1922. *The Journal and Essays of John Woolman*. New York: Macmillan.

Gunther, Gerald, ed. 1969. *John Marshall's Defense of McCulloch v. Maryland*. Stanford, CA: Stanford University Press.

Gutman, Herbert G. 1976. *The Black Family in Slavery and Freedom, 1750–1925*. New York: Pantheon.

———. 1975. *Slavery and the Numbers Game: A Critique of Time on the Cross*. Urbana: University of Illinois Press.

Hadden, Sally E. 1993. "Law Enforcement in a New Nation: Slave Patrols and Public Authority in the Old South, 1700–1865." Ph.D. dissertation, Department of History, Harvard University, Cambridge, MA.

Hahn, Steven. 1983. *The Roots of Southern Populism: Yeomen Farmers and the Transformation of the Georgia Backcountry*. New York: Oxford University Press.

Hall, Gwendolyn Midlo. 1992. *Africans in Colonial Louisiana: The Development of Afro-Creole Culture in the Eighteenth Century*. Baton Rouge: Louisiana State University Press.

Hall, Kermit L.; William M. Wicek; and Paul Finkelman. 1996. *American Legal History: Cases and Materials*. New York: Oxford University Press.

Hall, Mark. 1982. "The Proslavery Thought of J. D. B. DeBow: A Practical Man's Guide to Economics." *Southern Studies* 21 (Spring): 97–104.

Hamer, Philip M. 1935. "British Consuls and the Negro Seamen's Acts, 1850–1860." *Journal of Southern History* 1 (2): 138–168.

———. 1935. "Great Britain, the United States, and the Negro Seamen's Acts, 1822–1848." *Journal of Southern History* 1 (1): 3–28.

Hamilton, Alexander; James Madison; and John Jay. 1961. *The Federalist Papers*. Edited by Clinton L. Rossiter. New York: Mentor Books.

Hamilton, Holman. 1964. *Prologue to Conflict: The Crisis and Compromise of 1850*. Lexington: University of Kentucky Press.

Hancock, Harold B. 1973. "Mary Ann Shadd: Negro Editor, Educator, and Lawyer." *Delaware History* 15 (3): 187–194.

Hansen, Debra Gold. 1993. *Strained Sisterhood: Gender and Class in the Boston Female Anti-Slavery Society*. Amherst: University of Massachusetts Press.

Harding, Walter. 1982. *The Days of Henry Thoreau: A Biography*. New York: Dover Publications.

Harlan, Louis R. 1972. *Booker T. Washington: The Making of a Black Leader*. New York: Oxford University Press.

Harlow, Ralph Volney. 1939. *Gerrit Smith: Philanthropist and Reformer*. New York: Henry Holt.

Harper, Ida Husted. 1899. *The Life and Work of Susan B. Anthony*. Indianapolis, IN: Bowen-Merrill.

Harrington, Spencer. 1993. "Bones and Bureaucrats: New York City's Great Cemetery Imbroglio." *Archaeology* 2: 28–38.

Harris, Julia Collier. 1918. *The Life and Letters of Joel Chandler Harris*. New York: Houghton Mifflin.

Harrison, Lowell. 1949. "Thomas Roderick Dew: Philosopher of the Old South." *Virginia Magazine of History and Biography* 57 (October): 390–404.

Hatch, Alden. 1969. *The Byrds of Virginia*. New York: Holt, Rinehart and Winston.

Hatcher, William E. 1908. *John Jasper: The Unmatched Negro Philosopher and Preacher*. New York: F. H. Revell.

Haviland, Laura S. 1881. *A Woman's Life-Work: Labors and Experiences of Laura S. Haviland*. Chicago: Publishing Association of Friends.

Hayden, J. Carleton. 1971. "Conversion and Control: Dilemma of Episcopalians in Providing for the Religious Instructions of Slaves, Charleston, South Carolina, 1845–1860." *Historical Magazine of the Protestant Episcopal Church* 40 (June 2): 143–171.

Hays, Elinor Rice. 1961. *Morning Star: A Biography of Lucy Stone, 1818–1893*. New York: Harcourt, Brace and World.

Haywood, Jacquelyn S. 1974. *The American Missionary Association in Louisiana during Reconstruction*. Ph.D. dissertation, Department of History, University of California–Los Angeles. Ann Arbor, MI: University Microfilms.

Heimert, Alan. 1966. *Religion and the American Mind: From the Great Awakening to the Revolution*. Cambridge, MA: Harvard University Press.

Heitmann, John Alfred. 1987. *The Modernization of the Louisiana Sugar Industry, 1830–1910*. Baton Rouge: Louisiana State University Press.

Helper, Hinton R. 1968. *The Impending Crisis of the South and How to Meet It*. Edited by George Frederickson. 1857. Reprint, Cambridge, MA: Harvard University Press.

Henshaw, Henry W. 1910. "Slavery." In *Handbook of American Indians North of Mexico*. Edited by Frederick W. Hodge. Washington, DC: Bureau of American Ethnology.

Hersh, Blanche Glassman. 1978. *The Slavery of Sex: Feminist Abolitionist in America*. Urbana: University of Illinois Press.

Higginbotham, A. Leon. 1978. *In the Matter of Color: Race and the American Legal Process*. New York: Oxford University Press.

Hine, Darlene Clark; Elsa Barkley Brown; and Rosalyn Terborg-Penn, eds. 1993. *Black Women in America: An Historical Encyclopedia*. Brooklyn, NY: Carlson.

Hinks, Peter P. 1997. *To Awaken My Afflicted Brethren: David Walker and the Problem of Antebellum Slave Resistance*. University Park: Pennsylvania State University Press.

Hinton, Richard J., ed. 1898. *Poems by Richard Realf: Poet, Soldier, Workman*. New York: Funk and Wagnalls.

Hodges, Graham, ed. 1996. *The Black Loyalist Directory: African Americans in Exile after the American Revolution*. New York: Garland.

Holmes, Jack D. L. 1970. "The Abortive Slave Revolt at Pointe Coupee Louisiana, 1795." *Louisiana History* 11: 341–362.

Holmes, Urban. 1930. "A Study of Negro Onomastics." *American Speech* 5: 463–467.

Holt, Michael F. 1992. *Political Parties and American Political Development from the Age of Jackson to the Age of Lincoln*. Baton Rouge: Louisiana State University Press.

Howard, John Henry. 1827. *The Laws of the British Colonies in the West Indies and Other Parts of America Concerning Real and Personal Property and Manumission of Slaves, with a View of the Constitution of Each Colony*. London: Joseph Butterworth and Son.

Howe, Marc A. DeWolfe. 1932. "Thomas Wentworth Higginson." *Dictionary of American Biography*. Edited by Dumas Malone. New York: Charles Scribner's and Sons.

Hoyt, Edwin. 1970. *The Amistad Affair*. New York: Abelard-Schuman.

Hudson, Harold Gossie. 1976. "John Chavis." In *Dictionary of Negro Biography*. Edited by Rayford W. Logan and Michael R. Winston. New York: Norton.

Huggins, Nathan Irvin. 1977. *Black Odyssey: The Afro-American Ordeal in Slavery*. New York: Pantheon Books.

Jacoway, Elizabeth. 1980. *Yankee Missionaries in the South: The Penn School Experiment*. Baton Rouge: Louisiana State University Press.

James, Isaac. 1954. *"The Sun Do Move": The Story of the Life of John Jasper*. Richmond, VA: Whittet and Shepperson.

Jay, William. 1853. "Introductory Remarks to the Reproof of the American Church Contained in the Recent *History of the Protestant Episcopal Church in America* by the Bishop of Oxford." In *Miscellaneous Writings on Slavery*. Boston: John P. Jewett.

Jefferson, Thomas. 1955. *Notes on Virginia*. Edited by William Peden. Chapel Hill: University of North Carolina Press.

———. 1950–. *The Papers of Thomas Jefferson*. 20 vols. Edited by Julian P. Boyd. Princeton, NJ: Princeton University Press.

Jeffreys, M. D. W. 1948. "Names of American Negro Slaves." *American Anthropologist* 50: 571–573.

Jennings, Thelma. 1980. *The Nashville Convention: Southern Movement for Unity, 1848–1851*. Memphis, TN: Memphis State University Press.

Johannsen, Robert. 1991. *Lincoln, the South, and Slavery: The Political Dimension*. Baton Rouge: Louisiana State University Press.

Johnson, Clifton Herman. 1958. *The American Missionary Association, 1846–1861: A Study of Chris-*

tian Abolitionism. Ph.D. dissertation, Department of History, University of North Carolina at Chapel Hill. Ann Arbor, MI: University Microfilms.

Johnson, Harry H. 1910. *The Negro in the New World.* London: Methuen.

Johnson, Michael P., and James L. Roark. 1984. *Black Masters: A Free Family of Color in the Old South.* New York: W. W. Norton.

Johnson, Michael P., and James L. Roark, eds. 1984. *No Chariot Let Down: Charleston's Free People of Color on the Eve of the Civil War.* New York: Norton.

Johnson, Rossiter. 1879. "Richard Realf." *Lippincott's Magazine* 3: 293–300.

Johnson, Vicki Vaughn. 1992. *The Men and the Vision of the Southern Commercial Conventions, 1845–1871.* Columbia: University of Missouri Press.

Jones, Alfred Haworth. 1983. "Joel Chandler Harris: Tales of Uncle Remus." *American History Illustrated* 18 (3): 34–39.

Jones, Bessie, and Bess Lomax Hawes. 1987. *Step It Down: Games, Plays, Songs, and Stories from the Afro-American Heritage.* Athens: University of Georgia Press.

Jones, Howard. 1987. *Mutiny on the* Amistad: *The Saga of a Slave Revolt and Its Impact on American Abolition, Law, and Diplomacy.* New York: Oxford University Press.

———. 1977. *To the Webster-Ashburton Treaty: A Study in Anglo-American Relations, 1783–1843.* Chapel Hill: University of North Carolina Press.

Jones-Jackson, Patricia. 1987. *When Roots Die: Endangered Traditions on the Sea Islands.* Athens: University of Georgia Press.

Jordan, Winthrop D. 1968. *White over Black: American Attitudes toward the Negro, 1550–1812.* Baltimore: Penguin Books.

Jordon, Weymouth T. 1958. *Rebels in the Making: Planters' Conventions and Southern Propaganda.* Tuscaloosa, AL: Confederate Publishing.

Joyner, Charles. 1984. *Down by the Riverside: A South Carolina Slave Community.* Urbana: University of Illinois Press.

Karcher, Carolyn L. 1994. *The First Woman in the Republic: A Cultural Biography of Lydia Maria Child.* Durham, NC: Duke University Press.

Katz, William L. 1990. *Breaking the Chains: African-American Slave Resistance.* New York: Atheneum.

Keane, John. 1995. *Tom Paine: A Political Life.* London: Bloomsbury.

Keckley, Elizabeth. 1868. *Behind the Scenes: Thirty Years a Slave and Four Years in the White House.* New York: G. W. Carleton.

Keene, Jesse L. 1961. *The Peace Convention of 1861.* Tuscaloosa, AL: Confederate Publishing.

Kehoe, Alice Beck. 1992. *North American Indians: A Comprehensive Account.* Englewood Cliffs, NJ: Prentice-Hall.

Kelso, William M. 1984. *Kingsmill Plantations, 1619–1800: Archaeology of Country Life in Colonial Virginia.* San Diego: Academic Press.

Kemble, Frances Anne. 1863. *Journal of a Residence on a Georgian Plantation in 1838–1839.* New York: Harper and Brothers.

Kerr, Andrea Moore. 1992. *Lucy Stone: Speaking Out for Equality.* New Brunswick, NJ: Rutgers University Press.

Kim, Hyong-In. 1990. "Rural Slavery in Antebellum South Carolina and Early Choson Korea." Ph.D. dissertation. Department of History, University of New Mexico, Albuquerque, New Mexico.

King, Wilma. 1995. *Stolen Childhood: Slave Youth in Nineteenth Century America.* Bloomington: Indiana University Press.

Kirkham, Bruce E. 1977. *The Building of Uncle Tom's Cabin,* Knoxville: University of Tennessee Press.

Kirwan, Albert D. 1962. *John J. Crittenden: The Struggle for the Union.* Lexington: University of Kentucky Press.

Klein, Aaron E. 1971. *The Hidden Contributors: Black Scientists and Inventors in America.* New York: Doubleday and Company.

Klein, Herbert S. 1967. *Slavery in the Americas: A Comparative Study of Virginia and Cuba.* Chicago: University of Chicago Press.

Knight, Edgar W. 1930. "Notes on John Chavis." *North Carolina Historical Review* 7: 326–345.

Koger, Larry. 1985. *Black Slaveowners: Free Black Slave Masters in South Carolina, 1790–1860.* Jefferson, NC: McFarland.

Kolchin, Peter. 1993. *American Slavery, 1619–1877.* New York: Hill and Wang.

———. 1987. *Unfree Labor: American Slavery and Russian Serfdom.* Cambridge, MA: Harvard University Press.

Korn, Bertram Wallace. 1973. *Jews and Negro Slavery in the Old South.* In *Jews in the South.* Edited by Leonard Dinnerstein and Mary Dale Palsson. Baton Rouge: Louisiana State University Press.

Kotlikoff, Laurence J., and Sebastian Pinera. 1977. "The Old South's Stake in the Inter-Regional Movement of Slaves, 1850–1860." *Journal of Economic History* 37 (2): 434–450.

Kraditor, Aileen S. 1969. *Means and Ends in American Abolitionism: Garrison and His Critics on Strategy and Tactics, 1834–1850.* New York: Pantheon Books.

Kurland, Phillip B., and Lerner, Ralph. 1987. *The Founders' Constitution.* Chicago: University of Chicago Press.

Lambert, Frank. 1994. *Peddler in Divinity: George Whitefield and the Transatlantic Revivals.* Princeton, NJ: Princeton University Press.

Lane, Ann J., ed. 1971. *The Debate over Slavery: Stanley Elkins and His Critics.* Urbana: University of Illinois Press.

Lane, Margaret. 1972. *Frances Wright and the "Great Experiment."* Manchester, Eng.: Manchester University Press.

Larison, Cornelius Wilson. 1988. *Sylvia Dubois: A Biografy of the Slav Who Whipt Her Mistres and Gand Her Fredom.* Edited by Jared C. Lobdell. New York: Oxford University Press.

Lauber, Almon Wheeler. 1969. *Indian Slavery in Colonial Times within the Present Limits of the United States.* New York: AMS Press.

Laurie, Bruce. 1989. *Artisans into Workers: Labor in Nineteenth Century America.* New York: Noonday Press.

Leonard, Ira M., and Robert D. Parmet. 1971. *American Nativism, 1830–1860.* New York: Van Nostrand Reinhold.

Lerner, Gerda. 1964. *The Grimké Sisters from South Carolina.* Boston: Houghton Mifflin.

Levine, Lawrence W. 1977. *Black Culture and Black Consciousness: Afro-American Folk Thought from Slavery to Freedom.* Oxford: Oxford University Press.

Levine, Robert. 1997. *Martin R. Delany, Frederick Douglass, and the Politics of Representative Identity.* Chapel Hill: University of North Carolina Press.

Levy, Leonard W., and Dennis J. Mahoney, eds. 1987. *The Framing of the Constitution.* New York: Macmillan.

Lewis, David Levering. 1993. *W. E. B. DuBois: Biography of a Race.* New York: Henry Holt.

Lindsay, Arnett. 1920. "Diplomatic Relations between the United States and Great Britain Bearing on the Return of Negro Slaves, 1788–1828." *Journal of Negro History* 5: 261–278.

Littlefield, Daniel C. 1991. *Rice and Slaves.* Urbana: University of Illinois Press.

Lively, Donald E. 1992. *The Constitution and Race.* New York: Praeger.

Livermore, George. 1970. *An Historical Research Respecting the Opinions of the Founders of the Republic on Negroes as Slaves, as Citizens, and as Soldiers.* New York: Augustus M. Kelley.

Llowance, Mason I. Jr.; Ellen E. Westbrook; and R. C. DeProspo, eds. 1994. *The Stowe Debate: Rhetorical Strategies in Uncle Tom's Cabin.* Amherst: University of Massachusetts Press.

Lloyd, Arthur Young. 1939. *The Slavery Controversy, 1831–1860.* Chapel Hill: University of North Carolina Press.

Lloyd, Christopher. 1949. *The Navy and the Slave Trade.* London: Longmans.

Lofton, John. 1964. *Insurrection in South Carolina: The Turbulent World of Denmark Vesey.* Yellow Springs, OH: Antioch Press.

Logan, Shirley Wilson. 1995. *With Pen and Voice: A Critical Anthology of Nineteenth-Century African-American Women.* Carbondale: Southern Illinois University Press.

Loveland, Anne C. 1966. "Evangelicalism and 'Immediate Emancipation' in American Antislavery Thought." *Journal of Southern History* 32 (2): 172–188.

Lumpkin, Katharine Du Pre. 1974. *The Emancipation of Angelina Grimké.* Chapel Hill: University of North Carolina Press.

Luraghi, Raimondo. 1978. *The Rise and Fall of the Plantation South.* New York: New Viewpoints.

Lutz, Alma. 1968. *Crusade for Freedom: Women in the Antislavery Movement.* Boston: Beacon Press.

Mabee, Carlton. 1970. *Black Freedom: The Nonviolent Abolitionists from 1830 through the Civil War.* New York: Macmillan.

———. 1993. *Sojourner Truth: Slave, Prophet, Legend.* New York: New York University Press.

McAdoo, Bill. 1983. *Pre-Civil War Black Nationalism.* New York: David Walker Press.

McClendon, R. Earl. 1933. "The *Amistad* Claims: Inconsistencies of Policy." *Political Science Quarterly* 48: 386–412.

McCurry, Stephanie. 1995. *Masters of Small Worlds: Yeoman Households, Gender Relations, and the Political Culture of the Antebellum South Carolina Low Country.* New York: Oxford University Press.

McFeely, William S. 1991. *Frederick Douglass.* New York: W. W. Norton.

McGowan, James A. 1977. *Station Master on the Underground Railroad: The Life and Letters of Thomas Garrett.* Moylan, PA: Whimsie Press.

McManus, Edgar. 1966. *A History of Negro Slavery in New York.* Syracuse, NY: Syracuse University Press.

McNitt, Frank. 1972. *Navajo Wars: Military Campaigns, Slave Raids, and Reprisals.* Albuquerque: University of New Mexico Press.

McPherson, James. 1964. *The Struggle for Equality: Abolitionists and the Negro in the Civil War and Reconstruction.* Princeton, NJ: Princeton University Press.

McReynolds, Edwin C. 1988. *The Seminoles.* Norman: University of Oklahoma Press.

Maddex, Jack P., Jr. 1979. "'The Southern Apostasy' Revisited: The Significance of Proslavery Christianity." *Marxist Perspectives* 2 (Fall): 132–141.

Mails, Thomas E. 1992. *The Cherokee People: The*

Story of the Cherokees from Earliest Origins to Contemporary Times. Tulsa, OK: Council Oaks Books.

Maizlish, Stephen E. 1982. "The Meaning of Nativism and the Crisis of the Union; The Know Nothing Movement in the Antebellum North." In *Essays on American Antebellum Politics, 1840–1860.* Edited by Stephen E. Maizlish and John J. Kushma. College Station: Texas A & M University Press.

Malin, James C. 1942. *John Brown and the Legend of Fifty-six.* Philadelphia: American Philosophical Society.

Maltz, Earl M. 1990. *Civil Rights, the Constitution, and Congress, 1863–1869.* Lawrence: University Press of Kansas.

Manning, William, ed. 1942. *Diplomatic Correspondence of the United States: Canadian Relations, 1794–1860.* Washington, DC: Carnegie Endowment for International Peace.

Marambaud, Pierre. 1971. *William Byrd of Westover.* Charlottesville: University of Virginia Press.

Martin, Berbard, and Mark Spurrell. 1962. *The Journal of A Slave Trader, John Newton, 1750–1754.* London: Epworth Press.

Mason, Julian D., Jr., ed. 1989. *The Poems of Phillis Wheatley.* Chapel Hill: University of North Carolina Press.

Mathew, William M. 1988. *Edmund Ruffin and the Crisis of Slavery in the Old South: The Failure of Agricultural Reform.* Athens: University of Georgia Press.

Mathews, Donald G. 1977. *Religion in the Old South.* Chicago: University of Chicago Press.

May, Robert E. 1985. *John A. Quitman: Old South Crusader.* Baton Rouge: Louisiana State University Press.

———. 1973. *The Southern Dream of a Caribbean Empire, 1854–1861.* Baton Rouge: Louisiana State University Press.

Mayfield, John. 1979. *Rehearsal for Republicanism: Free Soil and the Politics of Antislavery.* Port Washington, NY: Kennikat Press.

Meade, George P. 1946. "A Negro Scientist of Slavery Days." *Scientific Monthly* 62: 317–326.

Meadows, Henry H. 1914. "The Police Control of the Slave in South Carolina." Unpublished manuscript, Emory University, Atlanta, GA.

Meier, August. 1963. *Negro Thought in America, 1880–1915.* Ann Arbor: University of Michigan Press.

Meltzer, Milton, and Patricia G. Holland, eds. 1982. *Lydia Maria Child: Selected Letters, 1817–1880.* Amherst: University of Massachusetts Press.

Mencken, H. L. 1955. *The American Language.* 4th edition. New York: Knopf.

Merrill, Walter M. 1963. *Against Wind and Tide: A Biography of William Lloyd Garrison.* Cambridge, MA: Harvard University Press.

Merritt, Elizabeth. 1923. *James Henry Hammond, 1807–1864.* Baltimore: Johns Hopkins University Press.

Miller, Edward A. 1995. *Gullah Statesman: Robert Smalls from Slavery to Congress, 1839–1915.* Columbia: University of South Carolina Press.

Miller, Floyd J. 1975. *The Search for a Black Nationality: Black Colonization and Emigration, 1787–1863.* Urbana: University of Illinois Press.

Miller, John C. 1977. *The Wolf by the Ears: Thomas Jefferson and Slavery.* New York: Norton.

Miller, M. Sammy. 1975. "Legend of a Kidnapper." *Crisis* 82 (April): 118–120.

Miller, Randall M., and John David Smith, eds. 1988. *Dictionary of Afro-American Slavery.* Westport, CT: Greenwood.

Miller, William Lee. 1996. *Arguing about Slavery: The Great Battle in the United States Congress.* New York: Knopf.

Mitchell, Betty. 1981. *Edmund Ruffin, a Biography.* Bloomington: Indiana University Press.

Mohr, Clarence L. 1986. *On the Threshold of Freedom: Masters and Slaves in Civil War Georgia.* Athens: University of Georgia Press.

Montgomery, Michael, ed. 1994. *The Crucible of Carolina: Essays in the Development of Gullah Language and Culture.* Athens: University of Georgia Press.

Mooney, James L., ed. 1991. *Dictionary of American Naval Fighting Ships.* Washington, DC: Naval Historical Center.

Moore, Wayne D. 1996. *Constitutional Rights and Powers of the People.* Princeton, NJ: Princeton University Press.

Morgan, Edmund. 1975. *American Slavery, American Freedom: The Ordeal of Colonial Virginia.* New York: Norton.

Morris, Christopher. 1988. "An Event in Community Organization: The Mississippi Slave Insurrection Scare of 1835." *Journal of Social History* 22 (3): 93–111.

Morris, Richard B. 1946. *Government and Labor in Early America.* New York: Columbia University Press.

Morris, Robert. 1981. *Reading, 'Riting, and Reconstruction: The Education of Freedmen in the South, 1861–1870.* Chicago: University of Chicago Press.

Morris, Thomas D. 1974. *Free Men All: The Personal Liberty Laws of the North, 1780–1861.* Baltimore: Johns Hopkins University Press.

———. 1996. *Southern Slavery and the Law, 1619–1860.* Chapel Hill: University of North Carolina Press.

Morrison, Chaplain W. 1967. *Democratic Politics and Sectionalism: The Wilmot Proviso Controversy.* Chapel Hill: University of North Carolina Press.

Morriss, Andrew P. 1995. "'This State Will Soon Have Plenty of Laws'—Lessons from One Hundred Years of Codification in Montana." *Montana Law Review* 56: 359–450.

Morton, Patricia, ed. 1996. *Discovering the Women in Slavery: Emancipating Perspectives on the American Past.* Athens: University of Georgia Press.

Moulton, Phillips P. "The Influence of the Writings of John Woolman." *Quaker History: The Bulletin of the Friends Historical Association* 61 (2): 3–13.

Mullin, Michael. 1992. *Africa in America: Slave Acculturation and Resistance in the American South and the British Caribbean, 1736–1831.* Urbana: University of Illinois Press.

Munroe, John A. 1979. *History of Delaware.* Newark: University of Delaware Press.

Murphy, Larry, J.; Gordon Melton; and Gary L. Ward, eds. 1993. *Encyclopedia of African-American Religions.* New York: Garland.

Myerson, Joel, ed. 1984. *The Transcendentalists: A Review of Research and Criticism.* New York: Modern Language Association of America.

Nash, Gary B. 1989. "New Light on Richard Allen: The Early Years of Freedom." *William and Mary Quarterly* 46 (2): 332–340.

Nash, Gary B., et al. 1994. *The American People: Creating a Nation and a Society.* New York: HarperCollins.

Nelson, William Edward. 1995. *The Fourteenth Amendment: From Political Principle to Judicial Doctrine.* Cambridge, MA: Harvard University Press.

Newman, Richard, ed. 1990. *Black Preacher to White America: The Collected Writings of Lemuel Haynes, 1774–1833.* Brooklyn, NY: Carlson.

Nichols, Charles H. 1963. *Many Thousand Gone: The Ex-Slaves' Account of Their Bondage and Freedom.* Bloomington: Indiana University Press.

Nott, Josiah Clark. 1849. *Connection between the Biblical and Physical History of Man.* New York: Bartlett and Welford.

Nott, Josiah Clark, and George R. Gliddon. 1857. *Indigenous Races of the Earth.* Philadelphia: Lippincott.

———. 1854. *Types of Mankind.* Philadelphia: Lippincott, Grambo, and Company.

Novak, John E., and Ronald D. Rotunda. 1991. *Constitutional Law.* St. Paul, MN: West Publishing.

Nye, Russell B. 1963. *Fettered Freedom: Civil Liberties and the Slave Controversy, 1830–1860.* East Lansing: Michigan State University Press.

Oakes, James. 1982. *The Ruling Race.* New York: Knopf.

Oates, Stephen B. 1990. *The Fires of Jubilee: Nat Turner's Fierce Rebellion.* New York: Harper and Row.

———. 1970. *To Purge This Land with Blood: A Biography of John Brown.* New York: Harper and Row.

Odum, Howard W. 1936. *Southern Regions of the United States.* Chapel Hill: North Carolina University Press.

Oglethorpe, James Edward. 1994. *The Publications of James Edward Oglethorpe.* Edited by Rodney M. Baine. Athens: University of Georgia Press.

Olmsted, Denison. 1846. *Memoir of Eli Whitney, Esq.* New York: Arno Press.

O'Neale, Sondra A. 1985. "Challenge to Wheatley's Critics: There Was No Other 'Game' in Town." *Journal of Negro Education* 54 (4): 500–511.

Onuf, Peter. 1987. *Statehood and Union: A History of the Northwest Ordinance.* Bloomington: Indiana University Press.

Owsley, Frank L. 1949. *Plain Folk of the Old South.* Baton Rouge: Louisiana State University Press.

Painter, Nell Irvin. 1988. "Martin R. Delany: Elitism and Black Nationalism." In *Black Leaders of the Nineteenth Century.* Edited by Leon Litwack and August Meier. Urbana: University of Illinois Press.

———. 1996. *Sojourner Truth: A Life, a Symbol.* New York: W. W. Norton.

Pasternak, Martin B. 1995. *Rise Now and Fly to Arms: The Life of Henry Highland Garnet.* New York: Garland.

Paustian, P. Robert. 1978. "The Evolution of Personal Naming Practices among American Blacks." *Names* 26 (1): 177–191.

Payne, Charles Edward. 1938. *Josiah B. Grinnell.* Iowa City: State Historical Society of Iowa.

Payne, Daniel Alexander. 1891. *History of the African Methodist Episcopal Church.* Nashville, TN: Publishing House of the A.M.E. Sunday School Union.

Pearson, Edward A. 1992. "From Stono to Vesey: Slavery, Resistance, and Ideology in South Carolina, 1739–1822." Ph.D. dissertation, Department of History, University of Wisconsin-Madison, Madison, Wisconsin.

Pease, Jane H. 1969. "The Freshness of Fanaticism: Abby Kelley Foster." Ph.D. dissertation, Department of History, University of Rochester, Rochester, New York.

Pease, Jane H., and William H. 1975. *The Fugitive Slave Law and Anthony Burns: A Problem of Law Enforcement.* Philadelphia: J. B. Lippincott.

———. 1990. *They Who Would be Free: Blacks' Search for Freedom, 1830–1861.* Chicago: University of Chicago Press.

Pease, William H., and Jane H. 1971. "The Negro Convention Movement." In *Key Issues in the Afro-American Experience*. Edited by Nathan I. Higgins et al. New York: Harcourt Brace Jovanovich.

Peck, Abraham J. 1987. "'That Other Peculiar Institution': Jews and Judaism in the Nineteenth Century South." *Modern Judaism* 7: 99–114.

Pemberton, Doris Hollis. 1983. *Juneteenth at Comanche Crossing*. Austin, TX: Eakin Publications.

Penick, James L., Jr. 1981. *The Great Western Land Pirate: John A. Murrell in Legend and History*. Columbia: University of Missouri Press.

Perdue, Charles L., et al. 1976. *Weevils in the Wheat: Interviews with Virginia Ex-Slaves*. Charlottesville: University Press of Virginia.

Perdue, Theda. 1979. "The Development of Plantation Slavery before Removal." In *The Cherokee Indian Nation, a Troubled History*. Edited by Duane H. King. Knoxville: University of Tennessee Press.

———. 1996. "Slavery." In *Encyclopedia of North American Indians*. Edited by Frederick E. Hoxie. New York: Houghton Mifflin.

———. 1979. *Slavery and the Evolution of Cherokee Society, 1540–1866*. Knoxville: University of Tennessee Press.

Perry, Michael. 1994. *The Constitution in the Courts: Law or Politics?* New York: Oxford University Press.

Perskey, Joseph. 1992. "Unequal Exchange and Dependency Theory in George Fitzhugh." *History of Political Economy* 24 (1) (Spring): 117–128.

Peterson, Merrill. 1987. *The Great Triumvirate: Webster, Clay, and Calhoun*. New York: Oxford University Press.

———. 1962. *The Jefferson Image in the American Mind*. New York: Oxford University Press.

Phillips, Ulrich B. 1918. *American Negro Slavery*. Gloucester, MA: D. Appleton and Company

Pinkney, Alphonso. 1976. *Red, Black, and Green: Black Nationalism in the United States*. Cambridge: Cambridge University Press.

Post, C. Gordon, ed. 1953. *A Disquisition on Government and Selections from the Discourse*. New York: Liberal Arts Press.

Potter, David M. 1976. *The Impending Crisis, 1848–1861*. New York: Harper and Row.

Price, Richard. 1983. *First Time: The Historical Vision of an Afro-American People*. Baltimore: Johns Hopkins University Press.

Puckett, Newbell N. 1938. "American Negro Names." *Journal of Negro History* 23: 35–48.

———. 1975. *Black Names in America*. Boston: G. K. Hall.

———. 1937. "Names of American Negro Slaves." In *Studies in the Science of Society*. Edited by G. P. Murdock. New Haven, CT: Yale University Press.

Pulis, John W., ed. 1997. *Moving On: Black Loyalists in the Afro-Atlantic World*. New York: Garland.

Quarles, Benjamin. 1974. *Allies For Freedom: Blacks and John Brown*. New York:

———. 1969. *Black Abolitionists*. New York: Oxford University Press.

———. 1968. *Frederick Douglass*. New York: Oxford University Press.

———. 1962. *Lincoln and the Negro*. New York: Oxford University Press.

———. 1961. *The Negro in the American Revolution*. Chapel Hill: University of North Carolina Press.

———. 1953. *The Negro in the Civil War*. Boston: Little, Brown.

Raboteau, Albert J. 1978. *Slave Religion*. New York: Oxford University Press.

Randell, Willard Sterne. 1993. *Thomas Jefferson: A Life*. New York: Henry Holt.

Rawick, George P., ed. 1972. *The American Slave: A Composite Autobiography*. Westport, CT: Greenwood.

Rayback, Joseph G. 1971. *Free Soil: The Election of 1848*. Lexington: University Press of Kentucky.

Realf, Richard. 1860. Testimony in "Mason Report." In U.S. Congress, Senate. *Committee Reports, 1859–60*. January 11–21: 91–113.

Ream, Debbie Williams. 1993. "Mine Eyes Have Seen the Glory." *American History Illustrated* 27 (1): 60–64.

Reidy, Joseph P. 1992. *From Slavery to Agrarian Capitalism in the Cotton Plantation South: Central Georgia, 1800–1880*. Chapel Hill: University of North Carolina Press.

Reimers, David M. 1965. *White Protestantism and the Negro*. New York: Oxford University Press.

Renehan, Edward J., Jr. 1995. *The Secret Six: The True Tale of the Men Who Conspired with John Brown*. New York: Crown.

Rhodes, Jane. 1992. "Breaking the Editorial Ice: Mary Ann Shadd Cary and the Provincial Freeman." Ph.D. dissertation, Department of History, University of North Carolina at Chapel Hill.

Richards, Leonard L. 1975. *"Gentlemen of Property and Standing": Anti-Abolition Mobs in Jacksonian America*. New York: Oxford University Press.

———. 1986. *The Life and Times of Congressman John Quincy Adams*. New York: Oxford University Press.

Richardson, Joe M. 1986. *Christian Reconstruction: The American Missionary Association and Southern Blacks, 1861–1890*. Athens: University of Georgia Press.

Richardson, Marilyn, ed. 1987. *Maria W. Stewart: America's First Black Woman Political Writer*. Bloomington: Indiana University Press.

Richardson, Robert D. 1986. *Henry Thoreau: A Life of the Mind*. Berkeley: University of California Press.

Rippon, John, ed., 1801. *The Baptist Annual Register*. London: Brown and James.

Robert, Joseph Clarke. 1941. *The Road from Monticello: A Study of the Virginia Slavery Debate of 1832*. Durham, NC: Duke University Press.

Roberts, John W. 1989. *From Trickster to Badman: The Black Folk Hero in Slavery and Freedom*. Philadelphia: University of Pennsylvania Press.

Roberts, Rita. 1994. "Patriotism and Political Criticism: The Evolution of Political Consciousness in the Mind of a Black Revolutionary Soldier." *Eighteenth Century Studies* 27 (Summer): 569–588.

Robinson, William H. 1981. *Phillis Wheatley: A Bio-Bibliography*. Boston: G. K. Hall.

———. 1984. *Phillis Wheatley and Her Writings*. New York: Garland.

Rodriguez, Junius Peter, Jr. 1992. "Ripe for Revolt: Louisiana and the Tradition of Slave Insurrection, 1803–1865." Ph.D. dissertation, Department of History, Auburn University, Auburn, Alabama.

Roediger, David R. 1991. *Wages of Whiteness: Race and the Making of the American Working Class*. London: Verso.

Roper, John Herbert. 1984. *U. B. Phillips: A Southern Mind*. Macon, GA: Mercer University Press.

Rose, Anne C. 1981. *Transcendentalism as a Social Movement, 1830–1850*. New Haven, CT: Yale University Press.

Rose, Willie Lee. 1964. *Rehearsal for Reconstruction: The Port Royal Experiment*. New York: Bobbs-Merrill.

Rossbach, Jeffrey. 1982. *Ambivalent Conspirators: John Brown, the Secret Six, and a Theory of Slave Violence*. Philadelphia: University of Pennsylvania Press.

Ruby, Robert H., and John A. Brown. 1993. *Indian Slavery in the Pacific Northwest*. Spokane, WA: Arthur H. Clark.

Russell, John H. 1916. "Colored Freeman as Slave Owners in Virginia." *Journal of Negro History* 1 (July): 233–242.

Saillant, John. 1994. "Lemuel Haynes' Black Republicanism and the American Republican Tradition, 1775–1820." *Journal of the Early Republic* 14 (3): 293–324.

Sallinger, Sharon. 1987. *"To Serve Well and Faithfully": Labor and Indentured Servants in Pennsylvania*. Cambridge: Cambridge University Press.

Salzman, Jack; David Lionel Smith; and Cornel West, eds. 1996. *Encyclopedia of African-American Culture and History*. New York: Macmillan Library Reference.

Scarupa, Harriet. 1995. "Learning from Ancestral Bones: New York's Exhumed African Past." *American Visions* (February/March): 18–21.

Schor, Joel. 1977. *Henry Highland Garnet: A Voice of Black Radicalism in the Nineteenth Century*. Westport, CT: Greenwood.

Schwarz, Philip J. 1996. *Slave Laws in Virginia*. Athens: University of Georgia Press.

———. 1988. *Twice Condemned: Slaves and the Criminal Laws of Virginia, 1705–1865*. Baton Rouge: Louisiana State University Press.

Schweninger, Loren. 1979. *James T. Rapier and Reconstruction*. Chicago: University of Chicago Press.

———. 1990. "John Carruthers Stanly and the Anomaly of Black Slaveholding." *North Carolina Historical Review* 67 (April): 159–192.

Scott, Donald M. 1979. "Abolition as a Sacred Vocation." In *Antislavery Reconsidered: New Perspectives on the Abolitionists*. Edited by Lewis Perry and Michael Fellman. Baton Rouge: Louisiana State University Press.

Scott, John Anthony. 1961. "On the Authenticity of Fanny Kemble's Journal of a Residence on a Georgian Plantation in 1838–1839." *Journal of Negro History* 46: 233–242.

Sekora, John, and Darwin Turner, eds. 1982. *The Art of Slave Narrative: Original Essays in Criticism and Theory*. Macomb: Western Illinois University Press.

Selby, John. 1977. *Dunmore*. Williamsburg: Virginia Independence Bicentennial Commission.

Sellin, J. T. 1976. *Slavery and the Penal System*. New York: Elsevier.

Sensbach, Jon. 1991. *A Separate Canaan: The Making of an Afro-Moravian World in North Carolina, 1763–1856*. Ann Arbor, MI: University Microfilms.

Sewell, Richard H. 1988. *The House Divided: Sectionalism and Civil War, 1848–1865*. Baltimore: Johns Hopkins University Press.

Shapiro, Herbert. 1984. "The Impact of the Aptheker Thesis: A Retrospective View of *American Negro Slave Revolts*." *Science and Society* 48: 52–73.

Shaw, George C. 1931. *John Chavis*. Binghamton, NY: Rail-Ballou Press.

Shewmaker, Kenneth, ed. 1990. *Daniel Webster: The "Completest Man."* Hanover, NH: University Press of New England.

Shore, Laurence. 1986. *Southern Capitalists: The Ideological Leadership of an Elite, 1832–1885*. Chapel Hill: University of North Carolina Press.

Shyllon, Folarin. 1977. *James Ramsay: The Unknown Abolitionist*. Edinburgh: Canongate.

Siebert, Wilbur H. 1898. *The Underground Railroad from Slavery to Freedom*. New York: Macmillan.

Silverman, Jason H. 1992. "Ashley Wilkes Revisited: The Immigrant as Slaveowner in the Old South." *Journal of Confederate History* 7: 123–135.

———. 1980. "Kentucky, Canada, and Extradition: The Jesse Happy Case." *Filson Club History* 54 (January): 50–60.

———. 1997. "'The Law of the Land Is the Law': Antebellum Jews, Slavery, and the Old South." In *Struggles in the Promised Land: Towards a History of Black-Jewish Relations in America.* Edited by Cornel West and Jack Salzman. New York: Oxford University Press.

———. 1985. *Unwelcome Guests: Canada West's Response to American Fugitive Slaves, 1800–1865.* Millwood, NY: Associated Faculty Press.

Simmons, William, J. 1968. *Men of Mark: Eminent, Progressive, and Rising.* New York: Arno.

Simpson, John Eddins. 1973. *Howell Cobb: The Politics of Ambition.* Chicago: Adams Press.

Singleton, Theresa. 1991. "The Archaeology of Slave Life." In *Before Freedom Came: African-American Life in the AnteBellum South.* Edited by Edward Campbell, Jr., and Kym Rice. Charlottesville: University Press of Virginia.

Singleton, Theresa A., ed. 1985. *The Archaeology of Slavery and Plantation Life.* Orlando, FL: Academic Press.

Skipper, Ottis Clark. 1958. *J. D. B. DeBow: Magazinist of the Old South.* Athens: University of Georgia Press.

Slaughter, Thomas P. 1991. *Bloody Dawn: The Christiana Riot and Racial Violence in the Antebellum North.* New York: Oxford University Press.

Smith, Abbot Emerson. 1947. *Colonists in Bondage: White Servitude and Convict Labor in America, 1607–1776.* Chapel Hill: University of North Carolina Press.

Smith, Craig R. 1989. *Defender of the Union: The Oratory of Daniel Webster.* New York: Greenwood.

Smith, Hilrie Shelton. 1972. *In His Image, But . . . Racism in Southern Religion, 1780–1910.* Durham, NC: Duke University Press.

Smith, John David. 1991. *An Old Creed for the New South: Proslavery Ideology and Historiography, 1865–1818.* Athens: University of Georgia Press.

Smith, John David, and John C. Inscoe, eds. 1993. *Ulrich Bonnell Phillips: A Southern Historian and His Critics.* Athens: University of Georgia Press.

Smith, Julia Floyd. 1985. *Slavery and Rice Culture in Low Country Georgia, 1750–1860.* Knoxville: University of Tennessee Press.

Smith, Page. 1976. *Jefferson: A Revealing Biography.* New York: American Heritage.

Smith, Venture. 1971. *A Narrative of the Life and Adventures of Venture Smith.* Boston: Beacon Press.

Snay, Mitchell. 1989. "American Thought and Southern Distinctiveness: The Southern Clergy and the Sanctification of Slaves." *Civil War History* 35 (4) (December): 311–328.

———. 1993. *Gospel of Disunion: Religion and Separatism in the Antebellum South.* Cambridge: Cambridge University Press.

Sobel, Mechal. 1987. *The World They Made Together: Black and White Values in Eighteenth-Century Virginia.* Princeton, NJ: Princeton University Press.

Soderlund, Jean R. 1994. "Priorities and Power: The Philadelphia Female Anti-Slavery Society." In *The Abolitionist Sisterhood: Women's Political Culture in Antebellum America.* Edited by Jean Fagan Yellin and John C. Van Horne. Ithaca, NY: Cornell University Press.

———. 1985. *Quakers and Slavery: A Divided Spirit.* Princeton, NJ: Princeton University Press.

Spain, August O. 1951. *The Political Theory of John C. Calhoun.* New York: Bookman Associates.

Spalding, Phinizy. 1977. *Oglethorpe in America.* Chicago: University of Chicago Press.

Spalding, Phinizy, and Harvey H. Jackson, eds. 1989. *Oglethorpe in Perspective: Georgia's Founder after Two Hundred Years.* Tuscaloosa: University of Alabama Press.

Stampp, Kenneth M. 1990. *America in 1857: A Nation on the Brink.* New York: Oxford University Press.

———. 1942. "An Analysis of T. R. Dew's *Review of the Debate in the Virginia Legislature.*" *Journal of Negro History* 27 (October): 380–387.

———. 1956. *The Peculiar Institution.* New York: Random House.

Stanley, A. Knighton. 1979. *The Children Is Crying: Congregationalism among Black People.* New York: Pilgrim Press.

Starling, Marion Wilson. 1981. *The Slave Narrative.* Boston: G. K. Hall.

Starobin, Robert S. 1970. *Denmark Vesey: The Slave Conspiracy of 1822.* Englewood Cliffs, NJ: Prentice-Hall.

Staudenraus, Philip J. 1961. *The African Colonization Movement, 1816–1865.* New York: Columbia University Press.

Stearns, Charles. 1969. *Narrative of Henry Box Brown.* Philadelphia: Rhetoric Publications.

Stephenson, Wendell. 1938. *Isaac Franklin: Slave Trader and Planter of the Old South.* Baton Rouge: Louisiana State University Press.

Stepto, Robert B. 1979. *From Behind the Veil: A Study of Afro-American Narrative.* Urbana: University of Illinois Press.

Sterkx, H. E. 1972. *The Free Negro in Ante-Bellum Louisiana*. Cranbury, NJ: Fairleigh Dickinson University.

Sterling, Dorothy. 1991. *Ahead of Her Time: Abby Kelley and the Politics of Anti-Slavery*. New York: W. W. Norton.

Sterling, Dorothy, ed. 1984. *We Are Your Sisters: Black Women in the Nineteenth Century*. New York: Norton.

Stevens, Charles Emery. 1973. *Anthony Burns: A History*. Williamstown, MA: Corner House Publishers.

Stevenson, Brenda. 1996. *Life in Black and White: Family and Community in the Slave South*. New York: Oxford University Press.

Stevenson, Brenda, ed. 1988. *The Journals of Charlotte Forten Grimké*. New York: Oxford University Press.

Stewart, James Brewer. 1992. *William Lloyd Garrison and the Challenge of Emancipation*. Arlington Heights, IL: Harlan Davidson.

Still, William. 1883. *The Underground Railroad*. Philadelphia: William Still.

Stiller, Richard. 1972. *Commune on the Frontier: The Story of Frances Wright*. New York: Thomas Y. Crowell.

Stimson, John Ward. 1903. "An Overlooked American Shelley." *Arena* 7: 15–26.

Stuckey, Sterling. 1988. "A Last Stern Struggle: Henry Highland Garnet and Liberation Theory." In *Black Leaders of the Nineteenth Century*. Edited by Leon Litwack and August Meier. Urbana: University of Illinois Press.

———. 1987. *Slave Culture: Nationalist Theory and the Foundations of Black America*. New York: Oxford University Press.

Sutch, Richard. 1975. "The Breeding of Slaves for Sale and the Westward Expansion of Slavery." In *Race and Slavery in the Western Hemisphere*. Edited by Stanley L. Engerman and Eugene D. Genovese. Princeton, NJ: Princeton University Press.

Suttles, Wayne, ed. 1990. *Handbook of North American Indians: Northwest Coast*. Washington, DC: Smithsonian Institution.

Swerdlow, Amy. 1994. "Abolition's Conservative Sisters: The Ladies' New York City Anti-Slavery Societies, 1834–1840." In *The Abolitionist Sisterhood: Women's Political Culture in Antebellum America*. Edited by Jean Fagan Yellin and John C. Van Horne. Ithaca, NY: Cornell University Press.

Swisher, Carl. 1974. *History of the Supreme Court of the United States: The Taney Period, 1836–1864*. New York: Macmillan.

———. 1936. *Roger B. Taney*. New York: MacMillan.

Syrett, John. 1971. "The Confiscation Acts: Efforts at Reconstruction during the Civil War." M.A. thesis, Department of History, University of Wisconsin, Madison.

Tadman, Michael. 1989. *Speculators and Slaves: Masters, Traders, and Slaves in the Old South*. Madison: University of Wisconsin Press.

Taylor, Robert M., Jr., ed. 1987. *The Northwest Ordinance 1787: A Bicentennial Handbook*. Indianapolis: Indiana Historical Society.

Thomas, Benjamin P. 1950. *Theodore Dwight Weld: Crusader for Freedom*. New Brunswick, NJ: Rutgers University Press.

Thomas, John L. 1963. *The Liberator: William Lloyd Garrison*. Boston: Little, Brown.

Thomas, Karen M. 1992. "Juneteenth Remembers Slavery, Celebrates Freedom." *Chicago Tribune*. June 18, final edition.

Thompson, Robert Farris. 1983. *Flash of the Spirit: African and Afro-American Art and Philosophy*. New York: Random House.

Thornton, John K. 1991. "African Dimensions of the Stono Rebellion." *American Historical Review* 96 (October): 1101–1113.

Thorpe, Earl. 1971. *Black Historians: A Critique*. New York: William Morrow.

Trudel, Marcel. 1990. *Dictionnaire des esclaves et de leurs propriétaires au Canada Français*. Ville LaSalle, Quebec: Éditions Hurtubise.

———. 1960. *L'esclavage au Canada Français*. Quebec: Les Presses Universitaires Laval.

Trueblood, David Elton. 1966. *The People Called Quakers*. Richmond, IN: Friends United Press.

Truth, Sojourner. 1991. *Narrative of Sojourner Truth: A Bondswoman of Olden Time*. Edited by Olive Gilbert. New York: Oxford University Press.

Turner, Lorenzo Dow. 1974. *Africanisms in the Gullah Dialect*. Ann Arbor: University of Michigan Press.

U.S. Congress. Senate. 1856. *Report of the Decisions of the Commissioner of Claims under the Convention of February 8, 1833, between the United States and Great Britain, Transmitted to the Senate by the President of the United States, August 11, 1856*. Senate Executive Document 103, 34th Congress, 1st sess. Washington, DC: Nicholson.

Venable, Austin L. 1942. "The Conflict between the Douglas and Yancey Forces in the Charleston Convention." *Journal of Southern History* 8 (May): 226–241.

———. 1945. "The Role of William L. Yancey in the Secession Movement." M.A. thesis, Department of History, Vanderbilt University, Nashville, Tennessee.

Venet, Wendy Hamand. 1991. *Neither Ballots nor Bullets: Women Abolitionists and the Civil War*. Charlottesville: University Press of Virginia.

Vlach, John Michael. 1993. *Back of the Big House: The Architecture of Plantation Slavery*. Chapel Hill: University of North Carolina Press.

Wade, Richard C. 1964. *Slavery in the Cities: The South, 1820–1860*. Oxford: Oxford University Press.

Wagenknecht, Edward. 1965. *Harriet Beecher Stowe: The Known and the Unknown*. New York: Oxford University Press.

Waklyn, Jon L. 1973. *The Politics of a Literary Man: William Gilmore Simms*. Westport, CT: Greenwood.

Walker, David. 1829. *David Walker's Appeal to the Colored Citizens of the World, 1829–1830, Its Setting and Its Meaning, together with the Full Text of the Third, and Last, Edition of the Appeal*. New York: Humanities Press.

Walker, James. 1976. *The Black Loyalists*. New York: Africana.

Walters, Ronald G. 1978. *American Reformers, 1815–1860*. New York: Hill and Wang.

Walther, Eric H. 1992. *The Fire-Eaters*. Baton Rouge: Louisiana State University Press.

Walton, Augustus Q. 1835. *A History of the Detection, Conviction, Life, and Designs of John A. Murel, the Great Western Land Pirate*. Athens, TN: G. White.

Washington, John E. 1942. *They Knew Lincoln*. New York: E. P. Dutton.

Watson, Charles S. 1993. *From Nationalism to Secessionism: The Changing Fiction of William Gilmore Simms*. Westport, CT: Greenwood.

Watt, James. 1995. "James Ramsay, 1733–1789: Naval Surgeon, Naval Chaplain, and Morning Star of the Antislavery Movement." *Mariner's Mirror* 81 (2): 156–170.

Weatherford, Jack. 1991. *Native Roots: How the Indians Enriched America*. New York: Crown Publishers.

Weinstein, Allen; Frank Otto Gatell; and David Sarasohn, eds. 1968. *American Negro Slavery: A Modern Reader*. New York: Oxford University Press.

Welch, Eloise Turner. 1976. "The Background and Development of the American Missionary Association's Decision to Educate Freedmen in the South, with Subsequent Repercussions." Ph.D. dissertation. Ann Arbor, MI: University Microfilms.

Wells, Tom Henderson. 1968. *The Slave Ship Wanderer*. Athens: University of Georgia Press.

Welsch, Roger L. 1981. *Omaha Tribal Myths and Legends*. Chicago: Swallow Press.

Wender, Herbert. 1930. *Southern Commercial Conventions, 1837–1859*. Baltimore: Johns Hopkins Press.

Wesley, Charles. 1970. *The Fifteenth Amendment and Black America, 1870–1970*. Washington, DC: Associated Publishers.

White, Deborah Gray. 1985. *Ar'n't I a Woman? Female Slaves in the Plantation South*. New York: Norton.

———. 1983. "Female Slaves: Sex Roles and Status in the Antebellum Plantation South." *Journal of Family History* 8 (Fall): 248–261.

Whitten, David O. 1981. *Andrew Durnford: A Black Sugar Planter in Antebellum Louisiana*. Natchitoches, LA: Northwestern State University.

Wiecek, William E. 1978. "Slavery and Abolition before the United States Supreme Court, 1820–1860." *Journal of American History* 65: 34–59.

———. 1977. *Sources of Anti-Slavery Constitutionalism*. Ithaca, NY: Cornell University Press.

Wiggins, William H. 1993. "Juneteenth: Tracking the Progress of an Emancipation Celebration." *American Visions* 8 (3) (June/July): 28–31.

———. 1987. *O Freedom! Afro-American Emancipation Celebrations*. Knoxville: University of Tennessee Press.

Wikramanayake, Marina. 1973. *A World in Shadow: The Free Black in Antebellum South Carolina*. Columbia: University of South Carolina Press.

Wilder, Daniel W. 1875. *The Annals of Kansas*. Topeka, KS: G. W. Martin.

Wiley, Bell I. 1938. *Southern Negroes, 1861–1865*. New Haven, CT: Yale University Press.

Wilkins, Thurman. 1988. *Cherokee Tragedy*. Norman: University of Oklahoma Press.

Williams, Carolyn. 1994. "The Female Antislavery Movement: Fighting against Racial Prejudice and Promoting Women's Rights in Antebellum America." In *The Abolitionist Sisterhood: Women's Political Culture in Antebellum America*. Edited by Jean Fagan Yellin and John C. Van Horne. Ithaca, NY: Cornell University Press.

———. 1991. "Religion, Race, and Gender in Antebellum American Radicalism: The Philadelphia Female Anti-Slavery Society, 1833–1870." Ph.D. dissertation, Department of History, University of California–Los Angeles.

Williams, Leonard F. 1972. *Richard Allen and Mother Bethel: African Methodist Episcopal Church*. Philadelphia: Historical Commission of Mother Bethel A.M.E.

Williams, Michael W., ed. 1993. *The African American Encyclopedia*. New York: Marshall Cavendish.

Williams, Russ E., ed. 1972. "Slave Patrol Ordinances of St. Tammany Parish, Louisiana, 1835–1838." *Louisiana History* 13: 399–412.

Williamson, Joel. 1980. *New People: Miscegenation and Mulattoes in the United States*. New York: Free Press.

Wilson, Carol. 1994. *Freedom at Risk: The Kidnapping of Free Blacks in America, 1780–1865*. Lexington: University of Kentucky Press.

Wilson, Ellen. 1976. *The Loyal Blacks*. New York: Capricorn Books.

Winks, Robin W. 1971. *The Blacks in Canada: A History*. New Haven, CT: Yale University Press.

Winthrop, Jordan. 1993. *Tumult and Silence at Second Creek: An Inquiry into a Civil War Slave Conspiracy*. Baton Rouge: Louisiana State University Press.

Wish, Harvey. 1941. "The Revival of the African Slave Trade in the United States, 1856–1860." *Mississippi Valley Historical Review* 27: 569–588.

Wish, Harvey, ed. 1960. *Antebellum: Writings of George Fitzhugh and Hinton Rowan Helper on Slavery*. New York: Capricorn Books.

Wood, Betty. 1984. *Slavery in Colonial Georgia, 1730–1775*. Athens: University of Georgia Press.

Wood, Peter. 1974. *Black Majority: Negroes in Colonial South Carolina from 1670 through the Stono Rebellion*. New York: Norton.

Woodson, Carter G. 1968. *The Education of the Negro Prior to 1861*. New York: Arno Press.

———. 1925. *Free Negro Owners of Slaves in the United States in 1830*. Washington, DC: Association for the Study of Negro Life and History.

Woodson, Carter G., ed. 1926. *The Mind of the Negro as Reflected in Letters Written during the Crisis, 1800–1860*. Washington, DC: Association for the Study of Negro Life and History.

Woodward, C. Vann. 1971. *Origins of the New South, 1877–1913*. Baton Rouge: Louisiana State University Press.

Woolman, John. 1922. *The Journal and Essays of John Woolman*. Edited by A. M. Gunmere. New York: Macmillan.

Wright, Frances. 1972. *Life, Letters, and Lectures, 1834–1844*. New York: Arno Press.

Wright, Louis B. 1940. *The First Gentlemen of Virginia*. San Marino, CA: Huntington Library.

Wright, Louis B., and Marion Tinling, eds. 1941. *The Secret Diary of William Byrd of Westover, 1709–1712*. Richmond, VA: Dietz Press.

Wyatt-Brown, Bertram. 1969. *Lewis Tappan and the Evangelical War against Slavery*. Cleveland: Case Western Reserve University Press.

Yang, Liwen. 1992. "John Brown's Role in the History of the Emancipation Movement of Black Americans." *Southern Studies* 3: 135–142.

Yellin, Jean Fagan. 1972. *The Intricate Knot: Black Figures in American Literature, 1776–1863*. New York: New York University Press.

Yellin, Jean Fagan, ed. 1987. *Incidents in the Life of a Slave Girl*. Cambridge, MA: Harvard University Press.

Yellin, Jean Fagan, and John C. Van Horne, eds. 1994. *The Abolitionist Sisterhood: Women's Political Culture in Antebellum America*. Ithaca, NY: Cornell University Press.

Yetman, Norman R. 1967. "The Background of the Slave Narrative Collection." *American Quarterly* 3: 535–553.

Zaborney, John J. 1997. "'They Are Out for Their Victuals and Clothes': Slave Hiring and Slave Family and Friendship Ties in Rural, Nineteenth-Century Virginia." In *New Directions in the African-American History of Virginia*. Edited by John Saillant. New York: Garland.

Zamir, Shamoon. 1995. *Dark Voices: W. E. B. DuBois and American Thought, 1888–1903*. Chicago: University of Chicago Press.

Zikmund, Barbara Brown, ed. 1984. *Hidden Histories in the United Church of Christ*. New York: United Church Press.

Zilversmit, Arthur. 1967. *The First Emancipation*. Chicago: University of Chicago Press.

~ILLUSTRATION CREDITS~

~INDEX~

Page numbers in boldface denote main entries.

black loyalists, 64–65, 85–86, 587
and Boers, 94–95
branding, 98
convict transportation, 194–195
Domesday Book, 219, 369
and Dutch slave trade, 232
early-medieval slave raiding, 225,
    368–369
and Egypt, 210, 381, 617
enslavement of Native Americans,
    33, 38
and Fédon's Rebellion, 266
and fugitive slaves in Canada, 32–33
and Gold Coast, 308
and Haiti, 152
Irish transportation, 225–226, 365,
    369–370
labor movement, 412
and Latin America, 8
laws, 447–448
proslavery arguments, **523–524**
Rom (Gypsy) slavery, 547
and seamen's acts, 567–568
textile industry, 126
and U.S. Southern nonslaveholders,
    471
Webster-Ashburton Treaty, 33,
    165–166, 686, **687–688**
See also British *headings*; Colonial
    expansion; Transatlantic slave
    trade
Great Popo. *See* Popo
Great Potato Famine, 226
Great Revival. *See* Second Great
    Awakening
Great Trek, 94–95, **311–312**, 647
Greece, ancient, xv–xvi, 6, **312–314**
    agriculture, 22
    and Cicero, 155
    concubinage, 182
    and early Christianity, 80
    gender, 298, 299
    Gortyn law code, 310
    Hesiod, 313, 340–341
    Homer, xv, 312, 313, 355–356, 578
    Isocrates, **371**
    Marxist analysis, 427
    names/naming, 455
    perioeci, 499–500
    Plato, xv, 314, 356, 510–511, 525,
        556, 595
    and proslavery arguments, 269, 525
    sexual abuse of slaves, 298
    slave rebellions, xvi, 48–49, 337,
        569–570
    Solon, iii, 600–601
    tattooing, 98, 629
    Theognis, 631–632
    war captives, xv, 48–49, 313, 355,
        356, 590
    See also Aristotle; Helots; Sparta

Greeley, Horace, 318, 338
Green, Beriah, 689
Green, Fletcher M., 121
Green, Shields, 104, 332
Green, William, 204, 582
Greene, Israel, 331–332
Greene, Nathaniel, 402
Grégoire, Abbé Henri-Baptiste, 204,
    314–315, 542, 671
Gregory I (Saint), **315–316**
Gregory of Nazianzus, 73, **316**
Gregory of Nyssa, 73
Gregory XVI (Pope), 153
Gregson v. Gilbert. See Zong incident
Grenada, 266, 427
Grenville, William, 301
Grew, Mary, 505
Grice, Hezekiah, 464
Griffiths, Julia, 473
Grimes, Leonard A., 114
Grimké, Angelina, 273, 274, **317**, 612,
    688
    *An Appeal to the Christian Women
        of the South*, 44–45, 317
    and female anti-slavery societies, 96,
        395, 505
    and Quakerism, 317, 318, 531
    and women's rights, 297, 700
Grimké, Francis J., 273
Grimké, Sarah Moore, 274, **317–318**,
    612, 688
    and female anti-slavery societies, 96,
        395, 505
    and Quakerism, 318, 531
    and women's rights, 297, 700
Grinnell, Josiah B., **318–319**
Griots, 225
Griqua people, 124, 432, 433
Grotius, Hugo, **319–320**
Group Areas Act (1950) (South
    Africa), 43
Groves v. Slaughter (U.S.), 626
Growth Without Development (U.S.),
    410
Grumettas, 263
Grundrisse, 256
Guadeloupe, 282, 405, 456
Guarocuya. *See* Enriquillo
Guatemala, 75, 398
Guerrero, Vincente, **320–321**, 466
Guinea Company (England), **321**,
    557
Guinean Company (Denmark), 208
Guineisk kompagni. See Guinean
    Company
Gulf countries, 15
Gullah, 16, 224, 297–298, **321–322**,
    567
Gullah Jack, **322–323**, 672
Guo Moruo, 187
Gurley, Ralph R., 28

Guthrie, John, 203
Gutman, Herbert G., 252, 265, 347,
    352, 353
Guy Rivers, 588
Guyana. *See* Berbice
Gypsy (Rom) slavery, **547–548**

Haciendas, 251, 437
Hadden, Sally, 495
Haggard, John, 144
Haida people, 36
Haiti, 16, 95, 162, 222, 315
    creole language, 198–199
    trickster tales, 650
    voodoo, 16, 152, 188, 213, 441,
        678–679
    See also Saint Domingue
Haitian Revolution, **325–328**,
    418–419
    and antislavery movements, 56
    and art, 52
    Christophe, 150–153, 162, 315,
        405, 505
    and Cuban slave market, 201
    Dessalines, 152, 213–215, 327, 419,
        505
    Dubois on, 227
    and Enlightenment, ix
    and French Revolution, 284, 325,
        327, 419
    and Napoleon, 327, 405–406, 456
    Pétion, 95, 152, 480, 504–505
    and proslavery arguments, 523
    Raimond, 480, 539
    and Raynal, 541, 542
    Rigaud, 327, 419, 480, 505,
        545–546
    and Sambo thesis, 564
    and slave rebellions, 205, 230, 305,
        327, 512
al-Hakam I (Caliph of Spain), 565
Hale, Edward Everett, **328**
Hale, John P., 280
Haley, Alex Palmer, 414
Ham, Curse of, 150, **328–329**, 526
Hammon, Jupiter, 255
Hammond, James Henry, **329–330**,
    526, 588
Hammond, Joshua, 148
Hammurabi Code, xiv, 63, 79, 98,
    330–331, 620
Hampton Institute (U.S.), 30, 42,
    685
Hampton, Wade, 304
Hancock, Ian, 547
Hanke, Lewis, 113, 545, 605
Hannen, James, 340
Hanson, John C., 423
Hanway, Castner, 148
Happy, Jesse, 32
Harding, Vincent, 47

Los Islands. *See* Îles de Loos
Lotus Sutra, 109, 111
Loughride, William, 318
Louis XIV (King of France), 168,
    291–292, 667
Louis XVIII (King of France), 457,
    571, 671, 673
Louisiana, 160, 168, 179, 224, 229
    and French slave trade, 285–286
    German Coast uprising (1811),
        304–305
    Pointe Coupee conspiracy, 511–512
    See also U.S. slavery
Louisiana Purchase (U.S.), 91, 380
Louis-Philippe (King of France), 169
Louverture, Toussaint, 152, 227, 326,
    418–419, 505, 539
    and Dessalines, 213, 214
    and Napoleon, 327, 405
    and Raynal, 542
Love, Alfred, 19
Lovejoy, Elijah P., 9, **420–421**
Lovejoy, Owen, 91
Lovejoy, Paul E., 13, 14, 239, 333,
    346, 348, 360, 563, 636
Lowell, James Russell, 614
Luanda, 112, 236–237, 518
Luba-Lunda, 136, 138
Lucullus, M. Terentius Varro, 608
Lugard, Frederick John Dealtry, 2,
    403, **421**
Luque, Hernando de, 27
Luraghi, Raimondo, 301
Lutheran Church, 209
Luz Maria, Martínez M., 350, 351
Lycurgus, **421–422**
Lyrics of Lowly Life, 413

Ma Tuan-lin, 147
Macaulay, Zachary, 17, 314, 671
Macedonia, 506
Macehualtin, 35
Maclean, George, 53
MacLeod, Murdo J., 138, 399
Maclure, William, 459
Macqueen, James, 522
Madagascar, 94, 144, 285, 429, 646
Madariaga, Salvador de, 95
Madeira, 13, 517, 618
Madison County Slave War, **423**
Madison, James, 9, 28, 173, 635
al-Maghili, 445–446
Magoffin, Beriah, 423
Mahdi (Egypt), 381
Mahfouz, Naguib, 349
Mahmud II (Ottoman Sultan), 378
Mails, Thomas E., 142
Makhweyane, 68
Malaria, 218
Mali, xvii, 305, **423–425**, 449
Malindi, 112

Mamluk sultanate, 261, 262
Mamluks, 262, 306, **425–426**, 483,
    484, 647
"The Man Without a Country," 328
Management of Slaves, 150
Mancipia, 595
Mandan people, 37
Mandela, Nelson, 43
Mandingo people, 308, 372, 594
Mandinka, 424
Mani Nzinga Nkuwu, 136
Manifest Destiny, 537
Mann, Horace, 205
Manning, Patrick, 133, 345, 591, 592
Mansfield, First Earl of. *See* Murray,
    William
Mansfield Park, 412
al-Mansur, 602
Mansur, Zubayr Rahma, 617
Manu, 618
Manuel, Moreno F., 350
Manuel I (King of Portugal), 12
Manumission, 4, 93–94, 279, **426–427**
    ancient world, xiv, 79, 313–314,
        431, 548, 552, 656
    and black slaveowners, 87, 89
    Dutch Caribbean, 230
    and early Christianity, 315–316
    French colonies, 410
    Indonesia, 367
    Latin America, 166–167, 202, 279,
        441, 491, 502, 606
    United States, 9, 87, 89, 172, 304,
        426
    See also Compensated emancipation
Marcus Aurelius (Roman emperor),
    182
Mare librum, 319
Maredudd (Prince of Wales), 368
Mariager, Peder, 208
Mariano Faliero, 26
*Maroon Societies: Rebel Slave Com-
    munities in the Americas*, 350
Maroon Wars (Jamaica), 64, 203, 253,
    587, 648–649
Maroons. *See* Fugitive slave communi-
    ties; Maroon Wars (Jamaica)
"Maroons within the Present Limits of
    the United States," 47
Marriage. *See* Slave family
Marronage. *See* Escape; Fugitive slave
    communities
Marschal, Andrew, 361
Marshall, John, 9, 630
Marshall, Thurgood, 634
Martellus, Henricus, 216
Martineau, Harriet, 588
Martinique, 282
Marx, Karl, 256, 270, 427, 428. *See
    also* Marxism
Marxism, **427–428**

and African historiography, 345
    on China, 145, 187
    and Engels, 346, 427
    Fox-Genovese, 276
    Genovese, 301–302
    on medieval Europe, xvii
    and modern world system model,
        177
    on wage slavery, 125, 269, 270, 681
Mary Barton, 412
Maryland, 121
Mas Gassis, Macram, 192
Mascarene Islands. *See* Mauritius;
    Réunion; Rodrigues
Masih, Iqbal, 191
Mason, Charles, 428
Mason-Dixon Line, **428–429**
Massachusetts, 176–177, 501
Massachusetts Anti-Slavery Society,
    60, 105, 143, 274, 408
Massachusetts Female Emancipation
    Society, 97
Massachusetts Kansas Committee,
    342
Master and Servant Acts (1842 and
    1856) (Cape Colony), 647
Masters and Lords, 177, 178
Masters and Slaves, 347
"Master-slave dialectic," 255–256
Masur, Gerhard, 95
Matamba, 237
Mathews, Donald G., 149
Mathews, John, 119
Matriarchal system, 144
Mattoso, Katia Queiros, 347, 351
Maude, H. E., 504
Mauritania, 517, 523, 642
    contemporary slavery in, 27, 191,
        192, 642
Mauritius, 166, 194, 285, **429–430**
Maximian, 63
Maxwell, Sir George, 404, 405
May, Robert E., 268
May, Samuel J., 41
May, Samuel, Jr., 612
Maya people, 35, 431, 432
Mayeque, 35
Mazehualob, 35
Mbanza Kongo, 14
Mbemba, Nzinga. *See* Afonso I
Mbiti, John S., 69
Mbundu people, 136, 137, 237
McCulloch v. Maryland (U.S.), 630,
    686
McDaniel, David, 115
McDonogh, John, 229
McFarlane, Milton, 203
McGowan, James A., 295
McKim, James Miller, 103, 281
Measles, 217
Mecca, 449, 483